READINGS IN AMERICAN POLITICS

Fourth Edition

READINGS IN AMERICAN POLITICS

Analysis and Perspectives

Fourth Edition

Ken Kollman

UNIVERSITY OF MICHIGAN

W. W. Norton & Company ■ New York ■ London

W. W. Norton & Company has been independent since its founding in 1923, when William Warder Norton and Mary D. Herter Norton first published lectures delivered at the People's Institute, the adult education division of New York City's Cooper Union. The firm soon expanded its program beyond the Institute, publishing books by celebrated academics from America and abroad. By mid-century, the two major pillars of Norton's publishing program—trade books and college texts—were firmly established. In the 1950s, the Norton family transferred control of the company to its employees, and today—with a staff of four hundred and a comparable number of trade, college, and professional titles published each year—W. W. Norton & Company stands as the largest and oldest publishing house owned wholly by its employees.

Editor: Pete Lesser
Associate editor: Samantha Held
Project Editor: Tenyia Lee
Production supervisor: Elizabeth Marotta
Composition by Westchester Publishing Services
Manufacturing by LSC Communications, Harrisonburg

Library of Congress Cataloging-in-Publication Data

W. W. Norton & Company, Inc., 500 Fifth Avenue, New York, N.Y. 10110-0017

www.wwnorton.com

W. W. Norton & Company Ltd., 15 Carlisle Street, London W1D 3BS

1 2 3 4 5 6 7 8 9 0

*To my amazing research collaborators over
the years: Scott, Pradeep, Allen, and John.*

CONTENTS

Preface   xiii
About the Editor   xvii

1 FUNDAMENTALS

1.1 JOHN LOCKE, from *The Second Treatise of Government*   1

1.2 MANCUR OLSON JR., from *The Logic of Collective Action: Public Goods and the Theory of Groups*   6

1.3 GARRETT HARDIN, "The Tragedy of the Commons," *Science*   24

1.4 D. RODERICK KIEWIET and MATHEW D. McCUBBINS, from *The Logic of Delegation: Congressional Parties and the Appropriations Process*   38

2 THE CONSTITUTION AND THE FOUNDING

2.1 BRUTUS, *The Antifederalist*, No. 1   51

2.2 JEREMY C. POPE and SHAWN TREIER, from "Voting for a Founding: Testing the Effect of Economic Interests at the Federal Convention of 1787," *The Journal of Politics*   60

2.3 ROBERT A. DAHL, from *How Democratic Is the American Constitution?*   70

3 FEDERALISM

3.1 CHRISTOPHER HAMMONS, from "State Constitutions, Religious Protection, and Federalism," *University of St. Thomas Journal of Law and Public Policy*   75

3.2 WILLIAM H. RIKER, from *Federalism: Origin, Operation, Significance* 82

3.3 *Arizona v. United States* (2012) 96

4 CIVIL RIGHTS AND CIVIL LIBERTIES

4.1 MICHAEL TESLER, from *Post-Racial or Most-Racial?: Race and Politics in the Obama Era* 109

4.2 *Brown v. Board of Education* (1954) 125

4.3 *District of Columbia v. Heller* (2008) 130

4.4 *Obergefell v. Hodges* (2015) 145

5 CONGRESS

5.1 DAVID R. MAYHEW, from *Congress: The Electoral Connection* 157

5.2 RICHARD F. FENNO JR., from *Home Style: House Members in Their Districts* 170

5.3 GARY W. COX and MATHEW D. McCUBBINS, from *Setting the Agenda: Responsible Party Government in the U.S. House of Representatives* 175

5.4 JUSTIN GRIMMER, SEAN WESTWOOD, and SOLOMON MESSING, from *The Impression of Influence: Legislator Communication, Representation, and Democratic Accountability* 195

6 THE PRESIDENCY

6.1 RICHARD E. NEUSTADT, from *Presidential Power and the Modern Presidents: The Politics of Leadership from Roosevelt to Reagan* 215

6.2 CHARLES M. CAMERON, from *Veto Bargaining: Presidents and the Politics of Negative Power* 224

6.3 BRANDICE CANES-WRONE, from *Who Leads Whom? Presidents, Policy, and the Public* 230

6.4 WILLIAM G. HOWELL, from *Power without Persuasion: The Politics of Direct Presidential Action* 251

6.5 SAMUEL KERNELL, from *Going Public: New Strategies of Presidential Leadership* 265

6.6 JAMES DRUCKMAN and LAWRENCE JACOBS, from *Who Governs: Presidents, Public Opinion, and Manipulation*   273

7 THE BUREAUCRACY

7.1 JAMES Q. WILSON, from *Bureaucracy: What Government Agencies Do and Why They Do It*   287

7.2 MATHEW D. McCUBBINS and THOMAS SCHWARTZ, "Congressional Oversight Overlooked: Police Patrols versus Fire Alarms," *American Journal of Political Science*   301

7.3 DANIEL P. CARPENTER, from *The Forging of Bureaucratic Autonomy: Reputations, Networks, and Policy Innovation in Executive Agencies, 1862–1928*   316

7.4 SUSAN L. MOFFITT, from *Making Public Policy: Participatory Bureaucracy in American Democracy*   321

7.5 SEAN GAILMARD and JOHN W. PATTY, from *Learning While Governing: Expertise and Accountability in the Executive Branch*   341

8 THE JUDICIARY

8.1 GERALD N. ROSENBERG, from *The Hollow Hope: Can Courts Bring about Social Change?*   349

8.2 *Marbury v. Madison* (1803)   356

8.3 *Lawrence v. Texas* (2003)   365

8.4 *National Federation of Independent Business v. Sebelius* (2012)   376

8.5 LEE EPSTEIN, ANDREW MARTIN, KEVIN QUINN, and JEFFREY SEGAL, from "Circuit Effects: How the Norm of Federal Judicial Experience Biases the Supreme Court," *University of Pennsylvania Law Review*   406

9 PUBLIC OPINION

9.1 ARTHUR LUPIA and MATHEW D. McCUBBINS, from *The Democratic Dilemma: Can Citizens Learn What They Need to Know?*   417

9.2 JOHN R. ZALLER, from *The Nature and Origins of Mass Opinion* 430

9.3 DONALD R. KINDER and CINDY D. KAM, from *Us Against Them: Enthnocentric Foundations of American Opinion* 435

9.4 KATHERINE J. CRAMER, from *The Politics of Resentment: Rural Consciousness in Wisconsin and the Rise of Scott Walker* 442

9.5 JAMES CAMPBELL, from *Polarized: Making Sense of a Divided America* 469

10 PARTICIPATION

10.1 JANELLE WONG, S. KARTHICK RAMAKRISHNAN, TAEKU LEE, and JANE JUNN, from *Asian American Political Participation: Emerging Constituents and Their Political Identities* 481

10.2 ROBERT D. PUTNAM, from *Bowling Alone: The Collapse and Revival of American Community* 489

11 INTEREST GROUPS

11.1 MARTIN GILENS, from *Affluence and Influence: Economic Inequality and Political Power in America* 493

11.2 KEN KOLLMAN, from *Outside Lobbying: Public Opinion and Interest Group Strategies* 501

11.3 LARRY M. BARTELS, from *Unequal Democracy: The Political Economy of the New Gilded Age* 516

12 POLITICAL PARTIES

12.1 JOHN H. ALDRICH, from *Why Parties? A Second Look* 525

12.2 ANGUS CAMPBELL, PHILIP E. CONVERSE, WARREN E. MILLER, and DONALD E. STOKES, from *The American Voter: An Abridgement* 541

12.3 MARTY COHEN, DAVID KAROL, HANS NOEL, and JOHN ZALLER, from *The Party Decides: Presidential Nominations Before and After Reform* 548

12.4 KEN KOLLMAN, "Who Drives the Party Bus?" 558

13 ELECTIONS

13.1 JOHN R. KOZA, BARRY FADEM, MARK GRUESKIN, MICHAEL S. MANDELL, ROBERT RICHIE, and JOSEPH F. ZIMMERMAN, from *Every Vote Equal: A State-Based Plan for Electing the President by National Popular Vote*   561

13.2 *Citizens United v. Federal Election Commission* (2010)   567

13.3 *Shelby County, Alabama v. Holder* (2013)   579

13.4 RICHARD L. FOX and JENNIFER L. LAWLESS, from "Gendered Perceptions and Political Candidacies: A Central Barrier to Women's Equality in Electoral Politics," *American Journal of Political Science*   586

13.5 CHRISTOPHER ACHEN and LARRY M. BARTELS, from *Democracy for Realists: Why Elections Do Not Produce Responsive Government*   601

14 THE MEDIA

14.1 MATTHEW A. BAUM, from *Soft News Goes to War: Public Opinion and American Foreign Policy in the New Media Age*   613

14.2 MARISA A. ABRAJANO, from *Campaigning to the New American Electorate: Advertising to Latino Voters*   617

15 POLICY

15.1 KENNETH SCHEVE and DAVID STASAVAGE, from *Taxing the Rich: A History of Fiscal Fairness in the United States and Europe*   629

15.2 SUZANNE METTLER, from *The Submerged State: How Invisible Government Policies Undermine American Democracy*   645

15.3 WALTER RUSSELL MEAD, from *Special Providence: American Foreign Policy and How It Changed the World*   659

Acknowledgments   663

PREFACE

This reader makes some of the most important work in political science and the subfield of American politics easily accessible to students in introductory courses. The selections included in this fourth edition were chosen to help accomplish several things: introduce students to fundamental concepts in political science and the study of American politics, such as collective-action problems, agenda-setting power, ideologies, and the median voter; provide specific insights into the workings of the major institutions and processes of American government; spur discussions on controversial topics, such as immigration, gay rights, campaign finance, and contemporary American foreign policy; and improve students' abilities to digest official government documents, such as Supreme Court cases.

The opening Fundamentals section introduces students to four crucial problems in politics:

1. *problem of maintaining individual liberty* under any form of government based on laws that constrain behavior;
2. *collective-action problems* among groups of people and how organizers and leaders of institutions can try to overcome such problems;
3. *common-resource problems*, which are variants of the standard collective-action problem but specifically refer to allocating scarce resources; and
4. *delegation (or principal–agent) problems*, which are ubiquitous in modern, democratic government, and require contract-like arrangements to solve.

The material in the Fundamentals section is a good foundation for students approaching the rest of the readings. With the above "problems" in mind, students will not only have a fresh perspective on classic selections, but will be able to analyze and make sense of more contemporary research. One can read Brutus's *Anti-Federalist* No. 1, for instance, with an eye toward common-resource problems. Brutus was concerned that an overpowering national government would oppress the states, and favored having a weak central government as it was under the Articles of Confederation. It is worth discussing the question: Was Brutus naïve about collective-action and common-resource problems inherent when the states compete for common resources? Did Brutus underestimate the potential role for centralized government to manage such problems? The selection from Robert Dahl offers criticisms of the solutions and compromises Madison and his fellow founders made when crafting the Constitution.

Many of the contemporary selections also have one or more of the "problems" from Chapter 1 as their backdrop. To take an example from Chapter 5 on Congress, the delegation problem is at the root of the arguments made by Cox and McCubbins on how (and why) partisan majorities grant agenda control to party leaders in Congress. And Wong et al's arguments in Chapter 10 focus on the ways Asian Americans have forged a collective identity across ethnicities to help solve internal collective-action problems. Students benefit greatly from seeing these theoretical threads in contemporary political science scholarship.

Quite a few of the readings provide grist for lively discussions on current events and policy controversies. Students will gain knowledge of legal arguments about gay marriage, health care reform, elections, education, and immigration, and they will confront arguments about the sustainability of recent trends in American foreign policy.

I use these readings when I teach. In preparing this fourth edition, I paid close attention to the suggestions from my students and other professors who assigned the previous edition. I hope you find these readings as useful as I do in understanding politics and, specifically, the American political system.

I owe special thanks to several people. For their wonderful feedback on previous editions, I thank:

Emily Acevedo, California State University, Los Angeles
E. Scott Adler, University of Colorado, Boulder
Tama Andrews, University of New Hampshire
John Aughenbaugh, Virginia Commonwealth University
Leslie Baker, Mississippi State University
Lauren Balasco, Pittsburg State University
Vilma Balmaceda, Nyack College
Paul Bellinger, Stephen F. Austin State University
Michael Berkman, Pennsylvania State University
Michael Berry, University of Colorado, Denver
Michael M. Binder, University of North Florida
Sarah Binder, George Washington University
Stephen Borrelli, University of Alabama
Matt Bosworth, Winona State University
Dan Cassino, Fairleigh Dickinson University
Devin Caughey, Massachusetts Institute of Technology
Helen Chang, Lehman College
Neil Chaturvedi, Seattle University
Jangsup Choi, Texas A&M University, Commerce

Mary Ann Clarke, Bryant University
Ann Cohen, CUNY, Hunter College
Martin Cohen, James Madison University
Jeff Colbert, Elon University
Richard S. Conley, University of Florida
Mark Croatti, American University
Paul R. DeHart, Texas State University
David Dulio, Oakland University
Justin Dyer, University of Missouri
Matthew Eshbaugh-Soha, University of North Texas
Andrew M. Essig, DeSales University
Emily Farris, Texas Christian University
Kathleen Ferraiolo, James Madison University
Emily R. Gill, Bradley University
Brad T. Gomez, Florida State University
Craig Goodman, Texas Tech University
Paul N. Goren, University of Minnesota
Lou Graziano, St. John's University
Andrew Green, Central College
Steven Greene, North Carolina State University
Richard Haesly, California State University, Long Beach
Thomas Halper, Baruch College
Danny Hayes, George Washington University
Audrey A. Haynes, University of Georgia
Diane J. Heith, St. John's University
Roberta Herzberg, Utah State University
Ronald J. Hrebenar, University of Utah
Ryan Hurl, University of Toronto Scarborough
Richard Jankowski, SUNY Fredonia
Dorothy James, Connecticut College
Marc James, Brock University
Kevin Jefferies, Alvin Community College
Jeff Jenkins, University of Virginia
Joel Johnson, Colorado State University, Pueblo
Timothy R. Johnson, University of Minnesota
Jennifer Jung-Kim, University of California, Los Angeles
David Lassen, University of Wisconsin, Madison
Christine Lipsmeyer, Texas A&M University
Alyx Mark, North Central College
Kenneth R. Mayer, University of Wisconsin, Madison
Corrine McConnaughy, Ohio State University
Ian McDonald, Duke University
Mark McKenzie, Texas Tech University
Bryan McQuide, Grand View University

Benjamin Melusky, Gettysburg College
Kristina Miler, University of Maryland
Fiona Miller, University of Toronto Mississauga
Nathan Mitchell, Prairie View A&M University
Ken Mulligan, Southern Illinois University
James Newman, Southeast Missouri State University
Sarah Niebler, Dickinson College
Timothy Nokken, Texas Tech University
Paul Nolette, Marquette University
Mikel Norris, Coastal Carolina University
Julie Pacheco, University of Iowa
Richard M. Pious, Barnard College
Taylor Price, University of Wisconsin, Madison
Nicholas Pyeatt, Pennsylvania State University, Altoona
Megan Remmel, Norwich University
Tim Reynolds, Alvin Community College
Kimberly Rice, Western Illinois University
Jason Roberts, University of North Carolina at Chapel Hill
Martin Saiz, California State University, Northridge
Dante Scala, University of New Hampshire
James Sheffield, University of Oklahoma
Sean M. Theriault, University of Texas at Austin
J. Alejandro Tirado, Texas Tech University
Terri Towner, Oakland University
Jessica Trounstine, University of California, Merced
Bob Turner, Skidmore College
Joseph Ura, Texas A&M University
Nicholas Valentino, University of Michigan
Justin Vaughn, Boise State University
Greg Vonnahme, University of Missouri, Kansas City
Charles Walcott, Virginia Tech
Harold M. Waller, McGill University
Kent Worcester, Marymount Manhattan College
Jeffrey S. Worsham, West Virginia University

Erin Ackerman and Ann Shin made possible the first edition, and Hannah Bozian helped with the second edition. Erica Mirabitur's dedicated work made the process smooth for the third edition, and she also helped with this latest version. Samantha Held was also instrumental in helping me pull together this fourth edition.

ABOUT THE EDITOR

KEN KOLLMAN is the Director of the Center for Political Studies, the Frederick G. L. Huetwell Professor, and Professor of Political Science and Research Professor in the Institute for Social Research at the University of Michigan. His research and teaching focus on political parties, elections, lobbying, and federal systems. He also regularly teaches the introductory American politics course at the University of Michigan. In addition to numerous articles, he has written *Perils of Centralization: Lessons from Church, State, and Corporation* (2013), *The Formation of National Party Systems: Federalism and Party Competition in Canada, Great Britain, India, and the United States* (with Pradeep Chhibber, 2004) and *Outside Lobbying: Public Opinion and Interest Group Strategies* (1998). Professor Kollman is also the author of an American government textbook published by W. W. Norton, *The American Political System*, now in its third edition.

READINGS IN
AMERICAN
POLITICS

Fourth Edition

1

FUNDAMENTALS

1.1

JOHN LOCKE

From *The Second Treatise of Government*

Locke's treatise forms part of the intellectual foundations of the American and French Revolutions, and of all modern democracies and democratic movements. He argues that people are born free and equal but that oppressive government tramples this "natural liberty." However, Locke explains, people can freely consent to having a government inhibit this liberty, and because they consent to being constrained, such a government can lead to "peace, safety, and public good."

OF THE BEGINNING OF POLITICAL SOCIETIES

95. Men being . . . by nature all free, equal, and independent, no one can be put out of this estate and subjected to the political power of another without his own consent. The only way whereby any one divests himself of his natural liberty and puts on the bonds of civil society is by agreeing with other men to join and unite into a community for their comfortable, safe, and peaceable living one amongst another, in a secure enjoyment of their properties and a greater security against any that are not of it. This any number of men may do, because it injures not the freedom of the rest; they are left as they were in the liberty of the state of nature. When any number of men have so consented to make one community or government, they are thereby presently incorporated and make one body politic wherein the majority have a right to act and conclude the rest.

From Thomas P. Peardon, ed., *The Second Treatise of Government* (New York: The Liberal Arts Press, 1952).

96. For when any number of men have, by the consent of every individual, made a community, they have thereby made that community one body, with a power to act as one body, which is only by the will and determination of the majority; for that which acts any community being only the consent of the individuals of it, and it being necessary to that which is one body to move one way, it is necessary the body should move that way whither the greater force carries it, which is the consent of the majority; or else it is impossible it should act or continue one body, one community, which the consent of every individual that united into it agreed that it should; and so every one is bound by that consent to be concluded by the majority. And therefore we see that in assemblies impowered to act by positive laws, where no number is set by that positive law which impowers them, the act of the majority passes for the act of the whole and, of course, determines, as having by the law of nature and reason the power of the whole.

97. And thus every man, by consenting with others to make one body politic under one government, puts himself under an obligation to every one of that society to submit to the determination of the majority and to be concluded by it; or else this original compact, whereby he with others incorporates into one society, would signify nothing, and be no compact, if he be left free and under no other ties than he was in before in the state of nature. For what appearance would there be of any compact? What new engagement if he were no further tied by any decrees of the society than he himself thought fit and did actually consent to? This would be still as great a liberty as he himself had before his compact, or any one else in the state of nature has who may submit himself and consent to any acts of it if he thinks fit.

98. For if the consent of the majority shall not in reason be received as the act of the whole and conclude every individual, nothing but the consent of every individual can make anything to be the act of the whole; but such a consent is next to impossible ever to be had if we consider the infirmities of health and avocations of business which in a number, though much less than that of a commonwealth, will necessarily keep many away from the public assembly. To which, if we add the variety of opinions and contrariety of interests which unavoidably happen in all collections of men, the coming into society upon such terms would be only like Cato's coming into the theatre only to go out again. Such a constitution as this would make the mighty leviathan of a shorter duration than the feeblest creatures, and not let it outlast the day it was born in; which cannot be supposed till we can think that rational creatures should desire and constitute societies only to be dissolved; for where the majority cannot conclude the rest, there they cannot act as one body, and consequently will be immediately dissolved again.

99. Whosoever, therefore, out of a state of nature unite into a community must be understood to give up all the power necessary to the ends for which they unite into society to the majority of the community, unless they expressly agreed in any number greater than the majority. And this is done by barely

agreeing to unite into one political society, which is all the compact that is, or needs be, between the individuals that enter into or make up a commonwealth. And thus that which begins and actually constitutes any political society is nothing but the consent of any number of freemen capable of a majority to unite and incorporate into such a society. And this is that, and that only, which did or could give beginning to any lawful government in the world.

■ ■ ■

OF THE ENDS OF POLITICAL SOCIETY AND GOVERNMENT

123. If man in the state of nature be so free, . . . if he be absolute lord of his own person and possessions, equal to the greatest, and subject to nobody, why will he part with his freedom, why will he give up his empire and subject himself to the dominion and control of any other power? To which it is obvious to answer that though in the state of nature he has such a right, yet the enjoyment of it is very uncertain and constantly exposed to the invasion of others; for all being kings as much as he, every man his equal, and the greater part no strict observers of equity and justice, the enjoyment of the property he has in this state is very unsafe, very unsecure. This makes him willing to quit a condition which, however free, is full of fears and continual dangers; and it is not without reason that he seeks out and is willing to join in society with others who are already united, or have a mind to unite, for the mutual preservation of their lives, liberties, and estates, which I call by the general name 'property.'

124. The great and chief end, therefore, of men's uniting into commonwealths and putting themselves under government is the preservation of their property. To which in the state of nature there are many things wanting:

First, there wants an established, settled, known law, received and allowed by common consent to be the standard of right and wrong and the common measure to decide all controversies between them; for though the law of nature be plain and intelligible to all rational creatures, yet men, being biased by their interest as well as ignorant for want of studying it, are not apt to allow of it as a law binding to them in the application of it to their particular cases.

125. Secondly, in the state of nature there wants a known and indifferent judge with authority to determine all differences according to the established law; for every one in that state being both judge and executioner of the law of nature, men being partial to themselves, passion and revenge is very apt to carry them too far and with too much heat in their own cases, as well as negligence and unconcernedness to make them too remiss in other men's.

126. Thirdly, in the state of nature there often wants power to back and support the sentence when right, and to give it due execution. They who by any injustice offend will seldom fail, where they are able, by force, to make good

their injustice; such resistance many times makes the punishment dangerous and frequently destructive to those who attempt it.

127. Thus mankind, notwithstanding all the privileges of the state of nature, being but in an ill condition while they remain in it, are quickly driven into society. Hence it comes to pass that we seldom find any number of men live any time together in this state. The inconveniences that they are therein exposed to by the irregular and uncertain exercise of the power every man has of punishing the transgressions of others make them take sanctuary under the established laws of government and therein seek the preservation of their property. It is this makes them so willingly give up every one his single power of punishing, to be exercised by such alone as shall be appointed to it amongst them; and by such rules as the community, or those authorized by them to that purpose, shall agree on. And in this we have the original right of both the legislative and executive power, as well as of the governments and societies themselves.

128. For in the state of nature, to omit the liberty he has of innocent delights, a man has two powers:

The first is to do whatsoever he thinks fit for the preservation of himself and others within the permission of the law of nature, by which law, common to them all, he and all the rest of mankind are one community, make up one society, distinct from all other creatures. And, were it not for the corruption and viciousness of degenerate men, there would be no need of any other, no necessity that men should separate from this great and natural community and by positive agreements combine into smaller and divided associations.

The other power a man has in the state of nature is the power to punish the crimes committed against that law. Both these he gives up when he joins in a private, if I may so call it, or particular politic society and incorporates into any commonwealth separate from the rest of mankind.

129. The first power, viz., of doing whatsoever he thought fit for the preservation of himself and the rest of mankind, he gives up to be regulated by laws made by the society, so far forth as the preservation of himself and the rest of that society shall require; which laws of the society in many things confine the liberty he had by the law of nature.

130. Secondly, the power of punishing he wholly gives up, and engages his natural force—which he might before employ in the execution of the law of nature by his own single authority, as he thought fit—to assist the executive power of the society, as the law thereof shall require; for being now in a new state, wherein he is to enjoy many conveniences from the labor, assistance, and society of others in the same community as well as protection from its whole strength, he is to part also with as much of his natural liberty, in providing for himself, as the good, prosperity, and safety of the society shall require, which is not only necessary, but just, since the other members of the society do the like.

131. But though men when they enter into society give up the equality, liberty, and executive power they had in the state of nature into the hands of the

society, to be so far disposed of by the legislative as the good of the society shall require, yet it being only with an intention in every one the better to preserve himself, his liberty and property—for no rational creature can be supposed to change his condition with an intention to be worse—the power of the society, or legislative constituted by them, can never be supposed to extend farther than the common good, but is obliged to secure every one's property by providing against those three defects above-mentioned that made the state of nature so unsafe and uneasy. And so whoever has the legislative or supreme power of any commonwealth is bound to govern by established standing laws, promulgated and known to the people, and not by extemporary decrees; by indifferent and upright judges who are to decide controversies by those laws; and to employ the force of the community at home only in the execution of such laws, or abroad to prevent or redress foreign injuries, and secure the community from inroads and invasion. And all this to be directed to no other end but the peace, safety, and public good of the people.

1.2

From *The Logic of Collective Action: Public Goods and the Theory of Groups*

Olson introduces us to the concept of the collective action problem. This "problem" arises when individuals have incentives to free-ride off the contributions of others, reaping the benefits of some action without paying any of the costs. In describing the collective action problem and how groups or organizations can overcome it, Olson strongly challenges the widely held notion that having common interests is a sufficient condition for a political group to form.

I. A THEORY OF GROUPS AND ORGANIZATIONS

A. The Purpose of Organization

Since most (though by no means all) of the action taken by or on behalf of groups of individuals is taken through organizations, it will be helpful to consider organizations in a general or theoretical way.[1] The logical place to begin any systematic study of organizations is with their purpose. But there are all types and shapes and sizes of organizations, even of economic organizations, and there is then some question whether there is any single purpose that would be characteristic of organizations generally. One purpose that is nonetheless characteristic of most organizations, and surely of practically all organizations with an important economic aspect, is the furtherance of the interests of their members. That would seem obvious, at least from the economist's perspective. To be sure, some organizations may out of ignorance fail to further their members' interests, and others may be enticed into serving only the ends of the leadership.[2] But organizations often perish if they do nothing to further the interests of their members, and this factor must severely limit the number of organizations that fail to serve their members.

The idea that organizations or associations exist to further the interests of their members is hardly novel, nor peculiar to economics; it goes back at least to Aristotle, who wrote, "Men journey together with a view to particular advantage, and by way of providing some particular thing needed for the purposes of life, and similarly the political association seems to have come

From Mancur Olson Jr., *The Logic of Collective Action: Public Goods and the Theory of Groups* (Cambridge, MA: Harvard University Press, 1971).

together originally, and to continue in existence, for the sake of the *general advantages* it brings."[3] More recently Professor Leon Festinger, a social psychologist, pointed out that "the attraction of group membership is not so much in sheer belonging, but rather in attaining something by means of this membership."[4] The late Harold Laski, a political scientist, took it for granted that "associations exist to fulfill purposes which a group of men have in common."[5]

The kinds of organizations that are the focus of this study are *expected* to further the interests of their members.[6] Labor unions are expected to strive for higher wages and better working conditions for their members; farm organizations are expected to strive for favorable legislation for their members; cartels are expected to strive for higher prices for participating firms; the corporation is expected to further the interests of its stockholders;[7] and the state is expected to further the common interests of its citizens (though in this nationalistic age the state often has interests and ambitions apart from those of its citizens).

Notice that the interests that all of these diverse types of organizations are expected to further are for the most part *common interests:* the union members' common interest in higher wages, the farmers' common interest in favorable legislation, the cartel members' common interest in higher prices, the stockholders' common interest in higher dividends and stock prices, the citizens' common interest in good government. It is not an accident that the diverse types of organizations listed are all supposed to work primarily for the *common* interests of their members. Purely personal or individual interests can be advanced, and usually advanced most efficiently, by individual, unorganized action. There is obviously no purpose in having an organization when individual, unorganized action can serve the interests of the individual as well as or better than an organization; there would, for example, be no point in forming an organization simply to play solitaire. But when a number of individuals have a common or collective interest—when they share a single purpose or objective—individual, unorganized action (as we shall soon see) will either not be able to advance that common interest at all, or will not be able to advance that interest adequately. Organizations can therefore perform a function when there are common or group interests, and though organizations often also serve purely personal, individual interests, their characteristic and primary function is to advance the common interests of groups of individuals.

The assumption that organizations typically exist to further the common interests of groups of people is implicit in most of the literature about organizations, and two of the writers already cited make this assumption explicit: Harold Laski emphasized that organizations exist to achieve purposes or interests which "a group of men have in common," and Aristotle apparently had a similar notion in mind when he argued that political associations are created and maintained because of the "general advantages" they bring. R. M. MacIver also made this point explicitly when he said that "every organization presupposes an interest which its members all share."[8]

Even when unorganized groups are discussed, at least in treatments of "pressure groups" and "group theory," the word "group" is used in such a way that it means "a number of individuals with a common interest." It would of course be reasonable to label even a number of people selected at random (and thus without any common interest or unifying characteristic) as a "group"; but most discussions of group behavior seem to deal mainly with groups that do have common interests. As Arthur Bentley, the founder of the "group theory" of modern political science, put it, "there is no group without its interest."[9] The social psychologist Raymond Cattell was equally explicit, and stated that "every group has its interest."[10] This is also the way the word "group" will be used here.

Just as those who belong to an organization or a group can be presumed to have a common interest,[11] so they obviously also have purely individual interests, different from those of the others in the organization or group. All of the members of a labor union, for example, have a common interest in higher wages, but at the same time each worker has a unique interest in his personal income, which depends not only on the rate of wages but also on the length of time that he works.

B. Public Goods and Large Groups

The combination of individual interests and common interests in an organization suggests an analogy with a competitive market. The firms in a perfectly competitive industry, for example, have a common interest in a higher price for the industry's product. Since a uniform price must prevail in such a market, a firm cannot expect a higher price for itself unless all of the other firms in the industry also have this higher price. But a firm in a competitive market also has an interest in selling as much as it can, until the cost of producing another unit exceeds the price of that unit. In this there is no common interest; each firm's interest is directly opposed to that of every other firm, for the more other firms sell, the lower the price and income for any given firm. In short, while all firms have a common interest in a higher price, they have antagonistic interests where output is concerned. This can be illustrated with a simple supply-and-demand model. For the sake of a simple argument, assume that a perfectly competitive industry is momentarily in a disequilibrium position, with price exceeding marginal cost for all firms at their present output. Suppose, too, that all of the adjustments will be made by the firms already in the industry rather than by new entrants, and that the industry is on an inelastic portion of its demand curve. Since price exceeds marginal cost for all firms, output will increase. But as all firms increase production, the price falls; indeed, since the industry demand curve is by assumption inelastic, the total revenue of the industry will decline. Apparently each firm finds that with price exceeding marginal cost, it pays to increase its output, but the result is that each firm gets a smaller profit. Some economists in an earlier day may have questioned this result,[12] but the fact that profit-maximizing firms in a perfectly competitive industry can act contrary to their interests as a group is now widely understood and accepted.[13] A group of profit-maximizing firms can act to reduce their aggregate profits because in perfect competition each firm is, by definition, so small that it can ignore the effect of its output on price. Each firm finds it to its advantage to increase output to the point where marginal cost equals price and to ignore the effects of its extra output on the position of the industry. It is true that the net result is that all firms are worse off, but this does not mean that every firm has not maximized its profits. If a firm, foreseeing the fall in price resulting from the increase in industry output, were to restrict its own output, it would lose more than ever, for its price would fall quite as much in any case and it would have a smaller output as well. A firm in a perfectly competitive market gets only a small part of the benefit (of a small share of the industry's extra revenue) resulting from a reduction in that firm's output.

For these reasons it is now generally understood that if the firms in an industry are maximizing profits, the profits for the industry as a whole will be less than they might otherwise be.[14] And almost everyone would agree that this theoretical conclusion fits the facts for markets characterized by pure competition. The important point is that this is true because, though all the firms have a common interest in a higher price for the industry's product, it is in the interest of each firm that the other firms pay the cost—in terms of the necessary reduction in output—needed to obtain a higher price.

About the only thing that keeps prices from falling in accordance with the process just described in perfectly competitive markets is outside intervention. Government price supports, tariffs, cartel agreements, and the like may keep the firms in a competitive market from acting contrary to their interests. Such aid or intervention is quite common. It is then important to ask how it comes about. How does a competitive industry obtain government assistance in maintaining the price of its product?

Consider a hypothetical, competitive industry, and suppose that most of the producers in that industry desire a tariff, a price-support program, or some other government intervention to increase the price for their product. To obtain any such assistance from the government the producers in this industry will presumably have to organize a lobbying organization; they will have to become an active pressure group.[15] This lobbying organization may have to conduct a considerable campaign. If significant resistance is encountered, a great amount of money will be required.[16] Public relations experts will be needed to influence the newspapers, and some advertising may be necessary. Professional organizers will probably be needed to organize "spontaneous grass roots" meetings among the distressed producers in the industry, and to get those in the industry to write letters to their congressmen.[17] The campaign for the government assistance will take the time of some of the producers in the industry, as well as their money.

There is a striking parallel between the problem the perfectly competitive industry faces as it strives to obtain government assistance, and the problem it faces in the marketplace when the firms increase output and bring about a fall in price. *Just as it was not rational for a particular producer to restrict his output in order that there might be a higher price for the product of his industry, so it would not be rational for him to sacrifice his time and money to support a lobbying organization to obtain government assistance for the industry. In neither case would it be in the interest of the individual producer to assume any of the costs himself. A lobbying organization, or indeed a labor union or any other organization, working in the interest of a large group of firms or workers in some industry, would get no assistance from the rational, self-interested individuals in that industry.* This would be true even if everyone in the industry were absolutely convinced that the proposed program was in their interest (though in fact some might think otherwise and make the organization's task yet more difficult).[18]

Although the lobbying organization is only one example of the logical analogy between the organization and the market, it is of some practical importance. There are many powerful and well-financed lobbies with mass support in existence now, but these lobbying organizations do not get that support because of their legislative achievements. The most powerful lobbying organizations now obtain their funds and their following for other reasons.

Some critics may argue that the rational person will indeed support a large organization, like a lobbying organization, that works in his interest, because he knows that if he does not, others will not do so either, and then the organization will fail, and he will be without the benefit that the organization could have provided. This argument shows the need for the analogy with the perfectly competitive market. For it would be quite as reasonable to argue that prices will never fall below the levels a monopoly would have charged in a perfectly competitive market, because if one firm increased its output, other firms would also, and the price would fall; but each firm could foresee this, so it would not start a chain of price-destroying increases in output. In fact, it does not work out this way in a competitive market; nor in a large organization. When the number of firms involved is large, no one will notice the effect on price if one firm increases its output, and so no one will change his plans because of it. Similarly, in a large organization, the loss of one dues payer will not noticeably increase the burden for any other one dues payer, and so a rational person would not believe that if he were to withdraw from an organization he would drive others to do so.

The foregoing argument must at the least have some relevance to economic organizations that are mainly means through which individuals attempt to obtain the same things they obtain through their activities in the market. Labor unions, for example, are organizations through which workers strive to get the same things they get with their individual efforts in the market—higher wages, better working conditions, and the like. It would be strange indeed if the workers did not confront some of the same problems in the union that they meet in the market, since their efforts in both places have some of the same purposes.

However similar the purposes may be, critics may object that attitudes in organizations are not at all like those in markets. In organizations, an emotional or ideological element is often also involved. Does this make the argument offered here practically irrelevant?

A most important type of organization—the national state—will serve to test this objection. Patriotism is probably the strongest non-economic motive for organizational allegiance in modern times. This age is sometimes called the age of nationalism. Many nations draw additional strength and unity from some powerful ideology, such as democracy or communism, as well as from a common religion, language, or cultural inheritance. The state not only has many such powerful sources of support; it also is very important economically. Almost any government is economically beneficial to its citizens, in that the law and order it provides is a prerequisite of all civilized economic activity. But despite the force of patriotism, the appeal of the national ideology, the bond of a common culture, and the indispensability of the system of law and order, no major state in modern history has been able to support itself through voluntary dues or contributions. Philanthropic contributions are not even a significant source of revenue for most countries. Taxes, *compulsory* payments by definition, are needed. Indeed, as the old saying indicates, their necessity is as certain as death itself.

If the state, with all of the emotional resources at its command, cannot finance its most basic and vital activities without resort to compulsion, it would seem that large private organizations might also have difficulty in getting the individuals in the groups whose interests they attempt to advance to make the necessary contributions voluntarily.[19]

The reason the state cannot survive on voluntary dues or payments, but must rely on taxation, is that the most fundamental services a nation-state provides are, in one important respect, like the higher price in a competitive market: they must be available to everyone if they are available to anyone. The basic and most elementary goods or services provided by government, like defense and police protection, and the system of law and order generally, are such that they go to everyone or practically everyone in the nation. It would obviously not be feasible, if indeed it were possible, to deny the protection provided by the military services, the police, and the courts to those who did not voluntarily pay their share of the costs of government, and taxation is accordingly necessary. The common or collective benefits provided by governments are usually called "public goods" by economists, and the concept of public goods is one of the oldest and most important ideas in the study of public finance. A common, collective, or public good is here defined as any good such that, if any person X_i in a group $X_1, \ldots, X_i, \ldots, X_n$ consumes it, it cannot feasibly be withheld from the others in that group.[20] In other words, those who do not purchase or pay for any of the public or collective good cannot be excluded or kept from sharing in the consumption of the good, as they can where noncollective goods are concerned.

Students of public finance have, however, neglected the fact that *the achievement of any common goal or the satisfaction of any common interest means that a public or collective good has been provided for that group.*[21] The very fact that a goal or purpose is *common* to a group means that no one in the group is excluded from the benefit or satisfaction brought about by its achievement. As the opening paragraphs of this chapter indicated, almost all groups and organizations have the purpose of serving the common interests of their members. As R. M. MacIver puts it, "Persons . . . have common interests in the degree to which they participate in a cause . . . which indivisibly embraces them all."[22] It is of the essence of an organization that it provides an inseparable, generalized benefit. It follows that the provision of public or collective goods is the fundamental function of organizations generally. A state is first of all an organization that provides public goods for its members, the citizens; and other types of organizations similarly provide collective goods for their members.

And just as a state cannot support itself by voluntary contributions, or by selling its basic services on the market, neither can other large organizations support themselves without providing some sanction, or some attraction distinct from the public good itself, that will lead individuals to help bear the burdens of maintaining the organization. The individual member of the typical large organization is in a position analogous to that of the firm in a perfectly competitive market, or the taxpayer in the state: his own efforts will not have a noticeable effect on the situation of his organization, and he can enjoy any improvements brought about by others whether or not he has worked in support of his organization.

There is no suggestion here that states or other organizations provide *only* public or collective goods. Governments often provide noncollective goods like electric power, for example, and they usually sell such goods on the market much as private firms would do. Moreover, as later parts of this study will argue, large organizations that are not able to make membership compulsory *must also* provide some noncollective goods in order to give potential members an incentive to join. Still, collective goods are the characteristic organizational goods, for ordinary noncollective goods can always be provided by individual action, and only where common purposes of collective goods are concerned is organization or group action ever indispensable.[23]

■   ■   ■

Nontechnical Summary of Section D

The technical part of this section has shown that certain small groups can provide themselves with collective goods without relying on coercion or any positive inducements apart from the collective good itself.[24] This is because in some small groups each of the members, or at least one of them, will find that his personal gain from having the collective good exceeds the total cost of providing some amount of that collective good; there are members who would be better off if the collective good were provided, even if they had to pay the entire cost of providing it themselves, than they would be if it were not provided. In such situations there is a presumption that the collective good will be provided. Such a situation will exist only when the benefit to the group from having the collective good exceeds the total cost by more than it exceeds the gain to one or more individuals in the group. Thus, in a very small group, where each member gets a substantial proportion of the total gain simply because there are few others in the group, a collective good can often be provided by the voluntary, self-interested action of the members of the group. In smaller groups marked by considerable degrees of inequality—that is, in groups of members of unequal "size" or extent of interest in the collective good—there is the greatest likelihood that a collective good will be provided; for the greater the interest in the collective good of any single member, the greater the likelihood that that member will get such a significant proportion of the total benefit from the collective good that he will gain from seeing that the good is provided, even if he has to pay all of the cost himself.

Even in the smallest groups, however, the collective good will not ordinarily be provided on an optimal scale. That is to say, the members of the group will not provide as much of the good as it would be in their common interest to provide. Only certain special institutional arrangements will give the individual members an incentive to purchase the amounts of the collective good that would add up to the amount that would be in the best interest of the group as a whole. This tendency toward suboptimality is due to the fact that a collective good is, by definition, such that other individuals in the group cannot be kept from consuming it once any individual in the group has provided it for himself. Since an individual member thus gets only part of the benefit of any expenditure he makes to obtain more of the collective good, he will discontinue his purchase of the collective good before the optimal amount for the group as a whole has been obtained. In addition, the amounts of the collective good that a member of the group receives free from other members will further reduce his incentive to provide more of that good at his own expense. Accordingly, *the larger the group, the farther it will fall short of providing an optimal amount of a collective good.*

This suboptimality or inefficiency will be somewhat less serious in groups composed of members of greatly different size or interest in the collective good. In such unequal groups, on the other hand, there is a tendency toward an arbitrary sharing of the burden of providing the collective good. The largest member, the member who would on his own provide the largest amount of the collective good, bears a disproportionate share of the burden of providing the collective good. The smaller member by definition gets a smaller fraction of the benefit of any amount of the collective good he provides than a larger member, and therefore has less incentive to provide additional amounts of the collective good. Once a smaller member has the amount of the collective good he gets free from the largest member, he has more than he would have purchased for himself, and has no incentive to obtain any of the collective good at his own expense. In small groups with common interests there is accordingly *a surprising tendency for the "exploitation" of the great by the small.*

The argument that small groups providing themselves with collective goods tend to provide suboptimal quantities of these goods, and that the burdens of providing them are borne in an arbitrary and disproportionate way, does not hold in all logically possible situations. Certain institutional or procedural arrangements can lead to different outcomes. The subject cannot be analyzed adequately in any brief discussion. For this reason, and because the main focus of this reading is on large groups, many of the complexities of small-group behavior have been neglected in this study. An argument of the kind just outlined could, however, fit some important practical situations rather well, and may serve the purpose of suggesting that a more detailed analysis of the kind outlined above could help to explain the apparent tendency for large countries to bear disproportionate shares of the burdens of multinational organizations, like the United Nations and NATO, and could help to explain some of the popularity of neutralism among smaller countries. Such an analysis would also tend to explain the continual complaints that international organizations and alliances are not given adequate (optimal) amounts of resources.[25] It would also suggest that neighboring local governments in metropolitan areas that provide collective goods (like commuter roads and education) that benefit individuals in two or more local government jurisdictions would tend to provide inadequate amounts of these services, and that the largest local government (e.g., the one representing the central city) would bear disproportionate shares of the burdens of providing them.[26] An analysis of the foregoing type might, finally, provide some additional insight into the phenomenon of price leadership, and particularly the possible disadvantages involved in being the largest firm in an industry.

The most important single point about small groups in the present context, however, is that they may very well be able to provide themselves with a collective good simply because of the attraction of the collective good to the individual members. In this, small groups differ from larger ones. The larger a group is, the farther it will fall short of obtaining an optimal supply of any collective good, and the less likely that it will act to obtain even a minimal amount of such a good. In short, the larger the group, the less it will further its common interests.

■　　■　　■

F. A Taxonomy of Groups

To be sure, there can also be many instances in inclusive or non-market groups in which individual members do take into account the reactions of other members to their actions when they decide what action to take—that is, instances in which there is the strategic interaction among members characteristic of oligopolistic industries in which mutual dependence is recognized. In groups of one size range at least, such strategic interaction must be relatively important. That is the size range where the group is not so small that one individual would find it profitable to purchase some of the collective good himself, but where the number in the group is nonetheless sufficiently small that each member's attempts or lack of attempts to obtain the collective good would bring about noticeable differences in the welfare of some, or all, of the others in the group. This can best be understood by assuming for a moment that an inclusive collective good is already being provided in such a group through a formal organization, and then asking what would happen if one member of the group were to cease paying his share of the cost of the good. If, in a reasonably small organization, a particular person stops paying for the collective good he enjoys, the costs will rise noticeably for each of the others in the group; accordingly, they may then refuse to continue making their contributions, and the collective good may no longer be provided. However, the first person could realize that this might be the result of his refusal to pay anything for the collective good, and that he would be worse off when the collective good is not provided than when it was provided and he met part of the cost. Accordingly he might continue making a contribution toward the purchase of the collective good. He might; or he might not. As in oligopoly in a market situation, the result is indeterminate. The rational member of such a group faces a strategic problem and while the Theory of Games and other types of analyses might prove very helpful, there seems to be no way at present of getting a general, valid, and determinate solution at the level of abstraction of this chapter.[27]

What is the range of this indeterminateness? In a small group in which a member gets such a large fraction of the total benefit that he would be better off if he paid the entire cost himself, rather than go without the good, there is some presumption that the collective good will be provided. In a group in which no one member got such a large benefit from the collective good that he had an interest in providing it even if he had to pay all of the cost, but in which the individual was still so important in terms of the whole group that his contribution or lack of contribution to the group objective had a noticeable effect on the costs or benefits of others in the group, the result is indeterminate.[28] By contrast, in a large group in which no single individual's contribution makes a perceptible difference to the group as a whole, or the burden or benefit of any single member of the group, it is certain that a collective good will *not* be provided unless there is coercion or some outside inducements that will lead the members of the large group to act in their common interest.[29]

The last distinction, between the group so large it definitely cannot provide itself with a collective good, and the oligopoly-sized group which may provide itself with a collective good, is particularly important. It depends upon whether any two or more members of the group have a perceptible interdependence, that is, on whether the contribution or lack of contribution of any one individual in the group will have a perceptible effect on the burden or benefit of any other individual or individuals in the group. Whether a group will have the possibility of providing itself with a collective good without coercion or outside inducements therefore depends to a striking degree upon the number of individuals in the group, since the larger the group, the less the likelihood that the contribution of any one will be perceptible. It is not, however, strictly accurate to say that it depends solely on the number of individuals in the group. The relation between the size of the group and the significance of an individual member cannot be defined quite that simply. A group which has members with highly unequal degrees of interest in a collective good, and which wants a collective good that is (at some level of provision) extremely valuable in relation to its cost, will be more apt to provide itself with a collective good than other groups with the same number of members. The same situation prevails in the study of market structure, where again the number of firms an industry can have and still remain oligopolistic (and have the possibility of supracompetitive returns) varies somewhat from case to case. The standard for determining whether a group will have the capacity to act, without coercion or outside inducements, in its group interest is (as it should be) the same for market and non-market groups: it depends on whether the individual actions of any one or more members in a group are noticeable to any other individuals in the group.[30] This is most obviously, but not exclusively, a function of the number in the group.

It is now possible to specify when either informal coordination or formal organization will be necessary to obtain a collective good. The smallest type of group—the group in which one or more members get such a large fraction of the total benefit that they find it worthwhile to see that the collective good is provided, even if they have to pay the entire cost—may get along without any group agreement or organization. A group agreement might be set up to spread the costs more widely or to step up the level of provision of the collective good. But since there is an incentive for unilateral and individual action to obtain the collective good, neither a formal organization nor even an informal group agreement is indispensable to obtain a collective good. In any group larger than this, on the other hand, no collective good can be obtained without some group agreement, coordination, or organization. In the intermediate or oligopoly-sized group, where two or more members must act simultaneously before a collective good can be obtained, there must be at least tacit coordination or organization. Moreover, the larger a group is, the more agreement and organization it will need. The larger the group, the greater the number that will usually have to be included in the group agreement or organization. It may not be necessary that the entire group be organized, since some subset of the whole group may be able to provide the collective good. But to establish a group agreement or organization will nonetheless always tend to be more difficult the larger the size of the group, for the larger the group the more difficult it will be to locate and organize even a subset of the group, and those in the subset will have an incentive to continue bargaining with the others in the group until the burden is widely shared, thereby adding to the expense of bargaining. In short, costs of organization are an increasing function of the number of individuals in the group. (Though the more members in the group the greater the total costs of organization, the costs of organization per person need not rise, for there are surely economies of scale in organization.) In certain cases a group will already be organized for some other purpose, and then these costs of organization are already being met. In such a case a group's capacity to provide itself with a collective good will be explained in part by whatever it was that originally enabled it to organize and maintain itself. This brings attention back again to the costs of organization and shows that these costs cannot be left out of the model, except for the smallest type of group in which unilateral action can provide a collective good. The costs of organization must be clearly distinguished from the type of cost that has previously been considered. The cost functions considered before involved only the direct resource costs of obtaining various levels of provision of a collective good. When there is no pre-existing organization of a group, and when the direct resource costs of a collective good it wants are more than any single individual could profitably bear, additional costs must be incurred to obtain an agreement about how the burden will be shared and to coordinate or organize the effort to obtain the collective good. These are the costs of communication among group members, the costs of any bargaining among them, and the costs of creating, staffing, and maintaining any formal group organization.

A group cannot get infinitesimally small quantities of a formal organization, or even of an informal group agreement; a group with a given number of members must have a certain minimal amount of organization or agreement if it is to have any at all. Thus there are significant initial or minimal costs of organization for each group. Any group that must organize to obtain a collective good, then, will find that it has a certain minimum organization cost that must be met, however little of the collective good it obtains. The greater the number in the group, the greater these minimal costs will be. When this minimal organizational cost is added to the other initial or minimal costs of a collective good, which arise from its previously mentioned technical characteristics, it is evident that the cost of the first unit of a collective good will be quite high in relation to the cost of some subsequent units. However immense the benefits of a collective good, the higher the absolute total costs of getting any amount of that good, the less likely it is that even a minimal amount of that good could be obtained without coercion or separate, outside incentives.

This means that there are now three separate but cumulative factors that keep larger groups from furthering their own interest. First, the larger the group, the smaller the fraction of the total group benefit any person acting in the group interest receives, and the less adequate the reward for any group-oriented action, and the farther the group falls short of getting an optimal supply of the collective good, even if it should get some. Second, since the larger the group, the smaller the share of the total benefit going to any individual, or to any (absolutely) small subset of members of the group, the less the likelihood that any small subset of the group, much less any single individual, will gain enough from getting the collective good to bear the burden of providing even a small amount of it; in other words, the larger the group the smaller the likelihood of oligopolistic interaction that might help obtain the good. Third, the larger the number of members in the group the greater the organization costs, and thus the higher the hurdle that must be jumped before any of the collective good at all can be obtained. For these reasons, the larger the group the farther it will fall short of providing an optimal supply of a collective good, and very large groups normally will not, in the absence of coercion or separate, outside incentives, provide themselves with even minimal amounts of a collective good.[31]

NOTES

1. Economists have for the most part neglected to develop theories of organizations, but there are a few works from an economic point of view on the subject. See, for example, three papers by Jacob Marschak, "Elements for a Theory of Teams," *Management Science*, I (January 1955), 127–137, "Towards an Economic Theory of Organization and Information," in *Decision Processes*, ed. R. M. Thrall, C. H. Combs, and R. L. Davis (New York: John Wiley, 1954), pp. 187–220, and "Efficient and Viable Organization Forms," in *Modern Organization Theory*, ed. Mason Haire (New York: John Wiley, 1959), pp. 307–320; two papers by R. Radner, "Application of Linear Programming to Team Decision Problems," *Management Science*, V (January 1959), 143–150, and "Team Decision Problems," *Annals of Mathematical Statistics*, XXXIII (September 1962), 857–881; C. B. McGuire, "Some Team Models of a Sales Organization," *Management Science*, VII (January 1961), 101–130; Oskar Morgenstern, *Prolegomena to a Theory of Organization* (Santa Monica, Calif.: RAND Research Memorandum 734, 1951); James G. March and Herbert A. Simon, *Organizations* (New York: John Wiley, 1958); Kenneth Boulding, *The Organizational Revolution* (New York: Harper, 1953).

2. Max Weber called attention to the case where an organization continues to exist for some time after it has become meaningless because some official is making a living out of it. See his *Theory of Social and Economic Organization*, trans. Talcott Parsons and A. M. Henderson (New York: Oxford University Press, 1947), p. 318.

3. Aristotle, *Ethics* viii.9.1160a.

4. Leon Festinger, "Group Attraction and Membership," in *Group Dynamics*, ed. Dorwin Cartwright and Alvin Zander (Evanston, Ill.: Row, Peterson, 1953), p. 93.

5. *A Grammar of Politics*, 4th ed. (London: George Allen & Unwin, 1939), p. 67.

6. Philanthropic and religious organizations are not necessarily expected to serve only the interests of their members; such organizations have other purposes that are considered more important, however much their members "need" to belong, or are improved or helped by belonging. But the complexity of such organizations need not be debated at length here, because this study will focus on organizations with a significant economic aspect. The emphasis here will have something in common with what Max Weber called the "associative group"; he called a group associative if "the orientation of social action with it rests on a rationally motivated agreement." Weber contrasted his "associative group" with the "communal group" which was centered on personal affection, erotic relationships, etc., like the family. (See Weber, pp. 136–139, and Grace Coyle, *Social Process in Organized Groups*, New York: Richard Smith, Inc., 1930, pp. 7–9.) The logic of the theory developed here can be extended to cover communal, religious, and

philanthropic organizations, but the theory is not particularly useful in studying such groups.

7. That is, its members. This study does not follow the terminological usage of those organization theorists who describe employees as "members" of the organization for which they work. Here it is more convenient to follow the language of everyday usage instead, and to distinguish the members of, say, a union from the employees of that union. Similarly, the members of the union will be considered employees of the corporation for which they work, whereas the members of the corporation are the common stockholders.

8. R. M. MacIver, "Interests," *Encyclopaedia of the Social Sciences*, VII (New York: Macmillan, 1932), p. 147.

9. Arthur Bentley, *The Process of Government* (Evanston, Ill.: Principia Press, 1949), p. 211. David B. Truman takes a similar approach; see his *The Governmental Process* (New York: Alfred A. Knopf, 1958), pp. 33–35. See also Sidney Verba, *Small Groups and Political Behavior* (Princeton, N.J.: Princeton University Press, 1961), pp. 12–13.

10. Raymond Cattell, "Concepts and Methods in the Measurement of Group Syntality," in *Small Groups*, ed. A. Paul Hare, Edgard F. Borgatta, and Robert F. Bales (New York: Alfred A. Knopf, 1955), p. 115.

11. Any organization or group will of course usually be divided into subgroups or factions that are opposed to one another. This fact does not weaken the assumption made here that organizations exist to serve the common interests of members, for the assumption does not imply that intragroup conflict is neglected. The opposing groups within an organization ordinarily have some interest in common (if not, why would they maintain the organization?), and the members of any subgroup or faction also have a separate common interest of their own. They will indeed often have a common purpose in defeating some other subgroup or faction. The approach used here does not neglect the conflict within groups and organizations, then, because it considers each organization as a unit only to the extent that it does in fact attempt to serve a common interest, and considers the various subgroups as the relevant units with common interests to analyze the factional strife.

12. See J. M. Clark, *The Economics of Overhead Costs* (Chicago: University of Chicago Press, 1923), p. 417, and Frank H. Knight, *Risk, Uncertainty and Profit* (Boston: Houghton Mifflin, 1921), p. 193.

13. Edward H. Chamberlin, *Monopolistic Competition*, 6th ed. (Cambridge, Mass.: Harvard University Press, 1950), p. 4.

14. For a fuller discussion of this question see Mancur Olson, Jr., and David McFarland, "The Restoration of Pure Monopoly and the Concept of the Industry, *Quarterly Journal of Economics*, LXXVI (November 1962), 613–631.

15. Robert Michels contends in his classic study that "democracy is inconceivable without organization," and that "the principle of organization is an absolutely essential condition for the political struggle of the masses." See his *Political Parties*, trans. Eden and Cedar Paul (New York: Dover Publications, 1959), pp. 21–22. See also Robert A. Brady, *Business as a System of Power* (New York: Columbia University Press, 1943), p. 193.

16. Alexander Heard, *The Costs of Democracy* (Chapel Hill: University of North Carolina Press, 1960), especially note 1, pp. 95–96. For example, in 1947 the National Association of Manufacturers spent over $4.6 million, and over a somewhat longer period the American Medical Association spent as much on a campaign against compulsory health insurance.

17. "If the full truth were ever known . . . lobbying, in all its ramifications, would prove to be a billion dollar industry." U.S. Congress, House, Select Committee on Lobbying Activities, *Report*, 81st Cong., 2nd Sess. (1950), as quoted in the *Congressional Quarterly Almanac*, 81st Cong., 2nd Sess., VI, 764–765.

18. For a logically possible but practically meaningless exception to the conclusion of this paragraph.

19. Sociologists as well as economists have observed that ideological motives alone are not sufficient to bring forth the continuing effort of large masses of people. Max Weber provides a notable example:

"All economic activity in a market economy is undertaken and carried through by individuals for their own ideal or material interests. This is naturally just as true when economic activity is oriented to the patterns of order of corporate groups . . .

"Even if an economic system were organized on a socialistic basis, there would be no fundamental difference in this respect . . . The structure of interests and the relevant situation might change; there would be other means of pursuing interests, but this fundamental factor would remain just as relevant as before. It is of course true that economic action which is oriented on purely ideological grounds to the interest of others does exist. But it is even more certain that the mass of men do not act in this way, and it is an induction from experience that they cannot do so and never will . . .

"In a market economy the interest in the maximization of income is necessarily the driving force of all economic activity." (Weber, pp. 319–320.)

Talcott Parsons and Neil Smelser go even further in postulating that "performance" throughout society is proportional to the "rewards" and "sanctions" involved. See their *Economy and Society* (Glencoe, Ill.: Free Press, 1954), pp. 50–69.

20. This simple definition focuses upon two points that are important in the present context. The first point is that most collective goods can only be defined with respect to some specific group. One collective good goes to one group of people, another collective good to another group; one may benefit the whole world, another only two specific people. Moreover, some goods are collective goods to those in one group and at the same time private goods to those in another, because some individuals can be kept from consuming them and others can't. Take for example the parade that is a collective good to all those who live in tall buildings overlooking the parade route, but which appears to be a private good to those who can see it only by buying a ticket, for a seat in the stands along the way. The second point is that once the relevant group has been defined, the definition used here, like Musgrave's, distinguishes collective good in terms of infeasibility of excluding potential consumers of the good. This approach is used because collective goods produced by organizations of all kinds seem to be such that exclusion is normally not feasible. To be sure, for some collective goods it is physically possible to practice exclusion. But, as Head has shown, it is not necessary that exclusion be technically impossible; it is only necessary that it be infeasible or uneconomic. Head has also shown most clearly that nonexcludability is only one of two basic elements in the traditional understanding of public goods. The other, he points out, is "jointness of supply." A good has "jointness" if making it available to one individual means that it can be easily or freely supplied to others as well. The polar case of jointness would be Samuelson's pure public good, which is a good such that additional consumption of it by one individual does not diminish the amount available to others. By the definition used here, jointness is not a necessary attribute of a public good. At least one type of collective good considered here exhibits no jointness whatever, and few if any would have the degree of jointness needed to qualify as pure public goods. Nonetheless, most

of the collective goods to be studied here do display a large measure of jointness. On the definition and importance of public goods, see John G. Head, "Public Goods and Public Policy," *Public Finance,* vol. XVII, no. 3 (1962), 197–219; Richard Musgrave, *The Theory of Public Finance* (New York: McGraw-Hill, 1959); Paul A. Samuelson, "The Pure Theory of Public Expenditure," "Diagrammatic Exposition of a Theory of Public Expenditure," and "Aspects of Public Expenditure Theories," in *Review of Economics and Statistics,* XXXVI (November 1954), 387–390, XXXVII (November 1955), 350–356, and XL (November 1958), 332–338. For somewhat different opinions about the usefulness of the concept of public goods, see Julius Margolis, "A Comment on the Pure Theory of Public Expenditure," *Review of Economics and Statistics,* XXXVII (November 1955), 347–349, and Gerhard Colm, "Theory of Public Expenditures," *Annals of the American Academy of Political and Social Science,* CLXXXIII (January 1936), 1–11.

21. There is no necessity that a public good to one group in a society is necessarily in the interest of the society as a whole. Just as a tariff could be a public good to the industry that sought it, so the removal of the tariff could be a public good to those who consumed the industry's product. This is equally true when the public-good concept is applied only to governments; for a military expenditure, or a tariff, or an immigration restriction that is a public good to one country could be a "public bad" to another country, and harmful to world society as a whole.

22. R. M. MacIver in *Encyclopaedia of the Social Sciences,* VII, 147.

23. It does not, however, follow that organized or coordinated group action is *always* necessary to obtain a collective good.

24. I am indebted to Professor John Rawls of the Department of Philosophy at Harvard University for reminding me of the fact that the philosopher David Hume sensed that small groups could achieve common purposes but large groups could not. Hume's argument is however somewhat different from my own. In A *Treatise of Human Nature,* Everyman edition (London: J. M. Dent, 1952), II, 239, Hume wrote: "There is no quality in human nature which causes more fatal errors in our conduct, than that which leads us to prefer whatever is present to the distant and remote, and makes us desire objects more according to their situation than their intrinsic value. Two neighbours may agree to drain a meadow, which they possess in common: because it is easy for them to know each other's mind; and each must perceive, that the immediate consequence of his failing in his part, is the abandoning of the whole project. But it is very difficult, and indeed impossible, that a thousand persons should agree in any such action; it being difficult for them to concert so complicated a design, and still more difficult for them to execute it; while each seeks a pretext to free himself of the trouble and expense, and would lay the whole burden on others. Political society easily remedies both these inconveniences. Magistrates find an immediate interest in the interest of any considerable part of their subjects. They need consult nobody but themselves to form any scheme for promoting that interest. And as the failure of any one piece in the execution is connected, though not immediately, with the failure of the whole, they prevent that failure, because they find no interest in it, either immediate or remote. Thus, bridges are built, harbours opened, ramparts raised, canals formed, fleets equipped, and armies disciplined everywhere, by the care of government, which, though composed of men subject to all human infirmities, becomes, by one of the finest and most subtle inventions imaginable, a composition which is in some measure exempted from all these infirmities."

25. Some of the complexities of behavior in small groups are treated in Mancur Olson, Jr., and Richard Zeckhauser, "An Economic Theory of Alliances," *Review of Economics and Statistics,* XLVIII (August 1966), 266–279, and in "Collective Goods,

Comparative Advantage, and Alliance Efficiency," in *Issues of Defense Economics* (A Conference of the Universities-National Bureau-Committee for Economics Research), ed. Roland McKean (New York: National Bureau of Economic Research, 1967), pp. 25–48. [Footnote added in 1970.]

26. I am indebted to Alan Williams of York University in England, whose study of local government brought the importance of these sorts of spillovers among local govenments to my attention.

27. It is of incidental interest here to note also that oligopoly in the marketplace is in some respects akin to logrolling in the organization. If the "majority" that various interests in a legislature need is viewed as a collective good—something that a particular interest cannot obtain unless other interests also share it—then the parallel is quite close. The cost each special-interest legislator would like to avoid is the passage of the legislation desired by the other special-interest legislators, for if these interests gain from their legislation, often others, including his own constituents, may lose. But unless he is willing to vote for the legislation desired by the others, the particular special-interest legislator in question will not be able to get his own legislation passed. So his goal would be to work out a coalition with other special-interest legislators in which they would vote for exactly the legislation he wanted, and he in turn would give them as little in return as possible, by insisting that they moderate their legislative demands. But since every potential logroller has this same strategy, the result is indeterminate: the logs may be rolled or they may not. Every one of the interests will be better off if the logrolling is done than if it is not, but as individual interests strive for better legislative bargains the result of the competing strategies may be that no agreement is reached. This is quite similar to the situation oligopolistic groups are in, as they all desire a higher price and will all gain if they restrict output to get it, but they may not be able to agree on market shares.

28. The result is clearly indeterminate when F_4 is less than C/V_g at every point and it is also true that the group is not so large that no one member's actions have a noticeable effect.

29. One friendly critic has suggested that even a large pre-existing organization could continue providing a collective good simply by conducting a kind of plebiscite among its members, with the understanding that if there were not a unanimous or nearly unanimous pledge to contribute toward providing the collective good, this good would no longer be provided. This argument, if I understand it correctly, is mistaken. In such a situation, an individual would know that if others provided the collective good he would get the benefits whether he made any contribution or not. He would therefore have no incentive to make a pledge unless a completely unanimous set of pledges was required, or for some other reason his one pledge would decide whether or not the good would be provided. But if a pledge were required of every single member, or if for any other reason any one member could decide whether or not the group would get a collective good, this one member could deprive all of the others in the group of great gains. He would therefore be in a position to bargain for bribes. But since any other members of the group might gain just as much from the same holdout strategy, there is no likelihood that the collective good would be provided. See Buchanan and Tullock, pp. 96–116.

30. The noticeability of the actions of a single member of a group may be influenced by the arrangements the group itself sets up. A previously organized group, for example, might ensure that the contributions or lack of contributions of any member of the group, and the effect of each such member's course on the burden and benefit for others, would be advertised, thus ensuring that the group effort would not collapse from

imperfect knowledge. I therefore define "noticeability" in terms of the degree of knowledge, and the institutional arrangements, that actually exist in any given group, insetad of assuming a "natural noticeability" unaffected by any group advertising or other arrangements. This point, along with many other valuable comments, has been brought to my attention by Professor Jerome Rothenberg, who does, however, make much more of a group's assumed capacity to create "artificial noticeability" than I would want to do. I know of no practical example of a group or organization that has done much of anything, apart from improve information, to enhance the noticeability of an individual's actions in striving for a collective good.

31. There is one logically conceivable, but surely empirically trivial, case in which a large group could be provided with a very small amount of a collective good without coercion or outside incentives. If some very small group enjoyed a collective good so inexpensive that any one of the members would benefit by making sure that it was provided, even if he had to pay all of the cost, and if millions of people then entered the group, with the cost of the good nonetheless remaining constant, the large group could be provided with a little of this collective good. This is because by hypothesis in this example the costs have remained unchanged, so that one person still has an incentive to see that the good is provided. Even in such a case as this, however, it would still not be quite right to say that the large group was acting in its group interest, since the output of the collective good would be incredibly suboptimal. The optimal level of provision of the public good would increase each time an individual entered the group, since the unit cost of the collective good by hypothesis is constant, while the benefit from an additional unit of it increases with every entrant. Yet the original provider would have no incentive to provide more as the group expanded, unless he formed an organization to share costs with the others in this (now large) group. But that would entail incurring the considerable costs of a large organization, and there would be no way these costs could be covered through the voluntary and rational action of the individuals in the group. Thus, if the total benefit from a collective good exceeded its costs by the thousandfold or millionfold, it is logically possible that a large group could provide itself with some amount of that collective good, but the level of provision of the collective good in such a case would be only a minute fraction of the optimal level. It is not easy to think of practical examples of groups that would fit this description. . . . It would be easy to rule out even any such exceptional cases, however, simply by defining *all* groups that could provide themselves with some amount of a collective good as "small groups" (or by giving them other names), while putting all groups that could not provide themselves with a collective good in another class. But this easy route must be rejected, for that would make this part of the theory tautologous and thus incapable of refutation. Therefore the approach here has been to make the (surely reasonable) empirical hypothesis that the total costs of the collective goods wanted by large groups are large enough to exceed the value of the small fraction of the total benefit that an individual in a large group would get, so that he will not provide the good. There may be exceptions to this, as to any other empirical statement, and thus there may be instances in which large groups could provide themselves with (at most minute amounts of) collective goods through the voluntary and rational action of one of their members.

1.3

GARRETT HARDIN

"The Tragedy of the Commons"

In this powerful reading, Hardin builds on Olson's ideas to show the negative consequences that may ensue when people are not constrained in their acquisition of food, energy, land, water, minerals, and other natural resources. People pursuing their own interests can overdraw publicly owned resources, leading to a depletion of those resources. This argument is significant in the study of politics because many governmental institutions not only prevent the overdrawing of fixed resources, but also determine who has access to those resources.

> The population problem has no technical solution; it requires a fundamental extension in morality.

At the end of a thoughtful article on the future of nuclear war, Wiesner and York[1] concluded that: "Both sides in the arms race are . . . confronted by the dilemma of steadily increasing military power and steadily decreasing national security. *It is our considered professional judgment that this dilemma has no technical solution*. If the great powers continue to look for solutions in the area of science and technology only, the result will be to worsen the situation."

I would like to focus your attention not on the subject of the article (national security in a nuclear world) but on the kind of conclusion they reached, namely that there is no technical solution to the problem. An implicit and almost universal assumption of discussions published in professional and semipopular scientific journals is that the problem under discussion has a technical solution. A technical solution may be defined as one that requires a change only in the techniques of the natural sciences, demanding little or nothing in the way of change in human values or ideas of morality.

In our day (though not in earlier times) technical solutions are always welcome. Because of previous failures in prophecy, it takes courage to assert that a desired technical solution is not possible. Wiesner and York exhibited this courage; publishing in a science journal, they insisted that the solution to the problem was not to be found in the natural sciences. They cautiously qualified

From Garrett Hardin, "The Tragedy of the Commons," *Science* 162, no. 3859 (December 1968): 1243–48.

their statement with the phrase, "It is our considered professional judgment. . . ." Whether they were right or not is not the concern of the present article. Rather, the concern here is with the important concept of a class of human problems which can be called "no technical solution problems," and, more specifically, with the identification and discussion of one of these.

It is easy to show that the class is not a null class. Recall the game of tick-tack-toe. Consider the problem, "How can I win the game of tick-tack-toe?" It is well known that I cannot, if I assume (in keeping with the conventions of game theory) that my opponent understands the game perfectly. Put another way, there is no "technical solution" to the problem. I can win only by giving a radical meaning to the word "win." I can hit my opponent over the head; or I can drug him; or I can falsify the records. Every way in which I "win" involves, in some sense, an abandonment of the game, as we intuitively understand it. (I can also, of course, openly abandon the game—refuse to play it. This is what most adults do.)

The class of "No technical solution problems" has members. My thesis is that the "population problem," as conventionally conceived, is a member of this class. How it is conventionally conceived needs some comment. It is fair to say that most people who anguish over the population problem are trying to find a way to avoid the evils of overpopulation without relinquishing any of the privileges they now enjoy. They think that farming the seas or developing new strains of wheat will solve the problem—technologically. I try to show here that the solution they seek cannot be found. The population problem cannot be solved in a technical way, any more than can the problem of winning the game of tick-tack-toe.

WHAT SHALL WE MAXIMIZE?

Population, as Malthus said, naturally tends to grow "geometrically," or, as we would now say, exponentially. In a finite world this means that the per capita share of the world's goods must steadily decrease. Is ours a finite world?

A fair defense can be put forward for the view that the world is infinite; or that we do not know that it is not. But, in terms of the practical problems that we must face in the next few generations with the foreseeable technology, it is clear that we will greatly increase human misery if we do not, during the immediate future, assume that the world available to the terrestrial human population is finite. "Space" is no escape.[2]

A finite world can support only a finite population; therefore, population growth must eventually equal zero. (The case of perpetual wide fluctuations above and below zero is a trivial variant that need not be discussed.) When this condition is met, what will be the situation of mankind? Specifically, can Bentham's goal of "the greatest good for the greatest number" be realized?

No—for two reasons, each sufficient by itself. The first is a theoretical one. It is not mathematically possible to maximize for two (or more) variables at the same time. This was clearly stated by von Neumann and Morgenstern,[3] but the principle is implicit in the theory of partial differential equations, dating back at least to D'Alembert (1717–1783).

The second reason springs directly from biological facts. To live, any organism must have a source of energy (for example, food). This energy is utilized for two purposes: mere maintenance and work. For man, maintenance of life requires about 1600 kilocalories a day ("maintenance calories"). Anything that he does over and above merely staying alive will be defined as work, and is supported by "work calories" which he takes in. Work calories are used not only for what we call work in common speech; they are also required for all forms of enjoyment, from swimming and automobile racing to playing music and writing poetry. If our goal is to maximize population it is obvious what we must do: We must make the work calories per person approach as close to zero as possible. No gourmet meals, no vacations, no sports, no music, no literature, no art. . . . I think that everyone will grant, without argument or proof, that maximizing population does not maximize goods. Bentham's goal is impossible.

In reaching this conclusion I have made the usual assumption that it is the acquisition of energy that is the problem. The appearance of atomic energy has led some to question this assumption. However, given an infinite source of energy, population growth still produces an inescapable problem. The problem of the acquisition of energy is replaced by the problem of its dissipation, as J. H. Fremlin has so wittily shown.[4] The arithmetic signs in the analysis are, as it were, reversed; but Bentham's goal is still unobtainable.

The optimum population is, then, less than the maximum. The difficulty of defining the optimum is enormous; so far as I know, no one has seriously tackled this problem. Reaching an acceptable and stable solution will surely require more than one generation of hard analytical work—and much persuasion.

We want the maximum good per person; but what is good? To one person it is wilderness, to another it is ski lodges for thousands. To one it is estuaries to nourish ducks for hunters to shoot; to another it is factory land. Comparing one good with another is, we usually say, impossible because goods are incommensurable. Incommensurables cannot be compared.

Theoretically this may be true; but in real life incommensurables *are* commensurable. Only a criterion of judgment and a system of weighting are needed. In nature the criterion is survival. Is it better for a species to be small and hideable, or large and powerful? Natural selection commensurates the incommensurables. The compromise achieved depends on a natural weighting of the values of the variables.

Man must imitate this process. There is no doubt that in fact he already does, but unconsciously. It is when the hidden decisions are made explicit that the arguments begin. The problem for the years ahead is to work out an acceptable theory of weighting. Synergistic effects, nonlinear variation, and difficulties in discounting the future make the intellectual problem difficult, but not (in principle) insoluble.

Has any cultural group solved this practical problem at the present time, even on an intuitive level? One simple fact proves that none has: there is no prosperous population in the world today that has, and has had for some time, a growth rate of zero. Any people that has intuitively identified its optimum point will soon reach it, after which its growth rate becomes and remains zero.

Of course, a positive growth rate might be taken as evidence that a population is below its optimum. However, by any reasonable standards, the most rapidly growing populations on earth today are (in general) the most miserable. This association (which need not be invariable) casts doubt on the optimistic assumption that the positive growth rate of a population is evidence that it has yet to reach its optimum.

We can make little progress in working toward optimum population size until we explicitly exorcize the spirit of Adam Smith in the field of practical demography. In economic affairs, *The Wealth of Nations* (1776) popularized the "invisible hand," the idea that an individual who "intends only his own gain," is, as it were, "led by an invisible hand to promote . . . the public interest."[5] Adam Smith did not assert that this was invariably true, and perhaps neither did any of his followers. But he contributed to a dominant tendency of thought that has ever since interfered with positive action based on rational analysis, namely, the tendency to assume that decisions reached individually will, in fact, be the best decisions for an entire society. If this assumption is correct it justifies the continuance of our present policy of laissez-faire in reproduction. If it is correct we can assume that men will control their individual fecundity so as to produce the optimum population. If the assumption is not correct, we need to reexamine our individual freedoms to see which ones are defensible.

TRAGEDY OF FREEDOM IN A COMMONS

The rebuttal to the invisible hand in population control is to be found in a scenario first sketched in a little-known pamphlet[6] in 1833 by a mathematical amateur named William Forster Lloyd (1794–1852). We may well call it "the tragedy of the commons," using the word "tragedy" as the philosopher Whitehead used it:[7] "The essence of dramatic tragedy is not unhappiness. It resides in the solemnity of the remorseless working of things." He then goes on to say, "This inevitableness of destiny can only be illustrated in terms of human life by incidents which in fact involve unhappiness. For it is only by them that the futility of escape can be made evident in the drama."

The tragedy of the commons develops in this way. Picture a pasture open to all. It is to be expected that each herdsman will try to keep as many cattle as possible on the commons. Such an arrangement may work reasonably satisfactorily for centuries because tribal wars, poaching, and disease keep the numbers of both man and beast well below the carrying capacity of the land. Finally, however, comes the day of reckoning, that is, the day when the long-desired goal of social stability becomes a reality. At this point, the inherent logic of the commons remorselessly generates tragedy.

As a rational being, each herdsman seeks to maximize his gain. Explicitly or implicitly, more or less consciously, he asks, "What is the utility *to me* of adding one more animal to my herd?" This utility has one negative and one positive component.

1. The positive component is a function of the increment of one animal. Since the herdsman receives all the proceeds from the sale of the additional animal, the positive utility is nearly +1.
2. The negative component is a function of the additional overgrazing created by one more animal. Since, however, the effects of overgrazing are shared by all the herdsmen, the negative utility for any particular decision-making herdsman is only a fraction of –1.

Adding together the component partial utilities, the rational herdsman concludes that the only sensible course for him to pursue is to add another animal to his herd. And another; and another. . . . But this is the conclusion reached by each and every rational herdsman sharing a commons. Therein is the tragedy. Each man is locked into a system that compels him to increase his herd without limit—in a world that is limited. Ruin is the destination toward which all men rush, each pursuing his own best interest in a society that believes in the freedom of the commons. Freedom in a commons brings ruin to all.

Some would say that this is a platitude. Would that it were! In a sense, it was learned thousands of years ago, but natural selection favors the forces of psychological denial.[8] The individual benefits as an individual from his ability to deny the truth even though society as a whole, of which he is a part, suffers. Education can counteract the natural tendency to do the wrong thing, but the inexorable succession of generations requires that the basis for this knowledge be constantly refreshed.

A simple incident that occurred a few years ago in Leominster, Massachusetts, shows how perishable the knowledge is. During the Christmas shopping season the parking meters downtown were covered with plastic bags that bore tags reading: "Do not open until after Christmas. Free parking courtesy of the mayor and city council." In other words, facing the prospect of an increased demand for already scarce space, the city fathers reinstituted the system of the commons. (Cynically, we suspect that they gained more votes than they lost by this retrogressive act.)

In an approximate way, the logic of the commons has been understood for a long time, perhaps since the discovery of agriculture or the invention of private property in real estate. But it is understood mostly only in special cases which are not sufficiently generalized. Even at this late date, cattlemen leasing national land on the western ranges demonstrate no more than an ambivalent understanding, in constantly pressuring federal authorities to increase the head count to the point where overgrazing produces erosion and weed-dominance. Likewise, the oceans of the world continue to suffer from the survival of the philosophy of the commons. Maritime nations still respond automatically to the shibboleth of the "freedom of the seas." Professing to believe in the "inexhaustible resources of the oceans," they bring species after species of fish and whales closer to extinction.[9]

The National Parks present another instance of the working out of the tragedy of the commons. At present, they are open to all, without limit. The parks themselves are limited in extent—there is only one Yosemite Valley—whereas population seems to grow without limit. The values that visitors seek in the parks are steadily eroded. Plainly, we must soon cease to treat the parks as commons or they will be of no value to anyone.

What shall we do? We have several options. We might sell them off as private property. We might keep them as public property, but allocate the right to enter them. The allocation might be on the basis of wealth, by the use of an auction system. It might be on the basis of merit, as defined by some agreed-upon standards. It might be by lottery. Or it might be on a first-come, first-served basis, administered to long queues. These, I think, are all the reasonable possibilities. They are all objectionable. But we must choose—or acquiesce in the destruction of the commons that we call our National Parks.

POLLUTION

In a reverse way, the tragedy of the commons reappears in problems of pollution. Here it is not a question of taking something out of the commons, but of putting something in—sewage, or chemical, radioactive, and heat wastes into water; noxious and dangerous fumes into the air; and distracting and unpleasant advertising signs into the line of sight. The calculations of utility are much the same as before. The rational man finds that his share of the cost of the wastes he discharges into the commons is less than the cost of purifying his wastes before releasing them. Since this is true for everyone, we are locked into a system of "fouling our own nest," so long as we behave only as independent, rational, free-enterprisers.

The tragedy of the commons as a food basket is averted by private property, or something formally like it. But the air and waters surrounding us cannot readily be fenced, and so the tragedy of the commons as a cesspool must be prevented by different means, by coercive laws or taxing devices that make it cheaper for the polluter to treat his pollutants than to discharge them untreated. We have not progressed as far with the solution of this problem as we have with the first. Indeed, our particular concept of private property, which deters us from exhausting the positive resources of the earth, favors pollution. The owner of a factory on the bank of a stream—whose property extends to the middle of the stream—often has difficulty seeing why it is not his natural right to muddy the waters flowing past his door. The law, always behind the times, requires elaborate stitching and fitting to adapt it to this newly perceived aspect of the commons.

The pollution problem is a consequence of population. It did not much matter how a lonely American frontiersman disposed of his waste. "Flowing water purifies itself every 10 miles," my grandfather used to say, and the myth was near enough to the truth when he was a boy, for there were not too many people. But as population became denser, the natural chemical and biological recycling processes became overloaded, calling for a redefinition of property rights.

HOW TO LEGISLATE TEMPERANCE?

Analysis of the pollution problem as a function of population density uncovers a not generally recognized principle of morality, namely: *the morality of an act is a function of the state of the system at the time it is performed.*[10] Using the commons as a cesspool does not harm the general public under frontier conditions, because there is no public; the same behavior in a metropolis is unbearable. A hundred and fifty years ago a plainsman could kill an American bison, cut out only the tongue for his dinner, and discard the rest of the animal. He was not in any important sense being wasteful. Today, with only a few thousand bison left, we would be appalled at such behavior.

In passing, it is worth noting that the morality of an act cannot be determined from a photograph. One does not know whether a man killing an elephant or setting fire to the grassland is harming others until one knows the total system in which his act appears. "One picture is worth a thousand words," said an ancient Chinese; but it may take 10,000 words to validate it. It is as tempting to ecologists as it is to reformers in general to try to persuade others by way of the photographic shortcut. But the essense of an argument cannot be photographed: it must be presented rationally—in words.

That morality is system-sensitive escaped the attention of most codifiers of ethics in the past. "Thou shalt not . . ." is the form of traditional ethical directives which make no allowance for particular circumstances. The laws of our society follow the pattern of ancient ethics, and therefore are poorly suited to governing a complex, crowded, changeable world. Our epicyclic solution is to augment statutory law with administrative law. Since it is practically impossible to spell out all the conditions under which it is safe to burn trash in the backyard or to run an automobile without smog-control, by law we delegate the details to bureaus. The result is administrative law, which is rightly feared for an ancient reason—*Quis custodiet ipsos custodes?*—"Who shall watch the watchers themselves?" John Adams said that we must have "a government of laws and not men." Bureau administrators, trying to evaluate the morality of acts in the total system, are singularly liable to corruption, producing a government by men, not laws.

Prohibition is easy to legislate (though not necessarily to enforce);
do we legislate temperance? Experience indicates that it can be accomp
best through the mediation of administrative law. We limit possibilities u
essarily if we suppose that the sentiment of *Quis custodiet* denies us the
of administrative law. We should rather retain the phrase as a perpe
reminder of fearful dangers we cannot avoid. The great challenge facing
now is to invent the corrective feedbacks that are needed to keep custodia\
honest. We must find ways to legitimate the needed authority of both the custo
dians and the corrective feedbacks.

FREEDOM TO BREED IS INTOLERABLE

The tragedy of the commons is involved in population problems in another
way. In a world governed solely by the principle of "dog eat dog"—if indeed
there ever was such a world—how many children a family had would not be a
matter of public concern. Parents who bred too exuberantly would leave fewer
descendants, not more, because they would be unable to care adequately for
their children. David Lack and others have found that such a negative feedback
demonstrably controls the fecundity of birds.[11] But men are not birds, and have
not acted like them for millenniums, at least.

If each human family were dependent only on its own resources; *if* the children of improvident parents starved to death; *if*, thus, overbreeding brought its
own "punishment" to the germ line—*then* there would be no public interest in
controlling the breeding of families. But our society is deeply committed to the
welfare state,[12] and hence is confronted with another aspect of the tragedy of
the commons.

In a welfare state, how shall we deal with the family, the religion, the race,
or the class (or indeed any distinguishable and cohesive group) that adopts
overbreeding as a policy to secure its own aggrandizement?[13] To couple the
concept of freedom to breed with the belief that everyone born has an equal
right to the commons is to lock the world into a tragic course of action.

Unfortunately this is just the course of action that is being pursued by the
United Nations. In late 1967, some 30 nations agreed to the following:[14]

> The Universal Declaration of Human Rights describes the family as the
> natural and fundamental unit of society. It follows that any choice and
> decision with regard to the size of the family must irrevocably rest with
> the family itself, and cannot be made by anyone else.

It is painful to have to deny categorically the validity of this right; denying it,
one feels as uncomfortable as a resident of Salem, Massachusetts, who denied
the reality of witches in the 17th century. At the present time, in liberal quarters, something like a taboo acts to inhibit criticism of the United Nations.
There is a feeling that the United Nations is "our last and best hope," that we

shouldn't find fault with it; we shouldn't play into the hands of the archconservatives. However, let us not forget what Robert Louis Stevenson said: "The truth that is suppressed by friends is the readiest weapon of the enemy." If we love the truth we must openly deny the validity of the Universal Declaration of Human Rights, even though it is promoted by the United Nations. We should also join with Kingsley Davis[15] in attempting to get Planned Parenthood-World Population to see the error of its ways in embracing the same tragic ideal.

CONSCIENCE IS SELF-ELIMINATING

It is a mistake to think that we can control the breeding of mankind in the long run by an appeal to conscience. Charles Galton Darwin made this point when he spoke on the centennial of the publication of his grandfather's great book. The argument is straightforward and Darwinian.

People vary. Confronted with appeals to limit breeding, some people will undoubtedly respond to the plea more than others. Those who have more children will produce a larger fraction of the next generation than those with more susceptible consciences. The difference will be accentuated, generation by generation.

In C. G. Darwin's words: "It may well be that it would take hundreds of generations for the progenitive instinct to develop in this way, but if it should do so, nature would have taken her revenge, and the variety *Homo contracipiens* would become extinct and would be replaced by the variety *Homo progenitivus*."[16]

The argument assumes that conscience or the desire for children (no matter which) is hereditary—but hereditary only in the most general formal sense. The result will be the same whether the attitude is transmitted through germ cells, or exosomatically, to use A. J. Lotka's term. (If one denies the latter possibility as well as the former, then what's the point of education?) The argument has here been stated in the context of the population problem, but it applies equally well to any instance in which society appeals to an individual exploiting a commons to restrain himself for the general good—by means of his conscience. To make such an appeal is to set up a selective system that works toward the elimination of conscience from the race.

PATHOGENIC EFFECTS OF CONSCIENCE

The long-term disadvantage of an appeal to conscience should be enough to condemn it; but has serious short-term disadvantages as well. If we ask a man who is exploiting a commons to desist "in the name of conscience," what are we saying to him? What does he hear?—not only at the moment but also in the wee small hours of the night when, half asleep, he remembers not merely the words we used but also the nonverbal communication cues we gave him unawares? Sooner or later, consciously or subconsciously, he senses that he has received two communications, and that they are contradictory: (i) (intended communication) "If you don't do as we ask, we will openly condemn you for not acting like a responsible citizen"; (ii) (the unintended communication) "If you *do* behave as we ask, we will secretly condemn you for a simpleton who can be shamed into standing aside while the rest of us exploit the commons."

Everyman then is caught in what Bateson has called a "double bind." Bateson and his co-workers have made a plausible case for viewing the double bind as an important causative factor in the genesis of schizophrenia.[17] The double bind may not always be so damaging, but it always endangers the mental health of anyone to whom it is applied. "A bad conscience," said Nietzsche, "is a kind of illness."

To conjure up a conscience in others is tempting to anyone who wishes to extend his control beyond the legal limits. Leaders at the highest level succumb to this temptation. Has any President during the past generation failed to call on labor unions to moderate voluntarily their demands for higher wages, or to steel companies to honor voluntary guidelines on prices? I can recall none. The rhetoric used on such occasions is designed to produce feelings of guilt in non-cooperators.

For centuries it was assumed without proof that guilt was a valuable, perhaps even an indispensable, ingredient of the civilized life. Now, in this post-Freudian world, we doubt it.

Paul Goodman speaks from the modern point of view when he says: "No good has ever come from feeling guilty, neither intelligence, policy, nor compassion. The guilty do not pay attention to the object but only to themselves, and not even to their own interests, which might make sense, but to their anxieties."[18]

One does not have to be a professional psychiatrist to see the consequences of anxiety. We in the Western world are just emerging from a dreadful two-centuries-long Dark Ages of Eros that was sustained partly by prohibition laws, but perhaps more effectively by the anxiety-generating mechanisms of education. Alex Comfort has told the story well in *The Anxiety Makers*;[19] it is not a pretty one.

Since proof is difficult, we may even concede that the results of anxiety may sometimes, from certain points of view, be desirable. The larger question we should ask is whether, as a matter of policy, we should ever encourage the use of a technique the tendency (if not the intention) of which is psychologically pathogenic. We hear much talk these days of responsible parenthood; the coupled words are incorporated into the titles of some organizations devoted to birth control. Some people have proposed massive propaganda campaigns to instill responsibility into the nation's (or the world's) breeders. But what is the meaning of the word responsibility in this context? Is it not merely a synonym for the word conscience? When we use the word responsibility in the absence of substantial sanctions are we not trying to browbeat a free man in a commons into acting against his own interest? Responsibility is a verbal counterfeit for a substantial *quid pro quo*. It is an attempt to get something for nothing.

If the word responsibility is to be used at all, I suggest that it be in the sense Charles Frankel uses it.[20] "Responsibility," says this philosopher, "is the product of definite social arrangements." Notice that Frankel calls for social arrangements—not propaganda.

MUTUAL COERCION MUTUALLY AGREED UPON

The social arrangements that produce responsibility are arrangements that create coercion, of some sort. Consider bank-robbing. The man who takes money from a bank acts as if the bank were a commons. How do we prevent such action? Certainly not by trying to control his behavior solely by a verbal appeal to his sense of responsibility. Rather than rely on propaganda we follow Frankel's lead and insist that a bank is not a commons; we seek the definite social arrangements that will keep it from becoming a commons. That we thereby infringe on the freedom of would-be robbers we neither deny nor regret.

The morality of bank-robbing is particularly easy to understand because we accept complete prohibition of this activity. We are willing to say "Thou shalt not rob banks," without providing for exceptions. But temperance also can be created by coercion. Taxing is a good coercive device. To keep downtown shoppers temperate in their use of parking space we introduce parking meters for short periods, and traffic fines for longer ones. We need not actually forbid a citizen to park as long as he wants to; we need merely make it increasingly expensive for him to do so. Not prohibition, but carefully biased options are what we offer him. A Madison Avenue man might call this persuasion; I prefer the greater candor of the word coercion.

Coercion is a dirty word to most liberals now, but it need not forever be so. As with the four-letter words, its dirtiness can be cleansed away by exposure to the light, by saying it over and over without apology or embarrassment. To many, the word coercion implies arbitrary decisions of distant and irresponsible bureaucrats; but this is not a necessary part of its meaning. The only kind of coercion I recommend is mutual coercion, mutually agreed upon by the majority of the people affected.

To say that we mutually agree to coercion is not to say that we are required to enjoy it, or even to pretend we enjoy it. Who enjoys taxes? We all grumble about them. But we accept compulsory taxes because we recognize that voluntary taxes would favor the conscienceless. We institute and (grumblingly) support taxes and other coercive devices to escape the horror of the commons.

An alternative to the commons need not be perfectly just to be preferable. With real estate and other material goods, the alternative we have chosen is the institution of private property coupled with legal inheritance. Is this system perfectly just? As a genetically trained biologist I deny that it is. It seems to me that, if there are to be differences in individual inheritance, legal possession should be perfectly correlated with biological inheritance—that those who are biologically more fit to be the custodians of property and power should legally inherit more. But genetic recombination continually makes a mockery of the doctrine of "like father, like son" implicit in our laws of legal inheritance. An idiot can inherit millions, and a trust fund can keep his estate intact. We must admit that our legal system of private property plus inheritance is unjust—but we put up with it because we are not convinced, at the moment, that anyone has invented a better system. The alternative of the commons is too horrifying to contemplate. Injustice is preferable to total ruin.

It is one of the peculiarities of the warfare between reform and the status quo that it is thoughtlessly governed by a double standard. Whenever a reform measure is proposed it is often defeated when its opponents triumphantly discover a flaw in it. As Kingsley Davis has pointed out,[21] worshippers of the status quo sometimes imply that no reform is possible without unanimous agreement, an implication contrary to historical fact. As nearly as I can make out, automatic rejection of proposed reforms is based on one of two unconscious assumptions: (i) that the status quo is perfect; or (ii) that the choice we face is between reform and no action; if the proposed reform is imperfect, we presumably should take no action at all, while we wait for a perfect proposal.

But we can never do nothing. That which we have done for thousands of years is also action. It also produces evils. Once we are aware that the status quo is action, we can then compare its discoverable advantages and disadvantages with the predicted advantages and disadvantages of the proposed reform, discounting as best we can for our lack of experience. On the basis of such a comparison, we can make a rational decision which will not involve the unworkable assumption that only perfect systems are tolerable.

RECOGNITION OF NECESSITY

Perhaps the simplest summary of this analysis of man's population problems is this: the commons, if justifiable at all, is justifiable only under conditions of low-population density. As the human population has increased, the commons has had to be abandoned in one aspect after another.

First we abandoned the commons in food gathering, enclosing farm land and restricting pastures and hunting and fishing areas. These restrictions are still not complete throughout the world.

Somewhat later we saw that the commons as a place for waste disposal would also have to be abandoned. Restrictions on the disposal of domestic sewage are widely accepted in the Western world; we are still struggling to close the commons to pollution by automobiles, factories, insecticide sprayers, fertilizing operations, and atomic energy installations.

In a still more embryonic state is our recognition of the evils of the commons in matters of pleasure. There is almost no restriction on the propagation of sound waves in the public medium. The shopping public is assaulted with mindless music, without its consent. Our government is paying out billions of dollars to create supersonic transport which will disturb 50,000 people for every one person who is whisked from coast to coast 3 hours faster. Advertisers muddy the airwaves of radio and television and pollute the view of travelers. We are a long way from outlawing the commons in matters of pleasure. Is this because our Puritan inheritance makes us view pleasure as something of a sin, and plain (that is, the pollution of advertising) as the sign of virtue?

Every new enclosure of the commons involves the infringement of somebody's personal liberty. Infringements made in the distant past are accepted because no contemporary complains of a loss. It is the newly proposed infringements that we vigorously oppose; cries of "rights" and "freedom" fill the air. But what does "freedom" mean? When men mutually agreed to pass laws against robbing, mankind became more free, not less so. Individuals locked into the logic of the commons are free only to bring on universal ruin; once they see the necessity of mutual coercion, they become free to pursue other goals. I believe it was Hegel who said, "Freedom is the recognition of necessity."

The most important aspect of necessity that we must now recognize, is the necessity of abandoning the commons in breeding. No technical solution can rescue us from the misery of overpopulation. Freedom to breed will bring ruin to all. At the moment, to avoid hard decisions many of us are tempted to propagandize for conscience and responsible parenthood. The temptation must be resisted, because an appeal to independently acting consciences selects for the disappearance of all conscience in the long run, and an increase in anxiety in the short.

The only way we can preserve and nurture other and more precious freedoms is by relinquishing the freedom to breed, and that very soon. "Freedom is the recognition of necessity"—and it is the role of education to reveal to all the necessity of abandoning the freedom to breed. Only so, can we put an end to this aspect of the tragedy of the commons.

NOTES

1. J. B. Wiesner and H. F. York. *Sci. Amer.* 211 (No. 4), 27 (1964).

2. G. Hardin, *J. Hered.* 50, 68 (1959); S. von Hoernor, *Science* 137, 18 (1962).

3. J. von Neumann and O. Morgenstern, *Theory of Games and Economic Behavior* (Princeton Univ. Press, Princeton, N.J., 1947), p. 11.

4. J. H. Fremlin, *New Sci.*, No. 415 (1964), p. 285.

5. A. Smith, *The Wealth of Nations* (Modern Library, New York, 1937), p. 423.

6. W. F. Lloyd, *Two Lectures on the Checks to Population* (Oxford Univ. Press, Oxford, England, 1833), reprinted (in part) in *Population, Evolution, and Birth Control*, G. Hardin, Ed. (Freeman, San Francisco, 1964), p. 37.

7. A. N. Whitehead, *Science and the Modern World* (Mentor, New York, 1948), p. 17.

8. G. Hardin, Ed. *Population, Evolution, and Birth Control* (Freeman, San Francisco, 1964), p. 56.

9. S. McVay, *Sci. Amer.* 216 (No. 8), 13 (1966).

10. J. Fletcher, *Situation Ethics* (Westminster, Philadelphia, 1966).

11. D. Lack, *The Natural Regulation of Animal Numbers* (Clarendon Press, Oxford, 1954).

12. H. Girvetz, *From Wealth to Welfare* (Stanford Univ. Press, Stanford, Calif., 1950).

13. G. Hardin, *Perspec. Biol. Med.* 6, 366 (1963).

14. U. Thant, *Int. Planned Parenthood News*, No. 168 (February 1968), p. 3.

15. K. Davis, *Science* 158, 730 (1967).

16. S. Tax, Ed., *Evolution after Darwin* (Univ. of Chicago Press, Chicago, 1960), vol. 2, p. 469.

17. G. Bateson, D. D. Jackson, J. Haley, J. Weakland, *Behav. Sci.* 1, 251 (1956).

18. P. Goodman, *New York Rev. Books* 10 (No. 8), 22 (23 May 1968).

19. A. Comfort, *The Anxiety Makers* (Nelson, London, 1967).

20. C. Frankel, *The Case for Modern Man* (Harper, New York, 1955), p. 203.

21. J. D. Roslansky, *Genetics and the Future of Man* (Appleton-Century-Crofts, New York, 1966), p. 177.

1.4

D. RODERICK KIEWIET AND MATHEW D. McCUBBINS

From *The Logic of Delegation: Congressional Parties and the Appropriations Process*

Kiewiet and McCubbins describe the pervasive problem of delegation, sometimes called the principal-agent problem. This common "problem" occurs when there is a conflict of interest between the people who make decisions (principals) and the people hired by principals to carry out the decisions (agents). A key task of modern representative government is to ensure that decision makers have the means to manage the behavior of those implementing policies. For example, elected representatives rely on government agencies and bureaucrats to implement policies. How do elected officials control what government bureaucrats do?

COLLECTIVE ACTION AND DELEGATION

. . . The most familiar collective action problem is the prisoner's dilemma. It takes its name from the simple two-person game, but the social contexts in which most human interaction takes place tend to make *n*-person prisoners' dilemmas the more pervasive phenomenon. The crux of the dilemma is that individuals, in seeking to maximize their self-interest, have incentives to behave in ways that are inimical to the interests of the community as a whole (Hardin 1968). A good example of the dilemma is that of public goods (Olson 1965). The community would on net benefit from such a good, but those who do not contribute to its provision cannot be excluded from enjoying it. Everyone therefore has an incentive to free ride on the contributions of others. Even though the community may unanimously favor acquisition of the public good, little or no effort is expended to supply it. Rational individual choices produce irrational collective outcomes.

Collective action may also be stymied by a lack of coordination. In contrast to the prisoner's dilemma, where dominant strategies yield an inefficient equilibrium, other situations confront the community with multiple efficient equilibria. Members of the community are uncertain as to which strategies other members will pursue, and coordination may never be achieved. A simple coordination problem occurs when two cars enter an intersection simul-

From D. Roderick Kiewiet and Mathew D. McCubbins, *The Logic of Delegation: Congressional Parties and the Appropriations Process* (Chicago: University of Chicago Press, 1991).

taneously. Neither driver cares particularly who goes first; both are far more concerned about avoiding a collision. What frequently occurs, however, is a nerve-wracking *pas de deux* of false starts and sudden stops as the drivers make their way through the crossing. Even if everyone in the community would benefit from all alternatives under consideration, problems of coordination are exacerbated when different alternatives benefit some members relative to others.

▪　▪　▪

According to property rights theorists, the best response to collective action problems is to minimize their occurrence, something that is accomplished by relegating as much human activity as possible to the realm of the marketplace. Adam Smith argued long ago that the well-being of a community is better realized through individual market transactions than through the schemes of even the most benevolent planner. Much social benefit can also be derived from simple patterns of reciprocity. But there are limits to what can be achieved through voluntary trade and cooperation; uncoordinated, unorganized activity will get a community only so far. In most cases, the benefits of collective action are realized through organizations. It is in the context of organizations that collective action is most effectively coordinated, that prisoners' dilemmas are most readily overcome, and that stable social decisions are most likely to be reached.

The organizational bases of collective action are many—firms, bureaucracies, associations, committees, leagues, representative assemblies, to name a few. What the most prominent forms of organization have in common, however, is the delegation of authority to take action from the individual or individuals to whom it was originally endowed—the principal—to one or more agents. One major organizational theorist, in fact, defines organizations as "networks of overlapping or nested principal/agent relationships" (Tirole 1986, p. 181). Delegation from principals to agents is the key to the division of labor and development of specialization; tremendous gains accrue if tasks are delegated to those with the talent, training, and inclination to do them. This, when all is said and done, is what allows firms to profit, economies to grow, and governments to govern.

The underlings in an organization are obviously agents of their superiors, but the heads of organizations, such as coaches, firm managers, party leaders, are agents, too. Indeed, it is the delegation of authority to a central agent to lead or manage the organization that is the key to overcoming problems of collective action. Agents performing as leaders or managers must be endowed with the resources they need to discharge their duties effectively. In the case of congressional parties, leaders can exploit the prominence of their position to identify a focal point, thus solving problems of coordination by rallying support around one of possibly many acceptable alternatives. Their ability to structure the voting agenda, moreover, can overcome social choice instability.

In such a relationship the agent seeks to maximize his or her return subject to the constraints and incentives offered by the principal. The principal, conversely, seeks to structure the relationship with the agent so that the outcomes produced through the agent's efforts are the best the principal can achieve, given the choice to delegate in the first place. There is, then, a natural conflict of interest between the two. In economic settings this conflict is often over the amount of effort expended by the agent. In political settings it is more likely to be over the course of action the agent is to pursue. The policy agenda of agency bureaucrats, for example, can be quite at odds with the preferences of the elected officials who oversee them. As a consequence of this conflict of interest, the principal always experiences some reduction in welfare. First, he suffers agency losses that result from the agent behaving in ways other than those that best serve his interests. Second, the principal incurs agency costs in undertaking efforts to mitigate agency losses. Agency problems may be so great that they exceed the benefits to be derived from collection action, in which case the delegation should not occur.

The opportunistic behavior that is at the root of agency problems is by no means confined to principal/agent relationships. Individuals involved in market transactions have similar incentives to behave in a less than noble manner. Certain conditions that are generally present in principal/agent relationships, however, make it a particularly congenial environment for opportunism. These are the conditions of hidden action, hidden information, and a form of strategic vulnerability on the part of the principal that we refer to as Madison's dilemma.

Hidden Action and Hidden Information

In a wide variety of agency relationships, the agent possesses or acquires information that is either unavailable to the principal or prohibitively costly to obtain. The agent has incentives to use this information strategically or to simply keep it hidden—a situation referred to variously as the problem of truthful revelation or incentive incompatibility. In a firm, workers have information that is not available to management, such as how fast the assembly line can run before quality is compromised. They would prefer not to reveal this information, however, because they would rather not work at a breakneck pace. Another type of information that agents often have and principals do not is the agent's type (for example, knowledge of whether the agent is hardworking or lazy, talented or untalented, risk-averse or risk-acceptant). This variation on the hidden information problem is referred to as adverse selection.

Situations in which agents acquire information that is unavailable to the principal pervade public policy-making. The basis of Niskanen's (1971) argument as to how bureaus maximize the size of their budgets is that bureaucrats are privy to information about service delivery costs that is not available to elected politicians. Through their investigations, congressional committees uncover information that is not available to other members of the chamber.

Individual members, similarly, have better information than do congressional party leaders as to whether or not supporting the party's position might cause them trouble back home.

The second problem, that of hidden action, manifests itself in a variety of situations. Stockholders cannot observe whether the actions that firm managers take are in their best interest. Voters cannot observe whether the actions of elected representatives—their agents—are in their best interest. Hidden action is especially problematic when the agent's actions only partially determine outcomes, as in the case of team production or committee decisions, or when outcomes are partially determined by chance. In such cases, the principal is unable to infer the appropriateness of the agent's actions even from observed results.

Madison's Dilemma

Arguing for the separation of powers specified under the new Constitution, Madison wrote in *Federalist 51*, "In framing a government to be administered by men over men, the great difficulty lies in this: you must first enable the government to control the governed; and in the next place oblige it to control itself." Whatever their views about the document that was ultimately produced, members of the Constitutional Convention were keenly appreciative of Madison's observation. They had seen that under the Articles of Confederation the federal government had not been delegated enough authority to accomplish much of anything. Yet they feared that a government powerful enough to govern effectively would necessarily be powerful enough to oppress them.

In addition to problems of hidden action and hidden information, this third problem, one we call Madison's dilemma, is a potential pitfall in all institutions that rely upon delegation. The essence of the problem is that resources or authority granted to an agent for the purpose of advancing the interests of the principal can be turned against the principal. Although the problem is a general one of agency, it has long been recognized in liberal political theory as being of paramount importance when the agents involved are those in a position of leadership. Madison's dilemma is not a consequence of agents taking hidden action or acquiring hidden information, although these conditions can certainly make matters worse. Rather, it arises from agents exploiting the favorable strategic situation in which they have been placed.

In seeking to solve collective action problems, members of the community must be prescient in their delegation of authority to a central agent. If not, they may find that they would have been better off continuing to endure their problems than they are living with the solution their agent has achieved.

Collective Principals and Collective Agents

Problems of hidden action, hidden information, and Madison's dilemma are endemic to all agency relationships. There are additional hazards to delegation, however, when either collective principals or collective agents are involved. Specifically, the very same collective action problems that delegation is intended to overcome—prisoners' dilemmas, lack of coordination, and social choice instability—can reemerge to afflict either the collective agent or a collective principal. A collective principal may be unable to announce a single preference over its agent's actions or to offer a single contract governing compensation for the agent. A subset of the membership may strategically manipulate the decision-making process of the collective principal. Similarly, agents who are delegated management or leadership roles may use their agenda powers to do the same thing, thus leaving the collective principal vulnerable to a form of Madison's dilemma. A related consideration is that in appointing a new individual to a collective agent, such as a production team or a committee, that person's abilities and preferences cannot be evaluated in isolation. The principal must consider instead how the new agent will interact with existing members of the team or committee.

Distinct from the problems of collective principals and agents are problems specific to multiple principals and agents. An agent attempting to serve multiple principals often finds that any action he or she might take to benefit one principal injures another. Federal agencies are buffeted by conflicting pressures from their departments, the president, the courts, their interest group clients, as well as several congressional committees and subcommittees. Second, when there are multiple agents it is possible that they will collude against the principal. This can occur in a number of ways. Workers who break the curve, for example, are likely to be castigated by their fellow workers. The essence of "iron triangle" or "subgovernment" theories of public policy formation is that collusion between two sets of agents—federal agencies and the congressional committees that ostensibly oversee them—serves to undermine the welfare of the general public (their ultimate principal) rather than to promote it.

OVERCOMING AGENCY PROBLEMS

Agency losses can be contained, but only by undertaking measures that are themselves costly. There are four major classes of such measures: (1) contract design, (2) screening and selection mechanisms, (3) monitoring and reporting requirements, and (4) institutional checks.

Contract Design

Any contract between a principal and agent must satisfy the participation constraint. The agent's compensation must be at least as great as his or her opportunity costs, but less than the marginal benefit the principal derives from the actions of the agent. If this condition is not met, one side or the other will not be made better off by entering into the relationship and will decline to do so. Assuming that the participation constraint is satisfied, the principal's goal is to delegate tasks and responsibilities and to specify a corresponding schedule of compensation in such a way that the agent is motivated to best serve the principal's interests. Such contracts may specify negative rewards, or sanctions, particularly when the agent is capable of taking actions that are very harmful to the principal. In some situations, particularly when noncompliance with the principal's directives is hard to detect, the sanctions required to effect compliance are far greater in magnitude than the benefits that the principal derives from compliance.

Under conditions that usually exist in principal/agent relationships—hidden information and hidden action—designing compensation schedules is a tricky business. Examples abound of compensation schemes that create incentives for agent behavior other than that intended by the principal. If not otherwise constrained, brokers receiving a commission on trades churn through their clients' portfolios. Ford factory managers, no less creative than their celebrated Soviet counterparts, often met their quotas by surreptitiously building large numbers of automobiles prior to the official start of the production run (Halberstam 1986). Governmental agencies have an especially difficult time designing appropriate compensation schedules. Medicare administrators, for example, came to realize that simply reimbursing hospitals for all "reasonable" costs incurred in treating patients contributed to rapidly escalating claims. In 1982 they won congressional approval for a new system under which hospitals receive a fixed fee for treatment based upon the diagnosis related group (DRG) to which the patient has been assigned. In short order the system began to experience "DRG creep"; elderly Americans were succumbing to increasingly expensive diseases that often could be diagnosed only with the most advanced (and expensive) medical technology.

The problem of inappropriate incentives in compensation schemes can be mitigated by giving agents a residual claim on output. The compensation received by corporate executives, for example, is often in the form of profit sharing or other bonuses linked to the performance of the firm. Another example of this arrangement is sharecropping. Instead of charging a fixed rent, the landlord leases land to a tenant in return for a percentage of the crop. Compensation contracts of this form can be used in the public sector as well. In previous centuries, the king of France and other European monarchs garnered much of their revenue from "tax farmers," that is, individuals who were given the right to collect taxes in a particular geographic area so long as they surrendered an agreed-upon amount of the proceeds to the crown. The state of Ohio actually implemented this method for garnering revenue at the end of the Civil War; counties and cities were permitted to engage "tax inquisitors" who were empowered to find concealed taxable holdings (usually stocks and bank deposits) in return for a percentage of the proceeds.

Although such profit-sharing arrangements can help mitigate agency losses, they are hardly a panacea. They can be very expensive to the principal and do not necessarily remove all inappropriate incentives. In the realm of public policy, awarding agents a residual claim on output can have particularly obnoxious consequences; the interested student should be able to surmise why the institution of tax farming fell out of favor. Even if it were desirable to motivate public servants with a piece of the action, most important policy outputs are impossible to measure. How, for example, could the military establishment be awarded an incentive bonus that hinged upon whether or not they had had a good year?

Given the difficulties involved in designing optimal contracts prior to the establishment of an agency relationship, an alternative strategy for the principal may be to simply offer a compensation contract and, conditioned on the agent accepting it, to see how well he or she works out. There is, after all, no better information about how well an agent performs than his or her actual performance. Most employment contracts specify an initial probationary period (ranging from three or four days for waiters to three or four years for professors) and provide for periodic reviews after that. The principal can minimize the risk associated with this strategy by initially assigning an agent a modest set of tasks and responsibilities at a modest level of compensation. Those who perform well are rewarded by increasing the range of their authority and responsibility and, concomitantly, the level of their compensation. Agents who perform poorly will not similarly advance, or may even be demoted or dismissed. Like other strategies available to the principal, this one works best when agents can be induced to compete with each other. One of the major rationales for hierarchy in organizations is that it means there are more people seeking promotion to the next level than there are opportunities available.

Screening and Selection Mechanisms

A policy of hiring first and adjusting compensation later does nothing to address the problem of adverse selection discussed earlier; the offer of a given level of compensation attracts only those applicants whose opportunity costs are lower than the offer. This is not a damaging critique, however, because there is little that can be done about adverse selection simply by altering the terms of the compensation contract. The more telling problem is that information revealed by the agent's on-the-job performance, as valuable as it is, can be exceedingly expensive to obtain. Spence (1974) details several reasons why it can be so costly to sort out good agents from bad after they have been hired and why it pays both principals and agents to invest time and effort into avoiding bad matches in the first place:

> One might ask why the employer would not simply hire the person, determine his productivity, and then either fire him or adjust his wage or salary accordingly. There are several reasons why he will not do this. Frequently, he cannot. It may take time (even a long time) for the individual's real capabilities to become apparent. There may be a specific training required before the individual can handle certain kinds of jobs. There may be a contract and a contract period within which the individual cannot be fired and his salary cannot be adjusted. All of these factors tend to make the hiring decision an investment decision for the employer. Certain

costs incurred in hiring and in the early period of employment are sunk and cannot be recovered if the investment turns out badly. (p. 14)

To the extent they share in the benefits of minimizing agency losses and agency costs, both sides are better off if principals are able to identify those individuals who possess the appropriate talents, skills, and other personal characteristics prior to the establishment of the principal/agent relationship. The greater the investment entailed in the hiring decision, the more critical screening and selection mechanisms become. Thus Spence's arguments apply with even more force in the public sector than in the private. Congressional members appointed to committees do not serve a probationary period to see how well they work out. Civil Service employees, for all practical purposes, cannot be fired. And as incumbent presidents typically point out when running for reelection, the Oval Office is no place for on-the-job training.

But how are principals and agents able to find suitable matches when they lack the requisite information? Principals cannot observe agents' actual performance until after the commitment to hire them has been made. Potential agents, similarly, cannot know exactly what the job is like until they start doing it. This problem is compounded by the fact that both potential principals and potential agents frequently have an incentive to misrepresent their abilities and preferences. According to Spence, this informational gap is bridged by observing properties of each other that are reliable signals of the underlying qualities of interest. Many signals that employers attend to in the labor market are beyond the applicants' control, such as race, age, or gender, and for that reason can be illegitimate sources of discrimination. Other signals, however, the applicant has at least partial control over, such as appearing on time for the job interview, presenting a neat personal appearance, and expressing enthusiasm for the job.

Signaling is an important phenomenon in the political world as well. Congressional candidates who have served in an elected office before are far more likely to get elected than those who have not. A major reason for this is that their previous success signals to potential contributors that they are high-quality candidates. Congressional parties also tend not to name freshmen to the House Appropriations Committee. This is because freshmen have not been around long enough to demonstrate that they are the type of *homme sérieux* who has traditionally served on the committee—hardworking, respectful, and, whatever their ideological predilections, responsive to the needs of the party.

Monitoring and Reporting Requirements

Once a principal and agent have entered into a relationship, the most straightforward way to eliminate the conditions of hidden action and information would seem to be to institute procedures requiring agents to report whatever relevant information they have obtained and whatever actions they have taken. After all, hidden information is no longer hidden if you make the agent reveal it. On the basis of information provided by the agent, the principal can presumably tie the agent's compensation more directly to his or her actual conduct. As before, to the extent both sides share in a reduction in agency losses and agency costs, both principal and agent can be made better off.

In fact, reporting requirements are ubiquitous in both the private and public sectors. Employees fill out weekly progress reports for their supervisors, who in turn report to their supervisors on the status of their operations. Every year congressional committees, regulatory agencies, and executive departments report millions of pages of material on their hearings, investigations, and policy recommendations.

There are, however, costs entailed both in the agent's provision and in the principal's consumption of information. If nothing else, the transfer of information deflects time and attention away from tasks that they would otherwise be performing. Rather than require agents to report all relevant information, their reports should be at an optimal level of "coarsification." Unfortunately, this is difficult to modulate; a principal can either be starving for information or, more often, drowning in a sea of it. That hundreds of millions of dollars are invested annually in the design of management information systems attests to the difficulty of this problem.

The more serious drawback to reporting requirements, however, has already been broached, and that is the problem of truthful revelation or incentive incompatibility. The agent has incentives to shade things, to make reports that reflect favorably upon himself, or to reveal information in some other strategic manner. Employees may discover that energy, skill, and creativity applied to their weekly progress reports pays off much more handsomely than actually doing the job. Even if agents can somehow be constrained to be truthful in their reports, the principal will still not know what they are not reporting. For that reason principals typically supplement these requirements with what McCubbins and Schwartz (1984) have dubbed "police patrol" oversight— audits, investigations, and other direct methods of monitoring. To be effective, monitoring policies should be applied stochastically so as to preserve the element of surprise. Direct monitoring can cost the principal a great deal of time and effort. Anyone who has ever worked on a factory floor can attest to the fact that constant supervision is also demeaning and corrosive to the morale of both supervisor and supervisee.

Frequently an agent's actions affect individuals who are not a party to the original principal/agent contract. These individuals may be the intended beneficiaries of the agent's actions, as when an employee supplies a service to a customer on behalf of the firm's owners, or when bureaucrats deliver benefits to constituents on behalf of members of Congress or the president. Because affected third parties have an incentive to observe and to influence the actions of the agent, opportunities arise for oversight that is potentially less costly and more reliable than "police patrols." Instead of examining a sample of the agent's activities (or, more typically, the agent's reports about his or her activities), looking for inappropriate actions or improper use of information, the principal instead obtains information from the affected third parties. This McCubbins and Schwartz refer to as "fire alarm" oversight.

Fire alarm oversight offers several advantages. First, it allows the principal to gather information at lower cost; even when it is as costly as police patrol oversight, much of the cost is borne by the affected third parties. Second, it can yield better information. Under a realistic police patrol policy the principal examines only a small sample of the agent's actions and is therefore likely to miss violations. Under a well-designed fire alarm system, third parties can bring to the principal's attention any serious violation by the agent. More important, the affected third parties have incentives that are in accord with the principal's interests and not, as in the case of the agent, in conflict with them. Third, it is usually difficult to specify a priori a contract with the agent that unambiguously covers all contingencies, and consequently it is hard to tell whether an agent has violated the contract. In this situation, complaints by the affected third parties give principals the opportunity to spell out their goals more clearly.

Often it is no easier for affected third parties to oversee the agent's actions than it is for the principal. In such cases the principal can provide third parties with the means and the incentive to gather information and to report it to him. One common example is that of companies who post on the rear of their trucks an 800 number that motorists can call to report reckless driving by the vehicle's operator. Until 1874 the federal government awarded 25 percent of the fines and forfeiture collected to those who informed on fraudulent valuations by customs officers (Studenski and Krooss 1952, p. 170). Today several agencies of the federal government, including the Department of Defense, the Internal Revenue Service, and the Security and Exchange Commission, have taken similar measures by setting up fraud "hotlines" and advertising rewards for whistle-blowers. Although such programs have a number of operational problems, their deterrent effect may be substantial.

Alternatively, principals can set up a fire alarm system by requiring agents to notify third parties of any actions that affect them. According to McCubbins, Noll, and Weingast (1987), this requirement is a key feature of the Administrative Procedures Act of 1946. To comply with this legislation, an administrative agency must announce its intention to consider an issue well in advance of any decision. It must solicit comments and allow all interested parties to communicate their views. The agency must explicitly address any and all evidence presented and provide a rationalizable link between the evidence and its decisions. Such procedures, of course, do not necessarily remove inherent biases in agency decision making. But the mandated sequence of notice, comment, collection of evidence, and deliberation affords numerous opportunities for members of Congress to respond when an agency seeks to move in a direction that a key constituency group finds objectionable. This makes it very difficult for agencies to strategically manipulate congressional decisions by presenting a fait accompli, that is, a new policy with already mobilized supporters.

Institutional Checks

Most applications of the principal/agent framework in economics characterize the principal's problem as one of seeking to induce the agent to expend more effort. The assumption is that the harder they work, the more they produce. But agents are often in a position to do more harm to the principal than to simply withhold effort; embezzlement, insider trading, official corruption, abuse of authority, and coups d'etat are all testaments to this fact. Whenever an agent can take actions that might seriously jeopardize the principal's interests, the principal needs to thwart the agent's ability to pursue such courses of action unilaterally.

We refer to various countermeasures the principal may take in this regard as institutional checks. Operationally, institutional checks require that when authority has been delegated to an agent, there is at least one other agent with the authority to veto or to block the actions of that agent. The framers of the Constitution established many interlocking checks with the intention of constraining the more powerful central government they had created. Most firms also employ systems of checks. Large expenditures, for example, typically require the approval of both management and the comptroller. Some of the most check-laden institutions are universities. Granting tenure usually requires an overwhelmingly favorable vote in the department, the approval of the dean, the acquiescence of a university-wide ad hoc committee, and ratification by the trustees.

As Madison observed, ambition is best checked by ambition—agents positioned against each other should have countervailing interests. This is most readily accomplished by making the agents' compensation contingent on different standards, such as rewarding managers for increasing production but rewarding comptrollers for cutting costs. Checks can also be applied in information acquisition. Rather than striving for an unbiased source of information, a principal may do better obtaining biased reports from different agents who have conflicting incentives. The view that legal proceedings should be adversarial rather than administrative is based on the same logic. Conversely, checks are disabled when agents' incentives cease to be in conflict.

Checks are equivalent to what social choice theorists refer to as the presence of veto subgroups. The major theoretical results concerning the effects of veto subgroups are generally intuitive. First, the more veto subgroups (checks) there are, the harder it is to change the status quo. The status quo also becomes more difficult to change as preferences within veto subgroups become more homogeneous and as preferences between veto subgroups become more diverse. Checks, then, inhibit the ability of agents to take actions that the principal considers undesirable, but necessarily retard agents from taking desirable actions as well; security comes at the price of flexibility. The desirability of imposing checks on delegated authority thus increases with the utility the principal derives from the status quo and with the amount of danger posed by inappropriate agency actions.

REFERENCES

Halberstam, David. 1986. *The Reckoning*. New York, NY: William Morrow and Company.

Hardin, Garrett. 1968. "The Tragedy of the Commons." *Science* 162:1243–48.

McCubbins, Mathew, Roger Noll, and Barry Weingast. 1987. "Administrative Procedures as an Instrument of Political Control." *Journal of Law, Economics, and Organization* 3:243–77.

———, and Thomas Schwartz. 1984. "Congressional Oversight Overlooked: Police Patrols versus Fire Alarms." *American Journal of Political Science* 28:165–79.

Niskanen, William A. 1971. *Bureaucracy and Representative Government*. Chicago, IL: Aldine-Atherton.

Olson, Mancur. 1965. *The Logic of Collective Action*. Cambridge, MA: Harvard University Press.

Spence, A. Michael. 1974. *Market Signalling: Informational Transfer in Hiring and Related Screening Processes*. Cambridge, MA: Harvard University Press.

Studenski, Paul, and Herman Krooss. 1952. *Financial History of the United States*. New York, NY: McGraw-Hill.

Tirole, Jean. 1986. "Hierarchies and Bureaucracies: On the Role of Coercion in Organizations." *Journal of Law, Economics, and Organization* 2:181–214.

2

THE CONSTITUTION
AND THE FOUNDING

2.1

BRUTUS

The Antifederalist, No. 1

Brutus (a pseudonym used by an anonymous Antifederalist author or authors) argues against the Constitution, saying that it will grant too much power to the central, national government. In this essay, Brutus warns that if the national government were granted the powers described in the Constitution, it would eventually come to dominate the states and oppress the people.

To the Citizens of the State of New York.

When the public is called to investigate and decide upon a question in which not only the present members of the community are deeply interested, but upon which the happiness and misery of generations yet unborn is in great measure suspended, the benevolent mind cannot help feeling itself peculiarly interested in the result.

In this situation, I trust the feeble efforts of an individual, to lead the minds of the people to a wise and prudent determination, cannot fail of being acceptable to the candid and dispassionate part of the community. Encouraged by this consideration, I have been induced to offer my thoughts upon the present important crisis of our public affairs.

From Brutus, *The Antifederalist*, No. 1 (1787).

Perhaps this country never saw so critical a period in their political concerns. We have felt the feebleness of the ties by which these United-States are held together, and the want of sufficient energy in our present confederation, to manage, in some instances, our general concerns. Various expedients have been proposed to remedy these evils, but none have succeeded. At length a Convention of the states has been assembled, they have formed a constitution which will now, probably, be submitted to the people to ratify or reject, who are the fountain of all power, to whom alone it of right belongs to make or unmake constitutions, or forms of government, at their pleasure. The most important question that was ever proposed to your decision, or to the decision of any people under heaven, is before you, and you are to decide upon it by men of your own election, chosen specially for this purpose. If the constitution, offered to your acceptance, be a wise one, calculated to preserve the invaluable blessings of liberty, to secure the inestimable rights of mankind, and promote human happiness, then, if you accept it, you will lay a lasting foundation of happiness for millions yet unborn; generations to come will rise up and call you blessed. You may rejoice in the prospects of this vast extended continent becoming filled with freemen, who will assert the dignity of human nature. You may solace yourselves with the idea, that society, in this favoured land, will fast advance to the highest point of perfection; the human mind will expand in knowledge and virtue, and the golden age be, in some measure, realised. But if, on the other hand, this form of government contains principles that will lead to the subversion of liberty—if it tends to establish a despotism, or, what is worse, a tyrannic aristocracy; then, if you adopt it, this only remaining assylum for liberty will be shut up, and posterity will execrate your memory.

Momentous then is the question you have to determine, and you are called upon by every motive which should influence a noble and virtuous mind, to examine it well, and to make up a wise judgment. It is insisted, indeed, that this constitution must be received, be it ever so imperfect. If it has its defects, it is said, they can be best amended when they are experienced. But remember, when the people once part with power, they can seldom or never resume it again but by force. Many instances can be produced in which the people have voluntarily increased the powers of their rulers; but few, if any, in which rulers have willingly abridged their authority. This is a sufficient reason to induce you to be careful, in the first instance, how you deposit the powers of government.

With these few introductory remarks, I shall proceed to a consideration of this constitution:

The first question that presents itself on the subject is, whether a confederated government be the best for the United States or not? Or in other words, whether the thirteen United States should be reduced to one great republic, governed by one legislature, and under the direction of one executive and judicial; or whether they should continue thirteen confederated republics, under the direction and controul of a supreme federal head for certain defined national purposes only?

This enquiry is important, because, although the government reported by the convention does not go to a perfect and entire consolidation, yet it approaches so near to it, that it must, if executed, certainly and infallibly terminate in it.

This government is to possess absolute and uncontroulable power, legislative, executive and judicial, with respect to every object to which it extends, for by the last clause of section 8th, article 1st, it is declared "that the Congress shall have power to make all laws which shall be necessary and proper for carrying into execution the foregoing powers, and all other powers vested by this constitution, in the government of the United States; or in any department or office thereof." And by the 6th article, it is declared "that this constitution, and the laws of the United States, which shall be made in pursuance thereof, and the treaties made, or which shall be made, under the authority of the United States, shall be the supreme law of the land; and the judges in every state shall be bound thereby, any thing in the constitution, or law of any state to the contrary notwithstanding." It appears from these articles that there is no need of any intervention of the state governments, between the Congress and the people, to execute any one power vested in the general government, and that the constitution and laws of every state are nullified and declared void, so far as they are or shall be inconsistent with this constitution, or the laws made in pursuance of it, or with treaties made under the authority of the United States.—The government then, so far as it extends, is a complete one, and not a confederation. It is as much one complete government as that of New-York or Massachusetts, has as absolute and perfect powers to make and execute all laws, to appoint officers, institute courts, declare offences, and annex penalties, with respect to every object to which it extends, as any other in the world. So far therefore as its powers reach, all ideas of confederation are given up and lost. It is true this government is limited to certain objects, or to speak more properly, some small degree of power is still left to the states, but a little attention to the powers vested in the general government, will convince every candid man, that if it is capable of being executed, all that is reserved for the individual states must very soon be annihilated, except so far as they are barely necessary to the organization of the general government. The powers of the general legislature extend to every case that is of the least importance—there is nothing valuable to human nature, nothing dear to freemen, but what is within its power. It has authority to make laws which will affect the lives, the liberty, and property of every man in the United States; nor can the constitution or laws of any state, in any way prevent or impede the full and complete execution of every power given. The legislative power is competent to lay taxes, duties, imposts, and excises;—there is no limitation to this power, unless it be said that the clause which directs the use to which those taxes, and duties shall be applied, may be said to be a limitation: but this is no restriction of the power at all, for by this clause they are to be applied to pay the debts and provide for the common defence and general welfare of the

United States; but the legislature have authority to contract debts at their discretion; they are the sole judges of what is necessary to provide for the common defence, and they only are to determine what is for the general welfare; this power therefore is neither more nor less, than a power to lay and collect taxes, imposts, and excises, at their pleasure; not only [is] the power to lay taxes unlimited, as to the amount they may require, but it is perfect and absolute to raise them in any mode they please. No state legislature, or any power in the state governments, have any more to do in carrying this into effect, than the authority of one state has to do with that of another. In the business therefore of laying and collecting taxes, the idea of confederation is totally lost, and that of one entire republic is embraced. It is proper here to remark, that the authority to lay and collect taxes is the most important of any power that can be granted; it connects with it almost all other powers, or at least will in process of time draw all other after it; it is the great mean of protection, security, and defence, in a good government, and the great engine of oppression and tyranny in a bad one. This cannot fail of being the case, if we consider the contracted limits which are set by this constitution, to the late [state?] governments, on this article of raising money. No state can emit paper money—lay any duties, or imposts, on imports, or exports, but by consent of the Congress; and then the net produce shall be for the benefit of the United States: the only mean therefore left, for any state to support its government and discharge its debts, is by direct taxation; and the United States have also power to lay and collect taxes, in any way they please. Every one who has thought on the subject, must be convinced that but small sums of money can be collected in any country, by direct taxe[s], when the foederal government begins to exercise the right of taxation in all its parts, the legislatures of the several states will find it impossible to raise monies to support their governments. Without money they cannot be supported, and they must dwindle away, and, as before observed, their powers absorbed in that of the general government.

It might be here shewn, that the power in the federal legislative, to raise and support armies at pleasure, as well in peace as in war, and their controul over the militia, tend, not only to a consolidation of the government, but the destruction of liberty.—I shall not, however, dwell upon these, as a few observations upon the judicial power of this government, in addition to the preceding, will fully evince the truth of the position.

The judicial power of the United States is to be vested in a supreme court, and in such inferior courts as Congress may from time to time ordain and establish. The powers of these courts are very extensive; their jurisdiction comprehends all civil causes, except such as arise between citizens of the same state; and it extends to all cases in law and equity arising under the constitution. One inferior court must be established, I presume, in each state, at least, with the necessary executive officers appendant thereto. It is easy to see, that in the common course of things, these courts will eclipse the dignity, and take away from the respectability, of the state courts. These courts will be, in themselves, totally independent of the states, deriving their authority from the United States, and receiving from them fixed salaries; and in the course of human events it is to be expected, that they will swallow up all the powers of the courts in the respective states.

How far the clause in the 8th section of the 1st article may operate to do away all idea of confederated states, and to effect an entire consolidation of the whole into one general government, it is impossible to say. The powers given by this article are very general and comprehensive, and it may receive a construction to justify the passing almost any law. A power to make all laws, which shall be *necessary and proper*, for carrying into execution, all powers vested by the constitution in the government of the United States, or any department or officer thereof, is a power very comprehensive and definite [indefinite?], and may, for ought I know, be exercised in a such manner as entirely to abolish the state legislatures. Suppose the legislature of a state should pass a law to raise money to support their government and pay the state debt, may the Congress repeal this law, because it may prevent the collection of a tax which they may think proper and necessary to lay, to provide for the general welfare of the United States? For all laws made, in pursuance of this constitution, are the supreme lay of the land, and the judges in every state shall be bound thereby, any thing in the constitution or laws of the different states to the contrary notwithstanding.—By such a law, the government of a particular state might be overturned at one stroke, and thereby be deprived of every means of its support.

It is not meant, by stating this case, to insinuate that the constitution would warrant a law of this kind; or unnecessarily to alarm the fears of the people, by suggesting, that the federal legislature would be more likely to pass the limits assigned them by the constitution, than that of an individual state, further than they are less responsible to the people. But what is meant is, that the legislature of the United States are vested with the great and uncontroulable powers, of laying and collecting taxes, duties, imposts, and excises; of regulating trade, raising and supporting armies, organizing, arming, and disciplining the militia, instituting courts, and other general powers. And are by this clause invested with the power of making all laws, *proper and necessary*, for carrying all these into execution; and they may so exercise this power as entirely to annihilate all the state governments, and reduce this country to one single government. And if they may do it, it is pretty certain they will; for it will be found that the power retained by individual states, small as it is, will be a clog upon the wheels of the government of the United States; the latter therefore will be naturally inclined to remove it out of the way. Besides, it is a truth confirmed by the unerring experience of ages, that every man, and every body of men, invested with power, are ever disposed to increase it, and to acquire a superiority over every thing that stands in their way. This disposition, which is implanted in human nature, will operate in the federal legislature to lessen and ultimately to subvert the state authority, and having such advantages, will most certainly succeed, if the federal government succeeds at all. It must be very evident then, that what this constitution wants of being a complete consolidation of the several parts of the union into one complete government, possessed of perfect legislative, judicial, and executive powers, to all intents and purposes, it will necessarily acquire in its exercise and operation.

Let us now proceed to enquire, as I at first proposed, whether it be best the thirteen United States should be reduced to one great republic, or not? It is here taken for granted, that all agree in this, that whatever government we adopt, it ought to be a free one; that it should be so framed as to secure the liberty of the citizens of America, and such an one as to admit of a full, fair, and equal representation of the people. The question then will be, whether a government thus constituted, and founded on such principles, is practicable, and can be exercised over the whole United States, reduced into one state?

If respect is to be paid to the opinion of the greatest and wisest men who have ever thought or wrote on the science of government, we shall be constrained to conclude, that a free republic cannot succeed over a country of such immense extent, containing such a number of inhabitants, and these encreasing in such rapid progression as that of the whole United States. Among the many illustrious authorities which might be produced to this point, I shall content myself with quoting only two. The one is the baron de Montesquieu, spirit of laws, chap. xvi. vol. I [book VIII]. "It is natural to a republic to have only a small territory, otherwise it cannot long subsist. In a large republic there are men of large fortunes, and consequently of less moderation; there are trusts too great to be placed in any single subject; he has interest of his own; he soon begins to think that he may be happy, great and glorious, by oppressing his fellow citizens; and that he may raise himself to grandeur on the ruins of his country. In a large republic, the public good is sacrificed to a thousand views; it is subordinate to exceptions, and depends on accidents. In a small one, the interest of the public is easier perceived, better understood, and more within the reach of every citizen; abuses are of less extent, and of course are less protected." Of the same opinion is the marquis Beccarari.

History furnishes no example of a free republic, any thing like the extent of the United States. The Grecian republics were of small extent; so also was that of the Romans. Both of these, it is true, in process of time, extended their conquests over large territories of country; and the consequence was, that their governments were changed from that of free governments to those of the most tyrannical that ever existed in the world.

Not only the opinion of the greatest men, and the experience of mankind, are against the idea of an extensive republic, but a variety of reasons may be drawn from the reason and nature of things, against it. In every government, the will of the sovereign is the law. In despotic governments, the supreme authority being lodged in one, his will is law, and can be as easily expressed to a large extensive territory as to a small one. In a pure democracy the people are the sovereign, and their will is declared by themselves; for this purpose they must all come together to deliberate, and decide. This kind of government cannot be exercised, therefore, over a country of any considerable extent; it must be confined to a single city, or at least limited to such bounds as that the people can conveniently assemble, be able to debate, understand the subject submitted to them, and declare their opinion concerning it.

In a free republic, although all laws are derived from the consent of the people, yet the people do not declare their consent by themselves in person, but by representatives, chosen by them, who are supposed to know the minds of their constituents, and to be possessed of integrity to declare this mind.

In every free government, the people must give their assent to the laws by which they are governed. This is the true criterion between a free government and an arbitrary one. The former are ruled by the will of the whole, expressed in any manner they may agree upon; the latter by the will of one, or a few. If the people are to give their assent to the laws, by persons chosen and appointed by them, the manner of the choice and the number chosen, must be such, as to possess, be disposed, and consequently qualified to declare the sentiments of the people; for if they do not know, or are not disposed to speak the sentiments of the people, the people do not govern, but the sovereignty is in a few. Now, in a large extended country, it is impossible to have a representation, possessing the sentiments, and of integrity, to declare the minds of the people, without having it so numerous and unwieldly, as to be subject in great measure to the inconveniency of a democratic government.

The territory of the United States is of vast extent; it now contains near three millions of souls, and is capable of containing much more than ten times that number. Is it practicable for a country, so large and so numerous as they will soon become, to elect a representation, that will speak their sentiments, without their becoming so numerous as to be incapable of transacting public business? It certainly is not.

In a republic, the manners, sentiments, and interests of the people should be similar. If this be not the case, there will be a constant clashing of opinions; and the representatives of one part will be continually striving against those of the other. This will retard the operations of government, and prevent such conclusions as will promote the public good. If we apply this remark to the condition of the United States, we shall be convinced that it forbids that we should be one government. The United States includes a variety of climates. The productions of the different parts of the union are very variant, and their interests, of consequence, diverse. Their manners and habits differ as much as their climates and productions; and their sentiments are by no means coincident. The laws and customs of the several states are, in many respects, very diverse, and in some opposite; each would be in favor of its own interests and customs, and, of consequence, a legislature, formed of representatives from the respective parts, would not only be too numerous to act with any care or decision, but would be composed of such heterogenous and discordant principles, as would constantly be contending with each other.

The laws cannot be executed in a republic, of an extent equal to that of the United States, with promptitude.

The magistrates in every government must be supported in the execution of the laws, either by an armed force, maintained at the public expence for that purpose; or by the people turning out to aid the magistrate upon his command, in case of resistance.

In despotic governments, as well as in all the monarchies of Europe, standing armies are kept up to execute the commands of the prince or the magistrate, and are employed for this purpose when occasion requires: But they have always proved the destruction of liberty, and [are] abhorrent to the spirit of a free republic. In England, where they depend upon the parliament for their annual support, they have always been complained of as oppressive and unconstitutional, and are seldom employed in executing of the laws; never except on extraordinary occasions, and then under the direction of a civil magistrate.

A free republic will never keep a standing army to execute its laws. It must depend upon the support of its citizens. But when a government is to receive its support from the aid of the citizens, it must be so constructed as to have the confidence, respect, and affection of the people. Men who, upon the call of the magistrate, offer themselves to execute the laws, are influenced to do it either by affection to the government, or from fear; where a standing army is at hand to punish offenders, every man is actuated by the latter principle, and therefore, when the magistrate calls, will obey: but, where this is not the case, the government must rest for its support upon the confidence and respect which the people have for their government and laws. The body of the people being attached, the government will always be sufficient to support and execute its laws, and to operate upon the fears of any faction which may be opposed to it, not only to prevent an opposition to the execution of the laws themselves, but also to compel the most of them to aid the magistrate; but the people will not be likely to have such confidence in their rulers, in a republic so extensive as the United States, as necessary for these purposes. The confidence which the people have in their rulers, in a free republic, arises from their knowing them, from their being responsible to them for their conduct, and from the power they have of displacing them when they misbehave: but in a republic of the extent of this continent, the people in general would be acquainted with very few of their rulers: the people at large would know little of their proceedings, and it would be extremely difficult to change them. The people in Georgia and New-Hampshire would not know one another's mind, and therefore could not act in concert to enable them to effect a general change of representatives. The different parts of so extensive a country could not possibly be made acquainted with the conduct of their representatives, nor be informed of the reasons upon which measures were founded. The consequence will be, they will have no confidence in their legislature, suspect them of ambitious views, be jealous of every measure they adopt, and will not support the laws they pass. Hence the government will be nerveless and inefficient, and no way will be left to render it otherwise, but by establishing an armed force to execute the laws at the point of the bayonet—a government of all others the most to be dreaded.

In a republic of such vast extent as the United-States, the legislature cannot attend to the various concerns and wants of its different parts. It cannot be sufficiently numerous to be acquainted with the local condition and wants of the different districts, and if it could, it is impossible it should have sufficient time to attend to and provide for all the variety of cases of this nature, that would be continually arising.

In so extensive a republic, the great officers of government would soon become above the controul of the people, and abuse their power to the purpose of aggrandizing themselves, and oppressing them. The trust committed to the executive offices, in a country of the extent of the United-States, must be various and of magnitude. The command of all the troops and navy of the republic, the appointment of officers, the power of pardoning offences, the collecting of all the public revenues, and the power of expending them, with a number of other powers, must be lodged and exercised in every state, in the hands of a few. When these are attended with great honor and emolument, as they always will be in large states, so as greatly to interest men to pursue them, and to be proper objects for ambitious and designing men, such men will be ever restless in their pursuit after them. They will use the power, when they have acquired it, to the purposes of gratifying their own interest and ambition, and it is scarcely possible, in a very large republic, to call them to account for their misconduct, or to prevent their abuse of power.

These are some of the reasons by which it appears, that a free republic cannot long subsist over a country of the great extent of these states. If then this new constitution is calculated to consolidate the thirteen states into one, as it evidently is, it ought not to be adopted.

Though I am of opinion, that it is a sufficient objection to this government, to reject it, that it creates the whole union into one government, under the form of a republic, yet if this objection was obviated, there are exceptions to it, which are so material and fundamental, that they ought to determine every man, who is a friend to the liberty and happiness of mankind, not to adopt it. I beg the candid and dispassionate attention of my countrymen while I state these objections—they are such as have obtruded themselves upon my mind upon a careful attention to the matter, and such as I sincerely believe are well founded. There are many objections, of small moment, of which I shall take no notice—perfection is not to be expected in any thing that is the production of man—and if I did not in my conscience believe that this scheme was defective in the fundamental principles—in the foundation upon which a free and equal government must rest—I would hold my peace.

2.2

JEREMY C. POPE AND SHAWN TREIER

From "Voting for a Founding: Testing the Effect of Economic Interests at the Federal Convention of 1787"

A century ago Charles Beard made the famous argument that the Founders designed the Constitution to serve their individual economic interests and the interests of the upper class. Pope and Treier examine Beard's thesis using new data on the personal attributes of each of the Founders at the Constitutional Convention and the votes of those Founders on three main issues at the Convention: representation, the power of the president relative to Congress, and federalism. They find that Beard was partially right: individual Founders voted on these controversial issues often in keeping with the economic interests of their local areas and their families. But voting based on economic interests was uneven and depended on the specific issue at stake.

Understanding the voting patterns of the Federal Convention of 1787—more popularly known as the Constitutional Convention—has been a preoccupation of historians, political scientists, sociologists, and economists for well over one hundred years. There is inherent interest in the views of such famous statesmen as James Madison, Benjamin Franklin, and George Washington, among others, but social scientists want to go beyond simply learning their respective views or even measuring their issue positions to a clearer explanation of what interests or ideas could have motivated them. To tackle this complex problem, we must realize that the Convention proceeded in stages. The early period—May through July—focused on key issues for creating a new government: the nature of representation, the internal design of a new national government, and how power would be distributed between the national and the state governments. These decisions had to be resolved before the Committee of Detail could pull together a draft of the compromises. Only then could the delegates proceed to other matters like trade, war powers, and other issues.

Without disputing the key role of ideas and and philosophies of government (e.g., Lockean liberalism or republican virtue), we focus on interests that may have shaped debate. Charles Beard (1913) first offered an "economic," or interest-based, theory of the Convention, arguing it was a conflict between two classes:

From Jeremy C. Pope and Shawn Treier, "Voting for a Founding: Testing the Effect of Economic Interests at the Federal Convention of 1787," *The Journal of Politics* 77, no. 2 (April 2015): 519–34.

the "personalty" and the "realty." Though Beard's specific thesis has fallen out of favor, the spirit of explaining the Constitution by examining the relationship between key groups and the pattern of votes remains strong whether via a historical narrative or a social science model. . . . These efforts typically focus either on modeling coalitions (Jillson 2002; Slez and Martin 2007) or modeling the effect of economic interests on specific individual votes (Heckelman and Dougherty 2010; McGuire 2003). Our contribution is to attempt both elements simultaneously to test economic influence on the major dimensions of debate. . . . [Our] results suggest a picture of the Convention where economic interests matter. Beard's simplistic view of the Convention's interests may not hold, but a broader thesis about the importance of economic factors such as slavery, trade, and certain forms of wealth clearly is supported. . . . Economic interests indisputably mattered for the deep structure of preferences and voting at the Philadelphia Convention.

THEORIES OF THE CONVENTION

. . . Before we can ask which interests explain voting, we need to have a clear idea of the dimensions of the early debate so as to know what to model. Narrative histories often speak about a debate over "nationalism" and a stronger central government—Clinton Rossiter actually titles his chapter about the opening of the Convention the "Assault of the Nationalists" (1966, 159). The problem with this labeling is that it obscures multiple, distinct dimensions to nationalism: representation, the design of the new government, and the strength of the new government relative to the states.

It is well known that Madison believed representation should be proportional to the population of the states (Rossiter describes this issue as the "one large thing" that "divided them" [180]). And there is not a narrative account of the Convention, with which we are familiar, that does not emphasize representation as central to the first two months of debate (Beeman 2010; Bowen 1966; McDonald 1965; Rakove 1996; Roche 1961). But this dimension was hardly the only element of nationalization. Accounts that lump the powers and design of the national government in with representation are suggesting that multiple issues can be described using the same dimension. So when Rossiter describes the "assault of the nationalists," he is really talking about multiple dimensions of conflict. In fact, we know that delegates explicitly recognized some of these distinct dimensions. Beeman writes of George Read's (DE) beliefs that

> any new constitution ought to give the new government explicit supremacy over those governments of the individual states and that the new national legislature should have a veto over any state laws that might conflict with those of the central government. . . . But while Read was prepared to grant the central government sovereign power over the

individual states, he was unwilling to change the essential element of the Articles of Confederation that protected the sovereignty of those states. (2010, 72)

Equal state representation in the legislature was vital for Read. His position exemplifies how the debates had at least two distinct dimensions: proportional representation and the division of power between the national government and the states. What explains one dimension might have little to do with the other.

The discipline of building [a theory] of the Convention forces us to be clear about dimensions of debate, rather than simply treating them all as an example of "nationalism." . . . We are left with a situation where the best work on voting at the Convention suggests that there are multiple dimensions. . . .

As the first to explicitly offer an economic model of the Convention, Charles Beard is most famous for his simple thesis that the type of wealth mattered: personal wealth in liquid capital (the "personalty") worked against wealth in land and real estate (the "realty") to create a reformed constitution. Less well known is that Beard also offers some guidance on the dimensions of the Convention. In his sixth chapter, "The Constitution As An Economic Document," Beard lays out the case for how economic forces affected different dimensions of the document that would become the US Constitution. Beard opens this chapter with a discussion of how one needs to think about the Constitution and how *The Federalist* explains the economic content. Then he divides the rest of the chapter by several headings: "The Underlying Political Science of the Constitution," "The Structure of Government or the Balance of Powers," "The Powers Conferred Upon the Federal Government," and "Restrictions Laid Upon State Legislatures."

It is easy to see three dimensions that come out of this discussion: *representation;*[1] *national institutional design* or the balance of powers within the government; and *federalism* or the division between the federal government and the state governments. Beard's thesis appears to be that certain economic interests would take the same set of positions on all questions of reform: change the basis of representation to protect property rights; strengthen the national government's power; but also make sure property interests are powerful within that government by limiting the ability of a majority in the legislature to seize property.

▪ ▪ ▪

McDonald's (1958) landmark study demolished the consensus around Beard's ideas, revealing far more complexity in the economic patterns than Beard had contemplated—literally pointing to dozens of separate interests in play at the Convention. Today some historians dismiss an economic interpretation entirely (often focusing more on a cultural approach); however that was hardly the end of this type of explanation. . . . Instead of focusing on a simplistic version of two interests in opposition, McGuire (2003) conclusively demonstrates that several different "personal and constituent economic interests affected voting on particular issues" (91) and, that certain interests, like those living near centers of trade, were "more pro-national" (125). However, this work focuses on a small dataset of a few votes, which McGuire describes as "weak . . . and [leading to] imprecision in the estimated coefficients" (92);[2] furthermore, these votes occur later in the Convention, long after the basic structure had been decided. Heckelman and Dougherty (2010) come to a similar conclusion rejecting the narrow Beard thesis, but finding some support for economic motivations on a few key votes related to currency and debt issues.

. . . Though we have painstakingly reviewed the Convention records to increase our knowledge of delegate votes, there is *no* way to collect *all* of the positions necessary for a conventional model—many delegates never expressed a clear stand on a specific question. . . . Our principle could be described as "silence is more likely to indicate consent than dissent."

This assumption is similar to the strategy originally pursued by McDonald (1958). He assumes that because delegates from Pennsylvania rarely spoke— other than Morris and Franklin—the delegation was fairly unified. With his assumption in mind, we remind the reader that our model focuses on the first period of the Convention, running through vote 230 on July 26. This takes us through the moment that they have finished the major decisions on the structure of the plan and how it would be ratified. At this point the Committee of Detail takes up the draft and produces a document harmonizing all of the previous agreements. The Convention breaks until August 6 and then takes up the "details" that remain to be decided at this point. Scholars typically divide the convention into as many as five different periods (Jillson 2002; Slez and Martin 2007). Our purpose is to focus attention entirely on the first period of the Convention to explain the key decisions and major issues decided when they were still building the framework of the new government.

Discerning Individual Votes

All of the delegation votes are available, and some delegate votes are known clearly (because they are recorded in the notes). . . . We carefully went through the notes of the Convention to see where we could add information about specific individuals. . . .

. . . We examine the notes on the debates for any indication that a delegate supported or opposed a proposal, coding their positions to the specific roll call for the proposal (Farrand 1913). The most common form of approval or disapproval was to make a motion or second a motion on a question. For instance, we read that Mr. Read motioned and Mr. C.C. Pinckney seconded a motion to amend one of Randolph's proposals about the form of government (Farrand 1913, 35). Such motions and indications are scattered throughout the notes. In other cases delegates made a speech that clearly indicated support or opposition to a proposal. . . . Similar logical rules were employed throughout the process to analyze the positions of delegates.

■ ■ ■

VARIABLES

Our [theory] is designed to explain the two levels of voting—individual voting, but *within* delegations. Thus the [theory] characterizes both constituency and personal influences. . . . Our focus is on identifying which economic interests explained the deep structure of voting patterns at the Convention, but we control for noneconomic explanations as well. Throughout we focus on Beard's original ideas and their later extensions and tests.

State-Level Predictors

Several predictors fit into the model at each level of voting and are summarized in Table 1, including references for data sources. At the delegation level, the key variables are slave holdings, the percentage of the state that is rural, the estimated per capita real estate wealth, and the white population of the state.

■ ■ ■

Individual-Level Predictors

Coefficients on the delegation variables predict differences across the delegations. In contrast, coefficients on the individual-level variables predict commonalities across delegates. In that sense, the first part of the model is only about the differences across constituencies. In this second portion of the model we are asking what forces, regardless of the delegation's overall position, had a common influence across delegates? Table [1] again summarizes the key variables—the economic variables being slaves, distance from navigable water, public and private wealth holdings, land holdings, and occupation.

■ ■ ■

We have a series of tests—across multiple dimensions—for Beard's claims about economic interests. With all of these [statistical claims] in hand we . . . test Beard's specific ideas about the nature of what wealth mattered for voting but also which *types* of wealth predicted voting more generally. . . .

RESULTS

Small states pushing for an equal state vote in the upper chamber were intransigent. Rakove says "the supporters of the equal-state vote grew impervious to appeals for justice, however eloquent . . . On this issue there was little left to say" (1996, 70). . . . The small-state coalition was, in general, relatively unified

TABLE [1] Predictors of Delegation-Level Behavior and Delegate-Level Behavior

State Predictors	Source	Mean	SD	Maximum	Minimum
White state population	1790 census	236166.7	134188.4	4420000	46000
Slave holdings, per 100 whites	McGuire	26.3	28.6	76	0
Percentage rural	1790 census	95.1	4.8	100	86.5
State wealth	Pitkin	46637067.95	34068192.64	102145900.90	6233412.25
Individual Predictors					
Personal slave holdings	McGuire	37.9	67.0	300	0
Distance to water	McGuire	54.4	53.2	200	0
Private securities	McGuire	2405.5	9308.6	52000	0
Public securities	McGuire	1078.5	2098.8	10000	0
Agricultural land holdings	McDonald	0.56	0.5	1	0
Western land holdings	McDonald	0.22	0.42	1	0
Farmer	McGuire	0.1	0.3	1	0
Merchant	McGuire	0.1	0.3	1	0
Age	Biographies	44.1	11.9	81	26
Service in the revolution	McGuire	0.27	0.45	1	0
College	Heckelman and Dougherty	0.68	0.47	1	0
Hierarchical religion	Heckelman and Dougherty	0.68	0.47	1	0
Communitarian religion	Heckelman and Dougherty	0.17	0.38	1	0
English ancestry	McGuire & Biographies	0.49	0.51	1	0
Scottish ancestry	McGuire & Biographies	0.22	0.42	1	0

NOTE: Sources for each entry are listed at right. In the case of religion, we used Heckelman and Dougherty's classifications but then supplemented that with delegate biographies, chiefly Bradford (1982) and delegate biographies on the Library of Congress's website.

against shifting power away from the states and against proportional representation in the Senate—some delegates extremely so, like Lansing and Yates.[3] The large state coalition is less unified, especially on the question of centralization. Many delegates like Wilson, Hamilton, and Madison favor much more centralized power, but they were balanced by another set of delegates (especially from Georgia and South Carolina) far less supportive of a strong central government. The large states were simply less unified across dimensions.

. . . It is worth commenting on a few other notable individuals. . . . Madison, a leader of the federalist coalition at this point in history but shortly to become a leader of the anti-Federalist party, is clearly in the camp of leaders pushing for a stronger central government with greater proportional representation, though his position is not quite as extreme as some other prominent leaders on some dimensions. George Washington only spoke twice at the convention (though he did preside). But Madison records his vote on a few issues, and his position relative to the Virginia delegation is interesting. Like Madison, he favors proportional representation . . . , and he does appear to favor executive power over the legislature. . . . What must be clear, based on these results, is that the Convention was hardly a unified group even though it is sometimes described that way. And no delegate appears to have gotten their way on every single dimension. Wood notes that "Madison and Wilson lost the battles over the congressional veto of state laws and proportional representation in both houses, [but] they and the other Federalists . . . had essentially won the war over the basic nature of the central government" (2003, 158). Without disagreeing that the government's nature changed, these figures show complex preferences where no delegate or group dictated the result.

At the delegation level, the influence of slavery is obviously important. Delegations from slave states strongly favored proportional representation. . . . Delegations from states with relatively more slaves probably favored shifting power away from the states. . . . This is quite consistent with an interpretation that states with a more rural population feared shifting power away from the states and toward the national government. . . . Higher white-population states . . . favored a stronger national executive (relative to the legislature) *and* shifting power away from states to a national government.

Turning to the individual level . . . we begin again with slavery, and here the preference for proportional representation is also quite clear. Slave owners appear to have favored proportional representation . . . but at this level it becomes more clear that they opposed shifting power away from Congress to this new branch: the presidency. . . . The preference of southern states against a strong presidency can also be seen. . . . And, again, we see that the slave interest favored a stronger central government. Strikingly similar to the slave-owning interest, delegates living further from the coasts and trade favored reform on the representation and federalism dimensions but opposed creating a strong national executive.

Regarding . . . wealth . . . , holding private securities clearly predicts a preference for *both* a stronger central government *and* a stronger president within that government. Individual holdings in *public* securities are different; the only clear result is a preference *against* a stronger centralized government. This runs exactly opposite to expectations, not only in the sense that . . . Beard claimed that owners of public securities were "even more immediately concerned in the establishment of a stable national government" (1913, 32) than other forms of liquid wealth. Holdings in public securities actually predicted a preference for strong *state* governments. As for the type of delegate land holdings, they are influential only on the representation dimension. We find that holding agricultural land[4] predicts a strong preference *against* proportional representation. This prediction is clearly in the direction Beard suggested as holding farmland would have clearly placed delegates in Beard's "realty" class. Another prediction that goes as Beard would have suggested is holding western lands. Those who may have hoped to profit by speculation appeared to favor changing the basis of representation, though their preferences on the other variables are not as clear. . . . Merchants are more likely to support proportional representation . . . and centralized power . . . than farmers, but less likely to favor a stronger president at the expense of the Congress.

▪ ▪ ▪

DISCUSSION

The first few weeks of the Convention saw some of the most crucial decisions that would occur that Philadelphia summer, laying the foundation for a much stronger central government. Our aim was to test which interests mattered for which dimensions of debate in this early key period. . . . Where does this leave the economic thesis?

Beard's narrow thesis about two dominant interests finds little support. We find little evidence that anything like a "personalty" influence was powerful at the Convention in this period. In particular, our results contradict Beard's claim that those who held public securities were in a prime position to profit from the new government as they "brought their papers to the . . . Treasury to have them recorded and transformed into the stocks of the new government" (Beard 1913, 21). There are many specific points in the [theory] that reject Beard's narrow thesis. Those living near the coasts and closer to trade appear to have taken a dim view of the Constitution's proposed changes to representation. . . . Farmers appear to have favored most every element of the Constitution, and merchants appear to have a preference for weaker national power. Each of these findings, to some degree, contradicts Beard's claims, at least as they are applied to the Convention (we remind the reader that ratification is a separate issue we plan to take up in future research). However, his broader point about the importance of economic interests to voting—in this case to the preferences of the delegates and delegations—finds a great deal of support.

Beard's broad claim that "it was an economic document drawn with superb skill by men whose property interests were immediately at stake; and as such it appealed directly and unerringly to identical interests in the country at large" (1913, 188) gains a surprising amount of traction. It is not a complete explanation, but it sheds significant light on voting. While this analysis cannot speak to the motivations of those men, as Beard does, we do agree that economic interests played a clear and important role in organizing the deep structure of voting in Philadelphia. More rural delegations opposed giving power to a centralized government. Those living further from trade appear to have opposed strengthening the presidency. Private securities have a clear effect on both National Institutional Design and Federalism and, as suggested by Beard, that interest favored reform. Agricultural land owners were clearly voting against changing the basis of representation. . . . Beard gets enough correct that one cannot really dismiss his claims about the importance of economic interests—but one must consider different dimensions of the conflict.

We emphasize that this story is novel. . . . This is the first study to attempt a [theory] of interests across individual and delegation voting patterns in multiple dimensions. . . . We find that, in a sense, the historians were right. Beard's parsimonious claims were too simple. A multidimensional approach allows us to see which interests mattered on which dimensions. In fact every economic variable matters on some dimension, but the document ultimately created was far from a victory for any particular coalition, and economic interests hardly ruled the day in all cases.

The broader point may be that complexity was a key feature of the preferences. . . . When your coalitions are as complicated as this analysis shows, there is not likely to be one clear class that "won" at the Convention. . . . Small state delegates were, on average, less sympathetic to centralized power, but there were exceptions like Dickinson and Dayton who were about as enthusiastic on this point as many other delegates. And the large states were divided on some questions like the nature of the presidency and how far to push centralizing power. A few Southerners such as Baldwin and Pierce may have taken strongly pronational positions, but others like Rutledge and the Pinckneys were far more cautions. . . . It is an exaggeration to portray a tidy meeting of the minds in Philadelphia where demigods called "Founders" agreed on the set of principles that would guide the young nation.

Ironically for the slave interests, the government ultimately created was much stronger—and had the potential to become even stronger—than they probably imagined. The implicit alliance between slave holders and parochial interests living far from centers of trade may have won the debate over changing representation, but the new government and the president within that government became much more powerful than some slave owners preferred. This pattern certainly fits the received wisdom of a bundle of compromises. Simplistic views of what the "Founders" believed are far from the complex truth; a crucial historical event can only be approached with a rather complex explanation. The birth of the American government may not have been a result of one particular form of wealth or privilege dominating the debates, but it was the result of pluralism and compromise between representatives of different economic interests and ideas.

NOTES

1. Writing about the underlying political science, he references Madison on representation.

2. Though this self-criticism is far more applicable to his analysis of the Convention than it is of the ratification debates.

3. The results for this delegation suggest the model is capturing voting dynamics. The New York delegation median is approximately midway between the two factions in that state, leaning a bit more closely to Lansing and Yates. If the model were simply tying every delegate too closely to the state position, the delegates would be placed much closer together. Given that they are not, we are confident the model is working as we hope.

4. Note that this is distinct from actually working as a farmer.

REFERENCES

Beard, Charles A. 1913. *An Economic Interpretation of the Constitution of the United States*. New York: Macmillan.

Beeman, Richard. 2010. *Plain, Honest Men: The Making of the American Constitution*. New York: Random House.

Bowen, Catherine Drinker. 1966. *Miracle at Philadelphia: The Story of the Constitutional Convention May to September 1787*. New York: Back Bay Books.

Bradford, M. E. 1982. *A Worthy Company: Brief Lives of the Framers of the United States Constitution*. Marlborough, NH: Plymouth Rock Foundation.

Farrand, Max. 1913. *The Framing of the Constitution of the United States*. New Haven, CT: Yale University Press.

Heckelman, Jac C., and Keith L. Dougherty. 2010. "Personalty Interests at the Constitutional Convention: New Tests of the Beard Thesis." *Cliometrica* 4 (2): 207–28.

Jillson, Calvin C. 2002. *Constitution Making: Conflict and Consensus in the Federal Convention of 1787*. New York: Agathon Press.

McDonald, Forrest. 1958. *We the People*. Chicago: University of Chicago Press.

McDonald, Forrest. 1965. *E Pluribus Unum: The Formation of the American Republic 1776–1790*. New York: Houghton Mifflon.

McGuire, Robert A. 2003. *To Form a More Perfect Union: A New Economic Interpretation of the United States Constitution*. New York: Oxford University Press.

Rakove, Jack N. 1996. *Original Meanings: Politics and Ideas in the Making of the Constitution*. New York: Random House.

Roche, John P. 1961. "The Founding Fathers: A Reform Caucus in Action." *American Political Science Review* 55 (4): 799–816.

Rossiter, Clinton. 1966. *The Grand Convention*. New York: New American Library.

Slez, Adam, and John Levi Martin. 2007. "Political Action and Party Formation in the United States Constitutional Convention." *American Sociological Review* 72 (February): 42–67.

Wood, Gordon S. 2003. *The American Revolution: A History*. New York: Modern Library.

2.3

ROBERT A. DAHL

From *How Democratic Is the American Constitution?*

Dahl casts a critical eye on the American Constitution. He lists numerous problems with the document. Most important, it implicitly sanctioned slavery and set up two undemocratic institutions: the Supreme Court and the Senate. He concludes that it survived by allowing for mass elections to determine who controlled the national government, and thus was "democratic" enough to overcome its weaknesses.

UNDEMOCRATIC ELEMENTS IN THE FRAMERS' CONSTITUTION

. . . Judged from later, more democratic perspectives, the Constitution of the Framers contained at least seven important shortcomings.

Slavery

First, it neither forbade slavery nor empowered Congress to do so. In fact, the compromise on slavery not only denied Congress the effective power to prohibit the importation of slaves before 1808[1] but it gave constitutional sanction to one of the most morally objectionable byproducts of a morally repulsive institution: the Fugitive Slave laws, according to which a slave who managed to escape to a free state had to be returned to the slaveholder, whose property the slave remained.[2] That it took three-quarters of a century and a sanguinary civil war before slavery was abolished should at the least make us doubt whether the document of the Framers ought to be regarded as holy writ.

Suffrage

Second, the Constitution failed to guarantee the right of suffrage, leaving the qualifications of suffrage to the states.[3] It implicitly left in place the exclusion of half the population—women—as well as African Americans and Native Americans.[4] As we know, it took a century and a half before women were constitutionally guaranteed the right to vote, and nearly two centuries before a president and Congress could overcome the effective veto of a minority of

From Robert A. Dahl, *How Democratic Is the American Constitution?* (New Haven, CT: Yale University Press, 2001).

states in order to pass legislation intended to guarantee the voting rights of African Americans.

Election of the President

Third, the executive power was vested in a president whose selection, according to the intentions and design of the Framers, was to be insulated from both popular majorities and congressional control. As we'll see, the Framers' main design for achieving that purpose—a body of presidential electors composed of men of exceptional wisdom and virtue who would choose the chief executive unswayed by popular opinion—was almost immediately cast into the dustbin of history by leaders sympathetic with the growing democratic impulses of the American people, among them James Madison himself. Probably nothing the Framers did illustrates more sharply their inability to foresee the shape that politics would assume in a democratic republic. . . .

Choosing Senators

Fourth, senators were to be chosen not by the people but by the state legislatures, for a term of six years.[5] Although this arrangement fell short of the ambitions of delegates like Gouverneur Morris who wanted to construct an aristocratic upper house, it would help to ensure that senators would be less responsive to popular majorities and perhaps more sensitive to the needs of property holders. Members of the Senate would thus serve as a check on the Representatives, who were all subject to popular elections every two years.[6]

Equal Representation in the Senate

The attempt to create a Senate that would be a republican version of the aristocratic House of Lords was derailed, as we have seen, by a prolonged and bitter dispute over an entirely different question: Should the states be equally represented in Congress or should members of both houses be allocated according to population? This question not only gave rise to one of the most disruptive issues of the Convention, but it resulted in a fifth undemocratic feature of the Constitution. As a consequence of the famous—or from a democratic point of view, infamous—"Connecticut Compromise" each state was, as we have seen, awarded the same number of senators, without respect to population. Although this arrangement failed to protect the fundamental rights and interests of the most deprived minorities, some strategically placed and highly privileged minorities—slaveholders, for example—gained disproportionate power over government polices at the expense of less privileged minorities. . . .

Judicial Power

Sixth, the Constitution of the Framers failed to limit the powers of the judiciary to declare as unconstitutional laws that had been properly passed by Congress and signed by the president. What the delegates intended in the way of judicial review will remain forever unclear; probably many delegates were unclear in their own minds, and to the extent that they discussed the question at all, they were not in full agreement. But probably a majority accepted the view that the federal courts should rule on the constitutionality of state and federal laws in cases brought before them. Nevertheless, it is likely that a substantial majority intended that federal judges should not participate in making government laws and policies, a responsibility that clearly belonged not to the judiciary but to the legislative branch. Their opposition to any policy-making role for the judiciary is strongly indicated by their response to a proposal in the Virginia Plan that "the Executive and a convenient number of the National Judiciary, ought to compose a council of revision" empowered to veto acts of the National Legislature. Though this provision was vigorously defended by Madison and Mason, it was voted down, 6 states to 3.[7]

A judicial veto is one thing; judicial legislation is quite another. Whatever some of the delegates may have thought about the advisability of justices sharing with the executive the authority to veto laws passed by Congress, I am fairly certain that none would have given the slightest support to a proposal that judges should themselves have the power to legislate, to make national policy. However, the upshot of their work was that in the guise of reviewing the constitutionality of state and congressional actions or inactions, the federal judiciary would later engage in what in some instances could only be called judicial policy-making—or, if you like, judicial legislation.[8]

Congressional Power

Finally, the powers of Congress were limited in ways that could, and at times did, prevent the federal government from regulating or controlling the economy by means that all modern democratic governments have adopted. Without the power to tax incomes, for example, fiscal policy, not to say measures like Social Security, would be impossible. And regulatory actions—over railroad rates, air safety, food and drugs, banking, minimum wages, and many other policies—had no clear constitutional authorization. Although it would be anachronistic to charge the Framers with lack of foresight in these matters,[9] unless the Constitution could be altered by amendment or by heroic reinterpretation of its provisions—presumably by what I have just called judicial legislation—it would prevent representatives of later majorities from adopting the policies they believed were necessary to achieve efficiency, fairness, and security in a complex post-agrarian society.

Enlightened as the Framers' Constitution may have been by the standards of the eighteenth century, future generations with more democratic aspirations would find some of its undemocratic features objectionable—and even unacceptable. The public expression of these growing democratic aspirations was not long in coming.

Even Madison did not, and probably could not, predict the peaceful democratic revolution that was about to begin. For the American revolution was soon to enter into a new and unforeseen phase.

THE FRAMERS' CONSTITUTION MEETS EMERGENT DEMOCRATIC BELIEFS

We may tend to think of the American republic and its Constitution as solely the product of leaders inspired by extraordinary wisdom and virtue. Yet without a citizenry committed to republican principles of government and capable of governing themselves in accordance with those principles, the Constitution would soon have been little more than a piece of paper. As historical experience would reveal, in countries where democratic beliefs were fragile or absent, constitutions did indeed become little more than pieces of paper—soon violated, soon forgotten.

The American democratic republic was not created nor could it have been long maintained by leaders alone, gifted as they may have been. It was they, to be sure, who designed a framework suitable, as they thought, for a republic. But it was the American people, and the leaders responsive to them, who ensured that the new republic would rapidly become a *democratic* republic.

▪ ▪ ▪

I have little doubt that if the American Constitutional Convention had been held in 1820, a very different constitution would have emerged from the deliberations—although, I hasten to add, we can never know what shape that constitution might have taken. We can be reasonably sure, however, that the delegates would have attempted to provide more support for, and fewer barriers to, a democratic republic.

As to the undemocratic features of the constitution created in 1787, let me suggest four conclusions.

First, the aspects of the Constitution that are most defective from a democratic point of view do not necessarily all reflect the intentions of the Framers, insofar as we may surmise them. Though the flaws are traceable to their handiwork, they are in some cases flaws resulting from the inability of these superbly talented craftsmen to foresee how their carefully crafted instrument of government would work under the changing conditions that were to follow—and most of all, under the impact of the democratic revolution in which Americans were, and I hope still are, engaged.

Second, some of the undemocratic aspects of the original design also resulted from the logrolling and compromises that were necessary to achieve agreement. The Framers were not philosophers searching for a description of an ideal system. Nor—and we may be forever grateful to them for this—were they philosopher kings entrusted with the power to rule. They were practical men, eager to achieve a stronger national government, and as practical men they made compromises. Would the country have been better off if they had refused to do so? I doubt it. But in any case, they did compromise, and even today the Constitution bears the results of some of their concessions.

Third, undemocratic aspects that were more or less deliberately built into the Constitution overestimated the dangers of popular majorities—American popular majorities, at any rate—and underestimated the strength of the developing democratic commitment among Americans. As a result, in order to adapt the original framework more closely to the requirements of the emerging democratic republic, with the passage of time some of these aspects of the original Constitution were changed, sometimes by amendment, sometimes, as with political parties, by new institutions and practices.

Finally, though the defects seem to me serious and may grow even more serious with time, Americans are not much predisposed to consider another Constitution, nor is it clear what alternative arrangements would serve them better.

As a result, the beliefs of Americans in the legitimacy of their Constitution will remain, I think, in constant tension with their beliefs in the legitimacy of democracy.

For my part, I believe that the legitimacy of the Constitution ought to derive solely from its utility as an instrument of democratic government—nothing more, nothing less.

NOTES

1. Article I, Section 9. For an excellent account of the only full public debate over the slavery issue, see Joseph J. Ellis, *Founding Brothers: The Revolutionary Generation* (New York: Alfred A. Knopf, 2000), 81–119. The debate took place in the House of Representatives in March 1790 in response to petitions from Quakers in New York and Philadelphia "calling for the federal government to put an immediate end to the African slave trade" (81).

2. Article IV, Section 2.

3. Article I, Sections 2, 3.

4. For a magisterial study of the evolution of American citizenship, see Rogers Smith, *Civic Ideals: Conflicting Visions of Citizenship in U.S. History* (New Haven: Yale University Press, 1997). On the constitution's omission of citizenship for women, Native Americans, and African Americans, see 130–34.

5. Article I, Section 3.

6. By the same electorate as that for "the most numerous branch of the state legislature" (Article I, Section 2).

7. *Records*, 2: 83.

8. For evidence that the Supreme Court sometimes plays such a role, see my "Decision-Making in a Democracy: The Supreme Court as a National Policy-Maker," *Journal of Public Law 6*, no. 2, 279–95.

9. It is only fair to point out that given the political opposition to any increase in federal powers, the Framers may well have gone as far as they could go. Their major opponents, the Anti-Federalists, who saw the constitution as a threat to popular government at the state level, objected that the powers of Congress to regulate interstate commerce were excessive. Richard L. Perry, ed., *The Sources of Our Liberties: Documentary Origins of Individual Liberties in the United States Constitution and Bill of Rights* (New York: American Bar Association, 1959), 240.

3

FEDERALISM

3.1

CHRISTOPHER HAMMONS

From "State Constitutions, Religious Protection, and Federalism"

Interpretation of the "Establishment Clause" of the U.S. Constitution, which has to do with religious liberty and state intrusion, has been controversial. Aside from this passage, the Constitution is silent on religion. Hammons points out that state constitutions in the United States invoke religion and God much more frequently, and that constitution-making at the state level, even in contemporary times, has had a strong religious flavor. He makes the argument that the Founders of the U.S. Constitution likely considered religion to be mostly a state-level issue and thus favored keeping the national government out of decisions over regulation of religious institutions and practices.

Advocates of a strict separation of church and state make a compelling case that the agnostic and neutral language of the First Amendment is meant to shield people from public support of religion. These "separationists" contend that the United States Constitution does not provide any validation for religious belief in the public sphere. Traditional focus and interpretation of the First Amendment of the U.S. Constitution has resulted in a jurisprudence that interprets the religious clauses primarily as ensuring "freedom *from* religion" rather than protecting "freedom *for* religion." This has become the dominant mode of legal thought regarding religious liberty in the United States.

From Christopher Hammons, "State Constitutions, Religious Protection, and Federalism," *University of St. Thomas Journal of Law and Public Policy* 7, no. 22 (2013): 226–39.

Religious liberty clauses at the state level offer a different perspective. An analysis of early and current state constitutions reveals that our federal political system has a long tradition of accommodating religious liberty. Furthermore, these state constitutions often validate religion by invoking God as the foundation of order, liberty, and good government. Advocates of religious liberty might do better to focus their attention on state constitutions rather than their national counterpart. State constitutions avoid the agnostic and neutral language found in the U.S. Bill of Rights and typically offer stronger protection for religious liberty as well.

▪   ▪   ▪

To this end, advocates of religious liberty might consider pursuing a "federal" approach to religious freedom as a means of achieving a higher level of protection than is found in the U.S. Constitution. An examination of state constitutions provides compelling evidence that religious freedom, like many aspects of the Constitution, was meant to be dealt with largely at the state level.

. . . The U.S. Constitution depends heavily on state constitutions. The Constitution itself is a product of the state constitutional tradition and makes use of state constitutions to complete those issues where the U.S. Constitution is largely silent. Religion is one of these issues.

Religion is addressed most frequently, but not exclusively, in the preamble of most state constitutions. The purpose of a preamble at the beginning of a written constitution is largely philosophical. Preambles are not legally binding. Nor do they establish political institutions or policies. The main purpose of a constitutional preamble is to provide a statement of values and beliefs about the origin, operation, and purpose of government. In essence, constitutional preambles provide the basic beliefs of the constitutional framers.[1] The preamble to the United States Constitution is probably the best example of this:

> We the People of the United States, in Order to form a more perfect Union, establish Justice, insure domestic Tranquility, provide for the common defence, promote the general Welfare, and secure the Blessings of Liberty to ourselves and our Posterity, do ordain and establish this Constitution for the United States of America.[2]

In essence, the preamble addresses some of the most fundamental questions of political theory. In the case of the U.S. Constitution, the preamble provides the function of government (order, justice, peace, prosperity), the philosophical justification of government (preservation of liberty), and the source of governmental authority (the people of the United States).

A similar pattern is seen in state constitutions, although there are some striking differences. Since 1776, there have been 145 state constitutions used by the American states. The number is a product of a greater replacement rate among state constitutions and unique historical circumstances such as southern secession.[3] Almost all of the 145 state constitutions have a preamble. Only two current constitutions, New Hampshire and Virginia, do not. These two constitutions start with a Bill of Rights, which in many ways provides the same philosophical underpinnings of government but has the added impact of legal enforceability. Putting a Bill of Rights at the beginning of the document, rather than at the end, is a common pattern in state constitutions.[4]

State constitutional preambles frequently invoke God as the source of good government. The reference to God usually takes one of several forms—the Almighty, the Supreme Being, the Supreme Ruler, Divine Providence, or simply God. Perhaps more poetically, the South Carolina Constitution of 1868 professes its gratitude to the "Great Legislator of the Universe," while the Vermont Constitution of 1777 acknowledges the goodness of the "Great Governor of the Universe."[5]

Of the 145 constitutions used by the American states since 1776, eighty-nine constitutions or sixty-one percent contain references to God in their preambles. In most cases these preambles invoke God as the source of good government, appeal to God for help with good governance, or give thanks to God for the blessings of good government. The aforementioned Vermont Constitution of 1777, for example, gives thanks to the "Great Governor of the Universe" for the blessings of democratic government, noting that He alone "knows to what degree of earthly happiness mankind may attain by perfecting the arts of government."[6] The preamble to the Connecticut Constitution of 1818 acknowledges "with gratitude, the good providence of God, in having permitted [the people of Connecticut] to enjoy free government. . . ."[7] The North Carolina Constitution of 1868 states that the people of North Carolina are "grateful to Almighty God . . . for our civil, political, and religious liberties. . . ."[8]

While it is tempting to say that such references merely reflect the literary style of early American people or the unique colonial experience of the states formed during the Revolution, the pattern is not restricted to those constitutions drafted during the days of the early Republic. Of the fifty constitutions currently in use by the American states today, an astounding ninety percent mention God in their preamble. To this end, invocations of God in state constitutions are not just an artifact of the past.

For example, God is mentioned prominently in the preamble to the Wyoming Constitution, which gives thanks to "Almighty God for our civil, political, and religious liberties. . . ."[9] The current constitution of Wisconsin is "grateful to Almighty God for freedom. . . ."[10] Washington's Constitution gives thanks to the "Supreme Ruler of the Universe for our liberties. . . ."[11] While establishing their constitution, the people of Texas "humbly [invoke] the blessings of Almighty God. . . ."[12] Utah is "[g]rateful to Almighty God for life and liberty. . . ."[13] New York professes thanks to "Almighty God for our freedom. . . ."[14] Even California operates under a state constitution that invokes

God.[15] In total, forty-five of fifty current state constitutions mention God in the preamble. The distribution of the five states that do not mention God in their preambles—New Hampshire, Oregon, Vermont, Tennessee, and Virginia—indicate that there is no geographical or regional pattern for the references to God, or lack thereof, in state constitutions.

What state constitutions reveal is that unlike the national constitution, which is devoid of religious reference, previous and modern state constitutions explicitly invoke God in the preambles as the basis of good government, order, and liberty. This is part of a long constitutional tradition in the United States—a tradition that starts well over 150 years before the U.S. Constitution was drafted.[16]

▪   ▪   ▪

The Founding Generation . . . believed that religion was an important force for the preservation of the fledgling United States. This generation's argument went something like this: democratic government is based on the people; the people need virtue and morality to maintain self-government; religion provides the necessary moral compass and virtue for self-government; therefore, religion and good government are inherently linked. John Adams supported this argument through his comment that constitutional government would only work for "a moral and religious people." In connection, Benjamin Rush said that while all religions promote virtue, Christianity was most suited to virtuous government. Even those men that remained suspicious of organized religion, like Benjamin Franklin and Thomas Jefferson, still considered the teachings of Christ as valuable to a virtuous democratic system. Apparently to them the tenets of "love thy neighbor" and "thy brother's keeper" complemented the democratic ideal.

Because religion was viewed as a complementary part of good government, the fifty-five men who met in Philadelphia in 1787 harbored no opposition to religion as a positive social force. Instead, their disagreements centered on the extent to which government should sanction or endorse religion. This is why state constitutions play such an important role in our constitutional system. Well aware of the long religious traditions and stark denominational differences of each state, the Founders realized there was very little consensus on the degree, form, or doctrine of worship at the national level. This awareness led to there being minimal discussion of religion at the Constitutional Convention since most delegates recognized that any effort to centralize religious authority was not only unlikely, but contrary to the purpose of designing a *limited* national government.

As a result, the U.S. Constitution only references religion in three places. The first mention of religion is in the No Religious Test Clause found in Article VI, clause 3 of the U.S. Constitution.[17] This provision prohibits the requirement that officeholders adhere to or participate in a certain religion. However, it does not prohibit a person from holding office *because* they are religious.

The latter formulation would have been foreign to the Founding Fathers. This provision simply protects people from religious discrimination without being anti-religious in intent.

The second reference is found in Article II, § 1, which specifies the wording of the oath of office for the President of the United States. This oath, which takes into consideration that presidents may be religious, is required before the President begins execution of the office.[18] By its wording, it allows a president-elect to *affirm* rather than *swear* his duty to uphold the Constitution. This often overlooked provision is a nod toward Pennsylvania Quakers who were influential in Pennsylvania politics. It is designed to accommodate men whose religion would prevent them from swearing allegiance to anything other than God. Atheists and proponents of a strict separation of church and state incorrectly read the word "affirm" as providing a way of avoiding swearing an oath. Thus, they believe that it allows for a non-reliance on religion in upholding the Constitution. The fact that the alternative to "affirm" was originally included in the oath to *accommodate* religious people has been lost.

The third and most famous reference to religion in the U.S. Constitution is the Free Exercise Clause of the First Amendment. This clause states that "Congress shall make no law respecting an establishment of religion, or prohibiting the free exercise thereof. . . ."[19] The prohibition is telling to the extent that the restrictions are clearly directed toward the actions of the *national* government, with no mention of the states. This is because religion, like many other constitutional issues, was left to the jurisdiction of the states.

The wording of the First Amendment to the U.S. Constitution when contrasted with similar religious liberty amendments at the state level helps make the case that religion has a special status in American state constitutions that is absent in the national constitution. While the national constitution uses agnostic language which implies no government interference or endorsement of religion, most state constitutions take a markedly different approach to protecting religious liberty. Many state constitutions openly use the word "God" or make direct reference to the "Almighty" in their religious liberty clauses. For example, the New Hampshire Constitution states "[e]very individual has a natural and unalienable right to worship God according to the dictates of his own conscience, and reason; and no subject shall be hurt, molested, or restrained, in his [person] liberty, or estate, for worshipping God in the manner and season most agreeable to the dictates of his own conscience. . . ."[20] The Virginia Constitution reads:

> [t]hat religion or the duty which we owe to our Creator, and the manner of discharging it, can be directed only by reason and conviction, not by force or violence; and, therefore, all men are equally entitled to the free exercise of religion, according to the dictates of conscience; and that it is the mutual duty of all to practice Christian forbearance, love, and charity towards each other.[21]

The Nebraska Constitution reads "[a]ll persons have a natural and indefensible right to worship Almighty God according to the dictates of their own consciences."[22] The Oregon Constitution similarly declares "[a]ll men shall be secure in their Natural right, to worship Almighty God according to the dictates of their own conscience."[23]

All of the above provisions are still in effect today. It is interesting to think how different the legal debate over religious freedom in the United States would be if the First Amendment to the U.S. Constitution stated, "Congress shall make no law respecting an establishment of religion, or prohibiting the free worship of Almighty God." Such a statement would be an endorsement of religion. The specific reference to God in the provision would prevent the agnostic or atheistic interpretations that often accompany First Amendment legal cases today.

The frequent invocations of God in the preambles and in the religious liberty clauses of state constitutions indicate that religion, far from vanquished in American constitutionalism, is merely another aspect of our federal government intended for state jurisdiction. The fact that the references to God found in state constitutional preambles and religious liberty clauses are absent in the national constitution indicates that the state language is more than mere stylistic prose or eighteenth century tradition. If it were perfunctory language—merely stylistic window dressing for state constitutions—there would have been little resistance to including similar language at the national level as well. The absence of such language at the national level, and near ubiquity at the state level, means the religious invocations found in state constitutions had significant meaning that the Framers of the national constitution wished to avoid. In short, religion was one of the issues that was largely meant to be punted back to the states in our federal system.

▪ ▪ ▪

While the Free Exercise Clause can be incorporated and applied to the states, the Establishment Clause should be interpreted as jurisdictional with the intent to shield state religious practices from national interference. . . .

. . . It seems unlikely that the Court will adopt a "federal" perspective on the Establishment Clause anytime soon. Though there is a compelling case for such an interpretation, [researchers] contend that there are too many forces pushing against a change in the way the Court looks at the First Amendment. Many of the constituencies that are most interested in church-state issues—interest groups, local government, churches—benefit from the current interpretation of the First Amendment either through protection of their immediate interests or from the opportunity to foist controversial issues on the national government and hence avoid the ire of unhappy supporters. . . .

NOTES

1. Allan G. Tarr, *Understanding State Constitutions* 90 (2000).

2. U.S. Const. pmbl.

3. Christopher Hammons, "Was James Madison Wrong? Rethinking the American Preference for Short, Framework-Oriented Constitutions," 93 *Am. Pol. Sci. Rev.* 837 (1999).

4. Tarr, *supra* note 1, at 11.

5. S.C. Const. (1868); Vt. Const. (1777).

6. Vt. Const. pmbl. (1777).

7. Conn. Const. pmbl. (1818).

8. N.C. Const. pmbl. (1868).

9. Wyo. Const. pmbl. (1889).

10. Wis. Const. pmbl. (1848).

11. Wash. Const. pmbl. (1889).

12. Tex. Const. pmbl. (1876).

13. Utah Const. pmbl. (1895).

14. N.Y. Const. pmbl. (1777).

15. Cal. Const. pmbl. (1879).

16. Donald Lutz, *A Preface to American Political Theory* 113–140 (1992).

17. U.S. Const. art. VI, cl. 3.

18. U.S. Const. art. II, § 1.

19. U.S. Const. amend. 1.

20. N.H. Const. art. V.

21. Va. Const. art. I, § 16.

22. Neb. Const. art. I, § 4.

23. Or. Const. art. I, § 2.

3.2

WILLIAM H. RIKER

From *Federalism: Origin, Operation, Significance*

In this selection from his classic book on federalism, Riker offers a largely nega-tive view of American federalism. While the benefits of federalism can be iden-tified in theory, the costs have been steep in actual practice: through the 1960s the protection of privileged, wealthy minorities by state governments resulted in the oppression of poor, previously enslaved minorities.

IS THE FEDERAL BARGAIN WORTH KEEPING?

Up to this point this interpretation of federalism has been as simply descrip-tive as I have been able to keep it. The questions of whether or not federalism is superior to its contemporary alternative, unitary government, or its previ-ous alternative, imperialism; of whether or not federalism makes for good government or the good life; of whether or not federalism is an effective instrument of political integration—all these I have tried to keep out of the discussion in order to concentrate on the descriptive questions: What occa-sions federalism and what maintains it?

But most of the interest in federalism, both academic and popular, is about the further question: Is federalism worth keeping? And so in this final chap-ter we shall consider this moral question, not attempting to answer it but rather attempting to indicate some of the considerations that may properly enter into the answer.

Please note that I put the question "Is federalism worth keeping?" not "Is federalism worth starting?" If the argument has any validity at all, the latter question is trivial. In the drive for territorial expansion at the breakup of empire, one either needs to use the federal device to expand or one does not. Normative considerations presumably do not enter into calculation, once the decision to expand has been made. (Of course, that decision is itself normative; but, once it is made, the decision on the procedure of expansion is purely tech-nical. Since the normative question is usually settled by unconscious consen-sus, the salient question at the beginning of federalisms is typically the technical one.) But even if the original question of adopting federalism is purely technical,

From William H. Riker, *Federalism: Origin, Operation, Significance* (Boston: Little, Brown, 1964).

still, once federalism has been established and once a federalism has reached that degree of centralization previously described as category B, the question of whether or not it ought to be maintained is open. Presumably a society with a federal government in category B has attained sufficient unity that it is no longer necessary to use the federal device to keep the expanded society viable. So at that point a normative judgment can be made about whether or not to keep the institutions that originally permitted the expansion.

Of course, the question of whether or not federalism is worth keeping seldom arises as a matter of complete constitutional revision (e.g., in Austria and Germany after each of the world wars). More frequently, the question arises in a partial form; i.e., "What attitude ought one to adopt on this measure that will tend to reinforce (or break down) the guarantees of federalism?" In mature and stable federalisms such as the United States or Australia, where complete constitutional revision seems unlikely in the foreseeable future, there is nevertheless a frequent opportunity to decide constitutional questions on the basis of an attitude toward federalism and this is where the partial form of the question arises.[1] Whether the question arises in its partial form or in a proposal for full-scale constitutional revision is, however, irrelevant to the considerations involved in the answer. Hence, the evaluation of whether or not federalism is worth keeping need not be restrained by the infrequency of constitutional conventions. Rather it is a question that politicians in a mature federalism, especially politicians in a category B federalism, must think about almost every day.

The considerations that commonly enter into decisions on these questions are the arguments advanced in favor of maintaining (or abrogating) the guarantees to constituent units. In the following sections, we shall therefore examine these arguments and some of the evidence adduced in support of them.

I. Federalism and Freedom—The Theoretical Argument for Retention

Probably the commonest argument in public debate for support of the guarantees to constituent units is the assertion that federalism is a guarantee of freedom, followed by the prescription that, in order to preserve freedom, one must preserve federalism. Assuming, as most of us would, that freedom (whatever it is) is worth preserving, the prescription nevertheless depends on a purportedly descriptive assertion, which may or may not be true. In what way is federalism related to freedom?

The political traditions of most federally governed societies predispose most of their citizens to believe that their constitutional form (i.e., federalism) encourages a state of affairs (i.e., freedom) that is almost universally approved. And in the traditions of both Anglo-American and Latin-American federalisms this predisposition has been reinforced by the identification of the spirit of federalism with the notion of local self-government, which in turn is often identified with freedom.

But despite these predispositions of the tradition, there are also some *a priori* reasons to be skeptical about the truth of the assertion that federalism encourages freedom. There are, for example, a number of societies that keep a high degree of freedom without the use of federalism and, on the other hand, a number of federalisms simultaneously have been dictatorships. Local self-government and personal freedom both coexist with a highly centralized unitary government in Great Britain and the Vargas dictatorship in Brazil managed to coexist with federalism.

In the United States, moreover, we have even more reasons to be skeptical about the truth of the assertion when we observe that the most persistent exponents of "states' rights"—a doctrine that makes much of the freedom-encouraging features of federalism—have been those who use the doctrine as a veiled defense first of slavery, then of civil tyranny. Here it seems that federalism may have more to do with destroying freedom than with encouraging it.

Clearly the relationship, if any, between federalism and freedom is not immediately clear and deserves further investigation.

The traditional argument, which derives from *The Federalist* papers and which has been reiterated continually by advocates of states' rights in all federal systems, is the assertion that concentrated power is dangerous, a position best expressed in Acton's aphorism that power tends to corrupt and absolute power corrupts absolutely. Federalism is said to be a device to prevent absolute power and therefore to prevent tyranny. I do not think we need to take this argument very seriously. It is based on a wise saw that has the same standing in the study of politics that weather wisdom has in the study of meteorology. The aphorism is not true—indeed, sometimes its opposite is.[2] And indeed, even if it were true, there is no assurance that separating power is the appropriate way to prevent tyranny. The separation may actually promote tyranny by its constant frustration of majorities which, in their frustration, come to behave tyrannically.[3] So let us leave aside the traditional argument, which is at best folk wisdom, and examine the relationship between federalism and freedom *de novo*.

Of course, though we know fairly well what "federalism" means, we have at best a confused notion of what "freedom" means. So before we can go further, the word "freedom" must be defined. And many volumes have been written on this subject without conspicuous success in reaching agreement. Owing to the tradition of controversy over the meaning of this word, we do know, however, that one of the variables involved in the notion is the specific reference to persons. That is, one elementary question about freedom is: "freedom for whom?"

The question arises in this way: Given a society with a multiplicity of goals (and surely all societies with federal governments satisfy this assumption) and given the possibility that the achievement of goal A renders the achievement of another goal, B, unlikely or impossible. Then, when one speaks of freedom, one must specify whether one means freedom for the supporters of goal A or for those of goal B. If political life were conveniently arranged so that all feasible goals were compatible with one another, then this question could not arise. But usually we do not find such neat dovetailing of aspirations. And so in the presence of conflicting goals, a definition of freedom must always specify freedom for whom.

One convenient answer that some theories of freedom have offered is "the majority," which is unfortunately a highly artificial creation of rules of voting. Owing to this artificiality, therefore, other theories of freedom have suggested that freedom involves liberty for minorities to achieve their goals. The first kind of answer solves the problem in a somewhat arbitrary fashion, whereas the second kind begs the question completely.

But since this reading has no space to pursue the problem of the meaning of freedom, we shall merely assume the existence of two kinds, majoritarian and minoritarian, and then inquire whether or not it is theoretically true that federalism is a guarantee of either kind.

Considering, first, majoritarian freedom, it seems fairly obvious that federalism cannot at all be a guarantee of this kind of freedom; but rather can actually be an impediment. The effect of allowing ultimate decision at two different levels of government (which is the essence of the federal relationship) is that the losers at the national level may reverse the decision at the constituent level. Thus, the losers nationally may become the winners locally which of course negates the national decision in at least portions of the federal nation. Thereby, of course, the freedom of the national majority is infringed upon by local majorities.

A notorious example of such negation is the reversal of decision on civil rights for Negroes in the Southern and border states. The original national decision, taken by a narrow majority in the Civil War era, was soon reversed by local decisions in the South and along the border—where, of course, most Negroes lived. As a consequence, the Civil War decisions were thoroughly negated for most Negroes until sufficient numbers migrated northward and reawakened interest in again enforcing the old and, in recent years, frequently reaffirmed national decision.

To one who believes in the majoritarian notion of freedom, it is impossible to interpret federalism as other than a device for minority tyranny. At the present time in the United States (i.e., from roughly 1954 to that future time, if it ever comes, when most Negroes have full citizen rights) the chief question of public morals is whether or not the national decision will be enforced. To those who wish to enforce it, the plea for states' rights or for maintaining the guarantees of federalism is simply a hypocritical plea for the special privilege to disregard the national majority and, of course, to permit one minority, segregationist Southern whites, to tyrannize over another minority, the Southern Negroes. When freedom is defined as the right of self-direction for majorities, then the assertion that federalism promotes freedom is simply a hypocritical falsehood.

Considering, in the second place, minoritarian freedom, which is usually presented as the freedom of a minority to preserve its civil rights against a tyrannical majority, it is apparent, I shall argue, that for this kind of freedom federalism is, if not an impediment, still quite irrelevant.

Minoritarian freedom can be interpreted either as (1) the right of minorities to have a chance to become majorities and thus to make policy or (2) the right of minorities to make policy without becoming majorities. The first interpretation, i.e., the right to the chance to make policy, is in practice the maintenance of civil liberties so that prospective majorities will not be destroyed before they become such. The latter interpretation, though often set forth as the abstract ideal of freedom, is of course simply a rationale of confusion. Given, as previously, the existence of conflicting social goals, then the guarantee of the right of minorities to make policy merely assures the simultaneous existence of contradictory policies.

If minoritarian freedom is the right to have a chance to make policy, then federalism is undoubtedly an impediment to freedom in many circumstances and irrelevant to it in others. Federalism is a guarantee to constituent units of the *right* to make policy, not of the *chance* to make policy. Thus it grants far more than is necessary for freedom. The analysis works out as follows: Suppose the constituent unit granted the right to make policy agrees for the most part with the kind of policy that would be made by the national officials. Then the right to make policy means relatively little and in general federalism is irrelevant to the maintenance of freedom. Suppose, however, that the constituent unit does not so agree; then the right to make policy allows it to impinge on the right of local minorities to become majorities. This is exactly what has happened in the American South where, under its freedom to make policy, the local majority (which is a minority nationally) has deprived the local minority of its civil rights (even though that local minority has close links with the national majority). In short, federalism that grants *more* local autonomy than is necessary for freedom and civil liberty encourages local tyranny, even when freedom is narrowly interpreted as the grant of the right to minorities to have a chance to become majorities.

If, on the other hand, minoritarian freedom is the right to make policy, i.e., to allow minorities to create confusion, then federalism is again irrelevant to freedom in some circumstances and a positive hindrance to freedom in others. One may distinguish the circumstances according to whether or not it costs the society more to obtain uniformity than uniformity is worth. Consider an instance in which the cost of uniformity is greater than the reward: women's clothing. At numerous times in many societies sumptuary laws and laws against nudity have been passed and frequently they have been enforced only briefly. Presumably in such instances of laxity the cost of enforcement against numerous minorities of one is greater than the reward of uniformity. When enforcement costs more than the reward, federalism is irrelevant to freedom. If freedom is the grant to minorities of one of the right to decide, e.g., on physical decoration, then the right of constituent units to make policy they probably will not care to enforce against minorities is a meaningless grant. In such an instance, federalism has nothing to do with freedom, although it may guarantee tyranny.

But when national uniformity is worth more than confusion, then federalism is an impediment to freedom because it deprives the national majority of the chance to eliminate the excess costs of confusion. Consider, for example, the matter of civil rights for Negroes in the United States. The grant to constituent units to make policy on this question has meant at least the following consequences: For the last century approximately 10 percent of the people have been denied civil rights. Those so denied have been a kind of *lumpenproletariat* and hence a drain on the whole society. In short, the grant of autonomy to local majorities to create confused policies has resulted in a cost to the whole society that is probably greater than the cost of uniformity. At least, so the present restiveness of the national majority toward Southern whites' practices of tyranny so indicates. In such an instance, we may infer that, when the costs of the consequences of federalism are greater than the costs of enforcing uniformity, local tyrannies are also national tyrannies because they prevent national majorities from reducing costs. For example, the national costs of putting up with the consequences of Southern bigotry are so great that the permission to enforce bigotry locally constitutes a cost on the whole nation, a cost which is presumably greater than the cost of enforcing desegregation. In this instance, therefore, federalism is an impediment to the freedom of everybody except segregationist whites in the South.

In summary, the abstract assertion that federalism is a guarantee of freedom is undoubtedly false. If this assertion is intended as a description of nature, then it is manifestly false, as shown by counterinstances of the coexistence of federalism and dictatorship. If it is, however, intended as a theoretical assertion about an abstract relationship undisturbed by other institutional arrangements, then it is still false. If freedom is interpreted in a majoritarian way, then the assertion is invariably false, for federalism is an impediment to freedom. If freedom is interpreted in a minoritarian way, then either federalism has nothing to do with freedom or federalism is again an impediment to freedom.

II. The High Cost of Uniformity—The Practical Argument for Retention

The most frequently presented practical argument for the maintenance of the federal guarantees to the constituent units is that the cost of national decision making is greater than the reward that might be obtained from it. This argument is usually presented as a defense of expediency (e.g., that it would cost more in prospective civil disturbance to integrate the schools of Mississippi than can presently be gained from this action). But sometimes it is also presented as a moral good (e.g., that a positive value is obtained from diversity of culture). (The latter was a favorite argument of Justice Holmes, who interpreted the states as laboratories for solving public problems.) In either form, however, this argument is essentially an economic one involving a kind of cost analysis of constitutional forms.[4]

National decision making is in the abstract more efficient than local decision making on every issue. That is, assuming uniformity is itself costless, it is cheaper on any subject of legislation to have a uniform rule, which is made by a majority, than not to have uniformity. There are at least two strong theoretical reasons for this circumstance. For one thing there is some saving in uniformity; and for another, there is less likelihood of a minority imposing high external costs on the majority. Considering the first and lesser reason, it is apparent that there is some saving in personal learning to have something like nationally uniform rules of the road. If a red light meant different things in different localities it is highly likely that the cost of enforcement of road rules would increase enormously. But the more important saving through uniformity is the minimization of the external costs imposed on individuals when minorities are allowed to legislate a minority policy. These costs are, of course, very high when two minority policies are in direct conflict. But even when they do not seem to be in direct conflict, external costs may still be inordinately high. Consider the sum of the costs to individuals when there are different minimum wages in different localities. There is then much likelihood of capital flow from the high-wage localities to the low-wage localities for all those industries in which labor represents a high proportion of the cost. Aside from the imposition of a nationally uniform minimum wage, the only way that high-wage localities may counter this capital flow is by reducing the minimum wage level. Thus the localities with the low minimum wage are permitted to set this wage nationally. For all the localities that would like to have the high wage, the imposition of the low wage is, of course, a high external cost. Since only the lowest-wage locality will be satisfied, all other localities will suffer these external costs. The obvious way to reduce this cost is to impose a national policy. It is this possibility that accounts for the greater efficiency of uniform rules. The only circumstances in which the uniform policy would not reduce external costs over local policies would be when the low-wage locality constituted a national majority. But in this case, the supposedly local policy is in fact imposed by a national majority and is thus a uniform policy. Hence in all cases a uniform policy is cheaper from the point of view of external costs than a non-uniform policy.

Or consider the savings from uniformity in the regulation of morality rather than the regulation of the economy. Given the possibility of variation in divorce codes among constituent units, divorce may be easier to obtain in one jurisdiction than in another. Then, so long as some provision like the full faith and credit clause of the United States Constitution exists—and all federalisms have something like it—it follows that the code that will in fact regulate is the one with easiest divorce. We have an excellent example of this in the United States, where the national scandal of excessively large numbers of divorces and the concomitant scandal of ill-considered marriages are both the consequences of a variation in divorce codes. The existence of a few jurisdictions that grant divorces on the most trivial grounds and after only the briefest periods of residence are sufficient to render nugatory the more restrictive grounds and longer residence requirements of most other states. Thus the different moral standards of a few states, the codes of which seem to have been motivated more by a concern for tourist business than by any convictions one way or another about family stability, have the effect of imposing easy divorce on all jurisdictions. The external costs of the existence of what most citizens of most states regard as low moral standards are thus very high for the probably overwhelming majority that opposes easy divorce. Uniformity of divorce laws could materially lighten these costs for the majority, although it might raise costs for Nevada lawyers.

It seems clear on the basis of both theory and example that uniform national decision making is invariably more efficient, i.e., less costly in undesired impositions on other people, than is local decision making. This is simply to say that decisions made by a majority hurt fewer people than do decisions made by minorities. Since constituent governments are invariably minorities in the nation, the maintenance of federal guarantees to constituent units assures that the whole society must bear some extra and unnecessary external costs.

So far, however, we have considered the cost of decision making only in a vacuum. Even if national decision making is clearly more efficient in decreasing external costs, it still may be more expensive than local decision making because of (1) costs of decision making and (2) costs of enforcement.

Costs of decision making are those incurred in the process of assembling a coalition of the size necessary to make a decision. As the requirements increase from minorities (e.g., majorities in a constituent unit) to majorities (i.e., a national majority), the cost of making side-payments to reluctant members (i.e., logrolling) and of negotiating with all prospective members increases greatly. The cost of national decision making may well be greater than the rewards obtained from eliminating anarchy. Consider, for example, standards of beach clothing for females. Possibly a majority of people in the United States are offended by the appearance of bikinis and, were the decision costless, they would be glad to prohibit them. But, in fact, the decision is not costless. Some effort must be expended on defining what is offensive and what is not; more effort must be expended on finding the people who make up this majority; and finally additional effort must be expended on bringing them together in a group for action. In this imaginary example, the cost of decision is clearly very high, whereas the sum of the rewards to the majority is probably relatively low. Quite possibly the decision costs exceed the rewards.

Costs of enforcement are those incurred in the process of enforcing a majority decision against a recalcitrant minority. These costs vary with (1) the relative size of the minority, (2) the intensity of feeling of the minority, and (3) the ability of the minority to resist enforcement. It makes a difference for the existence of a national policy of prohibition, for example, whether or not most of the people are convinced teetotalers. In the United States during the prohibition era, the minority of regular users of alcohol was almost as large as the group of teetotalers, if indeed not larger. Hence enforcement was exceptionally costly. In India, on the other hand, where a much larger proportion

of the population consists of teetotalers and where the indigenous pharmaco-
poeia includes a variety of drugs with physiological and social effects similar
to those of alcohol, the enforcement of prohibition is relatively less costly.
Again it makes a difference for the existence of a national policy of assessing
an income tax whether or not the prosperous and the rich believe deeply that
they should not be taxed. Thus, in the United States, the prosperous and the
rich accept the basic notion of the tax and hence usually obey the exact letter
of the law. The existence of this attitude means that enforcement officers are
freed to pursue the minority of dishonest taxpayers. Hence the income tax
works pretty well as the basic tax of the nation. In India, on the other hand,
the justice of the tax is not as widely acknowledged by the prosperous and
rich. Hence enforcement agents must spend most of their efforts on what
would elsewhere be regarded as ordinary collection. As a consequence,
enforcement is costly and the income tax cannot be used as the basic tax system. Finally, it makes a difference for the existence of a national policy of
civil rights for depressed classes whether or not those who oppress them can
successfully defend the oppression both practically and philosophically.
Again compare India and the United States, in both of which national decisions have repeatedly condemned the oppression of in one case the Scheduled Castes and in the other case Negroes. In both cases there are good
practical devices to avoid enforcement; e.g., the relative unanimity of the
rural upper classes on the desirability of resistance. In both cases there are
also good philosophical grounds to resist enforcement; e.g., the doctrine of
states' rights in the United States and the doctrines of Hinduism in India. But
the outlook for enforcement of the national policy is much better in the
United States than in India simply because (1) the unanimity of the rural
upper classes is nationwide in India whereas in the United States it is breaking down and indeed is limited to two or three very recalcitrant states and (2)
the doctrine of states' rights is increasingly regarded as a sham for oppression whereas, owing to the new nationalism, the doctrines of Hinduism are
held to even more tenaciously than before. Negroes are likely to obtain civil
rights sooner than untouchables simply because the ability of their oppres-
sors to resist enforcement is less.

In this analysis of the costs of national decision making in relation to decision making by constituent units, we have thus identified three kinds of charges:

1. the profits of uniformity, symbolized by "U"; which are invariably positive in sign because majority decision is always better than anarchy;
2. the costs of making decisions, symbolized by "D," which are invariably negative in sign because it is more costly to assemble a majority
   than a minority; and
3. the costs of enforcement of decisions, symbolized by "E," which are
   also invariably negative in sign because the existence of a majority
   implies the existence of a minority that must be coerced.

The practical argument in favor of maintaining the federal guarantees to the constituent units is that $U+D+E\leq0$. Of course, this argument cannot be uttered generally for it would mean the desirability of the dissolution of the federalism. Rather, it must be uttered in particular instances and where it is asserted after a rough assessment of the values of U, D, and E. Since the argument cannot be asserted generally except as a proposal for civil war, one wonders about what kind of instances it seems reasonable in. In short, what kinds of circumstances minimize the sum of U, D, and E?

It is impossible, of course, to offer an exhaustive list; but one can specify some typical circumstances. As for minimizing U, which of course increases the likelihood that the inequation $U+D+E\leq0$ will hold, the most important circumstance probably is that the policy field will be fairly low on the preference schedules of most of the members of the prospective majority. If most people don't care much whether or not policy in a specific area (e.g., women's beachwear) is anarchic, then the positive value of U will be low. The issue of whether or not to maintain the federal guarantee to constituent units does not, however, arise when U is low, for to say U is low is to say it concerns something to which most people are close to indifferent. So the problem is: In what circumstances, when U is high, is—$(D+E)$ higher?

What minimizes D is the existence of numerous territorial minorities, each of whose schedules of preference is quite different from others. The fact that these minorities are territorially based gives them some strength to insist on obtaining their preferences and the fact that their preference schedules are different renders the bargaining process expensive. India is a federalism in which, *a priori*, one might expect D to be very low in many areas of public policy.

What minimizes E is the intensity of feeling of a minority, a defensive sense that their separateness is both under attack and worth preserving. Coupled with this sense of separateness must also be a large territorial and population base so that the minority actually has some strength to resist enforcement. Canada is a federalism in which, *a priori*, one might expect E to be very low in many areas of public policy.

The practical argument for the maintenance of the federal guarantees to the constituent units, *viz.*, that $U+D+E\leq0$, is clearly dependent upon the calculations of politicians and citizens about the magnitudes of U, D, and E in particular sets of circumstances. In general, if there are numerous areas *of importance* in which it is agreed that the inequation $U+D+E\leq0$ holds, then the argument in favor of maintaining the guarantees is good. If not, then the argument fails. For me, the argument is reasonable and impressive with respect to such federalisms as Canada and India, but it is specious and unreasonable with respect to such federalisms as the United States, Germany, Austria, and Australia.

III. Abrogating the Guarantees

The main theoretical argument in favor of abrogating the federal guarantees to constituent units has already been developed in connection with arguments for maintaining them: Decisions made by constituent units are invariably minority decisions that impose high external costs on the national majority. This assertion is wholly irrefutable on the level of theory, although it may be shown, as I have also indicated, that in particular instances it may cost more to remove the external costs than is saved with uniformity. But even though the assertion is theoretically irrefutable some effort has been expended in showing that it is not necessarily true in all circumstances. Cohen and Grodzins, for example, have attempted to show that state fiscal policies in the United States do not always conflict with national policies.[5] And they did indeed show that the state policies are less sharply in conflict with national policy than had previously been believed.[6] But to show that the anarchy of numerous minority decisions does not impose external costs as high as Hansen and Perloff believed is also to admit that external costs do exist. Indeed, the chief significance of Cohen and Grodzins' work is that they found a way to measure them. The existence of external costs is an invitation to eliminate them, which is the chief theoretical argument in favor of abrogating the guarantees.

Unfortunately the theoretical arguments, though theoretically decisive, are practically uncertain because of the uncertainty surrounding the magnitudes of U, D, and E. Hence, to decide in particular instances whether or not to abrogate the guarantees it is necessary to examine the cultural and institutional setting of the constitution. The appropriate questions are: Who benefits by the imposition of external costs on others? or, What minority is allowed by the federal device to impose its rules on the majority? According as one disapproves or approves of the values and purposes of these minorities, one favors or opposes the abrogation of the guarantees. One does not decide on the merits of federalism by an examination of federalism in the abstract, but rather on its actual meaning for particular societies.

What minorities benefit from the grant to make policy in:

The United States?
The main beneficiary throughout American history has been the Southern whites, who have been given the freedom to oppress Negroes, first as slaves and later as a depressed caste. Other minorities have from time to time also managed to obtain some of these benefits; e.g., special business interests have been allowed to regulate themselves, especially in the era from about 1890 to 1936, by means of the judicial doctrine of dual federalism, which eliminated both state and national regulation of such matters as wage rates and hours of labor. But the significance of federal benefits to economic interests pales beside the significance of benefits to the Southern segregationist whites. The judgment to be passed on federalism in the United States is therefore a judgment on the values of segregation and racial oppression.

Canada?

The main beneficiary in Canada from the beginning has been the French-speaking minority, whose dissidence was the original occasion for adopting federalism and is the justification for retaining it today. Secondarily, as in the United States, commercial interests have also benefited by escaping regulation. But since the French Canadians have no particular alliance with business, economic conservatives have benefited less in Canada than in the United States (where Southern segregationists have a tacit alliance with economic conservatives). That is, the French speakers have seen less reason to rig the competitive market to the advantage of owners (as against workers or consumers) because very few French Canadians have been owners.

Brazil?

The most significant minority benefiting from Brazilian federalism is the class of large landowners, especially in the relatively underdeveloped north and east. Although Brazilian federalism lacks the tone of racism associated with federalism in the United States, the social consequences are the same: the maintenance of a class of poor and inefficient farm laborers for the presumed benefit of agrarian landlords.

India?

Indian federalism is probably too youthful to identify the main beneficiaries of the privilege of minority decision making. But two kinds of minorities have tended to emphasize states' rights: non-Hindi-speaking groups (who, together, are of course a majority) and landlords in the least-developed agricultural areas.

Australia?

Since no single minority has been able to exploit the advantages of minority decision exclusively or for long periods of time, it is difficult to identify the main beneficiary. Nevertheless, it seems that commercial interests have been granted freedom from regulation more than any other group.

Germany?

Originally, federalism was intended to grant the right of minority decision to the non-Prussian southwest. But the significance of this minority has declined in the successive transformations of German federalism so that today it is difficult to specify who, if anyone, benefits most.

The foregoing survey of several federal systems suggests the wide variety of kinds of minorities that may benefit especially from the privilege to legislate. The kind of minorities that appears most frequently on this list is business and agricultural owners. It is not difficult to understand why. In capitalistic nations conflicting economic interests are engaged constantly in an effort

TABLE [1] Main Beneficiaries of Federalism

	Capitalists	Landlords	Linguistic Minorities	Racists
United States	X	X		X
Canada	X		X	
Mexico		X		
Brazil	X	X		
Argentina	X	X		
Australia	X			
India		X	X	
Switzerland	X		X	
Germany	X			
Yugoslavia			X	
Soviet Union			X	

to rig the competitive system in their favor. Those groups which constitute national majorities, e.g., workers, farm laborers, consumers, etc., are those which might be expected to benefit most from majoritarian decision processes. To allow minoritarian processes is, therefore, to deprive the very large groups of their chance to influence outcomes. Of course, the minority most likely to benefit from the chance to manipulate the market is that of the owners, business or agricultural according to whether the nation is primarily industrial or agrarian.

But it is not always or only the owners who benefit, for, as the brief survey indicates, linguistic or racist minorities may also thrive on federalism. One possible classification of federalism, especially appropriate for passing judgment on the desirability of retaining federalism, is by the main beneficiaries of the chance of minorities to legislate for the whole. A moral judgment must be passed in each instance and for comparative purposes I submit a list [Table 1] of the main characteristics of the main federalisms. It is notable that the federalism of the United States is unique in fostering racism.

IV. Is Federalism Worth Keeping?

One seldom has the opportunity to rewrite whole constitutions so the question of keeping or abandoning federalism can seldom arise. But a related question does frequently arise: What ought to be one's posture toward federalism? Should one always attempt to maintain or abrogate the guarantees to the constituent units?

In pure theory, the answer is that what one ought to seek to abrogate for federalism is a system of minority decision that imposes high external costs on everybody other than the minority. But practically the answer is not so clear, for the costs of decision and enforcement may outweigh the advantages of majoritarianism when the minority favored by federalism is passionate in its convictions.

Since the actual calculation of rewards and costs from abrogating federal guarantees is simply a rough "more or less" necessarily calculated by interested parties, one probably cannot even use a cost analysis in judging actual federalisms. Rather one must look to what they do and determine what minorities they favor. If one approves the goals and values of the privileged minority, one should approve the federalism. Thus, if in the United States one approves of Southern white racists, then one should approve of American federalism. If, on the other hand, one disapproves of the values of the privileged minority, one should disapprove of federalism. Thus, if in the United States one disapproves of racism, one should disapprove of federalism.

NOTES

1. For a concrete example of such an occasion, consider the creation (in 1935) of the unemployment insurance system as an adjunct to the social security system. President Roosevelt, apparently out of a concern for federalism, personally decided to assign the unemployment insurance and employment service to the states, at least so his advisor Tugwell tells us. (Rexford Tugwell, "The Experimental Roosevelt," *The Political Quarterly*, Vol. 21 (1950) pp. 239–62, at p. 241.) In turning down the advice of experts, Roosevelt personally preserved, at least in a small way, the constitutional guarantees of federalism. Whether or not he was wise to do so is, of course, another matter. Since the federal part of this system has been quietly and selectively administered, whereas the state part has been the center of much political turbulence and has often been charged with inefficiency, the experts were probably right from an administrative point of view. But constitutional considerations may be more important than administrative ones. What concerns us here, however, is not the correctness or incorrectness of Roosevelt's action, but simply the opportunity he had to decide a policy question on the basis of an interpretation of federalism.

2. See Arnold Rogow and Harold Lasswell, *Power, Corruption and Rectitude* (New York: Prentice-Hall, 1963).

3. See William H. Riker, *Democracy in the United States* (New York: Macmillan, 1953) Chapter 4.

4. An earlier attempt to apply a quasi-economic analysis to the costs of federalism is: J. Roland Pennock, "Federal and Unitary Government—Disharmony and Frustration," *Behavioral Science*, Vol. 4 (1959) pp. 147–57. This article contains an *ad hoc* and tendentious model from which calculations are made of the "harmony (or lessened frustration) which it is the peculiar genius of federalism to achieve." By conveniently ignoring what are here called external costs, e.g., those imposed on the majority when the minority is permitted to make rules, the author finds that federalism lessens the frustrations of a minority, which, of course, no one has ever denied. The unanswered question is: At whose expense is the frustration relieved?

5. Jacob Cohen and Morton Grodzins, "How Much Economic Sharing in American Federalism," *American Political Science Review*, Vol. 57 (1963) pp. 5–23.

6. Alvin Hansen and Harvey Perloff, *State and Local Finance in the National Economy* (New York: Norton, 1944).

3.3

Arizona v. United States (2012)

This decision struck down three provisions of Arizona law intended to give state police greater powers to enforce laws regarding immigration status. Justice Anthony Kennedy, in his majority opinion, affirms the power of the national government relative to the states. To the majority, the supremacy clause of the Constitution means that states "may not enter, in any respect, an area the Federal Government has reserved for itself." Since the national government passed laws regulating immigration, states like Arizona cannot have their own immigration policies.

JUSTICE KENNEDY delivered the opinion of the Court.

I

To address pressing issues related to the large number of aliens within its borders who do not have a lawful right to be in this country, the State of Arizona in 2010 enacted a statute called the Support Our Law Enforcement and Safe Neighborhoods Act. The law is often referred to as S.B. 1070, the version introduced in the state senate. Its stated purpose is to "discourage and deter the unlawful entry and presence of aliens and economic activity by persons unlawfully present in the United States." Ariz. Rev. Stat. Ann. §11-1051 (West 2012). The law's provisions establish an official state policy of "attrition through enforcement." *Ibid.* The question before the Court is whether federal law preempts and renders invalid four separate provisions of the state law.

The United States filed this suit against Arizona, seeking to enjoin S.B. 1070 as preempted. Four provisions of the law are at issue here. Two create new state offenses. Section 3 makes failure to comply with federal alien registration requirements a state misdemeanor. Section 5, in relevant part, makes it a misdemeanor for an unauthorized alien to seek or engage in work in the State; this provision is referred to as §5(C). Two other provisions give specific arrest authority and investigative duties with respect to certain aliens to state and local law enforcement officers. Section 6 authorizes officers to arrest without a warrant a person "the officer has probable cause to believe . . . has committed any public offense that makes the person removable from the

From *Arizona v. United States*, 567 U.S. ___ (2012).

United States." §13–3883(A)(5). Section 2(B) provides that officers who conduct a stop, detention, or arrest must in some circumstances make efforts to verify the person's immigration status with the Federal Government.

The United States District Court for the District of Arizona issued a preliminary injunction preventing the four provisions at issue from taking effect. The Court of Appeals for the Ninth Circuit affirmed. It agreed that the United States had established a likelihood of success on its preemption claims. The Court of Appeals was unanimous in its conclusion that §§3 and 5(C) were likely preempted. Judge Bea dissented from the decision to uphold the preliminary injunction against §§2(B) and 6. This Court granted certiorari to resolve important questions concerning the interaction of state and federal power with respect to the law of immigration and alien status.

II

A

The Government of the United States has broad, undoubted power over the subject of immigration and the status of aliens. This authority rests, in part, on the National Government's constitutional power to "establish an uniform Rule of Naturalization," U.S. Const., Art. I, §8, cl. 4, and its inherent power as sovereign to control and conduct relations with foreign nations. *United States v. Curtiss-Wright Export Corp.* (1936).

The federal power to determine immigration policy is well settled. Immigration policy can affect trade, investment, tourism, and diplomatic relations for the entire Nation, as well as the perceptions and expectations of aliens in this country who seek the full protection of its laws. Perceived mistreatment of aliens in the United States may lead to harmful reciprocal treatment of American citizens abroad. It is fundamental that foreign countries concerned about the status, safety, and security of their nationals in the United States must be able to confer and communicate on this subject with one national sovereign, not the 50 separate States. This Court has reaffirmed that "[o]ne of the most important and delicate of all international relationships . . . has to do with the protection of the just rights of a country's own nationals when those nationals are in another country." *Hines v. Davidowitz* (1941).

Federal governance of immigration and alien status is extensive and complex. Congress has specified categories of aliens who may not be admitted to the United States. Unlawful entry and unlawful reentry into the country are federal offenses. Once here, aliens are required to register with the Federal Government and to carry proof of status on their person. Failure to do so is a federal misdemeanor. Federal law also authorizes States to deny noncitizens a range of public benefits, and it imposes sanctions on employers who hire unauthorized workers. Congress has specified which aliens may be removed from the United States and the procedures for doing so. Aliens may be removed if they were inadmissible at the time of entry, have been convicted of certain crimes, or meet other criteria set by federal law. Removal is a civil, not criminal, matter. A principal feature of the removal system is the broad discretion exercised by immigration officials. Federal officials, as an initial matter, must decide whether it makes sense to pursue removal at all. If removal proceedings commence, aliens may seek asylum and other discretionary relief allowing them to remain in the country or at least to leave without formal removal.

Discretion in the enforcement of immigration law embraces immediate human concerns. Unauthorized workers trying to support their families, for example, likely pose less danger than alien smugglers or aliens who commit a serious crime. The equities of an individual case may turn on many factors, including whether the alien has children born in the United States, long ties to the community, or a record of distinguished military service. Some discretionary decisions involve policy choices that bear on this Nation's international relations. Returning an alien to his own country may be deemed inappropriate even where he has committed a removable offense or fails to meet the criteria for admission. The foreign state may be mired in civil war, complicit in political persecution, or enduring conditions that create a real risk that the alien or his family will be harmed upon return. The dynamic nature of relations with other countries requires the Executive Branch to ensure that enforcement policies are consistent with this Nation's foreign policy with respect to these and other realities.

Agencies in the Department of Homeland Security play a major role in enforcing the country's immigration laws. United States Customs and Border Protection (CBP) is responsible for determining the admissibility of aliens and securing the country's borders. In 2010, CBP's Border Patrol apprehended almost half a million people. Immigration and Customs Enforcement (ICE), a second agency, "conducts criminal investigations involving the enforcement of immigration-related statutes." ICE also operates the Law Enforcement Support Center. LESC, as the Center is known, provides immigration status information to federal, state, and local officials around the clock. ICE officers are responsible "for the identification, apprehension, and removal of illegal aliens from the United States." Hundreds of thousands of aliens are removed by the Federal Government every year.

B

The pervasiveness of federal regulation does not diminish the importance of immigration policy to the States. Arizona bears many of the consequences of unlawful immigration. Hundreds of thousands of deportable aliens are apprehended in Arizona each year. Unauthorized aliens who remain in the State comprise, by one estimate, almost 6 percent of the population. And in the State's most populous county, these aliens are reported to be responsible for a disproportionate share of serious crime.

Statistics alone do not capture the full extent of Arizona's concerns. Accounts in the record suggest there is an "epidemic of crime, safety risks, serious property damage, and environmental problems" associated with the influx of illegal migration across private land near the Mexican border. Brief for Petitioners 6. Phoenix is a major city of the United States, yet signs along an interstate highway 30 miles to the south warn the public to stay away. One reads, "DANGER—PUBLIC WARNING—TRAVEL NOT REC-OMMENDED / Active Drug and Human Smuggling Area / Visitors May Encounter Armed Criminals and Smuggling Vehicles Traveling at High Rates of Speed." The problems posed to the State by illegal immigration must not be underestimated.

These concerns are the background for the formal legal analysis that follows. The issue is whether, under preemption principles, federal law permits Arizona to implement the state-law provisions in dispute.

III

Federalism, central to the constitutional design, adopts the principle that both the National and State Governments have elements of sovereignty the other is bound to respect. From the existence of two sovereigns follows the possibility that laws can be in conflict or at cross-purposes. The Supremacy Clause provides a clear rule that federal law "shall be the supreme Law of the Land; and the Judges in every State shall be bound thereby, any Thing in the Constitution or Laws of any State to the Contrary notwithstanding." Art. VI, cl. 2. Under this principle, Congress has the power to preempt state law. There is no doubt that Congress may withdraw specified powers from the States by enacting a statute containing an express preemption provision.

State law must also give way to federal law in at least two other circumstances. First, the States are precluded from regulating conduct in a field that Congress, acting within its proper authority, has determined must be regulated by its exclusive governance. The intent to displace state law altogether can be inferred from a framework of regulation "so pervasive . . . that Congress left no room for the States to supplement it" or where there is a "federal interest . . . so dominant that the federal system will be assumed to preclude enforcement of state laws on the same subject." *Rice v. Santa Fe Elevator Corp.* (1947).

Second, state laws are preempted when they conflict with federal law. This includes cases where "compliance with both federal and state regulations is a physical impossibility," *Florida Lime & Avocado Growers, Inc. v. Paul* (1963), and those instances where the challenged state law "stands as an obstacle to the accomplishment and execution of the full purposes and objectives of Congress," *Hines*, 312 U.S., at 67. In preemption analysis, courts should assume that "the historic police powers of the States" are not superseded "unless that was the clear and manifest purpose of Congress." *Rice*, supra, at 230.

The four challenged provisions of the state law each must be examined under these preemption principles.

IV

A

Section 3

Section 3 of S.B. 1070 creates a new state misdemeanor. It forbids the "willful failure to complete or carry an alien registration document . . . in violation of 8 United States Code section 1304(e) or 1306(a)." Ariz. Rev. Stat. Ann. §11-1509(A) (West Supp. 2011). In effect, §3 adds a state-law penalty for conduct proscribed by federal law. The United States contends that this state enforcement mechanism intrudes on the field of alien registration, a field in which Congress has left no room for States to regulate.

The Court discussed federal alien-registration requirements in *Hines v. Davidowitz* (1941). In 1940, as international conflict spread, Congress added to federal immigration law a "complete system for alien registration." Id., at 70. The new federal law struck a careful balance. It punished an alien's willful failure to register but did not require aliens to carry identification cards. There were also limits on the sharing of registration records and fingerprints. The Court found that Congress intended the federal plan for registration to be a "single integrated and all-embracing system." Id., at 74. Because this "complete scheme . . . for the registration of aliens" touched on foreign relations, it did not allow the States to "curtail or complement" federal law or to "enforce additional or auxiliary regulations." Id., at 66–67. As a consequence, the Court ruled that Pennsylvania could not enforce its own alien-registration program.

The present regime of federal regulation is not identical to the statutory framework considered in *Hines*, but it remains comprehensive. Federal law now includes a requirement that aliens carry proof of registration. Other aspects, however, have stayed the same. Aliens who remain in the country for more than 30 days must apply for registration and be fingerprinted. Detailed information is required, and any change of address has to be reported to the Federal Government. The statute continues to provide penalties for the willful failure to register.

The framework enacted by Congress leads to the conclusion here, as it did in *Hines*, that the Federal Government has occupied the field of alien registration. The federal statutory directives provide a full set of standards governing alien registration, including the punishment for noncompliance. It was designed as a "harmonious whole." *Hines*, supra, at 72. Where Congress occupies an entire field, as it has in the field of alien registration, even complementary state regulation is impermissible. Field preemption reflects a congressional decision to foreclose any state regulation in the area, even if it is parallel to federal standards.

Federal law makes a single sovereign responsible for maintaining a comprehensive and unified system to keep track of aliens within the Nation's borders. If §3 of the Arizona statute were valid, every State could give itself independent authority to prosecute federal registration violations, "diminish[ing] the

[Federal Government]'s control over enforcement" and "detract[ing] from the 'integrated scheme of regulation' created by Congress." *Wisconsin Dept. of Industry v. Gould Inc.* (1986). Even if a State may make violation of federal law a crime in some instances, it cannot do so in a field (like the field of alien registration) that has been occupied by federal law.

Arizona contends that §3 can survive preemption because the provision has the same aim as federal law and adopts its substantive standards. This argument not only ignores the basic premise of field preemption—that States may not enter, in any respect, an area the Federal Government has reserved for itself—but also is unpersuasive on its own terms. Permitting the State to impose its own penalties for the federal offenses here would conflict with the careful framework Congress adopted. Were §3 to come into force, the State would have the power to bring criminal charges against individuals for violating a federal law even in circumstances where federal officials in charge of the comprehensive scheme determine that prosecution would frustrate federal policies.

There is a further intrusion upon the federal scheme. Even where federal authorities believe prosecution is appropriate, there is an inconsistency between §3 and federal law with respect to penalties. Under federal law, the failure to carry registration papers is a misdemeanor that may be punished by a fine, imprisonment, or a term of probation. State law, by contrast, rules out probation as a possible sentence (and also eliminates the possibility of a pardon). This state framework of sanctions creates a conflict with the plan Congress put in place.

These specific conflicts between state and federal law simply underscore the reason for field preemption. As it did in *Hines*, the Court now concludes that, with respect to the subject of alien registration, Congress intended to preclude States from "complement[ing] the federal law, or enforc[ing] additional or auxiliary regulations." 312 U.S., at 66–67. Section 3 is preempted by federal law.

B

Section 5(C)

Unlike §3, which replicates federal statutory requirements, §5(C) enacts a state criminal prohibition where no federal counterpart exists. The provision makes it a state misdemeanor for "an unauthorized alien to knowingly apply for work, solicit work in a public place or perform work as an employee or independent contractor" in Arizona. Violations can be punished by a $2,500 fine and incarceration for up to six months. The United States contends that the provision upsets the balance struck by the Immigration Reform and Control Act of 1986 (IRCA) and must be preempted as an obstacle to the federal plan of regulation and control.

When there was no comprehensive federal program regulating the employment of unauthorized aliens, this Court found that a State had authority to pass its own laws on the subject. In 1971, for example, California passed a law imposing civil penalties on the employment of aliens who were "not entitled to lawful residence in the United States if such employment would have an adverse effect on lawful resident workers." 1971 Cal. Stats. ch. 1442, §1(a). The law was upheld against a preemption challenge in *De Canas v. Bica* (1976). *De Canas* recognized that "States possess broad authority under their police powers to regulate the employment relationship to protect workers within the State." Id., at 356. At that point, however, the Federal Government had expressed no more than "a peripheral concern with [the] employment of illegal entrants." Id., at 360.

Current federal law is substantially different from the regime that prevailed when *De Canas* was decided. Congress enacted IRCA as a comprehensive framework for "combating the employment of illegal aliens." *Hoffman Plastic Compounds, Inc. v. NLRB* (2002). The law makes it illegal for employers to knowingly hire, recruit, refer, or continue to employ unauthorized workers. It also requires every employer to verify the employment authorization status of prospective employees. These requirements are enforced through criminal penalties and an escalating series of civil penalties tied to the number of times an employer has violated the provisions.

This comprehensive framework does not impose federal criminal sanctions on the employee side (i.e., penalties on aliens who seek or engage in unauthorized work). Under federal law some civil penalties are imposed instead. With certain exceptions, aliens who accept unlawful employment are not eligible to have their status adjusted to that of a lawful permanent resident. Aliens also may be removed from the country for having engaged in unauthorized work. In addition to specifying these civil consequences, federal law makes it a crime for unauthorized workers to obtain employment through fraudulent means. Congress has made clear, however, that any information employees submit to indicate their work status "may not be used" for purposes other than prosecution under specified federal criminal statutes for fraud, perjury, and related conduct.

The legislative background of IRCA underscores the fact that Congress made a deliberate choice not to impose criminal penalties on aliens who seek, or engage in, unauthorized employment. A commission established by Congress to study immigration policy and to make recommendations concluded these penalties would be "unnecessary and unworkable." U.S. Immigration Policy and the National Interest: The Final Report and Recommendations of the Select Commission on Immigration and Refugee Policy with Supplemental Views by Commissioners (1981). Proposals to make unauthorized work a criminal offense were debated and discussed during the long process of drafting IRCA. But Congress rejected them. In the end, IRCA's framework reflects a considered judgment that making criminals out of aliens engaged in unauthorized work—aliens who already face the possibility of employer exploitation because of their removable status—would be inconsistent with federal policy and objectives.

IRCA's express preemption provision, which in most instances bars States from imposing penalties on employers of unauthorized aliens, is silent about whether additional penalties may be imposed against the employees themselves. But the existence of an "express preemption provisio[n] does not bar the ordinary working of conflict preemption principles" or impose a "special burden" that would make it more difficult to establish the preemption of laws falling outside the clause. *Geier v. American Honda Motor Co.* (2000).

The ordinary principles of preemption include the well-settled proposition that a state law is preempted where it "stands as an obstacle to the accomplishment and execution of the full purposes and objectives of Congress." *Hines*, at 67. Under §5(C) of S.B. 1070, Arizona law would interfere with the careful balance struck by Congress with respect to unauthorized employment of aliens. Although §5(C) attempts to achieve one of the same goals as federal law—the deterrence of unlawful employment—it involves a conflict in the method of enforcement. The Court has recognized that a "[c]onflict in technique can be fully as disruptive to the system Congress enacted as conflict in overt policy." *Motor Coach Employees v. Lockridge* (1971). The correct instruction to draw from the text, structure, and history of IRCA is that Congress decided it would be inappropriate to impose criminal penalties on aliens who seek or engage in unauthorized employment. It follows that a state law to the contrary is an obstacle to the regulatory system Congress chose. Section 5(C) is preempted by federal law.

C

Section 6

Section 6 of S.B. 1070 provides that a state officer, "without a warrant, may arrest a person if the officer has probable cause to believe . . . [the person] has committed any public offense that makes [him] removable from the United States." Ariz. Rev. Stat. Ann. §13-3883(A)(5) (West Supp. 2011). The United States argues that arrests authorized by this statute would be an obstacle to the removal system Congress created.

As a general rule, it is not a crime for a removable alien to remain present in the United States. When the police stop someone based on nothing more than possible removability, the usual predicate for an arrest is absent. When an alien is suspected of being removable, a federal official issues an administrative document called a Notice to Appear. The form does not authorize an arrest. Instead, it gives the alien information about the proceedings, including the time and date of the removal hearing. If an alien fails to appear, an *in absentia* order may direct removal.

The federal statutory structure instructs when it is appropriate to arrest an alien during the removal process. For example, the Attorney General can exercise discretion to issue a warrant for an alien's arrest and detention "pending a decision on whether the alien is to be removed from the United States." 8 U.S.C. §1226(a). And if an alien is ordered removed after a hearing, the Attor-

ney General will issue a warrant. In both instances, the warrants are executed by federal officers who have received training in the enforcement of
immigration law. If no federal warrant has been issued, those officers have
more limited authority. They may arrest an alien for being "in the United
States in violation of any [immigration] law or regulation," for example, but
only where the alien "is likely to escape before a warrant can be obtained."
§1357(a)(2).

Section 6 attempts to provide state officers even greater authority to arrest
aliens on the basis of possible removability than Congress has given trained
federal immigration officers. Under state law, officers who believe an alien is
removable by reason of some "public offense" would have the power to conduct an arrest on that basis regardless of whether a federal warrant has been
issued or the alien is likely to escape. This state authority could be exercised
without any input from the Federal Government about whether an arrest
is warranted in a particular case. This would allow the State to achieve its
own immigration policy. The result could be unnecessary harassment of
some aliens (for instance, a veteran, college student, or someone assisting
with a criminal investigation) whom federal officials determine should not
be removed.

This is not the system Congress created. Federal law specifies limited circumstances in which state officers may perform the functions of an immigration officer. A principal example is when the Attorney General has granted that
authority to specific officers in a formal agreement with a state or local government. Officers covered by these agreements are subject to the Attorney General's direction and supervision. There are significant complexities involved in
enforcing federal immigration law, including the determination of whether a
person is removable. As a result, the agreements reached with the Attorney
General must contain written certification that officers have received
adequate training to carry out the duties of an immigration officer.

By authorizing state officers to decide whether an alien should be detained
for being removable, §6 violates the principle that the removal process is
entrusted to the discretion of the Federal Government. A decision on removability requires a determination of whether it is appropriate to allow a foreign
national to continue living in the United States. Decisions of this nature touch
on foreign relations and must be made with one voice.

In defense of §6, Arizona notes a federal statute permitting state officers to
"cooperate with the Attorney General in the identification, apprehension, detention, or removal of aliens not lawfully present in the United States." 8 U.S.C.
§1357(g)(10)(B). There may be some ambiguity as to what constitutes cooperation under the federal law; but no coherent understanding of the term would
incorporate the unilateral decision of state officers to arrest an alien for being
removable, absent any request, approval, or other instruction from the Federal Government. The Department of Homeland Security gives examples of
what would constitute cooperation under federal law. These include situations

where States participate in a joint task force with federal officers, provide operational support in executing a warrant, or allow federal immigration officials to gain access to detainees held in state facilities. State officials also can assist the Federal Government by responding to requests for information about when an alien will be released from their custody. But the unilateral state action to detain authorized by §6 goes far beyond these measures, defeating any need for real cooperation.

Congress has put in place a system in which state officers may not make warrantless arrests of aliens based on possible removability except in specific, limited circumstances. By nonetheless authorizing state and local officers to engage in these enforcement activities as a general matter, §6 creates an obstacle to the full purposes and objectives of Congress. Section 6 is preempted by federal law.

D

Section 2(B)

Section 2(B) of S.B. 1070 requires state officers to make a "reasonable attempt . . . to determine the immigration status" of any person they stop, detain, or arrest on some other legitimate basis if "reasonable suspicion exists that the person is an alien and is unlawfully present in the United States." Ariz. Rev. Stat. Ann. §11-1051(B) (West 2012). The law also provides that "[a]ny person who is arrested shall have the person's immigration status determined before the person is released." *Ibid.* The accepted way to perform these status checks is to contact ICE, which maintains a database of immigration records.

Three limits are built into the state provision. First, a detainee is presumed not to be an alien unlawfully present in the United States if he or she provides a valid Arizona driver's license or similar identification. Second, officers "may not consider race, color or national origin . . . except to the extent permitted by the United States [and] Arizona Constitution[s]." *Ibid.* Third, the provisions must be "implemented in a manner consistent with federal law regulating immigration, protecting the civil rights of all persons and respecting the privileges and immunities of United States citizens." §11-1051(L) (West 2012).

The United States and its amici contend that, even with these limits, the State's verification requirements pose an obstacle to the framework Congress put in place. The first concern is the mandatory nature of the status checks. The second is the possibility of prolonged detention while the checks are being performed.

1. Consultation between federal and state officials is an important feature of the immigration system. Congress has made clear that no formal agreement or special training needs to be in place for state officers to "communicate with the [Federal Government] regarding the immigration status of any

individual, including reporting knowledge that a particular alien is not lawfully present in the United States." 8 U.S.C. §1357(g)(10)(A). And Congress has obligated ICE to respond to any request made by state officials for verification of a person's citizenship or immigration status. ICE's Law Enforcement Support Center operates "24 hours a day, seven days a week, 365 days a year" and provides, among other things, "immigration status, identity information and real-time assistance to local, state and federal law enforcement agencies." ICE, Fact Sheet: Law Enforcement Support Center (May 29, 2012), online at http:// www.ice.gov/news/library/factsheets/lesc.htm. LESC responded to more than one million requests for information in 2009 alone. App. 93.

The United States argues that making status verification mandatory interferes with the federal immigration scheme. It is true that §2(B) does not allow state officers to consider federal enforcement priorities in deciding whether to contact ICE about someone they have detained. In other words, the officers must make an inquiry even in cases where it seems unlikely that the Attorney General would have the alien removed. This might be the case, for example, when an alien is an elderly veteran with significant and longstanding ties to the community.

Congress has done nothing to suggest it is inappropriate to communicate with ICE in these situations, however. Indeed, it has encouraged the sharing of information about possible immigration violations. A federal statute regulating the public benefits provided to qualified aliens in fact instructs that "no State or local government entity may be prohibited, or in any way restricted, from sending to or receiving from [ICE] information regarding the immigration status, lawful or unlawful, of an alien in the United States." §1644. The federal scheme thus leaves room for a policy requiring state officials to contact ICE as a routine matter.

2.   Some who support the challenge to §2(B) argue that, in practice, state officers will be required to delay the release of some detainees for no reason other than to verify their immigration status. Detaining individuals solely to verify their immigration status would raise constitutional concerns. And it would disrupt the federal framework to put state officers in the position of holding aliens in custody for possible unlawful presence without federal direction and supervision. The program put in place by Congress does not allow state or local officers to adopt this enforcement mechanism.

But §2(B) could be read to avoid these concerns. To take one example, a person might be stopped for jaywalking in Tucson and be unable to produce identification. The first sentence of §2(B) instructs officers to make a "reasonable" attempt to verify his immigration status with ICE if there is reasonable suspicion that his presence in the United States is unlawful. The state courts may conclude that, unless the person continues to be suspected of some crime for which he may be detained by state officers, it would not be reasonable to prolong the stop for the immigration inquiry.

To take another example, a person might be held pending release on a charge of driving under the influence of alcohol. As this goes beyond a mere stop, the arrestee (unlike the jaywalker) would appear to be subject to the categorical requirement in the second sentence of §2(B) that "[a]ny person who is arrested shall have the person's immigration status determined before [he] is released." State courts may read this as an instruction to initiate a status check every time someone is arrested, or in some subset of those cases, rather than as a command to hold the person until the check is complete no matter the circumstances. Even if the law is read as an instruction to complete a check while the person is in custody, moreover, it is not clear at this stage and on this record that the verification process would result in prolonged detention.

However the law is interpreted, if §2(B) only requires state officers to conduct a status check during the course of an authorized, lawful detention or after a detainee has been released, the provision likely would survive preemption—at least absent some showing that it has other consequences that are adverse to federal law and its objectives. There is no need in this case to address whether reasonable suspicion of illegal entry or another immigration crime would be a legitimate basis for prolonging a detention, or whether this too would be preempted by federal law.

The nature and timing of this case counsel caution in evaluating the validity of §2(B). The Federal Government has brought suit against a sovereign State to challenge the provision even before the law has gone into effect. There is a basic uncertainty about what the law means and how it will be enforced. At this stage, without the benefit of a definitive interpretation from the state courts, it would be inappropriate to assume §2(B) will be construed in a way that creates a conflict with federal law. As a result, the United States cannot prevail in its current challenge. This opinion does not foreclose other preemption and constitutional challenges to the law as interpreted and applied after it goes into effect.

V

Immigration policy shapes the destiny of the Nation. On May 24, 2012, at one of this Nation's most distinguished museums of history, a dozen immigrants stood before the tattered flag that inspired Francis Scott Key to write the National Anthem. There they took the oath to become American citizens. These naturalization ceremonies bring together men and women of different origins who now share a common destiny. They swear a common oath to renounce fidelity to foreign princes, to defend the Constitution, and to bear arms on behalf of the country when required by law. The history of the United States is in part made of the stories, talents, and lasting contributions of those who crossed oceans and deserts to come here.

The National Government has significant power to regulate immigration. With power comes responsibility, and the sound exercise of national power over immigration depends on the Nation's meeting its responsibility to base its laws on a political will informed by searching, thoughtful, rational civic discourse. Arizona may have understandable frustrations with the problems caused by illegal immigration while that process continues, but the State may not pursue policies that undermine federal law.

▪ ▪ ▪

The United States has established that §§3, 5(C), and 6 of S.B. 1070 are preempted. It was improper, however, to enjoin §2(B) before the state courts had an opportunity to construe it and without some showing that enforcement of the provision in fact conflicts with federal immigration law and its objectives.

The judgment of the Court of Appeals for the Ninth Circuit is affirmed in part and reversed in part. The case is remanded for further proceedings consistent with this opinion.

It is so ordered.

JUSTICE KAGAN took no part in the consideration or decision of this case.

4

CIVIL RIGHTS AND
CIVIL LIBERTIES

4.1

MICHAEL TESLER

From *Post-Racial or Most-Racial?:*
Race and Politics in the Obama Era

Using extensive survey data on political attitudes among African Americans, Latinos, Asian Americans, and whites, Tesler demonstrates that white Americans and members of several racial minority groups were deeply split in their attitudes toward Barack Obama and toward the two major political parties during the Obama presidency. The evidence shows striking gaps in support across racial groups and indicates that a substantial portion of the political polarization of American society stemmed from differences based on race.

BLACK-WHITE RACIAL DIVIDE IN OBAMA APPROVAL

. . . The black-white racial divide in 2012 presidential voting was about ten percentage points larger in 2012 than it was from 1988 to 2004. Merely looking at presidential voting understates the unique nature of the racial divide in public opinion about President Obama. Democratic presidential candidates received nearly 90 percent of the black vote in pre-Obama presidential elections from 1988 to 2004. That overwhelming black support created a ceiling

From Michael Tesler, *Post-Racial or Most-Racial?: Race and Politics in the Obama Era* (Chicago: University of Chicago Press, 2016).

effect, which made it impossible for any Democratic presidential candidate to perform much better among this group. African Americans, however, have not been nearly as uniform in their approval of Democratic presidents' job performances. President Clinton, whose popularity among African Americans was considered at the time to be "exceptionally strong" (Tate 1994, 207), had an approval rating near 70 percent in three national surveys of black Americans commissioned during the first two years of his presidency. Consequently, the black-white racial divide in President Clinton's pooled approval ratings from the 1994–2000 ANES surveys (thirty percentage points) was considerably smaller than the forty-five-percentage-point divide in black and white Americans' support for Democratic presidential candidates between 1988 and 2004.

Barack Obama's approval ratings, however, were more divided by color than Bill Clinton's. Black Americans were about fifty percentage points more likely to approve of Barack Obama than whites in Gallup polls conducted throughout most of his presidency (see [Figure 1]). The black-white racial divide in presidential approval was also more than fifty percentage points in the 2012 American National Election Study (ANES), with 92 percent of African Americans approving of Barack Obama's job performance in that survey compared to 40 percent of whites. Moreover, President Clinton's approval rating among blacks often increased and decreased in accordance with his white support. That is, when whites' opinions of Bill Clinton changed, so did those of blacks. President Obama's black approval rating, by contrast, was much more stable. Figure [1], which plots Obama's weekly Gallup approval rating by race, shows that President Obama's support from African Americans held pretty steady at around 90 percent approval throughout most of his first term in office. Meanwhile, white Americans fit the more usual pattern of presidential approval (Mueller 1973; Brody 1991; Green, Palmquist, and Schickler 2002; Sides and Vavreck 2013), whereby their support for Obama waned over time. With President Obama's white approval gradually declining during the course of his presidency, and his black support holding relatively constant, the racial divide in presidential approval increased from forty-two percentage points in 2009 to fifty points in 2010 and fifty-three points in 2014.

Kinder and Dale-Riddle (2012, 152) suggested that Barack Obama's unwavering support from African Americans was rooted in racial group consciousness: "Support for the president among African Americans," they wrote, "is perhaps, an affirmation of group solidarity; standing with the president an expression of racial pride." That contention seems hard to argue with, too. After all, group consciousness is one of the most important determinants of black public opinion and political behavior (Gurin, Hatchett, and Jackson 1989; Dawson 1994, 2001; Tate 1994; Kinder and Sanders 1996; Kinder and Winter 2001; Sears and Savalei 2006; Sniderman and Piazza 2002; Harris-Lacewell 2004; Kinder and Dale-Riddle 2012). Racial group identification was also a significant predictor of black support for presidential candidates like

FIGURE [1] President Obama's First-Term Weekly Approval Rating, by Race

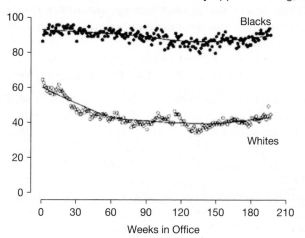

SOURCE: Gallup's weekly tracking polls.

Jesse Jackson and Barack Obama (Dawson 1994; Tate 1994; Tesler and Sears 2010; Kinder and Dale-Riddle 2012). And, perhaps most important for our purposes, in-group consciousness shaped prior presidents' black approval ratings. As Michael Dawson (1994, 162) noted, "Historically, African Americans' perceptions of the relationship between racial group interests and the current administration have helped determine African American presidential approval."

We can also leverage the oversample of African Americans in the 2012 ANES survey to more directly determine whether Barack Obama's unusually strong black support was a byproduct of in-group solidarity. Racial group thermometers are one of many indicators of in-group favoritism (Sears and Savalei 2009), and Kinder and Dale-Riddle (2012, 188–89) used thermometer ratings of blacks to test the effects of "racial group solidarity" on African Americans' support for Jesse Jackson in 1988 and Barack Obama in 2008. . . .

. . . The results . . . suggest that Barack Obama's atypically strong support from African Americans was rooted in racial group consciousness. . . . The black thermometer was weakly related to African Americans' strong approval of Bill Clinton's job performance in pooled 1994–2000 ANES surveys. In the 2012 ANES, however, the black thermometer was a highly significant ($p < .001$) predictor of African Americans' strong support for Barack Obama. . . . Obama's greater popularity among African Americans (80 percent strongly approving compared to 66 percent strongly approving of Clinton) was most pronounced among racially conscious African Americans. Indeed, African Americans who rated their own group most favorably were about twenty percentage points more likely to strongly approve of President Obama than President Clinton. Consistent with that finding, there was a very similar pattern with black respondents' thermometer ratings of Bill Clinton and Barack Obama. That is, African Americans' warmer feelings toward President Obama than President Clinton were also most pronounced among blacks who rated their own group most favorably.

■ ■ ■

All told, then, presidential assessments were increasingly divided by and over race during Barack Obama's presidency. The racial divide in Barack Obama's presidential approval ratings was about twenty to twenty-five percentage points greater than it had been for Bill Clinton. Moreover, this divide in support for President Obama was especially prominent between racially resentful whites, who, as shown in prior chapters and elsewhere (Tesler and Sears 2010), were more opposed to Obama than high-profile white Democrats and racially conscious blacks who had a stronger affinity for President Obama than they had for white Democrats like Bill Clinton.

■ ■ ■

THE GROWING BLACK-WHITE RACIAL DIVIDE IN OBAMA-ERA MACROPARTISANSHIP

Barack Obama's presidency marked a potential turning point in the well-documented black-white racial divide in party identification. As discussed in chapter 1, the percentage of African Americans who identified with the Democratic Party gradually declined by roughly twenty percentage points from 1968 to 2004 (Hajnal and Lee 2011; Luks and Elms 2005). Luks and Elms (2005, 737) further argue that the increased willingness of young African Americans to identify as Republicans and Independents from 1973 to 1994 stemmed in part from the reluctance of recent Democratic administrations to intervene on behalf of racial progress the way that their presidential predecessors did during the civil rights era. This conclusion suggests that the ongoing generational replacement of older African Americans, who came of age when the party leadership was more active in support of racial equality, with younger blacks who came of age under a Democratic Party that generally heeded its electoral temptation of racial silence, would have further accelerated the black exodus from the Democratic Party in the years prior to Barack Obama's election.

Hajnal and Lee (2011, 141), however, wisely concluded their trend analysis of black partisanship by posing the question, "Does a black president mean the end of the decline in African American attachment to the Democratic Party?" There are reasons to believe that it might have. For starters, . . . health care results . . . indicate that Barack Obama's strong connection to the issue polarized public opinion by both racial attitudes *and* race. Moreover, . . . the changing effects of racial attitudes on white support for Hillary Clinton from

2008 to 2012 were very similar to the dynamic effects of race. We might, therefore, expect the spillover of racialization into partisan attachments, as shown with racial attitudes in chapter 7, to have also taken the form of a growing black-white racial divide in Obama-era party identification. Indeed, prior research showed that Jesse Jackson's 1984 primary campaign for the Democratic presidential nomination immediately polarized southern partisanship by both racial attitudes and race (Sears, Citrin, and Kosterman 1987).

We also saw that racial group consciousness undergirded African Americans' extraordinarily strong support for Barack Obama (see also Kinder and Dale-Riddle 2012). African Americans, especially those with high levels of in-group consciousness, may therefore have been increasingly drawn to the Democratic Party because a black president whom they overwhelmingly supported led it. That suspected movement of racially conscious African Americans to the Democratic Party in the Obama era would have inevitably caused a growing black-white racial divide in macropartisanship. The chapter's third major hypothesis, then, is that the large pre-Obama black-white racial divide in party identification grew even wider in the Age of Obama.

The huge pre-Obama racial divide in Democratic Party identification did, in fact, grow significantly wider during [and] after Barack Obama's rise to prominence. Figure [2] leverages the oversamples of African Americans in the 2008 and 2012 ANES surveys to show how the black-white divide in party identification changed in those two Obama-era surveys from its 1988–2004 baseline percentage. African Americans' identification with the Democratic Party was ten percentage points higher in 2012 than it was in the pooled pre-Obama ANES surveys. Meanwhile, white identification with the Democratic Party decreased by about four percentage points over that time period. As a result of those divergent trends, the black-white divide in macropartisanship expanded significantly in the Age of Obama.

Aside from the ANES results, a number of other commercial and academic surveys confirm that the black-white divide in party identification increased substantially during the Obama era. Figure [2] also uses Co-operative Congressional Election Study (CCES) data, which included at least two thousand black respondents in every one of its biennial election year surveys, to show that black identification with the Democratic Party increased by about nine percentage points from 2006 to 2012. At the same time, though, the percentage of white Democrats decreased by one to two percentage points from 2006 to 2012 in the CCES. Thus, the black-white divide in macropartisanship increased by double digits in CCES surveys. Survey data collected by Pew and Gallup throughout Barack Obama's presidency also suggested that the black-white divide in Democratic Party identification increased by as much as ten percentage points from before to after Barack Obama ran for president (Pew Research Center 2011, 2012; Newport 2013; Jones 2014; Hajnal and Lee 2011).

One likely reason African Americans became significantly more Democratic during this time period was that Barack Obama's rise to prominence

FIGURE [2] Democratic Party Identification by Race

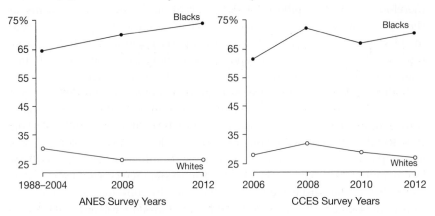

NOTE: Democratic-leaning Independents are not included in the figures.
SOURCES: American National Election Studies (ANES) cumulative file; 2012 ANES;
Cooperative Congressional Election Study (CCES) 2006; CCES 2008; and CCES 2012.

signaled his party might become more supportive of African American interests. Consistent with that expectation, African Americans saw a much larger
divide between Barack Obama and Mitt Romney in their support for "aid to
blacks" than they saw between prior Democratic and Republican presidential
candidates. That increase in perceived Democratic support for black interests could have been especially important for our purposes of explaining the
increase in black partisanship because racial identity measures liked linked
fate—the notion that one's personal well-being is directly affected by the
well-being of the larger black community—were only "relatively small" predictors of Democratic partisanship in the National Black Election Studies
conducted during the 1980s and 1990s (Hajnal and Lee 2011, 134). In other
words, having an African American president from the Democratic Party in the
White House, who was perceived as more supportive of black interests than
his predecessors, could have made group consciousness a more important
determinant of African Americans' party identifications than it had been in
the pre-Obama era.

■ ■ ■

African Americans grew increasingly Democratic during the Obama era
in large part because of racial group solidarity. That is, African Americans
who rated blacks most favorably were most likely to migrate to Barack Obama's
Democratic Party. Those results . . . , also suggest that attitudes about African
Americans drove the growing black-white divide in Obama-era party identification: White Americans who harbored out-group resentment toward blacks
became increasingly Republican, whereas African Americans who rated their

own racial group most favorably became more Democratic. The upshot was a growing polarization of mass partisanship by and over race.

THE GROWING WHITE-LATINO DIVIDE IN OBAMA-ERA PARTY IDENTIFICATION

This growing Obama-era divide in party identification by and over race was not too surprising. After all, the racial divide in approval of Barack Obama's presidency was exceptionally large, with that chasm greatest between racially conscious blacks and racially resentful whites. It makes perfect sense, according to the spillover of racialization hypothesis, for those same patterns to have reproduced themselves in the Obama-era partisan attachments of black and white Americans.

The growing partisan divide between whites and Latinos in the Age of Obama was more unexpected, though. As can be seen in Figure [3], the percentage of respondents who identified as Democrats in the Pew Hispanic Center's National Surveys of Latinos increased from 31 percent in both 2003 and 2007 all the way to 48 percent in 2012. In other words, Latinos were even more likely than African Americans to move to the Democratic Party in the Age of Obama. Given the trends in white partisanship shown in Figure [2], which revealed a slight decline in white Americans' Democratic Party identifications, the divide between whites and Latinos in macropartisanship increased by as much as twenty percentage points during Barack Obama's presidency.

Unlike African Americans' greater Democratic identification in the Obama era, it is difficult to make the case that Barack Obama, and the spillover of

FIGURE [3]   Percentage of Latinos Identifying as Democrats, 2003–12

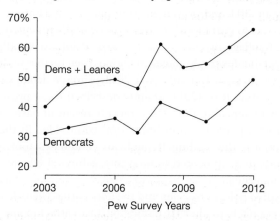

Pew Survey Years

SOURCES: Pew Hispanic Center National Surveys; percentages accessed from Roper Center's iPOLL databank.

racialization from mass assessments of his presidency into related political opinions, was directly responsible for this growing white-Latino partisan divide. To be sure, Barack Obama was very popular with Latinos throughout most of his presidency. Yet, that popularity was not nearly as strong or stable as his black support. President Obama's Hispanic approval ratings in weekly Gallup polls eroded over the first three years of his presidency and dipped slightly below 50 percent in several 2011 surveys. Moreover, the exit polls suggest that Bill Clinton won an even larger share of the two-party Latino vote in his presidential elections than Barack Obama did in his victories. And Bill Clinton's longstanding support from Latinos was cited as a major reason why Hillary Clinton decisively won the Hispanic vote against Barack Obama in the 2008 presidential primaries (Barreto et al. 2008; Tesler and Sears 2010).

Rather than their affinity for President Obama, Latinos' growing identification with the Democratic Party was more likely rooted in the Republican Party's increasingly hostile rhetoric and policy positions toward minorities during Obama's presidency. Or as Stanford political scientist Gary Segura said in a 2012 PBS interview, "The president has widely disappointed Latino voters through the failure to pursue immigration reform through unprecedented deportations. But he can credibly claim to be better than the alternative when the alternative is saying horrible things." These "horrible things," perhaps most notably, included Republicans' and Tea Partiers' frequent portrayals of Latino immigrants and immigration as a threat to Americans and American culture (Parker and Barreto 2013, 166; Skocpol and Williamson 2012, 76).

Such sentiments were also prevalent in Republican-sponsored state and national policies. Arizona's SB 1070, which the Obama administration challenged in court because it allowed for the racial profiling of Latinos based on the suspicion that they could be undocumented immigrants, was passed into law in 2010 almost entirely with Republican votes. Barack Obama and the Republican Party also clashed over the DREAM Act—a policy supported by the president in 2011 and prevented from passing by House Republicans in 2012—which was to grant legal status to young undocumented immigrants if they attended college or enlisted in the armed forces. Finally, Republican presidential candidates surely alienated Latinos even further with their rhetoric and policy positions in the 2011 and 2012 primary debates. Collingwood, Barreto, and Garcia-Rios (2014, 4) aptly described these presidential candidates' strategy to appeal to the GOP's "racially resentful base" in 2012: "In an effort to attract a perceived anti-immigrant voting bloc in the conservative primary elections, the leading Republican candidates took very hardline stances against undocumented immigrants, bilingual education, and bilingual voting materials."

Those hardline policy positions and the anti-Latino rhetoric that accompanied them were likely to alter Hispanics' partisan attachments. In fact, prior research shows that Republicans' strong support for California's Proposition

187—a 1994 ballot initiative that rendered undocumented immigrants ineligible for such public services as health care and education—helped shift the partisan attachments of Latinos in the Golden State toward the Democrats (Bowler, Nicholson, and Segura 2006; Barreto and Ramirez 2013).

Polling data suggests that Latinos were paying attention to these partisan developments. Hispanics increasingly thought that the Democratic Party cared more about Latinos than Republicans did during Barack Obama's presidency. Figure [4], for example, shows that 55 percent of the Latino respondents surveyed by the Pew Hispanic Center in 2012 thought that the Democratic Party had more concern for Latinos than the Republican Party—an increase of more than twenty percentage points since 2007. Likewise, only 33 percent of respondents in a 2012 national survey of Latinos commissioned by CNN said that the Republican Party "is generally doing a good job these days of reaching out to blacks, Hispanics, and other minorities." That figure was down eighteen percentage points from the 51 percent of Latinos who thought Republicans were doing a good job of reaching out to minorities in a 2000 CNN Poll. Meanwhile, the percentage of Latinos who thought the Democratic Party was doing a good job with minorities slightly increased from 75 percent in 2000 to 77 percent in 2012. National surveys conducted in 2012 by the polling firm Latino Decisions also showed that Latinos were at least forty percentage points more likely to say that the Democratic Party was doing "a good job" in its outreach to Hispanic voters than they were to say the Republican Party was doing a good job of reaching out to their ethnic group.

FIGURE [4] Percentage of Latinos Who Say the Democratic Party Has More Concern for Hispanics Than the Republican Party, 2004–12

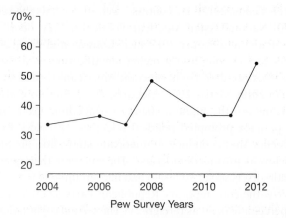

Pew Survey Years

SOURCES: Pew Hispanic Center National Surveys; percentages accessed from Roper Center's iPOLL databank.

With the Democratic Party increasingly viewed as the party more supportive of Latino interests in the Age of Obama, we might expect the relationship
between Hispanic in-group consciousness and Democratic Party identification to have increased over time. After all, . . . the effect of black-thermometer
ratings on African Americans' partisan attachments increased significantly
after Barack Obama's ascendancy signaled that his party may be more supportive of "aid to blacks." Moreover, and also like African Americans, in-group
consciousness has long been an important predictor of Latinos' political attitudes and behavior (DeSipio 1996; Sanchez 2006; Barreto 2010; Hajnal and
Lee 2011; Masuoka and Junn 2013). The chapter's fifth hypothesis, then, is
that Latinos' in-group identifications may have been activated by the perceived growing distance between the parties in their concern for Hispanics.

■ ■ ■

ASIAN AMERICANS AND REPUBLICANS
AS THE PARTY OF WHITE PEOPLE

Asian Americans' support for the Democratic Party . . . has increased dramati-
cally in the past two decades. In 1992, when the exit polls first reported Asian
Americans' vote choices, this group decisively preferred George H. W. Bush to
Bill Clinton (55 percent to 31 percent, respectively). Asian American support for
Democratic presidential candidates, however, has increased in every subsequent
election. So much so, that Barack Obama won 74 percent of the two-party Asian
American vote in 2012. That growing Democratic support extended to party
identification, as well. National surveys of Asian Americans conducted by the
Pew Research Center in 2012 and 2013 found that 50 percent and 64 percent of
Asians identified as Democrats or leaned Democratic in those respective polls
(Pew Research Center 2013). By contrast, well under half the respondents in
the 2000–2001 National Asian American Political Survey identified or leaned
Democratic (Bowler and Segura 2012; Lien, Conway, and Wong 2004).

Asian Americans' strong and growing identification with the Democratic
Party is somewhat peculiar. Higher-income Americans tend to support Repub-
licans (Gelman 2010; Bartels 2008; McCarty, Poole, and Rosenthal 2006), and
Asian Americans are the highest-earning racial/ethnic group in the United
States. This paradox prompted political scientists Alexander Kuo, Neil Malhotra, and Cecilia Mo to conduct an important study, fittingly titled "Why Do
Asian Americans Identify as Democrats?" The answer to their question, according to these authors, is social exclusion and intergroup solidarity. That is, "Asian
Americans view the contemporary Republican Party as excluding them from
society and perceiving them as foreign. . . . The second explanation [intergroup
solidarity], which is not mutually exclusive, is that Asian Americans believe
they have common interests with other ethnic minority groups that have been
longstanding constituencies within the Democratic Party, and thus align them-

selves with these groups rather than whites" (Kuo, Malhotra, and Mo 2014, 3–4). Kuo, Malhotra, and Mo (2014) support those hypotheses with some inge-nious experiments. Most notably, they found that priming social exclusion with the use of insensitive white lab administrators who questioned their partici-pants' citizenship before entering the laboratory shifted Asian Americans' par-tisan preferences thirteen percentage points more Democratic.

Like our analyses of Latino partisanship above, those social exclusion find-ings suggest that Asian Americans largely viewed the contemporary Repub-lican Party as the party of whites. We might, therefore, expect attitudes about white Americans to have also been important determinants of Asian Ameri-cans' partisan attachments. Unfortunately, the data for testing that hypoth-esis is not nearly as good as the data used to assess the changing impact on racial group thermometer ratings on the partisan attachments of whites, African Americans, and Latinos. The ANES, for example, includes only a tiny number of Asian Americans in their election-year surveys. Nevertheless, we can still glean some insights into how Asian Americans' thermometer ratings of various racial and ethnic groups impacted their partisan attachments in the 2011–12 CCAP survey because this massive survey of forty-four thousand respondents included more than eight hundred Asian Americans. At the same time, though, the CCAP's nationally representative Internet survey may not be representative of minority populations. Indeed, minority panelists who volunteer to take Internet surveys administered in English, such as the CCAP, are unlikely to reflect the full variation in these groups' political opinions. So, some caution is required in interpreting the results.

■   ■   ■

The large effects of antiwhite attitudes on Asian Americans' support for the Democratic Party seem to fit into that "party of whites" paradigm as well. Moreover, those strong effects of antiwhite affect are consistent with the con-tention by Kuo, Malhotra, and Mo (2014) that social exclusion of Asian Ameri-cans by whites drives support for the Democratic Party. . . . Intergroup solidarity also leads Asian Americans to identify with the Democratic Party. For, as can be seen, warmer thermometer ratings of blacks were also strongly linked to Asian Americans' identification with the Democratic Party. Finally, Asian Americans' thermometer ratings of their own group were not signifi-cantly related to their partisan attachments—a result similar to Hajnal and Lee's (2011) contention that racial identity has a weaker effect on Asian American partisanship than it does for Latinos.

There, unfortunately, has been very little work on the partisan attachments of Native Americans. So, we cannot similarly place the large effects of the white thermometer on their party identifications into a broader context. However, given the results for Asian Americans and Latinos, these findings suggest that Native Americans may have also viewed the modern Republican Party as the party of whites.

CONCLUDING REMARKS

The results . . . , in combination with the earlier findings . . . , suggest that the growing black-white divide in Obama-era political opinions was in large part about President Obama and attitudes toward African Americans. The exceptionally large black-white divide in Barack Obama's presidential approval ratings was most pronounced among racially resentful whites and racially conscious blacks. So, too, was the expanding racial divide in macropartisanship, as attitudes about African Americans became an increasingly important determinant of both black and white Americans' partisan identifications in the Age of Obama.

The growing number of Latinos and Asian Americans who identified as Democrats in the Obama era, however, seems to have been more about social exclusion and attitudes toward whites than it was about President Obama and feelings toward blacks. To be sure, Barack Obama's Democratic presidency and the hostile reaction to it from his partisan opponents likely contributed to minority groups' enhanced image of Republicans as the party of white people. A clear majority of Latinos, for example, thought that race was a factor in opposition to his presidency in a 2009 Pew poll (63 percent); and most of the Latinos (61 percent) in a 2010 ABC survey thought that the Tea Party Movement was based to some degree on racial prejudice toward the president. Barack Obama's ascendancy also helped give rise to the more ethnocentric elements of the Republican Party, such as the Tea Party (Parker and Barreto 2013), who were most opposed to immigration. Yet, unlike the growing black-white racial divide in Obama-era party identification, the partisan preferences of Latinos and Asian Americans would have most likely moved further away from white Americans even if Barack Obama had not been elected president in 2008. For, as mentioned earlier, Latinos preferred Hillary Clinton by a large margin to Barack Obama in the 2008 presidential primaries.

Minority voters' overwhelming support for Democrats could, therefore, continue into the foreseeable future. In fact, political commentators argued long before Barack Obama's presidential candidacy that the growing non-white electorate will inevitably lead to a longstanding Democratic majority in national politics (e.g., Judis and Teixeira 2004). Some astute academic commentators, however, have pushed back on this common "demographics as destiny" argument (Vavreck 2014; Bartels 2014; Piston 2014). Asian American and Latino voters, they point out, may not be as solidly Democratic as is often assumed. In keeping with that contention, Hajnal and Lee (2011) showed that these groups' party attachments are less crystallized than black and white partisanship. . . .

Conversely, Republicans could also stave off electoral defeat in the years ahead by turning out more whites and/or winning a larger share of their votes. Republican elites, in fact, regularly debated during Barack Obama's second term in office whether the party's best bet to retake the White House was to reach out to minorities or to pursue this white voter strategy (Edsall 2013; Trende 2013; Brownstein 2013). Republican strategist Sean Trende (2013) summarized the latter approach's potential: "It's entirely possible that as our nation becomes more diverse, our political coalitions will increasingly fracture along racial/ethnic lines rather than ideological ones. . . . I don't see any compelling reason why these trends can't continue, and why a Republican couldn't begin to approach Ronald Reagan's 30-point win with whites from 1984 in a more neutral environment than Reagan enjoyed."

There's some social scientific evidence to support that argument, too. Just drawing attention to the country's changing demographics in a survey experiment significantly increased the percentage of white Independents who expressed prejudiced attitudes, took conservative policy positions, and identified as Republicans (Craig and Richeson 2014a, 2014b). Ryan Enos's (2014, 2015) innovative work on racial threat similarly shows that increased contact with racial and ethnic minorities in Chicago and Boston, respectively, led whites to express more ethnocentric attitudes, turn out to vote in higher numbers, and support Republican candidates at greater rates. As a result of such studies, Larry Bartels (2014) concluded: "The changing American polity may come to look more like [Republican] Texas than like the multicultural Democratic stronghold of California. In an increasingly diverse America, identity politics will continue to cut both ways."

Finally, . . . Republicans could be quite constrained in their minority outreach after Barack Obama leaves office. . . . Rank-and-file Republicans were more racially conservative during his presidency than they had been in modern times. Consequently, it may be increasingly difficult for a Republican candidate to reach out to minorities and still win his or her party's presidential nomination. Mitt Romney, after all, had to take a very hard-line on immigration during the presidential primaries to curry favor with his party's base (Collingwood, Barreto, and Garcia-Rios 2014). . . . Internal divisions between congressional Republicans in the Obama era came down in large part to how racially resentful their constituents were. A majority of Republicans in the House of Representatives could, therefore, fear that reaching out to minorities will cost them their jobs. . . . The Republicans' most viable option going forward might be to try to mobilize and win more white votes. If so, then mass politics might grow even more divided by color in the post-Obama era.

REFERENCES

Barreto, Matt A. 2010. *Ethnic Cues: The Role of Shared Ethnicity in Latino Political Participation*. Ann Arbor: University of Michigan Press.

Barreto, Matt A., Luis R. Fraga, Sylvia Manzano, Valerie Martinez-Ebers, and Gary M. Segura. 2008. "'Should They Dance with the One Who Brung 'Em?' Latinos and the 2008 Presidential Election." *PS: Political Science and Politics* 61 (4): 753–61.

Barreto, Matt A., and Ricardo Ramirez. 2013. "Anti-Immigrant Politics and Lessons for the GOP from California." *Latino Decisions Blog.* http://www.latinodecisions.com/blog/2013/09/20/anti-immigrant-politics-and-lessons-for-the-gop-from-california/.

Bartels, Larry. M. 2008. *Unequal Democracy: The Political Economy of the New Gilded Age.* New York: Russell Sage Foundation.

———. 2014. "Can the Republican Party Thrive on White Identity?" *Monkey Cage.* http://www.washingtonpost.com/blogs/monkey-cage/wp/2014/04/16/can-the-republican-party-thrive-on-white-identity/.

Bowler, Shaun, Stephen P. Nicholson, and Gary M. Segura. 2006. "Earthquakes and Aftershocks: Race, Direct Democracy, and Partisan Change." *American Journal of Political Science* 50 (1): 146–59.

Bowler, Shaun, and Gary Segura. 2012. *The Future Is Ours: Minority Politics, Political Behavior, and the Multiracial Era of American Politics.* Washington, DC: CQ Press.

Brody, Richard A. 1991. *Assessing the President: The Media, Elite Opinion, and Public Support.* Stanford: Stanford University Press.

Brownstein, Ronald. 2013. "Bad Bet: Why the Republicans Can't Win with Whites Alone." *National Journal*, September 5. http://www.nationaljournal.com/magazine/bad-bet-why-republicans-can-t-win-with-whites-alone-20130905.

Collingwood, Loren, Matt A. Barreto, and Sergio I. Garcia-Rios. 2014. "Revisiting Latino Voting: Cross-Racial Mobilization in the 2012 Election." Political Research Quarterly 67 (3): 632–45. doi:10.117/1065912914532374.

Craig, Maureen A., and Jennifer A. Richeson. 2014a. "More Diverse Yet Less Tolerant? How the Increasingly Diverse Racial Landscape Affects White Americans' Racial Attitudes." *Personality and Social Psychology Bulletin* 40: 750–61. doi:10.17177/0146167214524993.

Craig, Maureen A., and Jennifer A. Richeson. 2014b. "On the Precipice of a 'Majority-Minority' America Perceived Status Threat from the Racial Demographic Shift Affects White Americans' Political Ideology." *Psychological Science* 25 (6): 1189–97.

Dawson, Michael. 1994. *Behind the Mule: Race and Class in African American Politics.* Princeton, NJ: Princeton University Press.

———. 2001. Black Visions: *The Roots of Contemporary African American Political Ideologies.* Chicago: University of Chicago Press.

DeSipio, Louis. 1996. *Counting on the Latino Vote: Latinos as a New Electorate.* Charlottesville: University of Virginia Press.

Edsall, Thomas B. 2013. "Should the Republican Party Just Focus on White Voters?" *New York Times*, op-ed, July 3.

Enos, Ryan D. 2014. "Causal Effect of Intergroup Contact on Exclusionary Attitudes." *Proceedings of the National Academy of Sciences* III (10): 3699–704.

———. 2015. "What Tearing Down Public Housing Projects Teaches Us about the Effect of Racial Threat on Political Participation." *American Journal of Political Science* 59. doi:10.1111/ajps.12156.

Gelman, Andrew. 2010. *Red State, Blue State, Rich State, Poor State: Why Americans Vote the Way They Do.* Princeton, NJ: Princeton University Press.

Green, Donald, Bradley Palmquist, and Eric Schickler. 2002. *Partisan Hearts and Minds.* New Haven, CT: Yale University Press.

Gurin, Patricia, Shirley Hatchett, and James Jackson. 1989. *Hope and Independence: Blacks' Response to Electoral and Party Politics.* New York: Russell Sage Foundation.

Hajnal, Zoltan L., and Taeku Lee. 2011. *Why Americans Don't Join the Party: Race, Immigration, and the Failure (of Political Parties) to Engage the Electorate*. Princeton, NJ: Princeton University Press.

Harris-Lacewell, Melissa. 2004. *Barbershops, Bibles, and BET: Everyday Talk and Black Political Thought*. Princeton, NJ: Princeton University Press.

Jones, Jeffrey M. 2014. "U.S. Whites More Solidly Republican in Recent Years: Party Preferences More Polarized by Race and Ethnicity under Obama." http://www .gallup.com/poll/168059/whites-solidly-republican-recent-years.aspx.

Judis, John B., and Ruy Teixeira. 2004. *The Emerging Democratic Majority*. New York: Simon and Schuster.

Kinder, Donald R., and Allison Dale-Riddle. 2012. *The End of Race?* New Haven, CT: Yale University Press.

Kinder, Donald R., and Lynn M. Sanders. 1996. *Divided by Color: Racial Politics and Democratic Ideals*. Chicago: University of Chicago Press.

Kinder, Donald, and Nicholas Winter. 2001. "Exploring the Racial Divide: Blacks, Whites, and Opinion on National Policy." *American Journal of Political Science* 45: 439–56.

Kuo, Alexander, Neil A. Malhotra, and Cecilia Hyunjung Mo. 2014. "Why Do Asian Americans Identify as Democrats? Testing Theories of Social Exclusion and Intergroup Solidarity." Unpublished manuscript, Vanderbilt University.

Lien, Pei-Te, M. Margaret Conway, and Janelle Wong. 2004. *The Politics of Asian Americans*. New York: Routledge.

Luks, Samantha, and Laurel Elms. 2005. "African American Partisanship and the Legacy of the Civil Rights Movement: Generational, Regional, and Economic Influences on Democratic Identification, 1973–1994." *Political Psychology* 26: 735–54.

Masuoka, Natalie, and Jane Junn. 2013. *The Politics of Belonging: Race, Public Opinion, and Immigration*. Chicago: University of Chicago Press.

McCarty, Nolan, Keith T. Poole, and Howard Rosenthal. 2006. *Polarized America: The Dance of Ideology and Unequal Riches*. Cambridge, MA: MIT Press.

Mueller, John E. 1973. *War, Presidents and Public Opinion*. New York: Wiley.

Newport, Frank. 2013. "Democrats Racially Diverse; Republicans Mostly White: Democrats and Independents Grow More Diverse since 2008." http://www.gallup .com/poll/160373/democrats-racially-diverse-republicans-mostly-white.aspx.

Parker, Christopher S., and Matt A. Barreto. 2013. *Change They Can't Believe In: The Tea Party and Reactionary Politics in America*. Princeton, NJ: Princeton University Press.

Pew Research Center. 2011. "GOP Makes Big Gains among White Voters." July 22. http://www.people-press.org/2011/07/22/gop-makes-big-gains-among-white -voters/.

———. 2012. "Partisan Polarization Surges in Bush and Obama Years." June 4. http:// www.people-press.org/files/legacy-pdf/06-04-12%20Values%20Release.pdf.

———. 2013. "The Rise of Asian Americans." April 4. http://www.pewsocialtrends.org /files/2013/04/Asian-Americans-new-full-report-04-2013.pdf.

Piston, Spencer. 2014. "Lighter-Skinned Minorities Are More Likely to Support Republicans." *Monkey Cage*. http://www.washingtonpost.com/blogs/monkey-cage/wp /2014/09/17/lighter-skinned-minorities-are-more-likely-to-support-republicans/.

Sanchez, Gabriel R. 2006. "The Role of Group Consciousness in Latino Public Opinion." *Political Research Quarterly* 59 (3): 435–46.

Sears, David O., Jack Citrin, and Richard Kosterman. 1987. "Jesse Jackson and the Southern White Electorate in 1984." In *Blacks in Southern Politics*, edited by

Robert P. Steed, Laurence W. Moreland, and Tod A. Baker, 209–25. New York: Praeger.

Sears, David O., and Victoria Savalei. 2006. "The Political Color Line in America: Many Peoples of Color or Black Exceptionalism? *Political Psychology* 27: 895–924.

———. 2009. "Sharp or Blunt Instruments? Measuring Affect toward Ethnic and Racial Groups in Contemporary America." Paper presented at the annual meeting of the International Society for Political Psychology, Dublin, July 17.

Sides, John, and Lynn Vavreck 2013. *The Gamble: Choice and Chance in the 2012 Presidential Election*. Princeton, NJ: Princeton University Press.

Skocpol, Theda, and Vanessa Williamson. 2012. *The Tea Party and the Remaking of Republican Conservatism*. Oxford: Oxford University Press.

Sniderman, Paul M., and Thomas Piazza. 2002. *Black Pride and Black Prejudice*. Princeton, NJ: Princeton University Press.

Tate, Katherine. 1994. *From Protest to Politics: The New Black Voters in American Elections*. Cambridge, MA: Harvard University Press.

Tesler, Michael, and David O. Sears. 2010. *Obama's Race: The 2008 Election and the Dream of a Post-Racial America*. Chicago: University of Chicago Press.

Trende, Sean. 2013. "The Case of the Missing White Voters Revisited." June 21. *Real Clear Politics*. http://www.realclearpolitics.com/articles/2013/06/21/the_case_of_the _missing_white_voters_revisited_118893.html.

Vavreck, Lynn. 2014. "It's Not Too Late for Republicans to Win Latino Votes." *Upshot*. August 11. http://www.nytimes.com/2014/08/12/upshot/its-not-too-late-for-republicans -to-win-latino-votes.html?_r=0&abt=0002&abg=0.

4.2

Brown v. Board of Education (1954)

In one of the most important Supreme Court cases in American history, the justices unanimously and emphatically overturned the precedent from Plessy v. Ferguson *(1896), which had upheld the right of local communities and states to maintain separate public facilities for the races. "[I]n the field of public education," the Court declared, "the doctrine of 'separate but equal' has no place." This 1954 decision started the American legal system down a new path of active intervention in the racial policies of government at all levels.*

MR. CHIEF JUSTICE WARREN delivered the opinion of the Court.

These cases come to us from the States of Kansas, South Carolina, Virginia, and Delaware. They are premised on different facts and different local conditions, but a common legal question justifies their consideration together in this consolidated opinion.

In each of the cases, minors of the Negro race, through their legal representatives, seek the aid of the courts in obtaining admission to the public schools of their community on a nonsegregated basis. In each instance, they had been denied admission to schools attended by white children under laws requiring or permitting segregation according to race. This segregation was alleged to deprive the plaintiffs of the equal protection of the laws under the Fourteenth Amendment. In each of the cases other than the Delaware case, a three-judge federal district court denied relief to the plaintiffs on the so-called "separate but equal" doctrine announced by this Court in *Plessy v. Ferguson.* Under that doctrine, equality of treatment is accorded when the races are provided substantially equal facilities, even though these facilities be separate. In the Delaware case, the Supreme Court of Delaware adhered to that doctrine, but ordered that the plaintiffs be admitted to the white schools because of their superiority to the Negro schools.

The plaintiffs contend that segregated public schools are not "equal" and cannot be made "equal," and that hence they are deprived of the equal protection of the laws. Because of the obvious importance of the question presented, the Court took jurisdiction. Argument was heard in the 1952 Term,

•

From *Brown v. Board of Education*, 347 U.S. 483 (1954).

and reargument was heard this Term on certain questions propounded by the Court.

Reargument was largely devoted to the circumstances surrounding the adoption of the Fourteenth Amendment in 1868. It covered exhaustively consideration of the Amendment in Congress, ratification by the states, then-existing practices in racial segregation, and the views of proponents and opponents of the Amendment. This discussion and our own investigation convince us that, although these sources cast some light, it is not enough to resolve the problem with which we are faced. At best, they are inconclusive. The most avid proponents of the post-War Amendments undoubtedly intended them to remove all legal distinctions among "all persons born or naturalized in the United States." Their opponents, just as certainly, were antagonistic to both the letter and the spirit of the Amendments and wished them to have the most limited effect. What others in Congress and the state legislatures had in mind cannot be determined with any degree of certainty.

An additional reason for the inconclusive nature of the Amendment's history with respect to segregated schools is the status of public education at that time. In the South, the movement toward free common schools, supported by general taxation, had not yet taken hold. Education of white children was largely in the hands of private groups. Education of Negroes was almost nonexistent, and practically all of the race were illiterate. In fact, any education of Negroes was forbidden by law in some states. Today, in contrast, many Negroes have achieved outstanding success in the arts and sciences, as well as in the business and professional world. It is true that public school education at the time of the Amendment had advanced further in the North, but the effect of the Amendment on Northern States was generally ignored in the congressional debates. Even in the North, the conditions of public education did not approximate those existing today. The curriculum was usually rudimentary; ungraded schools were common in rural areas; the school term was but three months a year in many states, and compulsory school attendance was virtually unknown. As a consequence, it is not surprising that there should be so little in the history of the Fourteenth Amendment relating to its intended effect on public education.

In the first cases in this Court construing the Fourteenth Amendment, decided shortly after its adoption, the Court interpreted it as proscribing all state-imposed discriminations against the Negro race.[1] The doctrine of "separate but equal" did not make its appearance in this Court until 1896 in the case of *Plessy v. Ferguson*, involving not education but transportation.[2] American courts have since labored with the doctrine for over half a century. In this Court, there have been six cases involving the "separate but equal" doctrine in the field of public education. In *Cumming v. County Board of Education*, and *Gong Lum v. Rice*, the validity of the doctrine itself was not challenged. In more recent cases, all on the graduate school level, inequality was found in that specific benefits enjoyed by white students were denied to Negro students of the same educational qualifications. *Missouri ex rel. Gaines v. Canada*, *Sipuel v. Okla-*

homa, *Sweatt v. Painter, McLaurin v. Oklahoma State Regents*. In none of these cases was it necessary to reexamine the doctrine to grant relief to the Negro plaintiff. And in *Sweatt v. Painter, supra*, the Court expressly reserved decision on the question whether *Plessy v. Ferguson* should be held inapplicable to public education.

In the instant cases, that question is directly presented. Here, unlike *Sweatt v. Painter*, there are findings below that the Negro and white schools involved have been equalized, or are being equalized, with respect to buildings, curricula, qualifications and salaries of teachers, and other "tangible" factors. Our decision, therefore, cannot turn on merely a comparison of these tangible factors in the Negro and white schools involved in each of the cases. We must look instead to the effect of segregation itself on public education.

In approaching this problem, we cannot turn the clock back to 1868, when the Amendment was adopted, or even to 1896, when *Plessy v. Ferguson* was written. We must consider public education in the light of its full development and its present place in American life throughout the Nation. Only in this way can it be determined if segregation in public schools deprives these plaintiffs of the equal protection of the laws.

Today, education is perhaps the most important function of state and local governments. Compulsory school attendance laws and the great expenditures for education both demonstrate our recognition of the importance of education to our democratic society. It is required in the performance of our most basic public responsibilities, even service in the armed forces. It is the very foundation of good citizenship. Today it is a principal instrument in awakening the child to cultural values, in preparing him for later professional training, and in helping him to adjust normally to his environment. In these days, it is doubtful that any child may reasonably be expected to succeed in life if he is denied the opportunity of an education. Such an opportunity, where the state has undertaken to provide it, is a right which must be made available to all on equal terms.

We come then to the question presented: Does segregation of children in public schools solely on the basis of race, even though the physical facilities and other "tangible" factors may be equal, deprive the children of the minority group of equal educational opportunities? We believe that it does.

In *Sweatt v. Painter*, in finding that a segregated law school for Negroes could not provide them equal educational opportunities, this Court relied in large part on "those qualities which are incapable of objective measurement but which make for greatness in a law school." In *McLaurin v. Oklahoma State Regents*, the Court, in requiring that a Negro admitted to a white graduate school be treated like all other students, again resorted to intangible considerations: ". . . his ability to study, to engage in discussions and exchange views with other students, and, in general, to learn his profession." Such considerations apply with added force to children in grade and high schools. To separate them from others of similar age and qualifications solely because of their race generates a feeling of inferiority as to their status in the community that may affect their hearts and minds in a way unlikely ever to be undone. The effect of this separation on their educational opportunities was well stated by a finding in the Kansas case by a court which nevertheless felt compelled to rule against the Negro plaintiffs: Segregation of white and colored children in public schools has a detrimental effect upon the colored children. The impact is greater when it has the sanction of the law, for the policy of separating the races is usually interpreted as denoting the inferiority of the negro group. A sense of inferiority affects the motivation of a child to learn. Segregation with the sanction of law, therefore, has a tendency to [retard] the educational and mental development of negro children and to deprive them of some of the benefits they would receive in a racial[ly] integrated school system.[3] Whatever may have been the extent of psychological knowledge at the time of *Plessy v. Ferguson*, this finding is amply supported by modern authority. Any language in *Plessy v. Ferguson* contrary to this finding is rejected.

We conclude that, in the field of public education, the doctrine of "separate but equal" has no place. Separate educational facilities are inherently unequal. Therefore, we hold that the plaintiffs and others similarly situated for whom the actions have been brought are, by reason of the segregation complained of, deprived of the equal protection of the laws guaranteed by the Fourteenth Amendment. This disposition makes unnecessary any discussion whether such segregation also violates the Due Process Clause of the Fourteenth Amendment.[4]

Because these are class actions, because of the wide applicability of this decision, and because of the great variety of local conditions, the formulation of decrees in these cases presents problems of considerable complexity. On reargument, the consideration of appropriate relief was necessarily subordinated to the primary question—the constitutionality of segregation in public education. We have now announced that such segregation is a denial of the equal protection of the laws. In order that we may have the full assistance of the parties in formulating decrees, the cases will be restored to the docket, and the parties are requested to present further argument on Questions 4 and 5 previously propounded by the Court for the reargument this Term.[5] The Attorney General of the United States is again invited to participate. The Attorneys General of the states requiring or permitting segregation in public education will also be permitted to appear as *amici curiae* upon request to do so by September 15, 1954, and submission of briefs by October 1, 1954.

It is so ordered.

NOTES

1. *Slaughter-House Cases*, 16 Wall. 36, 67–72 (1873); *Strauder v. West Virginia*, 100 U.S. 303, 307–308 (1880): It ordains that no State shall deprive any person of life, liberty, or property, without due process of law, or deny to any person within its jurisdiction the equal protection of the laws. What is this but declaring that the law in the States shall be

the same for the black as for the white; that all persons, whether colored or white, shall stand equal before the laws of the States, and, in regard to the colored race, for whose protection the amendment was primarily designed, that no discrimination shall be made against them by law because of their color? The words of the amendment, it is true, are prohibitory, but they contain a necessary implication of a positive immunity, or right, most valuable to the colored race—the right to exemption from unfriendly legislation against them distinctively as colored—exemption from legal discriminations, implying inferiority in civil society, lessening the security of their enjoyment of the rights which others enjoy, and discriminations which are steps towards reducing them to the condition of a subject race.

2. The doctrine apparently originated in *Roberts v. City of Boston*, 59 Mass.198, 206 (1850), upholding school segregation against attack as being violative of a state constitutional guarantee of equality. Segregation in Boston public schools was eliminated in 1855. Mass.Acts 1855, c. 256. But elsewhere in the North, segregation in public education has persisted in some communities until recent years. It is apparent that such segregation has long been a nationwide problem, not merely one of sectional concern.

3. A similar finding was made in the Delaware case: I conclude from the testimony that, in our Delaware society, State-imposed segregation in education itself results in the Negro children, as a class, receiving educational opportunities which are substantially inferior to those available to white children otherwise similarly situated. 87 A.2d 862, 865.

4. See *Bolling v. Sharpe*, post, p. 497, concerning the Due Process Clause of the Fifth Amendment.

5. Assuming it is decided that segregation in public schools violates the Fourteenth Amendment, (a) would a decree necessarily follow providing that, within the limits set by normal geographic school districting, Negro children should forthwith be admitted to schools of their choice, or (b) may this Court, in the exercise of its equity powers, permit an effective gradual adjustment to be brought about from existing segregated systems to a system not based on color distinctions?

4.3

District of Columbia v. Heller (2008)

In the majority opinion from this controversial Supreme Court decision, Justice Antonin Scalia offers a view of the Second Amendment that interprets the right to bear arms as applying to individuals. He argues against the notion that the amendment was written to apply to the rights of collectives, like states or communities, to bear arms. Instead, the writers of the amendment intended the right to bear arms to be an individual right. Applying this reasoning, the Court struck down the Washington, D.C., law banning handguns as unconstitutional.

ON WRIT OF CERTIORARI TO THE UNITED STATES COURT OF APPEALS FOR THE DISTRICT OF COLUMBIA CIRCUIT

JUSTICE SCALIA delivered the opinion of the Court.

We consider whether a District of Columbia prohibition on the possession of usable handguns in the home violates the Second Amendment to the Constitution.

I

The District of Columbia generally prohibits the possession of handguns. It is a crime to carry an unregistered firearm, and the registration of handguns is prohibited. Wholly apart from that prohibition, no person may carry a handgun without a license, but the chief of police may issue licenses for one-year periods. District of Columbia law also requires residents to keep their lawfully owned firearms, such as registered long guns, "unloaded and dissembled or bound by a trigger lock or similar device" unless they are located in a place of business or are being used for lawful recreational activities.

Respondent Dick Heller is a D.C. special police officer authorized to carry a handgun while on duty at the Federal Judicial Center. He applied for a registration certificate for a handgun that he wished to keep at home, but the District refused. He thereafter filed a lawsuit in the Federal District Court for

From *District of Columbia v. Heller,* 554 U.S. 570 (2008).

the District of Columbia seeking, on Second Amendment grounds, to enjoin the city from enforcing the bar on the registration of handguns, the licensing requirement insofar as it prohibits the carrying of a firearm in the home without a license, and the trigger-lock requirement insofar as it prohibits the use of "functional firearms within the home." The District Court dismissed respondent's complaint, The Court of Appeals for the District of Columbia Circuit, construing his complaint as seeking the right to render a firearm operable and carry it about his home in that condition only when necessary for self-defense. It held that the Second Amendment protects an individual right to possess firearms and that the city's total ban on handguns, as well as its requirement that firearms in the home be kept nonfunctional even when necessary for self-defense, violated that right. The Court of Appeals directed the District Court to enter summary judgment for respondent.

We granted certiorari.

II

We turn first to the meaning of the Second Amendment.

A

The Second Amendment provides: "A well regulated Militia, being necessary to the security of a free State, the right of the people to keep and bear Arms, shall not be infringed." In interpreting this text, we are guided by the principle that "[t]he Constitution was written to be understood by the voters; its words and phrases were used in their normal and ordinary as distinguished from technical meaning." *United States* v. *Sprague*, Normal meaning may of course include an idiomatic meaning, but it excludes secret or technical meanings that would not have been known to ordinary citizens in the founding generation.

The two sides in this case have set out very different interpretations of the Amendment. Petitioners and today's dissenting Justices believe that it protects only the right to possess and carry a firearm in connection with militia service. Respondent argues that it protects an individual right to possess a firearm unconnected with service in a militia, and to use that arm for traditionally lawful purposes, such as self-defense within the home.

The Second Amendment is naturally divided into two parts: its prefatory clause and its operative clause. The former does not limit the latter grammatically, but rather announces a purpose. The Amendment could be rephrased, "Because a well regulated Militia is necessary to the security of a free State, the right of the people to keep and bear Arms shall not be infringed." Although this structure of the Second Amendment is unique in our Constitution, other legal documents of the founding era, particularly individual-rights provisions of state constitutions, commonly included a prefatory statement of purpose.

Logic demands that there be a link between the stated purpose and the command. The Second Amendment would be nonsensical if it read, "A well regulated Militia, being necessary to the security of a free State, the right of the people to petition for redress of grievances shall not be infringed." That requirement of logical connection may cause a prefatory clause to resolve an ambiguity in the operative clause. But apart from that clarifying function, a prefatory clause does not limit or expand the scope of the operative clause. Therefore, while we will begin our textual analysis with the operative clause, we will return to the prefatory clause to ensure that our reading of the operative clause is consistent with the announced purpose.

1. Operative Clause

A. "RIGHT OF THE PEOPLE." The first salient feature of the operative clause is that it codifies a "right of the people." The unamended Constitution and the Bill of Rights use the phrase "right of the people" two other times, in the First Amendment's Assembly-and-Petition Clause and in the Fourth Amendment's Search-and-Seizure Clause. The Ninth Amendment uses very similar terminology ("The enumeration in the Constitution, of certain rights, shall not be construed to deny or disparage others retained by the people"). All three of these instances unambiguously refer to individual rights, not "collective" rights, or rights that may be exercised only through participation in some corporate body.

Three provisions of the Constitution refer to "the people" in a context other than "rights"—the famous preamble ("We the people"), §2 of Article I (providing that "the people" will choose members of the House), and the Tenth Amendment (providing that those powers not given the Federal Government remain with "the States" or "the people"). Those provisions arguably refer to "the people" acting collectively—but they deal with the exercise or reservation of powers, not rights. Nowhere else in the Constitution does a "right" attributed to "the people" refer to anything other than an individual right.

This contrasts markedly with the phrase "the militia" in the prefatory clause. As we will describe below, the "militia" in colonial America consisted of a subset of "the people"—those who were male, able bodied, and within a certain age range. Reading the Second Amendment as protecting only the right to "keep and bear Arms" in an organized militia therefore fits poorly with the operative clause's description of the holder of that right as "the people."

We start therefore with a strong presumption that the Second Amendment right is exercised individually and belongs to all Americans.

B. "KEEP AND BEAR ARMS." We move now from the holder of the right—"the people"—to the substance of the right: "to keep and bear Arms."

Before addressing the verbs "keep" and "bear," we interpret their object: "Arms." The eighteenth-century meaning is no different from the meaning today. The 1773 edition of Samuel Johnson's dictionary defined "arms" as "weapons of offence, or armour of defence." Timothy Cunningham's important 1771 legal dictionary defined "arms" as "any thing that a man wears for his defence, or takes into his hands, or useth in wrath to cast at or strike another."

We turn to the phrases "keep arms" and "bear arms." Johnson defined "keep" as, most relevantly, "[t]o retain; not to lose," and "[t]o have in custody." Webster defined it as "[t]o hold; to retain in one's power or possession." No party has apprised us of an idiomatic meaning of "keep Arms." Thus, the most natural reading of "keep Arms" in the Second Amendment is to "have weapons."

"Keep arms" was simply a common way of referring to possessing arms, for militiamen and everyone else.

At the time of the founding, as now, to "bear" meant to "carry." When used with "arms," however, the term has a meaning that refers to carrying for a particular purpose—confrontation. In *Muscarello* v. *United States*, in the course of analyzing the meaning of "carries a firearm" in a federal criminal statute, Justice Ginsburg wrote that "[s]urely a most familiar meaning is, as the Constitution's Second Amendment . . . indicate[s]: 'wear, bear, or carry . . . upon the person or in the clothing or in a pocket, for the purpose . . . of being armed and ready for offensive or defensive action in a case of conflict with another person.'" We think that Justice Ginsburg accurately captured the natural meaning of "bear arms." Although the phrase implies that the carrying of the weapon is for the purpose of "offensive or defensive action," it in no way connotes participation in a structured military organization.

From our review of founding-era sources, we conclude that this natural meaning was also the meaning that "bear arms" had in the eighteenth century. In numerous instances, "bear arms" was unambiguously used to refer to the carrying of weapons outside of an organized militia. The most prominent examples are those most relevant to the Second Amendment: Nine state constitutional provisions written in the eighteenth century or the first two decades of the nineteenth, which enshrined a right of citizens to "bear arms in defense of themselves and the state" or "bear arms in defense of himself and the state." It is clear from those formulations that "bear arms" did not refer only to carrying a weapon in an organized military unit.

The phrase "bear Arms" also had at the time of the founding an idiomatic meaning that was significantly different from its natural meaning: "to serve as a soldier, do military service, fight" or "to wage war." But it *unequivocally* bore that idiomatic meaning only when followed by the preposition "against," which was in turn followed by the target of the hostilities.

In any event, the meaning of "bear arms" that petitioners and Justice Stevens propose is *not even* the (sometimes) idiomatic meaning. Rather, they manufacture a hybrid definition, whereby "bear arms" connotes the actual carrying of arms (and therefore is not really an idiom) but only in the service of an organized militia. No dictionary has ever adopted that definition, and we have been apprised of no source that indicates that it carried that meaning at the time of the founding. But it is easy to see why petitioners and the dissent are driven to the hybrid definition. Giving "bear Arms" its idiomatic meaning would cause the protected right to consist of the right to be a soldier or to wage war—an absurdity that no commentator has ever endorsed.

Petitioners justify their limitation of "bear arms" to the military context by pointing out the unremarkable fact that it was often used in that context—the same mistake they made with respect to "keep arms." It is especially unremarkable that the phrase was often used in a military context in the federal legal sources (such as records of congressional debate) that have been the focus of petitioners' inquiry. Those sources would have had little occasion to use it *except* in discussions about the standing army and the militia. Other legal sources frequently used "bear arms" in nonmilitary contexts. If one looks beyond legal sources, "bear arms" was frequently used in nonmilitary contexts.

Justice Stevens points to a study by *amici* supposedly showing that the phrase "bear arms" was most frequently used in the military context. Of course, as we have said, the fact that the phrase was commonly used in a particular context does not show that it is limited to that context, and, in any event, we have given many sources where the phrase was used in nonmilitary contexts. Moreover, the study's collection appears to include (who knows how many times) the idiomatic phrase "bear arms against," which is irrelevant. The *amici* also dismiss examples such as "bear arms . . . for the purpose of killing game" because those uses are "expressly qualified." That analysis is faulty. If "bear arms" means, as we think, simply the carrying of arms, a modifier can limit the purpose of the carriage. But if "bear arms" means, as the petitioners and the dissent think, the carrying of arms only for military purposes, one simply cannot add "for the purpose of killing game." The right "to carry arms in the militia for the purpose of killing game" is worthy of the mad hatter. Thus, these purposive qualifying phrases positively establish that "to bear arms" is not limited to military use.

Justice Stevens places great weight on James Madison's inclusion of a conscientious-objector clause in his original draft of the Second Amendment: "but no person religiously scrupulous of bearing arms, shall be compelled to render military service in person." He argues that this clause establishes that the drafters of the Second Amendment intended "bear Arms" to refer only to military service. In any case, what Justice Stevens would conclude from the deleted provision does not follow. It was not meant to exempt from military service those who objected to going to war but had no scruples about personal gunfights.

Finally, Justice Stevens suggests that "keep and bear Arms" was some sort of term of art, presumably akin to "hue and cry" or "cease and desist." Justice Stevens believes that the unitary meaning of "keep and bear Arms" is established by the Second Amendment's calling it a "right" (singular) rather than "rights" (plural). There is nothing to this. State constitutions of the founding period routinely grouped multiple (related) guarantees under a singular "right," and the First Amendment protects the "right [singular] of the people peaceably to assemble, and to petition the Government for a redress of grievances."

C. MEANING OF THE OPERATIVE CLAUSE.   Putting all of these textual elements together, we find that they guarantee the individual right to possess and carry weapons in case of confrontation. This meaning is strongly confirmed by the historical background of the Second Amendment. We look to this because it has always been widely understood that the Second Amendment, like the First and Fourth Amendments, codified a *pre-existing* right. The very text of the Second Amendment implicitly recognizes the pre-existence of the right and declares only that it "shall not be infringed." As we said in *United States* v. *Cruikshank*, "[t]his is not a right granted by the Constitution. Neither is it in any manner dependent upon that instrument for its existence. The Second Amendment declares that it shall not be infringed. . . ."

Between the Restoration and the Glorious Revolution, the Stuart Kings Charles II and James II succeeded in using select militias loyal to them to suppress political dissidents, in part by disarming their opponents. Under the auspices of the 1671 Game Act, for example, the Catholic James II had ordered general disarmaments of regions home to his Protestant enemies. These experiences caused Englishmen to be extremely wary of concentrated military forces run by the state and to be jealous of their arms. They accordingly obtained an assurance from William and Mary, in the Declaration of Right (which was codified as the English Bill of Rights), that Protestants would never be disarmed: "That the subjects which are Protestants may have arms for their defense suitable to their conditions and as allowed by law." This right has long been understood to be the predecessor to our Second Amendment. It was secured to them as individuals, according to "libertarian political principles," not as members of a fighting force.

And, of course, what the Stuarts had tried to do to their political enemies, George III had tried to do to the colonists. In the tumultuous decades of the 1760s and 1770s, the Crown began to disarm the inhabitants of the most rebellious areas. That provoked polemical reactions by Americans invoking their rights as Englishmen to keep arms.

There seems to us no doubt, on the basis of both text and history, that the Second Amendment conferred an individual right to keep and bear arms. Of course the right was not unlimited, just as the First Amendment's right of free speech was not. Thus, we do not read the Second Amendment to protect the right of citizens to carry arms for *any sort* of confrontation, just as we do not read the First Amendment to protect the right of citizens to speak for *any purpose*. Before turning to limitations upon the individual right, however, we must determine whether the prefatory clause of the Second Amendment comports with our interpretation of the operative clause.

2. Prefatory Clause

The prefatory clause reads: "A well regulated Militia, being necessary to the security of a free State. . . ."

A. "WELL-REGULATED MILITIA." In *United States* v. *Miller* (1939), we explained that "the Militia comprised all males physically capable of acting in concert for the common defense."

Petitioners take a seemingly narrower view of the militia, stating that "[m]ilitias are the state- and congressionally-regulated military forces described in the Militia Clauses." Although we agree with petitioners' interpretive assumption that "militia" means the same thing in Article I and the Second Amendment, we believe that petitioners identify the wrong thing, namely, the organized militia. Unlike armies and navies, which Congress is given the power to create, the militia is assumed by Article I already to be *in existence*. Congress is given the power to "provide for calling forth the militia," §8, cl. 15; and the power not to create, but to "organiz[e]" it—and not to organize "a" militia, which is what one would expect if the militia were to be a federal creation, but to organize "the" militia, connoting a body already in existence. To be sure, Congress need not conscript every able-bodied man into the militia, because nothing in Article I suggests that in exercising its power to organize, discipline, and arm the militia, Congress must focus upon the entire body. Although the militia consists of all able-bodied men, the federally organized militia may consist of a subset of them.

Finally, the adjective "well-regulated" implies nothing more than the imposition of proper discipline and training.

B. "SECURITY OF A FREE STATE." The phrase "security of a free state" meant "security of a free polity," not security of each of the several States as the dissent below argued. Joseph Story wrote in his treatise on the Constitution that "the word 'state' is used in various senses [and in] its most enlarged sense, it means the people composing a particular nation or community." Moreover, the other instances of "state" in the Constitution are typically accompanied by modifiers making clear that the reference is to the several States—"each state," "several states," "any state," "that state," "particular states," "one state," "no state." And the presence of the term "foreign state" in Article I and Article III shows that the word "state" did not have a single meaning in the Constitution.

3. Relationship between Prefatory Clause and Operative Clause

Does the preface fit with an operative clause that creates an individual right to keep and bear arms? It fits perfectly, once one knows the history that the founding generation knew and that we have described above. That history showed that the way tyrants had eliminated a militia consisting of all the able-bodied men was not by banning the militia but simply by taking away the people's arms, enabling a select militia or standing army to suppress political opponents.

The debate with respect to the right to keep and bear arms, as with other guarantees in the Bill of Rights, was not over whether it was desirable (all agreed that it was) but over whether it needed to be codified in the Constitution.

During the 1788 ratification debates, the fear that the federal government would disarm the people in order to impose rule through a standing army or select militia was pervasive in Antifederalist rhetoric. Federalists responded that because Congress was given no power to abridge the ancient right of individuals to keep and bear arms, such a force could never oppress the people. It was understood across the political spectrum that the right helped to secure the ideal of a citizen militia, which might be necessary to oppose an oppressive military force if the constitutional order broke down.

It is therefore entirely sensible that the Second Amendment's prefatory clause announces the purpose for which the right was codified: to prevent elimination of the militia. The prefatory clause does not suggest that preserving the militia was the only reason Americans valued the ancient right; most undoubtedly thought it even more important for self-defense and hunting. But the threat that the new Federal Government would destroy the citizens' militia by taking away their arms was the reason that right—unlike some other English rights—was codified in a written Constitution. Justice Breyer's assertion that individual self-defense is merely a "subsidiary interest" of the right to keep and bear arms, is profoundly mistaken. He bases that assertion solely upon the prologue—but that can only show that self-defense had little to do with the right's *codification;* it was the *central component* of the right itself.

B

Our interpretation is confirmed by analogous arms-bearing rights in state constitutions that preceded and immediately followed adoption of the Second Amendment. Four States adopted analogues to the Federal Second Amendment in the period between independence and the ratification of the Bill of Rights. Two of them—Pennsylvania and Vermont—clearly adopted individual rights unconnected to militia service.

We therefore believe that the most likely reading of all of these pre-Second Amendment state constitutional provisions is that they secured an individual right to bear arms for defensive purposes.

> [A]t least seven [states] unequivocally protected an individual citizen's right to self-defense is strong evidence that that is how the founding generation conceived of the right.

The historical narrative that petitioners must endorse would thus treat the Federal Second Amendment as an odd outlier, protecting a right unknown in state constitutions or at English common law, based on little more than an overreading of the prefatory clause.

C

Justice Stevens relies on the drafting history of the Second Amendment—the various proposals in the state conventions and the debates in Congress. It is dubious to rely on such history to interpret a text that was widely understood to codify a pre-existing right, rather than to fashion a new one. But even assuming that this legislative history is relevant, Justice Stevens flatly misreads the historical record.

It is true, as Justice Stevens says, that there was concern that the Federal Government would abolish the institution of the state militia. That concern found expression, however, *not* in the various Second Amendment precursors proposed in the State conventions, but in separate structural provisions that would have given the States concurrent and seemingly nonpreemptible authority to organize, discipline, and arm the militia when the Federal Government failed to do so. The Second Amendment precursors, by contrast, referred to the individual English right already codified in two (and probably four) State constitutions. The Federalist-dominated first Congress chose to reject virtually all major structural revisions favored by the Antifederalists, including the proposed militia amendments. Rather, it adopted primarily the popular and uncontroversial (though, in the Federalists' view, unnecessary) individual-rights amendments. The Second Amendment right, protecting only individuals' liberty to keep and carry arms, did nothing to assuage Antifederalists' concerns about federal control of the militia.

Justice Stevens thinks it significant that the Virginia, New York, and North Carolina Second Amendment proposals were "embedded . . . within a group of principles that are distinctly military in meaning," such as statements about the danger of standing armies. But so was the highly influential minority proposal in Pennsylvania, yet that proposal, with its reference to hunting, plainly referred to an individual right. Other than that erroneous point, Justice Stevens has brought forward absolutely no evidence that those proposals conferred only a right to carry arms in a militia.

D

We now address how the Second Amendment was interpreted from immediately after its ratification through the end of the nineteenth century.

1. Post-Ratification Commentary

Three important founding-era legal scholars interpreted the Second Amendment in published writings. All three understood it to protect an individual right unconnected with militia service.

St. George Tucker's version conceived of the right as necessary for self-defense. He equated that right, absent the religious and class-based restrictions, with the Second Amendment. He grouped the right with some of the individual rights included in the First Amendment and said that if "a law be passed by congress, prohibiting" any of those rights, it would "be the province of the judiciary to pronounce whether any such act were constitutional, or not; and if not, to acquit the accused . . . ." It is unlikely that Tucker was referring to a person's being "accused" of violating a law making it a crime to bear arms in a state militia.

In 1825, William Rawle, a prominent lawyer who had been a member of the Pennsylvania Assembly that ratified the Bill of Rights, published an influential treatise.

Rawle clearly differentiated between the people's right to bear arms and their service in a militia. Rawle further said that the Second Amendment right ought not "be abused to the disturbance of the public peace," such as by assembling with other armed individuals "for an unlawful purpose"—statements that make no sense if the right does not extend to *any* individual purpose.

Joseph Story published his famous Commentaries on the Constitution of the United States in 1833. Justice Stevens suggests that "[t]here is not so much as a whisper" in Story's explanation of the Second Amendment that favors the individual-rights view. That is wrong. Story explained that the English Bill of Rights had also included a "right to bear arms," a right that, as we have discussed, had nothing to do with militia service.

Story's Commentaries also cite as support Tucker and Rawle, both of whom clearly viewed the right as unconnected to militia service. In addition, in a shorter 1840 work Story wrote: "One of the ordinary modes, by which tyrants accomplish their purposes without resistance, is, by disarming the people, and making it an offence to keep arms, and by substituting a regular army in the stead of a resort to the militia."

2. Pre–Civil War Case Law

The nineteenth-century cases that interpreted the Second Amendment universally support an individual right unconnected to militia service. In *Houston* v. *Moore*, this Court held that States have concurrent power over the militia, at least where not pre-empted by Congress. In the famous fugitive-slave case of *Johnson* v. *Tompkins*, Baldwin, sitting as a circuit judge, cited both the Second Amendment and the Pennsylvania analogue for his conclusion that a citizen has "a right to carry arms in defence of his property or person, and to use them, if either were assailed with such force, numbers or violence as made it necessary for the protection or safety of either."

Many early nineteenth-century state cases indicated that the Second Amendment right to bear arms was an individual right unconnected to militia service, though subject to certain restrictions.

An 1829 decision [*United States* v. *Sheldon*] by the Supreme Court of Michigan said:

> The constitution of the United States also grants to the citizen the right to keep and bear arms. But the grant of this privilege cannot be construed into the right in him who keeps a gun to destroy his neighbor. No rights are intended to be granted by the constitution for an unlawful or unjustifiable purpose.

In *Nunn* v. *State*, the Georgia Supreme Court construed the Second Amendment as protecting the "*natural* right of self-defence" and therefore struck down a ban on carrying pistols openly. Its opinion perfectly captured the way in which the operative clause of the Second Amendment furthers the purpose announced in the prefatory clause.

3. Post–Civil War Legislation

In the aftermath of the Civil War, there was an outpouring of discussion of the Second Amendment in Congress and in public discourse, as people debated whether and how to secure constitutional rights for newly free slaves. Since those discussions took place 75 years after the ratification of the Second Amendment, they do not provide as much insight into its original meaning as earlier sources. Yet those born and educated in the early nineteenth century faced a widespread effort to limit arms ownership by a large number of citizens; their understanding of the origins and continuing significance of the Amendment is instructive.

Blacks were routinely disarmed by Southern States after the Civil War. Those who opposed these injustices frequently stated that they infringed blacks' constitutional right to keep and bear arms. Needless to say, the claim was not that blacks were being prohibited from carrying arms in an organized state militia.

Congress enacted the Freedmen's Bureau Act on July 16, 1866. Section 14 stated:

> [T]he right . . . to have full and equal benefit of all laws and proceedings concerning personal liberty, personal security, and the acquisition, enjoyment, and disposition of estate, real and personal, including the constitutional right to bear arms, shall be secured to and enjoyed by all the citizens . . . without respect to race or color, or previous condition of slavery. . . .

The understanding that the Second Amendment gave freed blacks the right to keep and bear arms was reflected in congressional discussion of the bill, with even an opponent of it saying that the founding generation "were for every man bearing his arms about him and keeping them in his house, his castle, for his own defense."

It was plainly the understanding in the post–Civil War Congress that the Second Amendment protected an individual right to use arms for self-defense.

4. Post–Civil War Commentators

Every late-nineteenth-century legal scholar that we have read interpreted the Second Amendment to secure an individual right unconnected with militia service. The most famous was the judge and professor Thomas Cooley, who wrote a massively popular 1868 Treatise on Constitutional Limitations. Concerning the Second Amendment it said:

Among the other defences to personal liberty should be mentioned the right of the people to keep and bear arms . . . . The alternative to a standing army is 'a well-regulated militia,' but this cannot exist unless the people are trained to bearing arms. How far it is in the power of the legislature to regulate this right, we shall not undertake to say, as happily there has been very little occasion to discuss that subject by the courts.

All other post–Civil War nineteenth-century sources we have found concurred with Cooley.

E

We now ask whether any of our precedents forecloses the conclusions we have reached about the meaning of the Second Amendment.

United States v. *Cruikshank,* in the course of vacating the convictions of members of a white mob for depriving blacks of their right to keep and bear arms, held that the Second Amendment does not by its own force apply to anyone other than the Federal Government. The opinion explained that the right "is not a right granted by the Constitution [or] in any manner dependent upon that instrument for its existence. The second amendment . . . means no more than that it shall not be infringed by Congress." The limited discussion of the Second Amendment in *Cruikshank* supports, if anything, the individual-rights interpretation.

Presser v. *Illinois* (1886) held that the right to keep and bear arms was not violated by a law that forbade "bodies of men to associate together as military organizations, or to drill or parade with arms in cities and towns unless authorized by law." Justice Stevens presses *Presser* into service to support his view that the right to bear arms is limited to service in the militia by joining *Presser's* brief discussion of the Second Amendment with a later portion of the opinion making the seemingly relevant (to the Second Amendment) point that the plaintiff was not a member of the state militia. Unfortunately for Justice Stevens' argument, that later portion deals with the *Fourteenth Amendment;* it was the *Fourteenth Amendment* to which the plaintiff's nonmembership in the militia was relevant. Thus, Justice Stevens' statement that *Presser* "suggested that . . . nothing in the Constitution protected the use of arms outside the context of a militia," is simply wrong. *Presser* said nothing about the Second Amendment's meaning or scope, beyond the fact that it does not prevent the prohibition of private paramilitary organizations.

Justice Stevens places overwhelming reliance upon this Court's decision in *United States* v. *Miller* (1939) . "[H]undreds of judges," we are told, "have relied on the view of the amendment we endorsed there," and "[e]ven if the textual and historical arguments on both sides of the issue were evenly balanced, respect for the well-settled views of all of our predecessors on this Court, and for the rule of law itself . . . would prevent most jurists from endorsing such a dramatic upheaval in the law," And what is, according to Justice Stevens, the holding of *Miller* that demands such obeisance? That the Second Amendment "protects the right to keep and bear arms for certain military purposes, but that it does not curtail the legislature's power to regulate the nonmilitary use and ownership of weapons."

Nothing so clearly demonstrates the weakness of Justice Stevens' case. *Miller* did not hold that and cannot possibly be read to have held that. The judgment in the case upheld against a Second Amendment challenge two men's federal convictions for transporting an unregistered short-barreled shotgun in interstate commerce, in violation of the National Firearms Act. It is entirely clear that the Court's basis for saying that the Second Amendment did not apply was *not* that the defendants were "bear[ing] arms" not "for . . . military purposes" but for "nonmilitary use." Rather, it was that the *type of weapon at issue* was not eligible for Second Amendment protection. Beyond that, the opinion provided no explanation of the content of the right.

Justice Stevens can say again and again that *Miller* did "not turn on the difference between muskets and sawed-off shotguns, it turned, rather, on the basic difference between the military and nonmilitary use and possession of guns," but the words of the opinion prove otherwise. The most Justice Stevens can plausibly claim for *Miller* is that it declined to decide the nature of the Second Amendment right.

It is particularly wrongheaded to read *Miller* for more than what it said, because the case did not even purport to be a thorough examination of the Second Amendment.

We conclude that nothing in our precedents forecloses our adoption of the original understanding of the Second Amendment. It should be unsurprising that such a significant matter has been for so long judicially unresolved. For most of our history, the Bill of Rights was not thought applicable to the States, and the Federal Government did not significantly regulate the possession of firearms by law-abiding citizens. Other provisions of the Bill of Rights have similarly remained unilluminated for lengthy periods. It is demonstrably not true that, as Justice Stevens claims, "for most of our history, the invalidity of Second-Amendment-based objections to firearms regulations has been well settled and uncontroversial." For most of our history the question did not present itself.

III

Like most rights, the right secured by the Second Amendment is not unlimited. Commentators and courts routinely explained that the right was not a right to keep and carry any weapon whatsoever in any manner whatsoever and for whatever purpose. Although we do not undertake an exhaustive historical analysis today of the full scope of the Second Amendment, nothing in our opinion should be taken to cast doubt on longstanding prohibitions on the possession of firearms by felons and the mentally ill, or laws forbidding the carrying of firearms in sensitive places such as schools and government buildings, or laws imposing conditions and qualifications on the commercial sale of arms.

IV

We turn finally to the law at issue here. As we have said, the law totally bans handgun possession in the home. It also requires that any lawful firearm in the home be disassembled or bound by a trigger lock at all times, rendering it inoperable.

As the quotations earlier in this opinion demonstrate, the inherent right of self-defense has been central to the Second Amendment right. The handgun ban amounts to a prohibition of an entire class of "arms" that is overwhelmingly chosen by American society for that lawful purpose. The prohibition extends, moreover, to the home, where the need for defense of self, family, and property is most acute. Under any of the standards of scrutiny that we have applied to enumerated constitutional rights, banning from the home "the most preferred firearm in the nation to 'keep' and use for protection of one's home and family," would fail constitutional muster.

Few laws in the history of our Nation have come close to the severe restriction of the District's handgun ban.

It is no answer to say, as petitioners do, that it is permissible to ban the possession of handguns so long as the possession of other firearms (i.e., long guns) is allowed. It is enough to note, as we have observed, that the American people have considered the handgun to be the quintessential self-defense weapon. There are many reasons that a citizen may prefer a handgun for home defense: It is easier to store in a location that is readily accessible in an emergency; it cannot easily be redirected or wrestled away by an attacker; it is easier to use for those without the upper-body strength to lift and aim a long gun; it can be pointed at a burglar with one hand while the other hand dials the police. Whatever the reason, handguns are the most popular weapon chosen by Americans for self-defense in the home, and a complete prohibition of their use is invalid.

We must also address the District's requirement (as applied to respondent's handgun) that firearms in the home be rendered and kept inoperable at all times. This makes it impossible for citizens to use them for the core lawful purpose of self-defense and is hence unconstitutional.

In sum, we hold that the District's ban on handgun possession in the home violates the Second Amendment, as does its prohibition against rendering any lawful firearm in the home operable for the purpose of immediate self-defense. Assuming that Heller is not disqualified from the exercise of Second Amendment rights, the District must permit him to register his handgun and must issue him a license to carry it in the home.

We are aware of the problem of handgun violence in this country, and we take seriously the concerns raised by the many *amici* who believe that prohibition of handgun ownership is a solution. The Constitution leaves the District of Columbia a variety of tools for combating that problem, including some measures regulating handguns. But the enshrinement of constitutional rights necessarily takes certain policy choices off the table. These include the absolute prohibition of handguns held and used for self-defense in the home. Undoubtedly some think that the Second Amendment is outmoded in a society where our standing army is the pride of our Nation, where well-trained police forces provide personal security, and where gun violence is a serious problem. That is perhaps debatable, but what is not debatable is that it is not the role of this Court to pronounce the Second Amendment extinct.

We affirm the judgment of the Court of Appeals.

It is so ordered.

4.4

Obergefell v. Hodges (2015)

This landmark Supreme Court case decided two issues. First, writing for the majority of the Court, Justice Anthony Kennedy affirmed that denying same-sex couples the right to marry denies them a fundamental right guaranteed by the Constitution, and therefore no state can deny such couples the same rights of marriage granted to opposite-sex couples. Second, Kennedy holds that no state can deny any same-sex married couple from another state the same rights granted to opposite-sex married couples. Thus, states must fully recognize same-sex marriages sanctioned by other states.

JUSTICE KENNEDY delivered the opinion of the Court.

The Constitution promises liberty to all within its reach, a liberty that includes certain specific rights that allow persons, within a lawful realm, to define and express their identity. The petitioners in these cases seek to find that liberty by marrying someone of the same sex and having their marriages deemed lawful on the same terms and conditions as marriages between persons of the opposite sex.

I

These cases come from Michigan, Kentucky, Ohio, and Tennessee, States that define marriage as a union between one man and one woman. . . . The petitioners are 14 same-sex couples and two men whose same-sex partners are deceased. The respondents are state officials responsible for enforcing the laws in question. The petitioners claim the respondents violate the Fourteenth Amendment by denying them the right to marry or to have their marriages, lawfully performed in another State, given full recognition.

. . . The Court of Appeals held that a State has no constitutional obligation to license same-sex marriages or to recognize same-sex marriages performed out of State.

The petitioners sought certiorari. This Court granted review, limited to two questions. . . . The first, presented by the cases from Michigan and Kentucky,

From *Obergefell v. Hodges*, 576 U.S. ___ (2015).

is whether the Fourteenth Amendment requires a State to license a marriage between two people of the same sex. The second, presented by the cases from Ohio, Tennessee, and, again, Kentucky, is whether the Fourteenth Amendment requires a State to recognize a same-sex marriage licensed and performed in a State which does grant that right.

II

A

From their beginning to their most recent page, the annals of human history reveal the transcendent importance of marriage. The lifelong union of a man and a woman always has promised nobility and dignity to all persons, without regard to their station in life. Marriage is sacred to those who live by their religions and offers unique fulfillment to those who find meaning in the secular realm. Its dynamic allows two people to find a life that could not be found alone, for a marriage becomes greater than just the two persons. Rising from the most basic human needs, marriage is essential to our most profound hopes and aspirations.

The centrality of marriage to the human condition makes it unsurprising that the institution has existed for millennia and across civilizations. . . . There are untold references to the beauty of marriage in religious and philosophical texts spanning time, cultures, and faiths, as well as in art and literature in all their forms. It is fair and necessary to say these references were based on the understanding that marriage is a union between two persons of the opposite sex.

That history is the beginning of these cases. The respondents say it should be the end as well. To them, it would demean a timeless institution if the concept and lawful status of marriage were extended to two persons of the same sex. Marriage, in their view, is by its nature a gender-differentiated union of man and woman. This view long has been held—and continues to be held—in good faith by reasonable and sincere people here and throughout the world.

The petitioners acknowledge this history but contend that these cases cannot end there. Were their intent to demean the revered idea and reality of marriage, the petitioners' claims would be of a different order. But that is neither their purpose nor their submission. To the contrary, it is the enduring importance of marriage that underlies the petitioners' contentions. This, they say, is their whole point. Far from seeking to devalue marriage, the petitioners seek it for themselves because of their respect—and need—for its privileges and responsibilities. And their immutable nature dictates that same-sex marriage is their only real path to this profound commitment.

Recounting the circumstances of three of these cases illustrates the urgency of the petitioners' cause from their perspective. Petitioner James Obergefell, a plaintiff in the Ohio case, met John Arthur over two decades ago. They fell in love and started a life together, establishing a lasting, committed relation. In 2011, however, Arthur was diagnosed with amyotrophic lateral sclerosis, or

ALS. This debilitating disease is progressive, with no known cure. Two years ago, Obergefell and Arthur decided to commit to one another, resolving to marry before Arthur died. To fulfill their mutual promise, they traveled from Ohio to Maryland, where same-sex marriage was legal. It was difficult for Arthur to move, and so the couple were wed inside a medical transport plane as it remained on the tarmac in Baltimore. Three months later, Arthur died. Ohio law does not permit Obergefell to be listed as the surviving spouse on Arthur's death certificate. By statute, they must remain strangers even in death, a state-imposed separation Obergefell deems "hurtful for the rest of time." App. in No. 14–556 etc., p. 38. He brought suit to be shown as the surviving spouse on Arthur's death certificate.

April DeBoer and Jayne Rowse are co-plaintiffs in the case from Michigan. They celebrated a commitment ceremony to honor their permanent relation in 2007. They both work as nurses, DeBoer in a neonatal unit and Rowse in an emergency unit. In 2009, DeBoer and Rowse fostered and then adopted a baby boy. Later that same year, they welcomed another son into their family. The new baby, born prematurely and abandoned by his biological mother, required around-the-clock care. The next year, a baby girl with special needs joined their family. Michigan, however, permits only opposite-sex married couples or single individuals to adopt, so each child can have only one woman as his or her legal parent. If an emergency were to arise, schools and hospitals may treat the three children as if they had only one parent. And, were tragedy to befall either DeBoer or Rowse, the other would have no legal rights over the children she had not been permitted to adopt. This couple seeks relief from the continuing uncertainty their unmarried status creates in their lives.

Army Reserve Sergeant First Class Ijpe DeKoe and his partner Thomas Kostura, co-plaintiffs in the Tennessee case, fell in love. In 2011, DeKoe received orders to deploy to Afghanistan. Before leaving, he and Kostura married in New York. A week later, DeKoe began his deployment, which lasted for almost a year. When he returned, the two settled in Tennessee, where DeKoe works full-time for the Army Reserve. Their lawful marriage is stripped from them whenever they reside in Tennessee, returning and disappearing as they travel across state lines. DeKoe, who served this Nation to preserve the freedom the Constitution protects, must endure a substantial burden.

The cases now before the Court involve other petitioners as well, each with their own experiences. Their stories reveal that they seek not to denigrate marriage but rather to live their lives, or honor their spouses' memory, joined by its bond.

B

The ancient origins of marriage confirm its centrality, but it has not stood in isolation from developments in law and society. The history of marriage is one of both continuity and change. That institution—even as confined to opposite-sex relations—has evolved over time.

For example, marriage was once viewed as an arrangement by the couple's parents based on political, religious, and financial concerns; but by the time of the Nation's founding it was understood to be a voluntary contract between a man and a woman. . . . As the role and status of women changed, the institution further evolved. Under the centuries-old doctrine of coverture, a married man and woman were treated by the State as a single, male-dominated legal entity. . . . As women gained legal, political, and property rights, and as society began to understand that women have their own equal dignity, the law of coverture was abandoned. . . . These and other developments in the institution of marriage over the past centuries were not mere superficial changes. Rather, they worked deep transformations in its structure, affecting aspects of marriage long viewed by many as essential. . . .

These new insights have strengthened, not weakened, the institution of marriage. Indeed, changed understandings of marriage are characteristic of a Nation where new dimensions of freedom become apparent to new generations, often through perspectives that begin in pleas or protests and then are considered in the political sphere and the judicial process.

This dynamic can be seen in the Nation's experiences with the rights of gays and lesbians. Until the mid-20th century, same-sex intimacy long had been condemned as immoral by the state itself in most Western nations, a belief often embodied in the criminal law. For this reason, among others, many persons did not deem homosexuals to have dignity in their own distinct identity. A truthful declaration by same-sex couples of what was in their hearts had to remain unspoken. Even when a greater awareness of the humanity and integrity of homosexual persons came in the period after World War II, the argument that gays and lesbians had a just claim to dignity was in conflict with both law and widespread social conventions. Same-sex intimacy remained a crime in many States. Gays and lesbians were prohibited from most government employment, barred from military service, excluded under immigration laws, targeted by police, and burdened in their rights to associate. . . .

For much of the 20th century, moreover, homosexuality was treated as an illness. When the American Psychiatric Association published the first Diagnostic and Statistical Manual of Mental Disorders in 1952, homosexuality was classified as a mental disorder, a position adhered to until 1973. . . . Only in more recent years have psychiatrists and others recognized that sexual orientation is both a normal expression of human sexuality and immutable. . . .

In the late 20th century, following substantial cultural and political developments, same-sex couples began to lead more open and public lives and to establish families. This development was followed by a quite extensive discussion of the issue in both governmental and private sectors and by a shift in public attitudes toward greater tolerance. As a result, questions about the rights of gays and lesbians soon reached the courts, where the issue could be discussed in the formal discourse of the law.

This Court first gave detailed consideration to the legal status of homosexuals in *Bowers v. Hardwick*, 478 U.S. 186 (1986). There it upheld the constitutionality of a Georgia law deemed to criminalize certain homosexual acts. Ten years later, in *Romer v. Evans*, 517 U.S. 620 (1996), the Court invalidated an amendment to Colorado's Constitution that sought to foreclose any branch or political subdivision of the State from protecting persons against discrimination based on sexual orientation. Then, in 2003, the Court overruled *Bowers*, holding that laws making same-sex intimacy a crime "demea[n] the lives of homosexual persons." *Lawrence v. Texas*, 539 U. S. 558, 575.

Against this background, the legal question of same-sex marriage arose. . . .

Numerous cases about same-sex marriage have reached the United States Courts of Appeals in recent years. In accordance with the judicial duty to base their decisions on principled reasons and neutral discussions, without scornful or disparaging commentary, courts have written a substantial body of law considering all sides of these issues. That case law helps to explain and formulate the underlying principles this Court now must consider. With the exception of the opinion here under review and one other, see *Citizens for Equal Protection v. Bruning*, 455 F. 3d 859, 864–868 (CA8 2006), the Courts of Appeals have held that excluding same-sex couples from marriage violates the Constitution. There also have been many thoughtful District Court decisions addressing same-sex marriage—and most of them, too, have concluded same-sex couples must be allowed to marry. In addition the highest courts of many States have contributed to this ongoing dialogue in decisions interpreting their own State Constitutions. . . .

After years of litigation, legislation, referenda, and the discussions that attended these public acts, the States are now divided on the issue of same-sex marriage. . . .

III

Under the Due Process Clause of the Fourteenth Amendment, no State shall "deprive any person of life, liberty, or property, without due process of law." The fundamental liberties protected by this Clause include most of the rights enumerated in the Bill of Rights. . . . In addition these liberties extend to certain personal choices central to individual dignity and autonomy, including intimate choices that define personal identity and beliefs. . . .

The identification and protection of fundamental rights is an enduring part of the judicial duty to interpret the Constitution. That responsibility, however, "has not been reduced to any formula." . . . Rather, it requires courts to exercise reasoned judgment in identifying interests of the person so fundamental that the State must accord them its respect. . . . That process is guided by many of the same considerations relevant to analysis of other constitutional provisions that set forth broad principles rather than specific requirements. History and tradition guide and discipline this inquiry but do not set its outer boundaries. . . . That method respects our history and learns from it without allowing the past alone to rule the present.

The nature of injustice is that we may not always see it in our own times. The generations that wrote and ratified the Bill of Rights and the Fourteenth Amendment did not presume to know the extent of freedom in all of its dimensions, and so they entrusted to future generations a character protecting the right of all persons to enjoy liberty as we learn its meaning. When new insight reveals discord between the Constitution's central protections and a received legal stricture, a claim to liberty must be addressed.

Applying these established tenets, the Court has long held the right to marry is protected by the Constitution. In *Loving v. Virginia*, 388 U.S. 1, 12 (1967), which invalidated bans on interracial unions, a unanimous Court held marriage is "one of the vital personal rights essential to the orderly pursuit of happiness by free men." The Court reaffirmed that holding in *Zablocki v. Redhail*, 434 U.S. 374, 384 (1978), which held the right to marry was burdened by a law prohibiting fathers who were behind on child support from marrying. The Court again applied this principle in *Turner v. Safley*, 482 U.S. 78, 95 (1987), which held the right to marry was abridged by regulations limiting the privilege of prison inmates to marry. Over time and in other contexts, the Court has reiterated that the right to marry is fundamental under the Due Process Clause. . . .

It cannot be denied that this Court's cases describing the right to marry presumed a relationship involving opposite-sex partners. The Court, like many institutions, has made assumptions defined by the world and time of which it is a part. . . .

Still, there are other, more instructive precedents. This Court's cases have expressed constitutional principles of broader reach. In defining the right to marry these cases have identified essential attributes of that right based in history, tradition, and other constitutional liberties inherent in this intimate bond. . . .

This analysis compels the conclusion that same-sex couples may exercise the right to marry. The four principles and traditions to be discussed demonstrate that the reasons marriage is fundamental under the Constitution apply with equal force to same-sex couples.

A first premise of the Court's relevant precedents is that the right to personal choice regarding marriage is inherent in the concept of individual autonomy. This abiding connection between marriage and liberty is why *Loving* invalidated interracial marriage bans under the Due Process Clause. . . . Like choices concerning contraception, family relationships, procreation, and childrearing, all of which are protected by the Constitution, decisions concerning marriage are among the most intimate that an individual can make. . . . Indeed, the Court has noted it would be contradictory "to recognize a right of privacy with respect to other matters of family life and not with respect to the decision to enter the relationship that is the foundation of the family in our society." . . .

Choices about marriage shape an individual's destiny. . . .

The nature of marriage is that, through its enduring bond, two persons together can find other freedoms, such as expression, intimacy, and spirituality. This is true for all persons, whatever their sexual orientation. . . . There is dignity in the bond between two men or two women who seek to marry and in their autonomy to make such profound choices. . . .

A second principle in this Court's jurisprudence is that the right to marry is fundamental because it supports a two-person union unlike any other in its importance to the committed individuals. This point was central to *Griswold v. Connecticut*, which held the Constitution protects the right of married couples to use contraception. . . .

As this Court held in *Lawrence*, same-sex couples have the same right as opposite-sex couples to enjoy intimate association. *Lawrence* invalidated laws that made same-sex intimacy a criminal act. . . .

A third basis for protecting the right to marry is that it safeguards children and families and thus draws meaning from related rights of childrearing, procreation, and education. . . . Under the laws of the several States, some of marriage's protections for children and families are material. But marriage, also confers more profound benefits. . . . Marriage also affords the permanency and stability important to children's best interests. . . .

As all parties agree, many same-sex couples provide loving and nurturing homes to their children, whether biological or adopted. And hundreds of thousands of children are presently being raised by such couples. . . . Most States have allowed gays and lesbians to adopt, either as individuals or as couples, and many adopted and foster children have same-sex parents. . . . This provides powerful confirmation from the law itself that gays and lesbians can create loving, supportive families.

Excluding same-sex couples from marriage thus conflicts with a central premise of the right to marry. Without the recognition, stability, and predictability marriage offers, their children suffer the stigma of knowing their families are somehow lesser. They also suffer the significant material costs of being raised by unmarried parents, relegated through no fault of their own to a more difficult and uncertain family life. The marriage laws at issue here thus harm and humiliate the children of same-sex couples. . . .

That is not to say the right to marry is less meaningful for those who do not or cannot have children. An ability, desire, or promise to procreate is not and has not been a prerequisite for a valid marriage in any State. In light of precedent protecting the right of a married couple not to procreate, it cannot be said the Court or the States have conditioned the right to marry on the capacity or commitment to procreate. The constitutional marriage right has many aspects, of which childbearing is only one.

Fourth and finally, this Court's cases and the Nation's traditions make clear that marriage is a keystone of our social order. Alexis de Tocqueville recognized this truth on his travels through the United States almost two centuries ago:

> "There is certainly no country in the world where the tie of marriage is so much respected as in America . . . [W]hen the American retires from the turmoil of public life to the bosom of his family, he finds in it the image of order and of peace. . . . [H]e afterwards carries [that image] with him into public affairs." 1 Democracy in America 309 (H. Reeve transl., rev. ed. 1990)

For that reason, just as a couple vows to support each other, so does society pledge to support the couple, offering symbolic recognition and material benefits to protect and nourish the union. Indeed, while the States are in general free to vary the benefits they confer on all married couples, they have throughout our history made marriage the basis for an expanding list of governmental rights, benefits, and responsibilities. These aspects of marital status include: taxation; inheritance and property rights; rules of intestate succession; spousal privilege in the law of evidence; hospital access; medical decision-making authority; adoption rights; the rights and benefits of survivors; birth and death certificates; professional ethics rules; campaign finance restrictions; workers' compensation benefits; health insurance; and child custody, support, and visitation rules. . . .

There is no difference between same- and opposite-sex couples with respect to this principle. Yet by virtue of their exclusion from that institution, same-sex couples are denied the constellation of benefits that the States have linked to marriage. This harm results in more than just material burdens. Same-sex couples are consigned to an instability many opposite-sex couples would deem intolerable in their own lives. As the State itself makes marriage all the more precious by the significance it attaches to it, exclusion from that status has the effect of teaching that gays and lesbians are unequal in important respects. It demeans gays and lesbians for the State to lock them out of a central institution of the Nation's society. Same-sex couples, too, may aspire to the transcendent purposes of marriage and seek fulfillment in its highest meaning.

The limitation of marriage to opposite-sex couples may long have seemed natural and just, but its inconsistency with the central meaning of the fundamental right to marry is now manifest. With that knowledge must come the recognition that laws excluding same-sex couples from the marriage right impose stigma and injury of the kind prohibited by our basic charter.

■   ■   ■

The right to marry is fundamental as a matter of history and tradition, but rights come not from ancient sources alone. They rise, too, from a better informed understanding of how constitutional imperatives define a liberty that remains urgent in our own era. Many who deem same-sex marriage to be wrong reach that conclusion based on decent and honorable religious or philosophical premises, and neither they nor their beliefs are disparaged here. But when that sincere, personal opposition becomes enacted law and public policy, the necessary consequence is to put the imprimatur of the State itself on an exclusion that soon demeans or stigmatizes those whose own liberty is then denied. Under the Constitution, same-sex couples seek in marriage the same legal treatment as opposite-sex couples, and it would disparage their choices and diminish their personhood to deny them this right.

The right of same-sex couples to marry that is part of the liberty promised by the Fourteenth Amendment is derived, too, from that Amendment's guarantee of the equal protection of the laws. The Due Process Clause and the Equal Protection Clause are connected in a profound way, though they set forth independent principles. Rights implicit in liberty and rights secured by equal protection may rest on different precepts and are not always coextensive, yet in some instances each may be instructive as to the meaning and reach of the other. In any particular case one Clause may be thought to capture the essence of the right in a more accurate and comprehensive way, even as the two Clauses may converge in the identification and definition of the right. . . .

The Court's cases touching upon the right to marry reflect this dynamic. In *Loving* the Court invalidated a prohibition on interracial marriage under both the Equal Protection Clause and the Due Process Clause. The Court first declared the prohibition invalid because of its unequal treatment of interracial couples. . . . The reasons why marriage is a fundamental right became more clear and compelling from a full awareness and understanding of the hurt that resulted from laws barring interracial unions.

▪　　▪　　▪

It is now clear that the challenged laws burden the liberty of same-sex couples, and it must be further acknowledged that they abridge central precepts of equality. Here the marriage laws enforced by the respondents are in essence unequal: same-sex couples are denied all the benefits afforded to opposite-sex couples and are barred from exercising a fundamental right. Especially against a long history of disapproval of their relationships, this denial to same-sex couples of the right to marry works a grave and continuing harm. The imposition of this disability on gays and lesbians serves to disrespect and subordinate them. And the Equal Protection Clause, like the Due Process Clause, prohibits this unjustified infringement of the fundamental right to marry. . . .

These considerations lead to the conclusion that the right to marry is a fundamental right inherent in the liberty of the person, and under the Due Process and Equal Protection Clauses of the Fourteenth Amendment couples of the same-sex may not be deprived of that right and that liberty. The Court now holds that same-sex couples may exercise the fundamental right to marry. No longer may this liberty be denied to them. *Baker v. Nelson* must be and now is overruled, and the State laws challenged by Petitioners in these cases are now held invalid to the extent they exclude same-sex couples from civil marriage on the same terms and conditions as opposite-sex couples.

■   ■   ■

I V

. . . The petitioners' stories make clear the urgency of the issue they present to the Court. James Obergefell now asks whether Ohio can erase his marriage to John Arthur for all time. April DeBoer and Jayne Rowse now ask whether Michigan may continue to deny them the certainty and stability all mothers desire to protect their children, and for them and their children the childhood years will pass all too soon. Ijpe DeKoe and Thomas Kostura now ask whether Tennessee can deny to one who has served this Nation the basic dignity of recognizing his New York marriage. Properly presented with the petitioners' cases, the Court has a duty to address these claims and answer these questions.

Indeed, faced with a disagreement among the Courts of Appeals—a disagreement that caused impermissible geographic variation in the meaning of federal law—the Court granted review to determine whether same-sex couples may exercise the right to marry. Were the Court to uphold the challenged laws as constitutional, it would teach the Nation that these laws are in accord with our society's most basic compact. Were the Court to stay its hand to allow slower, case-by-case determination of the required availability of specific public benefits to same-sex couples, it still would deny gays and lesbians many rights and responsibilities intertwined with marriage.

The respondents also argue allowing same-sex couples to wed will harm marriage as an institution by leading to fewer opposite-sex marriages. This may occur, the respondents contend, because licensing same-sex marriage severs the connection between natural procreation and marriage. That argument, however, rests on a counterintuitive view of opposite-sex couple's decisionmaking processes regarding marriage and parenthood. Decisions about whether to marry and raise children are based on many personal, romantic, and practical considerations; and it is unrealistic to conclude that an opposite-sex couple would choose not to marry simply because same-sex couples may do so. . . . The respondents have not shown a foundation for the conclusion that allowing same-sex marriage will cause the harmful outcomes they describe. Indeed, with respect to this asserted basis for excluding same-sex couples from the right to marry, it is appropriate to observe these cases involve only the rights of two consenting adults whose marriages would pose no risk of harm to themselves or third parties.

Finally, it must be emphasized that religions, and those who adhere to religious doctrines, may continue to advocate with utmost, sincere conviction that, by divine precepts, same-sex marriage should not be condoned. The First Amendment ensures that religious organizations and persons are given proper protection as they seek to teach the principles that are so fulfilling and so central to their lives and faiths, and to their own deep aspirations to continue the family structure they have long revered. The same is true of those who oppose same-sex marriage for other reasons. In turn, those who believe allowing same-sex marriage is proper or indeed essential, whether as a matter of religious conviction or secular belief, may engage those who disagree with their view in an open and searching debate. The Constitution, however, does not permit the State to bar same-sex couples from marriage on the same terms as accorded to couples of the opposite sex.

V

These cases also present the question whether the Constitution requires States to recognize same-sex marriages validly performed out of State. As made clear by the case of Obergefell and Arthur, and by that of DeKoe and Kostura, the recognition bans inflict substantial and continuing harm on same-sex couples.

. . . Leaving the current state of affairs in place would maintain and promote instability and uncertainty. For some couples, even an ordinary drive into a neighboring State to visit family or friends risks causing severe hardship in the event of a spouse's hospitalization while across state lines. In light of the fact that many States already allow same-sex marriage—and hundreds of thousands of these marriages already have occurred—the disruption caused by the recognition bans is significant and ever-growing.

As counsel for the respondents acknowledged at argument, if States are required by the Constitution to issue marriage licenses to same-sex couples, the justifications for refusing to recognize those marriages performed elsewhere are undermined. . . . The Court, in this decision, holds same-sex couples may exercise the fundamental right to marry in all States. It follows that the Court also must hold—and it now does hold—that there is no lawful basis for a State to refuse to recognize a lawful same-sex marriage performed in another State on the ground of its same-sex character.

■　■　■

No union is more profound than marriage, for it embodies the highest ideals of love, fidelity, devotion, sacrifice, and family. In forming a marital union, two people become something greater than once they were. As some of the petitioners in these cases demonstrate, marriage embodies a love that may endure even past death. It would misunderstand these men and women to say they disrespect the idea of marriage. Their plea is that they do respect it, respect it so deeply that they seek to find its fulfillment for themselves. Their hope is not to be condemned to live in loneliness, excluded from one of civilization's oldest institutions. They ask for equal dignity in the eyes of the law. The Constitution grants them that right.

The judgment of the Court of Appeals for the Sixth Circuit is reversed.

It is so ordered.

5

CONGRESS

5.1

DAVID R. MAYHEW

From *Congress: The Electoral Connection*

In this classic work on Congress, Mayhew asks: What would Congress look like, and how would members of Congress behave, if members were solely interested in one thing: getting reelected? Mayhew says they would posture and preen, but also occasionally produce valuable legislation. In other words, it would look like the Congress we actually observe in the United States.

Mostly through personal experience on Capitol Hill, I have become convinced that scrutiny of purposive behavior offers the best route to an understanding of legislatures—or at least of the United States Congress. In the fashion of economics, I shall make a simple abstract assumption about human motivation and then speculate about the consequences of behavior based on that motivation. Specifically, I shall conjure up a vision of United States congressmen as single-minded seekers of reelection, see what kinds of activity that goal implies, and then speculate about how congressmen so motivated are likely to go about building and sustaining legislative institutions and making policy. At all points I shall try to match the abstract with the factual.

I find an emphasis on the reelection goal attractive for a number of reasons. First, I think it fits political reality rather well. Second, it puts the spotlight directly on men rather than on parties and pressure groups, which in the past have often entered discussions of American politics as analytic phantoms.

From David R. Mayhew, *Congress: The Electoral Connection* (New Haven, CT: Yale University Press, 1974).

Third, I think politics is best studied as a struggle among men to gain and maintain power and the consequences of that struggle. Fourth—and perhaps most important—the reelection quest establishes an accountability relationship with an electorate, and any serious thinking about democratic theory has to give a central place to the question of accountability. The abstract assumption notwithstanding, I regard this venture as an exercise in political science rather than economics. Leaving aside the fact that I have no economics expertise to display, I find that economists who study legislatures bring to bear interests different from those of political scientists. Not surprisingly the public finance scholars tend to look upon government as a device for spending money. I shall give some attention to spending, but also to other governmental activities such as the production of binding rules. And I shall touch upon such traditional subjects of political science as elections, parties, governmental structure, and regime stability. Another distinction here is that economics research tends to be infused with the normative assumption that policy decisions should be judged by how well they meet the standard of Pareto optimality. This is an assumption that I do not share and that I do not think most political scientists share. There will be no need here to set forth any alternative assumption. . . .

My subject of concern here is a single legislative institution, the United States Congress. In many ways, of course, the Congress is a unique or unusual body. It is probably the most highly "professionalized" of legislatures, in the sense that it promotes careerism among its members and gives them the salaries, staff, and other resources to sustain careers. Its parties are exceptionally diffuse. It is widely thought to be especially "strong" among legislatures as a checker of executive power. Like most Latin American legislatures but unlike most European ones, it labors in the shadow of a separately elected executive. My decision to focus on the Congress flows from a belief that there is something to be gained in an intensive analysis of a particular and important institution. But there is something general to be gained as well, for the exceptionalist argument should not be carried too far. In a good many ways the Congress is just one in a large family of legislative bodies. I shall find it useful at various points in the analysis to invoke comparisons with European parliaments and with American state legislatures and city councils. I shall ponder the question of what "functions" the Congress performs or is capable of performing—a question that can be answered only with the records of other legislatures in mind. Functions to be given special attention are those of legislating, overseeing the executive, expressing public opinion, and servicing constituents. No functional capabilities can be automatically assumed.[1] Indeed the very term *legislature* is an unfortunate one because it confuses structure and function. Accordingly I shall here on use the more awkward but more neutral term *representative assembly* to refer to members of the class of entities inhabited by the United States House and Senate. Whatever the noun, the identifying characteristics of institutions in the class have been well stated by Loewenberg: it is true of all such entities that (1) "their members are formally equal to each other in status, distinguishing parliaments from hierarchically ordered organizations," and (2) "the authority of their members depends on their claim to representing the rest of the community, in some sense of that protean concept, representation."[2]

The following discussion will take the form of an extended theoretical essay. Perforce it will raise more questions than it answers. As is the custom in mono-causal ventures, it will no doubt carry arguments to the point of exaggeration; finally, of course, I shall be satisfied to explain a significant part of the variance rather than all of it. What the discussion will yield, I hope, is a picture of what the United States Congress looks like if the reelection quest is examined seriously.

▪   ▪   ▪

The ultimate concern here is not how probable it is that legislators will lose their seats but whether there is a connection between what they do in office and their need to be reelected. It is possible to conceive of an assembly in which no member ever comes close to losing a seat but in which the need to be reelected is what inspires members' behavior. It would be an assembly with no saints or fools in it, an assembly packed with skilled politicians going about their business. When we say "Congressman Smith is unbeatable," we do not mean that there is nothing he could do that would lose him his seat. Rather we mean, "Congressman Smith is unbeatable as long as he continues to do the things he is doing." If he stopped answering his mail, or stopped visiting his district, or began voting randomly on roll calls, or shifted his vote record eighty points on the ADA scale, he would bring on primary or November election troubles in a hurry. It is difficult to offer conclusive proof that this last statement is true, for there is no congressman willing to make the experiment. But normal political activity among politicians with healthy electoral margins should not be confused with inactivity. What characterizes "safe" congressmen is not that they are beyond electoral reach, but that their efforts are very likely to bring them uninterrupted electoral success.

Whether congressmen think their activities have electoral impact, and whether in fact they have impact, are of course two separate questions. Of the former there can be little doubt that the answer is yes. In fact in their own minds successful politicians probably overestimate the impact they are having. Kingdon found in his Wisconsin candidates a "congratulation-rationalization effect," a tendency for winners to take personal credit for their victories and for losers to assign their losses to forces beyond their control. The actual impact of politicians' activities is more difficult to assess. The evidence on the point is soft and scattered. It is hard to find variance in activities undertaken, for there are no politicians who consciously try to lose. There is no doubt that the electorate's general awareness of what is going on in Congress is something less than robust. Yet the argument here will be that congressmen's activities in fact do have electoral impact. Pieces of evidence will be brought in as the discussion proceeds.

The next step here is to offer a brief conceptual treatment of the relation between congressmen and their electorates. In the Downsian analysis what national party leaders must worry about is voters' "expected party differential." But to congressmen this is in practice irrelevant, for reasons specified earlier. A congressman's attention must rather be devoted to what can be called an "expected incumbent differential." Let us define this "expected incumbent differential" as any difference perceived by a relevant political actor between what an incumbent congressman is likely to do if returned to office and what any possible challenger (in primary or general election) would be likely to do. And let us define "relevant political actor" here as anyone who has a resource that might be used in the election in question. At the ballot box the only usable resources are votes, but there are resources that can be translated into votes: money, the ability to make persuasive endorsements, organizational skills, and so on. By this definition a "relevant political actor" need not be a constituent; one of the most important resources, money, flows all over the country in congressional campaign years.

It must be emphasized that the average voter has only the haziest awareness of what an incumbent congressman is actually doing in office. But an incumbent has to be concerned about actors who do form impressions about him, and especially about actors who can marshal resources other than their own votes. Senator Robert C. Byrd (D., W.Va.) has a "little list" of 2,545 West Virginians he regularly keeps in touch with. A congressman's assistant interviewed for a Nader profile in 1972 refers to the "thought leadership" back in the district. Of campaign resources one of the most vital is money. An incumbent not only has to assure that his own election funds are adequate, he has to try to minimize the probability that actors will bankroll an expensive campaign against him. There is the story that during the first Nixon term Senator James B. Pearson (R., Kans.) was told he would face a well-financed opponent in his 1972 primary if he did not display more party regularity in his voting. Availability of money can affect strength of opposition candidacy in both primary and general elections.

Another resource of significance is organizational expertise, probably more important than money among labor union offerings. Simple ability to do electioneering footwork is a resource the invoking of which may give campaigns an interesting twist. Leut-hold found in studying ten 1962 House elections in the San Francisco area that 50 percent of campaign workers held college degrees (as against 12 percent of the Bay area population), and that the workers were more issue oriented than the general population. The need to attract workers may induce candidates to traffic in issues more than they otherwise would. Former Congressman Allard K. Lowenstein (D., N.Y.) has as his key invokable resource a corps of student volunteers who will follow him from district to district, making him an unusually mobile candidate.

Still another highly important resource is the ability to make persuasive endorsements. Manhattan candidates angle for the imprimatur of the *New York Times*. New Hampshire politics rotates around endorsements of the *Manchester Union Leader*. Labor union committees circulate their approved lists.

Chicago Democratic politicians seek the endorsement of the mayor. In the San Francisco area and elsewhere House candidates try to score points by winning endorsements from officials of the opposite party. As Neustadt argues, the influence of the president over congressmen (of both parties) varies with his public prestige and with his perceived ability to punish and reward. One presidential tool is the endorsement, which can be carefully calibrated according to level of fervor, and which can be given to congressmen or to challengers running against congressmen. In the 1970 election Senator Charles Goodell (R., N.Y.), who had achieved public salience by attacking the Nixon administration, was apparently done in by the resources called forth by that attack; the vice president implicitly endorsed his Conservative opponent, and the administration acted to channel normally Republican money away from Goodell.

What a congressman has to try to do is to insure that in primary and general elections the resource balance (with all other deployed resources finally translated into votes) favors himself rather than somebody else. To maneuver successfully he must remain constantly aware of what political actors' incumbent differential readings are, and he must act in a fashion to inspire readings that favor himself. Complicating his task is the problem of slack resources. That is, only a very small proportion of the resources (other than votes) that are conceivably deployable in congressional campaigns are ever in fact deployed. But there is no sure way of telling who will suddenly become aroused and with what consequence. For example, just after the 1948 election the American Medical Association, unnerved by the medical program of the Attlee Government in Britain and by Democratic campaign promises here to institute national health insurance, decided to venture into politics. By 1950 congressmen on record as supporters of health insurance found themselves confronted by a million-dollar AMA advertising drive, local "healing arts committees" making candidate endorsements, and even doctors sending out campaign literature with their monthly bills. By 1952 it was widely believed that the AMA had decided some elections, and few congressmen were still mentioning health insurance.

In all his calculations the congressman must keep in mind that he is serving two electorates rather than one—a November electorate and a primary electorate nested inside it but not a representative sample of it. From the standpoint of the politician a primary is just another election to be survived. A typical scientific poll of a constituency yields a congressman information on the public standing of possible challengers in the other party but also in his own party. A threat is a threat. For an incumbent with a firm "supporting coalition" of elite groups in his party the primary electorate is normally quiescent. But there can be sudden turbulence. And it sometimes happens that the median views of primary and November electorates are so divergent on salient issues that a congressman finds it difficult to hold both electorates at once. This has been a recurrent problem among California Republicans.

A final conceptual point has to do with whether congressmen's behavior should be characterized as "maximizing" behavior. Does it make sense to visualize the congressman as a maximizer of vote percentage in elections—November or primary or, with some complex trade-off, both? For two reasons the answer is probably no. The first has to do with his goal itself, which is to stay in office rather than to win all the popular vote. More precisely his goal is to stay in office over a number of future elections, which does mean that "winning comfortably" in any one of them (except the last) is more desirable than winning by a narrow plurality. The logic here is that a narrow victory (in primary or general election) is a sign of weakness that can inspire hostile political actors to deploy resources intensively the next time around. By this reasoning the higher the election percentages the better. No doubt any congressman would engage in an act to raise his November figure from 80 percent to 90 percent if he could be absolutely sure that the act would accomplish the end (without affecting his primary percentage) and if it could be undertaken at low personal cost. But still, trying to "win comfortably" is not the same as trying to win all the popular vote. As the personal cost (e.g., expenditure of personal energy) of a hypothetical "sure gain" rises, the congressman at the 55 percent November level is more likely to be willing to pay it than his colleague at the 80 percent level.

▪ ▪ ▪

Whether they are safe or marginal, cautious or audacious, congressmen must constantly engage in activities related to reelection. There will be differences in emphasis, but all members share the root need to do things—indeed, to do things day in and day out during their terms. The next step here is to present a typology, a short list of the *kinds* of activities congressmen find it electorally useful to engage in. The case will be that there are three basic kinds of activities. . . .

One activity is *advertising,* defined here as any effort to disseminate one's name among constituents in such a fashion as to create a favorable image but in messages having little or no issue content. A successful congressman builds what amounts to a brand name, which may have a generalized electoral value for other politicians in the same family. The personal qualities to emphasize are experience, knowledge, responsiveness, concern, sincerity, independence, and the like. Just getting one's name across is difficult enough; only about half the electorate, if asked, can supply their House members' names. It helps a congressman to be known. "In the main, recognition carries a positive valence; to be perceived at all is to be perceived favorably." A vital advantage enjoyed by House incumbents is that they are much better known among voters than their November challengers. They are better known because they spend a great deal of time, energy, and money trying to make themselves better known. There are standard routines—frequent visits to the constituency, nonpolitical speeches to home audiences, the sending out of infant care booklets and letters of condolence and congratulation. Of 158 House members questioned in the mid-1960s, 121 said that they regularly sent newsletters to their constituents; 48 wrote separate news or opinion columns for newspapers; 82 regularly reported to their constituencies by radio or television; 89 regularly sent out mail questionnaires. Some routines are less standard. Congressman George E. Shipley (D., Ill.) claims to have met personally about half his constituents (i.e., some 200,000 people). For over twenty years Congressman Charles C. Diggs, Jr. (D., Mich.) has run a radio program featuring himself as a "combination disc jockey-commentator and minister." Congressman Daniel J. Flood (D., Pa.) is "famous for appearing unannounced and often uninvited at wedding anniversaries and other events." Anniversaries and other events aside, congressional advertising is done largely at public expense. Use of the franking privilege has mushroomed in recent years; in early 1973 one estimate predicted that House and Senate members would send out about 476 million pieces of mail in the year 1974, at a public cost of $38.1 million—or about 900,000 pieces per member with a subsidy of $70,000 per member. By far the heaviest mailroom traffic comes in Octobers of even-numbered years. There are some differences between House and Senate members in the ways they go about getting their names across. House members are free to blanket their constituencies with mailings for all boxholders; senators are not. But senators find it easier to appear on national television—for example, in short reaction statements on the nightly news shows. Advertising is a staple congressional activity, and there is no end to it. For each member there are always new voters to be apprised of his worthiness and old voters to be reminded of it.

A second activity may be called *credit claiming*, defined here as acting so as to generate a belief in a relevant political actor (or actors) that one is personally responsible for causing the government, or some unit thereof, to do something that the actor (or actors) considers desirable. The political logic of this, from the congressman's point of view, is that an actor who believes that a member can make pleasing things happen will no doubt wish to keep him in office so that he can make pleasing things happen in the future. The emphasis here is on individual accomplishment (rather than, say, party or governmental accomplishment) and on the congressman as doer (rather than as, say, expounder of constituency views). Credit claiming is highly important to congressmen, with the consequence that much of congressional life is a relentless search for opportunities to engage in it.

Where can credit be found? If there were only one congressman rather than 535, the answer would in principle be simple enough. Credit (or blame) would attach in Downsian fashion to the doings of the government as a whole. But there are 535. Hence it becomes necessary for each congressman to try to peel off pieces of governmental accomplishment for which he can believably generate a sense of responsibility. For the average congressman the staple way of doing this is to traffic in what may be called "particularized benefits." Particularized governmental benefits, as the term will be used here, have two properties: (1) Each benefit is given out to a specific individual, group, or geographical constituency, the recipient unit being of a scale that allows a single congressman to be recognized (by relevant political actors and other congressmen) as the claimant for the benefit (other congressmen being perceived as indifferent or hostile). (2) Each benefit is given out in apparently ad hoc fashion (unlike, say, social security checks) with a congressman apparently having a hand in the allocation. A particularized benefit can normally be regarded as a member of a class. That is, a benefit given out to an individual, group, or constituency can normally be looked upon by congressmen as one of a class of similar benefits given out to sizable numbers of individuals, groups, or constituencies. Hence the impression can arise that a congressman is getting "his share" of whatever it is the government is offering. (The classes may be vaguely defined. Some state legislatures deal in what their members call "local legislation.")

In sheer volume the bulk of particularized benefits come under the heading of "casework"—the thousands of favors congressional offices perform for suppliants in ways that normally do not require legislative action. High school students ask for essay materials, soldiers for emergency leaves, pensioners for location of missing checks, local governments for grant information, and on and on. Each office has skilled professionals who can play the bureaucracy like an organ—pushing the right pedals to produce the desired effects. But many benefits require new legislation, or at least they require important allocative decisions on matters covered by existent legislation. Here the congressman fills the traditional role of supplier of goods to the home district. It is a believable role; when a member claims credit for a benefit on the order of a dam, he may well receive it. Shiny construction projects seem especially useful. In the decades before 1934, tariff duties for local industries were a major commodity. In recent years awards given under grant-in-aid programs have become more useful as they have become more numerous. Some quests for credit are ingenious; in 1971 the story broke that congressmen had been earmarking foreign aid money for specific projects in Israel in order to win favor with home constituents. It should be said of constituency benefits that congressmen are quite capable of taking the initiative in drumming them up; that is, there can be no automatic assumption that a congressman's activity is the result of pressures brought to bear by organized interests. Fenno shows the importance of member initiative in his discussion of the House Interior Committee.

A final point here has to do with geography. The examples given so far are all of benefits conferred upon home constituencies or recipients therein (the latter including the home residents who applauded the Israeli projects). But the properties of particularized benefits were carefully specified so as not to exclude the possibility that some benefits may be given to recipients outside the home constituencies. Some probably are. Narrowly drawn tax loopholes qualify as particularized benefits, and some of them are probably conferred upon recipients outside the home districts. (It is difficult to find solid evidence on the point.) Campaign contributions flow into districts from the outside, so it would not be surprising to find that benefits go where the resources are.

How much particularized benefits count for at the polls is extraordinarily difficult to say. But it would be hard to find a congressman who thinks he can afford to wait around until precise information is available. The lore is that they count—furthermore, given home expectations, that they must be supplied in regular quantities for a member to stay electorally even with the board. Awareness of favors may spread beyond their recipients, building for a member a general reputation as a good provider. "Rivers Delivers." "He Can Do More For Massachusetts." A good example of Capitol Hill lore on electoral impact is given in this account of the activities of Congressman Frank Thompson, Jr. (D., N.J., 4th district):

> In 1966, the 4th was altered drastically by redistricting; it lost Burlington County and gained Hunterdon, Warren, and Sussex. Thompson's performance at the polls since 1966 is a case study of how an incumbent congressman, out of line with his district's ideological persuasions, can become unbeatable. In 1966, Thompson carried Mercer by 23,000 votes and lost the three new counties by 4,600, winning reelection with 56% of the votes. He then survived a district-wide drop in his vote two years later. In 1970, the Congressman carried Mercer County by 20,000 votes and the rest of the district by 6,000, finishing with 58%. The drop in Mercer resulted from the attempt of his hard-line conservative opponent to exploit the racial unrest which had developed in Trenton. But for four years Thompson had been making friends in Hunterdon, Warren, and Sussex, busy doing the kind of chores that congressmen do. In this case, Thompson concerned himself with the interests of dairy farmers at the Department of Agriculture. The results of his efforts were clear when the results came in from the 4th's northern counties.

So much for particularized benefits. But is credit available elsewhere? For governmental accomplishments beyond the scale of those already discussed? The general answer is that the prime mover role is a hard one to play on larger matters—at least before broad electorates. A claim, after all, has to be credible. If a congressman goes before an audience and says, "I am responsible for passing a bill to curb inflation," or "I am responsible for the highway program," hardly anyone will believe him. There are two reasons why people may be skeptical of such claims. First, there is a numbers problem. On an accomplishment of a sort that probably engaged the supportive interest of more than one member it is reasonable to suppose that credit should be apportioned among them. But second, there is an overwhelming problem of information costs. For typical voters Capitol Hill is a distant and mysterious place; few have anything like a working knowledge of its maneuverings. Hence there is no easy way of knowing whether a congressman is staking a valid claim or not. The odds are that the information problem cuts in different ways on different kinds of issues. On particularized benefits it may work in a congressman's favor; he may get credit for the dam he had nothing to do with building. Sprinkling a district with dams, after all, is something a congressman is supposed to be able to do. But on larger matters it may work against him. For a voter lacking an easy way to sort out valid from invalid claims the sensible recourse is skepticism. Hence it is unlikely that congressmen get much mileage out of credit claiming on larger matters before broad electorates.

Yet there is an obvious and important qualification here. For many congressmen credit claiming on non-particularized matters is possible in specialized subject areas because of the congressional division of labor. The term "governmental unit" in the original definition of credit claiming is broad enough to include committees, subcommittees, and the two houses of Congress itself. Thus many congressmen can believably claim credit for blocking bills in subcommittee, adding on amendments in committee, and so on. The audience for transactions of this sort is usually small. But it may include important political actors (e.g., an interest group, the president, the *New York Times*, Ralph Nader) who are capable of both paying Capitol Hill information costs and deploying electoral resources. There is a well-documented example of this in Fenno's treatment of post office politics in the 1960s. The postal employee unions used to watch very closely the activities of the House and Senate Post Office Committees and supply valuable electoral resources (money, volunteer work) to members who did their bidding on salary bills. Of course there are many examples of this kind of undertaking, and there is more to be said about it.

The third activity congressmen engage in may be called *position taking*, defined here as the public enunciation of a judgmental statement on anything likely to be of interest to political actors. The statement may take the form of a roll call vote. The most important classes of judgmental statements are those prescribing American governmental ends (a vote cast against the war; a statement that "the war should be ended immediately") or governmental means (a statement that "the way to end the war is to take it to the United Nations"). The judgments may be implicit rather than explicit, as in: "I will support the president on this matter." But judgments may range far beyond these classes to take in implicit or explicit statements on what almost anybody should do or how he should do it: "The great Polish scientist Copernicus has been unjustly neglected"; "The way for Israel to achieve peace is to give up the Sinai." The congressman as position taker is a speaker rather than a doer. The electoral requirement is not that he make pleasing things happen but that he make pleasing judgmental statements. The position itself is the political commodity. Especially on matters where governmental responsibility is widely diffused it is not surprising that political actors should fall back on positions as tests of incumbent virtue. For voters ignorant of congressional processes the recourse is an easy one. The following comment by one of Clapp's House interviewees is highly revealing: "Recently, I went home and began to talk about the ——— act. I was pleased to have sponsored that bill, but it soon dawned on me that the point wasn't getting through at all. What was getting through was that the act might be a help to people. I changed the emphasis: I didn't mention my role particularly, but stressed my support of the legislation."

The ways in which positions can be registered are numerous and often imaginative. There are floor addresses ranging from weighty orations to mass-produced "nationality day statements." There are speeches before home groups, television appearances, letters, newsletters, press releases, ghostwritten books, *Playboy* articles, even interviews with political scientists. On occasion congressmen generate what amount to petitions; whether or not to sign the 1956 Southern Manifesto defying school desegregation rulings was an important decision for southern members. Outside the roll call process the congressman is usually able to tailor his positions to suit his audiences. A solid consensus in the constituency calls for ringing declarations; for years the late Senator James K. Vardaman (D., Miss.) campaigned on a proposal to repeal the Fifteenth Amendment. Division or uncertainty in the constituency calls for waffling; in the late 1960s a congressman had to be a poor politician indeed not to be able to come up with an inoffensive statement on Vietnam ("We must have peace with honor at the earliest possible moment consistent with the national interest"). On a controversial issue a Capitol Hill office normally prepares two form letters to send out to constituent letter writers—one for the pros and one (not directly contradictory) for the antis. Handling discrete audiences in person requires simple agility, a talent well demonstrated in this selection from a Nader profile:

> "You may find this difficult to understand," said Democrat Edward R. Roybal, the Mexican-American representative from California's thirtieth district, "but sometimes I wind up making a patriotic speech one afternoon and later on that same day an anti-war speech. In the patriotic speech I speak of past wars but I also speak of the need to prevent more wars. My positions are not inconsistent; I just approach different people differently." Roybal went on to depict the diversity of crowds he speaks to: one afternoon he is surrounded by balding men wearing Veterans' caps and holding American flags; a few hours later he speaks to a crowd of Chicano youths, angry over American involvement in Vietnam. Such a diverse constituency, Roybal believes, calls for different methods of expressing one's convictions.

Indeed it does. Versatility of this sort is occasionally possible in roll call voting. For example a congressman may vote one way on recommittal and the other on final passage, leaving it unclear just how he stands on a bill. Members who cast identical votes on a measure may give different reasons for having done so. Yet it is on roll calls that the crunch comes; there is no way for a member to avoid making a record on hundreds of issues, some of which are controversial in the home constituencies. Of course, most roll call positions considered in isolation are not likely to cause much of a ripple at home. But broad voting patterns can and do; member "ratings" calculated by the Americans for Democratic Action, Americans for Constitutional Action, and other outfits are used as guidelines in the deploying of electoral resources. And particular issues often have their alert publics. Some national interest groups watch the votes of all congressmen on single issues and ostentatiously try to reward or punish members for their positions; over the years some notable examples of such interest groups have been the Anti-Saloon League, the early Farm Bureau, the American Legion, the American Medical Association, and the National Rifle Association. On rare occasions single roll calls achieve a rather high salience among the public generally. This seems especially true of the Senate, which every now and then winds up for what might be called a "showdown vote," with pressures on all sides, presidential involvement, media attention given to individual senators' positions, and suspense about the outcome. Examples are the votes on the nuclear test-ban treaty in 1963, civil rights cloture in 1964, civil rights cloture again in 1965, the Haynsworth appointment in 1969, the Carswell appointment in 1970, and the ABM in 1970. Controversies on roll calls like these are often relived in subsequent campaigns, the southern Senate elections of 1970 with their Haynsworth and Carswell issues being cases in point.

Probably the best position-taking strategy for most congressmen at most times is to be conservative—to cling to their own positions of the past where possible and to reach for new ones with great caution where necessary. Yet in an earlier discussion of strategy the suggestion was made that it might be rational for members in electoral danger to resort to innovation. The form of innovation available is entrepreneurial position taking, its logic being that for a member facing defeat with his old array of positions it makes good sense to gamble on some new ones. It may be that congressional marginals fulfill an important function here as issue pioneers—experimenters who test out new issues and thereby show other politicians which ones are usable. An example of such a pioneer is Senator Warren Magnuson (D., Wash.), who responded to a surprisingly narrow victory in 1962 by reaching for a reputation in the area of consumer affairs. Another example is Senator Ernest Hollings (D., S.C.), a servant of a shaky and racially heterogeneous southern constituency who launched "hunger" as an issue in 1969—at once pointing to a problem and giving it a useful nonracial definition. One of the most successful issue entrepreneurs of recent decades was the late Senator Joseph McCarthy (R., Wis.); it was all there—the close primary in 1946, the fear of defeat in 1952, the desperate casting about for an issue, the famous 1950 dinner at the Colony Restaurant where suggestions were tendered, the decision that "Communism" might just do the trick.

NOTES

1. "But it is equally true, though only of late and slowly beginning to be acknowledged, that a numerous assembly is as little fitted for the direct business of legislation as for that of administration." John Stuart Mill, *Considerations on Representative Government* (Chicago: Regency, 1962), p. 104.

2. Gerhard Loewenberg, "The Role of Parliaments in Modern Political Systems," in Loewenberg (ed.), *Modern Parliaments: Change or Decline?* (Chicago: Aldine-Atherton, 1971), p. 3.

5.2

RICHARD F. FENNO Jr.

From *Home Style: House Members in Their Districts*

Fenno's study of members of Congress leads him to consider four groups of peo-
ple that a typical representative considers subsets of his or her constituency: (1)
all people in the district, (2) those who tend to vote for the representative in gen-
eral elections, (3) those who ardently support and vote for the representative in
primary elections, and (4) those who contribute money and time to the represen-
tative's reelection. These groups are like concentric circles surrounding the repre-
sentative, and he or she has to pay careful attention to all four of these groups.

What does a House member see when looking at his or her constituency?
Kaleidoscopic variety, no doubt. That is why there can be no one "correct"
way of slicing up and classifying member perceptions—only "helpful" ways.
Most helpful to me has been the member's view of a constituency as a nest
of concentric circles. In one form or another, in one expression or another, in
one degree or another, this bull's-eye perception is shared by all House members. It is helpful to us for the same reason it is common to them. It is a perception constructed out of the necessities of political life.

THE GEOGRAPHICAL CONSTITUENCY: THE DISTRICT

The largest of the concentric circles represents the House member's most
encompassing view of his or her constituency. It is "the district," the entity to
which, from which, and within which the member travels. It is the entity whose
boundaries have been fixed by state legislative enactment or by court decision.
It includes the entire population within those boundaries. Because it is a legal
entity, we could refer to it as the legal constituency. We capture more of what
the member has in mind when conjuring up "my district," however, if we think
of it as the *geographical constituency*. We then retain the idea that the district is
a legally bounded space, and emphasize that it is located in a particular place.

The Washington community is often described as a group of people all of
whom come from somewhere else. The House of Representatives, by design,

From Richard F. Fenno Jr., *Home Style: House Members in Their Districts* (New York: Pearson Longman, 2003).

epitomizes this characteristic; and its members function with a heightened sense of their ties to another place. There are, of course, constant reminders. The member's district is, after all, "the Tenth District of *California*." Inside the chamber, he is "the gentleman from *California*." In the media, he is "Representative Smith (D. *California*)." So it is not surprising that when you ask a member, "What kind of district do you have?" the answer often begins with, and nearly always includes, a geographical, space-and-place perception. Thus, the district is seen as "the largest in the state, twenty-eight counties in the southeastern corner," or "three layers of suburbs to the west of the city, a square with the northwest corner cut out," or "a core district, the core of the city." If the boundaries have been changed by a recent redistricting, the geography of "the new district" will be compared to that of "the old district": "I picked up five northern counties and lost two on the eastern edge. The new district is a lot more spread out."

If one essential aspect of "the geographical constituency" is seen as its location and boundaries, another is its internal makeup. And House members describe their districts' internal makeup using political science's most familiar demographic and political variables: socioeconomic structure, ideology, ethnicity, residential patterns, religion, partisanship, stability, diversity, etc. Every congressman, in his mind's eye, sees his geographical constituency in terms of some special configuration of such variables.

■   ■   ■

THE REELECTION CONSTITUENCY: THE SUPPORTERS

Each congressman does perceive an explicitly political constituency nested within his geographical constituency. It is composed of those people in the district who he thinks vote for him. We shall call it his *reelection constituency*. But, because all members do not perceive their support in coalitional terms and because all members do see support in reelection terms, we shall use the more universal language.[1] As they move about "the district," House members continually draw the distinction between those people who vote for them and those who do not: "I do well here"; "I run poorly here"; "This group supports me"; "This group does not." By distinguishing supporters from nonsupporters, they articulate their fundamental political perception.

House members use two reference points—one cross-sectional, the other longitudinal—in shaping this perception. First, by a process of inclusion and exclusion, they come to a rough approximation of the upper and lower ranges of the reelection constituency. That is to say, there are some votes a member believes he nearly always gets. There are other votes he believes he almost never gets. Among those he thinks he usually gets, the perceived partisan component of the electorate is always a basic element. Every member begins with a perception of his partisan support—estimated by registration figures or poll data, and by political demography.

> It's a good Democratic district now—59 percent registered Democrats. And for the first time I feel safe. . . . I used to brag that my old district was the wealthiest, best-educated district in the country represented by a Democrat. But I wasn't a bit sad to give up the wealthy part of the district and pick up all those poor, ill-educated good Democrats in the new part of the district.

When the partisan composition of the district is clearly insufficient for reelection, members express ideas about the nature of their cross-party supporters.

> My district registers only 37 percent Republican. And they have no place else to go. My problem is, how can I get enough Democratic votes to win the general election. . . . Civil servants, bank clerks, insurance salesmen, bricklayers, carpenters, the craft unions; these have been the mainstream of my Democratic support—middle class and working class. . . . The hard hats are the people most likely to vote for me. That's my lucrative territory—not the liberal, intellectual wing [of the Democratic party].

Every member has some idea of the people most likely to join his reelection constituency, his "lucrative territory." During a campaign, these people will often be "targeted" and subjected to special recruiting or activating efforts.

A congressman's sense of the people least likely to join his reelection constituency is usually as well developed as his sense for his "lucrative territory." Comments like "I'll never carry this town"; "This part of the district is hopeless"; "I've never been able to crack these space industry guys"; "I'd love to get the pickup truck vote, but I never do" punctuate his travels in the district. If a member chooses to attack "the special interests" in his district, it is from these perceived never-supporters that the objects of his attacks will come.

▪ ▪ ▪

Thinking about "last time's" electoral margin, if it was an apparently safe one, should assuage a good deal of a representative's uncertainty about his reelection constituency. And it does. But it does not produce certainty. Far from it. Most House members will have experienced, at some point in their careers, "the fight of my life"—a testing election they felt especially hard-pressed to win. When members recall their testing elections they dwell on the immense organizational and personal efforts required to win.

THE PRIMARY CONSTITUENCY: THE STRONGEST SUPPORTERS

In thinking about their political condition, House members make distinctions *within* their reelection constituency, thus giving us a third, still smaller perceptual circle. Having distinguished between their nonsupporters and their supporters, they further distinguish between their weak supporters and their strong supporters. Weak supporters come in both the routine and the temporary varieties. Routine supporters do no more than vote for the member, often simply following party identification. Temporary supporters back the member as the best available alternative "this time," as "the lesser of two evils." Strong supporters display an intensity capable of producing additional political activity, and they tender their support "through thick and thin," regardless of who the challenger may be. Within each reelection constituency, then, nests a smaller constituency perceived as "my strongest supporters," "my loyalists," "my true believers," "my political base," "my hard core," "my nucleus," "my tough nut," "my bread basket." We shall think of these people as the ones each congressman believes would provide his last line of electoral defense in a primary contest, and label them the *primary constituency*.[2] We do not mean this label to include all the people who vote for him in a primary, only those from whom he expects a special solidity of support in a primary election.

A protected congressional seat is one protected as much from primary defeat as from general election defeat. And a primary constituency is something every congressman must have one of.

▪   ▪   ▪

THE PERSONAL CONSTITUENCY: THE INTIMATES

Within the primary constituency, House members perceive still a fourth, and final, concentric circle. These are the few individuals whose relationship with the member is so personal and so intimate that their relevance cannot be captured by any description of "very strongest supporters." Some of them are his closest political advisers and confidants. Others are people from whom he draws emotional sustenance for his political work. They are all people with whom the congressman has shared some crucial experience—usually early in his career, and often the "testing election." Times of relaxation are thick with reminiscence. Fellow feeling is heavily "we few, we happy few, we band of brothers." Sometimes a staff assistant is among these intimates; sometimes not. Sometimes the member's spouse is involved, but not always. These are the people, if any, to whom he has entrusted his political career. He can meet with all of them in one place, face to face, as he cannot with any of his other constituencies. He knows them by name, as individuals. He thinks of them as his friends. "A guy is lucky in politics," said one congressman. "He's carried here by his friends and he is kept here by his friends. That gives you a nice feeling." We shall think of these politically and emotionally supportive friends as the member's *personal constituency*.

▪   ▪   ▪

CONCLUSION

Each member of Congress perceives four concentric constituencies: geographic, reelection, primary, and personal. This is not the only way a member sees his or her "constituency"; but it is one way. It is a set of perceptions that emphasizes the context in which, and the strategies by which, the House member seeks electoral support. It is a complicated context, one featuring varying scopes of support and varying intensities of support. The strategies developed for getting and keeping electoral support involve the manipulation of these scopes and intensities. . . .

A perceptual analysis of congressional constituencies both complicates and clarifies efforts of political science to understand the relationship between congressman and constituency. It complicates matters both conceptually and statistically. For example, political scientists have a heavy investment in role conceptions that distinguish between the "trustee" who follows his independent judgment and the "delegate" who follows the wishes of his constituency. But we now must ask, which constituency? And we cannot be content with a conceptual scheme that provides only two answers to this question: "the district" and "the nation."[3] More frequent, we think, than this kind of choice is one in which the congressman must choose among constituencies *within* the district. Also, when studies of party voting conclude that a member of Congress can vote independently because he or she "knows the constituency isn't looking,"[4] we need to ask again, which constituency? One of the several constituencies may very well be looking.

NOTES

1. John Kingdon, *Candidates for Office: Beliefs and Strategies* (New York: Random House, 1966), chap. 3. In her study of congressional challengers in New York, Linda Fowler finds that some did not perceive or think in terms of an electoral "coalition." Linda Fowler, "The Cycle of Defeat: Recruitment of Congressional Challengers," unpublished manuscript, University of Rochester, 1977. When asked to describe his "supporters," one congressman in my group answered, "That's very hard to evaluate. I never thought in terms of groups. . . . I never thought of my support as coming from groups. The middle group, I guess, homeowners. It's very hard to say." The importance of the reelection constituency is well argued (though not subsequently employed) in Aage Clausen, *How Congressmen Decide: A Policy Focus* (New York: St. Martin's, 1973), p. 126.

2. The term is from Leo Snowiss, "Congressional Recruitment and Representation," *American Political Science Review* 60 (September 1966): 629–639.

3. For example, see Roger Davidson, *The Role of the Congressman* (New York: Pegasus, 1973).

4. David Stokes and Warren Miller, "Party Government and the Saliency of Congress," *Public Opinion Quarterly* 26 (Winter 1962): 531–546.

5.3

GARY W. COX AND MATHEW D. McCUBBINS

From *Setting the Agenda: Responsible Party Government in the U.S. House of Representatives*

The majority party in the House of Representatives closely controls legislative business, but to do so the party needs the cooperation of its members. How do majority political parties in Congress keep their coalitions together to pass legislation? Cox and McCubbins argue that party leaders, first, offer plum committee assignments and pork barrel benefits to rank-and-file members, and second, keep tight control over the agenda to ensure that no bills are voted upon that would potentially divide the party.

PROCEDURAL CARTEL THEORY

> The job of speaker is not to expedite legislation that runs counter to the wishes of the majority of his majority.
>
> —Speaker Dennis Hastert (R-IL)[1]

In this chapter, we present and discuss the assumptions that undergird procedural cartel theory. To provide a context for comparison, however, we first briefly survey the literature on partisan legislative organization.

Theories of Partisan Legislative Organization

Much of the literature on legislative organization focuses on why political parties are created within legislatures in the first place. We divide extant explanations into those that hinge primarily on the internal legislative payoffs to forming parties and those that hinge primarily on the external electoral payoffs. We then turn to survey the literature on how parties are organized and what parties do.

Why Are There Parties in Legislatures?

PARTIES ARE CREATED TO SOLVE INTERNAL COLLECTIVE ACTION PROBLEMS. One line of theorizing about why parties exist is similar to the distributive line of argument regarding committees. Absent any organization (other than a voting

From Gary W. Cox and Mathew D. McCubbins, *Setting the Agenda: Responsible Party Government in the U.S. House of Representatives* (New York: Cambridge University Press, 2005).

rule for floor decisions), legislators face a chaotic and unpredictable agenda. They cannot be sure that the legislature will not vote tomorrow to strip them of benefits conferred today. Nor is it clear how to ensure that the benefits are conferred to begin with, given a world where any legislator can move any amendment at any time.

In order to deal with the unpredictability—and unprofitability—of the unorganized legislature, legislators form political parties to bind themselves together in durable coalitions. Gains from legislative trade that could not be accrued without parties are thus accrued.

PARTIES ARE CREATED TO SOLVE EXTERNAL COLLECTIVE ACTION PROBLEMS. An alternative theory views legislative parties as being formed primarily to accrue electoral gains. Modern political parties facing mass electorates, similar to modern corporations facing mass markets, have a strong incentive to fashion and maintain a brand name. Such brand names are, however, public goods to all politicians running under the party's label. Thus, parties arise in order to ensure that the usual problems of providing and maintaining public goods are overcome—and in particular to internalize electoral externalities that would otherwise arise.

How Are Parties Organized?

If parties exist to solve collective action problems, as seems the main tenet in the literature, then how do they organize to solve these problems? The literature has several suggestions, which we now survey.

PARTIES AS FIRMS. Many scholars envision parties as being similar to the firms depicted in the literature on industrial organization (cf. Alchian and Demsetz 1972; Tirole 1988), in that they involve delegation to central agents (party leaders) in order to reduce transaction costs and ameliorate collective action problems. Scholars in this tradition implicitly accept the industrial organization literature's focus on hierarchical firms with single chief executive officers.

PARTIES AS PARTNERSHIPS. In the case of the political party, we believe a more fruitful analogy is to partnerships, such as law or accountancy firms, in which various gradations of senior partners provide overall strategic and tactical direction to the firm. The "senior partners" in our story—at least as regards the majority party—will be committee and subcommittee chairs, majority party floor leaders, campaign finance committee chairs, and the like. Agenda-setting and other powers are distributed across the offices held by these senior partners rather than fully concentrated in the hands of the speaker, just as the right to recruit new clients and take on new jobs is distributed among the senior partners in a law or accountancy firm, rather than fully concentrated in the hands of the firm's president. Similarly, just as the job of ensuring that no senior partner's actions impinge too unfavorably on a law firm's overall reputation falls not just on the firm's president but also on the other senior partners collectively, so too the job of policing committee chairs falls partly to the speaker and partly to informal politics centered on the party caucus.

What Do Parties Do?

Once organized, what do parties do to mitigate the collective action problems that are assumed to be the reason for their existence?

PARTIES AS FLOOR VOTING COALITIONS.   Some partisan theories view parties primarily as floor voting coalitions. In such theories, the central issue is the degree to which parties can discipline their members, ensuring a cohesive voting bloc on the floor, even when there are internal disagreements over policy.

The best-known model that seeks to explain variations in American parties' ability to discipline their members, and hence enact programs, is the conditional party government model of Aldrich (1995), Rohde (1991), and Aldrich and Rohde (2001). In this model, majority party backbenchers delegate more power to their party leaders, when preferences vary less within each party and more between the parties. Party government is thus conditional on a sufficient disagreement in preferences between the parties (relative to their internal disagreements) arising. When this condition is met, American parties act more in accord with the traditional model of responsible party government.

PARTIES AS PROCEDURAL COALITIONS.   Other partisan theories, including our own, view parties primarily as procedural coalitions. For such theories, the central issue is the majority party's ability to control the legislative agenda, defined as the set of bills considered and voted on the floor.

How Do Majority Parties Control the Agenda?

Strict party discipline, at least on important votes, is one method for the majority party or coalition to control legislative outcomes. When party leaders have the means to impose discipline on their backbenchers, agenda control is attained by the extension of the will of the party leadership. But, where discipline is costly, other methods may be substituted. In considering these other methods, there is an important distinction to be made between positive and negative agenda power. Positive agenda power is the ability to push bills through the legislative process to a final-passage vote on the floor. Negative agenda power is the ability to block bills from reaching a final passage vote on the floor. Formal and informal models of legislative parties differ in whether they depict parties as controlling the agenda via the allocation of proposal rights (positive agenda power) or veto rights (negative agenda power).

PARTIES AS ALLOCATING PROPOSAL RIGHTS.   Two examples of theories in which proposal rights are the key resource allocated by parties to their members are Laver and Shepsle's (1996) model of ministerial government and Diermeier and Feddersen's (1998) model of the vote of confidence. In a common interpretation of Laver and Shepsle's model, multiparty coalition governments allocate ministerial portfolios to their various member parties, with each minister then possessing both positive and negative agenda power in his respective jurisdiction. Thus, each minister can make proposals directly to the assembly, without needing cabinet clearance. In Diermeier and Feddersen's model, coalitions of legislators allocate increased "recognition probabilities" to their members, thereby increasing their ability to make proposals. Once recognized, a given member of a coalition again needs no preclearance by other members of the coalition for his proposals: They go straight to a final-passage vote in the plenary.

PARTIES AS ALLOCATING VETO RIGHTS.   An alternative view of parties is that they allocate negative agenda power, or veto rights, among their members. Tsebelis (2002) takes this view of parliamentary coalitions. Rather than view individual parties as possessing both negative and positive agenda power across a range of issues (those under the jurisdiction of the party's ministers), Tsebelis views parties as possessing a general veto over the entire range of issues the coalition must face—therefore no coalition partner possesses unilateral proposal power. Similarly, Cox and McCubbins (2002) view majority parties primarily as allocating veto (or delaying) power to various offices held by their senior partners, such as committee chairs and speakers, thus necessarily lessening the proposal power of any given party member or subset of members.

Procedural Cartel Theory

In this section, we list the assumptions and motivating principles of procedural cartel theory. Assumptions 1–5 are from our previous book, *Legislative Leviathan*, and are defended at length in the second edition of that volume. Assumption 6 is new to this reading, and, accordingly, we expand on it here. . . . After elaborating the assumptions of our theory, we sketch some of the intuitions that have steered our research (. . .) and conclude. . . . In subsequent chapters, we will present and test simplified and formalized models consistent with the broader theory presented here.

> **Assumption 1:** Members of Congress seek reelection to the House, internal advancement within the House, good public policy, and majority status.

In our previous work (Cox and McCubbins 1993), our formal statement of members' goals included three of the motivations just discussed: reelection, internal advancement, and majority status.[2] Key to our approach was the assumption that majority status confers substantial benefits. In particular, advancement to committee chairs and other key posts in the House is possible only if one's party gains a majority, and advancement of one's legislative projects is greatly facilitated by majority status.[3] Thus, majority status is arguably an essential gateway to internal advancement and policy goals. The more substantial the benefits of majority status are, the more incentive they provide to the senior partners in a given party to pursue majority status—hence to undertake the sorts of agenda-setting actions that we describe in the remainder of the reading.

> **Assumption 2:** The reputation (or brand name) of a member's party affects both the member's personal probability of reelection and, more substantially, the party's probability of securing a majority.

We have discussed this premise at length in our previous work (see Cox and McCubbins 1993, Chapter 5). To the extent that this assumption holds, a political party's reputation is a *public good* to all candidates sharing the party's label. More specifically, if a party's reputation improves or worsens, all members benefit or suffer together, regardless of whether they contributed to the improvement or worsening.

> **Assumption 3:** A party's reputation depends significantly on its record of legislative accomplishment.

The policies with which a particular party and its leaders are associated—both those it promotes and those it opposes—can significantly affect the party's reputation. A recent example of this is the budget battle waged between Speaker of the House Newt Gingrich and President Bill Clinton in 1995. This battle led to the opening of the new fiscal year without a federal budget, causing the closure of nonessential government services. For present purposes, the important point about this budgetary stand-off is simply that it led to a sharp reduction in the popularity of congressional Republicans and their leaders, as measured by thermometer ratings in mass surveys (Jacobson 1996). In other words, in this instance a leader's legislative policy—that of refusing to compromise on the budget—led directly to a decline in the party's overall popularity.

We assume that this anecdote points to a more general phenomenon, in which legislative actions taken by various members of the party can affect the overall party's reputation on the margin. There is some disagreement about how much and how quickly party identification incorporates new events and evaluations. For our purposes, we need simply to assert a position similar to that adopted by V. O. Key (1966), in which parties' legislative actions *do* consequentially affect voters' behavior. Whether the path by which legislative actions influence votes is through party reputations (party identification) or through some shorter-term partisan pathways is less important.

> **Assumption 4:** Legislating—hence compiling favorable records of legislative accomplishment—is akin to team production and entails overcoming an array of cooperation and coordination problems.

Achieving their goals—reelection, internal advancement, and majority status—requires passage of legislation, yet legislators' ability to accomplish things on their own is quite limited. Legislation must be accepted by majorities in both houses of Congress and be signed by the president to become law.[4] To get through even one house, moreover, a bill needs to get scarce floor time and the support of a majority coalition, both of which are costly and difficult to achieve. Legislating thus requires that members somehow join forces, cooperate, and engage in "team production" (Alchian and Demsetz 1972).

Team production, however, means confronting and overcoming a variety of collective action and coordination problems. For example, all members would like to spend more money on their own districts than might be optimal from their party's perspective (Cox and McCubbins 1993); all members would like to have free access to floor time, but the result could be that nothing can get done reliably; divergent national, regional, and partisan interests might lead members to pursue different policies in the absence of some coordinating mechanism. Most important for our theory, as noted above, the party label itself is a public good (for party members) that is subject to free-rider problems. Managing the party label is the primary collective action problem that members of a party must solve, and their collective goal of solving this and other collective action problems is the sense in which they are members of a partnership.

> **Assumption 5:** The primary means by which a (majority) party regulates its members' actions, in order to overcome problems of team production in the legislative process, is by delegating to a central authority.

Though other solutions for collective action problems exist, the most common solution seems to be delegation to a central authority—an idea that appears in a wide variety of literatures.[5] Three common elements in all these works are that the central authority to whom power is delegated monitors individual behavior, controls carrots and sticks with which to reward and punish individuals, and is motivated to solve the collective action problem(s) faced by the group. Along these lines, the core point of our previous book (Cox and McCubbins 1993) is that majority party members delegate to party leaders the authority to manage legislative resources and the legislative process in order to solve the cooperation and coordination problems they face, including maintaining the value of the party label.[6]

How are party leaders motivated to use their delegated powers for collective, rather than purely personal, gain? We argue that members wishing to hold important offices in the House (such as the speakership and committee chairs) know that the only realistic route to getting these offices is for their party to attain a majority of seats and for them to be in sufficiently good standing with their caucus to be (re)nominated for such offices.[7] Thus, the more valuable are the top posts going to the majority party's senior members, the more motivated are those members to ensure the party's continued majority status (and their own good standing).

As noted in the previous chapter, we believe that political parties are more fruitfully analogized to legal or accountancy partnerships than to strictly hierarchical single-leader firms (or armies). Thus, when we speak of delegation to a central authority, we do not mean literally to a single person but instead to a group of "senior partners."

> **Assumption 6:** The key resource that majority parties delegate to their senior partners is the power to set the legislative agenda; the majority party forms a procedural cartel that collectively monopolizes agenda-setting power.

This is our key assumption, and our point of departure from most of the previous literature. A *procedural cartel* is a coalition of legislators who constitute a majority in the assembly, share a common label (at least in the United States), and cartelize the agenda via the following basic strategy. First, the cartel creates (or, more typically, inherits) a set of offices endowed with special agenda-setting powers. In the case of the U.S. House, the main agenda-setting offices are the committee chairs, slots on the Rules Committee, and the speakership.[8] Second, the cartel ensures that its members get all, or nearly all, of the agenda-setting offices.[9] Third, cartel members expect those appointed to agenda-setting offices to *always* obey "the first commandment of party leadership"—*Thou shalt not aid bills that will split thy party*—and to sometimes obey the second commandment—*Thou shalt aid bills that most in thy party like.* Fourth, cartel members expect rank-and-file members to support the agenda-setting decisions rendered by officeholders when those decisions are made in conformity to the expectations just noted. Fifth, the cartel's leadership takes action to maintain cooperation and coordination within the cartel.

We use the term "cartel" because procedural cartels, like economic cartels, seek to establish a collective monopoly on a particular resource (in this case, agenda-setting power), seek to restrict supply of products made with this resource (in this case, bills that are placed on the floor agenda), and face problems of free-riding (in this case, members reluctant to vote for a party measure when such a vote will not sell well back home, or members eager to use their delegated agenda powers for personal gain). We have also used the term "legislative leviathan" to describe party organizations within legislatures, in order to emphasize their sometimes considerable degree of centralized authority.[10] Indeed, even during their relatively decentralized periods, parties in the U.S. House have been more hierarchical and stable than the typical economic cartel. Even though neither term's connotations are fully satisfactory, in this reading we will refer to party organizations as forming procedural cartels (and we will stress the analogy of a group of senior partners directing a law or accountancy firm rather than of a CEO running a corporation or a general commanding an army).

How Does the Majority Cartelize the Agenda?

In this section, we reconsider the defining features of "procedural cartels," as mentioned in Assumption 6. At this point, we wish only to argue that these features *plausibly* characterize the modern (i.e., post-Reed) House of Representatives; we will return to them in greater detail later in the reading.

The Structure of Agenda-Setting Offices

An initial question is whether there exist offices endowed with special agenda-setting powers in the House and whether these offices' powers were in some sense chosen by the majority party. By "special agenda-setting powers," or agenda power for short, we refer to any *special* ability to determine which bills are considered on the floor and under what procedures. Because any member can participate in an attempt to discharge a bill, we would not count "the ability to participate in a discharge attempt" as an "agenda power" in our sense. Such an ability is not special; it is general. In contrast, only members of the Rules Committee can participate in fashioning special rules,[11] and only chairs can delay bills merely by not scheduling them—to mention two examples of agenda power as we define it.

Given this definition, there obviously do exist offices in the House endowed with agenda power. As noted previously, the most important of these include the committee and subcommittee chairs, the seats on the Rules Committee, and the speakership.

Did the majority party in some sense choose the level of agenda power delegated to the various agenda-setting offices? Yes, in two senses.

First, the House adopts rules anew in each Congress. These rules are proposed by the majority party and are usually adopted on a straight party-line vote. Thus, among other things, the majority chooses (or reaffirms) the delegation of agenda power in those rules.

Second, the modern structure of agenda power in the House was erected in the period 1880–94 to enable the majority party to legislate, even against the wishes of the minority. . . . We will show that the House's rules have not, since 1894, changed so as to erase the majority party advantages accrued in this period. In particular, the minority party's ability to delay has not been restored, nor has the central position of the Rules Committee been significantly altered.[12] The powers of the speaker have waxed and waned, but when they have changed, they have simply been redistributed within the majority party, not allocated to any minority party members. In this sense, the majority party chose the structure of agenda power and the majority's overall advantage has remained largely constant since the 1890s (a claim we defend at length). . . .

Who Gets the Agenda-Setting Offices?

A second question is whether the majority party sets up a procedure for select-ing the occupants of the agenda-setting offices that is likely to lead in principle, and does lead in practice, to its members winning most of the agenda-setting offices. The answer in practice is clear: the majority party secures all chairs, the speakership, and a super-proportional share of seats on the Rules Commit-tee. It also secures super-proportional shares on the major committees that enjoy privileged access to the floor and on conference committees (which also exercise special agenda-setting powers) (Cox and McCubbins 1993).

As for the procedures regulating access to the House's agenda-setting posts, they all include an initial stage in which each party decides on nominees for the various posts, followed by a choice between, or ratification of, the parties' nominees in the House. The choice of a speaker is largely unregulated, as this is the first vote in each Congress and occurs before the adoption of rules. The choice of all other agenda-setting posts—committee positions of various sorts—is regulated. In particular, since 1917 the procedure has been as fol-lows. First, the majority party informs the minority of how many seats each party will receive on each committee. Second, each party submits a slate specifying its nominees for its designated committee positions. Third, the two party slates are combined into a single resolution that is then voted up or down (since 1917 it has not been permissible to amend the slates on the floor). Given these procedures, it is not surprising that the majority party has never failed to secure a monopoly on chairs, the speakership, and a disproportion-ally large share of seats on the control and conference committees.[13]

Fiduciary Behavior of Officeholders

A third question is whether party members expect that party officeholders will exercise their official powers partly for the benefit of the party, rather than purely to pursue personal goals, and whether officeholders who do not act as expected are sanctioned in some way. Since agenda cartelization entails delegation of authority from party backbenchers to party leaders, carteliza-tion creates the possibility of mischief by party leaders (i.e., not serving the collective interests of the party). Much of the literature implicitly adopts a strict standard by which to judge when officeholders act in the interest of their party, according to which they must aid legislation favored by significant majorities of their party. For example, the well-known accounts of Judge Smith's tenure on the Rules Committee point out—quite accurately—that he frequently obstructed legislation desired by large portions of his own party, and they conclude from this that Smith was acting in pursuit of his own or his faction's interests, not his party's.

Delay or outright obstruction of bills that significant portions of one's party want to turn into "party issues" represents an agency loss, but it does not mean that the persons in question have utterly abandoned representing or serving their party. After all, the wets in Thatcher's government delayed and obstructed when they could, and many other examples of hard bargaining over tough issues in coalition governments involve such tactics. Are we to conclude from every instance of persistent obstruction by elements of the governing coalition that the coalition is entirely toothless?

We think that would be premature. There are less stringent standards that might serve as "lines in the sand" demarcating behavior that is minimally fiduciary from behavior that is treasonous. Here, we wish to characterize such a standard, one that we believe has been expected of officeholders in the House at least since the late nineteenth century. This standard focuses on crimes of commission—pushing legislation one's party mostly dislikes—not on crimes of omission—failing to aid (or actively blocking) legislation one's party mostly likes. Crimes of commission increase in seriousness (1) with the proportion of the party that dislikes it and (2) if the bill actually passes. As a specific benchmark, *we claim that officeholders are expected never to push bills that would pass despite the opposition of a majority of their party.* We call such an event—passage of a bill against the votes of a majority of a given party— a *roll* of that party. If the majority's officeholders are not held to even the minimal standard of not using their powers to roll their own party, then they do indeed look like nonpartisan figures willing (and able with impunity) to build shifting coalitions in support of their projects.

An example of a violator of our proposed standard is Representative Phil Gramm (D-TX) who, during the negotiations leading to the first Reagan budget, clearly used his position in a way intended to roll his own party. In this specific instance, Democratic party leaders branded Gramm's behavior as unconscionable after they discovered it and took quick actions to sanction him, including stripping him of the posts he had abused (Roberts 1983a).[14]

Other similar examples can be cited. In 1924, eight Republicans on the Rules Committee cooperated on the passage of a strengthened discharge procedure, which most majority party members opposed; six of them were removed from the committee in the next Congress (in which the offending rule was also eviscerated cf. Hasbrouck 1927: 163–4). In 1975, Chairman Richard Ichord of the Internal Security Committee, a longtime thorn in the side of liberal Democrats, found that the committee had essentially been disestablished, due largely to actions taken in the Democratic Caucus (Jacobs 1995). In all these cases, the majority party caucus essentially *denied renomination* to wayward officeholders. There was no House vote needed to ratify the majority's decision; moreover, it would have been difficult to reject those decisions in the House, given that each party's slate of committee nominations is unamendable under House rules. To the extent that threats to deny renomination are credible, they induce officeholders to abandon, or at least sweeten, bills that substantial portions of their party dislike.

Our position is that these anecdotes generalize. In any period of congressional history, an officeholder behaving as Gramm did would have met with comparable reactions. In any period, it would be common knowledge that the standard of "not conspiring, explicitly or implicitly, with the enemy to roll one's own party" would apply to officeholders and that violators of this standard could expect to lose their offices and/or face other sanctions.

Many in the congressional literature seem to believe that sanctions against officeholders, especially against committee chairs, were simply not feasible in the period from 1937 to 1960. If this were so, then one should expect that Southern Democrats in this period used their agenda powers with impunity to push bills that they and the Republicans agreed on. Such "conservative coalition" bills, moving policy rightward, would have provoked splits in committees chaired by Southerners—with Northern Democrats outvoted by a combination of Southern Democrats and Republicans. Moreover, such bills would easily have made it to the floor, with the help of a Rules Committee often seen as controlled by the conservative coalition in this period. Once on the floor, conservative coalition bills would have *both* split the majority party *and* passed. Passage would follow as long as the number of conservative Southern Democrats plus regular Republicans exceeded the number of Northern Democrats plus liberal Republicans. Put another way, as long as the policy being changed lay to the left of the House median, the conservative coalition would have outvoted a majority of the Democratic Party. We assess the impact of the conservative coalition in detail, and evaluate these predictions. . . . For now, suffice it to say that we do not find significant evidence of Southern Democrats defecting from their party and joining with Republicans to successfully push an agenda unpalatable to Northern Democrats.

Loyalty from the Rank and File

A final question is: how does a procedural cartel ensure that its rank-and-file members support the agenda-setting decisions of its officeholders, even though at least some members' short-term interests would be better served by voting against those decisions? A key to the answer is that votes taken on procedural decisions (e.g., a vote to ratify a special rule proposed by the Rules Committee or to sustain a decision rendered by the speaker) are more obscure to constituents than are ordinary substantive votes (cf. Froman and Ripley 1965). If a member votes for a bill her constituents oppose on final passage, she runs a clear risk. If she supports a special rule filled with arcane boilerplate that helps ensure the bill's success, she runs a smaller risk.[15] Thus, party pressures can affect members' decisions on procedure more than their decisions on substance, even though all legislators know that procedural motions directly affect substantive outcomes.[16]

Another key point is that the cartel does not need the loyalty of every member on every vote. Often, it needs only enough votes to snatch victory from the jaws of defeat on close and important votes (cf. King and Zeckhauser 2003). This is a much more limited and manageable task than enforcing some minimum standard of cohesion across the board, which some mistakenly take to be what any "partisan" model must predict.

Is there evidence that cartels in the U.S. House do demand loyalty? Alexander (1970 [1916]: 210) notes that, soon after Reed's elevation of the Rules Committee to its modern status, members chafed under the expectation that "one must support whatever the Rules Committee brought forward or become irregular." More recently, Republican Whip Tom DeLay (R-TX) has made the party's expectations regarding behavior on procedural motions clear to his freshmen (Burger 1995).

To buttress such anecdotal evidence that majority parties do expect loyalty on key procedural votes, one can also point to more systematic evidence that the majority party's rank and file support their officeholders' agenda-setting decisions, while minority party members oppose them. First, after the packing of the Rules Committee in 1961 (and especially after the procedural reforms of 1973), members have voted with their parties significantly more than would be expected on the basis of their left–right position on a wide range of procedural and organizational votes (Cox and Poole 2002).[17] Second, in the postreform Congress, majority party members have been prone to support special rules, even when they then vote against the bill in question, while minority party members have exhibited the opposite tendency (Sinclair 2002). Sinclair's interpretation of this evidence is that majority party members are supporting their leaders' agenda-setting decisions, even when they oppose the substance of the proposals aided by the special rule in question, while minority party members oppose the Rules Committee's resolutions, even when they support the measure being aided. Third, more evidence of parties' influence over their members' voting behavior is reviewed. . . .

In addition, party leaders reward party members' loyalty on key votes, and especially on "agenda votes" in which the leaders of the two parties take opposing positions.[18] More loyal members are more likely to be appointed to the most desirable committees and to have committee transfers granted than are less loyal party members (Cox and McCubbins 1993, Chapter 7).

In summary, majority party leaders make clear their expectations of loyalty on certain key procedural votes; there is evidence that party pressures are greater on such votes; and there is evidence that more loyal members get better committee assignments. These findings are all consistent with a picture in which majority party leaders both *expect* and *get* "loyalty on the margin," enough to make the difference between winning and losing on close votes (King and Zeckhauser 2003).

Nevertheless, it is the very costliness of enforcing discipline in the U.S. House that helps to explain why U.S. parties principally rely on controlling the legislative agenda to achieve their legislative goals. In the model of responsible party government (American Political Science Association 1950), parties ensure cohesive voting blocs through a combination of control over nominations and disciplining their members. U.S. parties, however, have relatively weak nominating powers. Similarly, discipline is weaker in the United States than in some other countries. This puts more emphasis on agenda control, or influencing the bills and motions on which members must vote, as the single most powerful mechanism by which legislative outcomes can be affected in the U.S. House. By using agenda control, the party can prevent votes on which its disciplinary abilities would be strained or broken.

What about Quitting the Party?

In the discussion of fiduciary behavior and loyalty . . . , we did not address the issue of why members of a cartel do not quit their party, join the other side, and form a new cartel (with a better share of the spoils for themselves). In particular, one might wonder why centrist members cannot extract a better deal. Why are not all the committee chairs centrists, for example? Alternatively, why are not centrist chairs free to exercise agenda power in any way they see fit, subject only to majoritarian and not specifically partisan constraints?

There are three points we would urge in answer to this line of inquiry. First, it is rare for a single member to be pivotal (Senator James Jeffords in May 2001 being the most notable exception). Typically several members must simultaneously switch parties in order to bring down the current cartel. Potential defectors must thus *coordinate*, not just in the sense of jumping at the same time but also in the sense of negotiating, *before* actually defecting, with their prospective new partners over the division of the spoils.[19]

Second, and more important, it is ex ante costly to switch parties. The Grenvillite faction in late eighteenth-century English politics could pivot freely, little constrained by electoral considerations, because they literally owned their seats. In the modern U.S. House, however, elections are partisan, and party labels count for a lot. When a member switches party labels, can he communicate that fact—and at what cost—to his constituents? How many voters in his former party will continue out of habit or loyalty to support that party? How many voters in the new party will remember that he used to be in the other party and refuse to support him on that ground? Among those voters who do learn of the member's switch, how many will view it as purely opportunistic, making the representative seem unreliable? Can he combat such ideas at low cost? How many names on the member's donor list will stop contributing? Who has been planning to run for the other party and how will they react to the incumbent's switch? All these questions about electoral ramifications—and more besides—would have to be considered by prospective defectors, at least if they are prudent.

Third, it is ex post costly to switch parties. Grose and Yoshinaka (2003) report "that incumbent legislators who switch parties have poorer showings after their switch in both general and primary election contests." Moreover, if one regresses the number of terms remaining in a legislator's career in

Congress t on her seniority (i.e., the number of terms already served through Congress t) and a dummy variable equal to 1 if the member switched parties in Congress t, one finds the switched party dummy variable to have a statistically significant coefficient of roughly –3. In other words, by one crude estimate, the cost of switching parties is three fewer terms in the House than would otherwise be expected, given a member's current seniority.[20]

These various costs help explain why actual party switching has been rare in the House and Senate. To the extent that the exogenous electoral costs of switching are large, moreover, it would follow that the threat of switching parties would not be as effective as it would be in a pure spatial representation of politics.

CONCLUSION

. . . [W]e have laid out the main assumptions underpinning our theory of legislative parties. In our view, U.S. legislators seek not just reelection but also advancement in the internal hierarchy of posts within the House, good public policy, and majority status for their parties. Their parties compete in mass elections, as business firms compete in mass markets, by developing brand names. The value of a party's brand name depends on its legislative record of accomplishment. Thus, a key problem for majority parties is to manage the legislative process, in order to secure the best possible record, hence contributing to the best possible reputation.

This much was already evident in our original exploration of congressional organization, *Legislative Leviathan*. In this reading, we develop several additional themes.

First, we portray agenda control as the key to the majority party's influence over the legislative process. In the responsible party government model, the primary mechanisms by which a party overcomes collective action problems, so that it can enact a program, are screening candidates and disciplining legislators. In the U.S. context, however, both screening and discipline are—although utilized to some extent—relatively costly. This raises the importance of a third technique to manage conflicts between collective and individual goals; controlling the agenda so that the sharpest conflicts are never even considered on the floor.

How does a legislative majority party work to control the agenda? The mechanism is similar to that portrayed in *Legislative Leviathan*. Certain members of the party—whom we have here dubbed the "senior partners"—are given valuable offices wielding substantial agenda-setting powers. In order to secure their party's (re)nomination for these offices, senior partners are expected to obey a minimal commandment of party loyalty—namely, not using their official powers in order to promote bills that will, if considered on the floor, lead to serious splits in the party (operationalized as *rolls* in the coming chapters). The rank and file, meanwhile, are also expected to obey a minimal commandment of party loyalty—namely, supporting their officeholders' agenda-setting decisions, especially on the more procedurally arcane (yet substantively critical) votes. Their incentive to support such procedural maneuvers is the prospect of better internal advancement and a greater chance of majority status for the party as a whole.

Analogizing parties to partnerships is our second main point of departure from *Legislative Leviathan,* where we more often focused on the speaker and the top few leaders rather than the entire set of party members holding agenda-setting offices. Law and accountancy partnerships are designed to allow their senior partners considerable autonomy. By stressing the analogy to a partnership and the importance of agenda power, our approach naturally raises the question of how specific agenda powers are distributed among senior partners.

There are many theoretical possibilities, such as allocating *all* agenda power to the top party leader, allocating proposal power(s) to various senior partners, or allocating veto power(s) to various senior partners. We have argued that, whatever the details of agenda-power allocation, all majority parties in the U.S. House since adoption of Reed's Rules have structured agenda power in such a way that it is very difficult to roll them.

Closely related to the issue of what powers are distributed to which senior partners is the question of what standards of behavior those partners are expected to uphold. At one theoretical extreme, senior partners may have no fiduciary responsibilities to their parties. Agenda power is clearly allocated in these models but officeholders are then free to act in pursuit of their own interests, with neither formal checks (e.g., the necessity of securing their party's renomination) nor informal norms to constrain them. At the other theoretical extreme, senior partners may be expected completely to subordinate their personal goals to the party's. This is implicitly the case, for example, in Ranney's (1951) or the American Political Science Association's (1950) portrayal of responsible party government. Agenda power is not mentioned in such models, but officeholders are clearly enjoined to marshal their parties behind a coherent party platform.

We have opted for a theoretical middle ground of sorts, in which the norm to which senior partners are held depends on the internal homogeneity of the party. If the party is extremely heterogeneous (perhaps similar to a multiparty coalition government in other countries), then only a minimal standard can be realistically enforced: that of not using one's official powers to push legislation that will roll the party. As the party becomes more homogeneous, its senior partners are held to a higher standard, in which they must also use their official posts to help push legislation that most in the party support. Thus, for example, Jamie Whitten (D-MI) continued as chair of the powerful Appropriations Committee in the 1970s because he considerably increased his willingness to cooperate with the party leadership in pushing through Democratic priorities, even those he personally found distasteful (Crook and Hibbing 1985).

Why does the fiduciary standard become higher for more homogeneous parties? This prediction is entailed by our theory because procedural cartels, as we describe them, primarily distribute veto power among the senior partners of the party. Distributing veto power necessarily interferes with pushing through an ambitious program of legislation, as each senior partner with a veto in a particular policy area has to be brought on board. Thus, the ability of a procedural cartel to legislate necessarily depends on how similar their senior partners' preferences are.

Even when a majority's senior partners disagree on a wide range of issues, however, it becomes no easier to roll the majority party (i.e., pass bills that most majority party members dislike) because some senior partner or partners with relevant veto power will derail the bill. Thus, even internally divided majority parties do not surrender their *negative* agenda-setting power. They simply avoid bills that cannot be passed and move on to bills that can be passed, which tend to be less ideological and more porcine. The minority benefits from the internal divisions of the majority, in the sense that the bills the senior partners can agree on are less likely to have a clear ideological bite to them, hence less likely to roll the minority. But the minority is no more successful in dismantling the majority's previous accomplishments than before. Nor does it benefit by receiving a larger share of chairs, of staff, or of pork.

Because negative agenda power is the bedrock and "first story" of party government, in our view, most of this reading considers the consequences of such power. We return to the "second story" of party government, and discuss when a majority party might wish to build up such a story by readjusting the mix of positive and negative agenda power.

NOTES

1. Quoted in Babington (2004).

2. We did not there formally incorporate the third of Fenno's (1973) famous trio of goals: the pursuit of good public policy. . . . [H]owever, we adapt the standard spatial model of policy making for much of our argument, and this model is sufficiently abstract so that one can easily read personal policy goals into it. Thus, one can add the pursuit of policy as one of the goals that is consistent with the model we present here—although we do not insist on that interpretation.

3. As an example of the importance of majority status for members' legislative projects, consider the statements that Representative Ralph Hall made as he switched from being a member of the Democratic minority to being a member of the Republican majority: "This is the first time, I've just been zeroed out [by the Appropriations Committee]. . . . I've always said that if being a Democrat hurt my district, I'd either resign, retire or switch parties. . . . And it hurt my district this time [because I was denied funds]" (Wolf 2004).

4. Alternatively, of course, a bill can be vetoed, and the veto can be overridden by two thirds of both houses.

5. Among the other solutions suggested in the literature are preplay communication, repeated play, and property rights (Tirole 1988; Friedman 1971).

6. Describing the authority associated with party leadership, Dennis Hastert stated, "So I have two functions. One is governmental, the other political. The governmental function is to run the House, move legislation through, make sure the chairmen and the committees are all operating smoothly.... The other function is political. I have to recruit the best possible candidates for Congress and make sure they have the financial and other resources they need to run or, if they're already in Congress, to make sure they have enough to stave off potential challengers" (Hastert 2004: 181–2).

7. Speaker Dennis Hastert clearly recognized the importance of majority status and being in good standing with his party. He emphasized, "Stripped to its essentials, my job is to run the House and make sure we [Republicans] hold the House" (Hastert 2004: 181).

8. Although the speakership is a constitutional office, its agenda-setting powers, as well as those of the other offices mentioned, are stipulated in House rules and precedents. The cartel controls the allocation of agenda power to the various offices to the extent that it can control votes on the adoption of rules.

9. In the United States, the cartel ensures a near-monopoly on agenda-setting offices to the extent that it can control the relevant votes on the floor (on election of the speaker and appointment of committees). To aid in controlling these floor votes, the cartel establishes an intracartel procedure to decide on the nominee for speaker and on a slate of committee appointments.

10. The role of the majority party has also been analogized to former Soviet Congresses. Indeed, as Hastert (2004: 250) notes, "Representative David Obey . . . compares the way the House is run today to 'the old Soviet Congresses—stamp of approval and ratify' rather than using your own judgment. Well, Obey was here when Democrats ran the place. . . . Talk about rubber stamps and domination by a party that had lots of votes and squish room. They were ruthless. They did things like the old Soviet Congresses, such as removing offenders from their hideaway offices, grabbing their office furniture, and taking their parking spots away."

11. A "special rule" is a resolution reported by the Rules Committee that regulates the consideration of a bill or resolution.

12. We are talking here about the powers of the Rules Committee, not its membership.

13. Decrying this monopoly power of the majority party, Dennis Hastert stated, "The truth is that since the last time we had a majority in 1954 only one Republican, Missouri's Bill Emerson, had ever stood on the House Floor—and he stood there as a page. We [the Republicans] had been in the wilderness so long that nobody remembered anything about being in the leadership. We didn't even know where the special back rooms were; we didn't even know where the *keys* to those rooms were" (Hastert 2004: 118).

14. A number of his coconspirators, the so-called Boll Weevils, were also punished by then-Speaker Tip O'Neill. For example, John Breaux of Louisiana and Roy Dyson of Maryland failed to win spots on the Budget and Appropriations committees, respectively (Roberts 1983a). In Breaux's place, the Democratic Party awarded the Budget Committee position to Martin Frost, a Texas Democrat who had "proven himself to be a national Democrat" (Roberts 1983b). Although G. V. Montgomery of Mississippi was reelected chairman of Veterans' Affairs, he lost 53 votes in the party caucus and remarked that conservatives would henceforth likely be more cooperative with their party leaders in Congress (Roberts 1983a).

15. In Arnold's (1990) terms, procedural votes are less "traceable."

16. Nokken's (2004) analysis demonstrates that departing members of Congress in lame duck sessions increasingly vote with their party (as opposed to their constituency). The explanation for this phenomenon is that when constituency constraints are severed (as they are in this situation), members vote with their party in hopes that the party will reward them for their loyalty by aiding them in their future career moves.

17. Quantitatively, Cox and Poole estimate about five to 10 votes switching on key procedural votes, which is consistent with qualitative evidence regarding vest pocket votes.

18. Loyalty is always important in committee assignments, but during times of high homogeneity within the majority party, there may be an increased premium placed on legislative competence. High levels of intraparty homogeneity decrease the relative importance of high loyalty and increase the importance of competence (Wawro 2000, Crook and Hibbing 1985).

19. The Jeffords case is informative here, as it demonstrates the costs of negotiating a defection. The Democrats gave Senator Jeffords the chairmanship of the Environment and Public Works Committee as an inducement to switch parties, which required Harry Reid to give up his status as the ranking Democrat on the committee (Lancaster 2001).

20. The analysis covers only the 80th through 100th Congresses. It is a crude estimate for two main reasons. First, the (negative) correlation between whether a member switches parties and how long that member continues in the House may be only partly due to switching being bad per se. Perhaps members who switched had very poor electoral prospects, had they remained in their parties, and switched for this reason. So far as we know, however, there is no systematic evidence that party switchers did face greater electoral risks than the typical nonswitching member. Indeed, Ansolabehere, Snyder, and Stewart (2001) find qualitative evidence that discomfort with being ideological misfits accounts for legislators' switching; however, Castle and Fett (2000: 236–7) find that switching is more likely the more ideologically out of step a member is with his copartisans, controlling for a measure of primary electoral risk. Second, our data do not include the full number of terms served by members whose careers continue past the 100th Congress. For these members, the number of terms remaining is coded as zero. As there were no members who switched parties in the 100th Congress, this defect of the data biases our estimate of the cost of switching downward. In other words, if we knew the correct total terms remaining for all members whose careers reached the 100th Congress, the difference between switchers and nonswitchers would be even larger than we report here.

BIBLIOGRAPHY

Alchian, Armen, and Harold Demsetz. 1972. "Production, Information Costs, and Economic Organization." *The American Economic Review* 62: 777–95.

Aldrich, John H. 1995. *Why Parties? The Origin and Transformation of Party Politics in America.* Chicago: University of Chicago Press.

Aldrich, John H., and David W. Rohde. 2001. "The Logic of Conditional Party Government." In *Congress Reconsidered*, 7th ed., eds. Lawrence C. Dodd and Bruce I. Oppenheimer, 269–92. Washington, DC: Congressional Quarterly.

Alexander, DeAlva Stanwood. 1970 [1916]. *History and Procedure of the House of Representatives.* New York: Houghton Mifflin Company.

American Political Science Association. 1950. *Toward a More Responsible Party System: A Report*. New York: Rinehart.

Ansolabehere, Stephen, James Snyder, and Charles Stewart. 2001. "The Effects of Party and Preferences on Congressional Roll-Call Voting." *Legislative Studies Quarterly* 26: 533–72.

Arnold, R. Douglas. 1990. *The Logic of Congressional Action*. New Haven, CT: Yale University Press.

Babington, Charles. 2004. "Hastert Launches a Partisan Policy." Downloaded 11/27/04 from: www.washingtonpost.com.

Burger, Timothy. 1995. "After a Defeat, House Leaders Must Regroup." *Roll Call*, July 17.

Castle, David, and Patrick Fett. 2000. "Member Goals and Party Switching in the U.S. Congress." In *Congress on Display, Congress at Work*, ed. William T. Bianco, 231–42. Ann Arbor: University of Michigan Press.

Cox, Gary W., and Mathew D. McCubbins. 1993. *Legislative Leviathan: Party Government in the House*. Berkeley: University of California Press.

———. 2002. "Agenda Power in the U.S. House of Representatives, 1877 to 1986." In *Party, Process, and Political Change in Congress: New Perspectives on the History of Congress*, eds. David Brady and Mathew D. McCubbins. Stanford, CA: Stanford University Press.

Cox, Gary W., and Keith T. Poole. 2002. "On Measuring Partisanship in Roll-Call Voting: The U.S. House of Representatives, 1877–1999." *American Journal of Political Science* 46: 477–89.

Crook, Sara Brandes, and John R. Hibbing. 1985. "Congressional Reform and Party Discipline: The Effects of Changes in the Seniority System on Party Loyalty in the U.S. House of Representatives." *British Journal of Political Science* 15: 207–26.

Diermeier, Daniel, and Timothy J. Feddersen. 1998. "Cohesion in Legislatures and the Vote of Confidence Procedure." *American Political Science Review* 92: 611–21.

Fenno, Richard F. 1973. *Congressmen in Committees*. Boston: Little, Brown.

Friedman, James. 1971. "A Non-cooperative Equilibrium for Supergames." *Review of Economic Studies* 38: 1–12.

Froman, Lewis A., Jr., and Randall B. Ripley. 1965. "Conditions for Party Leadership: The Case of the House Democrats." *American Political Science Review* 59: 52–63.

Grose, Christian, and Antoine Yoshinaka. 2003. "The Electoral Consequences of Party Switching by Incumbent Members of Congress, Incumbent Legislators Who Switched Parties, 1947–2000." *Legislative Studies Quarterly* 27(1): 55–75.

Hasbrouck, Paul DeWitt. 1927. *Party Government in the House of Representatives*. New York: Macmillan.

Hastert, Dennis. 2004. *Speaker: Lessons from Forty Years in Coaching and Politics*. Washington, DC: Regnery.

Jacobs, John. 1995. *A Rage for Justice*. Berkeley: University of California Press.

Jacobson, Gary C. 1996. "The 1994 House Elections in Perspective." *Political Science Quarterly* 111: 203–23.

Key, V. O. 1966. *The Responsible Electorate*. Cambridge, MA: Harvard University Press.

King, David C., and Richard Zeckhauser. 2003. "Congressional Vote Options." *Legislative Studies Quarterly* 28: 387–411.

Lancaster, John. 2001. "Senate Republicans Try to Regroup: GOP Caucus Unites Behind Lott as Leader in the Wake of Jeffords's Defection," *The Washington Post*, May 26, p. A.18

Laver, Michael, and Kenneth A. Shepsle. 1996. *Making and Breaking Governments: Cabinets and Legislatures in Parliamentary Democracies*. Cambridge and New York: Cambridge University Press.

Nokken, Timothy P. 2004. "Roll Call Behavior in the Absence of Electoral Constraints: Shirking in Lame Duck Sessions of the House of Representatives, 1879–1933." Unpublished paper.

Ranney, Austin. 1951. "Toward A More Responsible Two-Party System: A Commentary." *American Political Science Review* 45: 488–99.

Roberts, Steven V. 1983a. "The Democrats Get Even." *New York Times*, January 9, p. E1.

———. 1983b. "Democrats Reward Loyalty in Giving Assignments," *New York Times*, January 6, p. A25.

Rohde, David W. 1991. *Parties and Leaders in the Postreform House*. Chicago: University of Chicago Press.

Sinclair, Barbara. 2002. "Do Parties Matter?" In *Party, Process, and Political Change: New Perspectives on the History of Congress*, eds. David Brady and Mathew D. McCubbins, 36–63. Stanford, CA: Stanford University Press.

Tirole, Jean. 1988. *The Theory of Industrial Organization*. Cambridge, MA: MIT Press.

Tsebelis, George. 2002. *Veto Players: How Political Institutions Work*. Princeton, NJ: Princeton University Press.

Wawro, Gregory. 2000. *Legislative Entrepreneurship in the U.S. House of Representatives*. Ann Arbor: University of Michigan Press.

Wolf, Jim. 2004. "Veteran Texas Democrat Switches to Republicans." Washington, DC: Reuters.

5.4

JUSTIN GRIMMER, SEAN WESTWOOD, AND SOLOMON MESSING

From *The Impression of Influence: Legislator Communication, Representation, and Democratic Accountability*

In this extensive study, researchers Grimmer, Westwood, and Messing analyzed words used by members of the House of Representatives in hundreds of thousands of press releases to claim credit for national government spending in their electoral districts. Approximately 20 percent of all press releases by members of the lower house of Congress mention some kind of federal spending in their district, with the member taking some credit. There is, however, considerable variation across representatives in this credit-claiming behavior, and evidence shows that at key moments following a Democratic-led fiscal stimulus, Republicans stopped taking credit and started criticizing government spending overall.

HOW LEGISLATORS CREATE AN IMPRESSION OF INFLUENCE

A long time Democratic member of Congress, Bart Stupak has strong incentives to cultivate an impression of influence over spending. This is partly because of his district's demographics. As industry has fled northern Michigan, Stupak's working class district has become increasingly reliant on federal investments to sustain the few jobs that remain. It is also because Stupak represents a swing district: in 2000 and 2004 it voted for George W. Bush, but in 2008 the district narrowly swung to Barack Obama. To win reelection Stupak needs a personal vote—that is, support not based on partisan affiliation or ideological positions—to win over both political independents and moderate Republicans.

Stupak creates an impression of influence, in part, by making regular appearances at new federal projects in the district. For example, he was on Mackinac Island on May 31, 2008 to participate in a groundbreaking ceremony for a new hospital. At the ceremony, Stupak praised the federal investment in the hospital asserting that it was "a vast improvement on the old facility."[1] Stupak's office also regularly issued press releases claiming credit

From Justin Grimmer, Sean Westwood, and Solomon Messing, *The Impression of Influence: Legislator Communication, Representation, and Democratic Accountability* (Princeton, NJ: Princeton University Press, 2015).

for federal projects in the district. One press release "announced that the U.S. Department of Agriculture's (USDA) Rural Development fund has approved a loan of $440,000 to Calumet Township for improvements to the Township's wastewater system."[2] In a different press release Stupak "announced [that] Northern Michigan University in Marquette has received $673,462 for the university's Electrical Power Technician job training program."[3] And in another he "announced three grants totaling $80,000 for the cities of Beaverton and Gladwin to purchase vehicles for public safety."[4] In still another statement Stupak asserted that he "was able to secure $3.4 million for a wide variety of vital projects for northern Michigan communities and facilities" in an Appropriations bill.[5] His office's credit claiming efforts translated into local news coverage. One story broadcasted that Stupak announced "$750,000 grant . . . award to Central Michigan University."[6] Another story explained how "the city of Gladwin has received two grants totaling $65,000 to assist local businesses" and included a quote from Stupak who explained that "we must do everything we can to help create and save jobs in our communities."[7]

Stupak uses the press releases to cultivate an impression among constituents that he is influential in delivering money to the district. And the hope is that this impression of influence will lead to electoral support. . . . Stupak's strategic response to his district reflects a broader pattern in who claims credit for spending and what projects they claim credit for obtaining. Legislators' incentives to cultivate an impression of influence vary across districts and, therefore, so too does their credit claiming behavior. The incentive to credit claim can arise from district demographics—such as median income or level of education—and from the partisan composition of the district.

We also demonstrate what legislators claim credit for securing. Legislators do claim credit for spending that actually occurs in the district and cut ribbons at new facilities. But they also claim credit for action taken throughout the appropriations process that are far removed from actual expenditures—including requesting that expenditures be included in spending bills. Legislators also claim credit broadly. Not only do they tout earmarks secured during the appropriations process, they also claim credit for grants allocated by executive agencies, where legislators have only indirect influence. And we show that legislators tend to announce relatively small grants. In some instances legislators tend to announce expenditures that are as small as $1,000. More typical expenditures are only slightly larger, with the usual expenditure announced providing only pennies per capita in the district.

. . . Communication is essential for understanding how representation occurs around spending and why actual spending and projects in a district provide only an incomplete picture of how legislators use particularistic projects to cultivate a personal vote. This picture is incomplete, in part, because legislators differ in how closely they strive to be associated with spending.[8] Some legislators work hard to be closely associated with projects. Other legislators avoid an association with spending projects and instead focus on policy work. It is also incomplete because legislators claim credit for projects long before they reach the district and even when the chance of the spending actually occurring in the district is small. As a result, the credit that legislators receive does not necessarily have a strong relationship to the actual levels of spending or the actual number of new projects. . . . A strong relationship between money and credit is not necessary for more effective representation.

To demonstrate how legislators use the spending process to create an impression of influence we analyze a new and large collection of House press releases—every press release, from each House office, from 2005 to 2010. This collection is comprised of nearly 170,000 press releases. To analyze the abundance of text, we make use of statistical tools applied to text, which facilitate efficient analysis of extremely large text collections.[9] Applying these tools, we measure how often legislators claim credit for spending and what legislators claim credit for delivering to the district. With the measures of legislators' credit claiming behavior in hand, we provide comprehensive evidence of how legislators create an impression of influence.

Before examining evidence of legislators' credit claiming, however, we want to emphasize that this chapter is not intended to demonstrate the causal effect of various district characteristics on legislators' rhetorical choices. Like many other studies of how legislators engage constituents, we lack a strong identification strategy to examine how district characteristics alter legislators' strategies.[10] Measuring causal effects is all the more challenging because we analyze several facets of district demand each of which are intertwined, with some features being causal consequences of others. Rather than provide causal estimates of the effect of district characteristics or institutional activities on credit claiming frequency, we instead document the systematic relationship between characteristics of districts and legislators' strategies. While the simple comparisons that we make in this chapter are insufficient to establish the causal effect of district characteristics on legislators' strategies, they are sufficient to establish an important descriptive fact: legislators who represent different types of districts adopt different types of strategies.[11] And building on this descriptive fact in subsequent chapters, we use a series of experiments to demonstrate the causal effect of legislators' credit claiming statements on constituent credit allocation and the personal vote.

Measuring Legislators' Credit Claiming Propensity

To measure how legislators cultivate an impression of influence we use an original collection of congressional press releases. Press releases may seem an odd choice for analyzing congressional communication, but there is growing evidence that press releases provide a reliable source for studying how members of Congress communicate with constituents. Using a collection of Senate press releases, Grimmer[12] shows that press releases broadly reflect senators' priorities in Washington and that the content of press releases [is] likely to reach constituents. Press releases commonly affect the content of newspaper stories and are sometimes run verbatim in local papers.

Press releases are also a medium in which legislators regularly claim credit for spending. Press releases can be issued on any day and on any topic and are thus particularly useful for legislators who may want to announce a new grant or expenditure. Floor speeches are less useful for studying credit claiming because legislators rarely claim credit for money on the House or Senate floor.[13] Newsletters are another potentially useful source for studying how members of Congress claim credit for spending.[14] The prominence of franked mail makes it a potentially useful place for legislators to cultivate support with constituents, but only a few newsletters are sent each year so they are unable to reflect legislators' broader credit claiming efforts.[15]

One of the virtues of press releases is that they are plentiful and therefore likely to capture how members of Congress cultivate a relationship with constituents. But this virtue is also a problem, because the abundance of text makes analyzing the corpus of press releases costly. The vast number of these press releases render an individual analysis and classification of each item practically impossible. Simply reading and attaching a label to each press release would be an immense task. Even at the extremely fast rate of one press release read every two minutes, classifying all the documents three times would require over 16,800 hours of a coder's labor.

The usual alternatives are not ideal for studying how members of Congress cultivate support. Scholars of congressional communication commonly analyze only a small sample of legislators,[16] but the small samples often make it difficult to detect relationships that are present among all members of Congress. Further, the specific samples usually include only behavior from a particular year[17] or particular set of policy debates.[18] The small samples provide valuable insights from the time periods studied, but are inappropriate for reaching more general conclusions.

Rather than rely on only a sub-sample of press releases, we analyze the entire collection of press releases using computational methods that ease the cost of analysis.[19] We make use of supervised learning methods to efficiently classify the content of our press releases.[20] Supervised learning methods begin like traditional manual content analysis. The first step is to manually classify a sample of the press releases. But then the sample of press releases are used to train—or supervise—statistical algorithms that classify the remaining documents. The end product is a set of labeled documents that, if the classification is performed accurately, allow us to analyze the entire collection of press releases as if they were hand labeled.

To classify the press releases we began with a four part coding scheme, developed from the classic typology of congressional action advanced in Mayhew[21] and then refined with our team of three coders. To refine our scheme we made two pilot attempts at coding documents. We used an existing coding scheme, assigned our coders to classify a set of documents, and then met with the coders to diagnose ambiguity and to clarify disagreements. After two rounds, agreement improved substantially and we settled on our final coding scheme. All the press releases that we use to train our models were labeled *after* we settled on a coding scheme, ensuring we are not artificially inflating our agreement rates.

The first category in our coding scheme—the target category—is for *credit claiming* press releases. Building on the definition of credit claiming advanced in Mayhew,[22] we define a credit claiming press release as one that explicitly announces an expenditure targeted to the district. Credit claiming includes tax expenditures—that is, tax breaks that are targeted at particular districts. Because we are interested in *particularistic* expenditures, we exclude expenditures that are national in scope, such as a legislator discussing spending on a war. The focus on district categories ensures that our study of legislators' credit claiming aligns with the type of district-level spending that comprises a large literature on how legislators use spending to cultivate support.[23]

The second category describes *egregious-earmark* press releases. These press releases discuss earmarks and particularistic spending, but criticize such legislation rather than claim credit for it. Disaggregating this category in our coding protocol helps ensure that our classifier distinguishes these linguistically similar press releases. The vast majority of the egregious-earmark press releases come from Jeff Flake (R-AZ), a conservative legislator known for his opposition to government spending projects. In a similar style to William Proxmire's Golden Fleece awards, Flake used creative messages to highlight spending he viewed as inappropriate. One press release criticized spending aimed at addressing abandoned mines. In it, Flake stated that "With this earmark, taxpayers are quite literally getting the shaft."[24]

The remaining categories describe other types of messages that have little relationship with spending. Our third category comprises *advertising* press releases and press releases that honor the achievements of local constituents . . . Press releases in this category commonly include those announcing winners of congressional art contests or announcing nominations for the service academies. The fourth category [is] *position taking* press releases. This category includes press releases in which a legislator touts a position on a prominent policy debate, claims credit for passing legislation that does not fall into the previous categories, or explicitly attacks the other party.

With this coding scheme, we asked our team of three coders to classify 800 sampled press releases—a number that we chose to balance the accuracy of our statistical models against the cost of hand coding documents.[25] Our coders displayed extremely high accuracy. Across all documents, at least one pair of coders agreed on 98% of documents and all three coders agreed 68% of the time. Agreement is even higher if we focus on just the credit claiming press releases—with all three coders agreeing 87% on whether a press release claims credit for an expenditure or not. Across categories we have an extremely high level of agreement, with a Krippendorff's Alpha of 0.66.

A further indication of our coders' reliability is that words that we expect to be associated with credit claiming messages are much more likely to occur in press releases that our coders labeled as credit claiming. The words that best distinguish credit claiming documents are: funding, million, announces, grant, funds, department, project, secured. As we will see below, each of these words is regularly used when legislators cultivate an impression of influence over spending that occurs in the district.[26]

Because we primarily focus on understanding credit claiming behavior, we use the hand labels to identify whether each press release claims credit or not. To train the statistical models, we first need to reconcile the three labels from our hand coders. Given the extremely high agreement, we used a voting procedure to determine each document's label and the modal code for each document is the final label.

With an accurate sample of hand-labeled documents, we are ready to train statistical models to classify all the remaining press releases. To classify all of the nearly 170,000 press releases from this relatively small sample of hand-coded documents we use an ensemble classifier, which combines a collection of prediction methods to predict whether each document is claiming credit. Ensemble methods are increasingly used in machine learning tasks.[27] This is because ensemble classifiers usually improve accuracy, while also making predictions more stable. Ensemble classifiers also facilitate learning about more complicated functional forms than any one of the constituent methods of the ensemble. We include five methods in our ensemble: a support vector machine (SVM), LASSO,[28] elastic net,[29] random forests, and Kernal Regularized Least Squares (KRLS).[30] Our ensemble of classifiers weights methods according to their predictive accuracy, which we assess using a cross-validation procedure.[31] The ensemble method attached weight to three of the constituent methods: 61% of the weight was given to random forest, 23% to elastic net, and 16% to SVM.

This ensemble method is accurate and is able to achieve very reliable, individually coded documents.[32] We assess the performance of our ensemble method by replicating our classification task using cross-validation.[33] We create our entire ensemble for a subset of hand-coded documents and then use the ensemble to classify the held-out, hand-coded documents. This method allows us to test the performance of our model against the "gold standard" of hand-labeled documents. It also demonstrates that the ensemble method is able to accurately replicate hand coding: 90% of our out-of-sample classifications agreed with the hand coders. Given that a document is credit claiming, we identified it at a high rate (67%) and given that we made a prediction that a document was credit claiming, it was very likely to actually be credit claiming (85%).[34]

Given this high accuracy rate, we trained our ensemble of classifiers on the full sample of hand coded press releases and applied it to our collection of 169,779 press releases. The product is that each press release is labeled as credit claiming or not. This reveals a relatively high rate of overall credit claiming—20.3% of all the press releases—over 34,000 press releases—are labeled as credit claiming press releases. This is in line with prior estimates of credit claiming in work on Senate press releases over a similar time period.[35]

The labeled documents are useful on their own, but our primary interest is in assessing legislators' credit claiming rate. We characterize the legislators' credit claiming rate with the proportion of press releases each legislator, in each year, allocated to credit claiming.[36] The simplest estimate of this proportion would just count the total number of a legislator's press releases that are credit claiming in a year and then divide by the total number of press releases from that year. But some House members issue only a few press releases in a year, causing the estimated proportion to be highly variable.[37] We introduce a small amount of smoothing—determined in a multilevel model—to obtain a less variable estimate of legislators' propensity to credit claiming (and to decrease the mean square error of our estimate of the credit claiming rate).[38] The smoothed estimates still provide accurate assessments of the proportion of press releases legislators dedicate to credit claiming. But (heuristically), they also ensure that we provide accurate predictions of future performance, not extreme predictions based on too few documents analyzed.

After smoothing, we now have a measure of the proportion of press releases from each representative in each year that claim credit for expenditures in the district.

Strategic Credit Claiming Rates

Using our measures of credit claiming, we characterize how often legislators claim credit for expenditures. Figure [1] summarizes the distribution of credit claiming propensities in the House of Representatives from 2005 to 2010. The density plot shows the substantial variation in how often legislators use credit claiming in their press releases and provides further face validity to our measures of credit claiming propensity. At one end of the extreme is Dan Burton (R-IN), who allocated only 0.5% of his press releases to credit claiming in 2008. Burton had strong electoral incentives to avoid credit claiming. He is a prominent conservative Republican who represents a heavily Republican district in central Indiana. In 2008, Burton faced a difficult challenge from John McGoff. McGoff alleged that Burton failed to fight against earmarks and pork, and that Burton's actions "are not the actions of a fiscally conservative congressman who cares about personal responsibility."[39] Mike Pence (R-IN) and Nancy Pelosi (D-CA) also allocated a similarly small share of their press releases to credit claiming, reflecting their pursuit of higher office and Washington activities. Pence (R-IN), who was chairman of the Republican Conference, worked to cultivate a reputation as a staunch fiscal conservative who supported earmark reform and successfully ran for governor of Indiana in 2012. Pelosi (D-CA) was minority leader in 2005 and 2006 and Speaker from 2007 to 2010, leading her to focus her attention on policy, with less space allocated to claiming credit for money spent in her district.

Moving along the distribution, we find legislators who allocate a larger share of their press releases to credit claiming. Bart Stupak, for example, allocates about a quarter of his press releases to credit claiming. More marginal Democrats—such as Chet Edwards (D-TX) and Rick Boucher (D-VA)—allocate an even larger share of their press releases to credit claiming statements. More marginal Republicans—such as Frank LoBiondo (R-NJ)—also allocate a larger share of their press releases to credit claiming in order to cultivate support with independents and even some Democrats.

And at the opposite extreme from Dan Burton is Hal Rogers (R-KY), who used 80.7% of his press releases in 2008 to claim credit for spending. Rogers, who has served on the Appropriations committee for nearly 30 years, was described in a *Washington Times* profile as using "his seat on the Appropriations Committee to protect one of his district's most important economic engines."[40] Rogers represents one of the poorest districts in the country, a rural district in Eastern Kentucky with few industries. Many of the industries that are in his district rely on federal contracts to stay open. And Rogers is not particularly ideological. He once remarked to his colleagues that "we can't afford a luxury like ideology." Perhaps it is not surprising that a *Lexington Herald-Leader* profile of Rogers proclaims that he is the "prince of pork."[41] Between the extreme examples of Dan Burton and Hal Rogers, representatives adopt distinctive strategies for associating themselves with spending in the dis-

FIGURE [1]   Substantial Variation in Credit Claiming Propensity

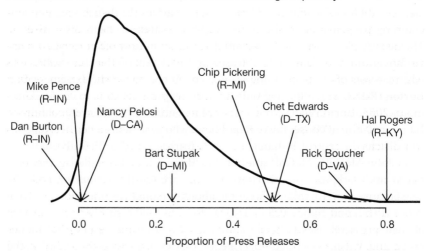

NOTE: This figure shows the substantial variability in credit claiming propensity across House members, as measured in the propartion of press releases that claim credit for spending.

trict. We now examine how characteristics of the district—and legislators' experience in Washington—covary with where legislators fall on this distribution.

The variation in legislators' credit claiming propensity is strategic and determined in part by a consideration of how legislators can cultivate support among constituents.[42] The decision calculus is straightforward: legislators tend to use credit claiming more often when it is valuable to them electorally and when alternative strategies are likely to be less effective. District demand for spending partially determines the value of claiming credit: when there is a greater need for spending there is likely a greater return on credit claiming efforts. Median district income will partially affect this perceived demand. Residents of low-income districts, like Stupak's Michigan district or Hal Rogers' Kentucky district, are more reliant on federal spending to build new infrastructure, to continue providing public services, and to create jobs.

The top plot in Figure [2] shows that legislators from low-income districts tend to claim credit more often than their colleagues who represent wealthier districts. In Figure [2] we plot the proportion of legislators' press releases allocated to credit claiming against median district income. We summarize the relationship with a simple nonparametric regression,[43] with cross-validation determining the amount of smoothing. The thick line in the top plot of Figure [2] summarizes the relationship between proportion of press releases allocated to credit claiming and median district income, while the gray band is a 95 percent confidence envelope.

This plot shows that representatives of the poorest districts consistently make the case that they exercise influence over the Appropriations process and deliver money to the district. And the expected proportion of press releases allocated to credit claiming decreases as the median district income increases, with the relationship relatively flat for higher levels of income. The nonparametric regression clearly shows that representatives of the poorest districts claim credit at a higher rate than other legislators. A simple parametric comparison provides a clear sense of the magnitude of this difference. Legislators who represent districts in the lowest quartile of income—districts with median incomes below $39,000—claim credit for spending in 4.6 percentage points more of their press releases than other representatives (95 percent confidence interval, [0.02, 0.07]) and 6.5 percentage points more than the representatives in the richest districts (95 percent confidence intervals, [0.04, 0.09]).

The bottom plot in Figure [2] shows a similar relationship with district education. Higher levels of education are obviously correlated with income and may also indicate that residents have different, more ideological, priorities. The horizontal axis has our measure of district education—the proportion of district constituents over 25 who hold a Bachelor's degree—and we place legislators' credit claiming rate on the vertical axis. Legislators' who represent well-educated districts allocate substantially less space to claiming credit for money. A seven percentage point increase in the proportion of residents with a Bachelor's degree is associated with a 4.5 percentage point decrease in credit claiming.

FIGURE [2] Proportion of Credit Claiming Press Releases Are Responsive to District Characteristics

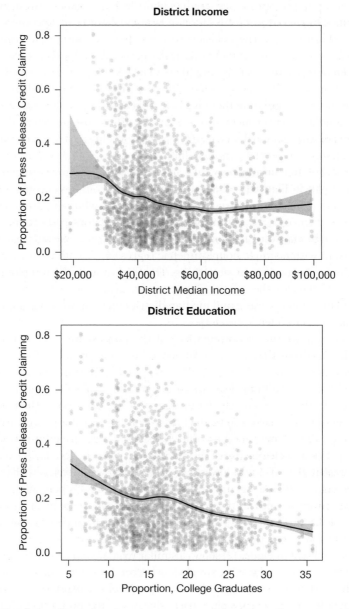

NOTE: This figure shows that the representatives of the poorest districts tend to claim credit for federal projects at a higher rate than representatives of richer districts and that representatives of districts with a lower percentage of college graduates tend to engage in credit claiming at a higher rate than representatives of districts with a higher percentage of college graduates.

What Legislators Claim Credit for Securing

So far we have shown that credit claiming rates matter because legislators have differential incentives to claim credit for spending that occurs in the district. As a result, legislators will have differential association with spending in their district. A second reason that credit claiming matters is that it expands the set of activities legislators can claim credit for performing. In this section we show that legislators regularly claim credit for expenditures that are still far from the district or allocated primarily through executive agencies. One approach to demonstrating what legislators claim credit for would be to develop a more complex coding scheme, have our coders reclassify documents, and then refit our supervised learning method to the collection of press releases. This method, however, is difficult to implement. More nuanced coding schemes pose a challenge for even experienced coders. They (the coders) tend to struggle to remember the rules, confuse terms, or overuse particular categories. It is also difficult to identify the categories of expenditures beforehand, as there are many and diverse ways that the government potentially can spend money.

Rather than define the categories beforehand, we use a statistical method that discovers a set of *topics*[44] and estimates how documents are divided across those topics. The particular model that we apply—Latent Dirichlet Allocation (LDA)—defines a topic to be a set of words that tend to occur together across documents. For example, words like highway, road, transportation, and bridge are likely to co-occur as members of Congress claim credit for highway expenditures. Unlike our supervised methods that require us to specify topics beforehand, LDA is an unsupervised method—that is, LDA discovers the topics that occur in documents. Given a set of topics, LDA then estimates the proportion of these topics that occur in each document. LDA allows us to identify simultaneously what legislators claim credit for securing and how often legislators discuss those particular topics.

We applied LDA to the credit claiming press releases that we identified in the previous section.[45] We set the number of topics at 25—a number that we arrived at using a substantive search from five to fifty topics. Following Quinn et al., we look for substantive topics that are not about particular subgroups, such as states.[46] On the one hand, if we had too few topics, the result was a merging of distinct spending topics—such as farming and highway expenditures. On the other hand, too many topics produced too many location-specific areas. Twenty-five topics represented an excellent middle ground between the two extremes, capturing distinct topic areas without too many area specific topics.

Table [1] presents the estimated topics and their frequency in representatives' credit claiming messages. The first column provides a short, one-word summary for each of the estimated topics. To obtain this summary, we read a random sample of about 10–15 press releases that have a large share of their content allocated to the topic.[47] The second column contains words that occur with a high frequency under each topic. The third column measures the proportion of documents that are allocated to each of the topics.

The topics in Table [1] reveal the diverse types of spending, which legislators claim credit for directing to their district. Detailed exploration shows the many stages in the appropriations process where legislators announce expenditures. This is evident in the most prevalent topic: *Requested appropriations.* These are expenditures that representatives have inserted into spending bills, but have yet to be allocated to the district. For example, in one press release Dave Camp (R-MI) "announced today that he was able to secure $2.5 million for widening M-72 from US-31 easterly 7.2 miles to Old M-72."[48] Later in this press release, Camp explains that the funding actually has "two more hurdles to clear to make sure the money is in the bill when it hits the President's desk: a vote in the Senate and a conference committee."[49] In a similar message, Mike Ross (D-AR) issued a press release stating that he "has successfully secured $5,122,000 for Millwood Lake in the Fiscal Year 2010 House Energy & Water Appropriations Bill. The bill passed the full U.S. House of Representatives July 16" and that he would "continue fighting for these important infrastructure dollars as they move through the appropriations process. Upon passage of the Energy & Water Appropriations Bill in the Senate, the measure will then go to a Conference Committee."[50] And Doc Hastings (R-WA) stated he "boosted federal funding for work on the Odessa Subaquifer for next year. This year Hastings has added $1 million, which when combined with the funding in the President's budget request, totals $1.185 million for Fiscal Year 2008" even though the funding had "been approved by the full House Appropriations Committee"—with a final passage vote in the House still needed.[51]

The prevalence of claiming credit for requests demonstrates that representatives believe they are able to use a broad set of actions to create an impression of influence over federal expenditures. Not only are legislators able to claim credit for spending once it has been finally approved, or when the expenditure actually occurs in the district, they also claim credit for inserting an expenditure into a bill. They even claim credit for merely requesting an expenditure for the district. Rather than claiming credit for actual spending, then, legislators claim credit for actions that they perform in Washington. Even if those actions only may lead to spending in the district at some future date.

The second most prevalent topic in credit claiming press releases covers *fire department* grants. Although legislators use these grants to create an impression that they influenced executive-branch spending in their district, they have only an indirect role in the fire department program. The fire department grants for which legislators claim credit are small, executive-branch expenditures made to local fire departments through the Assistant to Firefighter Grant Program (AFGP)—a FEMA-administered competitive grant program. . . . Such credit claiming occurs regularly, even though the grants

TABLE [1] Credit Claiming Topics

Labels	Key Words	Proportion
Requested appropriations	bill, funding, house, million, appropriations	0.08
Fire department grants	fire, grant, department, program, firefighters	0.08
Stimulus	recovery, funding, jobs, information, act,	0.06
Bureaucratic compliance	state, federal, congress, states, secretary	0.06
Transportation	transportation, project, airport, transit, million	0.06
Local education	education, school, students, program, college	0.05
Grants	rep, grant, news, county, release	0.05
Economic development	development, economic, business, jobs, county grants	0.05
Water projects	water, project, river, projects, corps	0.04
Justice grants	enforcement, law, police, program, justice	0.04
Rural grants	rural, agriculture, usda, development, county	0.04
HUD/Block grants	housing, program, grants, home, families	0.03
Tax credits	tax, act, small, credit, bill	0.03
Health care	health, care, services, veterans, medical	0.03
Disaster declarations	disaster, assistance, fema, federal, emergency	0.03
Winter heating	liheap, rep, Maine, funding, funds	0.03
National parks	national, park, Jersey, land, area	0.03
Defense construction	military, defense, million, air, army	0.03
University research	research, university, technology, center, science	0.03
New York projects	York, rep, hinchey, NY, federal	0.03
Energy projects	energy, renewable, efficiency, oil, fuel	0.02
Ribbon cutting/ Assistance	county, Florida, rep, office, north	0.02
Arkansas projects	Arkansas, Connecticut, state, Washington, rep	0.02
Local disaster declarations	rep, San, California, county, Maryland	0.02
Homeland security	security, homeland, border, million, emergency	0.02

NOTE: This table shows what legislators discuss in their credit claiming statements.

are relatively small. For example, Brian Higgins (D-NY) used a press release to "announce Walden Fire District will receive $75,259 in federal funding through the Assistance to Firefighters Grants Program (AFGP) for fiscal year 2005."[52] In another press release, Mike Rogers (R-AL), "congratulated the men and women of the Mount Olive Volunteer Fire Department and County Line Volunteer Fire Department today for receiving grants from the U.S. Department of Homeland Security." The press release went on to explain that "the Mount Olive Volunteer Fire Department should receive $26,125 in funding and the County Line Volunteer Fire Department should receive $16,957 in funding to help purchase operations and safety equipment."[53] Even smaller expenditures receive Rogers's attention: in one press release he "congratulated the men and women of the Daviston Volunteer Fire Department today for receiving a $9,975 grant from the U.S. Department of Homeland Security."[54] Even Appropriations cardinals claim credit for fire grants. David Obey—while chair of the Appropriations committee in 2007—issued a press release in which he "applauded the release of a $94,196 federal fire grant to the Antigo Fire Department."[55] Legislators' credit claiming over bureaucrats' funding decisions are not limited to fire grants. Table [1] shows that representatives take advantage of a wide array of expenditures allocated through grants. These grants include economic development grants for towns, Department of Justice grants for police, grants for rural economic development, and urban block grants to help cities function.

Legislators also claim credit for ensuring that wayward bureaucracies deliver necessary funds or encouraging congressional commissions to reconsider decisions to move funds away from the district.[56] For example, Tom Udall (D-NM) issued a press release to say that he and other members of the New Mexico delegation met "with members of the Base Realignment and Closure (BRAC) Commission." During this meeting, Udall says, they "tackled the flawed reasoning behind the Pentagon's decision to target Cannon Air Force Base for closure and expressed appreciation that the commission seems receptive to additional information that might save the base."[57] The credit claiming press releases can defend other military jobs. Maurice Hinchey (D-NY) stated that "in an effort to save local jobs, Congressman Maurice Hinchey (D-NY), a member of the House Appropriations Subcommittee on Defense, today formally announced that he will soon introduce a measure in Congress that would block a recent Pentagon decision to privatize hundreds of inherently government jobs at West Point."[58]

■　　■　　■

The evidence [presented here] shows why legislators' impression of influence over expenditures matters for understanding how legislators receive credit for particularistic spending in the district. Representatives differ in the extent to which they associate themselves with spending in the district. Some legislators have a strong incentive to pursue a personal vote—their reelection coalitions depend on winning the support of independents and even some opposing partisans. Other legislators, however, have a strong incentive to appeal to their copartisans, so they allocate a smaller share of their press releases to credit claiming. If representatives regularly attach themselves to spending in the district, then we expect (and we show in subsequent chapters) that representatives will be perceived as more efficacious at delivering money to the district. Legislators who do not engage in this credit claiming will not have the same association and will not receive the same benefit. Spending alone can help legislators cultivate a personal vote, but claiming credit makes it more likely that constituents will reward legislators for expenditures in the district.

We also show that the opportunity to claim credit extends far beyond money actually being spent in the district and for projects of many different sizes. Legislators claim credit for appropriations as they move through Congress. Even when money is far from being spent in the district or will not be spent for some time, legislators are able to claim credit for the spending. And legislators need not have a direct role in securing the money. Legislators are able to create an impression of influence across a variety of actions and the opportunities are expansive and regularly occurring. Further, the opportunities are only loosely constrained by the size of the expenditure or project.

When legislators engage in the types of credit claiming that we describe, . . . they shape their relationship with constituents.[59] Credit claiming efforts are one example of how legislators attempt to dictate the terms of evaluation to constituents. When legislators regularly claim credit for money spent in the district, they invite constituents to perform evaluations based on the extent and type of federal projects in the district, but when legislators avoid discussing spending, they encourage more ideological and partisan evaluations. This shift in evaluation may help explain the incumbency advantage and explain how legislators attempt to cultivate leeway.[60]

NOTES

1. Polk (2008).
2. Stupak (2007).
3. Stupak (2010b).
4. Stupak (2010a).
5. Stupak (2005).
6. Jankoviak (2009).
7. Staff (2010).
8. Stein and Bickers (1994).
9. Grimmer and Stewart (2013).
10. Caughey and Sekhon (2012); Sekhon and Titiunik (2012).
11. Grimmer (2013).
12. Grimmer (2013).
13. Grimmer (2013).

14. Lipinski (2004).

15. Lipinski (2004).

16. Schiller (2000); Lipinski (2004); Sulkin (2005); Sellers (2010).

17. Lipinski (2004); Sulkin (2005).

18. Sellers (2010).

19. Grimmer and Stewart (2013).

20. Hillard, Purpura, and Wilkerson (2008); Hopkins and King (2010).

21. Mayhew (1974).

22. Mayhew (1974).

23. Ferejohn (1974); Weingast, Shepsle, and Johnsen (1981); Levitt and Snyder (1997); Strömberg (2004); Chen and Malhotra (2007); Berry, Burden, and Howell (2010); Kriner and Reeves (2012).

24. Flake (2008).

25. Hopkins and King (2010); Jurafsky and Martin (2008).

26. To identify the words that are more likely to occur in press releases labeled credit claiming we use the *mutual information* between words in a document and their label. See Manning et al. (2008). Heuristically, mutual information measures how well a single word separates credit claiming press releases from other press releases— higher mutual information indicates that a word better separates categories than a word with lower mutual information.

27. Dietterich (2000); Hillard, Purpura, and Wilkerson (2008).

28. Hastie, Tibshirani, and Friedman (2001).

29. Hastie, Tibshirani, and Friedman (2001).

30. Hainmueller and Hazlett (2014).

31. van der Laan, Polley, and Hubbard (2007).

32. Hillard, Purpura, and Wilkerson (2008); Hopkins and King (2010).

33. Hasit, Tibshirani, and Friedman (2001).

34. These two measures are often known as *recall* and *precision*, respectively. To make the binary classification we had to determine a cutoff in the probability of being a credit claiming document. We did this to maximize an out-of-sample of measure of our performance—setting the threshold at 0.46. We have performed a wide array of robustness checks on the classification algorithm and our measures. Indeed, we replicate all the findings in this chapter without performing the binary classification, instead using the ensemble-weighted probability a press release is a credit claiming document.

35. Grimmer (2013).

36. Grimmer (2010).

37. Gelman and Hill (2007).

38. Gelman and Hill (2007). The smoothing was quite mild—the primary effect being to ensure that legislators who issued only a few press releases were not incorrectly labeled as sending press releases only from one category. Again, rerunning our analyses without smoothing yields the same results, though the estimates are more variable.

39. Munsey (2008).

40. Staff (2012).

41. Cheves (2005).

42. Mayhew (1974); Stein and Bickers (1997).

43. Cleveland (1979).

44. Blei, Ng, and Jordan (2003); Quinn et al. (2010); Grimmer (2010).

45. We estimated the model in MALLET.

46. Quinn et al. (2010).
47. Quinn et al. (2010).
48. Camp (2005).
49. Camp (2005).
50. Ross (2009).
51. Hastings (2007).
52. Higgins (2006).
53. Rogers (2008).
54. Rogers (2007).
55. Obey (2007).
56. Cain, Ferejohn, and Fiorina (1987).
57. Udall (2005).
58. Hinchey (2009).
59. Grimmer (2013).
60. Fenno (1978).

BIBLIOGRAPHY

Berry, Christopher R., Barry C. Burden, and William G. Howell. 2010. "The President and the Distribution of Federal Spending." *American Political Science Review* 104 (4): 783–99.

Blei, David, Andrew Ng, and Michael Jordan. 2003. "Latent Dirichlet Allocation." *Journal of Machine Learning and Research* 3: 993–1022.

Cain, Bruce, John Ferejohn, and Morris Fiorina. 1987. *The Personal Vote: Constituency Service and Electoral Independence.* Harvard University Press.

Camp, David. 2005. "Rep. Camp Secures $2.5 Million for M-72 Project." Representative Press Release.

Caughey, Devin, and Jasjeet Sekhon. 2012. "Regression Discontinuity Designs and Popular Elections: Implications of Pro-Incumbent Bias in Close U.S. House Races." *Political Analysis* 19 (4): 385–408.

Chen, Jowei, and Neil Malhotra. 2007. "The Law of k/n: The Effect of Chamber Size on Government Spending in Bicameral Legislatures." *American Political Science Review* 101 (4): 655–74.

Cheves, John. 2005. "Prince of Pork: Hal Rogers Hauls Home Tax Dollars by the Billions." *Lexington Herald-Leader.*

Cleveland, William S. 1979. "Robust Locally Weighted Regression and Scatter-plots." *Journal of the American Statistical Association* 74 (368): 829–36.

Dietterich, Thomas. 2000. "Ensemble Models in Machine Learning." *Multiple Classifier Systems* pp. 1–15.

Fenno, Richard. 1978. *Home Style: House Members in Their Districts.* Addison Wesley.

Ferejohn, John. 1974. *Pork Barrel Politics: Rivers and Harbors Legislation, 1947–1968.* Stanford University Press.

Flake, Jeff. 2008. "Rep. Flake Spotlights Egregious Earmark of the Week." Representative Press Release.

Gelman, Andrew, and Jennifer Hill. 2007. *Data Analysis Using Regression and Multilevel/Hierarchical Models.* Cambridge University Press.

Grimmer, Justin. 2010. "A Bayesian Hierarchical Topic Model for Political Texts: Measuring Expressed Agendas in Senate Press Releases." *Political Analysis* 18 (1): 1–35.

————. 2013. *Representational Style: What Legislators Say and Why It Matters.* Cambridge University Press.

Grimmer, Justin, and Brandon M. Stewart. 2013. "Text as Data: The Promise and Pitfalls of Automatic Content Analysis Methods for Political Texts." *Political Analysis* 21 (3): 267–97.

Hainmueller, Jens, and Chad Hazlett. 2014. "Kernel Regularized Least Squares: Reducing Misspecification Bias with a Flexible and Interpretable Machine Learning Approach." *Political Analysis.*

Hastie, Trevor, Robert Tibshirani, and Jerome Friedman. 2001. *The Elements of Statistical Learning.* Springer.

Hastings, Doc. 2007. "Rep. Hastings Secures $1.185 Million for Odessa Sub-aquifer." Representative Press Release.

Higgins, Brian. 2006. "Rep. Higgins Announces $75,259 for Walden Fire District." Representative Press Release.

Hillard, Dustin, Stephen Purpura, and John Wilkerson. 2008. "Computer-Assisted Topic Classification for Mixed-Methods Social Science Research." *Journal of Information Technology & Politics* 4 (4): 31–46.

Hinchey, Maurice. 2009. "Rep. Hinchey to Introduce Measure to Block Privatization of Government Jobs at West Point." Representative Press Release.

Hopkins, Daniel J., and Gary King. 2010. "A Method of Automated Nonparametric Content Analysis for Social Science." *American Journal of Political Science* 54 (1): 229–47.

Jankoviak, Shawna. 2009. "CMU Grant Will Expand Coverage." *Cheboygan News.* http://www.cheboygannews.com/article/20091105/NEWS/311059989.

Jurafsky, Danile, and James H. Martin. 2008. *Speech and Language Processing.* Pearson Prentice Hall.

Kriner, Douglas L., and Andrew Reeves. 2012. "The Influence of Federal Spending on Presidential Elections." *American Political Science Review* 106 (2): 348–66.

Levitt, Steven D., and James M. Snyder. 1997. "The Impact of Federal Spending on House Election Outcomes." *The Journal of Political Economy* 105 (1): 30–53.

Lipinski, Daniel. 2004. *Congressional Communication: Content and Consequences.* University of Michigan Press.

Manning, Christopher et al. 2008. *Introduction to Information Retrieval.* Cambridge University Press.

Mayhew, David. 1974. *Congress: The Electoral Connection.* Yale University Press.

Munsey, Patrick. 2008. "McGoff Launches Bid to Unseat Burton." *The Kokomo Perspective.* http://kokomoperspective.com/news/mcgoff-launches-bid-to-unseat-burton/article_003c0793-884f-5b1d-9774-d809bd0ed76c.html?mode=jqm.

Obey, David. 2007. "Rep. Obey Applauds Federal Grant to Help Firefighting Operations in Antigo." Representative Press Release.

Polk, Amy. 2008. "Community Leaders, Hospital Board Take Part in Hospital Groundbreaking." *Mackinac Island Town Crier.* http://www.mackinacislandnews.com/news/2008-05-31/front_page/022.html.

Quinn, Kevin et al. 2010. "How to Analyze Political Attention with Minimal Assumptions and Costs." *American Journal of Political Science* 54 (1): 209–28.

Rogers, Mike. 2007. "Rep. Rogers Announces $9,975 for Daviston Volunteer Fire Department." Representative Press Release.

————. 2008. "Rep. Rogers Announces $43,082 in Grants for Randolph County Fire Departments." Representative Press Release.

Ross, Mike. 2009. "Rep. Ross Secures $5,122,000 in House for Millwood Lake." Representative Press Release.

Schiller, Wendy. 2000. *Partners and Rivals: Representation in US Senate Delegations.* Princeton University Press.

Sekhon, Jasjeet S., and Rocio Titiunik. 2012. "When Natural Experiments are Neither Natural nor Experiments." *American Political Science Review* 106 (1): 35–57.

Sellers, Patrick. 2010. *Cycles of Spin: Strategic Communication in the US Congress.* Cambridge University Press.

Staff. 2010. "Gladwin Receives $65,000 in Grants." *Midland Daily News.* http://www.ourmidland.com/news/gladwin-receives-in-grants/article_bc61863c-c2bf-5b02-add2-529c5ff28d29.html.

———. 2012. "Harold 'Hal' Rogers, Profile." *The Washington Times.* http://www.washingtontimes.com/campaign-2012/candidates/harold-hal-rogers-208/.

Stein, Robert M., and Kenneth N. Bickers. 1994. "Congressional Elections and the Pork Barrel." *Journal of Politics* 56 (2): 377–99.

———. 1997. *Perpetuating the Pork Barrel: Policy Subsystems and American Democracy.* Cambridge University Press.

Strömberg, David. 2004. "Radio's Impact on Public Spending." *Quarterly Journal of Economics* 119 (1): 189–221.

Stupak, Bart. 2005. "North Michigan Receives $3.4 Million in Final Transportation Appropriations Bill." Representative Press Release.

———. 2007. "Calumet Township Receives $440,000 Loan for Water Infrastructure." Representative Press Release.

———. 2010a. "Rep. Stupak Announces Economic Impact Grants for Beaverton, Gladwin." Representative Press Release.

———. 2010b. "Rep. Stupak Announces Stimulus Funds for Northern Michigan University Job Training Program." Representative Press Release.

Sulkin, Tracy. 2005. *Issue Politics in Congress.* Cambridge University Press.

Udall, Tom. 2005. "New Mexico Lawmakers Tackle BRAC Recommendations with Three BRAC Commissioners." Representative Press Release.

van der Laan, Mark, Eric Polley, and Alan Hubbard. 2007. "Super Learner." *Statistical Applications in Genetics and Molecular Biology* 6 (1).

Weingast, Barry, Kenneth Shepsle, and Christopher Johnsen. 1981. "The Political Economy of Benefits and Costs: A Neoclassical Approach to Distributive Politics." *The Journal of Political Economy* 89 (4): 642–64.

6

THE PRESIDENCY

6.1

RICHARD E. NEUSTADT

From *Presidential Power and the Modern Presidents: The Politics of Leadership from Roosevelt to Reagan*

In leading a vast executive branch with millions of employees, the president can-not monitor all those who work for him, nor can he or she compel many people to act. This excerpt from the famous book by Neustadt makes the simple point that presidents lead by persuading others that their interests coincide with the president's interests. According to Neustadt, presidential power ebbs and flows with each president's credibility as a persuader.

THE POWER TO PERSUADE

. . . The Constitutional Convention of 1787 is supposed to have created a govern-ment of "separated powers." It did nothing of the sort. Rather, it created a gov-ernment of separated institutions *sharing* powers. "I am part of the legislative process," Eisenhower often said in 1959 as a reminder of his veto. Congress, the dispenser of authority and funds, is no less part of the administrative process. Federalism adds another set of separated institutions. The Bill of Rights adds others. Many public purposes can only be achieved by voluntary acts of private institutions; the press, for one, in Douglass Cater's phrase, is a "fourth branch of government." And with the coming of alliances abroad, the separate institutions of a London, or a Bonn, share in the making of American public policy.

From Richard E. Neustadt, *Presidential Power and the Modern Presidents: The Politics of Leader-ship from Roosevelt to Reagan* (New York: The Free Press, 1990).

What the Constitution separates our political parties do not combine. The parties are themselves composed of separated organizations sharing public authority. The authority consists of nominating powers. Our national parties are confederations of state and local party institutions, with a headquarters that represents the White House, more or less, if the party has a President in office. These confederacies manage presidential nominations. All other public offices depend upon electorates confined within the states. All other nominations are controlled within the states. The President and congressmen who bear one party's label are divided by dependence upon different sets of voters. The differences are sharpest at the stage of nomination. The White House has too small a share in nominating congressmen, and Congress has too little weight in nominating presidents for party to erase their constitutional separation. Party links are stronger than is frequently supposed, but nominating processes assure the separation.

The separateness of institutions and the sharing of authority prescribe the terms on which a President persuades. When one man shares authority with another, but does not gain or lose his job upon the other's whim, his willingness to act upon the urging of the other turns on whether he conceives the action right for him. The essence of a President's persuasive task is to convince such men that what the White House wants of them is what they ought to do for their sake and on their authority. (Sex matters not at all; for *man* read *woman*.)

Persuasive power, thus defined, amounts to more than charm or reasoned argument. These have their uses for a President, but these are not the whole of his resources. For the individuals he would induce to do what he wants done on their own responsibility will need or fear some acts by him on his responsibility. If they share his authority, he has some share in theirs. Presidential "powers" may be inconclusive when a President commands, but always remain relevant as he persuades. The status and authority inherent in his office reinforce his logic and his charm.

Status adds something to persuasiveness; authority adds still more. . . . In Walter Bagehot's charming phrase "no man can *argue* on his knees." Although there is no kneeling in this country, few men—and exceedingly few cabinet officers—are immune to the impulse to say "yes" to the President of the United States. It grows harder to say "no" when they are seated in his Oval Office at the White House, or in his study on the second floor, where almost tangibly he partakes of the aura of his physical surroundings. In Sawyer's case, moreover, the President possessed formal authority to intervene in many matters of concern to the secretary of commerce. These matters ranged from jurisdictional disputes among the defense agencies to legislation pending before Congress and, ultimately, to the tenure of the secretary, himself. . . .

A President's authority and status give him great advantages in dealing with the men he would persuade. Each "power" is a vantage point for him in the degree that other men have use for his authority. From the veto to appointments, from publicity to budgeting, and so down a long list, the White House now controls the most encompassing array of vantage points in the American political system. With hardly an exception, those who share in governing this country are aware that at some time, in some degree, the doing of *their* jobs, the furthering of *their* ambitions, may depend upon the President of the United States. Their need for presidential action, or their fear of it, is bound to be recurrent if not actually continuous. Their need or fear is his advantage.

A President's advantages are greater than mere listing of his "powers" might suggest. Those with whom he deals must deal with him until the last day of his term. Because they have continuing relationships with him, his future, while it lasts, supports his present influence. Even though there is no need or fear of him today, what he could do tomorrow may supply today's advantage. Continuing relationships may convert any "power," any aspect of his status, into vantage points in almost any case. When he induces other people to do what he wants done, a President can trade on their dependence now and later.

The President's advantages are checked by the advantages of others. Continuing relationships will pull in both directions. These are relationships of mutual dependence. A President depends upon the persons whom he would persuade; he has to reckon with his need or fear of them. They too will possess status, or authority, or both, else they would be of little use to him. Their vantage points confront his own; their power tempers his.

■　　■　　■

The power to persuade is the power to bargain. Status and authority yield bargaining advantages. But in a government of "separated institutions sharing powers," they yield them to all sides. With the array of vantage points at his disposal, a President may be far more persuasive than his logic or his charm could make him. But outcomes are not guaranteed by his advantages. There remain the counter pressures those whom he would influence can bring to bear on him from vantage points at their disposal. Command has limited utility; persuasion becomes give-and-take. It is well that the White House holds the vantage points it does. In such a business any President may need them all—and more.

II

This view of power as akin to bargaining is one we commonly accept in the sphere of congressional relations. Every textbook states and every legislative session demonstrates that save in times like the extraordinary Hundred Days of 1933—times virtually ruled out by definition at midcentury—a President will often be unable to obtain congressional action on his terms or even to halt action he opposes. The reverse is equally accepted: Congress often is frustrated by the President. Their formal powers are so intertwined that neither will accomplish very much, for very long, without the acquiescence of the other. By the same token, though, what one demands the other can resist. The stage is set for that great game, much like collective bargaining, in which each seeks to profit from the other's needs and fears. It is a game played catch-as-catch-can, case by case. And everybody knows the game, observers and participants alike.

■   ■   ■

In spheres of party politics the same thing follows, necessarily, from the confederal nature of our party organizations. Even in the case of national nominations a President's advantages are checked by those of others. In 1944 it is by no means clear that Roosevelt got his first choice as his running mate. In 1948 Truman, then the President, faced serious revolts against his nomination. In 1952 his intervention from the White House helped assure the choice of Adlai Stevenson, but it is far from clear that Truman could have done as much for any other candidate acceptable to him. In 1956 when Eisenhower was President, the record leaves obscure just who backed Harold Stassen's efforts to block Richard Nixon from renomination as vice president. But evidently everything did not go quite as Eisenhower wanted, whatever his intentions may have been. The outcomes in these instances bear all the marks of limits on command and of power checked by power that characterize congressional relations. Both in and out of politics these checks and limits seem to be quite widely understood.

Influence becomes still more a matter of give-and-take when Presidents attempt to deal with allied governments. A classic illustration is the long unhappy wrangle over Suez policy in 1956. In dealing with the British and the French before their military intervention, Eisenhower had his share of bargaining advantages but no effective power of command. His allies had their share of counterpressures, and they finally tried the most extreme of all: action despite him. His pressure then was instrumental in reversing them. But had the British government been on safe ground at home, Eisenhower's wishes might have made as little difference after intervention as before. Behind the decorum of diplomacy—which was not very decorous in the Suez affair—relationships among allies are not unlike relationships among state delegations at a national convention. Power is persuasion, and persuasion becomes bargaining. The concept is familiar to everyone who watches foreign policy.

In only one sphere is the concept unfamiliar: the sphere of executive relations. Perhaps because of civics textbooks and teaching in our schools, Americans instinctively resist the view that power in this sphere resembles power in all others. Even Washington reporters, White House aides, and congressmen are not immune to the illusion that administrative agencies comprise a single structure, "the" executive branch, where presidential word is law, or ought to be. . . . When a President seeks something from executive officials his persuasiveness is subject to the same sorts of limitations as in the case of congressmen, or governors, or national committeemen, or private citizens, or foreign governments. There are no generic differences, no differences in kind and only sometimes in degree. The incidents preceding the dismissal of MacArthur and the incidents surrounding seizure of the steel mills make it plain that here as elsewhere influence derives from bargaining advantages; power is a give-and-take.

Like our governmental structure as a whole, the executive establishment consists of separated institutions sharing powers. The President heads one of these; cabinet officers, agency administrators, and military commanders head others. Below the departmental level, virtually independent bureau chiefs head many more. Under midcentury conditions, federal operations spill across dividing lines on organization charts; almost every policy entangles many agencies; almost every program calls for interagency collaboration. Everything somehow involves the President. But operating agencies owe their existence least of all to one another—and only in some part to him. Each has a separate statutory base; each has its statutes to administer; each deals with a different set of subcommittees at the Capitol. Each has its own peculiar set of clients, friends, and enemies outside the formal government. Each has a different set of specialized careerists inside its own bailiwick. Our Constitution gives the President the "take-care" clause and the appointive power. Our statutes give him central budgeting and a degree of personnel control. All agency administrators are responsible to him. But they also are responsible to Congress, to their clients, to their staffs, and to themselves. In short, they have five masters. Only after all of those do they owe any loyalty to each other.

"The members of the cabinet," Charles G. Dawes used to remark, "are a president's natural enemies." Dawes had been Harding's budget director, Coolidge's vice president, and Hoover's ambassador to London; he also had been General Pershing's chief assistant for supply in World War I. The words are highly colored, but Dawes knew whereof he spoke. The men who have to serve so many masters cannot help but be somewhat the "enemy" of any one of them. By the same token, any master wanting service is in some degree the "enemy" of such a servant. A President is likely to want loyal support but not to relish trouble on his doorstep. Yet the more his cabinet members cleave to him, the more they may need help from him in fending off the wrath of rival masters. Help, though, is synonymous with trouble. Many a cabinet officer, with loyalty ill rewarded by his lights and help withheld, has come to view the White House as innately hostile to department heads. Dawes's dictum can be turned around.

A senior presidential aide remarked to me in Eisenhower's time: "If some of these cabinet members would just take time out to stop and ask themselves, 'What would I want if I were President?' they wouldn't give him all the trouble he's been having." But even if they asked themselves the question, such officials often could not act upon the answer. Their personal attachment to the President is all too often overwhelmed by duty to their other masters.

Executive officials are not equally advantaged in their dealings with a President. Nor are the same officials equally advantaged all the time. . . . The vantage points conferred upon officials by their own authority and status vary enormously. The variance is heightened by particulars of time and circumstance. In mid-October 1950, Truman, at a press conference, remarked of the man he had considered firing in August and would fire the next April for intolerable insubordination:

> Let me tell you something that will be good for your souls. It's a pity that you . . . can't understand the ideas of two intellectually honest men when they meet. General MacArthur . . . is a member of the Government of the United States. He is loyal to that Government. He is loyal to the President. He is loyal to the President in his foreign policy. . . . There is no disagreement between General MacArthur and myself.

MacArthur's status in and out of government was never higher than when Truman spoke those words. The words, once spoken, added to the general's credibility thereafter when he sought to use the press in his campaign against the President. And what had happened between August and October? Near victory had happened, together with that premature conference on postwar plans, the meeting at Wake Island.

If the bargaining advantages of a MacArthur fluctuate with changing circumstances, this is bound to be so with subordinates who have at their disposal fewer powers, lesser status, to fall back on. And when officials have no powers in their own right, or depend upon the President for status, their counterpressure may be limited indeed. White House aides, who fit both categories, are among the most responsive men of all, and for good reason. As a director of the budget once remarked to me, "Thank God I'm here and not across the street. If the President doesn't call me, I've got plenty I can do right here and plenty coming up to me, by rights, to justify my calling him. But those poor fellows over there, if the boss doesn't call them, doesn't ask them to do something, what *can* they do but sit?" Authority and status so conditional are frail reliances in resisting a President's own wants. Within the White House precincts, lifted eyebrows may suffice to set an aide in motion; command, coercion, even charm aside. But even in the White House a President does not monopolize effective power. Even there persuasion is akin to bargaining. A former Roosevelt aide once wrote of cabinet officers:

> Half of a President's suggestions, which theoretically carry the weight of orders, can be safely forgotten by a Cabinet member. And if the President asks about a suggestion a second time, he can be told that it is being investigated. If he asks a third time, a wise Cabinet officer will give him at least part of what he suggests. But only occasionally, except about the most important matters, do Presidents ever get around to asking three times.

The rule applies to staff as well as to the cabinet, and certainly has been applied *by* staff in Truman's time and Eisenhower's.

Some aides will have more vantage points than a selective memory. Sherman Adams, for example, as the assistant to the President under Eisenhower, scarcely deserved the appelation "White House aide" in the meaning of the term before his time or as applied to other members of the Eisenhower entourage. Although Adams was by no means "chief of staff" in any sense so sweeping—or so simple—as press commentaries often took for granted, he apparently became no more dependent on the President than Eisenhower on him. "I need him," said the President when Adams turned out to have been remarkably imprudent in the Goldfine case, and delegated to him, at least nominally, the decision on his own departure. This instance is extreme, but the tendency it illustrates is common enough. Any aide who demonstrates to others that he has the President's consistent confidence and a consistent part in presidential business will acquire so much business on his own account that he becomes in some sense independent of his chief. Nothing in the Constitution keeps a well-placed aide from converting status into power of his own, usable in some degree even against the President—an outcome not unknown in Truman's regime or, by all accounts, in Eisenhower's.

The more an officeholder's status and his powers stem from sources independent of the President, the stronger will be his potential pressure on the President. Department heads in general have more bargaining power than do most members of the White House staff; but bureau chiefs may have still more, and specialists at upper levels of established career services may have almost unlimited reserves of the enormous power which consists of sitting still.

■   ■   ■

In the right circumstances, of course, a President can have his way with any of these people. Chapter 2 includes three instances where circumstances were "right" and a presidential order was promptly carried out. But one need only note the favorable factors giving those three orders their self-executing quality to recognize that as between a President and his "subordinates," no less than others on whom he depends, real power is reciprocal and varies markedly with organization, subject matter, personality, and situation. The mere fact that persuasion is directed at executive officials signifies no necessary easing of his way. Any new congressman of the Administration's party, especially if narrowly elected, may turn out more amenable (though less useful) to the President than any seasoned bureau chief "downtown." *The probabilities of power do not derive from the literary theory of the Constitution.*

III

There is a widely held belief in the United States that were it not for folly or for knavery, a reasonable President would need no power other than the logic of his argument. No less a personage than Eisenhower has subscribed to that belief in many a campaign speech and press-conference remark. But faulty reasoning and bad intentions do not cause all quarrels with Presidents. The best of reasoning and of intent cannot compose them all. For in the first place, what the President wants will rarely seem a trifle to the people he wants it from. And in the second place, they will be bound to judge it by the standard of their own responsibilities, not his. However logical his argument according to his lights, their judgment may not bring them to his view.

Those who share in governing this country frequently appear to act as though they were in business for themselves. So, in a real though not entire sense, they are and have to be. When Truman and MacArthur fell to quarreling, for example, the stakes were no less than the substance of American foreign policy, the risks of greater war or military stalemate, the prerogatives of Presidents and field commanders, the pride of a proconsul and his place in history. Intertwined, inevitably, were other stakes as well: political stakes for men and factions of both parties; power stakes for interest groups with which they were or wished to be affiliated. And every stake was raised by the apparent discontent in the American public mood. There is no reason to suppose that in such circumstances men of large but differing responsibilities will see all things through the same glasses. On the contrary, it is to be expected that their views of what ought to be done and what they then should do will vary with the differing perspectives their particular responsibilities evoke. Since their duties are not vested in a "team" or a "collegium" but in themselves, as individuals, one must expect that they will see things for themselves. Moreover, when they are responsible to many masters and when an event or policy turns loyalty against loyalty—a day-by-day occurrence in the nature of the case—one must assume that those who have the duties to perform will choose the terms of reconciliation. This is the essence of their personal responsibility. When their own duties pull in opposite directions, who else but they can choose what they will do?

When Truman dismissed MacArthur, the latter lost three posts: the American command in the Far East, the Allied command for the occupation of Japan, and the United Nations command in Korea. He also lost his status as the senior officer on active duty in the United States armed forces. So long as he held those positions and that status, though, he had a duty to his troops, to his profession, to himself (the last is hard for any man to disentangle from the rest). As a public figure and a focus for men's hopes he had a duty to constituents at home, and in Korea and Japan. He owed a duty also to those other constituents, the UN governments contributing to his field forces. As a patriot he had a duty to his country. As an accountable official and an expert guide he stood at the call of Congress. As a military officer he had, besides, a duty to the President, his constitutional commander. Some of these duties may have manifested themselves in terms more tangible or more direct than others. But it would be nonsense to argue that the last negated all the rest, however much it might be claimed to override them. And it makes no more sense to think that anybody but MacArthur was effectively empowered to decide how he himself would reconcile the competing demands his duties made upon him.

▪ ▪ ▪

The essence of a President's persuasive task, with congressmen and everybody else, is to induce them to believe that what he wants of them is what their own appraisal of their own responsibilities requires them to do in their interest, not his. Because men may differ in their views on public policy, because differences in outlook stem from differences in duty—duty to one's office, one's constituents, oneself—that task is bound to be more like collective bargaining than like a reasoned argument among philosopher kings. Overtly or implicitly, hard bargaining has characterized all illustrations offered up to now. This is the reason why: Persuasion deals in the coin of self-interest with men who have some freedom to reject what they find counterfeit.

6.2

CHARLES M. CAMERON

From *Veto Bargaining: Presidents and the Politics of Negative Power*

*The president is the executive of the national government, but he has a key legis-
lative power that allows him to influence Congress: the veto. Cameron shows
how presidents can use the veto effectively to shape legislation. The threat of a
presidential veto can be enough; Congress will often write legislation specifically
to avoid a veto.*

"Presidential power" is a deceptive phrase. It suggests that the capacity to
shape policy is an attribute of the *president*, and a single attribute at that. But
power is not an attribute of an individual, like her height or weight. Instead,
"power" describes something about the outcome of a strategic interaction (a
"game"). In particular, a president has power in a game when its outcome
resembles what the president wants and he causes the outcome to be that way.[1]

This way of thinking about power shifts attention from the attributes of
presidents to the characteristics of the games they play. Among these many
games are the Supreme Court nominations game, the veto game, the executive
order game, the treaty ratification game, the legislative leadership game, the
agency supervision and management game, the commander-in-chief game,
the staffing game, the executive reorganization game, the opinion leadership
game, and the impeachment game. *Understanding the presidency means understanding these games.* I am tempted to add, "and that is all it means," but that
would be too strong. Skill, personality, and charisma seem to matter, or so
many people believe. But they always operate within the confines of specific
games and strategic circumstances. Understanding the games presidents play
is fundamental for understanding presidential power.

Presidents participate in so many games that it is hard to characterize them
in a simple way. Broadly speaking, though, when presidents interact with Congress, they often play *coordination games* or *bargaining games.* Loosely speaking, coordination games require many players to act in one of several possible
ways if they are to benefit themselves. If they do not all act in the same way,
they work at cross-purposes. The politics of such games involve selecting the
"focal points" coordinating the players' actions. A majority party setting its

From Charles M. Cameron, *Veto Bargaining: Presidents and the Politics of Negative Power* (New
York: Cambridge University Press, 2000).

legislative agenda in Congress is a prime example of this situation, because many players—across committees in both houses and in the leadership—must focus on a few priorities if they are to accomplish much. Oft times, the selection of focal points involves loose norms and improvisation rather than formal procedures specified in law or the Constitution; this lies outside what Neustadt called the "literary theory of the Constitution," though hardly outside the reach of social science.

In contrast, bargaining games require players to divide among themselves a "pie," or set of benefits. The politics of bargaining involves gambits increasing one's share of the pie. Examples include haggling over the content of laws, pulling and hauling to determine the direction and vigor of agency decisions, and bickering over the appointment of executive officials and judges. These activities all involve give-and-take across the branches of government. Many bargaining games in which the president participates are quite formal, with a structure specified by the Constitution, by law, or by norms of long-standing precedent.[2]

▪ ▪ ▪

PRESIDENTIAL BARGAINING GAMES: WHAT DO WE KNOW?

Given the importance of bargaining games for the contemporary presidency, an obvious question is: What does the empirical record tell us about presidential bargaining games? This seems like it should be an easy question to answer, but unfortunately it is not. The problem is that data on the *process* of bargaining—the number of vetoes, of nominees rejected by Congress, the number of oversight hearings, the number of policy proposals in State of the Union messages, the number of bills introduced in Congress, the number of executive orders reversed by Congress, and so on—are relatively easy to collect but hard to interpret (I'll explain why shortly). Conversely, data on the *outputs* from bargaining games—for example, the number and content of important laws, executive orders, and treaties, the intensity and import of bureaucratic action, the ideological tenor and meaning of court decisions—are very hard to collect but much easier to interpret.

Why are process measures so much harder to interpret compared to output measures? The problem is that power in bargaining games often operates through *anticipation*. Congress anticipates a veto if it goes too far: in order to avoid the veto, it trims back a policy initiative. No veto occurs, but the president's preferences have altered what Congress would have done if could have operated without constraint. In other words, the game's structure allows the president to exercise power over the outcome, even absent a veto. As a second example, suppose the president anticipates a torrent of opposition if he nominates a controversial activist to head a regulatory agency. Accordingly, he eschews the controversial nominee in favor of a more moderate one, though he would prefer to put the activist in charge if he could do so without cost. The nomination then flies through Congress. In this case, the structure of the game allows Congress to exercise some power over the nominee's ideology even with no direct evidence of this in the public record.

Situations like this involve the "second face of power," power operating through anticipated response.[3] These situations are notoriously difficult to study using process measures since participants maneuver to avoid the most easily measured consequences of disagreement.

How can one find the traces of power when the second face of power is at work? There are two methods: the first direct, the second indirect. The direct method involves measuring policy outputs and relating them to the actors' preferences. If the president actually exercises power over the output, even without taking visible action, then a switch from a liberal president to a conservative one should result in a change in policy, *ceteris paribus*. If one collects data on policy outputs and proxies for preference changes (e.g., partisan affiliation of the president and key congressional actors), and the policy outputs change in a clear and simple way in response to changes in the preference proxies, then one has strong circumstantial evidence of power being exercised. Obviously, one needs to control for confounding influences, but the principle is clear enough.[4]

The indirect approach is more convoluted. It begins with process data, such as vetoes, rejected nominees, reversed executive orders, and blocked agency initiatives. The problem is interpreting such data. In order for events like vetoes to occur, there must be policy disagreement between the actors. But this is only a *necessary* condition. It is certainly not a *sufficient* condition, as arguments about the second face of power indicate. Instead, a process marker like a veto, a rejected nominee or treaty, or a reversed executive order, represents the impact of policy disagreement, *plus something else beyond mere disagreement*. Let us call this additional element "Factor X."[5] The essence of the indirect approach is to build an explicit model of bargaining *incorporating Factor X*. Using this model, one can interpret the process measures and even draw conclusions about presidential power. Absent such a model, all that can be concluded from process measures like counts of vetoes is that policy disagreement occurred—a very weak conclusion since policy disagreement may not trigger a veto without Factor X.[6]

■   ■   ■

The Indirect Approach: Studying Veto Bargaining

Absent a model of vetoes (actual vetoes, not just veto power), any number of vetoes is equally compatible with little, some, or a great deal of presidential power over legislative outputs. No vetoes may mean that Congress has capitulated to the president, or the president has capitulated to Congress; or that Congress has made some compromises before submitting the bill to the president, who compromises somewhat by accepting it. Many vetoes are equally ambiguous. The lesson is a general one—data on process measures simply do not speak for themselves. The idea of the indirect approach is to combine process measures with explicit models of bargaining, in the hope the data will speak more distinctly.

Veto Threats

Matthews provides an elegant model of veto threats, beginning with a standard model of one-shot, take-it-or-leave-it bargaining over political issues.[7] Then he adds an explicit "Factor X"—congressional uncertainty about the president's policy preferences. In other words, Matthews assumes the president has a policy reputation, but the reputation is not so precise that Congress can predict with pinpoint accuracy the response of the president to every conceivable bill. Disagreement between the president and Congress, *plus* congressional uncertainty about how far it can push the president before triggering a veto, allows vetoes to occur within the model—they occur when the president turns out to be somewhat tougher (that is, more extreme) than Congress anticipated. Finally, Matthews allows the president to issue a veto threat before Congress writes a bill. Using quite sophisticated game theory, Matthews works out predictions about the behavior of Congress and president.

Within the confines of the model, one can evaluate the impact of the "institution" of the veto threat on presidential power. Broadly speaking, veto threats often enhance presidential power (relative to a world without veto threats), because they help the president and Congress strike bargains that they might not otherwise forge, for want of congressional concessions. Moreover, the concessions induced by threats often work to the advantage of the president.[8]

In our own research, my collaborators and I present systematic data on veto threats, congressional concessions after threats, and vetoes after threats, and use Matthews's model to interpret the data (and, to some extent, use the data to test the model).[9] The universe for the study consists of the 2,284 "nonminor" bills presented to the president between 1945 and 1992. We collected data on a random sample of 281 nonvetoed bills from the universe, stratified across three levels of "legislative significance" derived from an approach similar to Mayhew's. We also collected data on all vetoed bills in the universe, some 162 bills, for a total of 443 bills in all. We compiled data on threats and concessions from legislative histories of the bills, the public papers of the presidents, and newspaper accounts.

Statistical analysis of the data revealed the following patterns:

1. During unified government, veto threats rarely occur regardless of the significance of the legislation.
2. During divided government, veto threats occur frequently and increase in frequency with legislative significance. The frequency of veto threats for important legislation during divided government is surprisingly high: 34 percent of such bills received veto threats.

3. If a bill is not threatened, a veto is unlikely though not impossible.
4. If a bill is threatened, the probability of a veto increases dramatically, especially during divided government and at higher levels of legislative significance. But vetoes are not certain even after a threat.
5. Veto threats usually bring concessions.
6. Concessions deter vetoes. The bigger the concession the less likely a threatened bill is to be vetoed.

Although some of these findings lie outside the scope of Matthews's model (e.g., the importance of legislative significance), for the most part these findings strongly resemble what the model predicts. Thus, the model "explains" the data, in the sense that it provides a detailed causal mechanism for the process. If one combines the import of the model—veto threats often enhance presidential power—with the data on the actual frequency of threats, one obtains a picture in which veto threats assume considerable importance in the armamentarium of presidents serving in periods of divided party government.

NOTES

1. This conclusion follows from the canonical definition of power: "power is a causal relationship between preferences and outcomes." For a thorough discussion, see Jack Nagal, *The Descriptive Analysis of Power* (New Haven, CT: Yale University Press, 1975).

2. The distinction I am drawing between coordination and bargaining is rooted more in presidential politics than abstract game theory. For example, there are bargaining games in which coordination is critical (e.g., Nash bargaining games, with a multitude of equilibria). So I am not drawing a logical or mathematical distinction but instead pointing to the character of different activities.

3. Peter Bachrach and Morton Baratz, "The Two Faces of Power," *American Political Science Review* (1962) 56: 947–952.

4. This method of studying power is laid out in the classics of the power literature, see Robert A. Dahl, *Modern Political Analysis*, 2nd ed. (Englewood Cliffs, NJ: Prentice-Hall, 1970), and Jack Nagal, *The Descriptive Analysis of Power* (New Haven, CT: Yale University Press, 1975). It was first applied to studying presidential power in Terry Moe, "An Assessment of the Positive Theory of 'Congressional Dominance' of Bureaucracy," *Legislative Studies Quarterly* (1987) 12: 475, and Barry R. Weingast, and Mark J. Moran, "Bureaucracy Discretion or Congressional Control? Regulatory Policymaking by the Federal Trade Commission," *Journal of Political Economy* (1983) 91: 765–800.

5. For those who don't like suspense: "Factor X" often turns out to be some type of uncertainty, including uncertainty about what others will do (e.g., in the form of mixed strategies) or what they want (e.g., incomplete information about actors' preferences) and thus what they will do.

6. One cannot even conclude that vetoes are evidence of the most important or most intense disagreements. Drawing that conclusion requires a model of vetoes in which the statement is true; absent the model, it is not a valid inference.

7. Steven Matthews, "Veto Threats: Rhetoric in a Bargaining Game," *Quarterly Journal of Economics* (1989) 103: 347–369.

8. They don't always do so, for sometimes the concessions are inadequate to head off a veto. In this case, concessions don't actually advantage the president (neglecting veto overrides).

9. Charles M. Cameron, *Veto Bargaining: Presidents and the Politics of Negative Power* (New York: Cambridge University Press, 2000), and Charles Cameron, John S. Lapinski, and Charles Riemann, "Testing Formal Theories of Political Rhetoric," *Journal of Politics* (Winter 2000).

6.3

BRANDICE CANES-WRONE

From *Who Leads Whom? Presidents, Policy, and the Public*

Do presidents follow public opinion even when they believe it is wrong? Or do presidents do what they think is right even when doing so is unpopular? Canes-Wrone describes three important cases when presidents pandered; that is, they followed public opinion rather than do what they thought was the right thing to do. She argues that this happens often.

EXAMPLES OF POLICY PANDERING AND LEADERSHIP

Why did Jimmy Carter, a long-time proponent of expanding humanitarian assistance, suddenly propose to scale back the program? Why did Ronald Reagan, who was philosophically opposed to tax increases, recommend an unpopular one? And why did George H. W. Bush veto a bill extending unemployment benefits only to sign similar bills over the course of the following eight months?

. . . [T]he cases illustrate the behaviors of *policy pandering* and *policy leadership*. Pandering reflects circumstances in which a president supports a popular policy option despite the fact that he expects it to harm citizens' interests. Policy leadership, in comparison, occurs when a president endorses an unpopular option that he believes will advance societal welfare.

■   ■   ■

Case Selection

The primary motivation for developing the Conditional Pandering Theory was to assess the incentives of the president to pander to public opinion when forced to choose between endorsing a popular course of action or one he believes will produce a good outcome for society. Given this substantive aim, I focus the narrative analysis on executive decisions for which the president's beliefs regarding the optimal policy choice differed from those of the mass public. As previously discussed, the concept of policy pandering does not require that a president's beliefs regarding the optimal course of action are

From Brandice Canes-Wrone, *Who Leads Whom? Presidents, Policy, and the Public* (Chicago: University of Chicago Press, 2005).

necessarily correct. Accordingly, in the cases, the fact that a president deemed the mass citizenry to be misguided does not mean that the reader will necessarily agree with the president's assessment.

The need to ascertain the president's beliefs in relation to public opinion made the selection of cases contingent on the availability of historical evidence on these factors. Even so, I imposed a number of additional restrictions regarding the selection. First, to illustrate how the theoretical predictions vary according to the president's popularity relative to that of his likely competition, I ensured that one case concerned a president far ahead of his likely competition, one a president far behind, and one a president who could expect a tight race. . . . [A]t least one case involved a highly popular president, one an unpopular chief executive, and one a marginally popular president. Thus, in the narratives, presidential approval ratings are often employed as a proxy for a chief executive's popularity relative to that of his potential competition. Prior research establishes that this factor is correlated with a president's likelihood of retaining office (e.g., Brody and Sigelman 1983; Sigelman 1979). By comparison, trial heats are not particularly accurate assessments of a president's electoral prospects until the final months of a race; indeed, trial heats are not even routinely available throughout a president's term.

The second restriction is that the universe of potential cases was limited to the decisions of presidents since Nixon. The literature suggests that these presidents have been more likely than their predecessors to involve the mass public in policymaking (e.g., Kernell 1997; Skowronek 1993); the restriction enables showing that the Conditional Pandering Theory is germane to these presidencies. Third, to demonstrate that the theory is not limited in applicability to a given administration or personality, I selected a different chief executive for each case. Fourth, I chose only policy decisions that were significant enough to receive coverage in the *Congressional Quarterly Almanac*. This restriction was inspired by a desire to establish that the theory is relevant to relatively important policy decisions. Finally, the selection was influenced by the fact that presidents can more easily change public opinion in foreign as compared with domestic affairs. Because of this asymmetry, one might suppose that presidential pandering would be uncommon in foreign affairs and common in domestic matters. To demonstrate the relevance of the Conditional Pandering Theory across both domains, I illustrate the behavior of policy pandering with decisions involving foreign affairs and the behavior of policy leadership with decisions on domestic matters.

A substantial portion of each narrative is devoted to describing why seemingly plausible alternative explanations do not explain the sequence of events. This attention to alternative explanations is partially a function of the fact that one would not necessarily anticipate truth revelation by presidents and their advisors. Chief executives are not likely to admit, even in retrospect, that they followed public opinion despite having evidence suggesting the action would produce harmful effects. (Nor are presidents particularly likely to state that electoral motivations were what lead them to take an unpopular position, as occurs in the Conditional Pandering Theory when first-term presidents exercise policy leadership.) The narratives accordingly do not revolve around "smoking guns" of admissions by presidents but, instead, careful attention to their long-standing beliefs, public opinion, and possible alternative accounts.

President Carter and Foreign Aid: The Trustee Panders

Carter is reputed to have placed the public interest above other political objectives. For example, Erwin Hargrove (1988, 11) assesses in his biography of Carter: "The key of Carter's understanding of himself as a political leader was his belief that the essential responsibility of leadership was to articulate the good of the entire community rather than any part of it . . . Rather than being antipolitical or nonpolitical leadership, this was, for him, a different kind of leadership that eschewed the normal politician's preoccupation with representing private interests, bargaining, and short-term electoral goals." Similarly, Charles Jones (1988) characterizes Carter's regime as the "trusteeship presidency," in which the chief executive viewed himself as a trustee of the people and sought to enact policies he believed were in the public interest even when they were not politically expedient. Precisely because of this reputation, I illustrate the behavior of pandering with a case study that concerns President Carter. By establishing that the Conditional Pandering Theory has relevance for his policy decisions, I show it is applicable even to presidents who are not thought to cater to public opinion.

The case study focuses on Carter's budgetary proposal for the policy issue of humanitarian assistance in 1980, the year he ran for reelection. Upon taking office, Carter had pledged to switch U.S. policy toward communist containment in the Third World. Instead of responding militarily whenever conflicts over communism arose, Carter espoused a "preventive" approach. He sought to lessen the appeal of communism to the citizens of Third World nations by solving their underlying problems (e.g., Deibel 1987; Skidmore 1996). Development assistance comprised a key component of this preventive approach.

For the first three years of Carter's term, his proposals for humanitarian assistance, or economic aid, were consistent with this philosophy. In each year, Carter requested an increase and he invariably achieved one, even if not for the full amount he had requested. He pursued this expansion despite a lack of public support for the program; according to responses to the General Social Survey, throughout his administration over 65 percent of the populace believed the United States spent too much on foreign aid.[1]

Carter knew that his policy position was unpopular. He acknowledged as much during a call-in radio show he hosted during the first few months in office. Stating his policy stance to a caller, Carter began, "Well, John [the caller], I'm going to take a position that's not very popular, politically speaking."[2] Likewise, in a session with media representatives during the second year of the administration, Carter remarked, "I don't know of any issue that has less political support than that program itself, foreign aid in all its forms."[3]

Carter's lack of pandering over foreign aid during his first three years in office is consistent with his reputation for placing the public interest above other, more political objectives. His behavior also, however, comports with the Conditional Pandering Theory. The theory suggests that a president will not pander to public opinion if he does not soon face a contest for reelection or if he is highly popular or unpopular. In the early months of 1977 and 1978, when Carter submitted his foreign aid proposals as a part of his annual budgetary requests, the presidential election was relatively distant. By the outset of 1979, when Carter offered his humanitarian aid proposal for the following fiscal year, the electoral race was approaching but Carter's popularity was weak. His public approval ratings for the past year had averaged 43 percent, a very low level by historical standards. His decision to exercise policy leadership is thus consistent with the Conditional Pandering Theory.

Of course, that Carter's policymaking on foreign aid between 1977 and 1979 comports with the Conditional Pandering Theory does not eliminate the possibility that his actions were entirely the consequence of his character. For this reason, we focus on the humanitarian aid proposal Carter offered in 1980, when he reversed his previous position and recommended that the United States cut economic assistance. Specifically, in his budget of January 1980 (which was for fiscal year 1981), Carter proposed cutting economic assistance by 2 percent in nominal terms. The cut constituted a nominal decline of 26 percent relative to his recommendation in the previous budget. Moreover, given the inflation rate predicted by the administration, his request signified a real reduction of 11 percent from the appropriations of last year and 39 percent from his earlier proposal.

The descriptive summaries accompanying the numbers in Carter's budgets reflect the change in his policy position. The budget submitted in 1979 stated that it contained "increases in foreign aid with emphasis on long-term development of poor countries, and reducing widespread poverty." In contrast, the budget submitted in 1980 characterized the proposals for foreign affairs as "designed to help meet the near-term challenges to stability." This budget was also printed in the colors of Carter's reelection campaign, emphasizing the linkage between the document and election year politics (Hargrove 1988).

When Carter submitted his election-year budget, he had reason to believe the impending presidential race would be competitive. His approval ratings were respectable at 58 percent but not remarkably high by historical standards. Moreover, economists were forecasting an imminent recession that would cause double-digit inflation and an increase in unemployment. Carter knew that the recession, assuming it materialized, could cause him serious problems in his campaign for reelection. As a result, he very much wanted his budget to appeal to voters (Kaufman 1993, 168–69).

Carter's policy reversal on foreign aid helped to achieve this goal. By proposing a reduction in economic assistance, he ensured that his position on this program would be consonant with public opinion. According to a Roper survey taken the month before he submitted his budget, 72 percent of the population thought foreign assistance should be decreased.[4] Had Carter continued trying to expand economic aid, he would have handed challengers an easy issue on which to criticize him.

Thus consistent with the Conditional Pandering Theory, Carter switched his position in the direction of public opinion once he was marginally popular and soon faced a contest for reelection. He could reasonably expect that the effects of cutting economic assistance would not be known by voters before the election, particularly since appropriations bills are not typically enacted until summer at the earliest. Moreover, the anticipated competitiveness of the race meant that his policy choice might affect his likelihood of winning. As a result, Carter had an electoral incentive to take the popular position of cutting humanitarian assistance, even if he believed that increasing it was in America's long-term interest.

Among seemingly plausible alternative explanations, none receives support on careful examination. Perhaps the most natural justification, and one that would comport with Carter's reputation for pursuing the public interest, is that his beliefs about the value of humanitarian assistance had changed. In fact, as Michael Genovese (1994) observes, there is a good deal of evidence that Carter shifted from a "Wilsonian idealist" to a "Cold War confrontationist" as his term progressed. David Skidmore (1996) also describes this transformation in an analysis that is fittingly entitled *Reversing Course*. However, as these scholars acknowledge, the transformation began as early as 1978. Thus if the change in philosophy were the primary cause of Carter's policy reversal on foreign aid, the policy reversal should have occurred earlier.

Moreover, the budget that Carter proposed in his final month in office, after his electoral defeat, reiterated his commitment to a substantial growth in humanitarian assistance. He recommended increasing it by 26 percent in nominal terms, which, given the projected inflation rate, comprised a real increase of 12 percent. The justification Carter gave for this request in his Budget Message highlighted his continued belief in the importance of humanitarian assistance. He stated, "I believe in the need for higher levels of aid to achieve foreign policy objectives, promote economic growth, and help needy people abroad. Foreign aid is not politically popular and represents an easy target for budget reduction. But it is not a wise one." Carter's election-year proposal to decrease development assistance therefore cannot be attributed to a fundamental change in his convictions regarding the benefits of foreign aid.

Given that the policy shift cannot be ascribed to a change in Carter's convictions, I consider whether it can be attributed to factors specific to the time period in which it occurred. These alternative explanations include the macroeconomy, anticipated congressional behavior, and international events. I consider each in turn.

In January 1980, inflation was a major concern for President Carter and the public. During the past year, the consumer price index had increased by 12.4 percent and according to Gallup's Most Important Problem survey, 36 percent of citizens (a plurality of respondents) considered inflation to be the most important problem in the nation.[5] Carter accordingly designed his election-year budget with the goal of curbing inflation (Hargrove 1988, 102–3; Kaufman 1993, 168–69). One could therefore argue that he proposed to cut humanitarian aid in order to help reduce inflation.

The key problem with this argument is that Carter's overall budget was not all that fiscally conservative. As Hargrove (1988, 103) assesses, the budget reflected that Carter was "not, in the final analysis, a conservative prepared to launch a period of austerity." In fact, Carter's budget entailed real increases in other, more popular programs. For example, Carter proposed conspicuous growth in funding for federal health programs and ground transportation, issues on which a majority of the public supported higher spending.[6] It is therefore difficult to conclude that Carter's desire to curb inflation was the primary determinant of his decision to recommend reducing humanitarian assistance.

A separate potential explanation for the policy shift involves Carter's congressional relations. In 1979, Congress failed to enact a Foreign Aid Appropriations Bill. The funding for international assistance programs came from continuing resolutions, which appropriated almost 20 percent less than the president had requested for the programs. Given these events, one might conjecture that Carter's policy reversal resulted from a change in his bargaining strategy.

The evidence suggests, however, that Carter's proposal to reduce international assistance did not reflect a general adjustment in his approach to budgetary negotiations. In fact, in the same budget he proposed expanding programs for which Congress had in the previous year appropriated far less than he had requested. For example, in 1979 Carter obtained 23 percent less funding than he had proposed for the District of Columbia, but in 1980 he still requested 9 percent more than he had in the previous budgetary cycle. Likewise, Congress appropriated 9 percent less than Carter recommended for agricultural spending in 1979, yet in 1980 the president recommended an increase of 20 percent relative to his proposal of the previous year. Carter thus did not systematically lower his budgetary requests in response to previous failures to expand the programs.

In keeping with this evidence that Carter's legislative negotiations differed by policy area, I consider as a final rationale for his policy shift an explanation particular to foreign aid. Specifically, I examine the possibility that an international event induced the president to desire a lower level of humanitarian assistance. In 1979 there were two major international incidents that affected

U.S. interests: the abduction of American hostages in Iran in November 1979 and the Soviet invasion of Afghanistan in the following month. Ostensibly, these incidents could have affected Carter's beliefs concerning the value of bilateral assistance to the Soviet Union and Iran.

Regardless of the president's beliefs about such bilateral assistance, however, his proposal to reduce humanitarian aid could not be the consequence of them. As documented in the 1981 *Country Report on Human Rights Practices* prepared by the State Department, the United States offered no bilateral assistance to the Soviet Union or Iran in 1979.[7] Thus, Carter could not recommend cutting assistance to these countries.[8] A related possibility is that the Soviet invasion of Afghanistan and the Iranian hostage crisis induced the president to disfavor the use of humanitarian aid as a means of solving the problems of the Third World. Yet, as previously discussed, soon after the 1980 elections, Carter proposed a massive increase in humanitarian assistance. Thus the international events seem to have, if anything, strengthened the president's belief that humanitarian assistance would promote U.S. interests.[9]

In sum, Carter's policy reversal on foreign aid in 1980 cannot be attributed to a change in his belief system, the state of the economy, congressional relations, or to the major foreign events of the day. Nor is the shift consistent with his subsequent policy proposals on foreign aid. The decision does, however, comport with the Conditional Pandering Theory. When the election was distant or Carter's approval ratings were low, he pursued the course of action he believed to be in the public interest. Yet when the election was near and his public standing was such that he seemed likely to face a tight race, the president pandered to public opinion.

President Bush and Unemployment Benefits: Policy Leadership from Ahead and Pandering

Throughout the summer of 1991, President Bush looked likely to sail to reelection. His approval ratings had hit historically high levels in the wake of the Gulf War victory earlier that year and still hovered in the high 60s and low 70s.[10] Front-runners for the Democratic nomination decided one after another not to challenge the president. By September, Al Gore, Richard Gephardt, and Jay Rockefeller IV had all dropped out of the race. As Robert E. Denton and Mary E. Stuckey (1994, 19) surmise, "Bush simply seemed unbeatable."

This popularity was noteworthy given the lackluster economy over which the president was presiding. The gross national product (GNP) had increased only 0.4 percent during the second quarter of 1991, and this relatively meager growth followed nine months of GNP retraction.[11] As of June, the unemployment rate was approaching 7 percent.[12] Much of the unemployment involved middle-management workers who had been downsized by corporations. These managers were having a particularly difficult time finding alternative employment; many remained jobless at the time their unemployment benefits expired. The unemployment rate thus reflected a substantial number of workers who were not only out of work but also not receiving government assistance. For instance, in July 1991 unemployment compensation expired for 350,000 jobless Americans (Cohen 1997, 218).

It was in this environment that Congress enacted a series of bills extending unemployment benefits. The first of these bills to reach Bush's desk was HR 3201, which arrived August 17. The legislation provided up to 20 weeks of extra benefits through July 1992 at an estimated cost of $5.3 billion. The legislation specified that for the compensation to be distributed, the president had to declare a state of emergency. Bush signed the bill but did not declare an emergency, thereby preventing the expenditure of the benefits.

The second unemployment bill to reach Bush's desk was S 1722, entitled the Emergency Unemployment Compensation Act of 1991. The bill, which was passed by Congress on October 1, again offered up to 20 weeks of extended benefits and had an estimated cost of $6.4 billion. Unlike the earlier legislation, S 1722 did not allow the president the option of signing the legislation without obligating the additional benefits. Bush could thus either veto the bill or enact the temporary extension.[13]

Surveys conducted around the time that Congress passed S 1722 suggest the bill was quite popular. A *Los Angeles Times* poll taken September 21 through 25 found that 63 percent of respondents favored the legislation strongly or at least somewhat, and only 33 percent opposed it.[14] Likewise, a Harris poll conducted September 27 through October 2 found that only 37 percent of respondents would rate the president's opposition to the bill as "excellent" or "pretty good."[15] These survey data suggest that to the extent Bush wished to placate the mass public, he had an incentive to endorse the legislation.

Bush's incentives were not straightforward, however, because he did not believe that the extension of unemployment benefits would promote a strong economy. As David Mervin (1996, 87) describes, the president was "particularly averse to government interference in the economy." This belief repeatedly put him in conflict with the Democratic-controlled Congress. Nicholas Calio, who was in charge of Bush's legislative relations, describes how the White House perceived congressional efforts to control the economy: "There were many things that, in our view, Congress got involved in [which] it really shouldn't—in micro managing markets . . . There were a lot of things we felt needed to be stopped."[16]

The legislation S 1722, the Emergency Unemployment Compensation Act, was apparently one of those things. While the legislation was being considered, Bush openly referred to it as part of "a bunch of garbage" that the Democrats were sending his way.[17] In a news conference, he argued that the measure would ultimately harm taxpayers. Furthermore, he exhorted citizens to implore their representatives to "do something that the President can sign that will help us with unemployment benefits but will also protect the other taxpayer."[18] On October 11, Bush vetoed S 1722, declaring in an accompanying memorandum that it would "threaten economic recovery and its associated job creation." He continued, "the Congress has . . . ignored my call for passage of measures that will increase the nation's competitiveness, productivity and growth.[19]

For all of this strong language, Bush agreed to a measure quite similar to S 1722, HR 3575, less than two months later. HR 3575 extended unemployment benefits for up to 20 weeks through mid-June at an estimated cost of $5.3 billion. When the president signed the bill on November 15, his electoral vulnerability was much greater than it had been when he had vetoed S 1722. Headlines from the preceding weeks had declared "Democrats Find Bush Is Vulnerable" and "Democrat Hopefuls See Bush Weakness."[20] Correspondingly, his popularity ratings had dropped to 56 percent.[21]

The possibility that Bush switched his policy position for electoral reasons did not go unnoticed at the time. For example, Senator George Mitchell of Maine, referring to Bush's apparent reversal, asserted the president was in "panic city."[22] The administration rebuked such criticism and claimed the legislative negotiations had in fact culminated in a victory for the president over the details of how the unemployment benefits would be funded. According to the administration, the bill that Bush had originally vetoed would have increased the deficit and thus violated the 1990 Budget Act, which required that any new program not add to the deficit. The bill he signed, in comparison, supposedly paid for itself through tax increases on the wealthy, the renewal of an employer tax, and a new policy of income confiscation from individuals who defaulted on school loans.[23]

Such a justification for Bush's action would have been more credible had the president not soon thereafter approved another temporary extension of unemployment benefits, HR 4095, which many believed would increase the deficit. Bush signed this subsequent legislation on February 7, 1992, after his popularity ratings had been hovering in the mid-40s for the past month.[24] HR 4095 provided an additional thirteen weeks of benefits, paying for them primarily through a "surplus" that the Office of Management and Budget (OMB) predicted would arise from 1991 tax bills.[25] The Congressional Budget Office (CBO) disputed the prediction of a surplus, and critics ridiculed the forecast.[26] For example, Representative Thomas J. Downey, a Democrat from Long Island, chided that "Only in the land of Oz could you take a $350 billion deficit and find $2 billion in savings."[27]

The claim that Bush did not switch his position seemed even more disingenuous in July 1992. On July 3, when the president was running neck-and-neck with Bill Clinton and Ross Perot in the pre-election polls, the president signed HR 5260, which permanently changed the unemployment system by allowing nonemergency benefits to take effect more easily during times of high unemployment. As recently as April, Bush had opposed making such permanent changes to the system.[28] Even the day before signing HR 5260, the president had threatened to veto the permanent expansion.[29] The champion of the bill in Congress, Representative Thomas J. Downey, offered an explanation for Bush's actions during the brief House debate over the legislation. He predicted, "The President is going to sign this bill for two reasons. Unemployment is up, and his popularity is down."[30]

Does the variation in Bush's policy decisions over unemployment benefits correspond to the predictions of the Conditional Pandering Theory? The theory suggests that a president will endorse policies that he believes are in the public interest when he is quite popular relative to his likely electoral competition, when he is relatively unpopular, or when he does not soon face a contest for reelection. In this case, Bush supported an unpopular policy that he believed would advance a strong economy so long as his electoral prospects were strong. Once he seemed vulnerable, however, he changed course and issued popular decisions that did not reflect his belief that preventing government interference in the economy would harm it and, by consequence, societal welfare. This variation in executive behavior is exactly what the Conditional Pandering Theory would predict.

Some readers may take issue with the notion that Bush was trying to advance societal welfare by vetoing unemployment benefits. It is accordingly worth reemphasizing that the Conditional Pandering Theory does not require that a president is actually advancing citizens' interests, only that he believes he is doing so; the president can be wrong in this assessment. The preceding description of events documented that Bush believed economic recovery, as well as long-term growth, would be best advanced by limiting government interference in the macroeconomy. The question of whether these beliefs were accurate, or whether they are in part a function of ideological biases, is not paramount to analyzing the predicative power of the theory. In the concluding section of this reading, I return to the issue of whether presidents are likely to have better information than citizens do about the expected consequences of policies. For now, I have a more precise goal, which is to show that the Conditional Pandering does a better job at predicting the variation in Bush's policy decisions than seemingly likely alternative explanations.

To realize this goal, four alternative rationales are evaluated, the last two of which are evaluated jointly. First, I examine whether Bush altered his policy beliefs in response to economic events. Second, the possibility that his claims of policy consistency were correct is considered. Third, I analyze executive-legislative negotiations that occurred after Clinton had taken a clear lead in order to assess whether Bush's likelihood of pandering was simply greater the sooner the election; and fourth, whether this likelihood was greater the lower his chances of retaining office.

During the course of the executive-legislative negotiations over the extension of unemployment benefits, the unemployment rate itself varied noticeably. When the president vetoed an extension of benefits in October 1991, the Labor Department had just announced that the rate had dropped a tenth of a percentage point to 6.7 percent. A month later, when Bush approved a temporary extension, the rate had risen back up to 6.8 percent. Furthermore, at the subsequent bill signings in February and July, the rate was estimated to be 7.1

percent and 7.8 percent respectively. It therefore seems plausible that changes in the economic situation caused Bush to believe greater government intervention in the economy was warranted.

Yet the evidence suggests otherwise. In June 1991 the unemployment rate was 6.9 percent and legislation temporarily extending compensation to the jobless was already making its way through Congress. Bush, who was enjoying approval ratings in the mid-70s, did not lend support to the bill. Then in July 1992, Bush threatened to veto a permanent expansion of unemployment benefits even after the Labor Department had announced that the unemployment rate was 7.8 percent, the highest level in eight years.[31]

Finally, Bush never intimated that he reversed course because of changes in the economy. Instead, he consistently stated that his willingness to approve extensions of compensation depended on whether they would increase the deficit. For example, during a news conference in August 1991, he promoted Senator Dole's proposed extension of unemployment benefits, which was less expensive than the Democratic proposals, claiming that the Dole plan had "fiscal integrity."[32] At a fundraising luncheon in November, the president expounded his position further, declaring that:

> The Democratic leaders know that I've been ready since August to sign an extension, but to sign one as proposed by most of the Republicans in the Senate and House that lives within the budget agreement. We don't have to add to the ever-increasing deficit and still do what is compassionate and correct. They passed a bill. They wanted to embarrass me politically. I vetoed that bill . . . Unemployed workers deserve this kind of support, but we need a change in the Congress if we're going to do it in a way that lives within the budget agreement.[33]

These assertions comport with the ones Bush gave eight months later with regards to permanently extending unemployment compensation. When the president was asked by Congressman Robert H. Michel, the Minority Leader of the House, whether he might veto such legislation, Bush responded that he had a "certain custodianship for trying to support reasonable expenditures." He continued, "If [Democratic congressional members] send me something that we view and the leadership here views as too expensive, we'll have to send it back and urge them to get one down there that we can support."[34]

In sum, Bush's actions as well as rhetoric indicate that changes in the unemployment rate did not alter his fundamental beliefs about the appropriateness of extending benefits to the jobless. The president's rhetoric highlights a separate alternative explanation, however, which is that substantive differences among the assorted bills explain the variation in his willingness to sign them. The president's decisions could accordingly be construed as an example of what Cameron (2000) terms "veto bargaining." This rationale for the seemingly disparate decisions has some merit. In fact, had the legislative matter ended after Bush's approval of the extension of benefits in November 1991, it would be relatively straightforward to argue that his policy actions reflected an aversion to increasing the deficit.

The president's behavior in February 1992 suggests that this alternative explanation cannot completely account for his behavior, however. As discussed previously, the extension Bush approved in February paid for itself only under highly disputed assumptions about unexpected revenues. In fact, during a congressional hearing on the legislation, Republican House members recommended that the unemployment trust fund be taken off-budget so that it could not affect the official deficit.[35] Bush's ostensible fiscal restraint thus not only entailed questionable assumptions about unexpected surpluses but also coincided with Republicans recommending score-keeping changes in the accounting of unemployment benefits. Given these circumstances, Bush's supposed fiscal responsibility appears more superficial than substantial. His desire for restraint may well have been sincere, but this desire appears to have been superseded by an impetus to enact a popular policy once he was facing a competitive electoral contest.

The final alternative hypotheses I consider are that Bush was simply more likely to pander to public opinion as the election neared, independent of his popularity; and that he was simply more likely to pander as his popularity declined, and thus would have pandered even if the preelection polls had indicated he was quite likely to lose reelection. The events described thus far do not allow one to distinguish between these explanations and the Conditional Pandering Theory. However, subsequent events shed light on the matter.

Clinton took a substantial lead in the polls following the Democratic Party Convention in mid-July. Throughout the remainder of the race, Bush was consistently the underdog, trailing the competition by as much as twenty-five points and sustaining approval ratings no higher than 40 percent.[36] While Congress did not enact other unemployment legislation during this period, the chambers did pass several bills that involved substantial government regulation of the private sector.

That legislation included the Family and Medical Leave Act of 1992 (S 5), which Congress enacted on September 10, and the Cable Television Consumer Protection and Competition Act of 1992 (S 12), which was sent to the president on September 22. The first bill granted workers up to twelve weeks of unpaid leave in order to care for a new baby or sick relative.[37] The second aided competitors to the cable industry, as well as bestowed the federal government with the power to set rates for the lowest-priced cable package.[38] Each of these bills appealed to popular sentiment. For instance, in a survey of registered voters, 63 percent of respondents stated that they would support a law requiring businesses to grant up to three months of unpaid leave for a new child or medical emergency, while only 31 percent opposed such a law.[39] Likewise, a Harris survey found that 87 percent of the national adult population believed most cable companies could overcharge customers owing to a lack of competition, and 70 percent favored allowing local telephone companies to provide cable services so that the cable industry would be more competitive.[40]

Despite the popularity of the policy issues, Bush vetoed the bills. In each case, his expressed rationale for doing so was consistent with his belief that government interference in the economy would harm it. The president professed that the Family and Medical Leave Act, if enacted, would become a "government-dictated mandate that increases costs and loses jobs."[41] He predicted the cable bill would "cost the economy jobs, reduce consumer programming choices, and retard the deployment of growth-oriented investment critical to the future of our Nation's communications infrastructure."[42]

Bush issued each veto within seven weeks of the election, by which time Clinton held a convincing lead in the preelection polls. When Bush delivered the Family Leave veto on September 22, Clinton maintained a ten percentage point advantage according to the Gallup trial heat.[43] At the time of the Cable Bill veto, on October 3, Bush trailed by eleven to twelve percentage points.[44] That the president vetoed the bills under these conditions suggests that he did not continually pander to public opinion as the election approached or as his popularity declined relative to his electoral competition.

Instead, as predicted by the Conditional Pandering Theory, Bush endorsed the policies he believed to be the right ones when he was unpopular compared with his electoral opposition. In combination with his decisions on unemployment legislation, Bush's behavior illustrates the theoretically predicted relationship between the likelihood of pandering and presidential popularity. When he was highly popular or unpopular relative to his competition, he supported the policies he believed would produce the best outcomes for the nation, despite the proximity of the presidential election. Only when he was in the midst of a seemingly tight race did he enact popular laws that he did not believe would ultimately advance citizens' interests.

Reagan and the Contingency Tax Proposal: Policy Leadership from Behind

In the beginning of 1983, Reagan's personal popularity was quite low. Throughout the month of January, his approval ratings hovered in the mid-30s.[45] This lack of popularity reflected the economic situation. In the previous year, the GNP had fallen 1.8 percent, the largest annual reduction since 1946.[46] Unemployment stood at 10.8 percent, the highest level since 1950.[47]

Many economists, including ones working in the executive branch, believed the projection of large deficits for years to come was holding back an economic recovery. As of January 1983, the projected deficits for the next five years were in the range of $185 to $300 billion, approximately 7 percent of GNP. In comparison, the deficit of the last full year before Reagan entered office was $60 billion, around 2 percent of GNP.[48] Paul Volcker, the Chairman of the Federal Reserve, publicly expressed his concerns about the projected deficits in January. He observed, "We are exposed to fears of 'out-of-control' structural deficits, and the result is upward pressure on interest rates."[49] Martin Feldstein, chairman of the Council of Economic Advisors, agreed with Volcker that the projection of large deficits was boosting interest rates and therefore impeding an economic recovery, particularly in sectors dependent on borrowing, such as housing and automobiles.[50] Indeed, interest rates were quite high; the prime rate was 11 percent and the rate for a conventional home loan was 13.25 percent.[51]

Reagan was deeply concerned about the economy and, moreover, realized that he would not win reelection in 1984 unless conditions improved. He acknowledged that if his administration could not move the country into a recovery it "obviously . . . would be a sign" that he should retire after one term.[52] Reagan also recognized the projected deficits as a problem. For example, in an administration briefing in May 1982, he claimed that "the only thing that's keeping the interest rates up and preventing a speedier recovery is the lack of confidence on the part of the private sector that government will stay the course" by progressing toward a balanced budget.[53]

Curbing the deficit was not a simple matter for the president, however. He desired significant increases in defense spending and the preservation of his recently enacted income tax cuts (e.g., Dallek 1984, 105; Feldstein 1994, 26 and 36–37). Furthermore, Reagan did not want to obtain the needed reductions through changes to Medicare, Social Security, or federal employee retirement programs, which together constituted a majority of the budget (Dallek 1984, 72–73). The president was willing, indeed wanted, to decrease spending on social welfare programs (e.g., Hogan 1990, 225), but congressional leaders had indicated that they would be unwilling to curtail these programs substantially.[54]

It was in this setting that Reagan proposed standby taxes that would be triggered in a couple of years if the deficit did not decline by then; specifically, the taxes were scheduled to take effect on October 1, 1985, if the estimated deficit for fiscal year 1986 turned out to be greater than 2½ percent of the GNP and Congress had approved the president's spending cuts. The taxes included an excise fee on oil of approximately five dollars a barrel as well as an increase in corporate and personal income tax payments of approximately 1 percent of taxable income.[55] Reagan promoted this proposal in his State of the Union address, a radio address, and several targeted addresses during the first two months of 1983.[56]

The evidence suggests that Reagan believed the policy was in citizens' interests because it would help to control the deficit and thereby improve the economy by reducing interest rates. Martin Feldstein, who helped to design the plan along with Reagan's domestic policy adviser Ed Harper, describes how the president came to espouse the idea. Feldstein recounts that the president supported the policy over the objections of others within the White House because, ultimately, he "recognized the need to project declining deficits and an eventual budget balance" (Feldstein 1994, 28). The president's statements support this assertion. For example, in remarks to the St. Louis Regional Commerce and Growth Association on February 1, the president promoted the standby tax proposal by claiming that "it will reassure many of those out in the money markets today that we do mean to control inflation and interest rates."[57]

Despite Reagan's public espousal of the policy, it was quite unpopular. In fact, survey data suggest it was even less popular than the option of eliminating Reagan's income tax reductions. When citizens were asked whether they would support "a standby program of increased personal and business taxes—as well as a special tax on oil" for the years 1986–88 in order to reduce the budget deficit, 60 percent opposed the proposal.[58] In comparison, only 39 percent of the population believed that "July's tax cut should be put into effect despite the size of the government deficit."[59]

Reagan's promotion of the contingency tax proposal is thus not a case of a president following public opinion. Instead, consistent with the Conditional Pandering Theory, Reagan advocated a policy he believed would serve the public interest even though it was unpopular. As documented earlier, the president knew that without an economic recovery, he would be unlikely to win reelection. He believed that the standby taxes, if enacted, would help the economy and thereby increase his likelihood of winning the upcoming race. His electoral incentive was therefore to promote the proposal despite its lack of popular support.

Of course, it remains plausible that Reagan's behavior was consistent with the Conditional Pandering Theory but that he promoted the proposal for other reasons. I discuss three plausible alternative explanations: that Reagan had a propensity to follow his policy beliefs regardless of the political circumstances; that the president was somehow catering to his conservative base; and that he was playing blame-game politics with the Democrats over who was responsible for the budget deficit. None of these explanations is corroborated under scrutiny.

A seemingly credible rationale for Reagan's behavior is that he generally advocated policies he thought were in the public interest, regardless of their popularity. Indeed, this claim receives some support from officials who worked for him. For example, Edwin Meese III, Reagan's attorney general from February 1985 through August 1988, observes that "Reagan was remarkably steadfast when pursuing his key objectives" (Meese 1992, 330). Martin Anderson, the chief domestic and policy adviser to the president in 1981 and 1982, similarly assesses that Reagan would "never alter his course" when he felt strongly about a decision (Pemberton 1997, 110).

Notwithstanding Reagan's dedication to his beliefs, there is evidence that he was not above catering to public opinion. For example, he was more than willing to fire agency heads who became unpopular while following his agenda. William Pemberton (1997, 121) notes that after the White House pressured Ann Gorsuch Burford to resign her post as head of the Environmental

Protection Agency, she "felt betrayed" by the president because he had "abandoned her when she came under fire for carrying out his policy." Likewise, when James Watt, Reagan's first Secretary of Interior, told the president that he would probably have to fire Watt at some point because of the unpopular agenda Watt would be implementing, "Reagan, eyes sparkling with laughter, replied, 'I will'" (Pemberton 1997, 119).

Robert Dallek (1984, 33) reconciles the apparent tension between Reagan's faithfulness to his beliefs and capacity to make tactical modifications. "If Goldwater was ready to stand or fall on principle," Dallek observes, "Reagan, in his determination to be liked and to gain his personal goals, will compromise." As this assessment and Reagan's dealings with his officials imply, the president's support for the contingency taxes cannot be attributed to a universal unwillingness to take positions for purely political reasons.

Conclusion

The narratives on Carter's humanitarian assistance proposals, Bush's policy decisions on unemployment compensation, and Reagan's proposal for standby taxes establish that the Conditional Pandering Theory has explanatory power. In all of these analyses, the predictions of the theory were consistent with the president's policy decisions. Furthermore, the theory made sense of seemingly puzzling events; in each case a president switched positions and/or supported policies counter to his ideological leanings. In contrast, conventional explanations of presidential decision making—character, inside the beltway bargaining, and the appeasement of core constituencies, for example—did not account for the executive behavior.

NOTES

1. The survey asked, "We are faced with many problems in this country, none of which can be solved easily or inexpensively. I'm going to name some of these problems, and for each one I'd like you to tell me whether you think we're spending too much money on it, too little money, or about the right amount. Are we spending too much money, too little money, or about the right amount on foreign aid?"

2. Jimmy Carter, "'Ask President Carter' Remarks During a Telephone Call-in Program on the CBS Radio Network," March 5, 1977, *Public Papers of the Presidents of the United States, 1977 Book 1* (Washington, DC: Government Printing Office, 1977).

3. Jimmy Carter, "Remarks and a Question-and-Answer Session with a Group of Editors and News Directors," May 19, 1978, *Public Papers of the Presidents of the United States, 1978 Book 1* (Washington, DC: Government Printing Office, 1978).

4. Survey conducted December 1–8, 1979. The question wording is identical to that in note 1.

5. Survey conducted by the Gallup organization January 25–28, 1980. The survey asked the standard most important problem question, "What do you think is the most important problem in the nation today?" Responses were open-ended.

6. Carter proposed real increases of 9 percent in health programs and 4 percent in ground transportation. The public opinion data are from a Roper survey conducted

December 1–8, 1979. Respondents were asked the (by-now familiar) question, "We are faced with many problems in this country, none of which can be solved easily or inexpensively. I'm going to name some of these problems, and for each one I'd like you to tell me whether you think we're spending too much money on it, too little money or about the right amount." For health, the question ended with "improving and protecting the nation's health" and for ground transportation, it ended with "improving the public transportation." The responses suggest that 59 percent of adults believed the government was spending too little on health and that 50 percent believed too little was being spent on public transportation.

7. *Country Reports on Human Rights Practices,* report submitted to the Committee on Foreign Relations, U.S. Senate, and Committee on Foreign Affairs, U.S. House of Representatives, by the Department of State, February 2, 1981.

8. Carter did impose an embargo on the sale of grain to the Soviet Union, but this embargo did not affect appropriations for foreign assistance.

9. Nor did Carter shift his requests for humanitarian aid into security assistance; in nominal terms, Carter proposed a measly 0.002 percent increase in security aid.

10. Ragsdale (1998, 213).

11. Peter G. Gosselin, "Economy Rolling Again . . . But Slowly: Slight Gain in Gross National Product Worries Analysts," *Boston Globe,* July 27, 1991, 12.

12. U.S. Department of Labor, Bureau of Labor Statistics.

13. *Congressional Quarterly Almanac,* vol. 47 (1991), 304–8.

14. The question was: "Congress recently passed a bill to extend unemployment benefits beyond the regular 25-week period. To provide the 6.4 billion dollars needed to extend benefits, a budget emergency would have to be declared that President Bush says is not justified. Would you like to see Bush sign this bill into law, or do you think he should veto it?"

15. The question was: "Now let me ask you some specifics about President Bush. How would you rate him on . . . his opposition to a bill that would extend for 20 weeks unemployment insurance to unemployed workers whose benefits have run out . . . excellent, pretty good, only fair or poor?" The responses of "only fair" and "poor" are reported jointly by Harris, with 59 percent of the population assigning Bush one of these ratings.

16. Quoted in Mervin (1996, 114).

17. George Bush, "Remarks at a Republican Party Fundraising Dinner in East Brunswick, New Jersey," September 24, 1991, *Public Papers of the Presidents, 1991 Book 2* (Washington, DC: Government Printing Office, 1992).

18. George Bush, "The President's News Conference," October 4, 1991, *Public Papers of the Presidents, 1991 Book 2.*

19. George Bush, "Memorandum of Disapproval for the Emergency Unemployment Compensation Act of 1991," October 11, 1991, *Public Papers of the Presidents, 1991 Book 2.*

20. Andrew J. Glass, "Democrats Find Bush is Vulnerable," *Atlanta Journal and Constitution,* November 3, 1991, O5; Adam Pertman, "Democrat Hopefuls See Bush Weakness," *Boston Globe,* November 3, 1991, 213.

21. Ragsdale (1998, 213).

22. Michael Kranish, "Bush Bristles at Claims He Has Shifted," *Boston Globe,* November 17, 1991, 1.

23. *Congressional Quarterly Almanac,* vol. 48 (1992), 347–48.

24. Ragsdale (1998, 213).

25. *Congressional Quarterly Almanac,* vol. 48 (1992), 347.

26. Ibid.

27. To deal with the possibility that the additional unemployment compensation would add to the deficit, Congress voted to waive the 1990 Budget Act, which required that every new program pay for itself (*Congressional Quarterly Almanac,* vol. 48 [1992], 352).

28. Adam Clymer, "Bush Fights Long-Term Change in Jobless Benefits," *New York Times,* April 9, 1992, D20.

29. Adam Clymer, "Congress Passes Jobless Aid and Bush Says He Will Sign," *New York Times,* July 3, 1992, A13.

30. Ibid.

31. Jill Zuckman, "Bush Relents, Agrees to Sign Jobless Benefits Extension," *Congressional Quarterly Weekly,* July 4, 1992, 1961–62.

32. George Bush, "The President's News Conference," August 2, 1991, *Public Papers of the Presidents, 1991 Book 2.*

33. George Bush, "Remarks at a Bush-Quayle Fundraising Luncheon in New York City," November 12, 1991, *Public Papers of the Presidents, 1991 Book 2.*

34. George Bush, "Remarks and an Exchange with Reporters in a Meeting with the House Republican Conference on Health Care," July 2, 1992, *Public Papers of the Presidents, 1992–93 Book 1* (Washington, DC: Government Printing Office, 1993).

35. Ways and Means Committee Subcommittee on Human Resources Hearing. "Extending Unemployment Benefits." Panel of Congressional Witnesses, B-318 Rayburn House Office Building, January 23, 1992.

36. The 1992 Gallup Poll Presidential Candidate Trial Heats are available in the Roper Center for Public Opinion Research database on polls and surveys (commonly referred to as RPOLL). For Bush's approval ratings, see Ragsdale (1998, 213–14).

37. Jill Zuckman, "Family Leave Act Falls Again: Veto Override Fails in House," *Congressional Quarterly Weekly,* October 3, 1992, 3059.

38. Mike Mills, "Bush Asks for a Sign of Loyalty: Congress Changes the Channel," *Congressional Quarterly Weekly,* October 10, 1992, 3149–51.

39. NBC News and Wall Street Journal Poll conducted September 12–15, 1992. The survey asked: "Congress has passed a law that would require companies to give employees up to three months of unpaid leave for the birth or adoption of a child, or to care for a seriously ill family member, while protecting their job. Would you favor or oppose this law, even if it means additional costs for business?"

40. Harris survey conducted March 19–24, 1992. The first question was, "Here are some statements people have made about the cable television industry in America today. For each one, please tell me whether you agree or disagree. . . . Because most cable T.V. companies have local monopolies, they can charge too much for the service they provide." The second question was, "Would you favor or oppose changing the regulations so that your telephone company could provide cable television service in competition with the company that provides now?"

41. George Bush, "Remarks and an Exchange with Reporters on Family Leave Legislation," September 16, 1992, *Public Papers of the Presidents, 1992–93 Book 2.*

42. George Bush, "Letter to Congressional Leaders on Cable Television Legislation," September 17, 1992, *Public Papers of the Presidents, 1992–93 Book 2.*

43. Each of the following trial heats, conducted September 17–20 of registered voters and those who could vote without having yet registered, gave Clinton a ten-point lead. The questions were "If the (1992) presidential election were being held today, would you vote for the Republican ticket of George Bush and Dan Quayle or for the

Democratic ticket of Bill Clinton and Al Gore? (If Perot (vol.)/Other (vol.)/Don't know/ Refused, ask:) As of today, do you lean more to Bush and Quayle, the Republicans, or to Clinton and Gore, the Democrats?" and "If the (1992) presidential election were being held today, would you vote for the Republican ticket of George Bush and Dan Quayle or for the Democratic ticket of Bill Clinton and Al Gore?" In the first case, Clinton received support from 50 percent of respondents, and in the second, he received support from 44 percent.

44. These trial heats were conducted by the Gallup Organization on October 1–3 using the questions in the format of note 43. The only difference in the questions is that Ross Perot was explicitly mentioned as a candidate, a result of the fact that he had reentered the race. In the survey that did not urge the leaners to make a choice, Clinton was favored by 47 percent of respondents and Bush by 35 percent. In the survey that pushed the leaners to choose a candidate, Clinton received support from 44 percent of the respondents and Bush from 33 percent.

45. Ragsdale (1998, 210).

46. Anantole Kaletsky, "GNP in U.S. Fell 1.8% Last Year," *Financial Times* (London ed.), January 20, 1983, I1.

47. "Unemployment Claims Rose at End of the Year," *New York Times*, January 14, 1983, D15.

48. Jonathan Fuerbringer, "Do Deficits Impede Recovery?" *New York Times*, January 20, 1983, D1.

49. Volcker's statement was made at a meeting of the American Council for Capital Formation. Kenneth B. Noble, "Deficits Criticized by Volcker," *New York Times*, January 21, 1983, D3.

50. Fuerbringer, "Do Deficits Impede Recovery?"

51. "Current Interest Rates," *New York Times*, January 10, 1983, D7; Kenneth R. Harney, "Interest Rates May Rise Along with Economy," *Washington Post*, January 15, 1983, F1.

52. Rich Jaroslovsky, "Economic Upturn Aids President's Popularity, but It Is Not Panacea," *Wall Street Journal*, April 28, 1983, 1. Cited in Kernell (1997, 224).

53. Ronald Reagan, "Meeting with Editors from the Midwestern Region," May 10, 1982, *Public Papers of the Presidents, 1982 Book 1* (Washington, DC: Government Printing Office, 1983).

54. Hedrick Smith, "Deficit in the $185 Billion Range Expected in 1984 Reagan Budget," *New York Times*, January 18, 1983, A1.

55. Robert D. Hershey Jr., "President to Seek Contingent Taxes," *New York Times*, January 26, 1983, A15.

56. These addresses include the State of the Union on January 25, a national radio address entitled "Fiscal Year 1984 Budget" on January 29, "Remarks and a Question-and-Answer Session at the St. Louis Regional Commerce and Growth Association" on February 1, "Remarks and a Question-and-Answer Session via Satellite to the Young Presidents Organization" on February 14. All of these addresses are in the *Public Papers of the Presidents, 1983 Book 1* (Washington, DC: Government Printing Office, 1984).

57. Ibid.

58. Cambridge Reports, Research International survey conducted in January of 1983. The full question was "Last month, in his State of the Union and Budget Messages to Congress, President (Ronald) Reagan proposed the following actions as ways of reducing these budget deficits for the next few years. Please tell me whether you

would favor or oppose each of them. . . . Putting in effect a standby program of increased personal and business taxes—as well as a special tax on oil—for the years 1986–88."

59. Roper survey conducted January 8–22, 1983. The full question was, "A 5% cut in income taxes took effect in October 1981, and another 10% cut in income taxes took effect this past July. An additional 10% cut in income taxes is due to take effect this coming July. Do you think next July's tax cut should be put into effect despite the size of the government deficit, or do you think next July's tax cut should be cancelled to help reduce the deficit?"

REFERENCES

Brody, Richard A., and Lee Sigelman. 1983. "Presidential Popularity and Presidential Elections: An Update and Extension." *Public Opinion Quarterly* 47: 325–28.

Cameron, Charles M. 2000. *Veto Bargaining: President and the Politics of Negative Power.* Cambridge, UK: Cambridge University Press.

Cohen, Jeffrey E. 1997. *Presidential Responsiveness and Public Policy-Making: The Public and the Policies that Presidents Choose.* Ann Arbor: University of Michigan Press.

Dallek, Robert. 1984. *Ronald Reagan: The Politics of Symbolism.* Cambridge, MA: Harvard University Press.

Deibel, Terry L. 1987. *Presidents, Public Opinion, and Power: The Nixon, Carter and Reagan Years.* New York: Foreign Policy Association.

Denton, Robert E., Jr., and Mary E. Stuckey. 1994. "A Communication Model of Presidential Campaigns: A 1992 Overview." In *The 1992 Presidential Campaign: A Communication Perspective,* ed. Robert E. Denton, Jr., 1–42. Westport, CT: Praeger.

Feldstein, Martin. 1994. Introductory chapter of *American Economic Policy in the 1980s,* ed. Martin Feldstein, 1–79. Chicago: University of Chicago Press.

Genovese, Michael A. 1994. "Jimmy Carter and the Age of Limits: Presidential Power in a Time of Decline and Diffusion." In *The Presidency and Domestic Politics of Jimmy Carter,* ed. Herbert D. Rosenbaum and Alexej Ugrinsky, 187–221. Westport, CT: Greenwood Press.

Hargrove, Erwin C. 1988. *Jimmy Carter as President: Leadership and the Politics of the Public Good.* Baton Rouge: Louisiana State University Press.

Hogan, Joseph. 1990. *The Reagan Years: The Record in Presidential Leadership,* ed. Joseph Hogan. New York: Manchester University Press.

Jones, Charles O. 1988. *The Trusteeship Presidency: Jimmy Carter the United States Congress.* Baton Rouge: Louisiana State University Press.

Kaufman, Burton Ira. 1993. *The Presidency of James Earl Carter, Jr.* Lawrence: University Press of Kansas.

Kernell, Samuel. 1997. *Going Public: New Strategies of Presidential Leadership,* 3rd ed. Washington, DC: Congressional Quarterly Press.

Meese, Edwin III. 1992. *With Reagan: The Inside Story.* Washington, DC: Regnery Gateway.

Mervin, David. 1996. *George Bush and the Guardianship Presidency.* New York: St. Martin's Press.

Pemberton, William E. 1997. *Exit with Honor: The Life and Presidency of Ronald Reagan.* Armonk, NY: M. E. Sharpe.

Ragsdale, Lyn. 1998. *Vital Statistics on the Presidency: Washington to Clinton.* Washington, DC: Congressional Quarterly, Inc.

Sigelman, Lee. 1979. "Presidential Popularity and Presidential Elections." *Public Opinion Quarterly* 43: 532–34.

Skidmore, David. 1996. *Reversing Course: Carter's Foreign Policy, Domestic Politics, and the Failure of Reform.* Nashville, TN: Vanderbilt University Press.

Skowronek, Stephen. 1993. *The Politics Presidents Make: Leadership from John Adams to George Bush.* Cambridge, MA: Harvard University Press.

6.4

WILLIAM G. HOWELL

From *Power without Persuasion:*
The Politics of Direct Presidential Action

Presidents have increasingly used unilateral actions, such as executive orders, to make policy independent of Congress. Howell describes the trends in these unilateral actions and offers a historical explanation. Over the course of the twentieth century, both Congress and the Supreme Court permitted presidents more latitude because the problems they faced became more complicated.

PRESIDENTIAL POWER IN THE MODERN ERA

. . . Throughout the twentieth century, presidents have used their powers of unilateral action to intervene into a whole host of policy arenas. Examples abound:

- During World War II, Roosevelt issued dozens of executive orders that nationalized aviation plants, shipbuilding companies, thousands of coal companies, and a shell plant—all clear violations of the Fifth Amendment's "taking" clause. The courts overturned none of these actions.
- With executive order 9066, Roosevelt ordered the evacuation, relocation, and internment of over 110,000 Japanese Americans living on the West Coast.
- In 1948, Truman desegregated the military via executive order 9981.
- After congressional efforts to construct a program that would send American youth abroad to do charitable work faltered three years in a row, Kennedy unilaterally created the Peace Corps and then financed it using discretionary funds.
- Johnson instituted the first affirmative action policy with executive order 11246.
- Preempting Congress, Nixon used an executive order to design the Environmental Protection Agency not as an independent commission, as Congress would have liked, but as an agency beholden directly to the president.
- By subjecting government regulations to cost-benefit analyses wit .
  executive order 12291, Reagan centralized powers of regulatory review.

From William G. Howell, *Power without Persuasion: The Politics of Direct Presidential Action* (Princeton, NJ: Princeton University Press, 2003).

▪ In 1992, George Bush federalized the National Guard and used its members to quell the Los Angeles riots.

While the majority of unilateral directives may not resonate quite so loudly in the telling of American history, a growing proportion involve substantive policy matters. Rather than being simply "daily grist-of-the-mill diplomatic matter," presidential directives have become instruments by which presidents actually set all sorts of consequential domestic and foreign policy (Paige 1977). . . .

Between 1920 and 1998, presidents issued 10,203 executive orders, or roughly 130 annually. As might be expected, presidents issued more civil service orders than orders in any other policy arena. On average, presidents issued thirty-three such orders, most of which dealt with the management of government personnel. This proportion, however, declined precipitously after World War II, when executive orders were no longer used to perform such trivial administrative practices as exempting individuals from mandatory retirement requirements.

Outside of those orders relating directly to the civil service, each year presidents issued on average thirty-two orders in foreign affairs, another eight on social welfare policy, sixteen on regulations of the domestic economy, and fully thirty-three that concerned the management of public lands and energy policy, though the number in this last category has declined markedly over the past few decades. The majority of orders, it seems, have substantive policy content, both foreign and domestic.

These figures only concern executive orders, which represent but one tool among many that presidents have at their disposal. When negotiating with foreign countries, presidents can bypass the treaty ratification process by issuing executive agreements; not surprisingly, the ratio of executive agreements to treaties, which hovered between zero and one in the nineteenth century, now consistently exceeds thirty (King and Ragsdale 1988). If presidents choose to avoid the reporting requirements Congress has placed on executive orders, they can repackage their policies as executive memoranda, determinations, administrative directives, or proclamations. And if they prefer to keep their decisions entirely secret, they can issue national security directives, which neither Congress nor the public has an opportunity to review (Cooper 2002).

The U.S. Constitution does not explicitly recognize any of these policy vehicles. Over the years, presidents have invented them, citing national security or expediency as justification. Taken as a whole, though, they represent one of the most striking, and underappreciated, aspects of presidential power in the modern era. Born from a truly expansive reading of Article II powers, these policy mechanisms have radically impacted how public policy is made in America today. The president's powers of unilateral action exert just as much influence over public policy, and in some cases more, than the formal powers that presidency scholars have examined so carefully over the past several decades.

▪   ▪   ▪

If we want to account for the influence that presidents wield over the construction of public policy, we must begin to pay serious attention to the president's capacity to create law on his own.

"Presidential Power Is the Power to Persuade"

The image of presidents striking out on their own to conduct a war on terrorism or revamp civil rights policies or reconstruct the federal bureaucracy stands in stark relief to scholarly literatures that equate executive power with persuasion and, consequently, place presidents at the peripheries of the lawmaking process.

Richard Neustadt sets the terms by which every student of American politics has come to understand presidential power in the modern era. When thinking about presidents since FDR, Neustadt argues, "weak remains the word with which to start" (1991 [1960], xix). Presidents are much like Shakespearean kings, marked more by tragedy than grandeur. Each is held captive by world events, by competing domestic interests and foreign policy pressures, by his party, his cabinet, the media, a fickle public, and partisan Congress. To make matters worse, the president exercises little control over any of these matters—current events and the political actors who inhabit them regularly disregard his expressed wishes. As a result, the pursuit of the president's policy agenda is marked more by compromise than conviction; and his eventual success or failure (as determined by either the public at the next election or historians over time) ultimately rests with others, and their willingness to extend a helping hand.

The public now expects presidents to accomplish far more than their formal powers alone permit. This has been especially true since the New Deal, when the federal government took charge of the nation's economy, commerce, and the social welfare of its citizens. Now presidents must address almost every conceivable social and economic problem, from the impact of summer droughts on midwestern farmers to the spread of nuclear weapons in the former Soviet Union. Armed with little more than the powers to propose and veto legislation and recommend the appointment of bureaucrats and judges, however, modern presidents appear doomed to failure from the very beginning. As one recent treatise on presidential "greatness" puts it, "modern presidents bask in the honors of the more formidable office that emerged from the New Deal, but they find themselves navigating a treacherous and lonely path, subject to a volatile political process that makes popular and enduring achievement unlikely" (Landy and Milkis 2000, 197).

If a president is to enjoy any measure of success, Neustadt counsels, he must master the art of persuasion. Indeed, according to Neustadt, power and persuasion are synonymous. The ability to persuade, to convince other political actors that his interests are their own, defines political power and is the key to presidential achievement. Power is about bargaining and negotiating; about brokering deals and trading promises; and about cajoling legislators, bureaucrats, and justices to do things that the president cannot accomplish on his own. . . . The president wields influence when he manages to enhance his bargaining stature and build governing coalitions; and the principal way to accomplish as much, Neustadt claims, is to draw upon the bag of experiences, skills, and qualities that he brings to the office.

Intentionally or not, Neustadt set off a behavioral revolution. . . . Self-confidence, an instinct for power, an exalted reputation within the Washington community, and prestige among the general public were considered the foundations of presidential success. Without certain personal qualities, presidents could not hope to build the coalitions necessary for action. Power was contingent upon persuasion, and persuasion was a function of all the personal qualities individual presidents bore; and so, the argument ran, what the presidency was at any moment critically depended upon who filled the office.

By these scholars' accounts, a reliance on formal powers actually signals weakness. What distinguishes great presidents is not a willingness to act upon the formal powers of the presidency but an ability to rally support precisely when and where such formal powers are lacking. As Neustadt argues, formal powers constitute a "painful last resort, a forced response to the exhaustion of other remedies, suggestive less of mastery than of failure—the failure of attempts to gain an end by softer means" (1991 [1960], 24). Presidents who veto bill after bill (think Ford) do so because their powers to persuade have faltered. The presidents who effectively communicate (Reagan) or who garner strong professional reputations (Roosevelt) stand out in the eyes of history.

Although the notion of the personal presidency dominated the field for decades, its influence is on the decline. The principal reason is that it no longer matches up with the facts. The personal presidency became a popular theoretical notion just as the American presidency was experiencing tremendous growth and development as an institution: in its staffing, its budget, and the powers delegated to it by Congress. As time went on, it became increasingly clear that the field needed to take more seriously the formal structures and powers that define the modern presidency.

If the personal presidency literature is correct, executive power should rise and fall according to the personal qualities of each passing president. Presidential power should expand and contract according to the individual skills and reputations that each president brings to the office. The constituent elements of the personal presidency may be important. Prestige and reputation may matter. But if we are to build a theory of presidential power, it seems reasonable to start with its most striking developments during the modern era. And these developments have little to do with the personalities of the men who, since Roosevelt, have inhabited the White House.

By virtually any objective measure, the size and importance of the "presidential branch" has steadily increased over the past century (Hart 1995). According to Thomas Cronin, "for almost 150 years the executive power of the presidency has steadily expanded" (1989, 204). Edward Corwin echoes this sentiment, arguing that "taken by and large, the history of the Presidency is a history of aggrandizement" (1957, 238). How can such trends persist if presidential powers are fundamentally personal in nature? It cannot be that the caliber of presidents today is markedly higher than a century ago, and for that reason alone presidents have managed to exert more and more influence. Does it really make sense to say that successful twentieth-century presidents (e.g., the Roosevelts or Reagan) distinguish themselves from great nineteenth-century presidents (e.g., Jackson, Polk, or Lincoln) by exhibiting stronger personalities? And if not, how can we argue that the roots of modern presidential power are fundamentally personal in nature? While Neustadt may illuminate short-term fluctuations at the boundaries of presidential influence—skill in the art of persuasion surely plays some part in political power—he cannot possibly explain the general growth of presidential power.

During the past twenty years, scholars have revisited the more formal components of presidential power. Work on the institutional presidency has regained the stature it held in political science during the first half of the twentieth century. This work is far more rigorous than the personal presidency literature and, for that matter, the institutional literature's earlier incarnations. A science of politics is finally taking hold of presidential studies: empirical tests now are commonplace; theoretical assumptions are clearly specified; and hypotheses are subject to independent corroboration. Perhaps more important than its methodological contributions, though, the institutional literature has successfully refocused scholarly attention on the office of the presidency and the features that make it distinctly modern: its staff and budget, the powers and responsibilities delegated to it by Congress, and the growth of agencies and commissions that collect and process information within it.

Nothing in the institutional literature, however, fundamentally challenges Neustadt's original claim that "presidential power is the power to persuade" (1991 [1960], 11). Scholars continue to equate presidential power with an ability to bargain, negotiate, change minds, turn votes, and drive legislative agendas through Congress. Not surprisingly, the president remains secondary throughout this work. He continues to play second fiddle to the people who make real policy decisions: committee members writing bills, congressional representatives offering amendments, bureaucrats enforcing laws, judges deciding cases.

To legislate, to build a record of accomplishments about which to boast at the next election, and to find their place in history, presidents above all rely upon Congress—so the institutional literature argues. Without Congress's active support, and the endorsement of its members, presidents cannot hope to achieve much at all. . . . The struggle for votes is perennial; and success is always fleeting. Should Congress lock up, or turn away, the president has little or no recourse. Ultimately, presidents depend upon Congress to delegate authority, ratify executive decisions, and legislate when, and where, presidents cannot act at all.

▪ ▪ ▪

Because of his unique position within a system of separated powers, the president has numerous opportunities to take independent action, with or without the expressed consent of either Congress or the courts. Sometimes he does so by issuing executive orders, proclamations, or executive agreements; other times by handing down general memoranda to agency heads; and still other times by dispensing national security directives. The number of these unilateral directives, and of opportunities to use them, has literally skyrocketed during the modern era (Moe and Howell 1999a, 1999b). While presidents freely exercise these powers during periods of national crises, as the events following September 11th have made clear, they also rely upon executive orders and executive agreements during periods of relative calm, effecting policy changes that never would survive the legislative process. And to the extent that presidents use these "power tools of the presidency" more now than they did a century ago, the ability to act unilaterally speaks to what is distinctively "modern" about the modern presidency (Cooper 1997, 2002).

Rather than hoping to influence at the margins what other political actors do, the president can make all kinds of public policies without the formal consent of Congress. While the growth of the presidency as an institution (its staffs, budgets, departments, and agencies) augments presidential power, it is the ability to set policy unilaterally that deserves our immediate and sustained attention.

▪ ▪ ▪

Thinking about Unilateral Powers

From the beginning, it is worth highlighting what makes unilateral powers distinctive. For the ability to act unilaterally is unlike any other power formally granted the president. Two features stand out.

The most important is that the president moves policy first and thereby places upon Congress and the courts the burden of revising a new political landscape. Rather than waiting at the end of an extended legislative process to sign or veto a bill, the president simply sets new policy and leaves it up to Congress and the courts to respond. If they choose not to retaliate, either by passing a law or ruling against the president, then the president's order stands. Only by taking (or credibly threatening to take) positive action can either adjoining institution limit the president's unilateral powers.

. . . By moving first, and anticipating the moves of future actors, legislators of all stripes and in very different political systems influence the kinds of policies governments produce. . . . But gains to the president are twice over. While agenda setters in Congress only propose bills, the president moves first and creates legally binding public policies. And he does so without ever having to wait on coalitions subsequently forming, committee chairs cooperating, or party leaders endorsing.

The second important feature of unilateral powers is that the president acts alone. There is no need to rally majorities, compromise with adversaries, or wait for some interest group to bring a case to court. Rather than depending upon Congress to enact his legislative agendas, the president frequently can strike out on his own, occasionally catching even his closest advisors off guard (recall Clinton's unilateral decision to bomb Iraq in the fall of 1998, the day before his scheduled impeachment hearing in the House Judiciary Committee). As the chief of state, the modern president is in a unique position to lead, to define a national agenda, and to impose his will in more and more areas of governance.

■ ■ ■

The ability to move first and act alone, then, distinguishes unilateral powers from all other sources of influence. In this sense, Neustadt is turned upside-down, for unilateral action is the virtual antithesis of bargaining and persuading. Here, presidents just act; their power does not hinge upon their capacity to "convince [political actors] that what the White House wants of them is what they ought to do for their sake and for their authority" (Neustadt 1991 [1960], 30). To make policy, presidents need not secure the formal consent of Congress, the active support of bureaucrats, or the official approval of justices. Instead, presidents simply set public policy and dare others to counter. For as long as Congress lacks the votes (usually two-thirds of both chambers) to overturn him, the president can be confident that his policy will stand.

The presidency literature's traditional distinction between formal and informal powers does not contribute much insight here. Because the Constitution does not mandate them, powers of unilateral action cannot be considered formal. It is by reference to what presidents have done (or gotten away with) that these powers take form. But nor are these discretionary powers informal. They are not rooted in personal qualities that vary with each passing president. Rather, these powers emerge from specific institutional advantages within the office of the presidency itself: its structure, resources, and location in a system of separated powers. The promise of a sustained analysis of unilateral powers, then, is great. To the extent that presidents act unilaterally with increasing frequency and effect in the postwar era, an institutional theory of unilateral action enables scholars to see beyond Neustadt's original conception of presidential influence in the modern era.

The Tool Chest

. . . Presidents in more modern times have manufactured a number of policy instruments that give shape and meaning to . . . prerogative powers. The most common include executive orders, proclamations, national security directives, and executive agreements. There are few hard and fast rules about how policies are classified, affording presidents a fair measure of liberty to select the instrument that best serves their objectives. Still, some basic distinctions generally apply.

Among all unilateral directives, "executive orders combine the highest levels of substance, discretion, and direct presidential involvement" (Mayer 2001, 35). Executive orders, for the most part, instruct government officials and administrative agencies to take specific actions with regard to both domestic and foreign affairs. "Executive orders are directives issued by the president to officers of the executive branch, requiring them to take an action, stop a certain type of activity, alter policy, change management practices, or accept a delegation of authority under which they will henceforth be responsible for the implementation of law" (Cooper 2002, 16). But while presidents direct executive orders to subordinates within the executive branch, the impact of these orders is felt well beyond the boundaries of the federal government. . . . Through executive orders, presidents have dictated the terms by which government contractors hire and fire their employees, set restrictions on where American citizens can travel abroad, frozen the financial holdings of private parties, reset trade, tariffs, and determined the kinds of recreational activities that are allowed on public lands.

If executive orders are typically directed to officials within the federal government, presidential proclamations almost always target individuals and groups outside of the government. Because Article II of the Constitution does not endow the president with clear and immediate authority over private parties (as it does over the federal bureaucracy), it is not surprising that proclamations tend to be less consequential than executive orders, most involving ceremonial and commemorative affairs. There are, however, numerous exceptions, such as Nixon's 1971 proclamations and orders temporarily freezing all wages, rents, and prices as part of the national economic stabilization program; Ford's 1973 proclamation granting pardons to draft dodgers; and Carter's 1980 proclamations imposing new surcharges on imported oil.

■   ■   ■

Even the advent of the Cold War can be traced back to a national security directive. Issued in April 1950, N.S.C. 68 emphasized the historical importance of the mounting conflict between the United States and Soviet Union. The document, drafted by the director of the State Department's policy-planning staff, Paul Nitze, was a call to arms and defined the nation's military and political objectives as it waged an ongoing struggle against the world's only other superpower. . . . While it met some initial resistance within the Truman and Eisenhower administrations, N.S.C. 68, more than any other document, established the guiding doctrine for successive presidents' Cold War foreign policy.

Executive agreements stand apart from these other directives. While executive orders, proclamations, and (to a lesser degree) national security directives all are unilateral counterparts to legislation, executive agreements provide presidents with an alternative to the treaty ratification process. Rather than having to secure the consent of two-thirds of the Senate before entering into a bi- or multilateral agreement with foreign nations, presidents can use executive agreements to unilaterally commit the United States to deals involving such issues as international trade, ocean fishing rights, open air space, environmental standards, and immigration patterns. While most of these agreements concern very specific (and often technical) matters, the sheer number issued during the modern era has increased at such an astronomical rate that collectively they now constitute a vital means by which presidents unilaterally affect public policy.

When setting public policy, presidents frequently issue combinations of these various policy directives. To force the integration of schools in Little Rock, Arkansas, Eisenhower simultaneously issued a proclamation and an executive order. Carter relied upon a series of executive orders and executive agreements to negotiate the Iran Hostage Crisis. Presiding over World War II, the Korean War, and the Vietnam War, Roosevelt, Truman, Johnson, and Nixon all issued a wide array of secretive orders, national security directives and otherwise. Presidents frequently use executive orders, secretarial orders, and reorganization plans to create administrative agencies and then turn to other kinds of unilateral directives—for example, administrative directives, findings and determinations, and regulations—to monitor their behavior. The ease with which presidents can mix and match these unilateral directives to advance their policy goals is considerable.

The Legality of Unilateral Powers

The first Court challenge to a presidential order, *Little v. Barreme* (1804) concerned the legality of a seizure of a Danish ship, the *Flying Fish*. George Little, the captain of the *U.S.S. Boston,* had intercepted the ship at sea. At the time, Captain Little was complying with a John Adams presidential order that the Navy seize any and all ships sailing to or from French ports. Previously, however, Congress had only authorized the seizure of frigates sailing to French ports. Because the Danish brig was sailing *from* a French port and not *to* one (it was headed from Jérémie to St. Thomas), the Court for the first time had to resolve a discrepancy between a presidential order and congressional statute.

In a unanimous ruling written by Chief Justice John Marshall, the Court declared that had Adams' order stood alone, the Navy's actions would be constitutional. Because Congress had enacted a more restrictive statute, however, the Court was forced to rule in favor of the Danish captain. "Congressional policy announced in a statute necessarily prevails over inconsistent presidential orders. . . . Presidential orders, even those issued as Commander in Chief, are subject to restrictions by Congress." Marshall subsequently ordered Captain Little to pay damages. More importantly, though, Marshall established the clear principle that when an executive order blatantly conflicts with a law, the law prevails.

During the rest of the nineteenth century, the federal courts considered a host of challenges to unilateral directives issued by presidents, most of which involved military orders. It was not until the 1930s that the Supreme Court formally recognized the president's power to act unilaterally. Three cases—*United States v. Curtiss-Wright* (1936); *United States v. Belmont* (1937); and *United States v. Pink* (1942)—made the difference (Schubert 1973, 107).

Curtiss-Wright centrally involved the constitutionality of an executive agreement that forbade the sale of arms to countries involved in armed conflict. When it sold fifteen machine guns to the government of Bolivia, Curtiss-Wright Export Corporation was charged with violating the agreement. As part of its defense, the company argued that Congress had "abdicated its essential functions and delegated them to the Executive," and for that reason, the Court should overturn the executive agreement. Instead, the Supreme Court, in an oft-cited phrase, deemed the president the "sole organ of the federal government in the field of international relations" and upheld the constitutionality of this particular delegation of authority. Doing so, it formally recognized his legal right to issue executive agreements.

In *United States v. Belmont,* the Supreme Court extended this right to executive orders. When Russia reneged on debts owed to the United States in the 1930s, President Roosevelt seized Russian financial assets held in American banks. Arguing that Roosevelt's actions violated New York State law, a Russian investor asked the Court to overturn the executive order and to award compensation for his losses. The Court, however, refused. Doing so, it equated an executive order with federal law and reaffirmed its preeminence over state law.

The Supreme Court extended this reasoning to executive agreements in *United States v. Pink,* which again involved the seizure of Russian assets in American banks. This time, however, the focus concerned an exchange between the president and the Russian government known as the Litvinov Assignment. In a letter to Roosevelt, People's Commissar for Foreign Affairs Maxim Litvinov relinquished certain Russian claims to assets of Russian companies in New York banks. Roosevelt subsequently acknowledged the reassignment of property claims. In *Pink,* the question before the Court centered on the legal authority of this exchange. Ultimately, the Court ruled that because executive agreements have the same status as treaties, and because both override state laws, the plaintiffs could not use New York State law to try to recover their lost assets.

Collectively, *Curtiss-Wright, Belmont,* and *Pink* firmly established the president's authority to issue directives involving "external affairs." Their distinction between foreign and domestic policy, however, subsequently blurred. And for good reason. The list of exceptions to any definition of "foreign" or "domestic" policy is sufficiently long as to make the definitions themselves unworkable as elements of jurisprudence. "The original constitutional understanding that in domestic affairs Congress would make the law and presidents would see to its enforcement had never worked in practice and by the early 1990s it had largely been abandoned" (McDonald 1994, 314). The courts now fully recognize the president's power to issue executive orders and agreements that concern both foreign and domestic policy. Indeed, powers of unilateral action have become a veritable fixture of the American presidency in the modern era.

Writing Public Policy

Much can happen between the issuance of a presidential order and its implementation. Opportunities for shirking abound. Administrative agencies may read their mandates selectively; they may ignore especially objectionable provisions; they may report false or misleading information about initiatives' successes and failures. As we have already noted, the executive branch assuredly does not reduce to the president himself. Bureaucrats enjoy a fair measure of autonomy to do as they please.

Demanding a policy change does not make it so. As Neustadt himself forcefully argued, orders handed down from on high are not always self-executing (1991 [1960], 10–28). In 1948, for instance, Truman issued an executive order demanding the desegregation of the military, but decades passed before the outcome was finally realized. Presidents are engaged in a constant struggle to ensure compliance among members of the executive branch, and to advance the realization of their policy interests. Presidents appoint high-ranking officials who share their worldview, and whenever possible, presidents try to rally the support of their subordinates. This has important consequences for our understanding of presidential power; for when it comes to the implementation of public policy (whether enacted as a federal statute or issued as a unilateral directive), the power modern presidents wield very much depends upon their ability to persuade.

■ ■ ■

[W]hile presidents must build and sustain coalitions to pass laws, they can unilaterally issue policy directives over the vocal objections of congressional majorities. As one political observer instructs, "Forget Capitol Hill deliberations and back-room negotiations with industry titans. No need for endless debate and deal-making. For a president, an executive order can be as powerful as a law—and considerably easier to achieve." In the political fight over the content of public policy, presidents regularly exert power without persuasion.

■ ■ ■

CONCLUSION

▪   ▪   ▪

Macrotrends in Unilateral Policy Making

Since George Washington issued the Neutrality Proclamation in 1793, presidents have relied upon their unilateral powers to effect important policy changes. In the nineteenth century, Jefferson followed up with the Louisiana Purchase and Lincoln with the Emancipation Proclamation. In the early twentieth century, Theodore Roosevelt established the national parks system and Wilson issued more than 1,700 executive orders to guide the nation through World War I.

For the past fifty years, however, the trajectory of unilateral policy making has noticeably increased. While it was relatively rare, and for the most part inconsequential, during the eighteenth and nineteenth centuries, unilateral policy making has become an integral feature of the modern presidency. Presidents issue more unilateral directives today than ever before, steadily expanding their influence over all kinds of public policies, foreign and domestic. While there remain important fluctuations from year to year, and from administration to administration, the time-series of significant executive orders and executive agreements unmistakably rises.

In part, this is due to the overwhelming demands placed upon modern presidents. The public holds presidents responsible for all kinds of activities that previously either did not concern the federal government or rested solely within the domain of Congress. Presidents now develop policies on medical practices, racial discrimination, social welfare, labor and management relations, international trade, and education—areas that few presidents, prior to FDR, ever addressed. Indeed, it is difficult to think of a single area of governance that modern presidents can safely ignore. Modern presidents, in this sense, do more simply because the public expects them to.

In addition, presidential powers have expanded over the past half-century because the checks placed on them by Congress have subsided. As political parties have weakened, subcommittees have proliferated, and ideological divisions within Congress have heightened, Congress's ability to legislate has waned. So much so, in fact, that gridlock, while not constant, has become "a basic fact of U.S. lawmaking" (Krehbiel 1998, 4). This development has important implications for presidential power. As Congress weakens, the check it places on presidential power relaxes, and new opportunities arise for the president to strike out on his own. An expansion of presidential power then signals a shift in the overall division of powers—tipping the balance in favor of the president, and against Congress.

Two additional factors probably contributed to the overall increase in unilateral policy making during the latter half of the twentieth century. First, the time-series takes off in the late 1930s, just after the Supreme Court issued a series of rulings—*United States v. Curtiss-Wright* (1936); *United States v. Belmont* (1937); and *United States v. Pink* (1942)—that collectively fortified the president's legal authority to issue executive orders and executive agreements. With the official sanctioning of the Court, modern presidents proceeded with a greater measure of confidence when issuing executive orders and other unilateral directives. Second, many of these orders either created new administrative agencies or directed existing agencies to perform new functions. In this sense, the general trajectory of the significant executive order time-series maps the steady growth of the administrative state. Modern presidents did more simply because more needed to be done. Compared to their predecessors, modern presidents oversee more agencies that employ more employees that perform more tasks. As a consequence, it is little wonder that modern presidents rely upon the unilateral powers with greater frequency.

These trends, however, need not continue forever. There is nothing in the logic of the unilateral politics model that requires presidential power to increase monotonically over time. Quite the contrary, should a new consensus about policy matters emerge in Congress and legislative productivity displace gridlock, opportunities for presidents to act unilaterally may decline. Similarly, should executive actions attract heightened public scrutiny, judges may feel emboldened to overturn presidents with greater frequency.

BIBLIOGRAPHY

Cooper, Phillip. 2002. *By Order of the President: The Use and Abuse of Executive Direct Action.* Lawrence: University Press of Kansas.

———. 1997. "Power Tools for an Effective and Responsible Presidency." *Administration and Society* 29 (5): 529–56.

Corwin, Edward. 1957. *The President, Office and Powers, 1787–1948: History and Analysis of Practice and Opinion.* New York: New York University Press.

Cronin, Thomas. 1989. *Inventing the American Presidency.* Lawrence: University of Kansas Press.

Hart, John. 1995. *The Presidential Branch From Washington to Clinton.* Chatham, NJ: Chatham House Publishers, Inc.

King, Gary, and Lyn Ragsdale. 1988. *The Elusive Executive: Discovering Statistical Patterns in the Presidency.* Washington, DC: Congressional Quarterly Press.

Krehbiel, Keith. 1998. *Pivotal Politics: A Theory of U.S. Lawmaking.* Chicago: University of Chicago Press.

Landy, Marc, and Sidney Milkis. 2000. *Presidential Greatness.* Lawrence: University of Kansas Press.

Mayer, Kenneth. 2001. *With the Stroke of a Pen: Executive Orders and Presidential Power.* Princeton, NJ: Princeton University Press.

McDonald, Forrest. 1994. *The American Presidency: An Intellectual History.* Lawrence: University of Kansas Press.

Moe, Terry, and William Howell. 1999a. "The Presidential Power of Unilateral Action." *Journal of Law, Economics and Organization* 15 (1): 132–79.

———. 1999b. "Unilateral Action and Presidential Power: A Theory." *Presidential Studies Quarterly* 29 (4): 850–72.

Neustadt, Richard E. 1991 [1960]. *Presidential Power and the Modern Presidents.* New York: Free Press.

Paige, Joseph. 1977. *The Law Nobody Knows: Enlargement of the Constitution—Treaties and Executive Agreements.* New York: Vantage Press.

Schubert, Glendon. 1973. *The Presidency in the Courts.* New York: Da Capo Press.

6.5

SAMUEL KERNELL

From *Going Public: New Strategies of Presidential Leadership*

Over the course of the twentieth century, American presidents increasingly spoke directly to the people rather than to news reporters or through press releases. Today, presidents spend a lot of their time giving public speeches, but this behavior was rare 100 years ago. Kernell argues that this increase has given presidents more leverage when bargaining with Congress and makes sense in an age with a more educated population and improved means of travel and communication.

INTRODUCTION: GOING PUBLIC IN THEORY AND PRACTICE

I call the approach to presidential leadership that has come into vogue at the White House "going public." It is a strategy whereby a president promotes himself and his policies in Washington by appealing directly to the American public for support. Forcing compliance from fellow Washingtonians by going over their heads to enlist constituents' pressure is a tactic that was known but seldom attempted during the first half of the century. Theodore Roosevelt probably first enunciated the strategic principle of going public when he described the presidency as the "bully pulpit." Moreover, he occasionally put theory into practice with public appeals for his Progressive Party reforms. During the next thirty years, other presidents also periodically summoned public support to help them in their dealings with Congress. Perhaps the most famous such instance is Woodrow Wilson's ill-fated whistle-stop tour of the country on behalf of his League of Nations treaty. Equally noteworthy, historically, is Franklin D. Roosevelt's series of radio "fireside chats," which were designed less to subdue congressional opposition than to remind politicians of his continuing national mandate for the New Deal.

These historical instances are significant in large part because they are rare. Unlike Richard Nixon, who thought it important "to spread the White

From Samuel Kernell, *Going Public: New Strategies of Presidential Leadership* (Washington, DC: CQ Press, 2007).

House around" by traveling and speaking extensively,[1] these earlier presidents were largely confined to Washington and obliged to address the country through the nation's newspapers. The concept and legitimizing precedents of going public may have been established during these years, but the emergence of presidents who *routinely* did so to promote their policies outside Washington awaited the development of modern systems of transportation and mass communications. Going public should be appreciated as a strategic adaptation to the information age.

The regularity with which recent presidents have sought public backing for their Washington dealings has altered the way politicians both inside and outside the White House regard the office. . . .

Presidential Theory

Going public has become routine. This was not always the case. After World War I Congress refused to support President Wilson's League of Nations, a peace treaty the president himself had helped negotiate. In this instance Congress determined to amend the treaty and a president equally determined to finalize the agreement the other countries had ratified left him with little choice but to go public to try to marshal public opinion to force the Senate's agreement. Today our information-age presidents opt to go public regardless of the political climate in Washington.

There is another reason to systematically study this leadership strategy. Compared with many other aspects of the modern presidency, scholarship has only recently directed its attention toward this feature of the president's repertoire. Although going public had not become a keystone of presidential leadership in the 1950s and 1960s, when much of the influential scholarship on the subject was written, sufficient precedents were available for scholars to consider its potential for presidential leadership in the future.

Probably the main reason traditional presidential scholarship short-changed going public is its fundamental incompatibility with bargaining. Presidential power is the "power to bargain," Richard E. Neustadt taught a generation of students of the presidency.[2] When Neustadt published his definitive study of presidential leadership in 1960, the "bargaining president" had already become a centerpiece of pluralist theories of American politics. Nearly a decade earlier, Robert A. Dahl and Charles E. Lindblom had described the politician in America generically as "the human embodiment of a bargaining society." They made a special point to include the president in writing that despite his possessing "more hierarchical controls than any other single figure in the government . . . like everyone else . . . the President must bargain constantly."[3] Since Neustadt's landmark treatise, other major works on the presidency have reinforced and elaborated this theme.[4]

■   ■   ■

Going public entails public posturing. To the extent that it fixes the president's bargaining position, posturing makes subsequent compromise with other politicians more difficult. Because negotiators must be prepared to yield some of their clients' preferences to make a deal, bargaining proverbially proceeds best behind closed doors. Consider the difficulty Ronald Reagan's widely publicized challenge "My tax proposal is a line drawn in dirt" posed for subsequent budget negotiations in Washington.[5] Similarly, during his nationally televised State of the Union address in 1994, President Bill Clinton sought to repair his reputation as someone too willing to compromise away his principles by declaring to the assembled joint session of Congress, "If you send me [health care] legislation that does not guarantee every American private health insurance that can never be taken away, you will force me to take this pen, veto the legislation, and we'll come right back here and start all over again."[6] Not only did these declarations threaten to cut away any middle ground on which a compromise might be constructed, they probably stiffened the resolve of the president's adversaries, some of whom would later be needed to pass the administration's legislative program.

. . . [P]ossibly most injurious to bargaining, going public undermines the legitimacy of other politicians. It usurps their prerogatives of office, denies their role as representatives, and questions their claim to reflect the interests of their constituents. For a traditional bargaining stance with the president to be restored, these politicians would first have to reestablish parity, probably at a cost of conflict with the White House.[7]

Given these fundamental incompatibilities, one may further speculate that by spoiling the bargaining environment, going public renders the president's future influence ever more dependent upon his ability to generate popular support for himself and his policies. The degree to which a president draws upon public opinion determines the kind of leader he will be.

▪   ▪   ▪

THE GROWTH OF GOING PUBLIC

▪   ▪   ▪

Trends in Going Public

Going public can take a variety of forms. The most conspicuous is the formal, ceremonial occasion, such as an inaugural address or a State of the Union message, when official duty places the president prominently before the nation. Going public may, however, involve no more than a pregnant aside to a news reporter. This sort of casual, impromptu gesture eludes systematic analysis, but speeches, travel, and appearances—all of which take place in public view and therefore can be easily counted—form a good record of significant events with which to measure the rise of going public. Each of these nonexclusive activities can be further divided according to its locale or prominence.[8]

▪   ▪   ▪

FIGURE [1] Presidential Addresses, 1929–2003 (Yearly Averages for First Three Years of First Term)

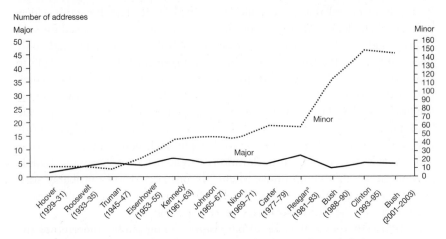

[a] Major addresses include television addresses only. With radio included, Reagan averaged twenty-four major addresses per year.

NOTE: To eliminate public activities inspired by concerns of reelection rather than governing, only the first three years have been tabulated. For this reason, Gerald Ford's record of public activities during his two and one-half years of office have been ignored.

SOURCES: Data for Hoover, Roosevelt, Truman, Eisenhower, Nixon, and Carter are from William W. Lammers, "Presidential Attention-Focusing Activities," in *The President and the American Public*, ed. Doris A. Graber (Philadelphia: Institute for the Study of Human Issues, 1982), Table 6-1, 152. Data for Kennedy, Johnson, Reagan, Bush, and Clinton are from *Public Papers of the Presidents* series. See also Samuel Kernell, "The Presidency and the People: The Modern Paradox," in *The Presidency and the Political System*, ed. Michael Nelson (Washington, DC: CQ Press, 1984), 242.

Figure [1] shows that until the 1960s, the average yearly numbers of major and minor addresses had grown steadily since Herbert Hoover's presidency. . . . The real explosion in presidential talk has occurred with minor addresses. Reagan, Carter, and Nixon on average surpassed Truman, Roosevelt, and Hoover by nearly fivefold in the use of such rhetoric. George H. W. Bush managed to double these already high levels of targeted addresses. During his first three years in office he averaged a minor address every three days. Clinton did Bush one better—a minor address nearly every other day, a pace almost matched by the younger Bush.

Public Appearances

Appearances are distinguished in Figures [2] and [3] by locale. . . . The number of public appearances outside the city generally reflects the president's non-Washington origins and divided party control of government.

FIGURE [2] Public Appearances by Presidents, 1929–2003 (Yearly Averages for First Three Years of First Term)

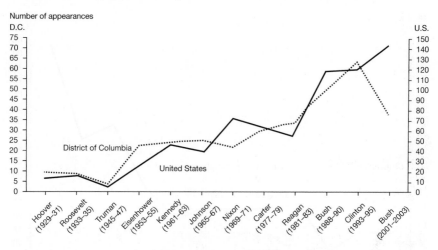

Number of appearances

NOTE: To eliminate public activities inspired by concerns of reelection rather than governing, only the first three years have been tabulated. For this reason, Gerald Ford's record of public activities during his two and one-half years of office have been ignored.

SOURCES: Data for Hoover, Roosevelt, Truman, Eisenhower, Nixon, and Carter are from William W. Lammers, "Presidential Attention-Focusing Activities," in *The President and the American Public*, ed. Doris A. Graber (Philadelphia: Institute for the Study of Human Issues, 1982), Table 6-2 and 6-3, 154–156. Data for Kennedy, Johnson, Reagan, Bush, and Clinton are from *Public Papers of the Presidents* series. See also Samuel Kernell, "The Presidency and the People: The Modern Paradox," in *The Presidency and the Political System*, ed. Michael Nelson (Washington, DC: CQ Press, 1984), 245.

Conclusion

. . . [T]he degree to which presidents go public determines the kind of leaders they will be. Modern presidents rely upon public opinion for their leadership in Washington to an extent unknown in the early 1950s. This makes for a style of leadership in the White House that was unknown to Robert A. Dahl and Charles E. Lindblom when they described the president as "an embodiment of a bargaining society" in the early 1950s or a few years later when Richard E. Neustadt predicated presidential power exclusively on bargaining.[9]

This proposition, claiming a change in the degree of going public and inferring a change in the character of leadership, is subject to rejoinder on two fronts. Because every president since Theodore Roosevelt has sought at some moment to rally public opinion to his side, and each in his public activity has drawn on the precedents and departed only marginally from the base lines of his immediate predecessor, one can easily miss the striking degree to which

FIGURE [3] Days of Political Travel by Presidents, 1929–2003 (Yearly Averages for First Three Years of First Term)

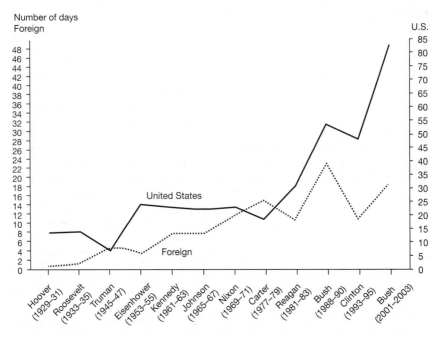

NOTE: To eliminate public activities inspired by concerns of reelection rather than governing, only the first three years have been tabulated. For this reason, Gerald Ford's record of public activities during his two and one-half years of office have been ignored. SOURCES: Data for Hoover, Roosevelt, Truman, Eisenhower, Nixon, and Carter are from William W. Lammers, "Presidential Attention-Focusing Activities," in *The President and the American Public*, ed. Doris A. Graber (Philadelphia: Institute for the Study of Human Issues, 1982), Table 6-5, 160. Data for Kennedy, Johnson, Reagan, Bush, and Clinton are from *Public Papers of the Presidents* series. See also Samuel Kernell, "The Presidency and the People: The Modern Paradox," in *The Presidency and the Political System*, ed. Michael Nelson (Washington, DC: CQ Press, 1984), 244.

presidents today go public compared with the presidents of the 1930s, 1940s, or even 1950s.

Moreover, I suspect that the increasing quantity of public activity has tended to be obscured by the varying quality of public rhetoric, which is always more memorable than the quantity. To those who compared Ronald Reagan's rhetorical talents with those of Franklin Roosevelt, little appears to have changed in the past fifty years.

■   ■   ■

Another counterargument accepts the trends examined in this chapter but holds that they have little bearing on the character of presidential leadership.

The president may be a more familiar face on television, and he may spend more time on the road, but his public relations have not reduced the role of bargaining in presidential leadership.

NOTES

1. These categories of going public correspond to those developed by William W. Lammers, who was the first to systematically examine trends in presidents' public activities (William W. Lammers, "Presidential Attention-Focusing Activities," in *The President and the American Public*, ed. Doris A. Graber [Philadelphia: Institute for the Study of Human Issues, 1982], 145–171).

To incorporate the research of Professor Lammers on the public activities of modern presidents, I adopted his coding scheme. I also consulted with him at the early stages of this study for his advice on how to code difficult cases. The present analysis, therefore, benefits from both his considerable research and good judgment.

2. The three general categories of public activities presented in Figures [1], [2], and [3] are intended to be neither mutually exclusive nor together an exhaustive classification of all public behavior. Press conferences . . . , purely ceremonial functions such as lighting the White House Christmas tree, vacation travel, and minor public activities such as White House receptions and brief remarks have been excluded from the analysis. The three categories of public activities are addresses, political travel, and appearances.

Addresses. Major addresses are those generally delivered in Washington, broadcast on television or radio, and focused on more than a narrow potential audience. Inaugural and State of the Union speeches are included in this group. Note that because of the extensive number of nationally broadcast radio addresses by President Reagan, I have separated his radio from his television addresses in Figure [1]. The major address totals for Presidents Bush and Clinton also exclude radio addresses. Omitted from major addresses are presidential press conferences and purely ceremonial functions (for example, calls to astronauts and Christmas tree lighting ceremonies). . . . [Regarding] the decline in the use of press conferences: Minor addresses are all nonmajor statements made outside the White House in which the president spoke more than one thousand words. Question-and-answer sessions, even if conducted outside a formal press conference setting, are excluded.

Political travel. To distinguish purely vacation travel from work-related travel, only those travel days that involved public political activity are included in Figure [3]. Moreover, to be coded as domestic political travel, the president must do more than engage in brief conversation with reporters. To be coded as political foreign travel, the travel day must include comments exceeding two hundred words, a meeting with a head of state, or attendance at an international conference, even if the president does not engage in public activity.

Appearances. Washington appearances take place away from the White House and the Executive Office Building and include all appearances in Washington and its surrounding suburbs. Brief comments with reporters are excluded from both Washington and U.S. appearances, but prepared remarks on arrival are included in the coding. Unlike Professor Lammers, who excluded President Carter's town meetings, I have coded them as constituting both days of travel and appearances.

3. As a cautionary note, in recent years the sources used to compile this list of television addresses appear to employ a more inclusive definition of "address to nation."

4. In Figures [1], [2], and [3], only the first three years have been tabulated in order to eliminate activities inspired by concerns for reelection rather than governing. Since Gerald Ford's tenure does not include three nonelection years, his record of public activities has been ignored.

5. Pierre Salinger, *With Kennedy* (New York: Doubleday, 1966), 138–144. For a discussion of other presidents' concerns with overexposure, see Godfrey Hodgson, *All Things to All Men* (New York: Simon & Schuster, 1980), 188–189.

6. Newton N. Minow, John Bartlow Martin, and Lee M. Mitchell, *Presidential Television* (New York: Basic Books, 1973), 65–68.

7. J. F. terHorst and Col. Ralph Albertazzie provide a lively chronology of presidential air travel in *The Flying White House* (New York: Coward, McCann, and Geoghegan, 1979).

8. "Hoover, with 37 Radio Talks in Past Year, Made a Record," *New York Times*, December 28, 1930, 1.

9. See Robert A. Dahl and Charles E. Lindblom, *Politics, Economics, and Welfare* (New York: Harper and Row, 1960); and Richard E. Neustadt, *Presidential Power* (New York: John Wiley and Sons, 1980).

6.6

JAMES DRUCKMAN AND LAWRENCE JACOBS

From *Who Governs: Presidents, Public Opinion, and Manipulation*

Recent presidents have collected public opinion data—often relying on private surveys not intended for public release—and used this information to craft public statements and policy decisions. Druckman and Jacobs analyzed presidential archives to better understand how different presidents used this public opinion information. In this selection, they compare Richard Nixon to Ronald Reagan and find evidence that Reagan more than Nixon paid careful attention to the attitudes of his own party's conservative constituencies. Nixon saw evidence in the polls that the Vietnam War was intensely polarizing, thus these polls moved him toward a middle ground in war policy to avoid antagonizing too many people.

HOW WHITE HOUSE STRATEGY DRIVES THE COLLECTION AND USE OF ITS POLLING

Presidents hunger for information about public opinion to enhance communication that will advance their political interests and improve their ability to move public attitudes. Despite its massive capacity for polling, the White House faces limits on how much and what kinds of polling data it can collect. Survey instruments have space constraints, and the collection and processing of data come with substantial financial and organizational costs. These constraints—combined with the intense political interests of presidents— pressure them to make choices and act as strategic gatherers of information rather than relying on arbitrarily assembled data.

Which public opinion data are most valuable to politicians? Previous research has not rigorously investigated why politicians decide to *collect* and *use* and which type is most strategically attractive (cf. Burstein 2003; Wlezien 2004).

Presidents tailor the information they collect and use to critical political circumstances—the proximity to Election Day, the coherence and salience of public attitudes toward specific problems or issues, changing political party dynamics, and the particular demands of domestic and foreign policy. The mix of challenges facing presidents shapes the distinctive contours of how they approach information gathering.

From James Druckman and Lawrence Jacobs, *Who Governs: Presidents, Public Opinion, and Manipulation* (Chicago: University of Chicago Press, 2015).

Its strategy regarding information shaped how the White House handled two of the most politically important types of polling data. The first type is the public's Ideological Identification—its aggregating of policy attitudes into one global measure of general ideological predisposition, which we refer to as *lumping*. The second type is the public's Policy Opinions—its disaggregated preferences for specific policies, which we refer to as *splitting*. In policy domains and electoral situations that politically threaten presidents, the White House is motivated to invest time in finding information on specific issues that the public ranks as important or salient; absent public scrutiny and the risk of damaging punishment during an approaching election, it is motivated to rely on less costly information related to general ideological orientation.

. . . We explore the distinctive approaches to lumping and splitting by Nixon and Reagan as they set about crafting their public presentations. Reagan invested most extensively in collecting and using data on both ideological orientations and policy preferences in order to stake out conservative positions that appealed to party activists and his strongest supporters while ducking land mines for swing voters. Nixon was less inclined to aggressively push a conservative agenda, preferring instead to hug the main contours of public opinion and selectively seize on opportunities to move to the right as conditions allowed.

We begin by exploring research on political representation to sketch potential political motivations for lumping and splitting and then proceed to analyze how and under what political and policy conditions Nixon and Reagan modulated their approach to information.

Lumping versus Splitting

Research on political representation has largely neglected how government officials track and use public opinion but nonetheless offers insights into the motivations that might affect how politicians approach information. Research by Erikson, MacKuen, and Stimson (2002, xxi, 289–91) indicates that "political leaders regularly ignore expressed public preferences on [specific policies] . . . knowing that the preferences arise from a weak grasp of the central facts." Instead, "it is the general public disposition, the mood, which policy makers must monitor." Kingdon (1984, 68–69, 153) similarly concludes that government officials rely on "general judgments about the state of public opinion," such as the sense of an "antigovernment mood in the country." This research suggests that politicians have incentives to act as lumpers who discount the public's specific policy preferences if they conclude that the public lacks the necessary information and attention to form specific views on individual policies and accurately scrutinize its specific positions. Under these conditions, politicians may focus on the electorate's mood—the coherent, homogenous direction that underlies all its considerations and views of apparently dissimilar policies.

In contrast to lumping, splitting is based on the assumption that the public's preferences for specific policies are—under certain circumstances—meaningful and likely to produce potentially damaging scrutiny of politicians' public positions. Under these conditions, investing resources in private polling to follow the public's policy preferences is worthwhile to strategic politicians (Monroe 1979, 1998; Page and Shapiro 1983; Geer 1991, 1996; Heith 1998, 2003; Manza and Cook 2002a, 2002b; Page 2002; Eisinger 2003; Wlezien 2004; Soroka and Wlezien 2005).

In addition to factoring in its appraisal of public opinion, the White House's collection and use of lumping or splitting data are also affected by its strategic circumstances and its perception of voter scrutiny and punishment. Politicians are motivated to invest resources in splitting on issues when they perceive risk in the face of an upcoming election (e.g., G. C. Wright 1989; Jacobs and Shapiro 2000; Canes-Wrone 2006; but cf. Rottinghaus 2010), the public's perception of particular policies as salient (Page and Shapiro 1983), the emergence of what are seen as intractable or threatening issues in foreign or domestic policy (Nincic 1990; Fiorina 1981; Kahneman and Tversky 1984), or the intensification of political party competition (Aldrich 1995; Carmines and Stimson 1989). This is consistent with previous research demonstrating that salient policies tend to generate greater government responsiveness to majority public opinion on those specific issues (Kuklinski and Elling 1977; Kuklinski and McCrone 1980; Page and Shapiro 1983; Wlezien 2004; Hill and Hurley 1999) and contribute to public attitudes that are more coherent and engaged in forming evaluations of candidates (Krosnick 1988, 1989, 1990; Iyengar 1990).

Absent the risk of unusual public scrutiny, politicians have incentives to rely on less costly information gleaned from Americans' general ideological orientation. In particular, lumping is a reasonable strategy when elections are not imminent and when issues and policy domains are less important to the public and do not involve intractable foreign or domestic challenges that are the subject of intense party competition. Under these conditions, the public's attitudes are typically less reliable, stable, and coherent (Zaller 1992; Druckman and Lupia 2000) and, as a result, pose a less direct threat to politicians.

The confluence of White House assessments of the public's relative attentiveness and knowledge and the risk of voter scrutiny and punishment suggests four general scenarios. The first two are when circumstances point the White House in one consistent direction toward either "Pure Splitting" (it perceives clear risks and demands information on the public's specific policy preferences) or "Pure Lumping" (it senses minimal political threats and is content to track the public's general conservative or liberal tilt). The third scenario is geared toward "Strategic Balancing" by engaging in both splitting and lumping to reduce risks while avoiding massive investments. The fourth scenario is for situations where presidents forgo opinion data of any sort owing to the certainty of their position or constraints on White House polling.

Lumping and Splitting Data

We examine the general question of whether, why, and how politicians collect and use different types of information on public opinion by studying the content of the survey research conducted by the Nixon and Reagan presidencies and their approaches to incorporating that research in their political strategies. In particular, we investigate the conditions under which the Nixon and Reagan White Houses engaged in lumping (i.e., focusing on the Ideological Identification measure) or splitting (i.e., focusing on Policy Opinion measures) by identifying the statistical associations between private polling data and presidential statements. More precisely, we pinpoint the relative effects of the two polling measures under different political conditions. Policy Opinion . . . reports the percentage of respondents taking a conservative position on specific issues—such as the percentage taking the conservative position in response to the question, "Are you in favor or not in favor of cutting federal spending?" . . .

Collection of these types of data provides a measure of White House attention to splitting. Ideological Identification, in contrast, reports the percentage of the public that self-identifies as generally conservative. The gathering of these data serves as an appropriate indicator of lumping even though the White House's construct differs from some previous work on lumping, such as Stimson's (1991) "public mood" measure. (We substituted Stimson's public mood measure in our analyses below and found quite similar results [for more details, see Druckman and Jacobs 2006].)

To detect White House decisions, we tracked presidential statements. We coded our Presidential Policy Positions measure on a five-point scale with higher scores indicating an increasingly conservative position. This allowed us to examine whether the statement data scale moves in congruent directions with the public opinion data scale. The lumping and splitting scenarios each predict a significant and positive relationship between the direction of the president's statements and his Ideological Identification and Policy Opinion data, respectively.

We created the data set by merging the presidential statement data with the public opinion data so that we have a potential observation for each issue during each month for Nixon and Reagan. . . . The data set also includes public opinion data on issue importance as that may condition lumping and splitting. Both Nixon and Reagan tracked issue importance by asking respondents to state the single most important problem facing the country—this measure reports the percentage who name a given issue.

Because the Nixon data covered forty-nine issues over forty-seven months, there is a potential for 2,303 observations for Nixon (assuming that he made a statement on every issue in each month [49 × 47]). The Reagan data spanned ninety-eight issues over ninety-seven months, leading to 9,506 potential observations. In practice, however, the presidents did not make a statement on every issue in every month. Nixon made a total of 1,288 statements on different policies in the given months; each of these 1,288 statements (or observations) represents the aggregated measures for each policy that he addressed during a given month (such as the conservative direction of all his statements on controlling inflation in January 1972 or fighting crime in February 1972). Reagan made a total of 3,261 statements on different policies in the given months.

In addition, neither president (especially Reagan) collected public opinion data on every issue over time; we analyzed the relationship between statements and public opinion data only when the public opinion data existed. The result is that the effective number of cases for each president was often substantially reduced, as we report below.

■ ■ ■

We integrate these quantitative analyses with archival research to explore the White House's intentions and strategies. This anchors our assumptions and interpretations in the actual internal deliberations within the Nixon and Reagan administrations. . . .

Strategic Investments in Information

We begin by examining four scenarios accounting for how the Nixon and Reagan teams engaged in lumping or splitting before public statements:

- Independence when the president had no opinion data of any sort
- Pure Splitting when the president had only Policy Opinion data
- Pure Lumping when the president had only Ideological Identification data
- Strategic Balancing when the president had both types of data

Table [1] reports the percentage and number of statements for each of these four scenarios. The rows identify statements for which a president had general data on Ideological Identification (or not), while the columns capture availability of the policy-specific Public Opinion data. (To be considered available, the data must have been collected by the White House at least one month prior to a statement.)

Indicative of the new era of presidents' investment in polling to fashion their public communications, Nixon and Reagan rarely spoke publicly without information on public opinion. Table [1] reveals that independence from public opinion data declined from 19 percent under Nixon (223 statements out of a total of 1,180) to zero under Reagan. In other words, Reagan made no statements without public opinion data on either the public's general ideological orientations or its specific policy preferences.

Although both presidents hungered for extensive polling that balanced its costs and benefits, they pursued distinctive strategic aims. Reagan aggressively sought out conservative positions while ducking land mines for swing voters, while Nixon was more hesitant about pursuing a conservative agenda.

Given their low costs, it is unsurprising that data on the public's general ideology (Ideological Identification) were extensively collected by both presidents. Table [1] shows that Nixon had data on Ideological Identification for

TABLE [1] Availability of Data on Policy Preferences and Ideological Orientation When Nixon and Reagan Made a Statement

	Policy Opinion Data Not Available		Policy Opinion Data Available		Total	
	Nixon	Reagan	Nixon	Reagan	Nixon	Reagan
	Independent		Pure Splitting			
Ideological identification data not available	19 (223)	0 (0)	5 (54)	0 (0)	24 (277)	0 (0)
	Pure Lumping		Strategic Balancing			
Ideological identification data available	39 (462)	18 (459)	37 (441)	82 (2,057)	76 (903)	100 (2,516)
Total	58 (685)	18 (459)	42 (495)	82 (2,057)	100 (1,180)	100 (2,516)

NOTE: Each cell reports the percentage (and absolute number) of statements for which Nixon or Reagan had a given type of data at least one month earlier.

76 percent, or 903, of his statements and that Reagan possessed it for all his statements. Both administrations collected data on the public's ideological orientations substantially more often than they did on the public's policy-specific preferences (Policy Opinions). This is in keeping with the White House's strategic allocation of resources: the low cost and simplicity of tracking the public's ideology made it a good investment for developing a readily available stream of information for crafting presidential statements.

The two Republican presidents did differ, however, on the extent to which they relied on a lumping strategy. Nixon most often pursued a pure lumping approach: he possessed *only* aggregated data on Ideological Identification for 39 percent of the president's public positions, while Reagan was half as likely to collect *only* aggregate information (i.e., for 18 percent of public positions). The strategic significance of this balance is revealing; as we discuss below, Reagan collected a broader scope of information in order to identify opportunities to move in conservative directions.

The higher cost and complexity of collecting polling data on specific policies create disincentives for the White House to invest in them. Nixon depended on polling data alone for only 5 percent of his statements, and Reagan never relied only on Policy Opinion results (he always had data on Ideological Identification).

Reflecting its efforts to expand the Republican coalition while holding on to swing voters, the Reagan White House invested far more heavily in collecting the maximum amount of information than did the Nixon administration.

Reagan possessed data on both ideology and specific policies for 82 percent of his statements, as compared to Nixon's 37 percent. Pursuing the strategic balancing strategy allowed both presidents (and, especially, Reagan) to minimize their political risks.

▪ ▪ ▪

We assess the substantive impact of Ideological Identification by looking at the change in Reagan's position when the public moved from 5 percent below the average conservativeness to 5 percent above its mean (i.e., the public becomes in total 10 percent more conservative). When these changes in public opinion occurred, Reagan moved his position on average in a conservative direction by 19 percent. This is an impressive, statistically significant effect: *White House poll reports of greater conservatism freed Reagan to adopt more conservative positions above and beyond what might be expected on the basis of other forces.* . . .

When Reagan invested in collecting data on the public's specific preferences, however, he resisted a full-bore ideological strategy; he favored the splitter strategy adopted by Nixon in order to carefully stake out public positions on particular policies. In particular, Nixon's and Reagan's public statements were influenced by White House polling on specific policies in cases where they possessed both Ideological Identification and Policy Opinion data. . . . As more of the public became conservative on *specific* policies, so did both presidents. . . . Although costly, the White House's collection of fuller information prompted Reagan (along with Nixon) to avoid a lumping strategy: Ideological Identification is incorrectly signed in a negative direction for Nixon and only marginally significant for Reagan. . . .

In sum, when White House polling was restricted to tracking Ideological Identification, these data had statistically significant effects on Reagan's statements. When the White House was able to invest in collecting both aggregated and disaggregated data, however, polling information on specific policies produced statistically significant effects, and these impacts were evident for both Nixon and Reagan. *Fuller information matters, and presidents capitalize on their costly investment in collecting detailed information on the public's detailed policy views.*

▪ ▪ ▪

The Conditioning Effects of the Election Cycle

The election cycle also conditions how presidents use their polling information. During his second term, when he no longer faced reelection, Reagan was not responsive to either Ideological Identification or Policy Opinion information in the area of foreign policy. This suggests that reelection and his drive to placate his conservative base spurred him to fashion his public positions on foreign affairs. . . . After he won a second term, the influence of party activists on his lame-duck term waned, a fact that interacted with important

changes in the prevailing reality—most notably, the thaw in US-Soviet relations and the coming collapse of the Soviet Union.

In short, Nixon and Reagan possessed similar polling capacities and even
similar polling expertise, but the particular political and policy circumstances
they faced prodded them to differentiate how they used the distinct types of
information at their disposal. Reagan was more geared than Nixon toward
appealing to general ideological conservatism. In addition to possibly reflecting variations in temperament and philosophies, the differences in how
Nixon and Reagan relied on polling information may also stem from changes
in the political parties and, especially, the growing influence of conservative
party activists within the Republican Party after the late 1970s (Aldrich 1995;
Jacobs and Shapiro 2000). Moreover, policy domains also conditioned the use
of different types of polling information: electoral risks and rewards are
more intense and direct in domestic than in foreign affairs, increasing the
political incentives to closely monitor public opinion in general and to give
careful consideration to the public's specific policy preference in particular.
Finally, electoral cycles influenced Reagan's pursuit of foreign policy, leading
to a less ideological approach after his reelection and greater independence
from his polling data.

Presidential Motivations for Collecting Policy Opinion Data

We have seen that presidents vary in how they use polling information given
the types of data available, the policy domain, and the timing during the election cycle. A basic question remains, however: *Why* do politicians choose to
make substantial investments in collecting polling data and particular types
of data?

The substantial rise of presidential polling after World War II coincides
with the unraveling of the New Deal coalition and a search for new means to
reliably track voters. At the same time, presidents and other political leaders
were less confident in long-standing gauges of public opinion—from Congress and political parties to interest groups (Eisinger 2003; Geer 1996).

In addition to adapting to general pressures, Nixon and Reagan faced distinct political incentives in deciding when to collect costly data on specific
policy issues. For Nixon, the key factor was the public's ranking of particular
issues as important. When voters saw an issue as important, Nixon was apt to
collect Policy Opinion data on that issue.

■ ■ ■

While Reagan's investment in Policy Opinion was not driven by salience, it
was informed by his dual political strategy of sustaining his appeal to swing
voters even as he aggressively pursued conservative policy goals. His public
statements were a third more conservative than Nixon's. These right-wing positions left Reagan exposed to potential backlash by median voters and help
account for his investment in tracking the public's specific policy preferences.

He collected twice as much Policy Opinion data when making a statement as did Nixon (82 vs. 42 percent . . .). This equipped him to anticipate broader public reactions before staking out a conservative ideological position.

Reagan's collection of Policy Opinion to calibrate his dual strategy of moving right while holding the center not only influenced his positions but also appears to have affected how he communicated. Reagan was twice as likely to make a public statement about a specific policy when he had polling data on it as opposed to when he lacked information on it; Nixon was equally prone to make a statement regardless of whether or not he possessed Policy Opinion data. This pattern holds up across policy domains and when issues are ranked as important.

Reagan collected Policy Opinion data for the strategic purpose of anticipating the impact of his publicly stated positions. This helped minimize the risk of alienating median voters even as he catered to economic and social conservatives. In contrast to Nixon, he was not influenced by the electoral motivations of responding to specific issues that the public ranked as important. Policy goals dominated his administration, and he turned to polls as a kind of early warning system to identify potential risks in talking about issues that were important to him and his allies and that he wanted to explain publicly. In short, the confluence of electoral and policy goals along with the differing costs of polling on ideology and specific policies explains Nixon's and Reagan's particular approaches to publicly stated positions.

Strategizing within the White House

Quantitative findings mesh with the White House's internal strategizing. For Nixon, the statistical analyses reflect the sustained effort of the president and senior officials to lock in the support of their conservative political base while simultaneously appealing to swing voters. Empirical evidence suggesting that Nixon responded to ideology on less important issues meshes with the advice of his aides to seize opportunities to appeal to his conservative "natural base" in order to dampen "right wing Republican unhappiness because we're not adequately cutting spending, welfare, etc. and they feel we're softening in Vietnam." Nixon was alarmed by criticism from prominent conservatives like Kevin Phillips and Pat Buchanan (who served in the White House) that "we basically had sold out all of our Republican conservative policies in our 'move to the left.'" Moreover, the diary of H. R. Haldeman records numerous meetings in which the president insisted that "we need the group enthusiasm of the right wing" and had to "maintain the conservative support." The administration, he demanded, had to "quit zigzagging and establish a cutting edge" in a "clear-cut," "tougher," "very hard direction" that "establish[es] an awareness of our philosophy to get the government cut down." He insisted: "There's no mileage politically for a conservative Administration in pushing how much we're spending, because the opposition will always spend more. . . . We can't gain on the liberals, but we can sure cool off the conservatives."

Archival records suggest that Nixon and his advisers collected and used their private polls on Ideological Identification to pinpoint where the public shared the conservatism of Nixon's political base. Nixon became convinced that, "based on polls, there are twice as many conservatives as Republicans." Haldeman's staff and other advisers believed that "the American people tend to categorize themselves as conservative more than as liberal." A study of Virginia in January 1972 paralleled the findings of a number of other state surveys: "voters' ratings of the candidates and themselves on the liberal-conservative continuum" showed that "Nixon is closest to the voters in terms of political ideology." On less salient issues, it appears that Nixon and his aides believed that conservative policy positions were critical to holding their political base.

Nixon and his senior advisers, however, accepted that centrist "split-ticket" voters were as important as the conservative base because they would provide the margin of victory. The president's team calculated that they could win over these voters by using his position on salient and popular issues.

Internal archival records reinforce our statistical results showing the White House's predisposition to track the public's policy preference on salient issues and to use that information in designing Nixon's statements; aides relied on their "polls on issues" to address the concern of "whether our position [on specific issues] has gone up or down in the eyes of the public." Nixon and his senior advisers were attuned to polling information on specific issues of *"particular importance to independent and swing voters."* Teeter ran multivariate models for the general electorate to support his argument that "ideology exerted little influence" on vote choice. Even as Nixon was pressured by his base, he and his advisers accepted that reelection depended on "monopolizing the center" and not "go[ing] all conservative." John Ehrlichman, the senior White House official in charge of domestic policy, counseled Nixon against "the pure conservative line which Phillips peddles" in favor of a "domestic course that is down the center" on policy issues.

Reagan's catering to the GOP political base as compared to swing voters contrasts with Nixon's strategy. Archival records of internal White House planning mesh with our earlier findings that Reagan aggressively pursued a strategy to advance the conservative policy goals that he and his allies embraced.

Reagan's fidelity to conservative policy goals was vividly displayed in the opening months of his administration when he knowingly contradicted the public's policy preferences as preparations were made for the inauguration and its initial proposals to set priorities and the public's impressions of the new president. At this critical opening juncture, Reagan's pollster (Richard Wirthlin) conducted extensive national polling to "test" the relationship between the public's policy preferences and Reagan's policy goal of "limit[ing] . . . government spending." Wirthlin urgently reported major public opposition to the president's proposals for cutting Social Security benefits. He dutifully reported to the White House's senior leadership in May 1981 that the president's Social

Security proposals had precipitated a threatening tag team—they were very salient and the president's "most unpopular position taken to date." Reagan's Social Security proposal, Wirthlin warned, was "the most potentially damaging issue we face" as it had quickly produced a "significant fall in the number of people who believe that [Reagan] cares about the needs of the elderly and poor" and a "rising feeling that the 49 billion dollar budget cuts will inevitably hurt the old and the sick" and "perhaps even the middle class." In the face of sustained public opposition, Reagan backed away. What stands out about Reagan, however, is that he persisted in many cases with policies that were unpopular with the general public but that he and his core supporters backed.

Archival records and empirical research reveal how Reagan pursued a strategy that was persistently conservative unless he wished to prevent a damaging backlash by swing voters; Nixon adopted an approach that was more sensitive to the median voter but alert for tactical opportunities to quell potential conservative revolts. As Nixon relied on his private polling to carefully track mainstream America, Reagan used his polling to cater to the diverse set of social, economic, and military conservative forces that formed his electoral coalition, pulling back (as in the case of Social Security reform) on the occasions where White House data detected significant defections among swing voters.

The Politics of Information Collection and Use

Previous research claimed that imperfect information instills uncertainty among politicians who tip-toe around voters to avoid alienating them and refrain from risking policy goals that vividly diverge from their opponent's (Shepsle 1972; Page 1978). Neglected is the extensive information about the type of public opinion that presidents have assembled to fit their political needs and used to minimize the risk of pursuing the policy goals that they and their loyalists favor.

Where past research on imperfect information concluded that politicians quell their policy goals to minimize risk, our original analysis finds that presidents scientifically map risk in order to narrow their responsiveness to the broad public to a few salient issues that voters scrutinize and to widen their discretion to pursue their policy goals. Reagan relied on his sophisticated polling to cater to conservatives until it flagged (as in the case of his far-reaching proposal to privatize Social Security) a substantial risk of alienating swing voters. Nixon took a more opportunistic approach of using his polling to pinpoint openings of voter disinterest to stake out conservative positions that quieted his restless base.

Leveraging their extensive polling information, presidents add a second precaution for pursuing policy goals—they attempt to shift the focus of voters to nonpolicy considerations related to personality. . . . The White House seeks to prime the president's image and to distract voters from scrutinizing his policy agenda.

REFERENCES

Aldrich, John H. 1995. *Why Parties? The Origin and Transformation of Political Parties in America*. Chicago: University of Chicago Press.

Burstein, Paul. 2003. "The Impact of Public Opinion on Public Policy: A Review and an Agenda." *Political Research Quarterly* 56, no. 1: 29–40.

Canes-Wrone, Brandice. 2006. *Who Leads Whom? Presidents, Policy, and the Public*. Chicago: University of Chicago Press.

Carmines, Edward, and James Stimson. 1989. *Issue Evolution: Race and the Transformation of American Politics*. Princeton, NJ: Princeton University Press.

Druckman, James, and Lawrence Jacobs. 2006. "Lumpers and Splitters: The Public Opinion Information That Politicians Collect and Use." *Public Opinion Quarterly* 70 (December): 453–76.

Druckman, James N., and Arthur Lupia. 2000. "Preference Formation." *Annual Review of Political Science* 3: 1–24.

Eisinger, Robert. 2003. *The Evolution of Presidential Polling*. New York: Cambridge University Press.

Erikson, Robert S., Michael B. MacKuen, and James A. Stimson. 2002. *The Macro Polity*. New York: Cambridge University Press.

Fiorina, Morris. 1981. *Retrospective Voting in American National Elections*. New Haven, CT: Yale University Press.

Geer, John G. 1991. "The Electorate's Partisan Evaluations: Evidence of a Continuing Democratic Edge." *Public Opinion Quarterly* 55, no. 2: 218–31.

———. 1996. *From Tea Leaves to Opinion Polls*. New York: Columbia University Press.

Heith, Diane. 1998. "Staffing the White House Public Opinion Apparatus: 1969–1988." *Public Opinion Quarterly* 62: 165–89.

———. 2003. "One for All: Using Focus Groups and Opinion Polls in the George H. W. Bush White House." *Congress and the Presidency* 30: 81–94.

Hill, Kim Quaile, and Patricia A. Hurley. 1999. "Dyadic Representation Reappraised." *American Journal of Political Science* 43: 109–37.

Iyengar, Shanto. 1990. "Shortcuts to Political Knowledge: The Role of Selective Attention and Accessibility." In *Information and Democratic Processes*, ed. John A. Ferejohn and James H. Kuklinski, 160–85. Urbana: University of Illinois Press.

Jacobs, Lawrence R., and Robert Y. Shapiro. 2000. *Politicians Don't Pander: Political Manipulation and the Loss of Democratic Responsiveness*. Chicago: University of Chicago Press.

Kahneman, Daniel, and Amos Tversky. 1984. "Choices, Values, and Frames." *American Psychologist* 39 (April): 341–50.

Kingdon, John W. 1984. *Agendas, Alternatives, and Public Policies*. Boston: Little, Brown.

Krosnick, Jon A. 1988. "The Role of Attitude Importance in Social Evaluation: A Study of Policy Preferences, Presidential Candidate Evaluations, and Voting Behavior." *Journal of Personality and Social Psychology* 55: 196–210.

———. 1989. "Attitude Importance and Attitude Accessibility." *Personality and Social Psychology Bulletin* 55: 297–308.

———. 1990. "Government Policy and Citizen Passion: A Study of Issue Publics in Contemporary America." *Political Behavior* 12: 59–92.

Kuklinski, James H., and Richard Elling. 1977. "Representational Role, Constituency Opinion, and Legislative Roll Call Behavior." *American Journal of Political Science* 21: 135–47.

Kuklinski, James H., and Donald J. McCrone. 1980. "Policy Salience and the Causal Structure of Representation." *American Politics Quarterly* 8: 139–64.

Manza, Jeff, and Fay Lomax Cook. 2002a. "A Democratic Polity? Three Views of Policy Responsiveness to Public Opinion in the United States." *American Politics Research* 30, no. 6: 630–67.

———. 2002b. "The Impact of Public Opinion on Public Policy: The State of the Debate." In *Navigating Public Opinion: Polls, Policy, and the Future of American Democracy*, ed. Jeff Manza, Fay Lomax Cook, and Benjamin I, 17–32. New York: Oxford University Press.

Monroe, Alan D. 1979. "Consistency between Policy Preferences and National Policy Decisions." *American Politics Quarterly* 7, no. 1: 3–18.

———. 1998. "Public Opinion and Public Policy, 1980–1993." *Public Opinion Quarterly* 62, no. 1: 6–28.

Nincic, Miroslav. 1990. "U.S. Soviet Policy and the Electoral Connection." *World Politics* 42: 370–96.

Page, Benjamin I. 1978. *Choices and Echoes in Presidential Elections.* Chicago: University of Chicago Press.

———. 2002. "The Semi-Sovereign Public." In *Navigating Public Opinion: Polls, Policy, and the Future of American Democracy*, ed. Jeff Manza, Fay Lomax Cook, and Benjamin I, 325–44. New York: Oxford University Press.

Page, Benjamin I., and Robert Y. Shapiro. 1983. "Effects of Public Opinion on Policy." *American Political Science Review* 77: 175–90.

Rottinghaus, Brandon. 2010. *The Provisional Pulpit: Modern Presidential Leadership of Public Opinion.* College Station: Texas A&M Press.

Shepsle, Kenneth A. 1972. "The Strategy of Ambiguity: Uncertainty and Electoral Competition." *American Political Science Review* 66, no. 2: 555–68.

Soroka, Stuart N., and Christopher Wlezien. 2005. "Opinion-Policy Dynamics: Public Preferences and Public Expenditure in the UK." *British Journal of Political Science* 35, no. 4: 665–89.

Stimson, James A. 1991. *Public Opinion in America: Moods, Cycles, and Swings.* Boulder, CO: Westview.

Wlezien, Christopher. 2004. "Patterns of Representation: Dynamics of Public Preferences and Policy." *Journal of Politics* 66: 1–24.

Wright, Gerald C. 1989. "Policy Voting in the U.S. Senate: Who Is Represented?" *Legislative Studies Quarterly* 14 (November): 465–86.

Zaller, John. 1992. *The Nature and Origins of Mass Opinion*. New York: Cambridge University Press.

7

THE BUREAUCRACY

7.1

JAMES Q. WILSON

From *Bureaucracy: What Government Agencies Do and Why They Do It*

Wilson writes convincingly that bureaucracies can vary greatly in their effectiveness. He pokes holes in standard complaints about bureaucracies by indicating how some of the inefficiencies that people complain about are either unavoidable or by design.

BUREAUCRACY AND THE PUBLIC INTEREST

The German army beat the French army in 1940; the Texas prisons for many years did a better job than did the Michigan prisons; Carver High School in Atlanta became a better school under Norris Hogans. These successes were the result of skilled executives who correctly identified the critical tasks of their organizations, distributed authority in a way appropriate to those tasks, infused their subordinates with a sense of mission, and acquired sufficient autonomy to permit them to get on with the job. The critical tasks were different in each case, and so the organizations differed in culture and patterns of authority, but all three were alike in one sense: incentives, culture, and authority were combined in a way that suited the task at hand.

By now, . . . the reader may find all this painfully obvious. If [these points] are obvious to the reader, then surely they are obvious to government officials.

From James Q. Wilson, *Bureaucracy: What Government Agencies Do and Why They Do It* (New York: Basic Books, 2006).

Intellectually perhaps they are. But whatever lip service may be given to the lessons . . . the daily incentives operating in the political world encourage a very different course of action.

Armies

Though the leadership and initiative of field officers and noncoms is of critical importance, the Pentagon is filled with generals who want to control combat from headquarters or from helicopters, using radios to gather information and computers to process it. Though the skill of the infantryman almost always has been a key to military success, the U.S. Army traditionally has put its best people in specialized units (intelligence, engineering, communications), leaving the leftovers for the infantry.[1] Though it has fought wars since 1945 everywhere except in Europe, the army continues to devote most of its planning to big-tank battles on the West German plains.

Prisons

The success of George Beto in the Texas DOC was there for everyone to see, but many observers gave the most favorable attention to prison executives who seemed to voice the best intentions (rehabilitation, prisoner self-governance) rather than the best accomplishments (safe, decent facilities).

Schools

Especially in big cities, many administrators keep principals weak and teachers busy filling out reports, all with an eye toward minimizing complaints from parents, auditors, interest groups, and the press. Teachers individually grumble that they are treated as robots instead of professionals, but collectively they usually oppose any steps—vouchers, merit pay, open enrollment, strengthened principals—that in fact have given teachers a larger role in designing curricula and managing their classrooms. Norris Hogans received little help from the Atlanta school system; politically, extra resources had to go to all schools "equally" rather than disproportionately to those schools that were improving the most.

These generals, wardens, administrators, and teachers have not been behaving irrationally; rather, they have been responding to the incentives and constraints that they encounter on a daily basis. Those incentives include the need to manage situations over which they have little control on the basis of a poorly defined or nonexistent sense of mission and in the face of a complex array of constraints that seems always to grow, never to shrink. Outside groups—elected officials, interest groups, professional associations, the media—demand a voice in the running of these agencies and make that demand effective by imposing rules on the agencies and demanding that all these rules be enforced all of the time. Moreover, habitual patterns of action—the lessons of the past, the memories of earlier struggles, the expectations of one's co-workers— narrow the area within which new courses of action are sought.

Bureaucrats often complain of "legislative micromanagement," and indeed it exists . . . with respect to the armed forces. There has been a dramatic increase in the number of hearings, reports, investigations, statutory amendments, and budgetary adjustments with which the Pentagon must deal.[2] But there also has been a sharp increase in presidential micromanagement. Herbert Kaufman notes that for a half century or more the White House has feared agency independence more than agency paralysis, and so it has multiplied the number of presidential staffers, central management offices, and requirements for higher-level reviews. Once you start along the path of congressional or White House control, the process acquires a momentum of its own. "As more constraints are imposed, rigidities fixing agencies in their established ways intensify. As a result, complaints that they do not respond to controls also intensify. Further controls, checkpoints, and clearances are therefore introduced."[3] Much the same story can be told with respect to the growing involvement of the courts in agency affairs.

With some conspicuous exceptions the result of this process has been to deflect the attention of agency executives away from how the tasks of their agencies get defined and toward the constraints that must be observed no matter what the tasks may be. Who then decides what tasks shall be performed? In a production agency with observable outputs and routinized work processes, the answer is relatively simple: The laws and regulations that created the agency also define its job. But in procedural, coping, and craft agencies, the answer seems to be nobody in particular and everybody in general. The operating-level workers define the tasks, occasionally by design, as in those cases where operator ideology makes a difference, but more commonly by accident, as in those instances where prior experiences, professional norms, situational and technological imperatives, and peer-group expectations shape the nature of the work.

From time to time a gifted executive appears at a politically propitious time and makes things happen differently. He or she creates a new institution that acquires a distinctive competence, a strong sense of mission, and an ability to achieve socially valued goals. The Army Corps of Engineers, the Social Security Administration, the Marine Corps, the Forest Service, the FBI: For many years after they were created, and in many instances still today, these agencies, along with a few others that could be mentioned, were a kind of elite service that stood as a living refutation of the proposition that "all bureaucrats are dim-witted paper-shufflers." And these are only the federal examples; at the local level one can find many school systems and police departments that have acquired a praiseworthy organizational character.

But one must ask whether today one could create from scratch the Marine Corps, or the FBI, or the Forest Service; possibly, but probably not. Who would dare suggest that a new agency come into being with its own personnel system (and thus with fewer opportunities for civil servants to get tenure), with a single dominant mission (and thus with little organizational deference to the myriad other goals outsiders would want it to serve), and with an arduous training regime designed to instill *esprit de corps* (and thus with less regard for those niceties and conveniences that sedentary people believe to be important)? Or how optimistic should we be that today we could organize a Social Security Administration in a way that would bring to Washington men and women of exceptional talent? Might not many of those people decide today that they do not want to risk running afoul of the conflict-of-interest laws, that they have no stomach for close media and congressional scrutiny, and that they would not accept the federal pay levels pegged to the salaries of members of Congress fearful of raising their own compensation?

It would be a folly of historical romanticism to imagine that great agencies were created in a golden age that is destined never to return, but it would be shortsighted to deny that we have paid a price for having emphasized rules and constraints to the neglect of tasks and mission. At the end of her careful review of the problems the SSA has had in managing disability insurance and supplemental security income, Martha Derthick makes the same point this way: "If the agencies repeatedly fall short, one ought at least to consider the possibility that there is a systematic mismatch between what they are instructed to do and their capacity to do it."[4] In recent years, when Congress has been creating new programs and modifying old ones at a dizzying rate, often on the basis of perfunctory hearings (or, as with the Senate's consideration of the 1988 drug bill, no hearings at all), a government agency capable of responding adequately to these endless changes would have to be versatile and adaptable, "capable of devising new routines or altering old ones very quickly." These qualities, she concludes, "are rarely found in large formal organizations."[5] I would only add that government agencies are far less flexible than formal organizations generally.

Things are not made much better by our national tendency to engage in bureaucrat-bashing. One has to have some perspective on this. It is true that bureaucracies prefer the present to the future, the known to the unknown, and the dominant mission to rival missions; many agencies in fact are skeptical of things that were "NIH"—Not Invented Here. Every social grouping, whether a neighborhood, a nation, or an organization, acquires a culture; changing that culture is like moving a cemetery: it is always difficult and some believe it is sacrilegious. It is also true, as many conservatives argue, that the government tries to do things that it is incapable of doing well, just as it is true, as many liberals allege, that the government in fact does many things well enough. As Charles Wolf has argued, both markets and governments have their imperfections; many things we might want to do collectively require us to choose between unsatisfactory alternatives.[6]

A Few Modest Suggestions that May Make a Small Difference

To do better we have to deregulate the government.[7] If deregulation of a market makes sense because it liberates the entrepreneurial energies of its members, then it is possible that deregulating the public sector also may help energize it.

The difference, of course, is that both the price system and the profit motive provide a discipline in markets that is absent in non-markets. Whether any useful substitutes for this discipline can be found for public-sector workers is not clear, though I will offer some suggestions. But even if we cannot expect the same results from deregulation in the two sectors we can agree at a minimum that detailed regulation, even of public employees, rarely is compatible with energy, pride in workmanship, and the exercise of initiative. The best evidence for this proposition, if any is needed, is that most people do not like working in an environment in which every action is second-guessed, every initiative viewed with suspicion, and every controversial decision denounced as malfeasance.

James Colvard, for many years a senior civilian manager in the navy, suggests that the government needs to emulate methods that work in the better parts of the private sector: "a bias toward action, small staffs, and a high level of delegation which is based on trust."[8] A panel of the National Academy of Public Administration (NAPA), consisting of sixteen senior government executives holding the rank of assistant secretary, issued a report making the same point:

> Over many years, government has become entwined in elaborate management control systems and the accretion of progressively more detailed administrative procedures. This development has not produced superior management. Instead, it has produced managerial overburden. . . . Procedures overwhelm substance. Organizations become discredited, along with their employees. . . . The critical elements of leadership in management appear to wither in the face of a preoccupation with process. The tools are endlessly "perfected"; the manager who is expected to use these tools believes himself to be ignored. . . . Management systems are not management. . . . The attitude of those who design and administer the rules . . . must be reoriented from a "control mentality" to one of "how can I help get the mission of this agency accomplished."[9]

But how can government "delegate" and "trust" and still maintain accountability? If it is a mistake to foster an ethos that encourages every bureaucrat to "go by the book," is it not an equally serious problem to allow zealots to engage in "mission madness," charging off to implement their private versions of some ambiguous public goal? (Steven Emerson has written a useful account of mission madness in some highly secret military intelligence and covert-action agencies.)[10] Given everything we know about the bureaucratic desire for autonomy and the political rewards of rule making, is there any reason to suppose that anybody will find it in his or her interest to abandon the "control mentality" and adopt the "mission accomplishment" mentality?

Possibly not. But it may be worth thinking about what a modestly deregulated government might look like. It might look as it once did, when some of the better federal agencies were created. At the time the Corps of Engineers, the Forest Service, and the FBI were founded much of the federal government was awash in political patronage, petty cabals, and episodic corruption. Organizing an elite service in those days may have been easier than doing so today, when the problems are less patronage and corruption than they are officiousness and complexity. But the keys to organizational success have not changed. The agencies were started by strong leaders who were able to command personal loyalty, define and instill a clear and powerful sense of mission, attract talented workers who believed they were joining something special, and make exacting demands on subordinates.

Today there is not much chance to create a new agency; almost every agency one can imagine already has been created. Even so, the lessons one learns from changing agencies confirm what can be inferred from studying their founding.

FIRST. Executives should understand the culture of their organizations—that is, what their subordinates believe constitute the core tasks of the agency—and the strengths and limitations of that culture. If members widely share and warmly endorse that culture the agency has a sense of mission. This permits the executive to economize on scarce incentives (people want to do certain tasks even when there are no special rewards for doing it); to state general objectives confident that subordinates will understand the appropriate ways of achieving them; and to delegate responsibility knowing that lower-level decisions probably will conform to higher-level expectations.

A good executive realizes that workers can make subtle, precise, and realistic judgments, but only if those judgments refer to a related, coherent set of behaviors. People cannot easily keep in mind many quite different things or strike reasonable balances among competing tasks. People want to know what is expected of them; they do not want to be told, in answer to this question, that "on the one hand this, but on the other hand that."

In defining a core mission and sorting out tasks that either fit or do not fit with this mission, executives must be aware of their many rivals for the right to define it. Operators with professional backgrounds will bring to the agency their skills but also their biases: Lawyers, economists, and engineers see the world in very different ways. You cannot hire them as if they were tools that in your skilled hands will perform exactly the task you set for them. Black and Decker may make tools like that, but Harvard and MIT do not. Worker peer groups also set expectations to which operators conform, especially when the operators work in a threatening, unpredictable, or confrontational environment. You may design the ideal patrol officer or schoolteacher, but unless you understand the demands made by the street and the classroom, your design will remain an artistic expression destined for the walls of some organizational museum.

These advantages of infusing an agency with a sense of mission are purchased at a price. An agency with a strong mission will give perfunctory attention, if any at all, to tasks that are not central to that mission. Diplomats in the State Department will have little interest in embassy security; intelligence officers in the CIA will not worry as much as they should about counterintelligence; narcotics agents in the DEA will minimize the importance of improper prescriptions written by physicians; power engineers in the TVA will not think as hard about environmental protection or conservation as about maximizing the efficiency of generating units; fighter pilots in the USAF will look at air transport as a homely stepchild; and navy admirals who earned their flag serving on aircraft carriers will not press zealously to expand the role of minesweepers.

If the organization must perform a diverse set of tasks, those tasks that are not part of the core mission will need special protection. This requires giving autonomy to the subordinate tasks subunit (e.g., by providing for them a special organizational niche) and creating a career track so that talented people performing non-mission tasks can rise to high rank in the agency. No single organization, however, can perform well a wide variety of tasks; inevitably some will be neglected. In this case, the wise executive will arrange to devolve the slighted tasks onto another agency, or to a wholly new organization created for the purpose. Running multitask conglomerates is as risky in the public as in the private sector. There are limits to the number of different jobs managers can manage. Moreover, conglomerate agencies rarely can develop a sense of mission; the cost of trying to do everything is that few things are done well. The turf-conscious executive who stoutly refuses to surrender any tasks, no matter how neglected, to another agency is courting disaster; in time the failure of his or her agency to perform some orphan task will lead to a political or organizational crisis. Long ago the State Department should have got out of the business of building embassies. Diplomats are good at many things, but supervising carpenters and plumbers is not one of them. Let agencies whose mission is construction—the Army Corps of Engineers or the navy's Seabees—build buildings.

SECOND. Negotiate with one's political superiors to get some agreement as to which are the *essential* constraints that must be observed by your agency and which the marginal constraints. This, frankly, may be impossible. The decentralization of authority in Congress (and in some state legislatures) and the unreliability of most expressions of presidential or gubernatorial backing are such that in most cases you will discover, by experience if not by precept, that all constraints are essential all of the time. But perhaps with effort some maneuvering room may be won. A few agencies obtained the right to use more flexible, less cumbersome personnel systems modeled on the China Lake experiment, and Congress has the power to broaden those opportunities. Perhaps some enlightened member of Congress will be able to get statutory authority for the equivalent of China Lake with respect to procurement regulations. An executive is well advised to spend time showing that member how to do it.

THIRD.   Match the distribution of authority and the control over resources to the tasks your organization is performing. In general, authority should be placed at the lowest level at which all essential elements of information are available. Bureaucracies will differ greatly in what level that may be. At one extreme are agencies such as the Internal Revenue Service or maximum-security prisons, in which uniformity of treatment and precision of control are so important as to make it necessary for there to be exacting, centrally determined rules for most tasks. At the other extreme are public schools, police departments, and armies, organizations in which operational uncertainties are so great that discretion must be given to (or if not given will be taken by) lower-level workers.

A good place in which to think through these matters is the area of weapons procurement. The overcentralization of design control is one of the many criticisms of such procurement on which all commentators seem agreed. Buying a new aircraft may be likened to remodeling one's home: You never know how much it will cost until you are done; you quickly find out that changing your mind midway through the work costs a lot of money; and you soon realize that decisions have to be made by people on the spot who can look at the pipes, wires, and joists. The Pentagon procures aircraft as if none of its members had ever built or remodeled a house. It does so because both it and its legislative superiors refuse to allow authority to flow down to the point where decisions rationally can be made.

The same analysis can be applied to public schools. As John Chubb and Terry Moe have shown, public and private schools differ in the locus of effective control.[11] At least in big cities, decisions in private schools that are made by headmasters or in Catholic schools that are made by small archdiocesan staffs are made in public schools by massive, cumbersome headquarters bureaucracies. Of course, there are perfectly understandable political reasons for this difference, but not very many good reasons for it. Many sympathetic critics of the public schools believe that the single most useful organizational change that could be made would be to have educational management decisions—on personnel, scheduling, and instructional matters—made at the school level.[12]

FOURTH.   Judge organizations by results. This reading has made it clear that what constitutes a valued result in government usually is a matter of dispute. But even when fairly clear performance standards exist, legislatures and executives often ignore them with unhappy results. William E. Turcotte compared how two state governments oversaw their state liquor monopolies. The state that applied clear standards to its liquor bureaucrats produced significantly more profit and lower administrative costs than did the state with unclear or conflicting standards.[13]

Even when results are hard to assess more can be done than is often the case. If someone set out to evaluate the output of a private school, hospital, or security service, he or she would have at least as much trouble as would someone trying to measure the output of a public school, hospital, or police department. Governments are not the only institutions with ambiguous products.

There are two ways to cope with the problem in government One . . . is to supply the service or product in a marketlike environment. Shift the burden of evaluation off the shoulders of professional evaluators and onto the shoulders of clients and customers, and let the latter vote with their feet. The "client" in these cases can be individual citizens or government agencies; what is important is that the client be able to choose from among rival suppliers.

But some public services cannot be supplied, or are never going to be supplied, by a market. We can imagine allowing parents to choose among schools but we cannot imagine letting them choose (at least for most purposes) among police departments or armies. In that case one should adopt the second way of evaluating a public service: carry out a demonstration project or conduct a field experiment. (I will use the two ideas interchangeably, though some scholars distinguish between them.)[14] An experiment is a planned alteration in a state of affairs designed to measure the effect of the intervention. It involves asking the question, "if I change X, what will happen to Y, having first made certain that everything else stays the same?" It sounds easy, but it is not.

A good experiment (bad ones are worse than no experiment at all) requires that one do the following: First, identify a course of action to be tested; call it the treatment. A "treatment" can be a police tactic, a school curriculum, or a welfare program. Second, decide what impact the treatment is intended to have; call this the outcome. The outcome can be a crime rate, an achievement score, a work effort, a housing condition, or an income level. Third, give the treatment to one group (the experimental group) and withhold it from another (the control group). A group might be a police precinct, a class of students, the tenants in a housing project, or people who meet some eligibility requirement (say, having low incomes). It is quite important how the membership in these groups is determined. It should be done randomly; that is, all eligible precincts, schools, tenants, or people should be randomly sorted into experimental and control groups. Random assignment means that all the characteristics of the members of the experimental and control groups are likely to be identical. Fourth, assess the condition of each group before and after the treatment. The first assessment describes the baseline condition, the second the outcome condition. This outcome assessment should continue for some time after the end of the treatment, because experience has shown that many treatments seem to have a short-term effect that quickly disappears. Fifth, make certain that the evaluation is done by people other than those providing the treatment. People like to believe that their efforts are worthwhile, so much so that perhaps unwittingly they will gather data in ways that make it look like the treatment worked even when it did not.[15]

The object of all this is to find out what works. Using this method we have discovered that tripling the number of patrol cars on a beat does not lower the crime rate; that foot patrol reduces the fear of crime but not (ordinarily) its incidence; and that arresting spouse-beaters reduces (for a while) future assaults more than does counseling the assaulters.[16] We have learned that giving people an income supplement (akin to the negative income tax) reduces work effort and in some cases encourages families to break up.[17] We have learned that giving special job training and support to welfare mothers, ex-offenders, and school drop-outs produces sizable gains in the employment records of the welfare recipients but no gain for the ex-offenders and school drop-outs.[18] We have learned that a housing allowance program increases the welfare of poor families even though it does not improve the stock of housing. We have learned that more flexible pay and classification systems greatly bene-fit the managers of navy research centers and improve the work atmosphere at the centers.

There also have been many failed or flawed management experiments. In the 1930s, Herbert Simon carried out what may have been the first serious such experiment when he tried to find out how to improve the performance of welfare workers in the California State Relief Administration. Though elegantly designed, the experimental changes proved so controversial and the political environment of the agency so unstable that it is not clear that any useful inferences can be drawn from the project.[19] The attempt to eval-uate educational vouchers at Alum Rock was undercut by the political need to restrict participation by private schools. . . . There are countless other "stud-ies" that are evaluations in name only; in reality they are self-congratulatory conclusions written by program administrators. The administrative world is a political world, not a scientific laboratory, and evaluators of administration must come to terms with that fact. Often there are no mutually acceptable terms. But where reasonable terms can be struck it is possible to learn more than untutored experience can tell us about what works.

Such dry and dusty research projects probably seem thin fare to people who want Big Answers to Big Questions such as "How can we curb rampant bureaucracy?" or "How can we unleash the creative talents of our dedicated public servants?" But public management is not an arena in which to find Big Answers; it is a world of settled institutions designed to allow imperfect people to use flawed procedures to cope with insoluble problems.

FIFTH.   The fifth and final bit of advice flows directly from the limits on judging agencies by their results. All organizations seek the stability and com-fort that comes from relying on standard operating procedures—"SOPs." When results are unknown or equivocal, bureaus will have no incentive to alter those SOPs so as better to achieve their goals, only an incentive to modify them to con-form to externally imposed constraints. The SOPs will represent an internally defined equilibrium that reconciles the situational imperatives, professional norms, bureaucratic ideologies, peer-group expectations, and (if present) leadership demands unique to that agency. The only way to minimize the adverse effect of allowing human affairs to be managed by organizations driven by their autonomous SOPs is to keep the number, size, and authority of such organizations as small as possible. If none of the four preceding bits of advice work, the reader must confront the realization that there are no solutions for the bureaucracy problem that are not also "solutions" to the government problem. More precisely: All complex organizations display bureaucratic problems of confusion, red tape, and the avoidance of responsibility. Those problems are much greater in government bureaucracies because government itself is the institutionalization of confusion (arising out of the need to moderate competing demands); of red tape (arising out of the need to satisfy demands that cannot be moderated); and of avoided responsibility (arising out of the desire to retain power by minimizing criticism).

In short, you can have less bureaucracy only if you have less government. Many, if not most, of the difficulties we experience in dealing with government agencies arise from the agencies being part of a fragmented and open political system. If an agency is to have a sense of mission, if constraints are to be minimized, if authority is to be decentralized, if officials are to be judged on the basis of the outputs they produce rather than the inputs they consume, then legislators, judges, and lobbyists will have to act against their own interests. They will have to say "no" to influential constituents, forgo the opportunity to expand their own influence, and take seriously the task of judging the organizational feasibility as well as the political popularity of a proposed new program. It is hard to imagine this happening, partly because politicians and judges have no incentive to make it happen and partly because there are certain tasks a democratic government must undertake even if they cannot be performed efficiently. The greatest mistake citizens can make when they complain of "the bureaucracy" is to suppose that their frustrations arise simply out of management problems; they do not—they arise out of governance problems.

Bureaucracy and the American Regime

The central feature of the American constitutional system—the separation of powers—exacerbates many of these problems. The governments of the United States were not designed to be efficient or powerful, but to be tolerable and malleable. Those who devised these arrangements always assumed that the federal government would exercise few and limited powers. As long as that assumption was correct (which it was for a century and a half) the quality of public administration was not a serious problem except in the minds of those reformers (Woodrow Wilson was probably the first) who desired to rationalize government in order to rationalize society. The founders knew that the separation of powers would make it so difficult to start a new program or to create a new agency that it was hardly necessary to think about how those agencies would be administered. As a result, the Constitution is virtually silent on what kind of administration we should have. At least until the Civil War thrust the problem on us, scarcely anyone in the country would have known what you were talking about if you spoke of the "problem of administration."

Matters were very different in much of Europe. Kings and princes long had ruled; when their authority was captured by parliaments, the tradition of ruling was already well established. From the first the ministers of the parliamentary regimes thought about the problems of administration because in those countries there was something to administer. The centralization of executive authority in the hands of a prime minister and the exclusion (by and large) of parliament from much say in executive affairs facilitated the process of controlling the administrative agencies and bending them to some central will. The constitutions of many European states easily could have been written by a school of management.

Today, the United States at every level has big and active governments. Some people worry that a constitutional system well-designed to preserve liberty when governments were small is poorly designed to implement policy now that governments are large. The contrast between how the United States and the nations of Western Europe manage environmental and industrial regulation . . . is illuminating: Here the separation of powers insures, if not causes, clumsy and adversarial regulation; there the unification of powers permits, if not causes, smooth and consensual regulation.

I am not convinced that the choice is that simple, however. It would take another book to judge the advantages and disadvantages of the separation of powers. The balance sheet on both sides of the ledger would contain many more entries than those that derive from a discussion of public administration. But even confining our attention to administration, there is more to be said for the American system than many of its critics admit.

America has a paradoxical bureaucracy unlike that found in almost any other advanced nation. The paradox is the existence in one set of institutions of two qualities ordinarily quite separate: the multiplication of rules and the opportunity for access. We have a system laden with rules; elsewhere that is a sure sign that the bureaucracy is aloof from the people, distant from their concerns, and preoccupied with the power and privileges of the bureaucrats—an elaborate, grinding machine that can crush the spirit of any who dare oppose it. We also have a system suffused with participation: advisory boards, citizen groups, neighborhood councils, congressional investigators, crusading journalists, and lawyers serving writs; elsewhere this popular involvement would be taken as evidence that the administrative system is no system at all, but a bungling, jerry-built contraption wallowing in inefficiency and shot through with corruption and favoritism.

That these two traits, rules and openness, could coexist would have astonished Max Weber and continues to astonish (or elude) many contemporary students of the subject. Public bureaucracy in this country is neither as rational and predictable as Weber hoped nor as crushing and mechanistic as he feared. It is rule-bound without being overpowering, participatory without being corrupt. This paradox exists partly because of the character and mores of the American people: They are too informal, spontaneous, and other-directed to be either neutral arbiters or passionless Gradgrinds. And partly it exists because of the nature of the regime: Our constitutional system, and above all the exceptional power enjoyed by the legislative branch, makes it impossible for us to have anything like a government by appointed experts but easy for individual citizens to obtain redress from the abuses of power. Anyone who wishes it otherwise would have to produce a wholly different regime, and curing the mischiefs of bureaucracy seems an inadequate reason for that. Parliamentary regimes that supply more consistent direction to their bureaucracies also supply more bureaucracy to their citizens. The fragmented American regime may produce chaotic government, but the coherent European regimes produce bigger governments.

In the meantime we live in a country that despite its baffling array of rules and regulations and the insatiable desire of some people to use government to rationalize society still makes it possible to get drinkable water instantly, put through a telephone call in seconds, deliver a letter in a day, and obtain a passport in a week. Our Social Security checks arrive on time. Some state prisons, and most of the federal ones, are reasonably decent and humane institutions. The great majority of Americans, cursing all the while, pay their taxes. One can stand on the deck of an aircraft carrier during night flight operations and watch two thousand nineteen-year-old boys faultlessly operate one of the most complex organizational systems ever created. There are not many places where all this happens. It is astonishing it can be made to happen at all.

NOTES

1. Arthur T. Hadley, *The Straw Giant* (New York: Random House, 1986), 53–57, 249–52.

2. CSIS, *U.S. Defense Acquisition: A Process in Trouble* (Washington, D.C.: Center for Strategic and International Studies, March 1987), 13–16.

3. Herbert Kaufman, *The Administrative Behavior of Federal Bureau Chiefs* (Washington, D.C.: The Brookings Institution, 1981), 192.

4. Martha Derthick, *Agency Under Stress: The Social Security Administration and American Government* (Washington, D.C.: Brookings Institution, 1990).

5. Ibid., chap. 3.

6. Charles Wolf, Jr., *Markets or Governments: Choosing Between Imperfect Alternatives* (Cambridge, MA: MIT Press, 1988).

7. I first saw this phrase in an essay by Constance Horner, then director of the federal Office of Personnel Management: "Beyond Mr. Gradgrind: The Case for Deregulating the Public Sector," *Policy Review* 44 (Spring 1988): 34–38. It also appears in Gary C. Bryner, *Bureaucratic Discretion* (New York: Pergamon Press, 1987), 215.

8. James Colvard, "Procurement: What Price Mistrust?" *Government Executive* (March 1985): 21.

9. NAPA, *Revitalizing Federal Management: Managers and Their Overburdened Systems* (Washington, DC: National Academy of Public Administration, November 1983), vii, viii, 8.

10. Steven Emerson, *Secret Warriors* (New York: G. P. Putnam's Sons, 1988).

11. John E. Chubb and Terry M. Moe, "Politics, Markets, and the Organization of Schools," *American Political Science Review* 82 (1988): 1065–87.

12. Chester E. Finn, Jr., "Decentralize, Deregulate, Empower," *Policy Review* (Summer 1986): 60; Edward A. Wynne, *A Year in the Life of an Excellent Elementary School* (Lancaster, PA: Technomic, 1993).

13. William E. Turcotte, "Control Systems, Performance, and Satisfaction in Two State Agencies," *Administrative Science Quarterly* 19 (1974): 60–73.

14. Richard P. Nathan, *Social Science in Government: Uses and Misuses* (New York: Basic Books, 1988), chap. 3.

15. Matters are, of course, a bit more complicated than this summary might suggest. There is a small library of books on evaluative research that go into these matters in more detail; a good place to begin is Richard P. Nathan, *Social Science in Government* (New York: Basic Books, 1988). On the political aspects of evaluation, see Henry J. Aaron, *Politics and the Professors* (Washington, DC: The Brookings Institution, 1978). On the technical side see Thomas D. Cook and Donald T. Campbell, *Quasi-Experimentation* (Chicago: Rand McNally, 1979). There is even a journal, *Evaluation Review*, specializing in these issues.

16. These projects were all done by the Police Foundation and are described in James Q. Wilson, *Thinking About Crime*, rev. ed. (New York: Basic Books, 1983).

17. See Joseph A. Pechman and P. Michael Timpane, eds., *Work Incentives and Income Guarantees* (Washington, D.C.: Brookings Institution, 1975); and R. Thayne Robson, ed., *Employment and Training R&D* (Kalamazoo, MI: Upjohn Institute for Employment Research, 1984).

18. Nathan, *Social Science,* chap. 5; and Manpower Demonstration Research Corporation, *Summary and Findings of the National Supported Work Demonstration* (Cambridge, MA: Ballinger, 1980).

19. Clarence E. Ridley and Herbert A. Simon, *Measuring Municipal Activities* (Chicago: International City Managers' Association, 1938).

7.2

MATHEW D. McCUBBINS AND THOMAS SCHWARTZ

"Congressional Oversight Overlooked: Police Patrols versus Fire Alarms"

In this classic article, McCubbins and Schwartz compare two kinds of oversight of executive agencies by Congress. Under the police patrol model, Congress provides resources for constant monitoring of bureaucratic behavior. Under the fire alarm model, Congress waits for complaints from constituents and groups in society about the bureaucracies and then holds them accountable. The fire alarm model is often the more efficient method of oversight.

Scholars often complain that Congress has neglected its oversight responsibility: despite a large and growing executive branch, Congress has done little or nothing to oversee administrative compliance with legislative goals. As a consequence, we are told, Congress has largely lost control of the executive branch: it has allowed the executive branch not only to grow but to grow irresponsible. In popular debate as well as congressional scholarship, this neglect of oversight has become a stylized fact: widely and dutifully reported, it is often bemoaned, sometimes explained, but almost never seriously questioned.[1]

We question it. What has appeared to scholars to be a neglect of oversight, we argue, really is a preference for one form of oversight over another, less-effective form. In so arguing, we develop a simple model of congressional choice of oversight policy, offer evidence to support the model, and draw from it further implications regarding bureaucratic discretion and regulatory legislation. More generally, we model the choice by policy makers of an optimal enforcement strategy, given opportunity costs, available technology, and human cognitive limits.

THE MODEL

Congressional oversight policy concerns whether, to what extent, and in what way Congress attempts to detect and remedy executive-branch violations of legislative goals. Our model of congressional choice of oversight policy rests on a distinction between two forms or techniques of oversight:

From Mathew D. McCubbins and Thomas Schwartz, "Congressional Oversight Overlooked: Police Patrols versus Fire Alarms," *American Journal of Political Science* 28, no. 1 (February 1984): 165–79.

Police-Patrol Oversight

Analogous to the use of real police patrols, police-patrol oversight is comparatively centralized, active, and direct: at its own initiative, Congress examines a
sample of executive-agency activities, with the aim of detecting and remedying any violations of legislative goals and, by its surveillance, discouraging
such violations. An agency's activities might be surveyed by any of a number
of means, such as reading documents, commissioning scientific studies, conducting field observations, and holding hearings to question officials and
affected citizens.

Fire-Alarm Oversight

Analogous to the use of real fire alarms, fire-alarm oversight is less centralized and involves less active and direct intervention than police-patrol oversight: instead of examining a sample of administrative decisions, looking for
violations of legislative goals, Congress establishes a system of rules, procedures,
and informal practices that enable individual citizens and organized interest
groups to examine administrative decisions (sometimes in prospect), to charge
executive agencies with violating congressional goals, and to seek remedies
from agencies, courts, and Congress itself. Some of these rules, procedures,
and practices afford citizens and interest groups access to information and
to administrative decision-making processes. Others give them standing to
challenge administrative decisions before agencies and courts, or help them
bring alleged violations to congressmen's attention. Still others facilitate collective action by comparatively disorganized interest groups. Congress's role
consists in creating and perfecting this decentralized system and, occasionally,
intervening in response to complaints. Instead of sniffing for fires, Congress
places fire-alarm boxes on street corners, builds neighborhood fire houses, and
sometimes dispatches its own hook-and-ladder in response to an alarm.

The distinction between police-patrol and fire-alarm oversight should not
be confused with the distinction that sometimes is drawn between *formal*
and *informal* oversight, which differ in that formal oversight activities have
oversight as their principal and official purpose, whereas informal oversight
activities are incidental to other official functions, such as appropriations
hearings. Both can involve direct and active surveillance rather than responses
to alarms. (See Dodd and Schott, 1979; Ogul, 1977.)

Our model consists of three assumptions:

Technological Assumption

Two forms of oversight are available to Congress: police-patrol oversight and
fire-alarm oversight. Congress can choose either form or a combination of the
two, making tradeoffs between them in two circumstances: (1) When writing
legislation, Congress can include police-patrol features, such as sunset review,

or fire-alarm features, such as requirements for public hearings. (2) When it evaluates an agency's performance, Congress can either call oversight hearings to patrol for violations of legislative goals or else wait for alarms to signal potential violations.

Motivational Assumption

A congressman seeks to take as much credit as possible for the net benefits enjoyed by his potential supporters—by citizens and interest groups, within his constituency and elsewhere, whose support can help him win reelection. This means, in part, that a congressman seeks to avoid as much blame as possible for the net costs borne by his potential supporters.

Institutional Assumption

Executive agencies act as agents of Congress and especially of those subcommittees on which they depend for authorizations and appropriations.

The Motivational Assumption is closely tied to Mayhew's celebrated reelection model (1974) and to the blame-shirking model of Fiorina (1982a). The Institutional Assumption is found in Baldwin (1975), Ferejohn (1981), Joskow (1974), McCubbins (1982a,b), and Mitnick (1980). Although not previously stated, the Technological Assumption seems to us to be uncontroversial.

That cannot be said of the Motivational Assumption, which depicts congressmen as pure politicians, single-mindedly pursuing reelection. To this picture one might object that real congressmen are not just politicians but statesmen, pursuing justice and the public interest, acting according to various moral and ideological principles, even at some cost to their reelection prospects.

We will argue, however, that if the Motivational Assumption were replaced by the assumption that congressmen act strictly as statesmen, our conclusions regarding oversight would still be derivable, although in a somewhat different way. Our analysis has less to do with specific legislative goals than with optimal strategies for enforcing compliance with legislative goals of any sort.

CONSEQUENCES

Three important consequences follow from our model:

Consequence 1

To the extent that they favor oversight activity of any sort, congressmen tend to prefer fire-alarm oversight to police-patrol oversight.

Our argument for Consequence 1 is that a congressman's objective, according to the Motivational Assumption, is to take as much credit as possible for net benefits enjoyed by his potential supporters and that he can do so more efficiently under a policy of fire-alarm oversight than under a police-patrol policy, for three reasons:

First, congressmen engaged in police-patrol oversight inevitably spend time examining a great many executive-branch actions that do not violate legislative goals or harm any potential supporters, at least not enough to occasion complaints. They might also spend time detecting and remedying arguable violations that nonetheless harm no potential supporters. For this they receive scant credit from their potential supporters. According to the Motivational Assumption, then, their time is largely wasted, so they incur opportunity costs. But under a fire-alarm policy, a congressman does not address concrete violations unless potential supporters have complained about them, in which case he can receive credit for intervening. So a unit of time spent on oversight is likely to yield more benefit for a congressman under a fire-alarm policy than under a policy-patrol policy. As a result, a fire-alarm policy enables congressmen to spend less time on oversight, leaving more time for other profitable activities, or to spend the same time on more personally profitable oversight activities—on addressing complaints by potential supporters. Justly or unjustly, time spent putting out visible fires gains one more credit than the same time spent sniffing for smoke.

Second, under a realistic police-patrol policy, congressmen examine only a small sample of executive-branch actions. As a result, they are likely to miss violations that harm their potential supporters, and so miss opportunities to take credit for redressing grievances, however fair the sample. Under a fire-alarm policy, by contrast, potential supporters can in most cases bring to congressmen's attention any violations that harm them and for which they have received no adequate remedy through the executive or judicial branch.

Third, although fire-alarm oversight can be as costly as police-patrol oversight, much of the cost is borne by the citizens and interest groups who sound alarms and by administrative agencies and courts rather than by congressmen themselves. A congressman's responsibility for such costs is sufficiently remote that he is not likely to be blamed for them by his potential supporters.

Consequence 2

Congress will not neglect its oversight responsibility. It will adopt an extensive and somewhat effective (even if imperfect) oversight policy.

This is because one of the two forms of oversight—the fire-alarm variety—serves congressmen's interests at little cost. When his potential supporters complain of a violation of legislative goals, a congressman gains credit if he eliminates the cause of the complaint. By virtue of the Institutional Assumption, he often can be reasonably effective in eliminating such causes. Beyond establishing and perfecting the system and addressing some complaints, fire-alarm oversight is almost costless to congressmen: others bear most of the cost.

Consequence 3

Congress will adopt an extensive and somewhat effective policy of fire-alarm oversight while largely neglecting police-patrol oversight.

This just summarizes Consequences 1 and 2.

MISPERCEPTION

Faced with an apparent fact he finds puzzling, unfortunate, or otherwise worthy of attention, a scientist has two alternatives: (a) to accept the fact and try to explain it, or (b) to question the *apparent* fact and try to explain its appearance. In the case at hand, students of Congress have, for the most part, chosen (a): they have uncritically agreed that Congress neglects its oversight responsibility and have tried to explain this neglect.

Here are the three main explanations found in the literature, along with a brief critical comment on each:

Complexity

Because public-policy issues are so complex, Congress has had to delegate authority over them to a large, complex, technically expert bureaucracy, whose actions it is unable effectively to oversee (Lowi, 1969; Ogul, 1977; Ripley, 1969; Seidman, 1975; Woll, 1977).

Comment

Given sufficient incentives, as Fiorina (1982a) observes, Congress has found the capacity to tackle a number of complex issues itself. A striking example is the tax code (Jaffe, 1973, pp. 1189–90). What is more, there is no evident reason why Congress should respond to the complexity of issues by creating a large, expert bureaucracy without also creating a large, expert congressional staff—one sufficiently large and expert, not only to help decide complex issues, but to help oversee a large, expert bureaucracy.

Good Government

To serve the public interest, Congress has established regulatory and other executive-branch agencies based on expertise and divorced from politics. Because these agencies are designed to serve the public interest, whereas Congress is influenced by special-interest lobbies, oversight not only is unnecessary but might be regarded as political meddling in processes that ought to remain nonpolitical (Lowi, 1969).

Comment

Whatever the original intent, it is no longer plausible in most cases to suppose that the public interest is best served by a bureaucracy unaccountable to Congress and, therefore, unaccountable to the electorate.

Decentralization

Because congressional decisions are made, for the most part, by a large number of small, relatively autonomous subcommittees with narrow jurisdictions, general oversight committees tend to be weak (Dodd and Schott, 1979).

Comment

At most this explains why congressional oversight responsibilities are not centralized. It does not explain why they are neglected. If anything, subcommittee specialization should enhance congressional oversight over individual agencies. Subcommittees controlling authorizations and appropriations might be in a better position to do oversight than so-called oversight committees.

Regarding the apparent fact that Congress neglects oversight, we choose alternative (b) over (a): what appears to be a neglect of oversight can be explained as a preference by congressmen for fire-alarm over police-patrol oversight. We have already argued that congressmen have this preference. Scholars who decry the neglect of oversight have, we suggest, focused on an single form of oversight: they have looked only for police-patrol oversight, ignoring the fire-alarm alternative—and therewith the major part of actual oversight activity. Observing a neglect of *police-patrol* oversight, they have mistakenly concluded that *oversight* is neglected.

It has been suggested to us that scholars who have remarked congressional neglect of oversight were using the word more narrowly than we are—that they were *defining* "oversight" to mean police-patrol oversight, contrary to our Technological Assumption.

To this we have three replies: First, established usage equates oversight with the task of detecting and remedying violations of legislative goals by the executive branch.[2] No technique for accomplishing this task can be ruled out by definition. Second, the definitional equation of oversight with police-patrol oversight reflects the odd view that it is less important for Congress to make a serious attempt to detect and remedy violations of legislative goals than to employ a specific technique for doing so. Third, it would be odd to have a name for one way of detecting and remedying executive-branch violations of legislative goals but none for the general task of detecting and remedying such violations.

It has also been suggested to us that fire-alarm activities were never conceived or intended to be a form of oversight, whatever their effects.

We agree that congressmen rarely if ever refer to fire-alarm activities as "oversight," a term officially applied to subcommittees engaged in direct surveillance—in police-patrol oversight. Still, there is no evident reason for congressmen to engage in most fire-alarm activities unless they aim thereby to detect and remedy certain administrative violations of legislative goals.

Those who equate oversight with police-patrol oversight might argue that redressing grievances against the executive branch is not the same as enforcing compliance with congressional goals: the goals congressmen pursue in answering alarms related to particular laws need not be the goals they had in mind when they enacted those laws.

We see no reason to believe, however, that acts of legislation reflect well-defined or unalterable legislative goals—especially in view of the classical voting paradox and similar anomalies (Arrow, 1963; Plott, 1967; Schwartz, 1970, 1981, 1982a). Rather, legislative goals are refined, elaborated, and even changed over time in response to new problems—including complaints against executive agencies—and to changes in preferences and political alignments. In answering fire alarms, congressmen not only enforce compliance with legislative goals; they help decide what those goals are.

Possibly those who bemoan congressional neglect of oversight would agree that fire-alarm oversight is extensively practiced but argue that it is not *effective*.

We have argued already that fire-alarm oversight is likely to be somewhat effective. The evidence presented two sections hence supports this conclusion.

Even granting that fire-alarm oversight is extensively practiced and *somewhat* effective, hence that Congress does not *neglect* its oversight responsibility, one might still wonder which form of oversight is the *more* effective. To this question we now turn.

THE GREATER EFFECTIVENESS OF FIRE-ALARM OVERSIGHT

We will argue that fire-alarm oversight is likely to be more effective, on balance, than police-patrol oversight. But this requires two qualifications: First, we do not contend that the most effective oversight policy is likely to contain no police-patrol features, only that fire-alarm techniques are likely to predominate. Second, we do not contend that a predominantly fire-alarm policy is more likely than a predominantly police-patrol policy to serve the public interest, only that it is likely to secure greater compliance with legislative goals; whether such compliance serves the public interest depends on what those goals are.

A predominantly fire-alarm oversight policy is likely to be more effective—to secure greater compliance with legislative goals—than a predominantly police-patrol policy for two main reasons:

First, legislative goals often are stated in such a vague way that it is hard to decide whether any violation has occurred unless some citizen or group registers a complaint. Such a complaint gives Congress the opportunity to spell out its goals more clearly—just as concrete cases and controversies give courts the opportunity to elucidate legal principles that would be hard to make precise in the abstract.

Second, whereas a fire-alarm policy would almost certainly pick up any violation of legislative goals that seriously harmed an organized group, a police-patrol policy would doubtless miss many such violations, since only a sample of executive-branch actions would be examined.

One who agrees with this point might still argue, on behalf of the greater efficacy of police-patrol oversight, that the citizens harmed by violations of legislative goals are not always represented by organized groups and, hence, cannot always sound a loud enough alarm to secure a redress of grievances.

Our reply is fourfold: First, nowadays even "disadvantaged" groups often have public spokesmen. Second, as we show in the following section, sometimes Congress passes legislation, as part of its fire-alarm policy, that helps comparatively disorganized groups to act collectively. Third, congressmen's extensive constituent-service activities provide even individual citizens with an effective voice against administrative agencies: case work is part (but only part) of the fire-alarm system. Finally, if the point is merely that fire-alarm oversight can be biased in various ways, then the same is true of police-patrol oversight; and although a good enough police-patrol policy would avoid bias, so would a good enough fire-alarm policy.

To be sure, fire-alarm oversight tends to be *particularistic* in the sense of Mayhew (1974): it arguably emphasizes the interests of individuals and interest groups more than those of the public at large. This is an important difference—the essential difference, we think, between the respective products of police-patrol and fire-alarm oversight. But whether it is a shortcoming of fire-alarm oversight depends on one's ideological point of view: even if fire-alarm oversight deemphasizes some public-interest concerns, it gives special emphasis to a concern for the interests and rights of individual citizens and small groups—a concern well founded in American political values.

Although our model refers only to Congress, we hazard to hypothesize that as most organizations grow and mature, their top policy makers adopt methods of control that are comparatively decentralized and incentive based. Such methods, we believe, will work more efficiently (relative to accepted policy goals) than direct, centralized surveillance. This is sufficiently plausible that we wonder why students of Congress have generally assumed that congressional oversight must be of the direct, centralized police-patrol variety. Part of the reason, perhaps, is that Congress itself applies the label "oversight" to subcommittees charged with police-patrol responsibilities.

As we stated earlier, Consequences 1–3 do not depend on our Motivational Assumption, which depicts congressmen as pure politicians rather than statesmen. This is because statesmen, wishing to secure compliance with their legislative goals, would presumably adopt the most effective oversight policy, and that is likely to be one in which fire-alarm techniques predominate.

EVIDENCE

Evidence for Consequence 3—and therewith our model—is plentiful and well known. Scholars who bemoan congressional neglect of oversight have not ignored this evidence. Rather, they have missed its significance: lacking the concept of fire-alarm oversight, they have failed to see the details of our fire-alarm system as instances of oversight activity. Here is a brief summary of the available evidence:

1. Under a fire-alarm system, complaints against administrative agencies are often brought to the attention of congressional subcommittees by lobbyists for organized groups, and to the attention of administrative agencies by congressional subcommittees. The functioning of this "subgovernmental triangle" has been well documented (Dodd and Oppenheimer, 1977; Fenno, 1966, 1973a,b; Goodwin, 1970; Ornstein, 1975; Ripley, 1969; Huitt, 1973; Matthews, 1960; Ripley and Franklin, 1976).

2. Congress has passed legislation to help comparatively disorganized groups to press their grievances against the federal government. McConnell (1966) shows how the Agriculture, Labor, and Commerce Departments act as lobbyists for farm, labor, and small-business interests. Congress has also created new programs, such as the Legal-Services Corporation, to organize and press the claims of comparatively voiceless citizens.

3. Constituent-service activities are not limited to unsnarling procedural knots. As part of the fire-alarm system, district staff and casework help individuals and groups—some of them otherwise powerless—to raise and redress grievances against decisions by administrative agencies. This casework component of legislative policy making has been examined only recently, with a primary focus on the electoral connection (Cain, Ferejohn, and Fiorina, 1979a,b; Fenno, 1978; Fiorina, 1977a; Mayhew, 1974; Parker and Davidson, 1979) and with a secondary focus on policy consequences (Fiorina, 1977a, 1982b; Fiorina and Noll, 1978, 1979a,b).

4. Often the fire-alarm system allows for the redress of grievances by administrative agencies and courts; Congress itself need not always get involved. To facilitate such redress, Congress has passed several laws, notably the Administrative Procedures Act of 1946 and the Environmental Procedures Act of 1969, that have substantially increased the number of groups with legal standing before administrative agencies and district courts regarding bureaucratic controversies (Lowi, 1969).[3] Congress has also, as in sections 4–7 of the Toxic Substances Control Act of 1976, increased the courts' powers to issue injunctions in response to alarms and has required administrative agencies to hold hearings, publish information, and invite public comment on agency decision making (McCubbins, 1982a).

5. There are numerous cases in which violations of legislative goals were brought to the attention of Congress, which responded with vigorous remedial measures. For example, Congress dismantled the Area Redevelopment Administration (ARA) in 1963, even though it had just been authorized in 1961. The ARA was encouraging industries to relocate in redevelopment areas despite clear provisions in the law to the contrary. Congress also can redefine or reaffirm its goals by

redefining or explicating the jurisdictional authority of an administrative agency. This happened with the Federal Trade Commission
when it first sought to regulate cigarette advertising, children's television, and funeral homes. Sometimes such congressional intervention
is legislatively mandated. Before taking action on a pending case, for
example, the National Labor Relations Board must consult with the
appropriate congressional committees.

6. The general impression that Congress neglects oversight, we have
argued, really is a perception that Congress neglects police-patrol
over-sight. That impression and the evidence adduced to support it
constitute further evidence for Consequences 1 and 3: they show that
congressmen tend to prefer an oversight policy in which fire-alarm
techniques predominate.

FURTHER IMPLICATIONS: HAS BUREAUCRATIC DISCRETION INCREASED?

Hand in glove with our stylized fact (neglect of oversight) goes another: Congress has increasingly relinquished its legislative authority to the executive
branch, allowing the bureaucracy to make law (Dodd and Schott, 1979; Hess,
1976; Lowi, 1969; Woll, 1977).[4]

Although Congress may, to some extent, have allowed the bureaucracy to
make law, it may also have devised a reasonably effective and noncostly way to
articulate and promulgate its own legislative goals—a way that depends on the
fire-alarm oversight system. It is convenient for Congress to adopt broad legislative mandates and give substantial rule-making authority to the bureaucracy. The problem with doing so, of course, is that the bureacracy might not
pursue Congress's goals. But citizens and interest groups can be counted on to
sound an alarm in most cases in which the bureaucracy has arguably violated
Congress's goals. Then Congress can intervene to rectify the violation. Congress has not necessarily relinquished legislative responsibility to anyone else.
It has just found a more efficient way to legislate.

When legislators try to write laws with sufficient detail and precision to preclude administrative discretion, they quickly run up against their own cognitive limits: beyond a certain point, human beings just cannot anticipate all the
contingencies that might arise. The attempt to legislate for all contingencies
can entail unintended (and undesired) consequences. In his classic study of
Anglo-American judicial reasoning, Levi (1948) makes this point about judges
(lawmakers of a sort), who lay down imprecise rules, which they subsequently
and gradually elaborate in response to concrete legal disputes. Oakeshott
(1973) makes a similar point about political activity of all sorts: it cannot be
based on precise, detailed blueprints, and so policy formulations can at best
be rough summaries of experience, requiring elaboration and judicious application case by case.

The ostensible shifting of legislative responsibility to the executive branch may simply be the responsible adoption of efficient legislative techniques and the responsible acceptance of human cognitive limits—both facilitated by the fire-alarm system.

FURTHER IMPLICATIONS: THE CHOICE OF REGULATORY POLICY

When it decides regulatory issues, Congress tends to choose one of two types of regulatory instrument: command-and-control instruments and incentive-based instruments. Congress faces a similar choice when it decides, not how to regulate society, but how to regulate the regulators—when it decides, in other words, on oversight policy. For police-patrol oversight is similar to command-and-control regulatory instruments, while fire-alarm oversight is similar to incentive-based instruments.

Offhand one might suppose that just as congressmen tend to prefer fire-alarm to police-patrol oversight policies, so they would tend to prefer incentive-based to command-and-control regulatory policies. Our observations, of course, do not support this supposition (Breyer, 1982; Fiorina, 1982a; Joskow and Noll, 1978; McCubbins, 1982a; McCubbins and Page, 1982; Schultze, 1977).

Paradoxically, Congress's very preference for fire-alarm oversight entails a preference for command-and-control regulatory policy. For command-and-control agencies are more susceptible of case-by-case congressional intervention in response to complaints, hence more susceptible of fire-alarm control, than are courts, taxing authorities, and private individuals and firms—the principal participants in incentive-based regulatory policy.

CONCLUSION

The widespread perception that Congress has neglected its oversight responsibility is a widespread mistake. Congressional scholars have focused their attention on police-patrol oversight. What has appeared to many of them to be a neglect of oversight is really a preference—an eminently rational one—for fire-alarm oversight. That a decentralized, incentive-based control mechanism has been found more effective, from its users' point view, than direct, centralized surveillance should come as no surprise.

Besides criticizing the received wisdom regarding congressional oversight, we hope to have highlighted a neglected way of looking at congressional behavior. Sometimes Congress appears to do little, leaving important policy decisions to the executive or judicial branch. But appearances can deceive. A perfectly reasonable way for Congress to pursue its objectives is by ensuring that fire alarms will be sounded, enabling courts, administrative agencies, and ultimately Congress itself to step in, whenever executive compliance with congressional objectives is called in question. In examining congressional policies and their impact, do not just ask how clear, detailed, or far-sighted congressional legislation is. Ask how likely it is that fire alarms will signal putative violations of legislative goals and how Congress is likely to respond to such alarms.

NOTES

1. See Bibby, 1966, 1968; Dodd and Schott, 1979; Fiorina, 1977a,b, 1982b; Hess, 1976; Huntington, 1973; Lowi, 1969; Mitnick, 1980; Ogul, 1976, 1977; Ripley, 1978; Scher, 1963; Seidman, 1975; Woll, 1977. The following remarks by Pearson (1975) succinctly exemplify this view: "Paradoxically, despite its importance, congressional oversight remains basically weak and ineffective" (p. 281). "Oversight is a vital yet neglected congressional function" (p. 288).

2. A 1977 report by the U.S. Senate Committee on Government Operations stated that "Oversight involves a wide range of congressional efforts to review and control policy implementation . . ." (pp. 4–5). According to Dodd and Schott (1979), "Oversight . . . involves attempts by Congress to review and control policy implementation" (p. 156). Ogul (1976) defines oversight as the process by which Congress determines, among other things, whether agencies are complying with congressional intent. See also Bibby, 1966; Harris, 1964; Lees, 1977; Lowi, 1969; Ripley, 1978; Woll, 1977.

3. Ferejohn (1974) provides a good example of how the decision-making procedures of the Army Corps of Engineers were expanded to include wilderness, wildlife, and environmental group interests by the passage of the 1969 Environmental Procedures Act.

4. On related points see Fiorina (1977b), Weingast and Moran (1981), McCubbins (1982a,b), and McCubbins and Page (1982). Weingast has argued that Congress employs a number of its constitutionally defined powers in a decentralized and often unobserved way in order to exercise control over the actions of administrative agencies (Calvert, Moran, and Weingast, 1982; Weingast and Moran, 1981).

REFERENCES

Arrow, Kenneth. 1963. *Social Choice and Individual Values*. 2nd ed. New York: Wiley.

Baldwin, John. 1975. *The Regulatory Agency and the Public Corporation: The Canadian Air Transport Industry*. Cambridge, MA: Ballinger.

Bibby, John. 1966. "Committee characteristics and legislative oversight of administration." *Midwest Journal of Political Science*, 10 (February 1966): 78–98.

———. 1968. "Congress' Neglected Function." In *Republican Papers*, edited by Melvin Laird. New York: Praeger.

Breyer, Stephen. 1982. *Regulation and Its Reform*. Cambridge, MA: Harvard University Press.

Cain, Bruce, John Ferejohn, and Morris Fiorina. 1979a. "The Roots of Legislator Popularity in Great Britain and the United States." Social Science Working Paper No. 288, California Institute of Technology, Pasadena, CA.

———. 1979b. "Casework Service in Great Britain and the United States." California Institute of Technology, Pasadena, CA: Mimeo.

Calvert, Randall, Mark Moran, and Barry Weingast. 1982. "Congressional Influence over Policymaking: The Case of the FTC." Paper presented at the annual meeting of the American Political Science Association, Chicago, September 1982.

Dodd, Lawrence, and Bruce Oppenheimer, eds. 1977. *Congress Reconsidered*. New York: Praeger.

Dodd, Lawrence, and Richard Schott. 1979. *Congress and the Administrative State*. New York: Wiley.

Fenno, Richard, Jr. 1966. *The Power of the Purse*. Boston: Little, Brown.

———. 1973a. *Congressmen in Committees*. Boston: Little, Brown.

———. 1973b. "The Internal Distribution of Influence: The House." In *The Congress and America's Future*, 2nd ed., edited by David Truman, 52–76. Englewood Cliffs, NJ: Prentice-Hall.

———. 1978. *Home Style*. Boston: Little, Brown.

Ferejohn, John. 1974. *Pork Barrel Politics*. Stanford, Calif.: Stanford University Press.

———. 1981. "A Note on the Structure of Administrative Agencies." California Institute of Technology, Pasadena, CA: Mimeo.

Fiorina, Morris, 1977a. *Congress: Keystone of the Washington Establishment*. New Haven, CT: Yale University Press.

———. 1977b. "Control of the Bureaucracy: A Mismatch of Incentives and Capabilities." Social Science Working Paper No. 182, California Institute of Technology, Pasadena, CA.

———. 1982a. "Legislative Choice of Regulatory Forms: Legal Process or Administrative Process?" *Public Choice* 39 (September 1982): 33–66.

———. 1982b. "Group Concentration and the Delegation of Legislative Authority." California Institute of Technology, Pasadena, CA: Mimeo.

Fiorina, Morris, and Roger Noll. 1978. "Voters, Bureaucrats and Legislators: A Rational Choice Perspective on the Growth of Bureaucracy", *Journal of Public Economics* 9 (June 1978): 239–54.

———. 1979a. "Voters, Legislators and Bureaucracy: Institutional Design in the Public Sector." In *Problemi di Administrazione Publica, Centro di Formazione e Studi per il Messogiorno*, Naples, Italy, Formes 4 (2): 69–89.

———. 1979b. "Majority Rule Models and Legislative Election." *Journal of Politics* 41: 1081–1104.

Goodwin, George, Jr. 1970. *The Little Legislatures*. Amherst: University of Massachusetts Press.

Harris, Joseph. 1964. *Congressional Control of Administration*. Washington, D.C.: Brookings.

Hess, Stephen. 1976. *Organizing the Presidency*. Washington, D.C.: Brookings.

Huitt, Ralph. 1973. "The Internal Distribution of Influence: The Senate." In *The Congress in America's Future*, 2nd ed., edited by David Truman, 77–101. Englewood Cliffs, NJ: Prentice-Hall.

Huntington, Samuel. 1973. "Congressional Responses to the Twentieth Century." In *The Congress in America's Future*, 2nd ed., edited by David Truman, 5–31. Englewood Cliffs, NJ: Prentice-Hall.

Jaffe, Louis. 1973. "The Illusion of the Ideal Administration." *Harvard Law Review* 86: 1183–99.

Joskow, Paul. 1974. "Inflation and Environmental Concern: Structural Change Is the Process of Public Utility Price Regulation." *Journal of Law and Economics* 17 (October 1974): 291–327.

Joskow, Paul, and Roger Noll. 1978. "Regulation in Theory and Practice: An Overview." California Institute of Technology, Social Science Working Paper No. 213, Pasadena, CA.

Lees, John D. 1977. "Legislatures and Oversight: A Review Article on a Neglected Area of Research." *Legislative Studies Quarterly* (May 1977): 193–208.

Levi, Edward. 1948. *Legal Reasoning.* Chicago: University of Chicago Press.

Lowi, Theodore. 1969. *The End of Liberalism.* New York: Norton.

Matthews, Donald. 1960. *U.S. Senators and Their World.* Chapel Hill: University of North Carolina Press.

Mayhew, David. 1974. *Congress: The Electoral Connection.* New Haven, CT: Yale University Press.

McConnell, Grant. 1966. *Private Power and American Democracy.* New York: Vintage Books.

McCubbins, Mathew. 1982a. "Rational Individual Behavior and Collective Irrationality: The Legislative Choice of Regulatory Forms." Ph.D. dissertation, California Institute of Technology, Pasadena, CA.

———. 1982b. "On the Form of Regulatory Intervention." Paper presented at the 1983 Annual Meeting of the Public Choice Society, Savannah, GA, March 24–26, 1983.

McCubbins, Mathew, and Talbot Page. 1982. "On the Failure of Environmental, Health and Safety Regulation." Paper presented at the 1983 Annual Meeting of the Midwest Political Science Association, Chicago, IL, April 20–23, 1983.

Mitnick, Barry. 1980. *The Political Economy of Regulation.* New York: Columbia University Press.

Oakeshott, Michael. 1973. "Political Education." In *Rationalism in Politics,* edited by Michael Oakeshott, 110–36. New York: Basic Books, 1962. Reprinted in *Freedom and Authority,* edited by Thomas Schwartz, 362–80. Encino, CA: Dickenson.

Ogul, Morris. 1976. *Congress Oversees the Bureaucracy.* Pittsburgh: University of Pittsburgh Press.

———. 1977. "Congressional Oversight: Structure and Incentives." In *Congress Reconsidered,* edited by Lawrence Dodd and Bruce Oppenheimer, 207–21. New York: Praeger.

Ornstein, Norman, ed. 1975. *Congress in Change.* New York: Praeger.

Parker, Glenn, and Roger Davidson. 1979. "Why Do Americans Love Their Congressmen So Much More than Their Congress?" *Legislative Studies Quarterly* 4 (February 1979): 53–62.

Pearson, James. 1975. "Oversight: A Vital Yet Neglected Congressional Function." *Kansas Law Review* 23: 277–88.

Plott, Charles. 1967. "A Notion of Equilibrium and Its Possibility under Majority Rules." *American Economic Review* 57 (September 1967): 787–806.

Ripley, Randall 1969. *Power in the Senate.* New York: St. Martin's.

———. 1978. *Congress: Process and Policy.* 2nd ed. New York: Norton.

Ripley, Randall, and Grace Franklin. 1976. *Congress, the Bureaucracy and Public Policy.* Homewood, IL: Dorsey.

Scher, Seymour. 1963. "Conditions for Legislative Control." *Journal of Politics* 25 (August 1963): 526–51.

Schultze, Charles. 1977. *The Public Use of Private Interest.* Washington, DC: Brookings.

Schwartz, Thomas. 1970. "On the Possibility of Rational Policy Evaluation." *Theory and Decision* 1 (October 1970): 89–106.

———. 1981. "The Universal-Instability Theorem." *Public Choice* 37 (3): 487–501.

————. 1982a. "A Really General Impossibility Theorem." *Quality and Quantity* 16 (December 1982): 493–505.

————. 1982b. "The Pork Barrel Paradox." University of Texas, Austin, TX: Mimeo.

Seidman, Harold. 1975. *Politics, Position, and Power: The Dynamics of Federal Organization.* New York: Oxford.

U.S. Senate. Committee on Government Operations. 1977. *Study on Federal Regulation, Vol. II, Congressional Oversight of Regulatory Agencies.* Washington, D.C.: Government Printing Office.

Weingast, Barry, and Mark Moran. 1981. "Bureaucratic Discretion of Congressional Control: Regulatory Policymaking by the Federal Trade Commission." Washington University, St. Louis: Center of the Study of American Business. Mimeo.

Woll, Peter. 1977. *American Bureaucracy.* New York: Norton.

7.3

DANIEL P. CARPENTER

From *The Forging of Bureaucratic Autonomy: Reputations, Networks, and Policy Innovation in Executive Agencies, 1862–1928*

Bureaucrats in the executive branch need some autonomy from politicians in order to do their work. Regulators of food and drugs, for example, should not be influenced by political pressure. After all, many of these bureaucrats have technical expertise or are in jobs that require impartial decisions. Carpenter argues that it took a long time for many bureaucratic positions to gain the appropriate amount of autonomy. Bureaucrats in the early twentieth century had to play their own political games to earn this autonomy, namely by cultivating their own loyal constituencies within industry and among the population.

Bureaucratic autonomy occurs when bureaucrats take actions consistent with their own wishes, actions to which politicians and organized interests defer even though they would prefer that other actions (or no action at all) be taken. Bureaucratic autonomy so defined is a common feature, though far from a universal one, of American government in the twentieth century. Agencies have at times created and developed policy with few, if any, constraints from legislative and executive overseers, and they have frequently coordinated organized interests as much as responded to them. To suggest that bureaucracies have policymaking autonomy may strike some readers as a controversial if not outlandish claim. Surely agencies lack the ability to take any action they desire in our system of representative government and rule of law. Yet I contend here that bureaucratic autonomy lies less in *fiat* than in *leverage*. Autonomy prevails when agencies can establish political legitimacy—a reputation for expertise, efficiency, or moral protection and a uniquely diverse complex of ties to organized interests and the media—and induce politicians to defer to the wishes of the agency even when they prefer otherwise. Under these conditions, politicians grant agency officials free rein in program building. They stand by while agency officials do away with some of their cherished programs and services. They even welcome agencies in shaping legislation itself.

■　■　■

From Daniel P. Carpenter, *The Forging of Bureaucratic Autonomy: Reputations, Networks, and Policy Innovation in Executive Agencies, 1862–1928* (Princeton, NJ: Princeton University Press, 2001).

THE POLITICS OF BUREAUCRATIC AUTONOMY

Bureaucrats are politicians, and bureaucracies are organizations of political actors. Autonomy arises when bureaucrats successfully practice a politics of legitimacy. It occurs when agency leaders build reputations for their organizations—reputations for efficacy, for uniqueness of service, for moral protection, and for expertise. It occurs, further, when they ground this reputation in a diverse coalition wrought from the multiple networks in which they are engaged. These coalitions, suspended in beliefs and in networks, and uncontrollable by politicians, are the stuff of autonomous bureaucratic policy innovation. This, I submit, is the basic lesson of the forging of bureaucratic autonomy in the United States. *Bureaucratic autonomy is politically forged.*

Contemporary political science—including an entire literature on bureaucracy that depends on "principal-agent" models of bureaucratic politics—assumes that the linkages between voters and policies occur through parties, elections, representatives, and the legislature. Yet the decisive steps in forging bureaucratic autonomy occurred when federal bureaucrats broke free from the traditional model of politics and established links directly to citizens and the new associations that increasingly claimed their allegiance. Long before the "iron triangles" of the New Deal Era, bureaucracies began to aggregate citizens and voters precisely when parties and politicians were having a difficult time doing so.

Because some agencies did this more successfully than others, the state-building achievement of the Progressive Era was concrete but limited. What emerged in the 1910s and 1920s was not a uniformly more powerful bureaucracy than existed three decades earlier. In pockets of the American state, relative autonomy conditioned upon political legitimacy materialized. Most other agencies lay dormant. Therein lies the puzzle of American state building. Why was the Department of Agriculture able to establish a foothold in writing significant legislation? Why was the Interior Department, with authority over public lands and ties to numerous western interests, unable to capitalize on the movements for conservation and western reclamation? Why were reformers in the Post Office Department able to eliminate systematically the positions of strong Republican identifiers in fourth-class offices at the very time when Republicans enjoyed hegemony in electoral politics? Why were postal officials able to grab all of the moral policing powers they wanted and resist political control of their use? Why was the USDA able to take its newfound authority in food and drug regulation and turn its fire on the very firms who most supported Republicans during the Progressive period?

The answer lies in the organizational properties of executive agencies at the turn of the century. Bureaucratic autonomy cannot exist apart from the organizational characteristics of the agencies that experience it. If it exists, bureaucratic autonomy *must* be premised not upon the popularity of a policy, not upon occasional administrative fiat, not upon a single well-heeled lobby, but upon the stable political legitimacy of the bureaucracy itself. To focus on organizational reputations is not, as I have emphasized, to divorce bureaucracies from politics. Instead, it is to reconceive politics as a process of coalition building and to acknowledge that in some circumstances bureaucrats can take the decisive initiative (at times, the *only* initiative) in building them. It is to these reputations—and the capacities and coalitions that supported them—that autonomous bureaucracies in America owe their origins.

■   ■   ■

The Poverty of Procedural Politics

The argument elaborated here poses several challenges to contemporary erudition on bureaucracies. Following the highly influential work of Mathew McCubbins, Roger Noll, and Barry Weingast, a generation of scholars has argued that an agency's "enacting coalition" of politicians can use administrative procedures to induce the agency to take exactly those actions that the coalition desires. These "procedural politics" theories suggest that most of the political action in bureaucratic politics occurs when the methods and processes for a given policy are set by politicians and the interests to which they respond. Hence bureaucratic politics does not really involve bureaucracies at all; "the administrative system is automatic."

The theory elaborated here suggests that procedural politics is unlikely to control agencies with stable political legitimacy. Agencies with esteemed officials who have publicly recognized capacity and expertise, and who have independent access to organized citizens, exercise power over the procedures of their agency. Autonomous agencies are powerful bargaining agents in procedural design. The more powerful constraint on administrative procedures is that legitimated agency officials can make it politically costly for politicians to constrain them. Partisans of the procedural-politics school of bureaucracy have discussed all sorts of mechanisms for controlling the bureaucracy without recognizing that these strategies have costs. In some respects, these amount to forfeiting the benefits of agency specialization. The argument here, however, is that when agencies have political legitimacy, the costs of control are *explicitly political and electoral.*

■   ■   ■

Congress, the Media, and Multiplicity

The role of general beliefs about agencies in bureaucratic reputations points to important changes in Congress and the media that enabled agencies to erect reputations. The building of bureaucratic reputations between Congress and executive departments found fertile soil in the Progressive period. Not only were bureau chiefs serving longer tenures, but members of Congress were investing more and more time in committees. As a result, agency officials and their overseers in Congress began to develop a mutual familiarity. The institutional memory of Congress grew, the abilities and interests of bureaus became clearer and more consistent, and uncertainty over the bureaucracy declined. The stability of these relations gave bureau chiefs an incentive to cultivate the trust of committee chairs and congressional party leaders, and some Progressive-Era program leaders adopted this strategy to great advantage.[1]

Perhaps the most important venue of bureaucratic reputation lay in the rapidly expanding media. At a time when broadcast news remained only an imaginary possibility, Americans received their political information from a highly variegated print industry. In this market the critical split was between the larger urban newspapers and related syndicates and the rural farm weeklies. In the urban newspapers arose the "muckraking" of Progressive reformers, whereas farm editors remained committed to a mix of populist and pro-agrarian sentiments. In part because these papers depended increasingly on the USDA and the Post Office for information and rate classification, both agencies were treated with favor by urban and rural presses. Yet the network advantages of the two agencies transcended mere resource dependence. Numerous Agriculture Department officials were close acquaintances with one or more rural newspaper editors. And newspaper editors, urban and rural, interacted frequently with postal officials over matters of rate classification. As a result of these ties, Progressive-Era citizens were better (and more favorably) informed about the USDA and Post Office than any other agencies in American government.

Reputations for Neutrality and Moral Protection

Traditionally, political scientists have expected greater autonomy where agencies can lay claim to expertise—especially where agencies possess a monopoly on information in a given area. A more interesting case of "policy" in this book emerges from "moral politics" during the culturally conservative Progressive Era. A key component of both the USDA's and the Post Office's march to autonomy was their linkages to Victorian moral reformers and their anti-adulteration campaigns, both in the adulteration of food and the adulteration of morals (through pornography and gambling). The Interior Department lacked any such connection to anti-adulteration themes. These moral reputations, and the framing of policy campaigns in terms of "protection" from "the evils of adulteration," served to enhance the agencies' esteem for national service. A core component of strong agency reputations is the mien of neutrality, impartiality, or orientation toward the public good. Where an agency's innovations appear patently to serve its own interests or those of a selected group or region, the political legitimacy necessary for autonomy is less likely to emerge.

In the case of postal state building, coalition building combined moralist Progressives, media organizations, agrarians, and corporate business. Each of these interests sought something different from the Post Office. Progressive Victorians wanted moral policing in the form of Comstockery, agrarians wanted expanded services in rural America and an alternative to institutions dominated by corporate industry, and business interests and the media (for different reasons) wanted an efficient national communications infrastructure. Each saw their interests met in the same programs. Without all four (and more) of these organizational forces, programs such as rural free delivery, parcels post, and postal savings would not have marked Progressive change as they did. More critically, without Anthony Comstock, August Machen, John Wanamaker, and other postal officials to bridge these forces and to create a multifaceted coalition, the possibility of institutional change would have been trifling.

The logic of multifaceted coalitions was demonstrated nowhere more powerfully than in the Department of Agriculture. Republican presidents, women's organizations, conservationists, congressional committees, agrarian organizations—all of these interests converged to influence policy change in areas as diverse as pharmaceutical regulation, forest preservation, and agricultural extension. The central point, again, is that the coalitions were nursed and maintained not by elected politicians but by middle-level bureaucrats. Far more than in Herbert Hoover's Department of Commerce, the "associational state" in America was established in the early-twentieth-century USDA. Unlike Commerce, moreover, the USDA exerted an immense influence on the groups in its coalitions.

■　■　■

The organizational flourishing that was characteristic of Progressive society offers one reason that the patterns of bureaucratic autonomy witnessed in this book are less likely to be observed in contemporary politics. To be sure, modern America is rife with organizations in the formal sense. The day-by-day embedment of Americans in organizations has waned, not strengthened, over the last few decades. The challenge of contemporary American state building, in this view, may demand more than "reinventing" American government.

NOTE

1. Jonathan N. Katz and Brian R. Sala, "Careerism, Committee Assignments, and the Electoral Connection," *American Political Science Review* 90 (March 1996): 21.

7.4

SUSAN L. MOFFITT

From *Making Public Policy:*
Participatory Bureaucracy in American Democracy

In this selection, Moffitt summarizes how bureaucracies often create public committees that permit people and groups from outside the government to comment on proposed regulations. She argues that these public committees allow bureaucratic leaders to learn from members of the public, but also to learn in public. The latter purpose, learning in public, has not been well understood by scholars of bureaucracy, but it has crucial benefits. Public committees are opportunities to show the processes by which bureaucratic leaders make decisions. They can enhance legitimacy for decisions and shield bureaucracies from charges of secrecy and unaccountability.

PORTALS OF DEMOCRACY IN AMERICAN BUREAUCRACY

"[K]nowledge is no longer an immobile solid; it has been liquefied; it is actively moving in all the currents of society itself."

—John Dewey[1]

"Advisory committees can be of great value. They contribute to the 'openness' of Governmental decision-making, and provide advice and information not otherwise available to the Government. Their functions range from providing policy advice on major national issues, to providing technical recommendations on particular problems."

—Federal Advisory Committees: Sixth Annual Report
of the President, 1978

"Imagine planning your day around your life, instead of your osteoarthritis pain," enticed Merck's advertising campaign for Vioxx, its blockbuster arthritis drug. The drug Merck promoted "for everyday victories" soon became a symbol of regulatory failure as evidence emerged linking Vioxx with serious cardiovascular side effects and deaths. At the beginning of Senate hearings

From Susan L. Moffitt, *Making Public Policy: Participatory Bureaucracy in American Democracy* (New York: Cambridge University Press, 2014).

convened in 2004 to investigate Vioxx's withdrawal from the market, Senator Charles Grassley (R-IA) alleged that the FDA had "allowed itself to be manipulated by Merck" and, more broadly, that "the FDA has a relationship with drug companies that is far too cozy."[2] The remedy for coziness with industry and for regulatory failure, Senator Grassley continued, would include "changes inside the FDA that [would] result in greater transparency and greater openness." In its 2007 review of American drug safety, the Institute of Medicine (IOM) similarly claimed, "the FDA's reputation has been hurt by a perceived lack of transparency and accountability to the public."[3] As part of its package of proposals to improve the agency's impaired reputation, the Institute of Medicine called on the FDA to make greater use of its public advisory committees—groups of nongovernmental medical practitioners, researchers, and stakeholder representatives that the FDA consults on matters such as drug approval and labeling—to supplement agency expertise and to enhance transparency in the drug approval process. These proposals suggested public engagement could render FDA decisions both more accountable and less prone to regulatory failure.

The FDA, however, *had* publicly reviewed and discussed Vioxx long before the drug's withdrawal, before Senator Grassley's rebuke, and before the Institute of Medicine's charge: the agency consulted with its Arthritis Drugs Advisory Committee about Vioxx's safety and efficacy both in 1999 and in 2001. Neither FDA staffers nor the firm sponsoring the drug served on the agency's drug advisory committees as voting members. Instead, the firm sponsoring the drug summarized evidence from drug trials and offered justifications for the drug's approval and labeling claims. Agency staffers presented their findings and concerns about drug applications in testimony before the committee as well. Both Vioxx meetings invited nonbinding advice from the committee in front of public audiences, and a portion of the 2001 deliberation included debate over whether Vioxx caused heart attacks and strokes.[4]

Public meetings like the ones convened by the FDA suggest potential portals for public participation in agency policymaking that can challenge key aspects of traditional bureaucratic administration. They can provide a public forum for agency critics, reveal details of agency decision making that an agency may prefer to keep private, produce information an agency may not want to consider, and compromise agency jurisdiction over the ultimate policy decision.[5] As part of public meetings convened in 2005 to discuss Vioxx's withdrawal from the market, a representative of the consumer advocacy group, Public Citizen, publicly charged that the FDA knew about cardiovascular risks associated with Cox-2 inhibitors such as Vioxx and failed to reveal that information promptly.[6] Long before Vioxx, AIDS activists and groups representing other disease sufferers started using FDA advisory committees to chastise the FDA publicly and viscerally. "The FDA is incapable of doing its job expeditiously," a member of the AIDS organization ACT-UP New York charged at the June 12, 1991 Antiviral Drugs Advisory Committee meeting reviewing the drug Foscavir. He continued in his address to the committee:

> Tell [FDA Commissioner] David Kessler, [Center for Drug Evaluation and Research Director] Carl Peck . . . that denying [Foscavir] to people who have nothing to lose because of their slow bureaucratic procedures is a moral outrage that this committee and the American public will not tolerate. Remind the FDA—and it is sick that they need to be reminded of this—but remind them that they work for us, the American taxpayers, and that we are dying because of their inefficiency.[7]

The conventional portrait of government bureaucrats depicts insatiable appetites for secrecy and exclusivity. This notorious closure fuels a fundamental and enduring tension facing American government: reconciling bureaucratic policy making with democratic accountability. Yet, bureaucrats in American agencies across the federal government frequently make their information public, open their policymaking processes to public advice, and, in doing so, expose themselves to public rebuke as in the case of Foscavir. If public participation poses a fundamental threat to bureaucratic power, why do bureaucrats open their doors to participation and *choose* to convene thousands of public meetings each year? Does public participation in agency policymaking, of the kind that emerged for the Vioxx review, improve policy outcomes and provide a portal for democratic governance, or does it merely yield an additional platform for industry influence and privilege in executive branch policymaking? More broadly, what effects does public participation have on bureaucratic administration, on policy outcomes, and on democratic accountability?

▪ ▪ ▪

"This is an idiotic policy," a member of the National Assessment Governing Board bluntly charged at the Board's May 2002 public meeting, referring to the portion of the No Child Left Behind Act (NCLB) that made the test questions on the National Assessment of Educational Progress more readily available to public inspection.[8]

Since 1969, the National Assessment of Educational Progress (NAEP) has been routinely testing and reporting nationally on student achievement in reading, math, science, and other subjects.[9] It has earned the reputation as the "gold standard" for measuring student achievement across the United States, a reputation that depends on producing valid measures of student achievement. Such validity stems from the assessment's design, which has historically precluded teachers from teaching to the test.

From the view of agency leadership at the National Center for Education Statistics (the government agency responsible for helping administer the assessment) along with some members of the National Assessment Governing

Board (the public board that sets policy for the assessment), provisions of NCLB designed to make National Assessment test questions more broadly accessible and transparent to the public threatened to jeopardize the assessment's integrity. Addressing the National Assessment Governing Board at its March 2002 meeting, the Acting Commissioner of the National Center for Education Statistics warned:

> [L]et's say, for example . . . someone got all the [NAEP] booklets and put them on a web site. Well, that would basically as far as I'm concerned shut down our ability to conduct that assessment.[10]

Similarly, the public Board's Executive Director warned at the May 2002 meeting that these new requirements could "bring NAEP to its knees" and possibly damage the statistical integrity of the test.[11] The Board Chairman echoed these worries, stating that it might be the responsibility of board members to speak about these concerns. He remarked that if it appeared this part of the law would jeopardize NAEP's integrity, it could be the Board's job to say "Stop."[12]

For the past fifty years, public participation through public committees has figured prominently in the National Assessment's governance, design, and operation. Public committees helped design the original NAEP in the early 1960s. Public committees have helped design and review the questions that NAEP poses on assessments. Public committees have governed the assessment's policy decisions ever since the assessment began. Unlike the advisory committees the FDA consults, public boards for the National Assessment enjoy binding policymaking authority over some policy tasks.[13] And the relationship between the Governing Board and the education statistics agency has, at times, been fraught.[14] Yet, the Board found itself at odds with a portion of the president's signature education policy initiative and in agreement with bureaucratic leadership in the National Center for Education Statistics, the government agency: to protect the statistical integrity of the National Assessment by shielding it from unfettered public access to assessment questions. The conventional portrait of public committees suggests that public participation can interfere with agencies' abilities to deploy their technical knowledge in policy implementation, and that a trade-off exists between democratic control and agency expertise. In the case of the National Assessment of Educational Progress, public participation has instead appeared to help protect and promote the statistical integrity of the assessment, combining public participation and aspects of closure. When does public participation enhance expertise and when does it compromise the technical integrity of agency policymaking? When do bureaucratic administration and democratic governance appear fundamentally at odds, and when can they be reconciled through participation that offers both?

The Tension between Bureaucratic Administration and American Democracy

[These] narratives invite us to rethink and refine ideas about whether and when expert knowledge creates tension between bureaucratic administration and democratic accountability. Both secrecy and expertise represent traditional hallmarks of bureaucratic administration[15] and provide the crux of the Vioxx puzzle. Given the power that exclusive expert knowledge and closure can confer, why would the FDA open its policymaking process to outside advisers and to an audience of spectators? One conventional response looks for elected officials' fingerprints on agency structures and processes that yield greater openness. The idea that government agencies possess and capitalize on exclusive expert information is foundational to theories of oversight and delegation that strive to explain when elected officials cede policymaking to bureaucrats and what structures and procedures elected officials construct to prevent bureaucrats' policies from straying far from elected officials' wishes.[16] Given bureaucrats' presumed appetites for secrecy, the power such secrecy can confer and the potential threat it poses to democratic governance, American elected officials and government reformers have repeatedly sought ways to induce bureaucrats to reveal otherwise private information and provide organized groups opportunities to monitor bureaucratic policymaking. This includes requirements to share government records, to conduct open government meetings, and to require public participation in rulemaking.[17] The ensuing political influence over agency work, however, can threaten agency expertise and impair the quality of policy outcomes. Aspects of political control, for instance, appear to come at the expense of drug safety.[18] Some versions of democratic accountability can compromise bureaucratic administration, and vice versa, thus yielding an apparent trade-off between the two.[19]

These concerns about the tension between bureaucratic policymaking, in which unelected civil servants make significant policy decisions, and democratic oversight that vests governing authority in the public have long been stitched into the fabric of American governance. This tension has taken on heightened significance, however, with the dramatic expansion and development of American bureaucracy since the nation's founding.[20] The American bureaucracy wields significant power, and some estimates suggest that agency administrators—not Congress or the president—create the majority of American laws through the rulemaking process.[21] With the growth of the American administrative state has come responsibility for policies, services, and decisions on which Americans' health, safety, and financial livelihood depend. Failures in bureaucratic expertise can produce devastating consequences.

Participatory Bureaucracy: Some Guiding Principles

When are federal-level bureaucrats more or less likely to seek public participation in agency policymaking? When is public participation more or less likely to support key features of bureaucratic administration: expertise and diverse support? [We should consider] bureaucrats as implementers broadly defined, who make policy in the course of implementation.[22] While putting policy into practice is a dynamic process,[23] knowledge and turf provide the backbones of bureaucratic task implementation. Considered in the context of U.S. federal-level policy, neither knowledge nor jurisdiction for task implementation is a general or fixed property of an agency. Instead, knowledge and turf vary by task. Conditions conducive to participatory bureaucracy thus depend on characteristics of a policy task, the fundamental unit of bureaucratic work.[24]

For instance, federal-level bureaucrats may have knowledge superior to family physicians on Vioxx's cardiovascular risks, but Merck might have better information than the bureaucrats, and researchers at the Cleveland Clinic might have better information yet. Instead of assuming monopoly information—on anyone's part—bureaucratic implementers confront a range of informational contexts, including when bureaucrats have more information, when outsiders have more information, when nobody has information, or when everyone is informed.[25] Government agencies also face a continuum of implementation contexts, ranging from fully in-house, such as a budget examination housed in the Office of Management and Budget, to well outside the agency's hierarchical reach. The federal government, for instance, enjoys relatively little formal authority over local public schools. The extent to which federal bureaucrats can implement policy in local school contexts typically depends on thousands of loosely connected implementers populating the vast governance space between the federal Department of Education and Valley View Elementary.

Consider the schema in Figure [1] that depicts variation on two crucial dimensions of implementation: information and turf. The horizontal axis represents the agency's information relative to task demands: the right side reflects full agency information, and the left side pegs at agency ignorance. The vertical axis represents a continuum from task independence to task interdependence. The top reflects full independence: the task is performed entirely within the agency's hierarchy. The bottom reflects fully interdependent implementations. Considerable scholarship on bureaucratic politics focuses on quadrants A and B, and with good reason. Quadrant A represents an ideal bureaucracy with perfect information and full authority over implementation, rather like Internal Revenue Service tax audits. This is where Weberian expertise and secrets may reside in harmony. In Quadrant B, bureaucrats enjoy authority over implementation, but their information is less complete relative to task demands. Here is where the tenets of Weberian power—technical knowledge and secrecy—may be at odds. The Atomic Energy Commission in the 1950s, for instance, enjoyed authority over the development of American nuclear power. When faced with insufficient information, the Commission engaged in private learning: talking behind closed doors with outsiders who had

FIGURE [1] Participation in American Bureaucracy by Task-Specific Information and Implementation Conditions

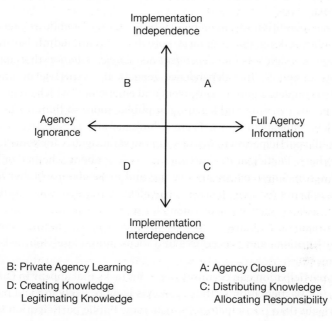

B: Private Agency Learning

D: Creating Knowledge
Legitimating Knowledge

A: Agency Closure

C: Distributing Knowledge
Allocating Responsibility

better information and more technical expertise than insiders.[26] Yet, Quadrant B is also where bureaucratic independence can allow bureaucrats to hide their ignorance: where secrecy enabled the Commission to avoid revealing their uncertainty over reactor safety, for instance. In his call for greater oversight of the Central Intelligence Agency in 1956, Senator Michael Mansfield (D-MT) lamented, "If we accept the idea of secrecy for secrecy's sake we will have no way of knowing whether we have a very fine intelligence service or a very poor one."[27] Secrecy can impair both expertise and democratic oversight.[28]

Task implementations that appear in Quadrants C and D foster greater incentives for bureaucrats not only to learn *from* the public but also to learn *in* public than in A and B. These are conditions of greater task interdependence, when bureaucrats depend fundamentally on implementers who reside outside the agency's hierarchical jurisdiction. To implement its task of ensuring drug safety and efficacy, for instance, the FDA depends on firms to gather and reveal appropriate information both to the FDA *and* to doctors and patients. The agency depends on physicians and patients to use therapies judiciously. It depends on firms and physicians to report adverse events to the agency. The FDA cannot command safe drug use: safety and efficacy are ultimately matters of practice that transcend the agency's organizational boundaries. While drug reviews present general conditions of interdependence, each drug review produces a different information and implementation context. . . .

Thus, one condition of participatory bureaucracy—public engagement in agency policymaking that supports both bureaucratic administration and democratic oversight—is *interdependent task implementation* that appears in Quadrants C and D. Interdependence renders the expertise or knowledge required for implementation contingent and emergent,[29] which creates incentives for public learning and learning *in* public, more so than for tasks with independent implementations. From a bureaucratic perspective, we would expect public participation to manifest in the same agency for some tasks but not for others. Participatory bureaucracy is less about whether or not the FDA reflects openness or closure overall, and more about whether and why openness appears for some tasks, such as drug reviews for novel indications, but not for others, such as drug reviews for supplemental indications. Participatory bureaucracy invites us to look beyond explanations that stop at the level of institutions and procedures and focus more closely on task-specific conditions.

Public participation can certainly occur for tasks that appear in Quadrants A and B, but participation in these contexts is more likely to yield participatory oversight than participatory bureaucracy. Public participation for tasks in Quadrants A and B [is] more likely to come at the expense of bureaucratic expertise and jurisdiction. The more that tasks are implemented in a traditional Weberian hierarchy—the more the tasks reside in Quadrants A and B—the less we would expect participatory bureaucracy to reconcile the democracy-bureaucracy tension, and the more we would expect the conventional trade-off, with more of one and less of another.[30] By some accounts, however, American government agency interdependence is both prevalent and expanding.[31] One estimate suggests that only 5 percent of "federal government activity" entails goods and services that government bureaucrats provide directly.[32] American government's reliance on third-party actors and public co-production renders public participation through public committees an increasingly feasible means of managing the bureaucracy-democracy tension.

However, complex tasks like those we would see in Quadrants C and D—such as regulator dependence on its regulatory target—can make agencies vulnerable to industry influence or capture,[33] which supports neither bureaucratic administration nor democratic oversight. Thus, a second condition for participatory bureaucracy is a public engagement process that yields *diverse expertise focused on implementation*. In the context of participatory bureaucracy, expert means possessing specialized knowledge that provides a baseline of knowledge or ability, but it does not inhere in fixed descriptive characteristics, such as being a woman or having a PhD. Instead, it can manifest from multiple sources, including the grassroots; and it depends on timing, location, and the nature of the policy task. Common critiques of participatory processes typically dichotomize "experts" and "public," defining expertise in terms of credentials or exclusive knowledge, and the public in terms of the mass that lacks formal credentials but has a potential interest in the issue. Participatory bureaucracy blurs the distinction between these categories. In participatory bureaucracy, disease sufferers may be expert in their ability to express how they are affected by disease, how they experienced pharmaceutical therapies, and their willingness to accept risk.[34] Expertise for participatory bureaucracy is not restricted to a particular profession or perspective, but evolves along with the implementation context: who is "expert" depends on the task.[35] Rather than dichotomies between the public and experts, participatory bureaucracy can embody significant overlap between the two.

Within the context of broadly defined expertise, diversity brings different *perspectives* and heuristics. This cognitive approach differs from traditional models of participation in bureaucratic policymaking that frame participation strictly as opportunities for communicating and advocating for particular *interests*.[36] Building on a broadly defined baseline of expertise, diverse perspectives and diverse cognitive heuristics render suboptimal policy decisions less likely. Suboptimal from the perspective of bureaucratic administration means policy outcomes that are costly to reverse and/or damaging to agency reputation.[37] Participatory bureaucracy is better equipped to manage the bureaucracy-democracy tension when it marshals diverse expertise keyed to the policy task. These conditions—diverse expertise focused on interdependent task implementation—render public participation amenable to supporting core elements of bureaucratic reputation: expertise and diverse support.[38]

Given the conditions it imposes on public participation, participatory bureaucracy clearly differs from participatory democracy's inclusiveness and empowerment.[39] Yet, participatory bureaucracy is amenable to democratic accountability when it "liquefies knowledge," to use Dewey's metaphor. Participatory bureaucracy that manages the bureaucracy-democracy tension is *indeterminate*: both the participatory process and its outcomes are fluid and evolving rather than fixed or foreordained. Participatory bureaucracy creates openness and access to policymaking that can expand beyond the scope of the particular task. Scholarship typically assesses the impact of participation on the individuals who participated in the policymaking process. Examples include Chicago's Alternative Policing Strategy that brought community members and police together to develop and implement priorities for the police, or environmental regulatory negotiations conducted through stakeholder participation.[40] The potential democratic contributions of participatory bureaucracy, however, exceed the scope of a singular decision or information exchange. Consistent with open-systems theories of organizations, participatory bureaucracy can transcend fixed jurisdictions and offer access to policymaking through visibility and through opportunities for engagement from governmental and nongovernmental sources.[41] The potential for accountability is ongoing: it does not end when the votes are cast and the meeting comes to an end. Open meetings can put knowledge into the public space that can, in turn, take on a life of its own. The promise of participatory bureaucracy resides in part in the ongoing portal it may create.

Skepticism toward participatory processes abounds. Imbalanced power can limit the extent and scope of participation and stifle discourse.[42] Insufficient connections between knowledge and subsequent action can limit the usefulness of public information for individual behavior or policy outcomes. Knowledge may drip rather than flow, and do so in ways that exacerbate political, social, and economic inequality. Yet, consider the counterfactuals of Quadrants A and B, where accountability may be even more remote *and* come at the expense of expert or competent implementation.

Participatory bureaucracy is not the sole solution for the bureaucracy-democracy tension, and can complement other governing approaches including representative bureaucracy and performance management. But it is distinct in notable ways. For one, bureaucrats may initiate, design, and administer participatory bureaucracy. Participatory bureaucracy is not necessarily imposed on the bureaucracy by elected officials. Rather than curtail agency autonomy, public participation creates room for government agencies to frame policy issues, shape alternatives for the public agenda, and cultivate favorable agency images. In this sense, participatory bureaucracy departs from congressional dominance views, which leave little room for bureaucratic autonomy and credit elected officials with institution building. While participatory bureaucracy offers room for representing interests, akin to pluralism or representative bureaucracy,[43] it also allows direct public access to information and policymaking, not just access mediated through representatives or groups.[44] Unlike pluralism and representative bureaucracy where the direction of influence and information flow is from t¹ e representatives to the policy decision, moreover, participatory bureaucracy can enable information to flow in multiple directions: from the agency to the various publics as well as from the public to the agency.[45] In contrast to some aspects of New Public Management,[46] participatory bureaucracy does not assume that the local level or the consumer has "better" information essential to policy implementation, just as it does not assume federal-level bureaucrats enjoy superior information. Information for implementation depends on the policy task.

Public participation's ability to manage the bureaucracy-democracy tension depends on the design of the policy task, on the design of participation, and on the broader context in which the policy is implemented and participation occurs. Managing the tension offers a potentially non-zero-sum approach to government administration. Instead of dichotomies between democratic governance and bureaucratic administration, between legislative and executive branch control, between public and private, or between public and expert, participatory bureaucracy offers potential complements. Rather than zero-sum, both elected officials and bureaucrats can reap rewards from permeable bureaucratic policymaking.[47] Both elected officials and bureaucrats can benefit from competent task implementation.[48] One way bureaucracy can abet competence is through public participation that assembles diverse expertise for interdependent task implementations.

Participatory bureaucracy shares several key features with the development of administrative expertise modeled in Gailmard and Patty's *Learning While Governing*. Both challenge the conventional assumption that bureaucrats enjoy superior or sufficient information relative to other policy actors. Both recognize the importance of information and authority for structuring bureaucratic incentives. Both recognize that bureaucratic expertise and democratic accountability are not necessarily at odds. Gailmard and Patty offer an important model for understanding organizational designs that induce bureaucrats to "acquire, share and elicit information," to use their terms.[49] Participatory bureaucracy focuses instead on task-specific variation in bureaucratic knowledge and jurisdiction that yield different incentives for learning *from* the public and learning *in* public across organizational and institutional arrangements. The analysis that follows suggests that systematic variation in task conditions goes far to explain some policy outcomes, whereas some prominent organizational and institutional differences do not.

The potential democratic mechanism in participatory bureaucracy also differs from principal-agent models. When learning in public liquefies knowledge, to use Dewey's metaphor, the potential for democratic accountability exceeds the scope of any singular policy decision. The transparency that can manifest from learning in public may assist democratic accountability not merely by holding the agency accountable but also by creating opportunities to hold other implementers outside the agency accountable upon whom task implementation depends. Accountability in participatory bureaucracy may manifest not only by holding the FDA solely responsible, for instance, but also by shining the spotlight on firms and inducing firms to behave in ways consistent with policy implementation.[50]

The policy conditions that make participatory bureaucracy promising, however, also render it fragile. Policies' interdependence can give way to imbalanced dependence, privilege, or even corruption. Emerging technologies and evolving expertise can expose nascent policies to unfounded attacks and equally unfounded sponsorship. The expansive, non-zero-sum potential of public knowledge generated through public participation can collide with zero-sum American politics. Appetites for secrecy persist. Public participation did not, for instance, prevent the arthritis drug Vioxx's post-marketing safety problems. Participatory bureaucracy is hard to pull off.

Given this mixed portrait of public participation in agency policymaking, this [reading] explores the following questions:

- When do different forms of public participation emerge: participatory oversight, private learning, and participatory bureaucracy?

- What are the implications of participatory bureaucracy for policy outcomes and bureaucratic reputations?
- What are the implications of participatory bureaucracy for democratic accountability?

Managing the challenge of expert bureaucratic administration amid democratic accountability confronts policymakers and implementers across policy domains, from pharmaceutical regulation, to education testing, to defense contracting, to financial services reform. The vast U.S. federal advisory committee system offers an enduring venue for examining public participation in agency policymaking, for assessing its potential to yield participatory bureaucracy, and for addressing this [reading's] guiding questions.

Participatory Bureaucracy through Public Advice

Federal public committees are uniquely positioned among forms of federal level public engagement, such as notice-and-comment procedures and freedom-of-information requests, to address the three guiding questions introduced in the previous section. Committees like the ones that contribute to policymaking for pharmaceutical regulation are part of a vast American system of public committees and represent a defining feature of the American administrative state.[51] Federal public boards and committees offer durable and prevalent venues for policy development and deliberation, with roughly 1,000 committees currently in operation across federal agencies, such as the FDA's Arthritis Drugs Advisory Committee. . . . Committees typically consist of individuals who are employed outside of government but who advise government agencies on topics ranging from aviation security to electronic medical records. Through the Federal Advisory Committee Act of 1972 and its amendments, common procedures govern advisory committee operations, including requirements for announcing meetings, setting committee agendas, transcribing meeting deliberations, and ensuring "balanced" committee membership. Although public meetings vary considerably, one common meeting format entails the agency presenting information on a policy, some nongovernmental individuals presenting information on that policy, some period of open public comment, and committee deliberation from members who are formally appointed to the public board and others in the room. Within the contours of Federal Advisory Committee Act provisions, committees vary considerably in terms of their meeting format, committee membership, meeting frequency, and their policy contributions.[52]

Federal public committees have the potential to make policy public in several ways. Committees are public in the sense that public officials—legislators, presidents, presidential appointees, bureaucrats—create them as portals for discussion and participation. Despite bureaucrats' legendary appetites for secrecy, government agencies have created nearly half of the approximately 1,000 federal advisory committees operating in 2010 and have played prominent roles in structuring many others, as Figure [2] illustrates.[53]

FIGURE [2] Count of Active Public Committees by Institutional Authority, 1974–2010

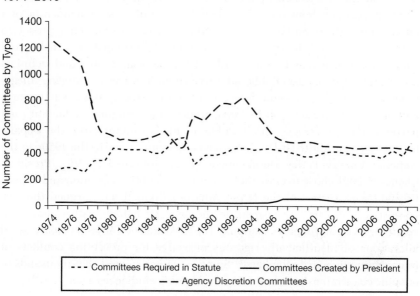

Committees are also public in the sense that they include members of the general public—individuals who work outside of government—in government policymaking.[54] This can provide individuals and interests a seat at government agencies' policymaking tables they would not otherwise enjoy.[55] Tens of thousands of people have served on public committees every year dating back to the 1950s. Some members serve as designated representatives of various interests. Other members serve as "special government employees" and are subject to government ethics provisions prohibiting conflicts of interest.

Committees are also public in the sense of promoting visibility: they can monitor and shine light on government agency policy processes. The Federal Advisory Committee Act contains provisions designed to promote committee transparency, such as requirements that advisory committees convene in public and make their meeting minutes publicly accessible, affording room for visibility and for knowledge to spread. Through their visibility, public committees can expand participation beyond the boundaries of the officially convened discussion: information and arguments from open public participation can disseminate to other sites of governance outside the agency.

Despite public committees' longevity and ubiquity in the landscape of American governance, they have faced steady criticism for failing to be sufficiently public or sufficiently participatory. Proponents argue public participation, in general, may legitimate policy, promote a capable citizenry, advance policy implementation, and generate new knowledge. Public committees, as one form of participation, may promote bureaucratic accountability to elected officials by allowing outsiders access to agency policymaking,[56] and can legitimize and encourage stable policy processes and outcomes.[57] Public participation in practice, however, habitually falls short of either a democratic or a bureaucratic ideal and has been described as "the most vilified approach to public involvement" in agency policymaking.[58] Participation can be constrained, opinions may become reinforced rather than evolve, and technical uncertainty can persist. Public advisory committees face enduring allegations of privileging particular interests, compromising agency expertise, promoting *secrecy* rather than transparency, or bringing validation, not participation, to agency work.[59] Public councils ranging from the Department of Justice Antitrust Division's advisory committees in the 1950s to the National Energy Policy Development Group convened by Vice President Cheney in 2001 chose to close their meetings to public inspection and to public audiences. Critics of the NASA Advisory Council have argued that the council operates as "spokesmen on the agency's behalf" rather than as a venue for meaningful participation.[60] The EPA's Science Advisory Board faced allegations of insufficiently rigorous measures for preventing conflicts of interest among board members.[61] Some estimates suggest that thousands of committee meetings are closed to general public audiences each year.[62]

■   ■   ■

Though transparency and public participation are typically cast as ways to curtail bureaucratic power, bureaucrats may benefit from and seek greater openness and engagement—and they may do so through public committees. Scholarship on public committees has helped us understand general committee operations and influence, committees' abilities to balance political and technical demands, elected officials' abilities to use committees as a way to monitor the bureaucracy, and representation on committees. Missing, however, is an account of public participation from a *bureaucratic perspective*: when public participation transforms into participatory bureaucracy and provides a potential means of managing the tension between democratic accountability and bureaucratic administration.

NOTES

1. John Dewey, *The School and Society and The Child and the Curriculum* (Chicago: University of Chicago Press, 1956), 25.

2. Statement of Senator Charles E. Grassley (R-IA), U.S. Congress, Senate, Committee on Finance, *FDA, Merck, and Vioxx: Putting Patient Safety First?* 108th Congress, 2nd Session, November 18, 2004 (Washington, DC: Government Printing Office, 2004), 3.

3. Institute of Medicine, *The Future of Drug Safety: Promoting and Protecting the Health of the Public* (Washington, DC: National Academy Press, 2007), 17.

4. Food and Drug Administration, "Arthritis Advisory Committee Meeting Transcript: Vioxx, April 20, 1999"; Food and Drug Administration, "Arthritis Advisory Committee Meeting Transcript: Vioxx, February 8, 2001."

5. Kenneth I. Kaitin, Ann Melville and Betsy Morris, "FDA Advisory Committees and the New Drug Approval Process," *Journal of Clinical Pharmacology* 29 (1989): 886–90; Steven J. Balla and John R. Wright, "Can Advisory Committees Facilitate Congressional Oversight of the Bureaucracy?" *Congress at Work, Congress on Display* (Ann Arbor: University of Michigan Press, 2000), 167–87; Steven J. Balla and John R. Wright, "Interest Groups, Advisory Committees, and Congressional Control of the Bureaucracy," *American Journal of Political Science* 45 (2001): 799–812.

6. See comments from Sidney Wolfe, "Food and Drug Administration, Joint Meeting of the Arthritis Advisory Committee and the Drug Safety and Risk Management Advisory Committee Transcript, Volume II, February 17, 2005," 240–41.

7. David Kessler was the FDA commissioner at the time. Carl Peck was the director of the Center for Drug Evaluation and Research, in charge of the drug review process. Statement of Derek Link, in Food and Drug Administration, "Antiviral Drugs Advisory Committee Transcript: Foscavir for treatment of cytomegalovirus retinitis in patients with AIDS, June 12, 1991," 6.

8. Author's field notes, May 17, 2002; see also National Assessment Governing Board, "Official Summary of Board Actions, Meeting of May 17–18, 2002," in August 2002 Briefing Book, 9–10; Lynn Olson, "Board Acts to Bring NAEP in Line with ESEA," *Education Week* 21 (2002): 22–24.

9. Assessments in Science, Writing, and Citizenship marked the first round of NAEP assessments, conducted in 1969–1970. Assessments in Reading and Literature began in 1970–1971, followed by assessments in Music and Social Studies in 1971–1972. The first assessment in Math was conducted in 1972–1973. See National Center for Education Statistics, *Directory of NAEP Publications* (Washington, DC: U.S. Department of Education, 1999).

10. See National Assessment Governing Board, "Board Meeting Transcript, March 1, 2002." Page numbers are not reported on pages of the transcript.

11. Author's field notes, May 18, 2002. Participants at the meeting discussed the "good faith effort" the Board and agency had undertaken to implement the law.

12. Author's field notes, May 18, 2002. For further discussion, see National Assessment Governing Board, "Official Summary of Board Actions, Meeting of May 17–18, 2002," in August 2002 Briefing Book, 10.

13. P.L. 103–382 stipulates that "Only sections 10, 11, and 12 of the Federal Advisory Committee Act shall apply with respect to the Board." Those sections bear on procedures for calling meetings, holding open meetings, transcript availability, and financial reporting.

14. A historical review concludes NAGB and NCES "usually have worked closely and harmoniously together" despite "certain tensions and disputes." See Maris Vinovskis, *Overseeing the Nation's Report Card: The Creation and Evolution of the National Assessment Governing Board* (Washington, DC: National Assessment Governing Board, 1998), 31.

15. Max Weber, *From Max Weber: Essays in Sociology* (New York: Oxford University Press, 1946), 233; Max Weber, *The Theory of Social and Economic Organizations* (London: Free Press of Glencoe, Collier-MacMillian Ltd., 1947), 339. This book defines secrecy as concealing information and defines transparency as revealing information, consistent with Sissela Bok, *Secrets: On the Ethics of Concealment and Revelation* (New York: Random House, 1983).

16. See Mathew McCubbins and Thomas Schwartz, "Congressional Oversight Overlooked: Police Patrols vs. Fire Alarms," *American Journal of Political Science* 28 (1984): 165–79; Mathew McCubbins, Roger Noll, and Barry Weingast, "Structure and

Process, Policy and Politics: Administrative Arrangements and the Political Control of Agencies," *Virginia Law Review* 75 (1989): 431–82; David Epstein and Sharyn O'Halloran, *Delegating Powers: A Transaction Cost Politics Approach to Policy Making under Separate Powers* (New York: Cambridge University Press, 1999); John Huber and Charles R. Shipan, *Deliberate Discretion: The Institutional Foundations of Bureaucratic Autonomy* (New York: Cambridge University Press, 2002).

17. On regulatory notice and comment procedures and its limitations, see Cornelius Kerwin, *Rulemaking* (Washington, DC: CQ Press, 2003), 62–66; Jason Webb Yackee and Susan Webb Yackee, "Bias Toward Business?" *Journal of Politics* 68 (2006): 128–39; Steven J. Balla, "Administrative Procedures and Political Control of the Bureaucracy," *American Political Science Review* 92 (1998): 663–73. On the Freedom of Information Act provisions, see Alasdair Roberts, *Blacked Out* (New York: Cambridge University Press, 2006), 13–18.

18. Politics can never be fully separate from administration. However, imposing deadlines on the FDA to review drugs quickly—one manifestation of political influence over agency policymaking—can compromise the quality of the agency's regulatory process by putting drugs on the market that are more likely to pose safety problems associated with adverse events and deaths. Daniel Carpenter, Jacqueline Chattopadhyay, Susan Moffitt, and Clayton Nall, "The Complications of Controlling Agency Time Discretion: FDA Review Deadlines and Postmarket Safety," *American Journal of Political Science* 56 (2012): 98–114.

19. Kathleen Bawn, "Political Control Versus Expertise: Congressional Choices About Administrative Procedures," *American Political Science Review* 89 (1995): 62–73.

20. Stephen Skowronek, *Building a New American State: The Expansion of National Administrative Capacities, 1877–1920* (Cambridge: Cambridge University Press, 1982); William T. Gormley, Jr. and Steven J. Balla, *Bureaucracy and Democracy: Accountability and Performance* (Washington, DC: CQ Press, 2007).

21. Kenneth F. Warren, *Administrative Law in the Political System*, 4th ed. (Boulder, CO: Westview Press, 2004), 282, cited in Susan Webb Yackee, "Lifecycle of Medical Product Rules Issued by the Food and Drug Administration," *Journal of Health Politics, Policy and Law* (Forthcoming). For comprehensive scholarship on bureaucratic power, see Daniel P. Carpenter, *Reputation and Power: Organizational Image and Pharmaceutical Regulation at the FDA* (Princeton, NJ: Princeton University Press, 2010).

22. Though this view of implementation as creating policy is typically attributed to grassroots implementation, it applies to federal-level implementers as well. On grassroots implementation, see Michael Lipsky, *Street-Level Bureaucracy: Dilemmas of the Individual in Public Services* (New York: Russell Sage Foundation, 1980).

23. On the factors affecting implementation, see David K. Cohen and Susan L. Moffitt, *The Ordeal of Equality: Did Federal Regulation Fix the Schools?* (Cambridge, MA: Harvard University Press, 2009), 17–44.

24. On the importance of tasks within an organizational context, see James Q. Wilson, *Bureaucracy: What Government Agencies Do and Why They Do It* (New York: Basic Books, 1989), 25–26. The discussion that follows does not aim to provide an optimal strategy for bureaucrats or for elected officials. Instead, it focuses on the conditions when participation is more or less likely to be consistent with key features of bureaucratic reputation.

25. For important work on the development of bureaucratic information and expertise, see Sean Gailmard and John W. Patty, *Learning While Governing: Expertise and Accountability in the Executive Branch* (Chicago: University of Chicago Press, 2012).

26. On the Atomic Energy Commission, see Brian Balogh, *Chain Reaction: Expert Debate and Public Participation in American Commercial Nuclear Power, 1945–1975* (New York: Cambridge University Press, 1991).

27. Comments of Senator Michael Mansfield, (D-MT), *Congressional Record* Senate, April 9, 1956, 5930.

28. Francis E. Rourke, *Secrecy and Publicity: Dilemmas of Democracy* (Baltimore, MD: Johns Hopkins Press, 1961) 5, 10–11, 138; Michel Crozier, *The Bureaucratic Phenomenon* (Chicago: University of Chicago Press, 1964), 153; Daniel Patrick Moynihan, *Secrecy: The American Experience* (New Haven, CT: Yale University Press, 1998); Kenneth J. Meier and John Bohte, *Politics and the Bureaucracy: Policymaking in the Fourth Branch of Government* (Belmont, CA: Thomson Wadsworth, 2007), 66; Harold Wilensky, *Organizational Intelligence* (New York: Basic Books, 1969), 144; Jeffrey Pfeffer and Gerald R. Salancik, *The External Control of Organizations* (New York: Harper and Row, 2003), 104.

29. For careful distinction between the concepts of complexity, difficulty, and uncertainty, see Scott E. Page, "Uncertainty, Difficulty and Complexity," *Journal of Theoretical Politics* 20 (2008): 115–49. Task interdependence is consistent with public administration's concept of co-production and viewing the public as a partner. John Clayton Thomas, *Citizen, Customer, Partner: Engaging the Public in Public Management* (New York: M.E. Sharpe, 2012), 10–12, 85–101; Jeffrey Brudney and Robert England, "Toward a Definition of the Co-Production Concept," *Public Administration Review* 43 (1983): 59–65; Sean P. Osborne, "Delivering Public Services: Time for a New Theory?" *Public Management Review* 12 (2010): 1–10.

30. For related discussion on this point, see Thomas, *Citizen, Customer, Partner,* 129–30.

31. Kenneth J. Meier and Laurence J. O'Toole, *Bureaucracy in a Democratic State: A Governance Perspective* (Baltimore, MD: Johns Hopkins University Press, 2006).

32. Lester M. Salamon, *The Tools of Government: A Guide to the New Governance* (New York: Oxford University Press, 2002), 4.

33. Nolan McCarty, "Complexity, Capacity and Capture," in *Preventing Regulatory Capture: Special Interest Influence and How to Limit It,* edited by Daniel Carpenter and David Moss (Cambridge: Cambridge University Press, 2013), 99–123.

34. Usable knowledge arises from many sources. Charles Lindblom and David K. Cohen, *Usable Knowledge: Social Science and Social Problem Solving* (New Haven, CT: Yale University Press, 1979). For related discussion, see p. 18 of Archon Fung and Erik Olin Wright, "Deepening Democracy: Innovations in Empowered Participatory Governance," *Politics and Society* 29 (2001): 5–41.

35. For more discussion on the relativity of capability for policy implementation, see Cohen and Moffitt, *Ordeal of Equality,* 17–44.

36. For a summary, see Meier and Bohte, *Politics and the Bureaucracy,* 198–205. On the distinction between representing interests and including diverse professional and social perspectives on public committees, see Mark B. Brown, "Fairly Balanced: The Politics of Representation on Government Advisory Committees," *Political Research Quarterly* 61 (2008): 547–60.

37. For a review on group decision making, see Daan van Knippenberg and Michaéla C. Schippers, "Work Group Diversity," *Annual Review of Psychology* 58 (2007): 515–41. On the ability of diverse perspectives to render suboptimal policy less likely, see Scott E. Page, *The Difference: How the Power of Diversity Creates Better Groups, Firms, Schools and Societies* (Princeton, NJ: Princeton University Press, 2007). On the impact of diverse perspectives on the quality of deliberation, see James Bohman, *Public Deliberation:*

Pluralism, Complexity and Democracy (Cambridge, MA: MIT Press, 1996). On costly reversals and agency reputation, see Daniel P. Carpenter, "Groups, the Media, Agency Waiting Costs and FDA Drug Approval," *American Journal of Political Science* 46 (2002): 490–505.

38. Bureaucrats benefit from diverse support for their programs and policies, instead of support limited to a single dominant group. Carpenter, *The Forging of Bureaucratic Autonomy*, 14, 32; Francis E. Rourke, *Bureaucracy, Politics and Public Policy*, 2nd ed. (Boston: Little, Brown & Co, 1976), 55.

39. Carol Pateman, *Participation and Democratic Theory* (Cambridge: Cambridge University Press, 1970).

40. Archon Fung, *Empowered Participation: Reinventing Urban Democracy* (Princeton, NJ: Princeton University Press, 2004), 3. On debate over the durability of policy made through negotiated rulemaking, see Cary Coglianese, "Assessing Consensus: The Promise and Performance of Negotiated Rulemaking," *Duke Law Journal* 46 (1997): 1255–1349; Laura Langbein, "Responsive Bureaus, Equity and Regulatory Negotiation," *Journal of Public Policy Analysis and Management* 21 (2002): 446–65. For a review of reg-neg, see Peter H. Schuck and Steven Kochevar, "Reg Neg Redux: The Career of a Procedural Reform," *Theoretical Inquiries in Law* 15 (2014).

41. Richard M. Cyert and James G. March, *A Behavioral Theory of the Firm* (Englewood Cliffs, NJ: Prentice-Hall, 1963); Pfeffer and Salancik, *The External Control of Organizations*; Karl Weick, "Educational Organizations as Loosely Coupled Systems," *Administrative Science Quarterly* 21 (1976): 1–19.

42. For a classic illustration of power represented through "blue ribbon" advisory committees at the local level, see Robert Dahl, *Who Governs? Democracy and Power in an American City* (New Haven, CT: Yale University Press, 1961), 124.

43. Representative bureaucracy focuses on having individuals who serve in government reflect the broader population in terms of gender, race, ethnicity, sexual orientation, and other descriptive characteristics. When bureaucracy embodies the interests and preferences of the populace, it can offer a defensible substitute for more direct democratic accountability and can impact subsequent policy decisions. Meier and O'Toole, *Bureaucracy in a Democratic State*, 67–92; Kenneth J. Meier, Eric Gonzalez Juenke, Robert D. Wrinkle, and J. L. Polinard, "Structural Choices and Representational Biases: The Post-Election Color of Representation," *American Journal of Political Science* 49 (2005): 758–68; Lael R. Keiser, Vicky M. Wilkins, Kenneth J. Meier, and Catherine A. Holland, "Lipstick and Logarithms: Gender, Institutional Context and Representative Bureaucracy," *American Political Science Review* 96 (2002): 553–64.

44. As Thomas argues, representative bureaucracy offers a top-down, hierarchical approach to bringing broader community voice into agency policymaking, in contrast to co-production forms of engagement. Thomas, *Citizen, Customer, Partner*, 20–29.

45. On this point, see Thomas, *Citizen, Customer, Partner*, 177.

46. For a consumer-oriented view, see David Osborne and Ted Gaebler, *Reinventing Government: How the Entrepreneurial Spirit Is Transforming the Public Sector* (Reading, MA: Addison-Wesley, 1992).

47. For related argument on the non-zero-sum potential of group engagement, see Jane J. Mansbridge, "A Deliberative Theory of Interest Representation," in *The Politics of Interests: Interest Groups Transformed*, edited by Mark P. Petracca (Boulder, CO: Westview Press, 1992), 32–57. In her discussion of public boards from the perspective of democratic accountability, Mansbridge distinguishes between unitary and adversary issues (conflicting or common interests) as key to understanding different partici-

patory arrangements. Jane J. Mansbridge, *Beyond Adversary Democracy* (Chicago: University of Chicago Press, 1983), ix–x of the revised preface.

48. Competently performing policy tasks can offer one expression of accountability. For an important theoretical approach that combines administrative balance and rationality to yield accountability, see Anthony Bertelli and Laurence E. Lynn Jr., *Madison's Managers: Public Administration and the Constitution* (Baltimore, MD: Johns Hopkins University Press, 2006).

49. Gailmard and Patty, *Learning While Governing*, 11.

50. Recall that the extent to which participatory bureaucracy yields competent task implementation can also support democratic accountability.

51. Rourke, *Bureaucracy, Politics and Public Policy*, 123. On committees that advise French pharmaceutical regulation, see Philippe Urfalino, *Le Grand Méchant Loup Pharmaceutique* (Paris: Les éditions Textuel, 2005).

52. In *Organizational Intelligence*, Harold Wilensky offers a useful summary of the range of ways the government may use advisory committees, including representing constituencies, testing ideas, channeling public attention, mobilizing policy support, and broadening participation in the policymaking process. Harold Wilensky, *Organizational Intelligence* (New York: Basic Books, 1969), 169–72. On the development and use of public committees in various policy domains, see Sheila Jasanoff, *The Fifth Branch: Science Advisors as Policy Makers* (Cambridge, MA: Harvard University Press, 1990); Stephen Hilgartner, *Science on Stage: Expert Advice as Public Drama* (Stanford, CA: Stanford University Press, 2000); Rourke. *Bureaucracy, Politics and Public Policy*, 121–24; David Truman, *The Governmental Process* (New York: Knopf, 1951), 458; Martha Derthick, *Policymaking for Social Security* (Washington, DC: Brookings Institution Press, 1979), 100–101; Herbert Kaufman, *The Administrative Behavior of Federal Bureau Chiefs* (Washington, DC: The Brookings Institution, 1981), 39–40; William T. Gormley Jr., *The Politics of Public Utility Regulation* (Pittsburgh, PA: University of Pittsburgh Press, 1983); Thomas A. Wolanin, *Presidential Advisory Committees: Truman to Nixon* (Madison: University of Wisconsin Press, 1975); Don K. Price, *Government and Science: Their Dynamic Relation in American Democracy* (New York: Oxford University Press, 1962) 130; Anthony Downs, *Inside Bureaucracy* (Boston: Little, Brown Downs, 1967), 207–8; Bruce L. R. Smith, *The Advisers: Scientists in the Policy Process* (Washington, DC: Brookings Institution Press, 1992), 8; Steven P. Croley and William F. Funk, "The Federal Advisory Committee Act and Good Government," *Yale Journal on Regulation* 14 (1997): 451–557.

53. Jasanoff, *The Fifth Branch*, 84–88; Derthick, *Policymaking for Social Security*, pp. 100–109. For a discussion of the ways in which committees are "public," see Wolanin, *Presidential Advisory Commissions*, 8–9.

54. For discussion on the state-society divide, see Jeffrey M. Sellers, "State-Society Relations," *The Sage Handbook of Governance*, edited by Mark Bevir (London: Sage, 2011), 124–41.

55. On the representation of interests on advisory committees, see Stéphane Lavertu, Daniel E. Walters, David L. Weimer, "Scientific Expertise and the Balance of Political Interests: MEDCAC and Medicare Coverage Decisions," *Journal of Public Administration Research and Theory* 22 (2012): 55–81.

56. Balla and Wright, "Can Advisory Committees Facilitate Congressional Oversight of the Bureaucracy?" 167–187.

57. Jasanoff, *The Fifth Branch*, 17; Hilgartner, *Science on Stage*; Heimann, *Acceptable Risks*, 154. Jasanoff discusses public committees' failures to achieve either democratic or technocratic ideals.

58. Thomas, *Citizen, Customer, Partner*, 173. Thomas notes that this critique "unfairly judges" some forms of participation.

59. For allegations of advisory committees creating barriers between government administration and the public, see U.S. Congress, Senate, *Advisory Committees*, Hearings before the Subcommittee on Intergovernmental Relations of the Committee on Government Operations, 92nd Congress, 1st Session, part 2 (Washington, DC: GPO, 1971), 497. The FDA's panel on cyclamates offers a well-known example of alleged validation.

60. Smith, *The Advisers*, 122.

61. U.S. General Accounting Office, *EPA's Science Advisory Board Panels: Improved Policies and Procedures Needed to Ensure Independence and Balance* (Washington, DC: GAO, 2001), 2.

62. Kevin D. Karty, "Closure and Capture in Federal Advisory Committees," *Business and Politics* 4 (2002): 213–38. However, other work suggests that most agencies "rarely close their meetings." See Croley and Funk, "The Federal Advisory Committee Act and Good Government," 505. Historically, peer review committees within the National Science Foundation and National Endowment for the Humanities constitute some of the most frequently closed committees.

7.5

SEAN GAILMARD AND JOHN W. PATTY

From *Learning While Governing: Expertise and Accountability in the Executive Branch*

Top leaders of government bureaucracies are typically appointed by elected offi-cials and share the political goals of the partisan politicians who appointed them. The people who work under these appointees are permanent government employ-ees and often have policy preferences at odds with their bosses. There is often tension between these two layers of bureaucracy. Gailmard and Patty argue that there is a mutually beneficial arrangement between politically appointed top bureaucrats and the more permanent government employees. The arrangement has three features: civil service protection for lower-level bureaucrats, some auton-omy for lower-level bureaucrats to become experts, and tolerance by the politi-cally appointed leaders of ideologically zealous bureaucrats below them.

DEVELOPING ADMINISTRATIVE EXPERTISE

A frequently cited justification for bureaucratic policymaking is that bureau-crats possess and utilize policy-relevant expertise above and beyond what one might reasonably expect of presidents, judges, and members of Congress. Expertise in matters as diverse and complicated as rail regulation, drug approval, resource management, monetary economics, traffic management on freeways, and flood control is not bestowed at birth; rather, it must be acquired or developed by individuals. In turn, those who divine the means to secure desired policy goals must have *incentives* to acquire that expertise. Especially in realms such as regulatory policymaking, developing a cadre of administrative experts is obviously more complicated than simply declaring that it should exist. Simply put, expert administration does not necessarily flow from legislative fiat: individually or collectively, bureaucrats cannot be compelled by statute to develop policy expertise.

We argue that incentives for administrative actors to acquire policy exper-tise result from the organizational structure and political position they occupy as created by political principals, in particular Congress. . . .

A natural "lever" to create the requisite incentives to acquire information takes the form of monetary rewards for doing so. This is well understood

From Sean Gailmard and John W. Patty, *Learning While Governing: Expertise and Accountability in the Executive Branch* (Chicago: University of Chicago Press, 2013), Chapter 2.

theoretically and often observed in for-profit enterprises, either explicitly or implicitly (e.g., commission pay for sales people to discover new sales opportunities). Yet monetary incentives for the acquisition of expertise are typically not offered by the federal government to agents in bureaucratic policymaking.

Under certain conditions, another lever to induce expertise development in the bureaucracy is policy discretion. If agents care about the content of policy, they will value the opportunity to influence it. That opportunity is simply policy discretion. If policy discretion is available to agents who demonstrate some degree of policy expertise, then policy discretion can operate as an incentive to acquire expertise.

The starting point of this logic is that the bureaucratic agent is a political actor in the sense of having preferences over the content of public policy like any other political actor. That is, we set aside the fiction that bureaucratic agents are politically neutral vessels who check their ideology at the door when they punch in for work. This accords with well-documented findings in political science and public administration that bureaucrats have important nonpecuniary motivations related to the content of the public policy in their purview.[1] This point is closely related to the concept of "public service motivation" in the public administration literature.[2] Essentially, we assume that public service motivation depends in part on the congruence between individual policy goals and organizational mission, and the ability of individuals to work on policy tasks they value.[3]

Because expertise development takes time, and because the "reward" of discretionary authority is conditioned on the agent's demonstration of expertise, the security and stability of a public servant's position in the bureaucracy is a central factor in determining the strength of incentives to invest in policymaking expertise. This logic elevates *civil service job protections* to a central role in the analysis of bureaucratic incentives. Such protections, which encompass a variety of restrictions on external and partisan attempts to sway individual bureaucrats' policy decisions (culminating in the mythical "life tenure" for bureaucrats), magnify the value of future policy discretion by increasing that confidence of today's public servants that they will indeed be able to actually utilize expanded authority won through their development of expertise. Thus, despite the limits they create on extrinsic incentives for bureaucratic responsiveness, civil service job protections benefit Congress because and when such protections induce policy-motivated bureaucrats to pursue careers in public service and develop policy-relevant expertise.

Although policy discretion and civil service protections combine to provide incentives for individuals motivated by policy to invest in expertise, they do not generate beneficial incentives "for free." Since these incentives only "work" for individuals with policy or ideological commitments, they create an inherent tension with the ideal of neutral competence. The classic ideal of "neutral competence" presumes that bureaucratic expertise is exogenous to politics and the place of the bureaucracy in it. In the eyes of Progressive-era progenitors of regulatory agencies, for example, able and fair-minded administrators stood by ready to apply scientific principles to policy.[4] But if agents in the bureaucracy do not obtain some chance to bend policy toward their preferred goals, they have no particular incentive to acquire policy expertise. But when public servants bend policy toward their vision of "the good," they bend it away from some other vision. If incentives are required to induce expertise development, and policy discretion serves this role, then expert administration cannot be neutral administration, available equally and without prejudice to fulfill whatever policy goals political principals might lay down.

A Theory of Delegation, Expertise, and Career Choices

We focus on a simple situation that nevertheless captures the issues we address clearly: a (unitary) legislative principal must choose how much discretionary policy-making authority to grant to a bureaucrat (e.g., through a statute delegating policy choices) whose policy preferences generally differ from those of the legislator. After receiving this statutory authority, the bureaucrat then decides whether to acquire policy-making expertise. After this, the bureaucrat uses the expertise she obtained from the legislature (if any) to make a policy decision. Then the bureaucrat may decide to leave public service. If she decides to leave, she is replaced by a new bureaucrat. If she does not decide to leave, she may be forced to do so anyway, if civil service job protections are less than perfect (as we will discuss in more detail), and again is replaced by a new bureaucrat. The legislative principal then observes whether the bureaucrat has remained in office and acquired expertise, and then the policy-making process repeats.

The bureaucrat's decisions in our theory are simple: whether to remain in public service and whether to invest in policy-making expertise. As we will argue, there are two possible outcomes. The first is a "regime of clerkship," as described by Carpenter (2001), in which bureaucrats neither acquire expertise nor seek prolonged employment in public service—similar to patterns under patronage job rotation or "spoils" systems. The second possible outcome is a regime of "politicized competence" in which some bureaucrats—those who care strongly about policy outcomes—invest in acquiring policy-making expertise and pursue a career in the civil service. This regime occurs when Congress can credibly commit itself to offering increased policy-making discretion in the future to bureaucrats who acquire expertise. This type of inducement leads to a selection effect in which only policy-motivated individuals pursue careers in public service, but (at least appear to) do so for the right reason: they acquire expertise in policy-making in pursuit of the ability to, at a later stage in their careers, affect public policy.

A key conclusion of the theory is that regimes of "politicized competence" require merit system protections against dismissal for purely partisan reasons. Without a sufficiently high level of assurance that one's job in the civil service is secure into the future (conditional on good performance, and not political cycles as in patronage regimes), the "offer" of discretion by the legislature to provide a "payment" for expertise development and self-selection into bureaucratic careers loses value. Merit system protection of job tenure removes some of a bureaucrat's risk from developing relationship-specific expertise because it increases the horizon over which this investment can pay off.

The "politicized competence" regime is interesting precisely because it describes a situation in which the bureaucrat obtains expertise and hence is able to make "better" policy decisions than Congress. Accordingly, the theory provides a strategic foundation for the bureaucratic informational advantage assumed in formal models on bureaucratic expertise and capacity.[5] More importantly, we address a tension in the principal–agent tradition of the relationship between legislative and bureaucratic branches of government. Specifically, if an agency problem exists, it must be understood as an agency problem that the legislature itself chose in the first place. By focusing on the endogenous development of agency policy preferences by self-selection into bureaucratic careers, we explore the value to a principal of effectively creating its own agency problem.

However, this alone is not enough to induce bureaucracies to invest in policy expertise, because it does not offer any positive benefit. The grant of policy discretion from the legislature, rationally chosen in response to expertise investment, fills this role. By allowing agents to bend policy to their liking, it offers "policy rents" for expertise development and a career in public service that only zealots value. A generalization of this argument is that the effects of personnel management administration and the politics of bureaucratic discretion are mutually dependent, and in this case, reinforcing. They are jointly sufficient and individually necessary to provide the bureaucrat an incentive to acquire task-specific expertise.

▪ ▪ ▪

The Bureaucrat's Policy Preferences

A bureaucrat is conceived in our theory as having two dimensions of policy preferences. First, he or she may have strong or weak preferences about policy outcomes. We refer to agents with strong preferences over policy outcomes as "zealots," and agents with weak policy preferences as "slackers." "Strong preferences over policy" are relative to the cost to an agent of investing in expertise. A zealot would be willing to incur nontrivial personal costs to make informed policy decisions because she cares enough about getting policy "right," in her own value system, to do so. A slacker would not be willing, even with unfettered authority, to incur personal cost to acquire policy-making expertise, because her utility difference from alternative policies is not large. This dimension reflects our interpretation of public service motivation: zealots have it, and slackers do not. Furthermore, zealots care about policy whether they are public servants or not. For instance, individuals who care about the right of labor unions to organize care about it whether they work to secure these rights at the National Labor Relations Board or whether they work in some unrelated private-sector occupation.

The second dimension of our representation of a bureaucrat's policy preferences describes the bureaucrat's ideal point—the policy outcome that he would choose given the authority and information to do so. . . .

▪ ▪ ▪

Expertise Development by Public Servants

The first set of questions we must tackle deal with expertise acquisition and career choices by bureaucrats. The theory offers a set of conclusions about these decisions, relating several of the parameters of the model with the emergence of expert and experienced bureaucrats. We present these in a sequential fashion. . . .

Discretion Inducement Conclusion

In the absence of direct monetary incentives, policy-making expertise will emerge only if such acquisition is rewarded through increased discretionary authority.

. . . The Discretion Inducement Conclusion is derived from the bureaucrat's decision calculus, which means that a fixed, positive level of discretionary authority serves at least partially as the proverbial carrot, a positive reward that is garnered from expertise acquisition. Put another way, according to the logic underlying the Discretion Inducement Conclusion, *the ability to use discretionary authority more effectively is a part of a zealot's motivation to acquire expertise.* Later in the chapter, we will discuss complementary conclusions based on the incentives of Congress in which the threat of loss of discretionary authority in the future upon failing to acquire expertise amplifies the bureaucrat's incentives underlying the Discretion Inducement Conclusion.

▪ ▪ ▪

Promotion Conclusion

Agencies will tend to experience lower rates of turnover when promotion leads to increased discretionary authority over policy choices.

The presumption that the remuneration from private employment exceeds that received by public servants (which is maintained throughout unless stated otherwise) is important. If public remuneration is sufficiently high, then bureaucratic turnover will tend to be low, regardless of the discretionary authority possessed by administrators. Such a conclusion hardly violates common sense, of course, but interestingly implies a positive effect of the relatively low rates of pay for experts within the public service. Namely, when a career in public service necessitates a sacrifice of non-policy-related rewards, one can be more confident that those who choose to pursue such a career are doing so for policy-related reasons. . . . [T]his is a double-edged sword from Congress's standpoint: successfully reducing turnover through the granting of discretionary authority correspondingly produces expertise development, but it occurs only by the actions of bureaucrats who may seek to implement policy outcomes distinct from those that Congress would most prefer.

■   ■   ■

Tenure Conclusion

Expertise development is promoted by increased job security. Furthermore, the importance of such protections is heightened when expertise is costlier to acquire.

The Tenure Conclusion summarizes one of the principal implications of the holdup problem for expertise development. Congress must be able to commit itself to retaining (and granting discretionary authority to) expert bureaucrats in order to provide sufficient incentive for acquisition of expertise. . . .

■   ■   ■

Expertise Promotion Conclusion

Congress and/or the president will support discretionary authority in a manner that induces expertise development only when the expertise is not prohibitively costly and the bureaucrat's preferences are not too divergent from those of the political principal in question.

The Expertise Promotion Conclusion leads to an ancillary finding about the substitutability of preference convergence and the cost of expertise acquisition: lowering the cost of acquiring expertise commensurately lowers the amount of discretion that Congress must offer as a reward to induce expertise development. This means that the expected cost of bureaucratic "drift" is smaller from the optimally designed Promotion Model, which implies that Congress is willing to pursue such an organizational strategy in the face of greater levels of preference divergence between it and the bureaucrat as the cost of expertise acquisition goes down. We refer to this theoretical conclusion as the *Political Substitution Conclusion.*

■   ■   ■

A central conclusion . . . is that Congress can induce expertise acquisition within an agency by, first, instituting relatively common civil service practices—notably, protection of job tenure and lower material rewards than an available outside option—and, second, granting bureaucrats some measure of control over policy issues they care about. Such a solution comes with an extra requirement: the bureaucrats who acquire expertise and make careers in public service are exactly those who have unusually strong policy preferences.

A corollary . . . conclusion about expertise acquisition is that neutral competence within administration is impossible in many situations. This failure, however, is not because "neutrality" itself is impossible, but because only those with a stake in policy can be induced (by the limited instruments available) to become experts. In other words, those public servants who would be neutral have no incentive to remain public servants. Furthermore, the approach to personnel management that would retain such individuals (e.g., direct remuneration for expertise) will not achieve neutral competence either—use of such incentives does not filter non-neutral servants out of the public service. Another way to view this . . . conclusions is that "politicized competence" (as is produced in the Promotion Model) is the best kind available in the long-run (i.e., in equilibrium). In this respect, expert bureaucratic policymaking is achieved through the creation—by Congress and for Congress—of an agency problem: significant discretion granted to agents with divergent policy goals. Congress creates (or at least should create) this agency problem precisely when the divergence of preferences serves the useful purpose of making expertise-development possible.

NOTES

1. Aberbach et al. (1981), Brehm and Gates (1997), Aberbach and Rockman (2000), and Golden (2000) consider the motivations and ideological bent of executive branch personnel.

2. Examples include Perry and Wise (1990), Perry (1997), Le Grand (2003), and Koehler and Rainey (2008).

3. A few recent contributions in this vein include Moynihan and Pandey (2007), Paarlberg and Perry (2007), and Gailmard (2010).

4. Nelson (1982); Skowronek (1982); Bertelli and Lynn (2006).

5. A nonexhaustive list of such works includes Calvert et al. (1989), Epstein and O'Halloran (1994, 1999), Gailmard (2002), Huber and Shipan (2002), and Huber and McCarty (2004).

BIBLIOGRAPHY

Aberbach, Joel D., Robert D. Putnam, and Bert A. Rockman. 1981. *Bureaucrats and Politicians in Western Democracies*, Cambridge, MA: Harvard University Press.

Aberbach, Joel D., and Bert A. Rockman. 2000. *In the Web of Politics: Three Decades of the U.S. Federal Executive*. Washington, DC: Brookings Institution Press.

Bertelli, Anthony M., and Laurence E. Lynn. 2006. *Madison's Managers: Public Administration and the Constitution*. Baltimore: Johns Hopkins University Press.

Brehm, John, and Scott Gates. 1997. *Working, Shirking, and Sabotage: Bureaucratic Response to a Democratic Public*. Ann Arbor: University of Michigan Press.

Calvert, Randall, Mathew McCubbins, and Barry Weingast. 1989. "A Theory of Political Control and Agency Discretion." *American Journal of Political Science* 33: 588–611.

Carpenter, Daniel P. 2001. *The Forging of Bureaucratic Autonomy: Reputations, Networks, and Policy Innovation in Executive Agencies, 1862–1928.* Princeton, NJ: Princeton University Press.

Epstein, David, and Sharyn O'Halloran. 1994. "Administrative Procedures, Information, and Agency Discretion: Slack vs. Flexibility." *American Journal of Political Science* 38 (3): 697–722.

———. 1999. *Delegating Powers: A Transaction Cost Politics Approach to Policy Making Under Separate Powers.* New York: Cambridge University Press.

Gailmard, Sean. 2002. "Expertise, Subversion, and Bureaucratic Discretion." *Journal of Law, Economics, and Organization* 18 (2): 536–55.

———. 2010. "Politics, Principal–Agent Problems, and Public Service Motivation." *International Public Management Journal* 13 (1): 35–45.

Golden, Marissa Martino. 2000. *What Motivates Bureaucrats? Politics and Administration during the Reagan Years.* New York: Columbia University Press.

Huber, John D., and Nolan McCarty. 2004. "Bureaucratic Capacity, Delegation, and Political Reform." *American Political Science Review* 98 (3): 481–94.

Huber, John D., and Charles R. Shipan. 2002. *Deliberate Discretion? The Institutional Foundations of Bureaucratic Autonomy.* New York: Cambridge University Press.

Koehler, Michael, and Hal G. Rainey. 2008. "Interdisciplinary Foundations of Public Service Motivation." In James Perry and Annie Hondegham eds., *Motivation in Public Management: The Call of Public Service,* 33–55. New York: Oxford University Press.

Le Grand, Julian. 2003. *Motivation, Agency, and Public Policy: Of Knights and Knaves, Pawns and Queens.* New York: Oxford University Press.

Moynihan, Donald P., and Sanjay K. Pandey. 2007. "The Role of Organizations in Fostering Public Service Motivation." *Public Administration Review* 67 (1): 40–53.

Nelson, William E. 1982. *The Roots of American Bureaucracy, 1830–1900.* Cambridge, MA: Harvard University Press.

Paarlberg, Laurie E., and James L. Perry. 2007. "Values Management." *American Review Public Administration* 37 (4): 387–408.

Perry, James L. 1997. "Antecedents of Public Service Motivation." *Journal of Public Administration Research and Theory* 7 (2): 181–97.

Perry, James L., and Lois Recascino Wise. 1990. "The Motivational Bases of Public Service." *Public Administration Review* 50 (3): 367–73.

Skowronek, Stephen. 1982. *Building a New American State.* New York: Cambridge University Press.

Volden, Craig. 2002. "A Formal Model of the Politics of Delegation in a Separation of Powers System." *American Journal of Political Science* 46 (1): 111–33.

8

THE JUDICIARY

8.1

GERALD N. ROSENBERG

From *The Hollow Hope: Can Courts Bring about Social Change?*

Rosenberg argues that courts in the United States are highly constrained in bring-ing about social change. Though many people think of the courts as "dynamic"—as drivers of social change—in Rosenberg's view, courts instead follow the other branches of government. They do not drive change but rather respond late to social changes and end up trying to catch up with trends in society.

INTRODUCTION

The Problem

■ ■ ■

To what degree, and under what conditions, can judicial processes be used to produce political and social change? What are the constraints that operate on them? What factors are important and why?

. . . Traditionally, most lawyers and legal scholars have focused on a related normative issue: whether courts *ought* to act. From the perspective of demo-cratic theory, that is an important and useful question. Yet since much of poli-tics is about who gets what, when, and how, and how that distribution is

From Gerald N. Rosenberg, *The Hollow Hope: Can Courts Bring about Social Change?* (Chicago: University of Chicago Press, 1991).

maintained, or changed, understanding to what extent, and under what conditions, courts can produce political and social change is of key importance.

. . . In the last several decades movements and groups advocating what I will shortly define as significant social reform have turned increasingly to the courts. Starting with the famous cases brought by the civil rights movement and spreading to issues raised by women's groups, environmental groups, political reformers, and others, American courts seemingly have become important producers of political and social change. Cases such as *Brown* (school desegregation) and *Roe* (abortion) are heralded as having produced major change. Further, such litigation has often occurred, and appears to have been most successful, when the other branches of government have failed to act. While officious government officials and rigid, unchanging institutions represent a real social force which may frustrate popular opinion, this litigation activity suggests that courts can produce significant social reform even when the other branches of government are inactive or opposed. Indeed, for many, part of what makes American democracy exceptional is that it includes the world's most powerful court system, protecting minorities and defending liberty, in the face of opposition from the democratically elected branches. Americans look to activist courts, then, as fulfilling an important role in the American scheme.[1] This view of the courts, although informed by recent historical experience, is essentially functional. It sees courts as powerful, vigorous, and potent proponents of change. I refer to this view of the role of the courts as the "Dynamic Court" view.

As attractive as the Dynamic Court view may be, one must guard against uncritical acceptance. Indeed, in a political system that gives sovereignty to the popular will and makes economic decisions through the market, it is not obvious why courts should have the effects it asserts. Maybe its attractiveness is based on something more than effects? Could it be that the self-understanding of the judiciary and legal profession leads to an overstatement of the role of the courts, a "mystification" of the judiciary? If judges see themselves as powerful; if the Bar views itself as influential, and insulated; if professional training in law schools inculcates students with such beliefs, might these factors inflate the self-importance of the judiciary? The Dynamic Court view may be supported, then, because it offers psychological payoffs to key actors by confirming self-images, not because it is correct.[2] And when this "mystification" is added to a normative belief in the courts as the guardian of fundamental rights and liberties—what Scheingold (1974) calls the "myth of rights"—the allure of the Dynamic Court view may grow.

Further, for all its "obviousness," the Dynamic Court view has a well-established functional and historical competitor. In fact, there is a long tradition of legal scholarship that views the federal judiciary, in Alexander Hamilton's famous language, as the "least dangerous" branch of government. Here, too, there is something of a truism about this claim. Courts, we know, lack both budgetary and physical powers. Because, in Hamilton's words, they lack power over either the "sword or the purse," their ability to produce political and social change is limited. In contrast to the first view, the "least dangerous" branch can do little more than point out how actions have fallen short of constitutional or legislative requirements and hope that appropriate action is taken. The strength of this view, of course, is that it leaves Americans free to govern themselves without interference from non-elected officials. I refer to this view of the courts as weak, ineffective, and powerless as the "Constrained Court" view.

The Constrained Court view fully acknowledges the role of popular preferences and social and economic resources in shaping outcomes. Yet it seems to rely excessively on a formal-process understanding of how change occurs in American politics. But the formal process doesn't always work, for social and political forces may be overly responsive to unevenly distributed resources. Bureaucratic inertia, too, can derail orderly, processional change. There is room, then, for courts to effectively correct the pathologies of the political process. Perhaps accurate at the founding of the political system, the Constrained Court view may miss growth and change in the American political system.

Clearly, these two views, and the aspirations they represent, are in conflict on a number of different dimensions. They differ not only on both the desirability and the effectiveness of court action, but also on the nature of American democracy. The Dynamic Court view gives courts an important place in the American political system while the older view sees courts as much less powerful than other more "political" branches and activities. The conflict is more than one of mere definition, for each view captures a very different part of American democracy. We Americans want courts to protect minorities and defend liberties, *and* to defer to elected officials. We want a robust political life *and* one that is just. Most of the time, these two visions do not clash. American legislatures do not habitually threaten liberties, and courts do not regularly invalidate the acts of elected officials or require certain actions to be taken. But the most interesting and relevant cases, such as *Brown* and *Roe*, occur when activist courts overrule and invalidate the actions of elected officials, or order actions beyond what elected officials are willing to do. What happens then? Are courts effective producers of change, as the Dynamic Court view suggests, or do their decisions do little more than point the way to a brighter, but perhaps unobtainable future? Once again, this conflict between two deeply held views about the role of the courts in the American political system has an obvious normative dimension that is worth debating.

▪ ▪ ▪

THE DYNAMIC AND THE CONSTRAINED COURT

▪ ▪ ▪

Structural Constraints: The Logic of the Constrained Court View

The view of courts as unable to produce significant social reform has a distinguished pedigree reaching back to the founders. Premised on the institutional structure of the American political system and the procedures and belief systems created by American law, it suggests that the conditions required for courts to produce significant social reform will seldom exist.

■   ■   ■

[T]he Constrained Court view holds that litigants asking courts for significant social reform are faced with powerful constraints. First, they must convince courts that the rights they are asserting are required by constitutional or statutory language. Given the limited nature of constitutional rights, the constraints of legal culture, and the general caution of the judiciary, this is no easy task. Second, courts are wary of stepping too far out of the political mainstream. Deferential to the federal government and potentially limited by congressional action, courts may be unwilling to take the heat generated by politically unpopular rulings. Third, if these two constraints are overcome and cases are decided favorably, litigants are faced with the task of implementing the decisions. Lacking powerful tools to force implementation, court decisions are often rendered useless given much opposition. Even if litigators seeking significant social reform win major victories in court, in implementation they often turn out to be worth very little. Borrowing the words of Justice Jackson from another context, the Constrained Court view holds that court litigation to produce significant social reform may amount to little more than "a teasing illusion like a munificent bequest in a pauper's will" (*Edwards v. California* 1941, 186).

Court Effectiveness: The Logic of the Dynamic Court View

The three constraints just presented are generated from the view of courts as unable to produce significant social reform. That view appears historically grounded and empirically plausible. Yet, on reflection, it has two main difficulties. First, it seems to overstate the limits on courts. After all, since the mid-twentieth century or so courts have been embroiled in controversies over significant social reform. Many lawyers, activists, and scholars have acted or written with the belief that the constraints are weak or non-existent and can easily be overcome. Indeed, the whole modern debate over judicial activism makes no sense if the Constrained Court view is correct. If courts are as impotent as the constraints suggest, then why has there been such political, academic, and judicial concern with the role of courts in modern America? Theory and practice are unaligned if the Constrained Court view is entirely correct. Second, examined carefully, its claim is that courts are *unlikely* to produce significant social reform; it does not deny the possibility. However, that doesn't help us understand when, and under what conditions, courts can produce significant social reform. The Constrained Court view is not the complete answer.

The Dynamic Court view may help. It maintains that courts can be effective producers of significant social reform. Its basic thrust is that not only are courts not as limited as the Constrained Court view suggests, but also, in some cases, they can be more effective than other governmental institutions in producing significant social reform.

Political, Institutional, and Economic Independence

▪   ▪   ▪

The Dynamic Court view provides a powerful alternative to the view of courts as the "least dangerous branch." Pointing to pathologies in the other branches, it places courts in a unique position to act. Acknowledging, perhaps, that the Constrained Court view was accurate at the Founding and for part of American history, it maintains that great change has occurred over the last few decades and that courts now have the tools to effectively produce significant social reform. Unlike the Constrained Court view, it is congruent with judicial activism and the modern use of the courts to produce significant social reform. While courts cannot solve all problems, the Dynamic Court view does see them as powerful and effective, unconstrained by the concentrations of power and bureaucratic inertia that stymie self-initiated change in the other branches.

▪   ▪   ▪

Yet for all their plausibility and surface appeal, and their seemingly accurate description of recent litigation, attempts to ground the Dynamic Court view empirically are not entirely satisfying. Unfortunately, studies of the sort referred to above neither completely validate it nor are particularly helpful in constructing hypotheses about courts' effectiveness in producing significant social reform. Often, they either focus on unrepresentative time periods, or on unimportant and noncontroversial cases, or they overstate their findings. In addition, many of the studies that support the Dynamic Court view are theoretical rather than empirical. They mistake what conceivably could happen with what actually has happened. Further, the empirical studies tend to examine only one case. The problem here, from the Constrained Court perspective, is that given the constraints on judges imposed by court rules and the legal culture, it is the rare judge who will become so actively engaged. Although the Dynamic Court view may be correct, the empirical evidence offered in its support does not seal the case.

▪   ▪   ▪

With special masters, again, actual case studies do not bear out claims on behalf of the Dynamic Court view. For example, introducing an edited compilation of seven studies of school desegregation, Kalodner concludes that "Masters have seldom if ever been effective in the effort to find a solution that is both acceptable and constitutional" (Kalodner 1978, 9). Reviewing the use of masters in six school desegregation cases, Kirp and Babcock explicitly reject Aronow's optimistic conclusions (Kirp and Babcock 1981, 395). Finally, a lengthy and detailed study of institutional reform litigation points out that under court rules the use of special masters must "be the exception and not the rule. Consequently, there cannot be reference to masters as a matter of course" (Special Project 1978, 808). While special masters may be helpful in some cases, overall their record of use appears of limited effectiveness. And the crucial question of under what conditions special masters will be effective is left unanswered.

The Dynamic Court view, then, though in large part an effective retort to the unbending constraints of the Constrained Court view, does not get us very far in understanding the conditions under which courts can produce significant social reform. While its logic of independence and equal access makes good sense, its lack of generalizable empirical support is unhelpful. In sum, while courts may be more effective in producing significant social reform than the constraints of the Constrained Court view allow, the Dynamic Court view does not definitively demonstrate when, and under what conditions, court efficacy can be found.

Conditions for Court Efficacy

The thrust of the Dynamic Court view is that its competitor oversimplifies reality by *under*stating court effectiveness. However, it appears that the Dynamic Court view likewise oversimplifies, by *over*stating court effectiveness. Further, the views appear to be in conflict. For example, the Dynamic Court view proposes court action in the face of hostile or inert political institutions while the constraints of the Constrained Court view tell us that in such situations success is least likely. Along with conflict, however, each view appears to convey something of the truth. On an intuitive level, opposition from political elites is not conducive to court effectiveness. On the other hand, judicial isolation from many pressures allows courts to act when other institutions wish to but cannot. Surely it is naive to expect courts to be able to solve political and economic problems that the other branches cannot. But it appears equally short-sighted to deny that since mid-century courts have played an important role in producing significant social reform. It may well be that while each view captures part of the truth, neither is fine-grained enough to capture the conditions under which courts can effectively produce significant social reform.

. . . I suggest that this is the case; the constraints of the Constrained Court view generally limit courts, but when political, social, and economic conditions have become supportive of change, courts can effectively produce significant social reform. . . . [T]he conditions enabling courts to produce significant social reform will seldom be present because courts are limited by three separate constraints built into the structure of the American political system:

1. The limited nature of constitutional rights . . .
2. The lack of judicial independence . . .
3. The judiciary's lack of powers of implementation . . .

However, when certain conditions are met, courts can be effective producers of significant social reform. These conditions occur when:

1. . . . There is ample legal precedent for change; *and,*
2. . . . There is support for change from substantial numbers in Congress and from the executive; *and,*
3. . . . There is either support from some citizens, or at least low levels of opposition from all citizens.

NOTES

1. Not everyone, however, thinks such liberal judicial activism is a good thing. It has spawned a wave of attacks on the judiciary ranging from Nathan Glazer's warning of the rise of an "imperial judiciary" to a spate of legislative proposals to remove court jurisdiction over a number of issues. See Glazer (1975); *An Imperial Judiciary* (1979). And, of course, Presidents Nixon and Reagan pledged to end judicial activism by appointing "strict constructionists" to the federal courts.

2. As McCann (1986, 114) suggests, in the public-interest movement, lawyers are "quite naturally the most ardent spokespersons" for the use of courts to produce change.

CASE REFERENCES

Edwards v. *California*, 314 U.S. 160 (1941).
Brown vs. Board of Education of Topeka, 347 U.S. 483 (1954).
Roe v. *Wade*, 410 U.S. 113 (1973).

REFERENCES

Aronow, Geoffrey F. 1980. "The Special Master in School Desegregation Cases: The Evolution of Roles in the Reformation of Public Institutions through Litigation." 7 *Hastings Const. L. Q.* 739.

Glazer, Nathan. 1975. "Towards an Imperial Judiciary?" *The Public Interest* (Fall): 104–23.

An Imperial Judiciary: Fact or Myth? 1979. Washington, DC: American Enterprise Institute.

Kalodner, Howard I. 1978. Introduction. In *Limits to Justice*. Eds. Howard I. Kalodner, and James J. Fishman. Cambridge, MA: Ballinger. 1–24.

Kirp, David L., and Gary Babcock. 1981. "Judge and Company: Court Appointed Masters, School Desegregation, and Institutional Reform. In "Symposium, Judicially Managed Institutional Reform." 32 *Alabama L. Rev.* 317.

McCann, Michael. 1986. *Taking Reform Seriously: Perspectives on Public Interest Liberalism*. Ithaca: Cornell University Press.

Scheingold, Stuart A. 1974. *The Politics of Rights: Lawyers, Public Policy, and Political Change*. New Haven, CT: Yale University Press.

Special Project. 1978. "The Remedial Process in Institutional Reform Litigation." 78 *Colum. L. Rev.* 784.

8.2

Marbury v. Madison (1803)

This foundational Supreme Court decision was a bold move by the Court to establish its central role in the national government. In writing this opinion, Chief Justice John Marshall laid out the case in favor of the Supreme Court having the final say in determining whether a law or action of the government is constitutional. By declaring that "it is emphatically the province and duty of the judicial department to say what the law is," this opinion establishes judicial review as a fundamental aspect of American government.

MR. CHIEF JUSTICE MARSHALL delivered the opinion of the Court.

At the last term, on the affidavits then read and filed with the clerk, a rule was granted in this case requiring the Secretary of State to show cause why a mandamus should not issue directing him to deliver to William Marbury his commission as a justice of the peace for the county of Washington, in the District of Columbia.

No cause has been shown, and the present motion is for a mandamus. The peculiar delicacy of this case, the novelty of some of its circumstances, and the real difficulty attending the points which occur in it require a complete exposition of the principles on which the opinion to be given by the Court is founded.

These principles have been, on the side of the applicant, very ably argued at the bar. In rendering the opinion of the Court, there will be some departure in form, though not in substance, from the points stated in that argument.

If he has a right, and that right has been violated, do the laws of his country afford him a remedy?

The very essence of civil liberty certainly consists in the right of every individual to claim the protection of the laws whenever he receives an injury. One of the first duties of government is to afford that protection. In Great Britain, the King himself is sued in the respectful form of a petition, and he never fails to comply with the judgment of his court.

The Government of the United States has been emphatically termed a government of laws, and not of men. It will certainly cease to deserve this high

From *Marbury v. Madison*, 5 U.S. 137 (1803).

appellation if the laws furnish no remedy for the violation of a vested legal right.

By the act concerning invalids, passed in June, 1794, the Secretary at War is ordered to place on the pension list all persons whose names are contained in a report previously made by him to Congress. If he should refuse to do so, would the wounded veteran be without remedy? Is it to be contended that where the law, in precise terms, directs the performance of an act in which an individual is interested, the law is incapable of securing obedience to its mandate? Is it on account of the character of the person against whom the complaint is made? Is it to be contended that the heads of departments are not amenable to the laws of their country?

Whatever the practice on particular occasions may be, the theory of this principle will certainly never be maintained. No act of the Legislature confers so extraordinary a privilege, nor can it derive countenance from the doctrines of the common law.

It follows, then, that the question whether the legality of an act of the head of a department be examinable in a court of justice or not must always depend on the nature of that act.

If some acts be examinable and others not, there must be some rule of law to guide the Court in the exercise of its jurisdiction.

In some instances, there may be difficulty in applying the rule to particular cases; but there cannot, it is believed, be much difficulty in laying down the rule.

The power of nominating to the Senate, and the power of appointing the person nominated, are political powers, to be exercised by the President according to his own discretion. When he has made an appointment, he has exercised his whole power, and his discretion has been completely applied to the case. If, by law, the officer be removable at the will of the President, then a new appointment may be immediately made, and the rights of the officer are terminated. But as a fact which has existed cannot be made never to have existed, the appointment cannot be annihilated, and consequently, if the officer is by law not removable at the will of the President, the rights he has acquired are protected by the law, and are not resumable by the President. They cannot be extinguished by Executive authority, and he has the privilege of asserting them in like manner as if they had been derived from any other source.

The question whether a right has vested or not is, in its nature, judicial, and must be tried by the judicial authority. If, for example, Mr. Marbury had taken the oaths of a magistrate and proceeded to act as one, in consequence of which a suit had been instituted against him in which his defence had depended on his being a magistrate; the validity of his appointment must have been determined by judicial authority.

So, if he conceives that, by virtue of his appointment, he has a legal right either to the commission which has been made out for him or to a copy of that commission, it is equally a question examinable in a court, and the decision of the Court upon it must depend on the opinion entertained of his appointment.

It is then the opinion of the Court:

That, by signing the commission of Mr. Marbury, the President of the United States appointed him a justice of peace for the County of Washington in the District of Columbia, and that the seal of the United States, affixed thereto by the Secretary of State, is conclusive testimony of the verity of the signature, and of the completion of the appointment, and that the appointment conferred on him a legal right to the office for the space of five years.

That, having this legal title to the office, he has a consequent right to the commission, a refusal to deliver which is a plain violation of that right, for which the laws of his country afford him a remedy.

It remains to be inquired whether, he is entitled to the remedy for which he applies.

With respect to the officer to whom it would be directed. The intimate political relation, subsisting between the President of the United States and the heads of departments, necessarily renders any legal investigation of the acts of one of those high officers peculiarly irksome, as well as delicate, and excites some hesitation with respect to the propriety of entering into such investigation. Impressions are often received without much reflection or examination, and it is not wonderful that, in such a case as this, the assertion by an individual of his legal claims in a court of justice, to which claims it is the duty of that court to attend, should, at first view, be considered [p170] by some as an attempt to intrude into the cabinet and to intermeddle with the prerogatives of the Executive.

It is scarcely necessary for the Court to disclaim all pretensions to such a jurisdiction. An extravagance so absurd and excessive could not have been entertained for a moment. The province of the Court is solely to decide on the rights of individuals, not to inquire how the Executive or Executive officers perform duties in which they have a discretion. Questions, in their nature political or which are, by the Constitution and laws, submitted to the Executive, can never be made in this court.

But, if this be not such a question; if so far from being an intrusion into the secrets of the cabinet, it respects a paper which, according to law, is upon record, and to a copy of which the law gives a right, on the payment of ten cents; if it be no intermeddling with a subject over which the Executive can be considered as having exercised any control; what is there in the exalted station of the officer which shall bar a citizen from asserting in a court of justice his legal rights, or shall forbid a court to listen to the claim or to issue a mandamus directing the performance of a duty not depending on Executive discretion, but on particular acts of Congress and the general principles of law?

If one of the heads of departments commits any illegal act under colour of his office by which an individual sustains an injury, it cannot be pretended that his office alone exempts him from being sued in the ordinary mode of proceeding, and being compelled to obey the judgment of the law. How then can his office exempt him from this particular mode of deciding on the legality of his conduct if the case be such a case as would, were any other individual the party complained of, authorize the process?

It is not by the office of the person to whom the writ is directed, but the nature of the thing to be done, that the propriety or impropriety of issuing a mandamus is to be determined. Where the head of a department acts in a case in which Executive discretion is to be exercised, in which he is the mere organ of Executive will, it is again repeated, that any application to a court to control, in any respect, his conduct, would be rejected without hesitation.

But where he is directed by law to do a certain act affecting the absolute rights of individuals, in the performance of which he is not placed under the particular direction of the President, and the performance of which the President cannot lawfully forbid, and therefore is never presumed to have forbidden—as for example, to record a commission, or a patent for land, which has received all the legal solemnities; or to give a copy of such record—in such cases, it is not perceived on what ground the Courts of the country are further excused from the duty of giving judgment that right to be done to an injured individual than if the same services were to be performed by a person not the head of a department.

This opinion seems not now for the first time to be taken up in this country.

It is true that the mandamus now moved for is not for the performance of an act expressly enjoined by statute.

It is to deliver a commission, on which subjects the acts of Congress are silent. This difference is not considered as affecting the case. It has already been stated that the applicant has, to that commission, a vested legal right of which the Executive cannot deprive him. He has been appointed to an office from which he is not removable at the will of the Executive, and, being so appointed, he has a right to the commission which the Secretary has received from the President for his use. The act of Congress does not, indeed, order the Secretary of State to send it to him, but it is placed in his hands for the person entitled to it, and cannot be more lawfully withheld by him than by another person.

This is a plain case of a mandamus, either to deliver the commission or a copy of it from the record, and it only remains to be inquired:

Whether it can issue from this Court.

The act to establish the judicial courts of the United States authorizes the Supreme Court to issue writs of mandamus, in cases warranted by the principles and usages of law, to any courts appointed, or persons holding office, under the authority of the United States.

The Secretary of State, being a person, holding an office under the authority of the United States, is precisely within the letter of the description, and if this Court is not authorized to issue a writ of mandamus to such an officer, it must be because the law is unconstitutional, and therefore absolutely incapable of conferring the authority and assigning the duties which its words purport to confer and assign.

The Constitution vests the whole judicial power of the United States in one Supreme Court, and such inferior courts as Congress shall, from time to time, ordain and establish. This power is expressly extended to all cases arising under the laws of the United States; and consequently, in some form, may be exercised over the present case, because the right claimed is given by a law of the United States.

In the distribution of this power. it is declared that the Supreme Court shall have original jurisdiction in all cases affecting ambassadors, other public ministers and consuls, and those in which a state shall be a party. In all other cases, the Supreme Court shall have appellate jurisdiction.

It has been insisted at the bar, that, as the original grant of jurisdiction to the Supreme and inferior courts is general, and the clause assigning original jurisdiction to the Supreme Court contains no negative or restrictive words, the power remains to the Legislature to assign original jurisdiction to that Court in other cases than those specified in the article which has been recited, provided those cases belong to the judicial power of the United States.

If it had been intended to leave it in the discretion of the Legislature to apportion the judicial power between the Supreme and inferior courts according to the will of that body, it would certainly have been useless to have proceeded further than to have defined the judicial power and the tribunals in which it should be vested. The subsequent part of the section is mere surplusage—is entirely without meaning—if such is to be the construction. If Congress remains at liberty to give this court appellate jurisdiction where the Constitution has declared their jurisdiction shall be original, and original jurisdiction where the Constitution has declared it shall be appellate, the distribution of jurisdiction made in the Constitution, is form without substance.

Affirmative words are often, in their operation, negative of other objects than those affirmed, and, in this case, a negative or exclusive sense must be given to them or they have no operation at all.

It cannot be presumed that any clause in the Constitution is intended to be without effect, and therefore such construction is inadmissible unless the words require it.

If the solicitude of the Convention respecting our peace with foreign powers induced a provision that the Supreme Court should take original jurisdiction in cases which might be supposed to affect them, yet the clause would have proceeded no further than to provide for such cases if no further restriction on the powers of Congress had been intended. That they should have appellate jurisdiction in all other cases, with such exceptions as Congress might make, is no restriction unless the words be deemed exclusive of original jurisdiction.

When an instrument organizing fundamentally a judicial system divides it into one Supreme and so many inferior courts as the Legislature may ordain and establish, then enumerates its powers, and proceeds so far to distribute them as to define the jurisdiction of the Supreme Court by declaring the cases in which it shall take original jurisdiction, and that in others it shall take appellate jurisdiction, the plain import of the words seems to be that, in one class of cases, its jurisdiction is original, and not appellate; in the other, it is appellate, and not original. If any other construction would render the clause inoperative, that is an additional reason for rejecting such other construction, and for adhering to the obvious meaning.

To enable this court then to issue a mandamus, it must be shown to be an exercise of appellate jurisdiction, or to be necessary to enable them to exercise appellate jurisdiction.

The authority, therefore, given to the Supreme Court by the act establishing the judicial courts of the United States to issue writs of mandamus to public officers appears not to be warranted by the Constitution, and it becomes necessary to inquire whether a jurisdiction so conferred can be exercised.

This original and supreme will organizes the government and assigns to different departments their respective powers. It may either stop here or establish certain limits not to be transcended by those departments.

The Government of the United States is of the latter description. The powers of the Legislature are defined and limited; and that those limits may not be mistaken or forgotten, the Constitution is written. To what purpose are powers limited, and to what purpose is that limitation committed to writing, if these limits may at any time be passed by those intended to be restrained? The distinction between a government with limited and unlimited powers is abolished if those limits do not confine the persons on whom they are imposed, and if acts prohibited and acts allowed are of equal obligation. It is a proposition too plain to be contested that the Constitution controls any legislative act repugnant to it, or that the Legislature may alter the Constitution by an ordinary act.

Between these alternatives there is no middle ground. The Constitution is either a superior, paramount law, unchangeable by ordinary means, or it is on a level with ordinary legislative acts, and, like other acts, is alterable when the legislature shall please to alter it.

If the former part of the alternative be true, then a legislative act contrary to the Constitution is not law; if the latter part be true, then written Constitutions are absurd attempts on the part of the people to limit a power in its own nature illimitable.

Certainly all those who have framed written Constitutions contemplate them as forming the fundamental and paramount law of the nation, and consequently the theory of every such government must be that an act of the Legislature repugnant to the Constitution is void.

This theory is essentially attached to a written Constitution, and is consequently to be considered by this Court as one of the fundamental principles of our society. It is not, therefore, to be lost sight of in the further consideration of this subject.

If an act of the Legislature repugnant to the Constitution is void, does it, notwithstanding its invalidity, bind the Courts and oblige them to give it effect? Or, in other words, though it be not law, does it constitute a rule as operative as if it was a law? This would be to overthrow in fact what was established in theory, and would seem, at first view, an absurdity too gross to be insisted on. It shall, however, receive a more attentive consideration.

It is emphatically the province and duty of the Judicial Department to say what the law is. Those who apply the rule to particular cases must, of necessity, expound and interpret that rule. If two laws conflict with each other, the Courts must decide on the operation of each.

So, if a law be in opposition to the Constitution, if both the law and the Constitution apply to a particular case, so that the Court must either decide that case conformably to the law, disregarding the Constitution, or conformably to the Constitution, disregarding the law, the Court must determine which of these conflicting rules governs the case. This is of the very essence of judicial duty.

If, then, the Courts are to regard the Constitution, and the Constitution is superior to any ordinary act of the Legislature, the Constitution, and not such ordinary act, must govern the case to which they both apply.

Those, then, who controvert the principle that the Constitution is to be considered in court as a paramount law are reduced to the necessity of maintaining that courts must close their eyes on the Constitution, and see only the law.

This doctrine would subvert the very foundation of all written Constitutions. It would declare that an act which, according to the principles and theory of our government, is entirely void, is yet, in practice, completely obligatory. It would declare that, if the Legislature shall do what is expressly forbidden, such act, notwithstanding the express prohibition, is in reality effectual. It would be giving to the Legislature a practical and real omnipotence with the same breath which professes to restrict their powers within narrow limits. It is prescribing limits, and declaring that those limits may be passed at pleasure.

That it thus reduces to nothing what we have deemed the greatest improvement on political institutions—a written Constitution, would of itself be sufficient, in America where written Constitutions have been viewed with so much reverence, for rejecting the construction. But the peculiar expressions of the Constitution of the United States furnish additional arguments in favour of its rejection.

The judicial power of the United States is extended to all cases arising under the Constitution.

Could it be the intention of those who gave this power to say that, in using it, the Constitution should not be looked into? That a case arising under the Constitution should be decided without examining the instrument under which it arises?

This is too extravagant to be maintained.

In some cases then, the Constitution must be looked into by the judges. And if they can open it at all, what part of it are they forbidden to read or to obey?

There are many other parts of the Constitution which serve to illustrate this subject.

It is declared that "no tax or duty shall be laid on articles exported from any State." Suppose a duty on the export of cotton, of tobacco, or of flour, and a suit instituted to recover it. Ought judgment to be rendered in such a case? ought the judges to close their eyes on the Constitution, and only see the law?

The Constitution declares that "no bill of attainder or *ex post facto* law shall be passed."

If, however, such a bill should be passed and a person should be prosecuted under it, must the Court condemn to death those victims whom the Constitution endeavours to preserve?

"No person," says the Constitution, "shall be convicted of treason unless on the testimony of two witnesses to the same overt act, or on confession in open court."

Here, the language of the Constitution is addressed especially to the Courts. It prescribes, directly for them, a rule of evidence not to be departed from. If the Legislature should change that rule, and declare one witness, or a confession out of court, sufficient for conviction, must the constitutional principle yield to the legislative act?

From these and many other selections which might be made, it is apparent that the framers of the Constitution contemplated that instrument as a rule for the government of courts, as well as of the Legislature.

Why otherwise does it direct the judges to take an oath to support it? This oath certainly applies in an especial manner to their conduct in their official character. How immoral to impose it on them if they were to be used as the instruments, and the knowing instruments, for violating what they swear to support!

The oath of office, too, imposed by the Legislature, is completely demonstrative of the legislative opinion on this subject. It is in these words: I do solemnly swear that I will administer justice without respect to persons, and do equal right to the poor and to the rich; and that I will faithfully and impartially discharge all the duties incumbent on me as according to the best of my abilities and understanding, agreeably to the Constitution and laws of the United States.

Why does a judge swear to discharge his duties agreeably to the Constitution of the United States if that Constitution forms no rule for his government? if it is closed upon him and cannot be inspected by him?

If such be the real state of things, this is worse than solemn mockery. To prescribe or to take this oath becomes equally a crime.

It is also not entirely unworthy of observation that, in declaring what shall be the supreme law of the land, the Constitution itself is first mentioned, and not the laws of the United States generally, but those only which shall be made in pursuance of the Constitution, have that rank.

Thus, the particular phraseology of the Constitution of the United States confirms and strengthens the principle, supposed to be essential to all written Constitutions, that a law repugnant to the Constitution is void, and that courts, as well as other departments, are bound by that instrument.

The rule must be discharged.

8.3

Lawrence v. Texas (2003)

In 2003, seventeen years after the Bowers v. Hardwick *decision that let stand state laws against sodomy, the Supreme Court reversed itself and declared that a Texas law banning homosexual sodomy was unconstitutional. The majority decided that state laws banning private sexual activity between consenting adults violated the constitutional right to privacy.*

JUSTICE KENNEDY delivered the opinion of the Court.

Liberty protects the person from unwarranted government intrusions into a dwelling or other private places. In our tradition the State is not omnipresent in the home. And there are other spheres of our lives and existence, outside the home, where the State should not be a dominant presence. Freedom extends beyond spatial bounds. Liberty presumes an autonomy of self that includes freedom of thought, belief, expression, and certain intimate conduct. The instant case involves liberty of the person both in its spatial and more transcendent dimensions.

I

The question before the Court is the validity of a Texas statute making it a crime for two persons of the same sex to engage in certain intimate sexual conduct.

In Houston, Texas, officers of the Harris County Police Department were dispatched to a private residence in response to a reported weapons disturbance. They entered an apartment where one of the petitioners, John Geddes Lawrence, resided. The right of the police to enter does not seem to have been questioned. The officers observed Lawrence and another man, Tyron Garner, engaging in a sexual act. The two petitioners were arrested, held in custody over night, and charged and convicted before a Justice of the Peace.

The complaints described their crime as "deviate sexual intercourse, namely anal sex, with a member of the same sex (man)." The applicable state law is Tex. Penal Code Ann. §21.06(a) (2003). It provides: "A person commits an

From *Lawrence v. Texas*, 539 U.S. 558 (2003).

offense if he engages in deviate sexual intercourse with another individual of the same sex." The statute defines "[d]eviate sexual intercourse" as follows:

"(A) any contact between any part of the genitals of one person and the mouth or anus of another person; or
"(B) the penetration of the genitals or the anus of another person with an object."

The petitioners exercised their right to a trial *de novo* in Harris County Criminal Court. They challenged the statute as a violation of the Equal Protection Clause of the Fourteenth Amendment and of a like provision of the Texas Constitution. Tex. Const., Art. 1, §3a. Those contentions were rejected. The petitioners, having entered a plea of *nolo contendere*, were each fined $200 and assessed court costs of $141.25.

The Court of Appeals for the Texas Fourteenth District considered the petitioners' federal constitutional arguments under both the Equal Protection and Due Process Clauses of the Fourteenth Amendment. After hearing the case en banc the court, in a divided opinion, rejected the constitutional arguments and affirmed the convictions. The majority opinion indicates that the Court of Appeals considered our decision in *Bowers v. Hardwick* (1986), to be controlling on the federal due process aspect of the case. *Bowers* then being authoritative, this was proper.

We granted certiorari, to consider three questions:

1. Whether Petitioners' criminal convictions under the Texas "Homosexual Conduct" law—which criminalizes sexual intimacy by samesex couples, but not identical behavior by different-sex couples—violate the Fourteenth Amendment guarantee of equal protection of laws?
2. Whether Petitioners' criminal convictions for adult consensual sexual intimacy in the home violate their vital interests in liberty and privacy protected by the Due Process Clause of the Fourteenth Amendment?
3. Whether *Bowers v. Hardwick*, should be overruled?

The petitioners were adults at the time of the alleged offense. Their conduct was in private and consensual.

II

We conclude the case should be resolved by determining whether the petitioners were free as adults to engage in the private conduct in the exercise of their liberty under the Due Process Clause of the Fourteenth Amendment to the Constitution. For this inquiry we deem it necessary to reconsider the Court's holding in *Bowers*.

There are broad statements of the substantive reach of liberty under the Due Process Clause in earlier cases, including *Pierce v. Society of Sisters* (1925), and *Meyer v. Nebraska* (1923); but the most pertinent beginning point is our decision in *Griswold v. Connecticut* (1965).

In *Griswold* the Court invalidated a state law prohibiting the use of drugs or devices of contraception and counseling or aiding and abetting the use of contraceptives. The Court described the protected interest as a right to privacy and placed emphasis on the marriage relation and the protected space of the marital bedroom.

After *Griswold* it was established that the right to make certain decisions regarding sexual conduct extends beyond the marital relationship. In *Eisenstadt v. Baird* (1972), the Court invalidated a law prohibiting the distribution of contraceptives to unmarried persons. The case was decided under the Equal Protection Clause; but with respect to unmarried persons, the Court went on to state the fundamental proposition that the law impaired the exercise of their personal rights. It quoted from the statement of the Court of Appeals finding the law to be in conflict with fundamental human rights, and it followed with this statement of its own:

> It is true that in *Griswold* the right of privacy in question inhered in the marital relationship. . . . If the right of privacy means anything, it is the right of the *individual*, married or single, to be free from unwarranted governmental intrusion into matters so fundamentally affecting a person as the decision whether to bear or beget a child.

The opinions in *Griswold* and *Eisenstadt* were part of the background for the decision in *Roe v. Wade* (1973). As is well known, the case involved a challenge to the Texas law prohibiting abortions, but the laws of other States were affected as well. Although the Court held the woman's rights were not absolute, her right to elect an abortion did have real and substantial protection as an exercise of her liberty under the Due Process Clause. The Court cited cases that protect spatial freedom and cases that go well beyond it. *Roe* recognized the right of a woman to make certain fundamental decisions affecting her destiny and confirmed once more that the protection of liberty under the Due Process Clause has a substantive dimension of fundamental significance in defining the rights of the person.

In *Carey v. Population Services Int'l* (1977), the Court confronted a New York law forbidding sale or distribution of contraceptive devices to persons under 16 years of age. Although there was no single opinion for the Court, the law was invalidated. Both *Eisenstadt* and *Carey*, as well as the holding and rationale in *Roe*, confirmed that the reasoning of *Griswold* could not be confined to the protection of rights of married adults. This was the state of the law with respect to some of the most relevant cases when the Court considered *Bowers v. Hardwick*.

The facts in *Bowers* had some similarities to the instant case. A police officer, whose right to enter seems not to have been in question, observed Hardwick, in his own bedroom, engaging in intimate sexual conduct with another adult male. The conduct was in violation of a Georgia statute making it a criminal offense to engage in sodomy. One difference between the two cases is that the Georgia statute prohibited the conduct whether or not the participants were of the same sex, while the Texas statute, as we have seen, applies only to participants of the same sex. Hardwick was not prosecuted, but he brought an action in federal court to declare the state statute invalid. He alleged he was a practicing homosexual and that the criminal prohibition violated rights guaranteed to him by the Constitution. The Court, in an opinion by Justice White, sustained the Georgia law. Chief Justice Burger and Justice Powell joined the opinion of the Court and filed separate, concurring opinions. Four Justices dissented. (opinion of Blackmun, J., joined by Brennan, Marshall, and Stevens, JJ.); (opinion of Stevens, J., joined by Brennan and Marshall, JJ.).

The Court began its substantive discussion in *Bowers* as follows: "The issue presented is whether the Federal Constitution confers a fundamental right upon homosexuals to engage in sodomy and hence invalidates the laws of the many States that still make such conduct illegal and have done so for a very long time." That statement, we now conclude, discloses the Court's own failure to appreciate the extent of the liberty at stake. To say that the issue in *Bowers* was simply the right to engage in certain sexual conduct demeans the claim the individual put forward, just as it would demean a married couple were it to be said marriage is simply about the right to have sexual intercourse. The laws involved in *Bowers* and here are, to be sure, statutes that purport to do no more than prohibit a particular sexual act. Their penalties and purposes, though, have more far-reaching consequences, touching upon the most private human conduct, sexual behavior, and in the most private of places, the home. The statutes do seek to control a personal relationship that, whether or not entitled to formal recognition in the law, is within the liberty of persons to choose without being punished as criminals.

This, as a general rule, should counsel against attempts by the State, or a court, to define the meaning of the relationship or to set its boundaries absent injury to a person or abuse of an institution the law protects. It suffices for us to acknowledge that adults may choose to enter upon this relationship in the confines of their homes and their own private lives and still retain their dignity as free persons. When sexuality finds overt expression in intimate conduct with another person, the conduct can be but one element in a personal bond that is more enduring. The liberty protected by the Constitution allows homosexual persons the right to make this choice.

Having misapprehended the claim of liberty there presented to it, and thus stating the claim to be whether there is a fundamental right to engage in consensual sodomy, the *Bowers* Court said: "Proscriptions against that conduct have ancient roots." In academic writings, and in many of the scholarly *amicus* briefs filed to assist the Court in this case, there are fundamental criticisms of the historical premises relied upon by the majority and concurring opinions in *Bowers*. We need not enter this debate in the attempt to reach a definitive historical judgment, but the following considerations counsel against adopting the definitive conclusions upon which *Bowers* placed such reliance.

At the outset it should be noted that there is no longstanding history in this country of laws directed at homosexual conduct as a distinct matter. Beginning in colonial times there were prohibitions of sodomy derived from the English criminal laws passed in the first instance by the Reformation Parliament of 1533. The English prohibition was understood to include relations between men and women as well as relations between men and men. Nineteenth-century commentators similarly read American sodomy, buggery, and crime-against-nature statutes as criminalizing certain relations between men and women and between men and men. The absence of legal prohibitions focusing on homosexual conduct may be explained in part by noting that according to some scholars the concept of the homosexual as a distinct category of person did not emerge until the late 19th century. Thus early American sodomy laws were not directed at homosexuals as such but instead sought to prohibit nonprocreative sexual activity more generally. This does not suggest approval of homosexual conduct. It does tend to show that this particular form of conduct was not thought of as a separate category from like conduct between heterosexual persons.

Laws prohibiting sodomy do not seem to have been enforced against consenting adults acting in private. A substantial number of sodomy prosecutions and convictions for which there are surviving records were for predatory acts against those who could not or did not consent, as in the case of a minor or the victim of an assault. As to these, one purpose for the prohibitions was to ensure there would be no lack of coverage if a predator committed a sexual assault that did not constitute rape as defined by the criminal law. Thus the model sodomy indictments presented in a 19th-century treatise, addressed the predatory acts of an adult man against a minor girl or minor boy. Instead of targeting relations between consenting adults in private, 19th-century sodomy prosecutions typically involved relations between men and minor girls or minor boys, relations between adults involving force, relations between adults implicating disparity in status, or relations between men and animals.

To the extent that there were any prosecutions for the acts in question, 19th-century evidence rules imposed a burden that would make a conviction more difficult to obtain even taking into account the problems always inherent in prosecuting consensual acts committed in private. Under then-prevailing standards, a man could not be convicted of sodomy based upon testimony of a consenting partner, because the partner was considered an accomplice. A partner's testimony, however, was admissible if he or she had not consented to the act or was a minor, and therefore incapable of consent. The rule may explain in part the infrequency of these prosecutions. In all events that infrequency makes it difficult to say that society approved of a rigorous and systematic punishment of the consensual acts committed in private and by adults.

The longstanding criminal prohibition of homosexual sodomy upon which the *Bowers* decision placed such reliance is as consistent with a general condemnation of nonprocreative sex as it is with an established tradition of prosecuting acts because of their homosexual character.

The policy of punishing consenting adults for private acts was not much discussed in the early legal literature. We can infer that one reason for this was the very private nature of the conduct. Despite the absence of prosecutions, there may have been periods in which there was public criticism of homosexuals as such and an insistence that the criminal laws be enforced to discourage their practices. But far from possessing "ancient roots," American laws targeting same-sex couples did not develop until the last third of the 20th century. The reported decisions concerning the prosecution of consensual, homosexual sodomy between adults for the years 1880–1995 are not always clear in the details, but a significant number involved conduct in a public place.

It was not until the 1970s that any State singled out same-sex relations for criminal prosecution, and only nine States have done so. Post-*Bowers* even some of these States did not adhere to the policy of suppressing homosexual conduct. Over the course of the last decades, States with same-sex prohibitions have moved toward abolishing them.

In summary, the historical grounds relied upon in *Bowers* are more complex than the majority opinion and the concurring opinion by Chief Justice Burger indicate. Their historical premises are not without doubt and, at the very least, are overstated.

It must be acknowledged, of course, that the Court in *Bowers* was making the broader point that for centuries there have been powerful voices to condemn homosexual conduct as immoral. The condemnation has been shaped by religious beliefs, conceptions of right and acceptable behavior, and respect for the traditional family. For many persons these are not trivial concerns but profound and deep convictions accepted as ethical and moral principles to which they aspire and which thus determine the course of their lives. These considerations do not answer the question before us, however. The issue is whether the majority may use the power of the State to enforce these views on the whole society through operation of the criminal law. "Our obligation is to define the liberty of all, not to mandate our own moral code." *Planned Parenthood of Southeastern Pa. v. Casey* (1992).

Chief Justice Burger joined the opinion for the Court in *Bowers* and further explained his views as follows: "Decisions of individuals relating to homosexual conduct have been subject to state intervention throughout the history of Western civilization. Condemnation of those practices is firmly rooted in Judeao-Christian moral and ethical standards." 478 U.S. 196. As with Justice White's assumptions about history, scholarship casts some doubt on the sweeping nature of the statement by Chief Justice Burger as it pertains to private homosexual conduct between consenting adults. In all events we think that our laws and traditions in the past half century are of most relevance here. These references show an emerging awareness that liberty gives substantial protection to adult persons in deciding how to conduct their private lives in matters pertaining to sex. "[H]istory and tradition are the starting point but not in all cases the ending point of the substantive due process inquiry." *County of Sacramento v. Lewis* (1998) (Kennedy, J., concurring).

This emerging recognition should have been apparent when *Bowers* was decided. In 1955 the American Law Institute promulgated the Model Penal Code and made clear that it did not recommend or provide for "criminal penalties for consensual sexual relations conducted in private." It justified its decision on three grounds: (1) The prohibitions undermined respect for the law by penalizing conduct many people engaged in; (2) the statutes regulated private conduct not harmful to others; and (3) the laws were arbitrarily enforced and thus invited the danger of blackmail. In 1961 Illinois changed its laws to conform to the Model Penal Code. Other States soon followed.

In *Bowers* the Court referred to the fact that before 1961 all 50 States had outlawed sodomy, and that at the time of the Court's decision 24 States and the District of Columbia had sodomy laws. Justice Powell pointed out that these prohibitions often were being ignored, however. Georgia, for instance, had not sought to enforce its law for decades.

The sweeping references by Chief Justice Burger to the history of Western civilization and to Judeo-Christian moral and ethical standards did not take account of other authorities pointing in an opposite direction. A committee advising the British Parliament recommended in 1957 repeal of laws punishing homosexual conduct. Parliament enacted the substance of those recommendations 10 years later.

Of even more importance, almost five years before *Bowers* was decided the European Court of Human Rights considered a case with parallels to *Bowers* and to today's case. An adult male resident in Northern Ireland alleged he was a practicing homosexual who desired to engage in consensual homosexual conduct. The laws of Northern Ireland forbade him that right. He alleged that he had been questioned, his home had been searched, and he feared criminal prosecution. The court held that the laws proscribing the conduct were invalid under the European Convention on Human Rights. Authoritative in all countries that are members of the Council of Europe (21 nations then, 45 nations now), the decision is at odds with the premise in *Bowers* that the claim put forward was insubstantial in our Western civilization.

In our own constitutional system the deficiencies in *Bowers* became even more apparent in the years following its announcement. The 25 States with laws prohibiting the relevant conduct referenced in the *Bowers* decision are reduced now to 13, of which 4 enforce their laws only against homosexual conduct. In those States where sodomy is still proscribed, whether for same-sex or heterosexual conduct, there is a pattern of nonenforcement with respect to consenting adults acting in private. The State of Texas admitted in 1994 that as of that date it had not prosecuted anyone under those circumstances.

Two principal cases decided after *Bowers* cast its holding into even more doubt. In *Planned Parenthood of Southeastern Pa. v. Casey,* the Court reaffirmed the substantive force of the liberty protected by the Due Process Clause. The *Casey* decision again confirmed that our laws and tradition afford constitutional protection to personal decisions relating to marriage, procreation, contraception, family relationships, child rearing, and education. In explaining the respect the Constitution demands for the autonomy of the person in making these choices, we stated as follows:

> These matters, involving the most intimate and personal choices a person may make in a lifetime, choices central to personal dignity and autonomy, are central to the liberty protected by the Fourteenth Amendment. At the heart of liberty is the right to define one's own concept of existence, of meaning, of the universe, and of the mystery of human life. Beliefs about these matters could not define the attributes of personhood were they formed under compulsion of the State. (Ibid.)

Persons in a homosexual relationship may seek autonomy for these purposes, just as heterosexual persons do. The decision in *Bowers* would deny them this right.

The second post-*Bowers* case of principal relevance is *Romer v. Evans* (1996). There the Court struck down class-based legislation directed at homosexuals as a violation of the Equal Protection Clause. *Romer* invalidated an amendment to Colorado's constitution which named as a solitary class persons who were homosexuals, lesbians, or bisexual either by "orientation, conduct, practices or relationships," and deprived them of protection under state antidiscrimination laws. We concluded that the provision was "born of animosity toward the class of persons affected" and further that it had no rational relation to a legitimate governmental purpose.

As an alternative argument in this case, counsel for the petitioners and some *amici* contend that *Romer* provides the basis for declaring the Texas statute invalid under the Equal Protection Clause. That is a tenable argument, but we conclude the instant case requires us to address whether *Bowers* itself has continuing validity. Were we to hold the statute invalid under the Equal Protection Clause some might question whether a prohibition would be valid if drawn differently, say, to prohibit the conduct both between same-sex and different-sex participants.

Equality of treatment and the due process right to demand respect for conduct protected by the substantive guarantee of liberty are linked in important respects, and a decision on the latter point advances both interests. If protected conduct is made criminal and the law which does so remains unexamined for its substantive validity, its stigma might remain even if it were not enforceable as drawn for equal protection reasons. When homosexual conduct is made criminal by the law of the State, that declaration in and of itself is an invitation to subject homosexual persons to discrimination both in the public and in the private spheres. The central holding of *Bowers* has been brought in question by this case, and it should be addressed. Its continuance as precedent demeans the lives of homosexual persons.

The stigma this criminal statute imposes, moreover, is not trivial. The offense, to be sure, is but a class C misdemeanor, a minor offense in the Texas legal system. Still, it remains a criminal offense with all that imports for the dignity of the persons charged. The petitioners will bear on their record the history of their criminal convictions. Just this Term we rejected various challenges to state laws requiring the registration of sex offenders. We are advised that if Texas convicted an adult for private, consensual homosexual conduct under the statute here in question the convicted person would come within the registration laws of at least four States were he or she to be subject to their jurisdiction. This underscores the consequential nature of the punishment and the state-sponsored condemnation attendant to the criminal prohibition. Furthermore, the Texas criminal conviction carries with it the other collateral consequences always following a conviction, such as notations on job application forms, to mention but one example.

The foundations of *Bowers* have sustained serious erosion from our recent decisions in *Casey* and *Romer*. When our precedent has been thus weakened, criticism from other sources is of greater significance. In the United States criticism of *Bowers* has been substantial and continuing, disapproving of its reasoning in all respects, not just as to its historical assumptions. The courts of five different States have declined to follow it in interpreting provisions in their own state constitutions parallel to the Due Process Clause of the Fourteenth Amendment.

To the extent *Bowers* relied on values we share with a wider civilization, it should be noted that the reasoning and holding in *Bowers* have been rejected elsewhere. The European Court of Human Rights has followed not *Bowers* but its own decision in *Dudgeon v. United Kingdom*. Other nations, too, have taken action consistent with an affirmation of the protected right of homosexual adults to engage in intimate, consensual conduct. The right the petitioners seek in this case has been accepted as an integral part of human freedom in many other countries. There has been no showing that in this country the governmental interest in circumscribing personal choice is somehow more legitimate or urgent.

The doctrine of *stare decisis* is essential to the respect accorded to the judgments of the Court and to the stability of the law. It is not, however, an inexorable command. In *Casey* we noted that when a Court is asked to overrule a precedent recognizing a constitutional liberty interest, individual or societal reliance on the existence of that liberty cautions with particular strength against reversing course. The holding in *Bowers*, however, has not induced detrimental reliance comparable to some instances where recognized individual rights are involved. Indeed, there has been no individual or societal reliance on *Bowers* of the sort that could counsel against overturning its holding once there are compelling reasons to do so. *Bowers* itself causes uncertainty, for the precedents before and after its issuance contradict its central holding.

The rationale of *Bowers* does not withstand careful analysis. In his dissenting opinion in *Bowers* Justice Stevens came to these conclusions:

> Our prior cases make two propositions abundantly clear. First, the fact that the governing majority in a State has traditionally viewed a particular practice as immoral is not a sufficient reason for upholding a law prohibiting the practice; neither history nor tradition could save a law prohibiting miscegenation from constitutional attack. Second, individual decisions by married persons, concerning the intimacies of their physical relationship, even when not intended to produce offspring, are a form of "liberty" protected by the Due Process Clause of the Fourteenth Amendment. Moreover, this protection extends to intimate choices by unmarried as well as married persons. (footnotes and citations omitted)

Justice Stevens's analysis, in our view, should have been controlling in *Bowers* and should control here.

Bowers was not correct when it was decided, and it is not correct today. It ought not to remain binding precedent. *Bowers v. Hardwick* should be and now is overruled.

The present case does not involve minors. It does not involve persons who might be injured or coerced or who are situated in relationships where consent might not easily be refused. It does not involve public conduct or prostitution. It does not involve whether the government must give formal recognition to any relationship that homosexual persons seek to enter. The case does involve two adults who, with full and mutual consent from each other, engaged in sexual practices common to a homosexual lifestyle. The petitioners are entitled to respect for their private lives. The State cannot demean their existence or control their destiny by making their private sexual conduct a crime. Their right to liberty under the Due Process Clause gives them the full right to engage in their conduct without intervention of the government. "It is a promise of the Constitution that there is a realm of personal liberty which the government may not enter." The Texas statute furthers no legitimate state interest which can justify its intrusion into the personal and private life of the individual.

Had those who drew and ratified the Due Process Clauses of the Fifth Amendment or the Fourteenth Amendment known the components of liberty in its manifold possibilities, they might have been more specific. They did not presume to have this insight. They knew times can blind us to certain truths and later generations can see that laws once thought necessary and proper in fact serve only to oppress. As the Constitution endures, persons in every generation can invoke its principles in their own search for greater freedom.

The judgment of the Court of Appeals for the Texas Fourteenth District is reversed, and the case is remanded for further proceedings not inconsistent with this opinion.

It is so ordered.

8.4

National Federation of Independent Business v. Sebelius (2012)

*In this controversial decision, the Supreme Court upheld nearly all of the Afford-
able Care Act, the signature health care law of the Obama administration. Chief
Justice John Roberts wrote the majority opinion and split legal hairs. Aspects of
the law, he wrote, violate the commerce clause of the Constitution, but can be
upheld because they are consistent with Congress's power to tax. One provision of
the law on funding for Medicaid was declared unconstitutional, while the remainder of the law was permitted to stand. This decision will undoubtedly have deep
political consequences for many years, not only because of the implications for
health care policy, but also because of the Chief Justice's indication of his discomfort with the current legal status of the commerce clause. That clause has been
widely seen as opening the door to greater national power relative to the states,
and Roberts, in this opinion, signals that he thinks that door is open too wide.*

CHIEF JUSTICE ROBERTS delivered the opinion of the Court.

Today we resolve constitutional challenges to two provisions of the Patient
Protection and Affordable Care Act of 2010: the individual mandate, which
requires individuals to purchase a health insurance policy providing a minimum level of coverage; and the Medicaid expansion, which gives funds to the
States on the condition that they provide specified health care to all citizens
whose income falls below a certain threshold. We do not consider whether the
Act embodies sound policies. That judgment is entrusted to the Nation's elected
leaders. We ask only whether Congress has the power under the Constitution to
enact the challenged provisions.

In our federal system, the National Government possesses only limited powers; the States and the people retain the remainder. Nearly two centuries ago,
Chief Justice Marshall observed that "the question respecting the extent of the
powers actually granted" to the Federal Government "is perpetually arising,
and will probably continue to arise, as long as our system shall exist." *McCulloch v. Maryland* (1819). In this case, we must again determine whether the Constitution grants Congress powers it now asserts, but which many States and
individuals believe it does not possess. Resolving this controversy requires us

From *National Federation of Independent Business v. Sebelius*, 567 U.S. _____ (2012).

to examine both the limits of the Government's power, and our own limited role in policing those boundaries.

The Federal Government "is acknowledged by all to be one of enumerated powers." *Ibid.* That is, rather than granting general authority to perform all the conceivable functions of government, the Constitution lists, or enumerates, the Federal Government's powers. Congress may, for example, "coin Money," "establish Post Offices," and "raise and support Armies." Art. I, §8, cls. 5, 7, 12. The enumeration of powers is also a limitation of powers, because "[t]he enumeration presupposes something not enumerated." *Gibbons v. Ogden* (1824). The Constitution's express conferral of some powers makes clear that it does not grant others. And the Federal Government "can exercise only the powers granted to it." *McCulloch, supra.*

Today, the restrictions on government power foremost in many Americans' minds are likely to be affirmative prohibitions, such as contained in the Bill of Rights. These affirmative prohibitions come into play, however, only where the Government possesses authority to act in the first place. If no enumerated power authorizes Congress to pass a certain law, that law may not be enacted, even if it does not violate any of the express prohibitions in the Bill of Rights or elsewhere in the Constitution.

Indeed, the Constitution did not initially include a Bill of Rights at least partly because the Framers felt the enumeration of powers sufficed to restrain the Government. As Alexander Hamilton put it, "the Constitution is itself in every rational sense, and to every useful purpose, A BILL OF RIGHTS." *The Federalist*, No. 84. And when the Bill of Rights was ratified, it made express what the enumeration of powers necessarily implied: "The powers not delegated to the United States by the Constitution . . . are reserved to the States respectively, or to the people." U. S. Const., Amdt. 10. The Federal Government has expanded dramatically over the past two centuries, but it still must show that a constitutional grant of power authorizes each of its actions.

The same does not apply to the States, because the Constitution is not the source of their power. The Constitution may restrict state governments—as it does, for example, by forbidding them to deny any person the equal protection of the laws. But where such prohibitions do not apply, state governments do not need constitutional authorization to act. The States thus can and do perform many of the vital functions of modern government—punishing street crime, running public schools, and zoning property for development, to name but a few—even though the Constitution's text does not authorize any government to do so. Our cases refer to this general power of governing, possessed by the States but not by the Federal Government, as the "police power."

"State sovereignty is not just an end in itself: Rather, federalism secures to citizens the liberties that derive from the diffusion of sovereign power." *New York v. United States* (1992). Because the police power is controlled by 50 different States instead of one national sovereign, the facets of governing that touch on citizens' daily lives are normally administered by smaller governments closer to the governed. The Framers thus ensured that powers which "in the ordinary course of affairs, concern the lives, liberties, and properties of the people" were held by governments more local and more accountable than a distant federal bureaucracy. *The Federalist*, No. 45 (J. Madison). The independent power of the States also serves as a check on the power of the Federal Government: "By denying any one government complete jurisdiction over all the concerns of public life, federalism protects the liberty of the individual from arbitrary power." *Bond v. United States* (2011).

This case concerns two powers that the Constitution does grant the Federal Government, but which must be read carefully to avoid creating a general federal authority akin to the police power. The Constitution authorizes Congress to "regulate Commerce with foreign Nations, and among the several States, and with the Indian Tribes." Art. I, §8, cl. 3. Our precedents read that to mean that Congress may regulate "the channels of interstate commerce," "persons or things in interstate commerce," and "those activities that substantially affect interstate commerce." *United States v. Morrison* (2000). The power over activities that substantially affect interstate commerce can be expansive. That power has been held to authorize federal regulation of such seemingly local matters as a farmer's decision to grow wheat for himself and his livestock, and a loan shark's extortionate collections from a neighborhood butcher shop.

Congress may also "lay and collect Taxes, Duties, Imposts and Excises, to pay the Debts and provide for the common Defence and general Welfare of the United States." U.S. Const., Art. I, §8, cl. 1. Put simply, Congress may tax and spend. This grant gives the Federal Government considerable influence even in areas where it cannot directly regulate. The Federal Government may enact a tax on an activity that it cannot authorize, forbid, or otherwise control. And in exercising its spending power, Congress may offer funds to the States, and may condition those offers on compliance with specified conditions. These offers may well induce the States to adopt policies that the Federal Government itself could not impose.

The reach of the Federal Government's enumerated powers is broader still because the Constitution authorizes Congress to "make all Laws which shall be necessary and proper for carrying into Execution the foregoing Powers." Art. I, §8, cl. 18. We have long read this provision to give Congress great latitude in exercising its powers: "Let the end be legitimate, let it be within the scope of the constitution, and all means which are appropriate, which are plainly adapted to that end, which are not prohibited, but consist with the letter and spirit of the constitution, are constitutional." *McCulloch*.

Our permissive reading of these powers is explained in part by a general reticence to invalidate the acts of the Nation's elected leaders. "Proper respect for a coordinate branch of the government" requires that we strike down an Act of Congress only if "the lack of constitutional authority to pass [the] act in question is clearly demonstrated." *United States v. Harris* (1883). Members of this Court are vested with the authority to interpret the law; we possess neither the expertise nor the prerogative to make policy judgments. Those decisions are entrusted to our Nation's elected leaders, who can be thrown out of office if the people disagree with them. It is not our job to protect the people from the consequences of their political choices.

Our deference in matters of policy cannot, however, become abdication in matters of law. "The powers of the legislature are defined and limited; and that those limits may not be mistaken, or forgotten, the constitution is written." *Marbury v. Madison* (1803). Our respect for Congress's policy judgments thus can never extend so far as to disavow restraints on federal power that the Constitution carefully constructed. "The peculiar circumstances of the moment may render a measure more or less wise, but cannot render it more or less constitutional." "Chief Justice John Marshall, A Friend of the Constitution No. V," *Alexandria Gazette*, July 5, 1819, in John Marshall's *Defense of McCulloch v. Maryland*. And there can be no question that it is the responsibility of this Court to enforce the limits on federal power by striking down acts of Congress that transgress those limits. *Marbury v. Madison, supra.*

The questions before us must be considered against the background of these basic principles.

I

In 2010, Congress enacted the Patient Protection and Affordable Care Act, 124 Stat. 119. The Act aims to increase the number of Americans covered by health insurance and decrease the cost of health care. The Act's 10 titles stretch over 900 pages and contain hundreds of provisions. This case concerns constitutional challenges to two key provisions, commonly referred to as the individual mandate and the Medicaid expansion.

The individual mandate requires most Americans to maintain "minimum essential" health insurance coverage. The mandate does not apply to some individuals, such as prisoners and undocumented aliens. Many individuals will receive the required coverage through their employer, or from a government program such as Medicaid or Medicare. But for individuals who are not exempt and do not receive health insurance through a third party, the means of satisfying the requirement is to purchase insurance from a private company.

Beginning in 2014, those who do not comply with the mandate must make a "[s]hared responsibility payment" to the Federal Government. That payment, which the Act describes as a "penalty," is calculated as a percentage of household income, subject to a floor based on a specified dollar amount and a ceiling based on the average annual premium the individual would have to pay for qualifying private health insurance. In 2016, for example, the penalty will be 2.5 percent of an individual's household income, but no less than $695 and no more than the average yearly premium for insurance that covers

60 percent of the cost of 10 specified services (e.g., prescription drugs and hospitalization). The Act provides that the penalty will be paid to the Internal Revenue Service [IRS] with an individual's taxes, and "shall be assessed and collected in the same manner" as tax penalties, such as the penalty for claiming too large an income tax refund. The Act, however, bars the IRS from using several of its normal enforcement tools, such as criminal prosecutions and levies. And some individuals who are subject to the mandate are nonetheless exempt from the penalty—for example, those with income below a certain threshold and members of Indian tribes.

On the day the President signed the Act into law, Florida and 12 other States filed a complaint in the Federal District Court for the Northern District of Florida. Those plaintiffs—who are both respondents and petitioners here, depending on the issue—were subsequently joined by 13 more States, several individuals, and the National Federation of Independent Business. The plaintiffs alleged, among other things, that the individual mandate provisions of the Act exceeded Congress's powers under Article I of the Constitution. The District Court agreed, holding that Congress lacked constitutional power to enact the individual mandate. The District Court determined that the individual mandate could not be severed from the remainder of the Act, and therefore struck down the Act in its entirety.

The Court of Appeals for the Eleventh Circuit affirmed in part and reversed in part. The court affirmed the District Court's holding that the individual mandate exceeds Congress's power. The panel unanimously agreed that the individual mandate did not impose a tax, and thus could not be authorized by Congress's power to "lay and collect Taxes." U.S. Const., Art. I, §8, cl. 1. A majority also held that the individual mandate was not supported by Congress's power to "regulate Commerce . . . among the several States." *Id.*, cl. 3. According to the majority, the Commerce Clause does not empower the Federal Government to order individuals to engage in commerce, and the Government's efforts to cast the individual mandate in a different light were unpersuasive. Judge Marcus dissented, reasoning that the individual mandate regulates economic activity that has a clear effect on interstate commerce.

Having held the individual mandate to be unconstitutional, the majority examined whether that provision could be severed from the remainder of the Act. The majority determined that, contrary to the District Court's view, it could. The court thus struck down only the individual mandate, leaving the Act's other provisions intact.

Other Courts of Appeals have also heard challenges to the individual mandate. The Sixth Circuit and the D.C. Circuit upheld the mandate as a valid exercise of Congress's commerce power. The Fourth Circuit determined that the Anti-Injunction Act prevents courts from considering the merits of that question. That statute bars suits "for the purpose of restraining the assessment or collection of any tax." A majority of the Fourth Circuit panel reasoned that the individual mandate's penalty is a tax within the meaning of the Anti-Injunction Act, because it is a financial assessment collected by the IRS through the normal means of taxation. The majority therefore determined that the plaintiffs could not challenge the individual mandate until after they paid the penalty.

The second provision of the Affordable Care Act directly challenged here is the Medicaid expansion. Enacted in 1965, Medicaid offers federal funding to States to assist pregnant women, children, needy families, the blind, the elderly, and the disabled in obtaining medical care. In order to receive that funding, States must comply with federal criteria governing matters such as who receives care and what services are provided at what cost. By 1982 every State had chosen to participate in Medicaid. Federal funds received through the Medicaid program have become a substantial part of state budgets, now constituting over 10 percent of most States' total revenue.

The Affordable Care Act expands the scope of the Medicaid program and increases the number of individuals the States must cover. For example, the Act requires state programs to provide Medicaid coverage to adults with incomes up to 133 percent of the federal poverty level, whereas many States now cover adults with children only if their income is considerably lower, and do not cover childless adults at all. The Act increases federal funding to cover the States' costs in expanding Medicaid coverage, although States will bear a portion of the costs on their own. If a State does not comply with the Act's new coverage requirements, it may lose not only the federal funding for those requirements, but all of its federal Medicaid funds.

Along with their challenge to the individual mandate, the state plaintiffs in the Eleventh Circuit argued that the Medicaid expansion exceeds Congress's constitutional powers. The Court of Appeals unanimously held that the Medicaid expansion is a valid exercise of Congress's power under the Spending Clause. And the court rejected the States' claim that the threatened loss of all federal Medicaid funding violates the Tenth Amendment by coercing them into complying with the Medicaid expansion. We granted *certiorari* to review the judgment of the Court of Appeals for the Eleventh Circuit with respect to both the individual mandate and the Medicaid expansion. Because no party supports the Eleventh Circuit's holding that the individual mandate can be completely severed from the remainder of the Affordable Care Act, we appointed an *amicus curiae* to defend that aspect of the judgment below. And because there is a reasonable argument that the Anti-Injunction Act deprives us of jurisdiction to hear challenges to the individual mandate, but no party supports that proposition, we appointed an *amicus curiae* to advance it.

II

Before turning to the merits, we need to be sure we have the authority to do so. The Anti-Injunction Act provides that "no suit for the purpose of restraining the assessment or collection of any tax shall be maintained in any court by any person, whether or not such person is the person against whom such tax was assessed." This statute protects the Government's ability to collect a consistent stream of revenue, by barring litigation to enjoin or otherwise obstruct the collection of taxes. Because of the Anti-Injunction Act, taxes can ordinarily be challenged only after they are paid, by suing for a refund.

The penalty for not complying with the Affordable Care Act's individual mandate first becomes enforceable in 2014. The present challenge to the mandate thus seeks to restrain the penalty's future collection. *Amicus* contends that the Internal Revenue Code treats the penalty as a tax, and that the Anti-Injunction Act therefore bars this suit.

The text of the pertinent statutes suggests otherwise. The Anti-Injunction Act applies to suits "for the purpose of restraining the assessment or collection of any *tax*." (emphasis added). Congress, however, chose to describe the "[s]hared responsibility payment" imposed on those who forgo health insurance not as a "tax," but as a "penalty." There is no immediate reason to think that a statute applying to "any tax" would apply to a "penalty."

Congress's decision to label this exaction a "penalty" rather than a "tax" is significant because the Affordable Care Act describes many other exactions it creates as "taxes." Where Congress uses certain language in one part of a statute and different language in another, it is generally presumed that Congress acts intentionally.

Amicus argues that even though Congress did not label the shared responsibility payment a tax, we should treat it as such under the Anti-Injunction Act because it functions like a tax. It is true that Congress cannot change whether an exaction is a tax or a penalty for constitutional purposes simply by describing it as one or the other. Congress may not, for example, expand its power under the Taxing Clause, or escape the Double Jeopardy Clause's constraint on criminal sanctions, by labeling a severe financial punishment a "tax."

The Anti-Injunction Act and the Affordable Care Act, however, are creatures of Congress's own creation. How they relate to each other is up to Congress, and the best evidence of Congress's intent is the statutory text. We have thus applied the Anti-Injunction Act to statutorily described "taxes" even where that label was inaccurate.

Congress can, of course, describe something as a penalty but direct that it nonetheless be treated as a tax for purposes of the Anti-Injunction Act. For example, 26 U.S.C. §6671(a) provides that "any reference in this title to 'tax' imposed by this title shall be deemed also to refer to the penalties and liabilities provided by" subchapter 68B of the Internal Revenue Code. Penalties in subchapter 68B are thus treated as taxes under Title 26, which includes the Anti-Injunction Act. The individual mandate, however, is not in subchapter 68B of the Code. Nor does any other provision state that references to taxes in Title 26 shall also be "deemed" to apply to the individual mandate.

Amicus attempts to show that Congress did render the Anti-Injunction Act applicable to the individual mandate, albeit by a more circuitous route. Section 5000A(g)(1) specifies that the penalty for not complying with the mandate "shall be assessed and collected in the same manner as an assessable penalty under subchapter B of chapter 68." Assessable penalties in subchapter 68B, in turn, "shall be assessed and collected in the same manner as taxes." According to *amicus*, by directing that the penalty be "assessed and collected in the same manner as taxes," §5000A(g)(1) made the Anti-Injunction Act applicable to this penalty.

The Government disagrees. It argues that §5000A(g)(1) does not direct courts to apply the Anti-Injunction Act, because §5000A(g) is a directive only to the Secretary of the Treasury to use the same "methodology and procedures" to collect the penalty that he uses to collect taxes. Brief for United States 32–33.

We think the Government has the better reading. As it observes, "Assessment" and "Collection" are chapters of the Internal Revenue Code providing the Secretary authority to assess and collect taxes, and generally specifying the means by which he shall do so. Section 5000A(g)(1)'s command that the penalty be "assessed and collected in the same manner" as taxes is best read as referring to those chapters and giving the Secretary the same authority and guidance with respect to the penalty. That interpretation is consistent with the remainder of §5000A(g), which instructs the Secretary on the tools he may use to collect the penalty. The Anti-Injunction Act, by contrast, says nothing about the procedures to be used in assessing and collecting taxes.

Amicus argues in the alternative that a different section of the Internal Revenue Code requires courts to treat the penalty as a tax under the Anti-Injunction Act. Section 6201(a) authorizes the Secretary to make "assessments of all taxes (including interest, additional amounts, additions to the tax, and *assessable penalties*)." (Emphasis added.) *Amicus* contends that the penalty must be a tax, because it is an assessable penalty and §6201(a) says that taxes include assessable penalties.

That argument has force only if §6201(a) is read in isolation. The Code contains many provisions treating taxes and assessable penalties as distinct terms. There would, for example, be no need for §6671(a) to deem "tax" to refer to certain assessable penalties if the Code already included all such penalties in the term "tax." Indeed, *amicus*'s earlier observation that the Code requires assessable penalties to be assessed and collected "in the same manner as taxes" makes little sense if assessable penalties are themselves taxes. In light of the Code's consistent distinction between the terms "tax" and "assessable penalty," we must accept the Government's interpretation: §6201(a) instructs the Secretary that his authority to assess taxes includes the authority to assess penalties, but it does not equate assessable penalties to taxes for other purposes.

The Affordable Care Act does not require that the penalty for failing to comply with the individual mandate be treated as a tax for purposes of the Anti-Injunction Act. The Anti-Injunction Act therefore does not apply to this suit, and we may proceed to the merits.

III

The Government advances two theories for the proposition that Congress had constitutional authority to enact the individual mandate. First, the Government argues that Congress had the power to enact the mandate under the Commerce Clause. Under that theory, Congress may order individuals to buy health insurance because the failure to do so affects interstate commerce, and could undercut the Affordable Care Act's other reforms. Second, the Government argues that if the commerce power does not support the mandate, we should nonetheless uphold it as an exercise of Congress's power to tax. According to the Government, even if Congress lacks the power to direct individuals to buy insurance, the only effect of the individual mandate is to raise taxes on those who do not do so, and thus the law may be upheld as a tax.

A

The Government's first argument is that the individual mandate is a valid exercise of Congress's power under the Commerce Clause and the Necessary and Proper Clause. According to the Government, the health care market is characterized by a significant cost-shifting problem. Everyone will eventually need health care at a time and to an extent they cannot predict, but if they do not have insurance, they often will not be able to pay for it. Because state and federal laws nonetheless require hospitals to provide a certain degree of care to individuals without regard to their ability to pay, hospitals end up receiving compensation for only a portion of the services they provide. To recoup the losses, hospitals pass on the cost to insurers through higher rates, and insurers, in turn, pass on the cost to policy holders in the form of higher premiums. Congress estimated that the cost of uncompensated care raises family health insurance premiums, on average, by over $1,000 per year.

In the Affordable Care Act, Congress addressed the problem of those who cannot obtain insurance coverage because of preexisting conditions or other health issues. It did so through the Act's "guaranteed-issue" and "community-rating" provisions. These provisions together prohibit insurance companies from denying coverage to those with such conditions or charging unhealthy individuals higher premiums than healthy individuals.

The guaranteed-issue and community-rating reforms do not, however, address the issue of healthy individuals who choose not to purchase insurance to cover potential health care needs. In fact, the reforms sharply exacerbate that problem, by providing an incentive for individuals to delay purchasing health insurance until they become sick, relying on the promise of guaranteed and affordable coverage. The reforms also threaten to impose massive new costs on insurers, who are required to accept unhealthy individuals but prohibited from charging them rates necessary to pay for their coverage. This will lead insurers to significantly increase premiums on everyone.

The individual mandate was Congress's solution to these problems. By requiring that individuals purchase health insurance, the mandate prevents cost-shifting by those who would otherwise go without it. In addition, the mandate forces into the insurance risk pool more healthy individuals, whose premiums on average will be higher than their health care expenses. This allows insurers to subsidize the costs of covering the unhealthy individuals the reforms require them to accept. The Government claims that Congress has power under the Commerce and Necessary and Proper Clauses to enact this solution.

1

The Government contends that the individual mandate is within Congress's power because the failure to purchase insurance "has a substantial and deleterious effect on interstate commerce" by creating the cost-shifting problem. Brief for United States 34. The path of our Commerce Clause decisions has not always run smooth, but it is now well established that Congress has broad authority under the Clause. We have recognized, for example, that "[t]he power of Congress over interstate commerce is not confined to the regulation of commerce among the states," but extends to activities that "have a substantial effect on interstate commerce." *United States v. Darby* (1941). Congress's power, moreover, is not limited to regulation of an activity that by itself substantially affects interstate commerce, but also extends to activities that do so only when aggregated with similar activities of others.

Given its expansive scope, it is no surprise that Congress has employed the commerce power in a wide variety of ways to address the pressing needs of the time. But Congress has never attempted to rely on that power to compel individuals not engaged in commerce to purchase an unwanted product. Legislative novelty is not necessarily fatal; there is a first time for everything. But sometimes "the most telling indication of [a] severe constitutional problem . . . is the lack of historical precedent" for Congress's action. *Free Enterprise Fund v. Public Company Accounting Oversight Bd.* (2010). At the very least, we should "pause to consider the implications of the Government's arguments" when confronted with such new conceptions of federal power. *United States v. Lopez* (1995).

The Constitution grants Congress the power to "*regulate* Commerce." Art. I, §8, cl. 3 (emphasis added). The power to regulate commerce presupposes the existence of commercial activity to be regulated. If the power to "regulate" something included the power to create it, many of the provisions in the Constitution would be superfluous. For example, the Constitution gives Congress the power to "coin Money," in addition to the power to "regulate the Value thereof." *Id.*, cl. 5. And it gives Congress the power to "raise and support Armies" and to "provide and maintain a Navy," in addition to the power to "make Rules for the Government and Regulation of the land and naval Forces." *Id.*, cls. 12–14. If the power to regulate the armed forces or the value of money included the power to bring the subject of the regulation into existence, the specific grant of such powers would have been unnecessary. The language of the Constitution reflects the natural understanding that the power to regulate assumes there is already something to be regulated.

Our precedent also reflects this understanding. As expansive as our cases construing the scope of the commerce power have been, they all have one thing in common: They uniformly describe the power as reaching "activity." It is nearly impossible to avoid the word when quoting them.

The individual mandate, however, does not regulate existing commercial activity. It instead compels individuals to become active in commerce by purchasing a product, on the ground that their failure to do so affects interstate commerce. Construing the Commerce Clause to permit Congress to regulate individuals precisely because they are doing nothing would open a new and potentially vast domain to congressional authority. Every day individuals do not do an infinite number of things. In some cases they decide not to do something; in others they simply fail to do it. Allowing Congress to justify federal regulation by pointing to the effect of inaction on commerce would bring countless decisions an individual could potentially make within the scope of federal regulation, and—under the Government's theory—empower Congress to make those decisions for him.

Applying the Government's logic to the familiar case of *Wickard v. Filburn* shows how far that logic would carry us from the notion of a government of limited powers. In *Wickard*, the Court famously upheld a federal penalty imposed on a farmer for growing wheat for consumption on his own farm. That amount of wheat caused the farmer to exceed his quota under a program designed to support the price of wheat by limiting supply. The Court rejected the farmer's argument that growing wheat for home consumption was beyond the reach of the commerce power. It did so on the ground that the farmer's decision to grow wheat for his own use allowed him to avoid purchasing wheat in the market. That decision, when considered in the aggregate along with similar decisions of others, would have had a substantial effect on the interstate market for wheat.

Wickard has long been regarded as "perhaps the most far reaching example of Commerce Clause authority over intrastate activity," *Lopez*, 514 U.S., but the Government's theory in this case would go much further. Under *Wickard* it is within Congress's power to regulate the marker for wheat by supporting its price. But price can be supported by increasing demand as well as by decreasing supply. The aggregated decisions of some consumers not to purchase wheat have a substantial effect on the price of wheat, just as decisions not to purchase health insurance have on the price of insurance. Congress can therefore command that those not buying wheat do so, just as it argues here that it may command that those not buying health insurance do so. The farmer in *Wickard* was at least actively engaged in the production of wheat, and the Government could regulate that activity because of its effect on commerce. The Government's theory here would effectively override that limitation, by establishing that individuals may be regulated under the Commerce Clause whenever enough of them are not doing something the Government would have them do.

Indeed, the Government's logic would justify a mandatory purchase to solve almost any problem. To consider a different example in the health care market, many Americans do not eat a balanced diet. That group makes up a larger percentage of the total population than those without health insurance. The failure of that group to have a healthy diet increases health care costs, to a greater extent than the failure of the uninsured to purchase insurance. Those increased costs are borne in part by other Americans who must pay more, just as the uninsured shift costs to the insured. Congress addressed the insurance problem by ordering everyone to buy insurance. Under the Government's theory, Congress could address the diet problem by ordering everyone to buy vegetables.

People, for reasons of their own, often fail to do things that would be good for them or good for society. Those failures—joined with the similar failures of others—can readily have a substantial effect on interstate commerce. Under the Government's logic, that authorizes Congress to use its commerce power to compel citizens to act as the Government would have them act.

That is not the country the Framers of our Constitution envisioned. James Madison explained that the Commerce Clause was "an addition which few oppose and from which no apprehensions are entertained." *The Federalist*, No. 45. While Congress's authority under the Commerce Clause has of course expanded with the growth of the national economy, our cases have "always recognized that the power to regulate commerce, though broad indeed, has limits." *Maryland v. Wirtz* (1968). The Government's theory would erode those limits, permitting Congress to reach beyond the natural extent of its authority, "everywhere extending the sphere of its activity and drawing all power into its impetuous vortex." *The Federalist*, No. 48 (J. Madison). Congress already enjoys vast power to regulate much of what we do. Accepting the Government's theory would give Congress the same license to regulate what we do not do, fundamentally changing the relation between the citizen and the Federal Government.

To an economist, perhaps, there is no difference between activity and inactivity; both have measurable economic effects on commerce. But the distinction between doing something and doing nothing would not have been lost on the Framers, who were "practical statesmen," not metaphysical philosophers. *Industrial Union Dept., AFL–CIO v. American Petroleum Institute* (1980). As we have explained, "the framers of the Constitution were not mere visionaries, toying with speculations or theories, but practical men, dealing with the facts of political life as they understood them, putting into form the government they were creating, and prescribing in language clear and intelligible the powers that government was to take." *South Carolina v. United*

States (1905). The Framers gave Congress the power to regulate commerce, not to compel it, and for over 200 years both our decisions and Congress's actions have reflected this understanding. There is no reason to depart from that understanding now.

The Government sees things differently. It argues that because sickness and injury are not only unpredictable but unavoidable, "the uninsured as a class are active in the market for health care, which they regularly seek and obtain." Brief for United States 50. The individual mandate "merely regulates how individuals finance and pay for that active participation—requiring that they do so through insurance, rather than through attempted self-insurance with the back-stop of shifting costs to others." *Ibid.*

The Government repeats the phrase "active in the market for health care" throughout its brief, but that concept has no constitutional significance. An individual who bought a car two years ago and may buy another in the future is not "active in the car market" in any pertinent sense. The phrase "active in the market" cannot obscure the fact that most of those regulated by the individual mandate are not currently engaged in any commercial activity involving health care, and that fact is fatal to the Government's effort to "regulate the uninsured as a class." Our precedents recognize Congress's power to regulate "class[es] of *activities*," *Gonzales v. Raich* (2005) (emphasis added), not classes of individuals, apart from any activity in which they are engaged.

The individual mandate's regulation of the uninsured as a class is, in fact, particularly divorced from any link to existing commercial activity. The mandate primarily affects healthy, often young adults who are less likely to need significant health care and have other priorities for spending their money. It is precisely because these individuals, as an actuarial class, incur relatively low health care costs that the mandate helps counter the effect of forcing insurance companies to cover others who impose greater costs than their premiums are allowed to reflect. If the individual mandate is targeted as a class, it is a class whose commercial inactivity rather than activity is its defining feature.

The Government, however, claims that this does not matter. The Government regards it as sufficient to trigger Congress's authority that almost all those who are uninsured will, at some unknown point in the future, engage in a health care transaction. Asserting that "[t]here is no temporal limitation in the Commerce Clause," the Government argues that because "[e]veryone subject to this regulation is in or will be in the health care market," they can be "regulated in advance." Tr. of Oral Arg. 109 (Mar. 27, 2012).

The proposition that Congress may dictate the conduct of an individual today because of prophesied future activity finds no support in our precedent. We have said that Congress can anticipate the effects on commerce of an economic activity. But we have never permitted Congress to anticipate that activity itself in order to regulate individuals not currently engaged in commerce. Each one of our cases, including those cited by Justice Ginsburg, *post*, involved preexisting economic activity.

Everyone will likely participate in the markets for food, clothing, transportation, shelter, or energy; that does not authorize Congress to direct them to purchase particular products in those or other markets today. The Commerce Clause is not a general license to regulate an individual from cradle to grave, simply because he will predictably engage in particular transactions. Any police power to regulate individuals as such, as opposed to their activities, remains vested in the States.

The Government argues that the individual mandate can be sustained as a sort of exception to this rule, because health insurance is a unique product. According to the Government, upholding the individual mandate would not justify mandatory purchases of items such as cars or broccoli because, as the Government puts it, "[h]ealth insurance is not purchased for its own sake like a car or broccoli; it is a means of financing health care consumption and covering universal risks." Reply Brief for United States 19. But cars and broccoli are no more purchased for their "own sake" than health insurance. They are purchased to cover the need for transportation and food.

The Government says that health insurance and health care financing are "inherently integrated." Brief for United States 41. But that does not mean the compelled purchase of the first is properly regarded as a regulation of the second. No matter how "inherently integrated" health insurance and health care consumption may be, they are not the same thing: They involve different transactions, entered into at different times, with different providers. And for most of those targeted by the mandate, significant health care needs will be years, or even decades, away. The proximity and degree of connection between the mandate and the subsequent commercial activity is too lacking to justify an exception of the sort urged by the Government. The individual mandate forces individuals into commerce precisely because they elected to refrain from commercial activity. Such a law cannot be sustained under a clause authorizing Congress to "regulate Commerce."

2

The Government next contends that Congress has the power under the Necessary and Proper Clause to enact the individual mandate because the mandate is an "integral part of a comprehensive scheme of economic regulation"—the guaranteed-issue and community-rating insurance reforms. Brief for United States 24. Under this argument, it is not necessary to consider the effect that an individual's inactivity may have on interstate commerce; it is enough that Congress regulate commercial activity in a way that requires regulation of inactivity to be effective.

The power to "make all Laws which shall be necessary and proper for carrying into Execution" the powers enumerated in the Constitution, Art. I, §8, cl. 18, vests Congress with authority to enact provisions "incidental to the [enumerated] power, and conducive to its beneficial exercise," *McCulloch*, 4 Wheat. Although the Clause gives Congress authority to "legislate on that vast mass of incidental powers which must be involved in the constitution," it does not license the exercise of any "great substantive and independent power[s]" beyond those specifically enumerated. *Id*. Instead, the Clause is "merely a declaration, for the removal of all uncertainty, that the means of carrying into execution those [powers] otherwise granted are included in the grant." *Kinsella v. United States* (1960).

As our jurisprudence under the Necessary and Proper Clause has developed, we have been very deferential to Congress's determination that a regulation is "necessary." We have thus upheld laws that are "'convenient, or useful' or 'conducive' to the authority's 'beneficial exercise.'" *United States v. Comstock* (2010). But we have also carried out our responsibility to declare unconstitutional those laws that undermine the structure of government established by the Constitution. Such laws, which are not "consist[ent] with the letter and spirit of the constitution," *McCulloch, supra*, are not "proper [means] for carrying into Execution" Congress's enumerated powers. Rather, they are, "in the words of *The Federalist*, 'merely acts of usurpation' which 'deserve to be treated as such.'" *Printz v. United States* (1997).

Applying these principles, the individual mandate cannot be sustained under the Necessary and Proper Clause as an essential component of the insurance reforms. Each of our prior cases upholding laws under that Clause involved exercises of authority derivative of, and in service to, a granted power. For example, we have upheld provisions permitting continued confinement of those already in federal custody when they could not be safely released, *Comstock, supra*; criminalizing bribes involving organizations receiving federal funds, *Sabri v. United States* (2004); and tolling state statutes of limitations while cases are pending in federal court, *Jinks v. Richland County* (2003). The individual mandate, by contrast, vests Congress with the extraordinary ability to create the necessary predicate to the exercise of an enumerated power.

This is in no way an authority that is "narrow in scope," *Comstock, supra,* or "incidental" to the exercise of the commerce power, *McCulloch, supra*. Rather, such a conception of the Necessary and Proper Clause would work a substantial expansion of federal authority. No longer would Congress be limited to regulating under the Commerce Clause those who by some preexisting activity bring themselves within the sphere of federal regulation. Instead, Congress could reach beyond the natural limit of its authority and draw within its regulatory scope those who otherwise would be outside of it. Even if the individual mandate is "necessary" to the Act's insurance reforms, such an expansion of federal power is not a "proper" means for making those reforms effective.

The Government relies primarily on our decision in *Gonzales v. Raich*. In *Raich*, we considered "comprehensive legislation to regulate the interstate market" in marijuana. Certain individuals sought an exemption from that regulation on the ground that they engaged in only intrastate possession and consumption. We denied any exemption, on the ground that marijuana is a fungible commodity, so that any marijuana could be readily diverted into the interstate market. Congress's attempt to regulate the interstate market for marijuana would therefore have been substantially undercut if it could not also regulate intrastate possession and consumption. *Id.* Accordingly, we recognized that "Congress was acting well within its authority" under the Necessary and Proper Clause even though its "regulation ensnare[d] some purely intrastate activity." *Id. Raich* thus did not involve the exercise of any "great substantive and independent power," *McCulloch, supra,* of the sort at issue here. Instead, it concerned only the constitutionality of "individual *applications* of a concededly valid statutory scheme." *Raich, supra* (emphasis added).

Just as the individual mandate cannot be sustained as a law regulating the substantial effects of the failure to purchase health insurance, neither can it be upheld as a "necessary and proper" component of the insurance reforms. The commerce power thus does not authorize the mandate.

B

That is not the end of the matter. Because the Commerce Clause does not support the individual mandate, it is necessary to turn to the Government's second argument: that the mandate may be upheld as within Congress's enumerated power to "lay and collect Taxes." Art. I, §8, cl. 1.

The Government's tax power argument asks us to view the statute differently than we did in considering its commerce power theory. In making its Commerce Clause argument, the Government defended the mandate as a regulation requiring individuals to purchase health insurance. The Government does not claim that the taxing power allows Congress to issue such a command. Instead, the Government asks us to read the mandate not as ordering individuals to buy insurance, but rather as imposing a tax on those who do not buy that product.

The text of a statute can sometimes have more than one possible meaning. To take a familiar example, a law that reads "no vehicles in the park" might, or might not, ban bicycles in the park. And it is well established that if a statute has two possible meanings, one of which violates the Constitution, courts should adopt the meaning that does not do so. Justice Story said 180 years ago: "No court ought, unless the terms of an act rendered it unavoidable, to give a construction to it which should involve a violation, however unintentional, of the constitution." *Parsons v. Bedford* (1830). Justice Holmes made the same point a century later: "[T]he rule is settled that as between two possible interpretations of a statute, by one of which it would be unconstitutional and by the other valid, our plain duty is to adopt that which will save the Act." *Blodgett v. Holden* (1927).

The most straightforward reading of the mandate is that it commands individuals to purchase insurance. After all, it states that individuals "shall" maintain health insurance. Congress thought it could enact such a command under the Commerce Clause, and the Government primarily defended the law on that basis. But, for the reasons explained above, the Commerce Clause does not give Congress that power. Under our precedent, it is therefore necessary to ask whether the Government's alternative reading of the statute—that it only imposes a tax on those without insurance—is a reasonable one.

Under the mandate, if an individual does not maintain health insurance, the only consequence is that he must make an additional payment to the IRS when he pays his taxes. That, according to the Government, means the mandate can be regarded as establishing a condition—not owning health insurance—that triggers a tax—the required payment to the IRS. Under that theory, the mandate is not a legal command to buy insurance. Rather, it makes going without insurance just another thing the Government taxes, like buying gasoline or earning income. And if the mandate is in effect just a tax hike on certain taxpayers who do not have health insurance, it may be within Congress's constitutional power to tax.

The question is not whether that is the most natural interpretation of the mandate, but only whether it is a "fairly possible" one. *Crowell v. Benson* (1932). As we have explained, "every reasonable construction must be resorted to, in order to save a statute from unconstitutionality." *Hooper v. California* (1895). The Government asks us to interpret the mandate as imposing a tax, if it would otherwise violate the Constitution. Granting the Act the full measure of deference owed to federal statutes, it can be so read, for the reasons set forth below.

C

The exaction the Affordable Care Act imposes on those without health insurance looks like a tax in many respects. The "[s]hared responsibility payment," as the statute entitles it, is paid into the Treasury by "taxpayer[s]" when they file their tax returns. It does not apply to individuals who do not pay federal income taxes because their household income is less than the filing threshold in the Internal Revenue Code. For taxpayers who do owe the payment, its amount is determined by such familiar factors as taxable income, number of dependents, and joint filing status. The requirement to pay is found in the Internal Revenue Code and enforced by the IRS, which—as we previously explained—must assess and collect it "in the same manner as taxes." This process yields the essential feature of any tax: it produces at least some revenue for the Government. Indeed, the payment is expected to raise about $4 billion per year by 2017.

It is of course true that the Act describes the payment as a "penalty," not a "tax." But while that label is fatal to the application of the Anti-Injunction Act, it does not determine whether the payment may be viewed as an exercise of Congress's taxing power. It is up to Congress whether to apply the Anti-Injunction Act to any particular statute, so it makes sense to be guided by Congress's choice of label on that question. That choice does not, however, control whether an exaction is within Congress's constitutional power to tax.

Our precedent reflects this: In 1922, we decided two challenges to the "Child Labor Tax" on the same day. In the first, we held that a suit to enjoin collection of the so-called tax was barred by the Anti-Injunction Act. Congress knew that suits to obstruct taxes had to await payment under the Anti-Injunction Act; Congress called the child labor tax a tax; Congress therefore intended the Anti-Injunction Act to apply. In the second case, however, we held that the same exaction, although labeled a tax, was not in fact authorized by Congress's taxing power. That constitutional question was not controlled by Congress's choice of label.

We have similarly held that exactions not labeled taxes nonetheless were authorized by Congress's power to tax. In the License Tax Cases, for example, we held that federal licenses to sell liquor and lottery tickets—for which the licensee had to pay a fee—could be sustained as exercises of the taxing power. And in *New York v. United States* we upheld as a tax a "surcharge" on out-of-state nuclear waste shipments, a portion of which was paid to the Federal Treasury. We thus ask whether the shared responsibility payment falls within Congress's taxing power, "[d]isregarding the designation of the exaction, and viewing its substance and application." *United States v. Constantine* (1935).

Our cases confirm this functional approach. For example, in *Bailey v. Drexel Furniture Co.* (1922), we focused on three practical characteristics of the so-called tax on employing child laborers that convinced us the "tax" was actually a penalty. First, the tax imposed an exceedingly heavy burden—10 percent of a company's net income—on those who employed children, no matter how small their infraction. Second, it imposed that exaction only on those who knowingly employed underage laborers. Such scienter requirements are typical of punitive statutes, because Congress often wishes to punish only those who intentionally break the law. Third, this "tax" was enforced in part by the Department of Labor, an agency responsible for punishing violations of labor laws, not collecting revenue.

The same analysis here suggests that the shared responsibility payment may for constitutional purposes be considered a tax, not a penalty: First, for most Americans the amount due will be far less than the price of insurance, and, by statute, it can never be more. It may often be a reasonable financial decision to make the payment rather than purchase insurance, unlike the "prohibitory" financial punishment in *Drexel Furniture*. Second, the individual mandate contains no scienter requirement. Third, the payment is collected solely by the IRS through the normal means of taxation—except that the Service is not allowed to use those means most suggestive of a punitive sanction, such as criminal prosecution. The reasons the Court in *Drexel Furniture* held that what was called a "tax" there was a penalty support the conclusion that what is called a "penalty" here may be viewed as a tax.

None of this is to say that the payment is not intended to affect individual conduct. Although the payment will raise considerable revenue, it is plainly designed to expand health insurance coverage. But taxes that seek to influence conduct are nothing new. Some of our earliest federal taxes sought to deter the purchase of imported manufactured goods in order to foster the growth of domestic industry. Today, federal and state taxes can compose more than half the retail price of cigarettes, not just to raise more money, but to encourage people to quit smoking. And we have upheld such obviously regulatory measures as taxes on selling marijuana and sawed-off shotguns. Indeed, "[e]very tax is in some measure regulatory. To some extent it interposes an economic impediment to the activity taxed as compared with others not taxed." *Sonzinsky v. United States* (1937). That §5000A seeks to shape decisions about whether to buy health insurance does not mean that it cannot be a valid exercise of the taxing power.

In distinguishing penalties from taxes, this Court has explained that "if the concept of penalty means anything, it means punishment for an unlawful act or omission." *United States v. Reorganized CF&I Fabricators of Utah, Inc.* (1996). While the individual mandate clearly aims to induce the purchase of health insurance, it need not be read to declare that failing to do so is unlawful. Neither the Act nor any other law attaches negative legal consequences to not buying health insurance, beyond requiring a payment to the IRS. The Government agrees with that reading, confirming that if someone chooses to pay rather than obtain health insurance, they have fully complied with the law.

Indeed, it is estimated that four million people each year will choose to pay the IRS rather than buy insurance. We would expect Congress to be troubled by that prospect if such conduct were unlawful. That Congress apparently regards such extensive failure to comply with the mandate as tolerable suggests that Congress did not think it was creating four million outlaws. It suggests instead that the shared responsibility payment merely imposes a tax citizens may lawfully choose to pay in lieu of buying health insurance.

The plaintiffs contend that Congress's choice of language—stating that individuals "shall" obtain insurance or pay a "penalty"—requires reading §5000A as punishing unlawful conduct, even if that interpretation would render the law unconstitutional. We have rejected a similar argument before. In *New York v. United States* we examined a statute providing that "[e]ach State shall be responsible for providing . . . for the disposal of . . . low-level radioactive waste." A State that shipped its waste to another State was exposed to surcharges by the receiving State, a portion of which would be paid over to the Federal Government. And a State that did not adhere to the statutory scheme faced "[p]enalties for failure to comply," including increases in the surcharge. *New York* urged us to read the statute as a federal command that the state legislature enact legislation to dispose of its waste, which would have violated the Constitution. To avoid that outcome, we interpreted the statute to impose only "a series of incentives" for the State to take responsibility for its waste. We then sustained the charge paid to the Federal Government as an exercise of the taxing power. We see no insurmountable obstacle to a similar approach here.

The joint dissenters argue that we cannot uphold §5000A as a tax because Congress did not "frame" it as such. In effect, they contend that even if the Constitution permits Congress to do exactly what we interpret this statute to do, the law must be struck down because Congress used the wrong labels. An example may help illustrate why labels should not control here. Suppose Congress enacted a statute providing that every taxpayer who owns a house without energy efficient windows must pay $50 to the IRS. The amount due is adjusted based on factors such as taxable income and joint filing status, and is paid along with the taxpayer's income tax return. Those whose income is below the filing threshold need not pay. The required payment is not called a "tax," a "penalty," or anything else. No one would doubt that this law imposed a tax, and was within Congress's power to tax. That conclusion should not change simply because Congress used the word "penalty" to describe the payment. Interpreting such a law to be a tax would hardly "[i]mpos[e] a tax through judicial legislation." Rather, it would give practical effect to the Legislature's enactment.

Our precedent demonstrates that Congress had the power to impose the exaction in §5000A under the taxing power, and that §5000A need not be read to do more than impose a tax. That is sufficient to sustain it. The "question of the constitutionality of action taken by Congress does not depend on recitals of the power which it undertakes to exercise." *Woods v. Cloyd W. Miller Co.* (1948).

Even if the taxing power enables Congress to impose a tax on not obtaining health insurance, any tax must still comply with other requirements in the Constitution. Plaintiffs argue that the shared responsibility payment does not do so, citing Article I, §9, clause 4. That clause provides: "No Capitation, or other direct, Tax shall be laid, unless in Proportion to the Census or Enumeration herein before directed to be taken." This requirement means that any "direct Tax" must be apportioned so that each State pays in proportion to its population. According to the plaintiffs, if the individual mandate imposes a tax, it is a direct tax, and it is unconstitutional because Congress made no effort to apportion it among the States.

Even when the Direct Tax Clause was written it was unclear what else, other than a capitation (also known as a "head tax" or a "poll tax"), might be a direct tax. Soon after the framing, Congress passed a tax on ownership of carriages, over James Madison's objection that it was an unapportioned direct tax. This Court upheld the tax, in part reasoning that apportioning such a tax would make little sense, because it would have required taxing carriage owners at dramatically different rates depending on how many carriages were in their home State. The Court was unanimous, and those Justices who wrote opinions either directly asserted or strongly suggested that only two forms of taxation were direct: capitations and land taxes.

That narrow view of what a direct tax might be persisted for a century. In 1880, for example, we explained that "direct taxes, within the meaning of the Constitution, are only capitation taxes, as expressed in that instrument, and taxes on real estate." *Springer v. United States* (1881). In 1895, we expanded our interpretation to include taxes on personal property and income from personal property, in the course of striking down aspects of the federal income tax. *Pollock v. Farmers' Loan & Trust Co.* (1895). That result was overturned by the Sixteenth Amendment, although we continued to consider taxes on personal property to be direct taxes.

A tax on going without health insurance does not fall within any recognized category of direct tax. It is not a capitation. Capitations are taxes paid by every person, "without regard to property, profession, or *any other circumstance*." *Hylton v. United States* (1796) (emphasis altered). The whole point of the shared responsibility payment is that it is triggered by specific circumstances—earning a certain amount of income but not obtaining health insurance. The payment is also plainly not a tax on the ownership of land or personal property. The shared responsibility payment is thus not a direct tax that must be apportioned among the several States.

There may, however, be a more fundamental objection to a tax on those who lack health insurance. Even if only a tax, the payment under §5000A(b) remains a burden that the Federal Government imposes for an omission, not an act. If it is troubling to interpret the Commerce Clause as authorizing Congress to regulate those who abstain from commerce, perhaps it should be similarly troubling to permit Congress to impose a tax for not doing something.

Three considerations allay this concern. First, and most importantly, it is abundantly clear the Constitution does not guarantee that individuals may avoid taxation through inactivity. A capitation, after all, is a tax that everyone must pay simply for existing, and capitations are expressly contemplated by the Constitution. The Court today holds that our Constitution protects us from federal regulation under the Commerce Clause so long as we abstain from the regulated activity. But from its creation, the Constitution has made no such promise with respect to taxes.

Whether the mandate can be upheld under the Commerce Clause is a question about the scope of federal authority. Its answer depends on whether Congress can exercise what all acknowledge to be the novel course of directing individuals to purchase insurance. Congress's use of the Taxing Clause to encourage buying something is, by contrast, not new. Tax incentives already promote, for example, purchasing homes and professional educations. Sustaining the mandate as a tax depends only on whether Congress has properly exercised its taxing power to encourage purchasing health insurance, not whether it can. Upholding the individual mandate under the Taxing Clause thus does not recognize any new federal power. It determines that Congress has used an existing one.

Second, Congress's ability to use its taxing power to influence conduct is not without limits. A few of our cases policed these limits aggressively, invalidating punitive exactions obviously designed to regulate behavior otherwise regarded at the time as beyond federal authority. More often and more recently we have declined to closely examine the regulatory motive or effect of revenue-raising measures. We have nonetheless maintained that "there comes a time in the extension of the penalizing features of the so-called tax when it loses its character as such and becomes a mere penalty with the characteristics of regulation and punishment." *Department of Revenue of Mont. v. Kurth Ranch* (1994) (quoting *Drexel Furniture, supra*).

We have already explained that the shared responsibility payment's practical characteristics pass muster as a tax under our narrowest interpretations of the taxing power. *Supra*. Because the tax at hand is within even those strict limits, we need not here decide the precise point at which an exaction becomes so punitive that the taxing power does not authorize it. It remains true, however, that the "power to tax is not the power to destroy while this Court sits." *Oklahoma Tax Comm'n v. Texas Co.* (1949).

Third, although the breadth of Congress's power to tax is greater than its power to regulate commerce, the taxing power does not give Congress the same degree of control over individual behavior. Once we recognize that Congress may regulate a particular decision under the Commerce Clause, the Federal Government can bring its full weight to bear. Congress may simply command individuals to do as it directs. An individual who disobeys may be subjected to criminal sanctions. Those sanctions can include not only fines and imprisonment, but all the attendant consequences of being branded a criminal: deprivation of otherwise protected civil rights, such as the right to bear arms or vote in elections; loss of employment opportunities; social stigma; and severe disabilities in other controversies, such as custody or immigration disputes.

By contrast, Congress's authority under the taxing power is limited to requiring an individual to pay money into the Federal Treasury, no more. If a tax is properly paid, the Government has no power to compel or punish individuals subject to it. We do not make light of the severe burden that taxation—especially taxation motivated by a regulatory purpose—can impose. But imposition of a tax nonetheless leaves an individual with a lawful choice to do or not do a certain act, so long as he is willing to pay a tax levied on that choice.

The Affordable Care Act's requirement that certain individuals pay a financial penalty for not obtaining health insurance may reasonably be characterized as a tax. Because the Constitution permits such a tax, it is not our role to forbid it, or to pass upon its wisdom or fairness.

D

Justice Ginsburg questions the necessity of rejecting the Government's commerce power argument, given that §5000A can be upheld under the taxing power. But the statute reads more naturally as a command to buy insurance than as a tax, and I would uphold it as a command if the Constitution allowed it. It is only because the Commerce Clause does not authorize such a command that it is necessary to reach the taxing power question. And it is only because we have a duty to construe a statute to save it, if fairly possible, that §5000A can be interpreted as a tax. Without deciding the Commerce Clause question, I would find no basis to adopt such a saving construction.

The Federal Government does not have the power to order people to buy health insurance. Section 5000A would therefore be unconstitutional if read as a command. The Federal Government does have the power to impose a tax on those without health insurance. Section 5000A is therefore constitutional, because it can reasonably be read as a tax.

IV

A

The States also contend that the Medicaid expansion exceeds Congress's authority under the Spending Clause. They claim that Congress is coercing the States to adopt the changes it wants by threatening to withhold all of a State's Medicaid grants, unless the State accepts the new expanded funding and complies with the conditions that come with it. This, they argue, violates the basic principle that the "Federal Government may not compel the States to enact or administer a federal regulatory program." *New York.*

There is no doubt that the Act dramatically increases state obligations under Medicaid. The current Medicaid program requires States to cover only certain discrete categories of needy individuals—pregnant women, children, needy families, the blind, the elderly, and the disabled. There is no mandatory coverage for most childless adults, and the States typically do not offer any such coverage. The States also enjoy considerable flexibility with respect to the coverage levels for parents of needy families. On average, States cover only those unemployed parents who make less than 37 percent of the federal poverty level, and only those employed parents who make less than 63 percent of the poverty line.

The Medicaid provisions of the Affordable Care Act, in contrast, require States to expand their Medicaid programs by 2014 to cover all individuals under the age of 65 with incomes below 133 percent of the federal poverty line. The Act also establishes a new "[e]ssential health benefits" package, which States must provide to all new Medicaid recipients—a level sufficient to satisfy a recipient's obligations under the individual mandate. The Affordable Care Act provides that the Federal Government will pay 100 percent of the costs of covering these newly eligible individuals through 2016. In the following years, the federal payment level gradually decreases, to a minimum of 90 percent. In light of the expansion in coverage mandated by the Act, the Federal Government estimates that its Medicaid spending will increase by approximately $100 billion per year, nearly 40 percent above current levels.

The Spending Clause grants Congress the power "to pay the Debts and provide for the . . . general Welfare of the United States." U.S. Const., Art. I, §8, cl. 1.

We have long recognized that Congress may use this power to grant federal funds to the States, and may condition such a grant upon the States' "taking certain actions that Congress could not require them to take." *College Savings Bank*, 527 U.S. Such measures "encourage a State to regulate in a particular way, [and] influenc[e] a State's policy choices." *New York, supra.* The conditions imposed by Congress ensure that the funds are used by the States to "provide for the . . . general Welfare" in the manner Congress intended.

At the same time, our cases have recognized limits on Congress's power under the Spending Clause to secure state compliance with federal objectives. "We have repeatedly characterized . . . Spending Clause legislation as 'much in the nature of a contract.'" *Barnes v. Gorman* (2002) (quoting *Pennhurst State School and Hospital v. Halderman* (1981)). The legitimacy of Congress's exercise of the spending power "thus rests on whether the State voluntarily and knowingly accepts the terms of the 'contract.'" *Pennhurst, supra.* Respecting this limitation is critical to ensuring that Spending Clause legislation does not undermine the status of the States as independent sovereigns in our federal system. That system "rests on what might at first seem a counterintuitive insight, that 'freedom is enhanced by the creation of two governments, not one.'" *Bond*, 564 U.S. (quoting *Alden v. Maine* (1999)). For this reason, "the Constitution has never been understood to confer upon Congress the ability to require the States to govern according to Congress's instructions." *New York, supra.* Otherwise, the two-government system established by the Framers would give way to a system that vests power in one central government, and individual liberty would suffer.

That insight has led this Court to strike down federal legislation that commandeers a State's legislative or administrative apparatus for federal purposes. It has also led us to scrutinize Spending Clause legislation to ensure that Congress is not using financial inducements to exert a "power akin to undue influence." *Steward Machine Co. v. Davis* (1937). Congress may use its spending power to create incentives for States to act in accordance with federal policies. But when "pressure turns into compulsion," *ibid.*, the legislation runs contrary to our system of federalism. "[T]he Constitution simply does not give Congress the authority to require the States to regulate." *New York.* That is true whether Congress directly commands a State to regulate or indirectly coerces a State to adopt a federal regulatory system as its own.

Permitting the Federal Government to force the States to implement a federal program would threaten the political accountability key to our federal system. "[W]here the Federal Government directs the States to regulate, it may be state officials who will bear the brunt of public disapproval, while the federal officials who devised the regulatory program may remain insulated from the electoral ramifications of their decision." *Id.* Spending Clause programs do not pose this danger when a State has a legitimate choice whether to accept the federal conditions in exchange for federal funds. In such a situation, state officials can fairly be held politically accountable for choosing to accept or refuse the federal offer. But when the State has no choice, the Federal Government can achieve its objectives without accountability, just as in *New York* and *Printz*. Indeed, this danger is heightened when Congress acts under the Spending Clause, because Congress can use that power to implement federal policy it could not impose directly under its enumerated powers.

We addressed such concerns in *Steward Machine*. That case involved a federal tax on employers that was abated if the businesses paid into a state unemployment plan that met certain federally specified conditions. An employer sued, alleging that the tax was impermissibly "driv[ing] the state legislatures under the whip of economic pressure into the enactment of unemployment compensation laws at the bidding of the central government." 301 U.S. We acknowledged the danger that the Federal Government might employ its taxing power to exert a "power akin to undue influence" upon the States. *Id.* But we observed that Congress adopted the challenged tax and abatement program to channel money to the States that would otherwise have gone into the Federal Treasury for use in providing national unemployment services. Congress was willing to direct businesses to instead pay the money into state programs only on the condition that the money be used for the same purposes. Predicating tax abatement on a State's adoption of a particular type of unemployment legislation was therefore a means to "safeguard [the Federal Government's] own treasury." *Id.* We held that "[i]n such circumstances, if in no others, inducement or persuasion does not go beyond the bounds of power." *Ibid.*

In rejecting the argument that the federal law was a "[weapon] of coercion, destroying or impairing the autonomy of the states," the Court noted that there was no reason to suppose that the State in that case acted other than through "her unfettered will." *Id.* Indeed, the State itself did "not offer a suggestion that in passing the unemployment law she was affected by duress." *Id.*

As our decision in *Steward Machine* confirms, Congress may attach appropriate conditions to federal taxing and spending programs to preserve its control over the use of federal funds. In the typical case, we look to the States to defend their prerogatives by adopting "the simple expedient of not yielding" to federal blandishments when they do not want to embrace the federal policies as their own. *Massachusetts v. Mellon* (1923). The States are separate and independent sovereigns. Sometimes they have to act like it.

The States, however, argue that the Medicaid expansion is far from the typical case. They object that Congress has "crossed the line distinguishing encouragement from coercion," *New York, supra,* in the way it has structured the funding: Instead of simply refusing to grant the new funds to States that will not accept the new conditions, Congress has also threatened to withhold those States' existing Medicaid funds. The States claim that this threat serves no purpose other than to force unwilling States to sign up for the dramatic expansion in health care coverage effected by the Act.

Given the nature of the threat and the programs at issue here, we must agree. We have upheld Congress's authority to condition the receipt of funds on the States' complying with restrictions on the use of those funds, because that is the means by which Congress ensures that the funds are spent according to its view of the "general Welfare." Conditions that do not here govern the use of the funds, however, cannot be justified on that basis. When, for example, such conditions take the form of threats to terminate other significant independent grants, the conditions are properly viewed as a means of pressuring the States to accept policy changes.

In *South Dakota v. Dole*, we considered a challenge to a federal law that threatened to withhold 5 percent of a State's federal highway funds if the State did not raise its drinking age to 21. The Court found that the condition was "directly related to one of the main purposes for which highway funds are expended—safe interstate travel." 483 U.S. At the same time, the condition was not a restriction on how the highway funds—set aside for specific highway improvement and maintenance efforts—were to be used.

We accordingly asked whether "the financial inducement offered by Congress" was "so coercive as to pass the point at which 'pressure turns into compulsion.'" *Id.* By "financial inducement" the Court meant the threat of losing 5 percent of highway funds; no new money was offered to the States to raise their drinking ages. We found that the inducement was not impermissibly coercive, because Congress was offering only "relatively mild encouragement to the States." *Dole*, 483 U.S. We observed that "all South Dakota would lose if she adheres to her chosen course as to a suitable minimum drinking age is 5 [percent]" of her highway funds. *Ibid.* In fact, the federal funds at stake constituted less than half of 1 percent of South Dakota's budget at the time. In consequence, "we conclude[d] that [the] encouragement to state action [was] a valid use of the spending power." *Ibid.* Whether to accept the drinking age change "remain[ed] the prerogative of the States not merely in theory but in fact." *Id.*

In this case, the financial "inducement" Congress has chosen is much more than "relatively mild encouragement"—it is a gun to the head. Section 1396c of the Medicaid Act provides that if a State's Medicaid plan does not comply with the Act's requirements, the Secretary of Health and Human Services may declare that "further payments will not be made to the State." A State that opts out of the Affordable Care Act's expansion in health care coverage thus stands to lose not merely "a relatively small percentage" of its existing Medicaid funding, but all of it. *Dole, supra.* Medicaid spending accounts for over 20 percent of the average State's total budget, with federal funds covering 50 to 83 percent of those costs. The Federal Government estimates that it will pay out approximately $3.3 trillion between 2010 and 2019 in order to cover the costs of pre-expansion Medicaid. In addition, the States have developed intricate statutory and administrative regimes over the course of many decades to implement their objectives under existing Medicaid. It is easy to see how the *Dole* Court could conclude that the threatened loss of less than half of 1 percent of South Dakota's budget left that State with a "preroga-tive" to reject Congress's desired policy, "not merely in theory but in fact." The threatened loss of over 10 percent of a State's overall budget, in contrast, is eco-nomic dragooning that leaves the States with no real option but to acquiesce in the Medicaid expansion.

Justice Ginsburg claims that *Dole* is distinguishable because here "Con-gress has not threatened to withhold funds earmarked for any other pro-gram." *Post.* But that begs the question: The States contend that the expansion is in reality a new program, and that Congress is forcing them to accept it by threatening the funds for the existing Medicaid program. We cannot agree that existing Medicaid and the expansion dictated by the Affordable Care Act are all one program simply because "Congress styled" them as such. *Post.* If the expansion is not properly viewed as a modification of the existing Medi-caid program, Congress's decision to so title it is irrelevant.

Here, the Government claims that the Medicaid expansion is properly viewed merely as a modification of the existing program because the States agreed that Congress could change the terms of Medicaid when they signed on in the first place. The Government observes that the Social Security Act, which includes the original Medicaid provisions, contains a clause expressly reserving "[t]he right to alter, amend, or repeal any provision" of that statute. So it does. But "if Congress intends to impose a condition on the grant of federal moneys, it must do so unambiguously." *Pennhurst.* A State confronted with statutory language reserving the right to "alter" or "amend" the pertinent pro-visions of the Social Security Act might reasonably assume that Congress was entitled to make adjustments to the Medicaid program as it developed. Con-gress has in fact done so, sometimes conditioning only the new funding, other times both old and new.

The Medicaid expansion, however, accomplishes a shift in kind, not merely degree. The original program was designed to cover medical services for four particular categories of the needy: the disabled, the blind, the elderly, and needy families with dependent children. Previous amendments to Medicaid eligibility merely altered and expanded the boundaries of these categories. Under the Affordable Care Act, Medicaid is transformed into a program to meet the health care needs of the entire nonelderly population with income below 133 percent of the poverty level. It is no longer a program to care for the neediest among us, but rather an element of a comprehensive national plan to provide universal health insurance coverage.

Indeed, the manner in which the expansion is structured indicates that while Congress may have styled the expansion a mere alteration of existing Medicaid, it recognized it was enlisting the States in a new health care program. Congress created a separate funding provision to cover the costs of providing services to any person made newly eligible by the expansion. While Congress pays 50 to 83 percent of the costs of covering individuals currently enrolled in Medicaid, once the expansion is fully implemented Congress will pay 90 percent of the costs for newly eligible persons. The conditions on use of the different funds are also distinct. Congress mandated that newly eligible persons receive a level of coverage that is less comprehensive than the traditional Medicaid benefit package.

As we have explained, "[t]hough Congress's power to legislate under the spending power is broad, it does not include surprising participating States with postacceptance or 'retroactive' conditions." *Pennhurst, supra.* A State could hardly anticipate that Congress's reservation of the right to "alter" or "amend" the Medicaid program included the power to transform it so dramatically.

Justice Ginsburg claims that in fact this expansion is no different from the previous changes to Medicaid, such that "a State would be hard put to complain that it lacked fair notice." *Post.* But the prior change she discusses—presumably the most dramatic alteration she could find—does not come close to working the transformation the expansion accomplishes. She highlights an amendment requiring States to cover pregnant women and increasing the number of eligible children. *Ibid.* But this modification can hardly be described as a major change in a program that—from its inception—provided health care for "families with dependent children." Previous Medicaid amendments simply do not fall into the same category as the one at stake here.

The Court in *Steward Machine* did not attempt to "fix the outermost line" where persuasion gives way to coercion. 301 U.S. The Court found it "[e]nough for present purposes that wherever the line may be, this statute is within it." *Ibid.* We have no need to fix the line either. It is enough for today that wherever that line may be, this statute is surely beyond it. Congress may not simply "conscript state [agencies] into the national bureaucratic army," *FERC v. Mississippi* (1982), and that is what it is attempting to do with the Medicaid expansion.

B

Nothing in our opinion precludes Congress from offering funds under the Affordable Care Act to expand the availability of health care, and requiring that States accepting such funds comply with the conditions on their use. What Congress is not free to do is to penalize States that choose not to participate in that new program by taking away their existing Medicaid funding. Section 1396c gives the Secretary of Health and Human Services the authority to do just that. It allows her to withhold all "further [Medicaid] payments . . . to the State" if she determines that the State is out of compliance with any Medicaid requirement, including those contained in the expansion. In light of the Court's holding, the Secretary cannot apply §1396c to withdraw existing Medicaid funds for failure to comply with the requirements set out in the expansion.

That fully remedies the constitutional violation we have identified. The chapter of the United States Code that contains §1396c includes a severability clause confirming that we need go no further. That clause specifies that "[i]f any provision of this chapter, or the application thereof to any person or circumstance, is held invalid, the remainder of the chapter, and the application of such provision to other persons or circumstances shall not be affected thereby." Today's holding does not affect the continued application of §1396c to the existing Medicaid program. Nor does it affect the Secretary's ability to withdraw funds provided under the Affordable Care Act if a State that has chosen to participate in the expansion fails to comply with the requirements of that Act.

This is not to say, as the joint dissent suggests, that we are "rewriting the Medicaid Expansion." *Post.* Instead, we determine, first, that §1396c is unconstitutional when applied to withdraw existing Medicaid funds from States that decline to comply with the expansion. We then follow Congress's explicit textual instruction to leave unaffected "the remainder of the chapter, and the application of [the challenged] provision to other persons or circumstances." When we invalidate an application of a statute because that application is unconstitutional, we are not "rewriting" the statute; we are merely enforcing the Constitution.

The question remains whether today's holding affects other provisions of the Affordable Care Act. In considering that question, "[w]e seek to determine what Congress would have intended in light of the Court's constitutional holding." *United States v. Booker* (2005). Our "touchstone for any decision about remedy is legislative intent, for a court cannot use its remedial powers to circumvent the intent of the legislature." *Ayotte v. Planned Parenthood of Northern New Eng.* (2006). The question here is whether Congress would have wanted the rest of the Act to stand, had it known that States would have a genuine choice whether to participate in the new Medicaid expansion. Unless it is "evident" that the answer is no, we must leave the rest of the Act intact. *Champlin Refining Co. v. Corporation Comm'n of Okla.* (1932).

We are confident that Congress would have wanted to preserve the rest of the Act. It is fair to say that Congress assumed that every State would participate in the Medicaid expansion, given that States had no real choice but to do so. The States contend that Congress enacted the rest of the Act with such full participation in mind; they point out that Congress made Medicaid a means for satisfying the mandate and enacted no other plan for providing coverage to many low-income individuals. According to the States, this means that the entire Act must fall.

We disagree. The Court today limits the financial pressure the Secretary may apply to induce States to accept the terms of the Medicaid expansion. As a practical matter, that means States may now choose to reject the expansion; that is the whole point. But that does not mean all or even any will. Some States may indeed decline to participate, either because they are unsure they will be able to afford their share of the new funding obligations, or because they are unwilling to commit the administrative resources necessary to support the expansion. Other States, however, may voluntarily sign up, finding the idea of expanding Medicaid coverage attractive, particularly given the level of federal funding the Act offers at the outset.

We have no way of knowing how many States will accept the terms of the expansion, but we do not believe Congress would have wanted the whole Act to fall, simply because some may choose not to participate. The other reforms Congress enacted, after all, will remain "fully operative as a law," *Champlin, supra,* and will still function in a way "consistent with Congress's basic objectives in enacting the statute," *Booker, supra.* Confident that Congress would not have intended anything different, we conclude that the rest of the Act need not fall in light of our constitutional holding.

■　■　■

The Affordable Care Act is constitutional in part and unconstitutional in part. The individual mandate cannot be upheld as an exercise of Congress's power under the Commerce Clause. That Clause authorizes Congress to regulate interstate commerce, not to order individuals to engage in it. In this case, however, it is reasonable to construe what Congress has done as increasing taxes on those who have a certain amount of income, but choose to go without health insurance. Such legislation is within Congress's power to tax.

As for the Medicaid expansion, that portion of the Affordable Care Act violates the Constitution by threatening existing Medicaid funding. Congress has no authority to order the States to regulate according to its instructions. Congress may offer the States grants and require the States to comply with accompanying conditions, but the States must have a genuine choice whether to accept the offer. The States are given no such choice in this case: They must either accept a basic change in the nature of Medicaid, or risk losing all Medicaid funding. The remedy for that constitutional violation is to preclude the Federal Government from imposing such a sanction. That remedy does not require striking down other portions of the Affordable Care Act.

The Framers created a Federal Government of limited powers, and assigned to this Court the duty of enforcing those limits. The Court does so today. But the Court does not express any opinion on the wisdom of the Affordable Care Act. Under the Constitution, that judgment is reserved to the people.

The judgment of the Court of Appeals for the Eleventh Circuit is affirmed in part and reversed in part.

It is so ordered.

8.5

LEE EPSTEIN, ANDREW MARTIN, KEVIN QUINN, AND JEFFREY SEGAL

From "Circuit Effects: How the Norm of Federal Judicial Experience Biases the Supreme Court"

Cases and justices both often make their way to the Supreme Court via the federal circuit courts. Epstein, Martin, Quinn, and Segal find strong evidence that Supreme Court justices who were appointed via this avenue tend to side consistently with their previous circuit courts. In fact, the authors report that in many circumstances these justices are twice as likely to side with the position of the circuit court where they previously served than are their fellow justices.

INTRODUCTION

■ ■ ■

On many . . . dimensions, the Roberts Court, as it is currently composed, is among the more homogeneous Courts in recent memory. Most noticeably, for the first time in American history all nine Justices came to their positions directly from U.S. courts of appeals.

While this "professionalization" of the Court is without precedent, it has been long in coming. Ever since President Dwight D. Eisenhower made clear that he "would use an appeals court appointment as a stepping stone to the Supreme Court," the vast majority of nominees have come from the federal circuits. Even more to the point, the Senate has not confirmed any Supreme Court nominee lacking circuit court experience since William H. Rehnquist in 1986. Of course, there was President George W. Bush's attempt in 2005 to appoint his White House counsel, Harriet Miers. Ironically enough, this nomination—so roundly criticized on the very ground that Miers had never served on the bench—may have solidified the practice of looking to the circuits for Supreme Court nominees. As one observer noted, "[t]he appointments of Chief Justice Roberts and Justice Alito, and contrastingly the rejection of Harriet Miers, reinforce a trend on the Court that nominees not only have prior judicial experience, but also federal appellate experience."

From Lee Epstein, Andrew Martin, Kevin Quinn, and Jeffrey Segal, "Circuit Effects: How the Norm of Federal Judicial Experience Biases the Supreme Court," *University of Pennsylvania Law Review* 157, no. 3 (2009): 833–80.

As new vacancies are likely to arise on the Court in the not-so-distant future, should the next presidential administration and the Senate continue to appoint Justices from the U.S. circuits? Commentators disagree on the best approach. Those who support this so-called "norm" of federal judicial experience point to any number of benefits. Two such benefits appearing on many lists are less contentious confirmation processes and, ultimately, superior products—Justices who reach decisions based on precedent or other neutral sources, and not on their own political preferences. Those opposed to the norm do not necessarily dispute these benefits but instead argue that the costs are substantial. They point to several disadvantages along these lines, perhaps one of the most pernicious being "circuit effects"—the possibility that federal-appellate-judges-turned-Supreme-Court-Justices are predisposed to affirm decisions coming from the circuits they just left.

In what follows, we weigh in on this debate, not by rehashing the existing arguments but rather by exploring them empirically. . . . On balance, we find that the benefits are virtually nonexistent—confirmation proceedings are no smoother for candidates coming from the circuits than for other nominees, and former appellate court judges are no more likely to follow precedent or to put aside their policy preferences than are Justices lacking judicial experience. The costs, on the other hand, are considerable. While we do not observe circuit effects in the form of Justices consistently biased toward all the U.S. courts of appeals, the data do reveal a clear predisposition on the part of former federal judges to rule in favor of their home courts. For some Justices the attachment is so strong that they are twice as likely to affirm decisions coming from the circuit on which they served than they are to affirm decisions coming from all other circuits.

Under any circumstances, circuit effects seem problematic; they suggest that when the President and senators follow the norm of federal judicial experience, the Justices they appoint are more likely to give the benefit of the doubt to some circuits than to others. But the problem of bias now transcends individual Justices. Because four of the nine current Justices served on the U.S. Court of Appeals for the District of Columbia, the norm has created a collective presumption in favor of decisions handed down by the D.C. Circuit judges. To provide but one example, while all other federal appellate court judges can expect the U.S. Supreme Court to reverse their decisions in about two out of every three disputes, those sitting on the D.C. Circuit actually enjoy a higher probability of being affirmed than reversed. Diluting this advantage . . . could take one of two forms: occasionally abandoning the practice of appointing federal judges to the Supreme Court, or selecting nominees from the range of circuits so that no single circuit is disproportionately represented.

I. THE ENTRENCHMENT OF THE NORM OF FEDERAL JUDICIAL EXPERIENCE

It is virtually indisputable that at least a practice, if not a norm, exists of appointing federal circuit court judges to the Supreme Court. As early as 1959 and as recently as 2008, commentators have acknowledged the grave hesitation of the President and senators alike to appoint anyone other than sitting judges, especially U.S. federal appellate court judges. Given empirical evidence in support of this claim, it should be noted that of the sixty-two nominations made between 1869 (when Congress established the first separate judgeships for the U.S. circuits) and 1952 (the last full year of the Truman administration), just 16% went to federal circuit court judges; since the onset of the Eisenhower administration in 1953, that figure increased to nearly 66%.

The demarcation of 1953 is no accident. Almost all scholars who have studied the increasing presence of circuit court judges on the Court claim that the practice's genesis lies in the 1950s, during the Eisenhower years, though disagreement arises over its origin. Some suggest that the instigators were members of Congress, who, in the wake of *Brown v. Board of Education* and other controversial decisions, pressured Eisenhower to appoint members of the bench. Sitting judges, the legislators claimed, would be more likely than politicians (such as Hugo Black or Earl Warren) or law professors (such as Felix Frankfurter) to respect precedent and to "base [their] decisions . . . upon 'law,' not 'sociology.'" Several members of Congress went so far as to propose legislation requiring all future appointees to have at least five years' judicial experience.

Other commentators point to President Eisenhower himself as the originator of the norm. They claim that after nominating Earl Warren as Chief Justice, Eisenhower deliberately "imposed" the criterion of judicial experience to distance himself from the overt "cronyism" that had characterized Franklin D. Roosevelt's and, especially, Harry Truman's approach to judicial selection.

II. THE BENEFITS OF THE NORM OF PRIOR JUDICIAL EXPERIENCE

Whatever the origins of the practice of appointing federal judges to the Supreme Court, it is impossible to refute David Yalof's claim that they are now the "darlings of the selection process." But should they remain so? . . .

A. The Confirmation Process

While analysts debate many features of the norm of federal judicial experience, virtually all agree that its entrenchment can be traced at least in part to the confirmation process: if Presidents want the Senate to confirm their nominees—as they invariably do—circuit judges are the safest bet. Should the President nominate "somebody who does not have a strong record of judicial experience," he may place himself and his candidate in a "vulnerable position."

Why? Commentators offer three explanations: (1) the public and politicians perceive federal appellate court judges as particularly well qualified for a seat on the Court; (2) organized interests are less likely to battle sitting federal judges; and, ultimately, (3) senators, even those who do not share the President's political affiliation, are more likely to support candidates elevated from the circuits. While each of these rationales seems plausible, none survives empirical scrutiny.

■ ■ ■

While it is true that qualifications are important to a successful confirmation, the data fail to show that appellate court judges are perceived as more meritorious than other nominees. . . .

. . . Whether owing to greater experience, expertise, or socialization, countless commentators have claimed that federal court judges do make superior nominees, or simply assume it to be true, but just as many systematic analyses refute it. In fact, perhaps because it represents something of an acid test for proponents of the norm of federal judicial experience, numerous scholars have tried but failed to establish a link between service in the circuits and judicial "greatness," however defined.

■ ■ ■

III. THE HOME COURT ADVANTAGE

Fifteen years ago, Lee Bollinger wrote, "I sense that, especially with the tendency exhibited over the past decades to give a high priority to prior judicial experience in making appointments to the bench, that we are heading towards a professionalized judiciary. . . . That . . . does not bode well for society." Bollinger may have been more right than he knew. If our analyses thus far suggest anything, it is that the advantages attributed to the norm of federal judicial experience lack evidentiary support. Actually, a serious downside already seems to have emerged: far from providing an objective evaluation of "judicial temperament and craftsmanship through the nominee's past judicial experience," the experiential norm may be providing evaluators with misinformation. Because "[t]he chance for promotion . . . is likely sufficient to induce behavior by lower court judges that they view as enhancing their chances for promotion," we are likely to get only a partial picture of the Justice who will eventually emerge on the Court.

But this is not the only potential downside. Another possibility centers on what we call "circuit effects." The general idea is that when former federal judges come to the Court, they may be favorably (or even unfavorably) predisposed to

the U.S. courts of appeals generally or toward their former circuits in particular. Either way, if circuit effects exist we might expect to find the judges-
turned-Justices affirming (or reversing) more frequently than they otherwise
would.

■   ■   ■

For former appellate court judges sitting on the Supreme Court, another
type of bias is possible: differential treatment of decisions coming out of
each Justice's former circuit versus all other circuits. While appellate court
judges with trial court experience receive cases only from districts within
their circuits, former appellate court judges sitting on the Supreme Court
hear cases from all circuits. Having worked with judges on their circuit for
months, years, or even decades, it is entirely possible that Justices will have
developed some attachment to their "home team" rather than to all circuits
generally. No doubt, to provide one example, Justice Alito occasionally
clashed with his former colleagues on the Third Circuit. Yet, seven of them,
assembled by Alito's "longtime friend" Judge Edward Becker, testified on Alito's behalf despite the obvious conflict of interest—an interest in retaining
"warm ties with a Supreme Court justice able to rule on their decisions that
are appealed to the nation's highest court." As one commentator noted, testimony of this sort was "extraordinary . . . for . . . sitting judges who will be
dealing with a colleague who could be positioned to uphold or overturn their
rulings."

In the case of Justice Alito, we might expect a positive circuit effect toward
his former colleagues, but it is entirely possible that such an effect does not
always work to the advantage of the home circuit. In fact, given the infa-
mously bad relations between some Supreme Court Justices and their former
colleagues—Justice Burger's clashes with liberals on the D.C. Circuit are
notorious—they may even work to the disadvantage of those courts.

In what follows, we explore the two forms of circuit effects: a general bias
toward the circuits and more specific biases toward the home courts. We find
no evidence of the former, but attachments to the Justices' former circuits are
quite substantial.

A. Bias Toward the Circuit Court

As a general matter and regardless of their career path, circuit court judges
tend to affirm lower court decisions. Precisely the opposite holds for Supreme
Court Justices.

Figure [1], which depicts the Justices' reversal rates, underscores the point.
With but two exceptions, Whittaker and Marshall, all Justices sitting since
1953 voted to reverse more often than not. This holds for Justices as ideologically diverse as Fortas and Goldberg on the left, Powell and O'Connor in the
middle, and Rehnquist and Scalia on the right; and it holds for the Court's
newest members, Alito and Roberts, neither of whom shows any indication of

FIGURE [1] Justices' Reversal Rates on Cases Coming from the U.S. Courts of Appeals

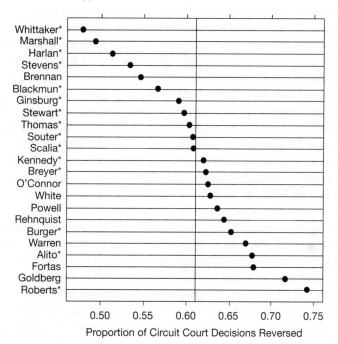

NOTE: The thin vertical line indicates the mean reversal rate. The data are for Justices starting their service on the Court since 1953 and include only cases that were orally argued.
*indicates former circuit court judges.

breaking with the long-standing tradition of reversal. Even more to the point, the reversal trend holds for Justices with federal judicial experience and those without it. While the former are less likely to reverse (0.59 versus 0.64), the difference is not statistically significant.

Why this regularity persists across time and areas of the law is not especially difficult to explain. Under most theories of judging on the Supreme Court, "reversal" is the more plausible forecast. Scholars who study the hierarchy of justice, for example, have noted that the threat of reversal is the only sanction available to Supreme Court Justices against errant circuit courts. Were the Justices to affirm all their decisions, the threat would lose its credibility.

The patterns become somewhat more interesting when we compare the treatment of cases coming to the Supreme Court from the circuits with those coming from all other courts (primarily state courts of last resort), while controlling for the ideological direction of the lower court's decision (either liberal or conservative). Under Judge Posner's logic, we might expect former circuit court judges to show a greater willingness to affirm appellate court rulings regardless of whether the decision below was left or right of center. In order to examine the factors affecting whether Justices voted to affirm the court below, we ran logistic regressions for each Justice on the type of court that had its ruling under review (federal appellate or another) and the ideological direction of the decision (liberal or conservative). The regressions show that for all but three of the Justices (Burton, Minton, and Reed), the ideological direction of the decision below was statistically significant. Put simply, regardless of whether the ruling comes from a state or federal court, liberal Justices vote to reverse conservative decisions and conservative Justices vote to reverse liberal decisions. Justices Alito and Ginsburg provide useful examples. If the decision of a circuit court is conservative, the probability that Alito will cast a vote to reverse is about 0.50; when it is a liberal decision, that figure jumps to nearly 0.80. Conversely, Ginsburg votes to reverse seven out of every ten conservative decisions coming before the Court but only five out of every ten liberal decisions.

Given the vast literature on the subject, ideological decision making of this sort is no surprise. Much more surprising . . . is that only four of the sixteen former circuit court judges show any bias toward the circuits—relative to the state supreme courts—and for two, Scalia and Thomas, the bias works against the circuits. That is, Justices Scalia and Thomas are significantly more likely to reverse a decision from the circuits than a comparable decision from the state courts—though the effect itself is reasonably small. Based on our estimates, Thomas, for example, reverses roughly four out of every ten conservative decisions coming from the circuits; that figure is closer to three out of every ten decisions coming from the states. On the other hand, five of the fifteen Justices without prior federal appellate experience exhibit some favoritism toward the circuits over all other courts, even after controlling for the ideological direction of the lower court decision: Justices Brennan, Clark, Douglas, Reed, and Powell.

B. Bias toward the Home-Court Circuit

While Justices Scalia, Thomas, and most of the others with appellate court experience show no favoritism toward the U.S. courts of appeals as a collective, a wholly different picture emerges when we focus on their former home courts. With only a few exceptions, Justices who served on the circuits behave in a significantly different manner toward their former court relative to all others.

Figure [2] vividly illustrates this point. There we depict the thirteen former appellate court judges appointed to the Supreme Court since 1953, along with a comparison of their reversal rates for the circuit on which they served against all other circuits. Note that for three Justices—Blackmun, Souter, and Stewart—the difference appears rather negligible. For the other ten Justices, however, a statistically significant difference emerges between the treatment of their former circuit and of the other appellate courts.

FIGURE [2]   Justices' Reversal Rates on Cases Coming from the U.S. Courts of Appeals on Which They Served and All Others

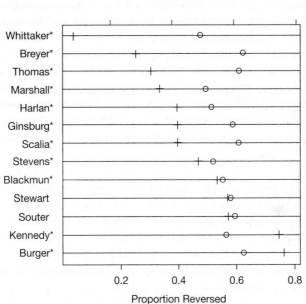

For eight of the ten Justices, the relationship is positive, meaning that they favored their former circuit (note that the crosses in Figure [2] are to the left of the circles). Take Ruth Bader Ginsburg, for example. Looking across all of the 946 decisions coming out of the U.S. courts of appeals that were reviewed by the Supreme Court since she joined the Court in 1994, Justice Ginsburg voted to affirm in about 40% and voted to reverse in 60%. The figures for the D.C. Circuit, where she served between 1980 and 1993 are nearly the mirror image: Justice Ginsburg voted to affirm in 58% and to reverse in 42%. Likewise, over the course of his career Justice. Thurgood Marshall voted to reverse federal appellate court decisions about as often as he voted to affirm them—except when it came to his former court, the Second Circuit. He voted to affirm more than six out of every ten cases coming from the Second Circuit. Then there is Charles Whittaker, who formerly sat on the Eighth Circuit. In only one of the dozen cases coming from the Eighth Circuit did he vote to reverse his former colleagues, though his overall reversal rate was about 50%.

For two of the ten Justices, the relationship is negative—meaning they were systematically biased against their circuit. . . .

Nonetheless, even after controlling for the ideological direction of the lower court decision, the basic patterns . . . remain. Of the thirteen Justices with federal judicial experience, only Justices Stewart, Souter, and Blackmun show no bias toward the former circuits; Justices Burger and Kennedy are significantly less favorably disposed to their home court; and the others are significantly more favorably disposed. Moreover, the size of the effect is nontrivial. . . . Consider Justice Breyer: If the First Circuit were to reach a decision favoring, say, the defendant in a criminal case or a plaintiff in an employment discrimination suit, the likelihood of Justice Breyer—a former member of that court—casting a vote to affirm is very high at $p = 0.69$. However, if a similar case were to come from another circuit, the odds that he would vote to affirm fall to well below $p = 0.50$.

Even more interesting, perhaps, are the cases of Justices Clarence Thomas and Antonin Scalia. As the analyses above indicate, both are significantly more likely to affirm decisions of state courts than the circuits; this is not so when it comes to their former home, the U.S. Court of Appeals for the District of Columbia. For cases in which the D.C. Circuit reached a conservative decision, the likelihood of Thomas casting a vote to reverse is only 0.20; for similarly conservative decision, the likelihood of Thomas casting a vote to reverse is only 0.20; for similarly conservative decisions coming out of all other circuits, the figure more than doubles, at 0.44. We can say the same of Justice Scalia—and, for that matter, another former member of the D.C. Circuit, Justice Ginsburg. . . . In fact, affirming decisions from their home court may be one of the few proclivities shared by Scalia and Thomas, on one side of the ideological spectrum, and Ginsburg, on the other.

CONCLUSION

From this analysis and all those preceding it, a clear conclusion emerges: the benefits of drawing Supreme Court Justices from the federal circuits are, at best, overstated, while the costs are, at minimum, understated. An obvious antidote is for the President to look to other pools for potential Court candidates. If confirmation is viewed as an important consideration, one can now feel reasonably certain that sitting federal judges are no less likely to face contentious proceedings than any other candidate; indeed, sitting judges may actually be more difficult to confirm. And if making high-quality appointments is a relevant criterion, the President can now legitimately claim that previous federal judicial experience is no guarantee that the candidate, as a Justice, will be more likely to follow precedent and less likely to follow his or her own political values, or even to go down in the annals as one of the "greats."

A less obvious, though no less plausible, remedy would be for appointers to work toward greater representation of the circuits on the Supreme Court.

Arlen Specter implicitly made this point in response to conflict-of-interest concerns that were raised when Justice Alito's colleagues from the Third Circuit testified on his behalf. No one should worry that Alito would be predisposed toward affirming the Third Circuit's rulings, Specter declared, because, "if confirmed, [Alito] would be one of nine people reviewing their cases."

This is true for the Third Circuit: Alito is the first and only Justice elevated from that court. It does not, however, hold for the First Circuit, on which two current Justices served (Souter and Breyer), nor for the D.C. Circuit, now with four representatives on the Supreme Court. In fact, our recommendation of greater diversity in circuit court representation follows from the D.C. Circuit's disproportionate presence on the current Court. Put simply, with its current status as something of a training camp for Supreme Court Justices, the Court of Appeals for the District of Columbia is now at a considerable advantage relative to the other eleven circuits.

9

PUBLIC OPINION

9.1

ARTHUR LUPIA AND MATHEW D. McCUBBINS

From *The Democratic Dilemma: Can Citizens Learn What They Need to Know?*

Some observers have concluded that Americans do not know enough about politics and government to make wise choices in voting and other political decisions. The "dilemma" in the title is that citizens are quite uninformed but are being asked to make weighty decisions, like who should be president. Lupia and McCubbins argue that most of the time, under normal conditions, citizens get enough information to make reasonable decisions.

> Knowledge will forever govern ignorance: And a people who mean to be their own Governors, must arm themselves with the power which knowledge gives. A popular Government, without popular information, or the means of acquiring it, is but a Prologue to a Farce or a Tragedy; or, perhaps both.
>
> —James Madison[1]

The founders of the American republic, and many of t[...] around the world, believed that democracy requires c[...] soned choices. Reasoned choice, in turn, requires that [...] sequences of their actions.

From Arthur Lupia and Mathew D. McCubbins, *The Democratic [...] What They Need to Know?* (New York: Cambridge University Press, 1[...]

Can voters, legislators, and jurors make reasoned choices? Many observers conclude that they cannot. The evidence for this conclusion is substantial—study after study documents the breadth and depth of citizen ignorance. Making matters worse is the fact that many people acquire what little information they have from thirty-minute news summaries, thirty-second political advertisements, or eight-second sound bites. From this evidence, it seems very likely that "Men of factious tempers, of local prejudices, or of sinister designs, may, by intrigue, by corruption, or by any other means, first obtain the suffrages, and then betray the interests, of the people" (Madison, *Federalist* 10).

It is widely believed that there is a mismatch between the requirements of democracy and most people's ability to meet these requirements. If this mismatch is too prevalent, then effective self-governance is impossible. The *democratic dilemma* is that the people who are called upon to make reasoned choices may not be capable of doing so.

[W]e concede that people lack political information. We also concede that this ignorance can allow people "of sinister designs" to deceive and betray the underinformed. We do not concede, however, that democracy *must* succumb to these threats. Rather, we conclude that:

- Reasoned choice does not require full information; rather, it requires the ability to predict the consequences of actions. We define this ability as knowledge.[2]
- People *choose* to disregard most of the information they could acquire and base virtually all of their decisions on remarkably little information.
- People often *substitute* the advice of others for the information they lack. This substitution can give people the capacity for reasoned choice.
- Relying on the advice of others involves tradeoffs. Although it decreases the costs of acquiring knowledge, it also introduces the possibility of deception.
- A person who wants to gain knowledge from the advice of others must choose to follow some advice while ignoring other advice. People make these choices in systematic and predictable ways.
- Political institutions can help people choose which advice to follow and which advice to ignore. Institutions do this when they *clarify* the incentives of advice givers.
- Understanding how people learn not only helps us better identify when presumed democratic dilemmas are real but also shows us how we might begin to resolve these dilemmas. . . .

EMOCRACY, DELEGATION, AND REASONED CHOICE

racy is a method of government based upon the choices of the people. dern democracies, the people elect or appoint others to represent them. Legislative assemblies, executives, commissions, judges, and juries are empowered by the people to make collective decisions on their behalf. These delegations form the foundation of democracy.

But there are dangers. As Dahl (1967: 21) warns, the principal danger is that uninformed decision makers, by failing to delegate well, will transform democracy into a *tyranny of experts:* "there are decisions that require me to *delegate* authority to others . . . but if I delegate, may I not, in practice, end up with a kind of aristocracy of experts, or even false experts?"

Must democracy become a tyranny of experts? Many observers answer yes, because those who delegate seem uninformed when compared with those to whom they delegate.

The principal democratic delegation, that of the people electing their governors, seems most susceptible to tyranny. Cicero's observation that "in the common people there is no wisdom, no penetration, no power of judgment" is an apt summary of modern voting studies (see Berelson 1952, Campbell et al. 1960, Converse 1964, Kinder and Sears 1985, Lane and Sears 1964, Luskin 1987, McClosky 1964, Neuman 1986, Schattschneider 1960, Schumpeter 1942, Zaller 1992, Zaller and Feldman 1992; for a survey, see Delli Carpini and Keeter 1996). Many scholars argue that voters, because of their obstinance or their inability to educate themselves, become the unwitting puppets of campaign and media puppet-masters (Bennett 1992, Sabato 1991). Iyengar (1987: 816) summarizes the literature on voting and elections: "the low level of political knowledge and the absence of ideological reasoning has lent credence to the charges that popular control of government is illusory." These studies suggest that voters who lack information cannot use elections to control their governors.

Other observers make similar arguments about elected representatives. Weber, for example, argues that legislators cannot control bureaucrats:

> Under normal conditions, the power position of a fully developed bureaucracy is always overtowering. The "political master" finds himself in the position of the "dilettante" who stands opposite the "expert," facing the trained official who stands within the management of administration. This holds whether the "master" whom the bureaucracy serves is a "people," equipped with the weapons of "legislative initiative," the "referendum," and the right to remove officials, or a parliament, elected on a more aristocratic or more "democratic" basis and equipped with the right to vote a lack of confidence, or with the actual authority to vote it. (Weber quoted in Gerth and Mills 1946: 232)

Niskanen (1971) continues that public officials' inability to contend with the complexities of modern legislation places them at the mercy of self-serving special interests and bureaucrats. Lowi (1979: xii) concludes, "actual policymaking will not come from voter preferences or congressional enactments but from a process of tripartite bargaining between the specialized administrators, relevant members of Congress, and the representatives of self-selected organized interests."

Jurors also seem to lack the information they need. Posner (1995: 52), for example, argues, "As American law and society become ever more complex, the jury's cognitive limitations will become ever more palpable and socially costly." Other observers characterize the legal system, not as a forum where citizens make reasoned choices, but as a stage for emotional appeals where style and deception overwhelm knowledge. As Abramson (1994: 3) laments,

> The gap between the complexity of modern litigation and the qualifica-
> tions of jurors has widened to frightening proportions. The average jury
> rarely understands the expert testimony in an anti-trust suit, a medical
> malpractice case, or an insanity defense. Nor do most jurors know the
> law or comprehend the judge's crash course of instructions on it. Trial
> by jury has thus become trial by ignorance.

Although the critiques of democracy's delegations are myriad and diverse, all have a common conclusion—*reasoned choice does not govern delegation.* As Schumpeter (1942: 262) argues, "the typical citizen drops down to a lower level of mental performance as soon as he enters the political field. He argues and analyzes in a way which he would readily recognize as infantile within the sphere of his real interests. He becomes a primitive again. His thinking is associative and affective. . . . [T]his may prove fatal to the nation."

If voters, legislators, and jurors lack the capability to delegate effectively, then democracy may be "but a prologue to a farce or a tragedy." Like the scholars just quoted, we find this possibility alarming. Unlike these scholars, however, we argue that the capabilities of the people and the requirements of democracy are not as mismatched as many critics would have us believe. In what follows, we will identify the conditions under which this mismatch does and does not exist.

A PREVIEW OF OUR THEORY

We argue that *limited information need not prevent people from making rea-
soned choices.* Of course, we are not the first analysts to make this type of argument. In the 1950s, for example, Berelson, Lazarfeld, and McPhee (1954) and Downs (1957) argued that voters rely on opinion leaders and political parties to overcome their information shortfalls. More recently, a generation of scholars has further countered the view that the "democratic citizen is expected to be well informed about political affairs" (Berelson, Lazarsfeld, and McPhee 1954: 308). Collectively, these scholars have demonstrated that voters can use a wide range of simple cues as substitutes for complex information. We concur with the basic insight of each of these studies—people can use substitutes for encyclopedic information.

However, we want to do more than argue that limited information need not prevent people from making reasoned choices. We want to argue that *there are specific conditions under which people who have limited information can make reasoned choices.* Therefore, in addition to showing that people *can* use cues, we want to answer questions about *when and how* people use cues, *when* cues are effective substitutes for detailed information, and *when* cues are detrimental. To understand who is (and who is not) capable of reasoned choice, we must be able to answer questions such as:

- When do people use simple cues?
- When do people ignore simple cues and seek more detailed information instead?
- When are simple cues sufficient for reasoned choice?
- When can people who offer simple cues manipulate or deceive those who use them?
- What factors determine why a person relies on some simple cues while ignoring many others?
- How do political institutions affect the use and effectiveness of simple cues?

To answer these questions, we construct theories of attention, persuasion, and delegation. . . . [O]ur theory has the rare advantage of being relevant to the usually separate debates on learning, communication, and choice held in cognitive science, economics, political science, and psychology. Next, we describe our theory and preview the answers it gives to the questions listed previously.

Knowledge and Information

We begin by developing a theory of attention. The purpose of our theory is to explain how humans cope with complexity and scarcity. As Simon (1979: 3) argues, "human thinking powers are very modest when compared with the complexities of the environments in which human beings live." Making matters worse is the fact that many of the resources people need to survive are scarce.

Ironically, for many political issues, information is not scarce; rather it is the cognitive resources that a person can use to process information that are scarce. For example, political information appears in the newspapers, in the mail, on community bulletin boards, and on television and radio and is relayed to us in person by friends and family. People often lack the time and energy needed to make sense of all this information. As a consequence, people often have only incomplete information. Fortunately, reasoned choice does not require complete information. Instead, it requires *knowledge: the ability to predict the consequences of actions.*[3]

Implicit in many critiques of democracy is the claim that people who lack *information* are incapable of reasoned choice. By contrast, we argue that people who lack information solve enormously complex problems every day. They do so by making effective use of the information available to them, sorting that which is useful from that which is not.

Information is useful only if it helps people avoid costly mistakes. By contrast, if more information does not lead people to change their decisions, then it provides no instrumental benefit and they should ignore it. Indeed, ignoring useless information is necessary for humans and other species to survive and prosper (Churchland and Sejnowski 1992).

Those who find such statements surprising should consider the almost boundless range of actions, both mundane and grand, for which people ignore available information. For example, people take medication without knowing all of the conditions under which it might be harmful. They also buy houses based on limited information about the neighborhoods around them and with little or no information about the neighbors. People make choices in this way not because the information is unavailable but because the costs of paying attention to it exceed the value of its use.[4]

Although reasoned choice does not require complete information, it does require the ability to predict the consequences of actions. In many cases, simple pieces of information can provide the knowledge people need. For example, to navigate a busy intersection successfully, you must *know* where all of the other cars are going to be sure that you can avoid crashing into them. Advocates of complete information might argue that successful automotive navigation requires as much information as you can gather about the intentions of other drivers and the speed, acceleration, direction, and mass of their cars. At many intersections, however, there is a simple substitute for *all* of this information—a traffic signal. At these intersections, traffic signals are substitutes for more complex information and reduce the amount of information required to make a reasoned choice. At intersections without working traffic signals or other simple cues, reasoned choices require more information. Using similar logic, it follows that limited information precludes reasoned choice only if people are stuck at complex political intersections and lack access to effective political traffic signals.

Persuasion, Enlightenment, and Deception

People who want to make reasoned choices need knowledge. There are two ways to acquire knowledge. The first way is to draw from personal experience. People who exercise this option use their own observations of the past to derive predictions about the future consequences of their actions. The second way is to learn from others. People who exercise this option substitute other people's observations of the past for the personal experience they lack.

In many political settings, only the second option is available. This is true because politics is often abstract and its consequences are remote. In these settings, personal experience does not provide sufficient knowledge for reasoned choice. For many political decisions, reasoned choice requires learning from others.

There are many explanations of how people learn from others. Indeed, a generation of scholars, starting with Knight, Simon, Berelson et al. and Downs, suggest numerous heuristics—simple means for generating information substitutes.[5] . . .

Individually, each of these explanations of how we learn from others is valuable and enlightening. Each reveals a source of the judgmental shortcuts that people undoubtedly use. However, as Sniderman, Brody, and Tetlock (1991: 70) argue, "The most serious risk is that . . . every correlation between independent and dependent variables [is] taken as evidence of a new judgmental shortcut." We agree. We need a theory that explains when or how people choose among the shortcuts listed in the preceding paragraph. To understand how people learn from others, we must be able to explain *how people choose whom to believe.*

▪ ▪ ▪

[N]otice that any attempt to learn from others leads to one of three possible outcomes.

- The first outcome is *enlightenment.* When someone furnishes us with knowledge, we become enlightened. Enlightenment, then, is the process of becoming enlightened. If we initially lack knowledge sufficient for reasoned choice and can obtain such knowledge only from others, then we can make reasoned decisions only if others enlighten us.
- The second outcome is *deception.* Deception is the process by which the testimony we hear reduces our ability to predict accurately the consequences of our actions. For example, we are deceived when someone lies to us *and* we believe that individual.
- The third outcome is that we *learn nothing.* When we learn nothing, our beliefs go unchanged and we gain no knowledge.

Both enlightenment and deception, in turn, require *persuasion: a successful attempt to change the beliefs of another.* The key to understanding whether people become enlightened or deceived by the testimony of others is to understand the conditions under which they can persuade one another.

Most scholars of communication and politics, dating back to Aristotle, focus on a speaker's *internal character* (e.g., honesty, ideology, or reputation) as a necessary condition for persuasion. If a speaker lacks the right character, then these scholars conclude that the speaker will not be persuasive. [W]e present a different set of necessary and sufficient conditions for persuasion. We argue that persuasion need not be contingent upon personal character; rather, *persuasion requires that a listener perceive a speaker to be both knowledgeable and trustworthy.* Although a perception of trust can arise from a positive evaluation of a speaker's character, we show that *external forces can substitute for character* and can thus generate persuasion in contexts where it would not otherwise occur.

An example of an external force that generates trust and persuasion is a listener's observation of a speaker's costly effort. From this observation, the listener can learn about the intensity of a speaker's preferences. This particular condition is also very much like the adage that actions speak louder than words. When speaker costs have this effect, they can provide a basis for trust by providing listeners with a window to speaker incentives.

To see how costly effort affects persuasion, consider the following situation. First, suppose that a listener knows a speaker to have one of three possible motivations—he is a conservative with intense preferences, a conservative with non-intense preferences, or a liberal with non-intense preferences. Second, suppose that the listener does not know which of the three motivations the speaker actually has. Third, suppose that the listener can make a reasoned choice only if he or she knows whether the speaker is liberal or conservative. Fourth, suppose that if the listener observes that the speaker paid a quarter of his or her income to affect a policy outcome, then the listener can conclude that the speaker has intense preferences. If all four suppositions are true, then the speaker's costly effort persuades the listener. As a result, the listener can make a reasoned choice because she can infer that the speaker is a conservative.

Another example of a trust-inducing external force is a penalty for lying. Penalties for lying, whether explicit, such as fines for perjury, or implicit, such as the loss of a valued reputation, can also generate trust by revealing a speaker's incentives. That is, although a listener may believe that a speaker has an interest in deception, the presence of a penalty for lying may lead the listener to believe that certain types of lies are prohibitively costly, rendering certain types of statements very likely to be true.

Our conditions for persuasion show when forces such as costly effort and penalties for lying are, and are not, effective substitutes for a speaker's character.[6] These conditions reveal that you do not necessarily learn more from people who are like you, nor do you learn more from people you like. This is why most people turn to financial advisors, instead of their mothers, when dealing with mutual funds, and back to Mom when seeking advice about child rearing.

Unlike most well-known theories of persuasion and strategic communication, our conditions for persuasion also clarify how and when people suffer as a result of substituting simple cues for complex information. For example, our theory allows us to identify conditions under which a speaker can deceive a listener (i.e., conditions under which a speaker lies *and* a listener believes the lie). These conditions are important because many critics of democracy claim that uninformed citizens are ripe for manipulation at the hands of slick political salesmen.

▪   ▪   ▪

More generally, our conditions for persuasion show why some statements are persuasive and others are not. The obvious reason for these differences is that statements vary in content. The less obvious reason is that the context under which a speaker makes a statement also affects persuasion considerably. Two people making precisely the same statement may not be equally persuasive if only one is subject to penalties for lying.

Our conditions for persuasion further imply that not everyone can persuade. People listen to some speakers and not others. They read some books and not others. They buy some products even though the manufacturers spend very little money on advertising while refusing to buy others supported by celebrity endorsements. Similarly, people respond to the advice of some experts or interest groups and not that of others. Our conditions for persuasion explain how people make these choices.

Our results also reveal the bounds on the effectiveness of the heuristics mentioned earlier. Consider, for example, the use of ideology as a heuristic. When there is a high correlation between a speaker's ideology and that speaker's knowledge and trustworthiness, then people are likely to find ideological cues useful. By contrast, when there is no clear correlation, ideology is useless. Similar arguments can be made about other heuristics, such as party, reputation, and likability. In sum, *concepts such as reputation, party, or ideology are useful heuristics only if they convey information about knowledge and trust. The converse of this statement is not true*—knowledge and trust are the fundamental factors that make cues persuasive; the other factors are not.

▪   ▪   ▪

Successful Delegation and the Institutions of Knowledge

. . . Two reasons are commonly cited for the failure of delegation: principals and agents have *conflicting interests* over the outcome of delegation, and agents have *expertise* regarding the consequences of the delegation that principals do not. When delegation occurs under these conditions, agents are free to take any action that suits them, irrespective of the consequences for the principal, and the principal cannot cause them to do otherwise.

We find that delegation succeeds if two conditions are satisfied: the knowledge condition and the incentive condition. The knowledge condition is satisfied in one of two ways. First, it is satisfied when the principal's personal experience allows her to distinguish beneficial from detrimental agent actions. Second, it is satisfied when the principal can obtain this knowledge from others. Therefore, the knowledge condition does not require the principal to know everything the agent knows; it requires only that the principal know enough to distinguish welfare-enhancing from welfare-decreasing agent actions.

The incentive condition is satisfied when the agent and the principal have at least some goals in common. In many cases, satisfaction of the knowledge condition is sufficient for satisfaction of the incentive condition: A principal who becomes enlightened with respect to the consequences of delegation either can motivate the agent to take actions that enhance her welfare or can reject the agent's actions that do not enhance her welfare.

We find that the outcome of delegation is not determined by whether or not the principal can match the agent's technical expertise. Instead, it is determined by the principal's ability to use the testimony of others effectively. If the principal has this ability, then delegation can succeed despite the information she lacks. If the principal lacks information about the agent and lacks the ability to learn from others, then delegation is doomed.

Moreover, we argue that, if democratic principals can create the context in which knowledgeable and persuasive speakers can inform them of the consequences of their agent's actions, then they can facilitate successful delegation. We argue that institutions, such as administrative procedure, rules of evidence, and statutory law, provide the context in which principals can learn about their agent's actions. Institutions can, if properly structured, offer principals a way to better judge their agent's actions. When institutions are poorly designed, or the incentives they induce are opaque, then the political consequence of limited information is likely to be failed delegation. By contrast, when these institutions properly and clearly structure incentives, then they facilitate enlightenment, reasoned choice, and successful delegation even in complex circumstances.

Conclusion

The mismatch between what delegation demands and citizens' capabilities constitutes the democratic dilemma. If people are not capable of reasoned political choices, then effective self-governance is an illusion. After observing that voters, legislators, and jurors are ignorant of many of the details of the decisions they face, many scholars and political commentators conclude that the illusion is real and argue for some type of reform. If their conclusion is correct, then effective self-governance may indeed require political reform. If their conclusion is incorrect, their reforms may restrain the truly competent and do more harm than good.

Other scholars have argued that people are quite capable of making complex decisions with very little information. They point to instances in which people use heuristics and conclude that such heuristics are sufficient for reasoned choice. If these conclusions are correct, then successful delegation does not require reform and the critics mentioned previously are akin to democracy's Chicken Littles. If, however, these latter conclusions are incorrect, then the optimistic scholars are akin to democracy's

Pollyannas, advocating the perpetuation of ineffective and harmful systems of governance.

Both sides of this debate recognize that people are often ignorant about the details of the choices they make. They also both recognize the existence of information shortcuts, cues, and heuristics. What is missing from this debate is an understanding of when ignorance of details prevents reasoned choice, how people choose among potential heuristics, and when these heuristics provide effective substitutes for the detailed information people lack. Only when we have these understandings will we be able to make constructive use of the common observation that people lack information. At that point, we can separate the Chicken Littles from the Pollyannas and build effective solutions to the democratic dilemma.

NOTES

1. From Hunt (1910: 103). Madison expressed similar beliefs in *Federalist 57* and in a speech before the Virginia Ratifying Convention, where he argued that it is necessary that the people possess the "virtue and intelligence to select men of virtue and wisdom" (Riemer 1986: 40).

2. There exists a centuries-old debate about what democracy *should* do. This debate has involved many great minds, is wide ranging, and is totally unresolved. We do not believe ourselves capable of resolving this debate. However, we strongly believe that we can make the debate more constructive. We can do so by clarifying the relationship between what information people have and what types of decisions they can make. Our reading is firmly about determining the capabilities of people who lack political information. It is designed to resolve debates about how much information voters, jurors, and legislators need in order to perform certain tasks. So, although our reading may help to clarify debates about what democracy should do, it will not resolve these debates.

We mention this because our relationship to the debate about what democracy should do motivates our definition of reasoned choice. Our definition of reasoned choice allows the reader to define an amount of knowledge that is required for reasoned choice. Some readers may argue that a reasoned choice requires knowledge of very technical matters, whereas others may argue that a reasoned choice requires less knowledge. Note that the difference between these viewpoints reduces to different views on what democracy should do. Therefore, our definition of reasoned choice is purposefully precise with respect to the relationship between information, knowledge, and choice and is purposefully vague with respect to most normative debates about what democracies *should* do.

3. For example, knowing which of two products is "better" than the other is often sufficient for us to make the same choice we would have made had we been completely informed about each product.

4. Furthermore, beyond being useless, some types of information cause people to make the wrong (i.e., welfare-reducing) choices when they would have otherwise made the right (i.e., welfare-increasing) ones with less information. For example, a person who votes for Jones instead of Smith because a newspaper endorses Jones may regret having attended to this additional information when Jones later opposes a policy that both she and Smith support.

5. Also, see Key (1966) and Tversky and Kahneman (1974).

6. A third external force that can induce a listener to trust a speaker arises when the speaker's statements are subject to some chance of being externally verified.

REFERENCES

Abramson, Jeffrey. 1994. *We, the Jury: The Jury System and the Ideal of Democracy.* New York: Basic Books.

Bennett, W. Lance. 1992. *The Governing Crisis: Media, Money, and Marketing in American Elections.* New York: St. Martin's Press.

Berelson, Bernard. 1952. "Democratic Theory and Public Opinion." *Public Opinion Quarterly* XVI: 313–30.

Berelson, Bernard, Paul F. Lazarfeld, and William N. McPhee. 1954. *Voting: A Study of Opinion Formation in a Presidential Campaign.* Chicago: University of Chicago Press.

Campbell, Angus, Philip E. Converse, Warren E. Miller, and Donald E. Stokes. 1960. *The American Voter.* New York: Wiley.

Churchland, Patricia S., and Terrence J. Sejnowski. 1992. *The Computational Brain.* Cambridge, MA: MIT Press.

Converse, Philip E. 1964. "The Nature of Belief Systems in Mass Publics." In *Ideology and Discontent,* edited by David E. Apter. New York: Free Press.

Dahl, Robert A. 1967. *Pluralist Democracy in the United States: Conflict and Consent.* Chicago: Rand McNally.

Delli Carpini, Michael X., and Scott Keeter. 1991. "Stability and Change in the United States Public's Knowledge of Politics." *Public Opinion Quarterly* 55: 583–612.

Downs, Anthony. 1957. *An Economic Theory of Democracy.* New York: Harper.

Gerth, H. H., and C. Wright Mills, eds. 1946. *From Max Weber: Essays in Sociology.* New York: Oxford University Press.

Hunt, Gaillard, ed. 1910. *The Writings of James Madison.* New York: Putnam.

Iyengar, Shanto. 1987. "Television News and Citizens' Explanations of National Affairs." *American Political Science Review* 81: 815–32.

Key, V. O. 1966. *The Responsible Electorate: Rationality in Presidential Voting, 1936–1960.* Cambridge, MA: Belknap Press of Harvard University Press.

Kinder, Donald R., and David O. Sears. 1985. "Public Opinion and Political Participation." In *Handbook of Social Psychology,* edited by G. Lindzey and E. Aronson. Reading, MA: Addison-Wesley.

Lane, Robert E., and David O. Sears. 1964. *Public Opinion.* Englewood Cliffs, NJ: Prentice-Hall.

Lowi, Theodore J. 1979. *The End of Liberalism: The Second Republic of the United States.* 2nd ed., New York: Norton.

Luskin, Robert C. 1987. "Measuring Political Sophistication." *American Journal of Political Science* 31: 856–99.

Madison, James. *Federalist.* In Clinton Rossiter, ed., *The Federalist Papers.* New York: Penguin.

McClosky, Herbert. 1964. "Consensus and Ideology in American Politics." *American Political Science Review* 58: 361–82.

Neuman, W. Russell. 1986. *The Paradox of Mass Politics: Knowledge and Opinion in the American Electorate.* Cambridge, Mass.: Harvard University Press.

Niskanen, William A. 1971. *Bureaucracy and Representative Government.* Chicago: Aldine-Atherton.

Posner, Richard. 1995. "Juries on Trial." *Commentary* 99: 49–52.

Riemer, Neal. 1986. *James Madison: Creating the American Constitution.* Washington, DC: Congressional Quarterly.

Sabato, Larry J. 1991. *Feeding Frenzy.* New York: Free Press.

Schattschneider, Elmer Eric. 1960. *The Semisovereign People: A Realist's View of Democracy in America.* New York: Holt, Rinehart and Winston.

Schumpeter, Joseph Alois. 1942. *Capitalism, Socialism, and Democracy.* New York: Harper.

Simon, Herbert A. 1979. *Models of Thought.* New Haven, CT: Yale University Press.

Sniderman, Paul M., Richard A. Brody, and Philip E. Tetlock. 1991. *Reasoning and Choice: Explorations in Political Psychology.* Cambridge: Cambridge University Press.

Tversky, Amos, and Daniel Kahneman. 1974. "Judgment under Uncertainty: Heuristics and Biases." *Science* 185: 1124–131.

Zaller, John. 1992. *The Nature and Origins of Mass Opinion.* Cambridge: Cambridge University Press.

Zaller, John, and Stanley Feldman. 1992. "A Simple Theory of the Survey Response: Answering Questions Versus Revealing Preferences." *American Journal of Political Science* 36: 579–616.

9.2

JOHN R. ZALLER

From *The Nature and Origins of Mass Opinion*

A large literature in political science examines what voters know and whether they have enough information to make informed choices in elections. Zaller proposes a model for how voters acquire information. Using this model, he argues that voters vary in the degree to which they are receptive to new information, depending on their underlying political predispositions and levels of knowledge about politics. His model lends insight into why some voters are swayed by public discourse and others stay firm in their attitudes.

HOW CITIZENS ACQUIRE INFORMATION AND CONVERT IT INTO PUBLIC OPINION

The comprehensive analysis of public opinion requires attention to two phenomena: how citizens learn about matters that are for the most part beyond their immediate experience, and how they convert the information they acquire into opinions.

. . . [I] propose a model of both phenomena. The model does not provide a fully accurate account of how people process information and form attitude statements. No model that is both parsimonious and testable on typical mass opinion data—the two most important constraints on my enterprise—could possibly do so. But the proposed model, as I hope to persuade the reader, does a plausible job of approximating what must actually occur, and a quite excellent job of accounting for the available survey evidence across a wide range of phenomena.

■ ■ ■

Some Definitions

I begin the statement of the model with definitions of primitive terms. The first is *consideration*, which is defined as any reason that might induce an individual to decide a political issue one way or the other.[1] Considerations, thus,

From John R. Zaller, *The Nature and Origins of Mass Opinion* (New York: Cambridge University Press, 1992).

are a compound of cognition and affect—that is, a belief concerning an object and an evaluation of the belief. . . .

Second, I define two types of political messages: persuasive messages and cueing messages. Persuasive messages are arguments or images providing a reason for taking a position or point of view; if accepted by an individual, they become considerations, as the term was just defined. . . .

Note that there is nothing in this account that implies that either political messages or the considerations that result from them must be coldly rational. On the contrary, messages may involve subtle or even subliminal images, and considerations may involve feelings or emotions. . . .

Cueing messages, which are the second type of message carried in elite discourse, consist of "contextual information" about the ideological or partisan implications of a persuasive message. The importance of cueing messages is that, as suggested by Converse (1964), they enable citizens to perceive relationships between the persuasive messages they receive and their political predispositions, which in turn permits them to respond critically to the persuasive messages.

▪ ▪ ▪

The Model

The model itself consists of four assertions, or axioms, about how individuals respond to political information they may encounter. Each is stated first as a general theoretical position and then elaborated and justified in more precise terms.

▪ ▪ ▪

A1. *RECEPTION AXIOM. The greater a person's level of cognitive engagement with an issue, the more likely he or she is to be exposed to and comprehend—in a word, to receive—political messages concerning that issue.*[2]

The messages people may receive include all types: that is, persuasive messages and cueing messages. . . .

Although cognitive engagement is the right specification for my model, it is a cumbersome and somewhat precious phrase. Therefore, I will, through most of the analysis that follows, use a simpler phrase, namely *political attentiveness* or *political awareness*. But cognitive engagement, political attentiveness, and political awareness are meant to convey the same meaning.

▪ ▪ ▪

A2. *RESISTANCE AXIOM. People tend to resist arguments that are inconsistent with their political predispositions, but they do so only to the extent that they possess the contextual information necessary to perceive a relationship between the message and their predispositions.*

The key to resistance, in this formulation, is *information* concerning the relationship between arguments and predispositions, where the requisite information is carried in cueing messages. According to the Reception Axiom, the probability of individuals acquiring cueing information depends on their levels of awareness of each given issue. Thus, A1 and A2 together imply that the likelihood of resisting persuasive communications that are inconsistent with one's political predispositions rises with a person's level of political attentiveness. Or, to put it the other way, politically inattentive persons will often be unaware of the implications of the persuasive communications they encounter, and so often end up "mistakenly" accepting them.

■ ■ ■

A3. ACCESSIBILITY AXIOM. The more recently a consideration has been called to mind or thought about, the less time it takes to retrieve that consideration or related considerations from memory and bring them to the top of the head for use.

Conversely, the longer it has been since a consideration or related idea has been activated, the less likely it is to be accessible at the top of the head; in the limit, a long unused set of considerations may be completely inaccessible, which is to say, forgotten.

This axiom appropriates for use in the model one of the best-established empirical regularities in cognitive psychology. General support for the basic idea is overwhelming and, as far as I can tell, undisputed. When an idea or concept has been recently used, seen, heard, or indirectly referenced, it is significantly more likely to be available for reuse than if it has not been recently activated.

■ ■ ■

A4. RESPONSE AXIOM. Individuals answer survey questions by averaging across the considerations that are immediately salient or accessible to them.

This axiom, which completes the statement of my proposed model, implies that persons who have been asked a survey question do not normally canvass their minds for all considerations relevant to the given issue; rather, they answer the question on the basis of whatever considerations are accessible "at the top of the head." In some cases, only a single consideration may be readily accessible, in which case individuals answer on the basis of that consideration; in other cases, two or more considerations may come quickly to mind, in which case people answer by averaging across accessible considerations.

An important feature of the Response Axiom is that it permits different people to respond to issue questions on the basis of different considerations— one, for example, emphasizing ideological concerns, another gut-level likes and dislikes, and yet another self-interest.

▪   ▪   ▪

Perhaps the most apt description of a survey response within the proposed model is "opinion statement." This term implies that the expression of opinion is genuine without also implying that it either represents prior reflection or is destined for a long half-life. The phrase "attitude report" has similar virtues.

Opinion statements, as conceived in my four-axiom model, are the outcome of a process in which people *receive* new information, decide whether to *accept* it, and then *sample* at the moment of answering questions. For convenience, therefore, I will refer to this process as the Receive-Accept-Sample, or RAS, Model.

How the Model Is Used

The model I have outlined consists of four very general claims about how people acquire information from the political environment (in the form of persuasive arguments and cues) and transform that information into survey responses.

▪   ▪   ▪

The argument to be made from the RAS model may be previewed as follows. It follows from the Response Axiom that the probability that a person will support or oppose a given policy depends on the mix of positive and negative considerations available in the person's mind at the moment of answering a question about it. If, for the moment, we overlook the probability of nonresponse (which occurs when no considerations are immediately salient in memory), and assume also that every consideration a person has internalized is as likely to be sampled as any other, then the probability of a liberal response by a given person is

$$Prob(Liberal\ response) = \frac{L}{L + C}$$

where L and C refer to the number of liberal and conservative considerations available in the person's mind. (I reiterate that here, as elsewhere in this book, liberal and conservative are simply *labels* for the directional thrust of ideas; a person may use a liberal consideration as the basis for a liberal response even though she is not, in any deeper sense, "a liberal.")

The balance of liberal and conservative considerations in people's minds depends on both society-level and individual-level variables. The key societal variables are the intensities of liberal and conservative information flows in the political environment with respect to a given issue. The key individual variables are political awareness and political predispositions. More aware persons will be exposed to more political communications (via the Reception

Axiom) but will be more selective in deciding which communications to internalize as considerations (via the Resistance Axiom). Thus, politically aware citizens will tend to fill their minds with large numbers of considerations, and these considerations will tend to be relatively consistent with one another and with the citizens' predispositions. Less aware persons will internalize fewer considerations and will be less consistent in doing so. As a result, more aware people will be more likely to be able to state opinions, and more likely to state opinions that are ideologically consistent with their predispositions.

NOTES

1. This term is a borrowing from Kelley (1983), who showed that individuals appear to make vote decisions in presidential elections on the basis of a net score across numerous competing "likes" and "dislikes" about the candidates, which he called "considerations."

2. These terms derive from McGuire, 1969.

REFERENCES

Converse, Philip. 1964. "The Nature of Belief Systems in Mass Publics." In *Ideology and Discontent*, edited by David Apter, 206–61. New York: Free Press.

Kelley, Stanley, Jr. 1983. *Interpreting Elections.* Princeton, NJ: Princeton University Press.

McGuire, William J. 1969. "The Nature of Attitudes and Attitude Change." In *Handbook of Social Psychology*, 2d ed. edited by G. Lindzey and E. Aronson, 136–314. Reading, MA.: Addison-Wesley.

9.3

DONALD R. KINDER AND CINDY D. KAM

From *Us Against Them: Ethnocentric Foundations of American Opinion*

In this excerpt from their book, Us Against Them: Ethnocentric Foundations of American Opinion, *Kinder and Kam show strong evidence that many Americans hold deep-seated prejudices against people who are of a different race. Furthermore, those prejudices are manifestations of ethnocentrism—seeing the world as "us and them." Ethnocentrism has meaningful political consequences. It can shape the different political attitudes and partisanship of people from different racial groups, affecting their voting behavior and the nature of their political participation.*

AMERICAN ETHNOCENTRISM TODAY

. . . [E]thnocentrism is an attitude that divides the world into two opposing camps. From an ethnocentric point of view, groups are either "friend" or they are "foe." Ethnocentrism is a general outlook on social difference; it is prejudice, broadly conceived.

■ ■ ■

Measuring Ethnocentrism

Ethnocentrism is commonly expressed through *stereotypes*. Stereotypes refer to the beliefs we possess about social groups—what we know or what we think we know about "poets, professors, professional wrestlers, and film stars" (Brown 1965, p. 188), among others. Stereotypes capture the characteristics that define a social group, that set it apart from others. Most often, such characteristics have to do with underlying dispositions—temperament, intelligence, trustworthiness—the deep core of human nature. When we say that "Jews are pushy" or that "blacks are lazy," we are trafficking in stereotypes.[1]

Stereotyping is often held up for reprimand, but it is an inevitable aspect of human cognition. To negotiate and make sense of the world, we need stereotypes. "Life is so short," as Gordon Allport once put it, "and the demands upon us for practical adjustments so great, that we cannot let our ignorance detain us in our daily transactions. We have to decide whether objects are good or

From Donald R. Kinder and Cindy D. Kam, *Us Against Them: Ethnocentric Foundations of American Opinion* (Chicago: University of Chicago Press, 2010), Chapter 3.

bad by classes. We cannot weigh each object in the world by itself. Rough and ready rubrics, however coarse and broad, have to suffice" (1954, p. 9).

If stereotypes are grounded in ordinary cognitive processes and if they reduce the social world to manageable size, they are, of course, very much a mixed blessing. For one thing, stereotypes exaggerate differences and sharpen boundaries: in-groups and out-groups appear more different from each other than they actually are. . . . For another, stereotypes tend to portray members of out-groups as though they were all the same: individual variation is flattened, anomalous cases are set aside. . . . Third, stereotypes are permeated by affect. To say that "Jews are pushy" or that "blacks are lazy" is not only to make a judgment but also to express an emotion. And fourth, stereotypes are easily activated and, once activated, influence judgment and behavior in a variety of ways.[2]

▪ ▪ ▪

How common is in-group favoritism in a fully modern setting? Do Americans attribute favorable characteristics more to their own group than they do to out-groups? Or, put the other way around, do they attribute undesirable characteristics less to their own group than they do to out-groups?

To answer these questions, consider Table [1]. There we have summarized results for a single characteristic (lazy versus hard-working) taken from a single survey (the 1992 NES). The columns of the table are defined by the group that is being rated. In the 1992 NES, the columns refer to ratings of whites, blacks, Hispanics, and Asians. The rows of the table are defined by the group that is providing the rating: ratings by whites, blacks, Hispanics,

TABLE [1]   In-Group Favoritism Expressed through Stereotypes (Lazy versus Hard-Working)

	Assessments of:			
Assessments by:	*Whites*	*Blacks*	*Hispanics*	*Asians*
Whites	0.32	−0.06	0.02	0.29
	(1627)	(1609)	(1538)	(1511)
Blacks	0.20	0.24	0.16	0.25
	(264)	(268)	(249)	(239)
Hispanics	0.33	−0.01	0.28	0.30
	(168)	(168)	(167)	(157)
Asians	0.38	−0.18	0.02	0.63
	(28)	(27)	(27)	(28)

NOTE: Table entry is the average assessment of each group, among respondents in each racial/ethnic group, on the lazy versus hard-working trait question. The trait assessments are coded from −1 (Nearly all are lazy) to +1 (Nearly all are hard-working). Number of observations appears in parentheses.
SOURCE: 1992 NES.

and Asians. The main elements of the table are mean scores on the trait, coded from –1 (almost all are lazy) to +1 (almost all are hard-working), with 0 representing the midpoint. A positive score indicates a favorable judgment, just as a negative score indicates an unfavorable judgment. The table also provides the number of cases (in parentheses) for each calculation. In some instances, this number is small (for Asian Americans, the number is perilously small).

Do whites, as predicted, attribute the characteristic of hard-working more to their own group than they do to blacks, Hispanics, and Asians? The first row of Table [1] shows that they do. Asian Americans display in-group favoritism too, and even more conspicuously (fourth row of Table [1]). The results for blacks and Hispanics are different, however. Both blacks and Hispanics see their own group as generally hard-working—but they generally see other groups as hard-working, too. As a result, in-group favoritism among black and Hispanic Americans is partial or limited. It shows up in just one respect. Black Americans believe blacks to be more hard-working than Hispanics, and Hispanics, returning the favor, believe that Hispanics are more hard-working than blacks.

The pattern of results shown in Table [1] is entirely general. It is just what we see elsewhere, in other NES and GSS surveys, and on other characteristics: intelligence, patriotism, self-reliance, trustworthiness, propensity for violence, and more. Everywhere we look, we find general in-group favoritism among white and Asian Americans, and partial in-group favoritism among black and Hispanic Americans.[3]

▪   ▪   ▪

Correlates of Ethnocentrism

Next we examine ethnocentrism's place among a standard set of social and political predispositions. We have argued that ethnocentrism represents a distinctive way of looking at the world. From an ethnocentric point of view, groups are either "friend" or "foe." As such, ethnocentrism might be correlated with other political predispositions—with certain varieties of conservatism, say— but it cannot be interchangeable with them. If that turned out to be true, then we would have no reason to proceed, no warrant for arguing that the understanding of public opinion has been diminished by the failure, up until now, to take ethnocentrism seriously. To see how closely ethnocentrism is associated with standard political predispositions, we rely on our primary measure of ethnocentrism, the one based on stereotypes (E), though the results would be no different were we to use the alternative measure based on group sentiment (E*).

We start with partisanship, first among equals when it comes to political predispositions. Most Americans think of themselves as Democrats or as Republicans. Party identification is a standing decision, a "durable attachment, not readily disturbed by passing events and personalities" (Campbell et al.

[1960] 1980, p. 151). And it is consequential: "To the average person, the affairs of government are remote and complex, and yet the average citizen is asked periodically to formulate opinions about these affairs. . . . In this dilemma, having the party symbol stamped on certain candidates, certain issue positions, certain interpretations of reality is of great psychological convenience" (Stokes 1966, pp. 126–27; also see Bartels 2000; Converse 1966; Green, Palmquist, and Schickler 2002). To the extent that the issues we take up in the chapters ahead—from the war on terrorism to affirmative action in college admissions—generate strong and durable disagreements between Democratic and Republican elites, we would expect Democrats and Republicans in the general public to disagree as well. Put differently, partisanship is likely to play an important part in our analysis of public opinion. True enough, but whatever part partisanship plays in opinion must be independent of the part ethnocentrism plays. As Table [2] reveals, partisanship and ethnocentrism are virtually uncorrelated.[4]

What about the relationship between ethnocentrism and views on the size and scope of government authority? Compared to citizens of other developed democracies, Americans are, on average, "suspicious of government, skeptical about the benefits of government authority, and impressed with the virtue of limiting government" (Kingdon 1999, p. 29). Moreover, differences among Americans on broad questions of governmental authority generate corresponding differences on a wide range of specific policy questions. Limited government is an important idea—but as Table [2] shows, it has no association with ethnocentrism.[5]

TABLE [2]   The Relationship between Ethnocentrism and Social and Political Predispositions

	Full sample	Whites	Blacks	Hispanics
Partisanship	−0.06	−0.00	0.02	0.03
	(4923)	(3931)	(598)	(394)
Limited government	−0.03	−0.09	−0.05	−0.02
	(4947)	(3951)	(604)	(392)
Egalitarianism	−0.19	−0.18	0.07	−0.02
	(4974)	(3964)	(609)	(401)
Ideological identification	−0.07	−0.07	0.02	0.03
	(4945)	(3951)	(599)	(395)
Social trust	−0.08	−0.17	−0.02	−0.07
	(4898)	(3901)	(602)	(395)

NOTE: Table entry is the Pearson correlation coefficient. Number of observations appears in parentheses.
SOURCES: 1992, 1996, 2000, and 2004 NES.

Alongside the American taste for limited government, and to some degree in opposition to it, is a preference for egalitarianism—what Tocqueville called the American "passion" for equality. Americans seem to take egalitarian beliefs—that everyone is fundamentally the same under the skin, that everyone deserves the same chance in life—seriously, and such general beliefs appear to influence what they think government should do (if anything) about poverty, health care, discrimination, and more. As might be expected, and as Table [2] shows, egalitarianism and ethnocentrism are negatively correlated. Ethnocentric Americans are inclined, slightly but consistently, to reject egalitarian principles.[6]

Next we consider ideological identification. It turns out that when asked directly, many American are willing to describe themselves in ideological terms—as liberals or (more often) as conservatives—and these descriptions appear to be, if not sophisticated or philosophical, politically meaningful. Self-identified liberals tend to favor redistributive policies and social change; self-identified conservatives tend to celebrate the market and express misgivings about racial integration (Conover and Feldman 1981; Levitin and Miller 1979). Liberals and conservatives also differ when it comes to ethnocentrism—Americans who think of themselves as conservative are a bit more ethnocentric, on average, than are those who think of themselves as liberal—though the difference is tiny, as shown in Table [2].[7]

■   ■   ■

In sum, partisanship, limited government, equality, ideological identification, and social trust are often treated as important ingredients in American public opinion. Our analysis of opinion will certainly take them into account. But the findings presented in Table [2] make clear that we can put away the worry that ethnocentrism brings nothing new to political analysis—that ethnocentrism is just another word for conservatism or anti-egalitarianism or the like. Ethnocentrism represents a distinctive outlook on social life, one that, . . . has a distinctive and independent impact on public opinion.

NOTES

1. On the definition of stereotype, see Allport (1954); McCauley, Stitt, and Segal (1980); and Stangor and Lange (1994).

2. For evidence on the power of stereotypes to shape judgment and behavior, see M. Brewer (1988); Devine (1989); Fazio and Dunton (1997); and Fiske (1998).

3. Other surveys include 1996 NES, 2000 NES, 2004 NES, 1990 GSS, and 2000 GSS.

4. Partisanship is measured with v923634, v960420, v000523, v043116. It ranges from 0 (strong Republican) to 1 (strong Democrat).

5. On this theme, see Tocqueville ([1848] 1994), Myrdal (1944), Lipset (1959), Hofstadter (1948), and especially Louis Hartz's *The Liberal Tradition in America* (1955). Limited government is measured by a three-item scale that has become a regular part of NES, thanks to research and development work by Gregory Markus (2001).

In 1992 NES, the limited government scale consists of an additive index of v925729–v925731. In 1996 NES, it consists of v961144–v961146. In 2000 NES, it is comprised of v0001420–v001422. In 2004 NES, it consists of v045150–v045152. The scale is fairly reliable (*alpha* averages 0.73 across the years). The index ranges from 0 (want more active government) to 1 (want less active government).

6. On the meaning and measurement of equality, see Feldman (1988); Kinder and Sanders (1996); Feldman and Zaller (1992); McClosky and Zaller (1984); Schlozman and Verba (1979); and Sears, Henry, and Kosterman (2000).

In 1992 NES, the egalitarianism scale consists of an additive index of v926024–v926029. In 1996 NES, it consists of v961229–v961234. In 2000 NES, it is comprised of v001521–v001526. In 2004 NES, it consists of v045212–v045217. The scale is reasonably reliable (*alpha* averages 0.70 across the years). The index ranges from 0 (not) to 1 (egalitarian).

7. Ideological identification is measured with v923509, v960365, v001368, and v045117. It ranges from 0 (extremely conservative) to 1 (extremely liberal).

REFERENCES

Allport, Gordon W. 1954. *The Nature of Prejudice*. Cambridge, MA: Addison-Wesley.

Bartels, Larry M. 2000. "Partisanship and Voting Behavior, 1952–1996." *American Journal of Political Science* 44 (1): 35–50.

Brewer, Marilynn B. 1988. "A Dual Process Model of Impression Formation." In *Advances in Social Cognition*, vol. 1, ed. T. K. Srull and R. S. Wyer, 1–36. Hillsdale, NJ: Erlbaum.

Brown, Roger. 1965. *Social Psychology*. New York: Free Press.

Campbell, Angus, Philip E. Converse, Warren E. Miller, and Donald E. Stokes. [1960] 1980. *The American Voter*, unabridged ed. Chicago: Midway Reprint.

Conover, Pamela, and Stanley Feldman. 1981. "The Origins and Meaning of Liberal/Conservative Self-Identification." *American Journal of Political Science* 25 (4): 617–45.

Converse, Philip E. 1966. "Information Flow and the Stability of Partisan Attitudes." In *Elections and the Political Order*, edited by Angus Campbell, Philip E. Converse, Donald Stokes, and Warren E. Miller, 136–57. New York: Wiley.

Devine, Patricia G. 1989. "Stereotypes and Prejudice: Their Automatic and Controlled Components." *Journal of Personality and Social Psychology* 56 (1): 5–18.

Fazio, Russell H., and B. C. Dunton. 1997. "Categorization by Race: The Impact of Automatic and Controlled Components of Racial Prejudice." *Journal of Experimental Social Psychology* 33: 451–70.

Feldman, Stanley. 1988. "Structure and Consistency in Public Opinion: The Role of Core Beliefs and Values." *American Journal of Political Science* 32 (2): 416–40.

Feldman, Stanley, and John R. Zaller. 1992. "The Political Culture of Ambivalence." *American Journal of Political Science* 36 (1): 268–307.

Fiske, Susan T. 1998. "Stereotyping, Prejudice, and Discrimination." In *Handbook of Social Psychology*, 4th ed., edited by Daniel Gilbert, Susan T. Fiske, and Gardner Lindzey, 357–411. Boston: McGraw-Hill.

Green, Donald P., Bradley Palmquist, and Eric Schickler. 2002. *Partisan Hearts and Minds*. New Haven, CT: Yale University Press.

Hartz, Louis, 1955. *The Liberal Tradition in America*. New York: Harcourt Brace.

Hofstadter, Richard. 1948. *The American Political Tradition and the Men Who Made It*. New York: Knopf.

Kinder, Donald R., and Lynn M. Sanders. 1996. *Divided by Color.* Chicago: University of Chicago Press.

Kingdon, John W. 1999. *America the Unusual.* Belmont, CA: Wadsworth.

Levitin, Teresa E., and Warren E. Miller. 1979. "Ideological Interpretations of Presidential Elections." *American Political Science Review* 73: 751–71.

Lipset, Seymour Martin. 1959. *Political Man: The Social Bases of Politics.* Baltimore: Johns Hopkins University Press.

Markus, Gregory B. 2001. "American Individualism Reconsidered." In *Citizens and Politics: Perspectives from Political Psychology,* edited by James H. Kuklinski, 401–32. New York: Cambridge University Press.

McCauley, C., C. L. Stitt, and M. Segal. 1980. "Stereotyping: From Prejudice to Prediction." *Psychological Bulletin* 87: 195–208.

McClosky, Herbert M., and John Zaller. 1984. *The American Ethos: Public Attitudes toward Capitalism and Democracy.* Cambridge, MA: Harvard University Press.

Myrdal, Gunnar. 1944. *An American Dilemma: The Negro Problem and Modern Democracy.* New York: Harper and Row.

Schlozman, Kay Lehman, and Sidney Verba. 1979. *Insult to Injury: Unemployment, Class, and Political Response.* Cambridge, MA: Harvard University Press.

Sears, David O., P. J. Henry, and Rick Kosterman. 2000. "Egalitarian Values and Contemporary Racial Politics." In *Racialized Politics,* edited by David O. Sears, Jim Sidanius, and Lawrence Bobo, 75–117. Chicago: University of Chicago Press.

Stangor, Charles, and James E. Lange. 1994. "Mental Representations on Social Groups: Advances in Understanding Stereotypes and Stereotyping." *Advances in Experimental Social Psychology* 26: 357–416.

Stokes, Donald E. 1966. "Party Loyalty and the Likelihood of Deviating Elections." In *Elections and the Political Order,* edited by Angus Campbell, Philip E. Converse, Warren E. Miller, and Donald E. Stokes, 125–35. New York: Wiley.

Tocqueville, Alexis de. [1848] 1994. *Democracy in America.* New York: Knopf.

9.4

KATHERINE J. CRAMER

From *The Politics of Resentment: Rural Consciousness in Wisconsin and the Rise of Scott Walker*

Cramer dove deep into the Wisconsin countryside to listen to people in rural areas talk about politics and government. In this striking reading, she reveals the complexities of political attitudes among rural people. Many of them feel alienated from government and shut out of national and state conversations about the future direction of the country. She argues that their attitudes, often simplified and ridiculed, and sometimes ignored, deserve to be taken seriously. These people may feel forgotten, but when they find candidates that appeal to them, they make big waves that can roil national and state politics.

REPUBLICAN AND RURAL: NOT JUST A CORRELATION

Scholars and political pundits have known for decades, over a century even, that there is a correlation between votes and rural-urban location in the United States. [Scholars know] very little about the way rural-versus-urban divides function *as a perspective* through which some people think about politics.

Since the mid-twentieth century, Wisconsin has looked pretty much like national electoral maps: blue cities and red rural places. In Wisconsin, the Democratic Party's success in the larger cities is due in part to stronger union organizing (Fowler 2008, 184) and the concentration of African Americans in those places. Also, some of the Republicanism in the rural areas may be a hold-over from anti–Democratic Party attitudes that rose up during World War I and II. Many Wisconsinites have German relatives somewhere in their family—43 percent of residents claimed German heritage in 2000 (Fowler 2008, 205). German American voters were strongly isolationist during World War I and II and, therefore, likely to vote against the Democrats, especially in rural areas, where unions had little influence (Fowler 2008).

Rural-urban divides have been an important part of Wisconsin's politics for at least a century. One of our famous quirks is that we were home to both

From Katherine J. Cramer, *The Politics of Resentment: Rural Consciousness in Wisconsin and the Rise of Scott Walker* (Chicago: University of Chicago Press, 2016).

Joe McCarthy and Bob La Follette, two decidedly different characters. McCarthy was the U.S. senator who is responsible for "McCarthyism"—the post–World War II anticommunist scare that led to the interrogations of many Americans, particularly government employees, people in the entertainment industry, and those involved in labor unions. La Follette, in contrast, is the father of Progressivism. He served in the U.S. House, the U.S. Senate, and was governor of the state in the first few decades of the twentieth century.

Some say that rural-urban tensions help explain how both of these folks were successful in the same state. Granted, the fact that La Follette and McCarthy were both from Wisconsin is a little less mysterious when you consider that they both started out as Republicans. Wisconsin was overwhelmingly Republican for much of the first half of the twentieth century (Epstein 1958). But the rural-urban divide helps solve part of the La Follette–McCarthy mystery, too. Both of them tapped into rural consciousness to win votes. When La Follette's Progressivism took hold, Wisconsin was mainly a nonmetropolitan state—as it is now. In that context, skepticism of party organizations among rural residents was a stronger force than was support of political machines among urban residents (Epstein 1958). Some scholars argue that McCarthy won his Senate seat by exploiting the skepticism that small-town residents had of globalization and distant institutions. Even the breakthrough of the modern Democratic Party—the election of Democrat William Proxmire to the Senate in a special election after McCarthy's death—is commonly understood as the result of Proxmire's successful appeal to "rural discontent" (Fowler 2008, 173). Also, he is the senator who devised the monthly Golden Fleece Award, an award he bestowed on a public official who had made an excessive government expenditure. Although a member of the Democratic Party, the party typically associated with "big government," he was a champion of government frugality.

For some time, then, there has been a correlation in Wisconsin, as in most of the United States, between rural and Republican. But that correlation is not inevitable and is not simply the result of people voting the same way their parents did. People have perspectives and understandings that make support for Republican candidates seem appropriate and natural.

. . . The perspective I am calling rural consciousness . . . had three main elements. First, rural consciousness was about perceptions of power, or who makes decisions and who decides what to even discuss. Second, it showed up with respect to perceptions of values and lifestyles. Third and finally, it involved perceptions of resources or who gets what.

These are the outlines of the rural consciousness I encountered. Every expression of this perspective did not sound exactly the same. As with all identities, people in particular places put their own twist on who they are. . . .

WHERE IS "RURAL" IN WISCONSIN?

. . . The two main metropolitan areas of the state . . . are Madison, the state capital and home to the flagship public university, and . . . Milwaukee, the main industrial area of the state. They are both located in the southern part of Wisconsin. The places outside these metro areas are sometimes referred to as "Outstate" or "out-state Wisconsin" (though this name annoys some people who live in those areas of the state) and the northern tier of the state, largely a tourist area, is typically called "up north."

This division of the state into Madison and Milwaukee versus the rest of the state was common knowledge to the people I encountered outside of Madison and Milwaukee. When talking about the big issues of the day, many of the people I visited in small towns automatically referred to this geography.

■ ■ ■

The rural consciousness perspective I heard was most common in communities one would readily identify as rural—lots of green space, few stoplights, and far from an urban center. But it also emerged in areas best described as nonmetro: more populous areas but beyond the major metro centers of Madison and Milwaukee. Rural consciousness was a matter of degree. Sometimes, for convenience, I use the term "rural" to refer broadly to all areas outside the two major metro areas in the state.

POWER

. . . The place-based sense of injustice among rural residents [could be] heard . . . in many of the groups I spent time with outside the Madison and Milwaukee areas. . . .

The rural consciousness perspective . . . was more than just identity as a rural person. Besides place identity, it encompassed perceptions of power, values and lifestyles, and resources. . . . When I heard people talking about rural consciousness in these conversations, they were often talking about several of these central elements.

. . . A good place to start is . . . education. [The] complaint that Wisconsin's funding formula for education unfairly hurt rural communities was a common concern across groups meeting in rural places. For example, on my first visit to [a] dice game group in central west Wisconsin, I started out with my "what are your big concerns here" question:

KJC: Anything—it can be any kind of concerns—I'll ask you more directly about the UW later on. What kind of issues? Partly the reason I want to know is that we do a phone survey at the UW and usually when we decide which topics to—

MARK: One thing we were bitching about yesterday is that you—is the state's penchant for unfunded mandates—what three times, two times they got a referenda in the community that was not wanted. And so now—they keep jamming the cost down to the county so they can avoid spending it on the state's nickel, that has to stop.

ERNIE: Things that are mandated should be paid for.

MARK: Yeah, the tax structure in this state is weird. I think that is a fundamental problem with the state is that they have to reorganize their tax structure. Local schools, local municipalities, and of course the state—what they're doing is they're just redirecting tax burden on the local taxes which ends up being more evident to the locals, so they more complain and then what ends up happening is they say it isn't their fault.

RICHARD: We don't have the economic base here to pay the kind of taxes that comes out of Madison. You know I mean down there if things go up 1 percent it doesn't—but 1 percent means a hell of a lot more here than it does in Madison or what Henry calls south of the Mason Dixon Line, the line east and west going through Wausau.

DALE: Or Portage [a city about an hour's drive north of Madison].

RICHARD: Well—

MARK: But I mean you know, right down to the tax form or the support form for the schools—why is a kid worth fourteen thousand dollars in Mequon [a suburban Milwaukee city] and what is he up here, Henry? Seven?

HENRY: Oh yeah—the consistency in schools that we're spending money— ridiculous. . . . Why don't they give each school X number of dollars per kid? If they want to spend eleven thousand dollars on a kid, tax the school district for the difference.

ERNIE: Have it averaged.

HENRY: Yeah, have it averaged. Everybody gets eight thousand dollars and if you want to spend eleven, tax the local district for it. Comprehensive plan.

MARK: This goes with the schools, in terms of facilities—facilities are gorgeous because they have the money to spend on it.

HENRY: If you take the state of Wisconsin and take a ruler and start at Green Bay and diagonally and just go fifty miles north of Madison, right over to the corner of the state, all your money lies in the south end of the state, your votes weight there. You're never going to get nothing changed to the north.

DAVE: That is absolutely correct.

HENRY: That's it.

MARK: That's not just the schools.

HENRY: We listen to the—being on the school board, we went several times to testify to the legislature to tell you that the formula was wrong, but they don't change it, because we haven't—if anybody on the south end would say change the formula for the schools, they never would get elected another two years and that's why all they are is looking for their own job.

Somebody makes a comment about the University of Wisconsin–Madison, and then Henry offers up his thoughts.

HENRY: And another thing, every time the state has a program, where do they, where do they implement it? Madison, Lake Geneva, in Milwaukee. They give everything to Milwaukee. You know all the programs in education—they want to try a new program, where do they put it? Milwaukee. Dead at the start. Why don't they put it out here where we can do something with it? Dead at the start.

RICHARD: Far as I can—like with—kept their schools up, Milwaukee let theirs fall down, and then they take our tax money to deal with the schools after we kept ours up. And they let theirs fall down.

HENRY: First of all, they oughta take that formula they give Milwaukee—they give Milwaukee a whole wad of money right off the top first and whatever is left, we divide by the other 425 schools in the state, which is wrong. Let Milwaukee do their own—get their fair—same share as we get, don't give a whole wad of it to them and then turn around and divide the rest among the rest of us.

In this conversation, the men complain about taxes and unfunded mandates—complaints that could come from someone in any type of municipality—but then they talk about this unfairness in terms of geography, namely, that a 1 percent tax increase "means a hell of a lot more here" than it does in the metro areas. They perceive that the decision making or the exercise of power in the major cities victimizes people in small towns by giving them less than their fair share of resources. In their eyes, decisions about funding for schools mean that small communities are the victims of distributive injustice.

Across the state, in a north-central tourist town, I asked a group of people at a diner counter early in the morning if they "feel like you're paying your fair share up here? Or heck no?"

NELSON: Well we'd like to keep more of our money for our school districts up here instead of sending it down below.

HELLEN [*The only other woman at the counter at that moment who is somewhat a little apologetic that she is about to leave me alone with them*]: I'm going to leave you with them.

KJC: Nice to meet you.

HELLEN: Good luck with these guys.

KJC: Oh thank you. So I'm sorry [to interrupt]—the schools. . . .

NELSON: They're taking so much of our money away from us. Want to close our schools and that sort of stuff, and the schools in Milwaukee and Madison and everyplace south of us, they've got all the foreign languages and everything else, and they got their curriculum is so much better than what we can give—because the fact that the state is not allowing us to have our money to educate our kids the way we should.

TREVOR: Talking about state schools? I thought that money came from here.

NELSON: Yeah—all of our money goes to Madison gets distributed back down to us.

KJC: A chunk of it—I don't know what percent but a good chunk of it.

NELSON: Yeah—the bureaucracy gets bigger and bigger. Their secretaries have to have secretaries . . .

PETE: Gotta figure with all the out-of-staters here, pay a lot of taxes.

NELSON: Oh sure—exactly true. People come up here to retire, the taxes eat 'em up. They have to move off [the lakes], but that's been their dream to get up here.

KJC: Oh no kidding.

NELSON: You know, as far as I'm concerned, I pay it, I don't protest, but I would like it if the city, the state would get fairer with the money. Why can't we have a foreign languages and that sort of stuff? Prepare for life after high school. They [kids from our community] get down to the colleges [which are almost all located south of this town], they are behind. . . .

Conversations about school funding often echoed the view that the rural areas were not getting their fair share. In such comments, people conveyed their identity as rural folks as well as their sense of injustice over the distribution of power and resources. I heard the claim that people in rural communities are helpless to change these funding formulas because no one downstate is listening to their concerns. They perceived that politicians and government in general are tone deaf to people outside the major cities.

Resentment about a lack of power compared to city people came through on many topics besides education. A group of people meeting in a gas station in a gorgeous hamlet on the Wisconsin River in southwest Wisconsin [was] very critical of what they saw as the state government's concern for tourists from the major cities and the Chicago area rather than themselves . . . :

GLENN: Just like everything else in Wisconsin, the most important thing to politicians in Wisconsin and in the state government is getting the tourists in here and the people out of Illinois. . . . You go to a boat landing around here and hell you can't unload your boat because there will be a dozen Illinois people there and they are top priority to the state and anybody with a supposed tourist label on 'em.

LARRY: Be there with their canoes, bring their food with 'em, their water, all they leave on the sand bars is shit.

[*Laughter*]

Four years later, their animosity toward the state government's neglect of their community's concerns came out as a complaint against unfunded mandates.

GEORGE: And where I see a lot of wasted money is garbage that I receive in the mail that doesn't have . . . I've been on the town board for about thirty-five years already . . .

KJC: Oh bless your heart.

GEORGE: And all the garbage I get, mail that doesn't even have anything to do with this area here whatsoever.

KJC: Huh. What kind of stuff?

GEORGE: Oh, from the state. Mandating everything, you know, do this, do that and our township doesn't have any curbs and gutters, there's so much stuff that the rural area doesn't even have that, you know, people in Milwaukee and Madison think, you know, that it's a big deal, but out here it's nothing.

As far as this group was concerned, city folks sent little to their community but junk mail and poop.

Even in a left-leaning group of retired women in an artsy community in northern Wisconsin, many of the members thought government paid no attention to their concerns.

KJC: OK, "How much attention do you feel the government pays to what the people think when it decides what to do? A good deal, some, or not much?"

[*Long pause*]

SUE: I think they're starting to get, that they're starting to listen with all this mess [the Great Recession].

KJC: Some. Yeah?

SUE: Before this I don't think. . . . I think it's changing.

DOROTHY: I think it's in the Beltway and out the Beltway. I mean Madison might listen to Madison people. Washington, DC, is a country unto itself. I know it; I spent time there. They haven't got a clue what the rest of the nation is up to, they're so absorbed studying their own belly button.

It is not a stretch to say that people in many places—not just rural areas—feel ignored by the government. But the complaints I heard in rural areas were not simply distrust of government—people in rural areas often perceived that government was *particularly* dismissive of the concerns of people in rural communities. Half of the groups outside the major metro areas expressed that belief. These attitudes were antigovernment thoughts, but they were rooted in residents' place identities.

. . . In a logging town in northwestern Wisconsin, during the run-up to the 2008 presidential election, I had this conversation with the two men remaining that morning out of a group that gathers in the back of the grocery store/gas station/liquor store/gift shop/hardware store:

KJC: Do you . . . what are your hopes for this presidential election? How would you like it to turn out in November?

Both of them laughed in response to the question before answering as follows:

SCOTT: Doesn't make any difference to me . . . Never has. I'm not a big political . . . I can't stand it because I've been around it for thirty-four years. County boards and stuff. I have no use for any of it. I'm sorry, I just—I'm sorry. That may be kind of a horseshit attitude, but I just, I'm sorry, I just don't.

KJC: A lot of people feel that way. The presidential candidates, you know, sometimes Wisconsin—

SCOTT: I can't see the difference it's gonna make up here anyway. We've been in a recession up here for thirty years, forty years. We don't know any different. People talk about recession, you oughta come up here.

KJC: Yeah?

SCOTT: Doesn't get any different.

Scott thought candidates did not care about his community and that his community, his place, had been ignored for decades. This was part of a widespread perception that small towns like his were generally overlooked. A group of women meeting for lunch in a central-west village on the day of the gubernatorial recall election in 2012 felt small communities like theirs had been "hung out to dry." I fumbled around with the question, but they ran with it.

KJC: Who do you think represents your concerns? I mean . . . do you . . . are there . . . does . . . do you feel like your state senator or state assembly person? Do you feel like anybody—

GLADYS: I think we are just hung out there to dry.

DOLORES: Great. I would agree with you. [*chuckles*]

KJC: That was the answer I feared, I mean—

DOLORES: There isn't anyone, I don't think, that really addresses the concerns of the smaller communities.

BEVERLY: No. I don't think so.

GLADYS: And being an agricultural dairy state, I understand that some of these farmers haven't got a lot more or maybe right in the same ballpark that they get for their milk that we got when we were farming twenty-three years ago and look at what else has gone up. The money it costs for the crops to go up . . . Nobody . . . We got the news. OK. "This big building burned in some area." It's all over the news. [But if] some farmer loses his barn, which is probably the same amount of money and the same catastrophe, it barely gets three seconds. It's not good.

Ignored by government and by the news media, these folks felt neglected by the powers that be. One way I noticed this was in the way they reacted to me. Several groups could not quite believe that I had made the effort to come "all the way from Madison" to talk with them. For example, in the town with the dice game in the central-west city, I spent time with a group that met up in the *early*, early morning at a gas station . . . :

KJC: Nice to meet you. Here's a football schedule for you—would you like one? Football schedule? Good for three years. Convenient, yeah? You're welcome. I would love to come back like January or February to talk to you guys again, could I?

["*Sure!*"]

MARK: I think we need more input out of Madison in your small areas. Even like your senators, and everything. I mean they've gotta get around to do things like this.

Even higher income people in places outside the Madison and Milwaukee metro areas expressed this kind of surprise. They saw themselves as less important than people in the metro areas in the eyes of politicians and other decision makers. For example, one group of professionals meeting for coffee every morning in a diner in a central Wisconsin city said they were surprised that I, a university employee from Madison, was taking the time to drive around the state to listen to people like them: "I think that we are impressed [that you come up here to visit with us]. Because most of us, particularly in a state like Wisconsin where politicians—none of the national ones come and see us—you know we only have ten electoral votes. I mean none of the politicians come to see us at all." The Downtown Athletic Club perceived that the focus of politicians on cities rather than rural areas was a fact of politics nationwide:

KJC: Well, what's your take on the presidential election?

JOHN: You don't even want to know.

[*Fred laughs*]

KJC: Yes, I do! Sure I do. I don't want to start any fights. I want to know what you think.

JOHN: I don't know. How's that?

KJC: Oh you, yes you do. Why don't you . . .

JOHN: You had the state of Ohio, what was it? No. Pennsylvania. Where four precincts voted nineteen thousand some odd to nothing. For Obama. That just doesn't make a lot of sense, does it?

FRED: I didn't hear that story.

KJC: A little fishy. I didn't either.

JOHN: There was like four or so precincts where Romney never got a vote. Not one. You would think that any precinct that there'd be one person contrary to the norm. And at least I would.

MATT: Yeah, makes you wonder there, don't it.

JOHN: But uh no, I don't know. The election? The president knew where to campaign. He campaigned in all the metropolitan areas. The cities and stuff. That's where all the vote was. If you looked at, I go back to Ohio cause that was the swing state they all talked about all the time, and if you look at it on the map, I'm going to say there's sixty-five counties and Romney—so characteristic throughout the whole nation won—the vast majority of territory, he did not win the cities. I mean that's . . . somebody was attacking—

FRED: By square miles he'd have won.

KJC: Here in Wisconsin, too, right?

JOHN: Easily. What the . . . what did they say? All you have to do is win eleven cities and you can win the election?

KJC: Really?

JOHN: Someone was just saying that. The populist . . . the vote is that manner [set up in a way] that if you win eleven cities, you can win the election. I don't know if that's true but. . . .

To me, much of what is getting talked about here is power, and that power comes in several layers. The most obvious example of this power is the ability of governments to force rural places to abide by laws they dislike. This is the classic definition of power—the ability of A to get B to do something B otherwise would not do (Dahl 1961). "Unfunded mandates" is one example. But there is another dimension of power getting talked about here, too: control over which concerns even get recognized and discussed (Bachrach and Baratz 1962). I heard people in rural areas say many times that all of the major decisions are made in the urban areas, by urban people, and dictated outward. They complained that authority flowed out from Madison and Milwaukee but never in reverse. They felt that they did not have the power to get people to listen to their concerns.

While the inability to get their concerns heard is a subtle instance of feeling powerless, it is nonetheless important. Power is partly about respect, recognition, and listening. People whose voices are never heard by decision makers have no power. When those in power listen to some group, they convey that they are worthy of attention and, implicitly, that they share their power.

Many of the people I spent time with in rural areas felt like their towns were drying up and blowing away because the spigot of resources had been turned off. In addition, though, there was also a sense that these more subtle forms of power had been denied them as well.

One member of a group of retired and working women meeting for breakfast in a rural, far northern resort community explained:

THERESA: As a former educator, I resented, highly, comments such as, "There is no education north of Highway 8 [a U.S. highway that runs East-West across the middle of the state]. These kids aren't—" and we send them

such absolutely excellent and well-prepared students there that they—
the attitude that the hick area of the state—was painful.

KJC: So who did you get that from? Recruiters?

THERESA: Professors.

KJC: Really? When they would visit?

THERESA: Yeah, or publish in newspaper articles or other, you know—and that
was a little distressful because I think northern Wisconsin feels a little far
away from Madison anyway. And we keep waving our hands and saying,
"Yoo-hoo, there's another half of a state up here! Up north is not Wausau
[the main city in the central part of the state]!"

This is not just alienation, or a lack of trust, or low efficacy with respect to
powerful institutions. These sentiments are tightly bound to a sense of place
identity. Simply put, many folks I met in small places identified as rural
people and equated membership in that category with being a person who is
systematically ignored and left out of the exercise of power.

VALUES AND LIFESTYLES

When people talked about public affairs from a rural consciousness perspective they were telling me that city people have a lack of listening skills, exhibit
a chronic lack of respect for the rural way of life, and regularly ignore rural
communities. Many people talked about this as part and parcel of a fundamental aspect of the rural-versus-urban divide: city people just don't seem to
get it. They don't understand rural life or pay attention to it.

Part of the reason people in rural areas felt misjudged by urbanites were
the widely known stereotypes of rural folks. Many rural residents believed
that city dwellers thought they were just "a bunch of rednecks," for example.
A third of groups ($N = 18$) in places with populations under ten thousand
assumed that public decision makers in the major metro areas held common
negative stereotypes of rural residents, such as "hicks," "country bumpkins,"
"rednecks," and uneducated folks (Creed and Ching 1997; Jarosz and Lawson
2002). One group that I interviewed even went so far as to call themselves the
"Mediocre Redneck Coffee Klatch."

They were defensive, but they were also proud. And they had their own stereotypes of city folk. Slightly more than a third of these groups ridiculed
urbanites' lack of common sense. Many of them made a point of emphasizing
that in contrast to city folk, they understood how to really hunt and fish and
knew what it was like to really interact with nature. Also, many people took
enormous pride in using their hands rather than what they saw as what most
city folks did for work: sitting behind a desk all day.

This combination of pride in one's group and sense that their group is
deprived relative to other groups is characteristic of group consciousness in
general. So notice that although many rural residents resented cities, they did

not necessarily want to live in one. Conversations in eleven of the twenty-one groups located in places with populations of less than ten thousand included comments to the effect that, despite the hardships of rural life, they preferred their lifestyles to rootless, fast-paced city living. "Down in the cities, they don't even know their neighbors most of 'em!" one man exclaimed to me. People took pride in the face-to-face nature of their interactions, as opposed to the bureaucracy and technology they perceived to be typical of urban life. For example, one woman in a small town explained to me that, in her community, people do not do inspections when selling a house. "It's seen as insulting," she said. "If I give you my word that the house is in good shape, why would you need to inspect it?"

This perception of differing lifestyles for rural and urban residents fed the belief that city dwellers could not make decent decisions on behalf of rural communities. Such concerns were more focused on differences in ways of life and values than on differences in partisanship—that, say, city folks were Democrats and rural folks were Republican. In particular, many rural residents perceived a different pace of life in cities and were downright mad about attempts to appeal to tourists by urbanizing their own towns. For example, in [a] group of loggers in [a] northwestern village, during my first visit, I asked a general anything-else-I-should-know question, and here's what the group offered up:

KJC: But is there something else I oughta know about—I don't know—your lives in [this town] or what is going on up here? I know you can learn a whole lot in half an hour, but this is really helpful, actually.

[*Long pause*]

SAM: Well it's a lot less rat race than Madison.

KJC: Yeah, really peaceful.

JOHNNY: Yeah it's nice. I wouldn't live anywhere else.

KJC: Yeah you want to stay here—I can see that.

SAM: Drives to work, his house within a mile you're in the country—I mean not that [far] even.

KJC: Aw, it's beautiful.

SAM: Yeah, it's a lot less hectic. When you grow up this way. I guess if you grow up in the city, people say they can't stand it here. But if you grow up here—

KJC: Well, I think even city people, when they come up here, it's just like, "Wow it's so relaxing!" or they'll say things like—

SAM: Then they want to change everything. Have you been to Minocqua [a popular northern tourist town]?

KJC: Yeah.

SAM: Or Hayward [another popular northern tourist town]?

KJC: Not in a long time.

SAM: Hayward was like [this town] twenty years ago, and now it's got Walmart.

KJC: Hayward has a Walmart?

SAM: McDonald's, Menards, Subway—you turn around, you make a little Madison. Just strip malls. Downtown turns into antique stores because everything is out at Walmart. Lost all your businesses. Like this was all stores [as he waves his arm at the boarded-up Main Street outside].

A few hours west of that group of loggers, I met up two times in the town hall with a handful of leaders from the local government and the public schools who would turn on the lights and the Mr. Coffee machine and huddle together there every morning. The men resented outsiders' desire to urbanize northern Wisconsin.

DEAN: What generally happens is that one or the other likes it here, either the husband likes it here or the wife, and the other just hates it because they want to go downtown every day, and shop. But if they wanna go shopping they have to drive twenty miles. So eventually, we've got like two- or three-million-dollar homes built, and they were there like five years, and one or the other of 'em didn't like it, and they sold out and went back to Florida.

KJC: Wow, did somebody buy that home? I mean, who's gonna? . . .

JACK: Oh yeah.

KJC: Really.

JACK: They had, you know, snowmobiles, all kinds of equipment, fishing rods and boats and all that, but she hated it here. Well, just to be in that party system in the city, and you come up here in the wintertime, there's nothing. I think that more spread between the very, very wealthy who move up here, and, it seems like to me, what we might call the middle class is shrinking, and the ones on the bottom. I don't have any facts, but that's the way I look at it.

Although most of the commentary about the contrast in urban and rural lifestyles was not overtly political, sometimes people did bring in politics directly. The men who gathered around the Mr. Coffee shared this:

FRANK: Well, we're very conservative in the Northwoods and they're very, very, very, very, very, very, very left in those cities. Just think if Madison and Milwaukee and La Crosse did not vote in an election. What would've happened? I mean our votes mean nothing because of the population and the votes [the large number of votes coming from cities, as opposed to small towns]. That's how I look at it. Same reason [upper] Michigan years ago wanted to leave lower Michigan. Form their own state.

KJC: So you feel like the show is pretty much run by the people—

FRANK: Oh yes, oh yeah. Yeah. We don't have any say.

KJC: So how about with the DNR [state Department of Natural Resources]? When you were working with the DNR?

FRANK [*sarcastically*]: Fine group of men. [*laughs*]

KJC: No, because the reason I ask is because connected with the state government did you feel like in your job you still didn't have much of a say—it was pretty much the folks in Madison telling you what you—

DEAN: You work long enough you have something political—we had decent working conditions—

AL: And that was the end of it. Now the governor appoints all the big shots and they don't know, before a guy had to work from the bottom all the way up and then become the head of the DNR. Now they just pick some guy off the street.

JACK: Oh yeah.

AL: A buddy of the governor and . . . That's the way I think about it. The DNR's changed.

Most of the people in this group were themselves elected officials or vocal commentators on public affairs. Their resentment toward the decisions people made in the cities had a clear partisan tone.

But when people talked about the inability of city dwellers to adequately represent rural concerns, partisanship was not front and center. Even for the group around the Mr. Coffee, they referenced "conservatism" not "Republicanism." There was a sense that urban residents lived differently. They were carving up the world into "us" and "them," but partisanship was not the key divider.

In addition, when they talked as if city people lived by different values, they were not emphasizing abortion, or gay marriage, or the things that are typically pointed to as the cultural issues that divide lower-income whites from the Democratic Party. Instead, the values they talked about were intertwined with economic concerns. When they talked about city folks being unable to understand rural life, those conversations were typically about how they had no understanding of the economic realities of rural life and how hard people had to work to make ends meet in small towns.

Here is one example of rural residents talking about how they struggled harder to get by than did people in cities. This exchange took place among a group of women meeting for lunch in the central-west town where the dice game takes place. They brought up the topic of health care and complained about politicians making choices out of step with ordinary people like themselves.

DOLORES: I have this feeling that—I don't know who mentioned this it might have been Bill Cosby—that if all of these senators and congressmen and all of these people took a cut in their wages, you know, and their benefits . . . and took the benefits that we have to take—

GLADYS: Yeah!

DOLORES: Live on the kind of salary that we have to live on, you know. They have no idea what small, rural America is like . . . small towns, you know! They couldn't begin to fathom what's it like to live on the incomes that we live on.

KJC: Do you feel that way about the state politicians too?
DOLORES: Up to a point. Yeah. You know, their thing is to win . . .

In a tiny town in the northwestern part of the state I met with a group of
people that gathers in the basement of the local church every Tuesday morning: stay-at-home moms and some kids, retirees, and people taking a break
from work. For a good chunk of time, the first time I met them, they complained about how disrespectful one of their state legislative representatives
was and about how clueless state inspectors are. One example they gave me
was the time an inspector checked the temperature of food in a salad bar in a
restaurant a few towns over by sticking her thermometer in the ice.

When I asked them what the University of Wisconsin–Madison does not do
well, they stated bluntly that people in Madison and Milwaukee have qualita-
tively different lifestyles than do people in the rural parts of the state.

KJC: What do you think the University of Wisconsin–Madison does not do
    well? When you think about [it] . . .
MARTHA: Represents our area. I mean we are like, we're strange to Madison.
    They want us to do everything for Madison's laws and the way they do
    things, but we totally live differently than the city people live. So they need
    to think more rural instead of all this city area.
DONNA: We can't afford to educate our children like they can in the cities.
    Simple as that. Don't have the advantages.
ETHEL: All the things they do, based on Madison and Milwaukee, never us.
MARTHA: Yeah, we don't have the advantages that they give their local people
    there, I think a lot of times. And it is probably because they don't under-
    stand how rural people live and what we deal with and our problems.
KJC: I think that's right. I think there is a whole lot of distance between—
    especially this corner of the state.
MARTHA: Oh we're, like, we're lost up here!
ROSEMARY: They don't even understand how we live in [our community]!
[*Laughter*]
MARTHA: Yeah that's right! It's very true. They won't even come and help us
    with our roads until you demand it.

In that conversation, in response to my question about the main concerns
in their community, they had talked about their representative in Madison as
someone unlike themselves, and about the state workers that regulated their
livelihoods as oblivious to the basics of their businesses. The sense of being
"strange to Madison" and living "differently than the city people live" was
about fundamental difference in lived experience. And much of that difference was tied to economics: "We don't have the advantages that they give
their local people there," Martha had said.

■   ■   ■

RESOURCES

When people in small towns claimed that they lived differently and had different values than city folks, they were often simultaneously claiming that they were people facing unique economic challenges. I want to hone in on their perceptions of economic injustice to show you the depth of these understandings. When people perceived that rural life was economically tough, this carried with it many complaints: about the injustice in the distribution of public dollars, unfair taxation, and more. Those complaints were intertwined with other aspects of rural consciousness, in particular, with their sense of being ignored and disrespected and of having fundamentally different values and lifestyles than city dwellers.

Here is a common narrative for how people wove these perceptions together: Rural life was a source of pride for many because it was different from urban living—it involved different lifestyles and values, including a special emphasis on hard work. That rural hard work ethic was a point of pride, but for many, it was a problem because in order to work hard, you needed a job, and rural communities were on the short end of the stick in terms of jobs. Why? Because rural communities had no power. Politicians and others with the ability to make the decisions to bring good-paying jobs to their communities paid no attention to their places.

In the rural communities I visited, I often heard people stating, as though a matter of fact, that jobs, wealth, and taxpayer dollars are in "the M&Ms," as people sometimes referred to Madison and Milwaukee. They complained that rural areas are being left on their own to fight a losing battle. Conversations in seventeen of the twenty-five groups outside the Madison and Milwaukee areas included statements conveying that their communities did not receive their fair share of resources and that metro residents did not understand this. Their comments conveyed that the rural-versus-urban distinction was *the* main way to characterize the distribution of taxation, wealth, and the cost of goods and services in the state. In short, many people in small towns perceived that their tax dollars are "sucked in" by Madison and spent on that city or Milwaukee, never to be seen again.

On this mapping, wealthy people live in the cities (cf. Bell 1992, 78). "Everybody in [the] northern [part of the state] makes money off of tourists . . . [the tourists] bring some of that fresh money up," one man in the diner group in the north-central tourist town told me. On a different visit to the same group, another man said simply, "When you get down in the city, people are making more money."

Many people equated the cities with wealth because they perceived that the cities are where the good jobs are. One man in the group meeting in the small town on the Wisconsin River explained to me during my first visit, "Our salaries are less than what they are in Madison, by far, our hourly wages. And I would think salaried jobs as well. People here don't make as much, but there again, it's—that's why we don't have . . . that's why a lot of our young people have gone someplace else." About four years later, I heard a similar conversation in that group:

RANDY: I'd like to see, you know, I'd like to see a lot of new young families move into town . . . That's one thing you do see is too many older, retired persons in your communities—to be real active it makes a difference . . .

GLENN: A lack of good-paying jobs for the younger people to live on. You know it takes money to live or play or anything else and you get into a town like this and the people who are on the boards and stuff are people who usually own their homes and have a job and their interests are more in the parks and the fire departments and different things like that where it takes jobs for these young people to keep 'em around. And, you got jobs, you get young people, you get homes being built, and you get things being done.

RANDY: That's the problem with rural America.

GLENN: Right.

RANDY: You start here, go down along the river or whatever, you pick any of these communities, we're fortunate in [this town] . . . we're fortunate here that we got two or three good industries in town which we're very fortunate to have.

[. . .]

GLENN: In any of these towns. You go around Madison, thirty-, forty-mile radius, the majority of 'em are driving to Madison you know and it's, you know, they want to live in a small town but they gotta have a job, a decent paying job. With four-dollar gas, that's gonna make it tough.

Along with complaints about gas prices, I often heard concerns about utility bills in rural areas. For example, in the breakfast group of women in a rural tourist town:

SALLY: The cost of the water and sewer here is outrageous compared to what they pay in Madison. So here is big rich Madison, with all the good high-paying jobs, getting the cheapest water, and we have people up here who have three months of employment [because of the short tourist season], what are they paying? And I feel like there should be more sharing—less taxes going to Madison to help offset—

DOROTHY: I just moved from [a city in the central part of the state]. A quarter of water in [that city] is seventy bucks . . . seventy dollars every *three* months for [that] water. Up here, which we constantly have been paying, every second month, the bill—and sometimes we're not here—is seventy dollars every *second* month.

A bit later in the conversation, they continued on this theme.

SALLY: You've also got to look at Madison and the growth of Madison. There's new sewers going in every single day, the result of the businesses. You go down there and you don't know where Madison starts and Mount Horeb—I mean it is just one big sewer. . . . Like Walmart, buy it in volume, get it cheaper. But I think we don't look at places here—I mean I was coming up here eighteen years ago with a business, and I was shocked at how little the people got for services here. You pay for your garbage collection here on top of paying high taxes. I mean Madison, I throw out sofas [and don't have to pay]. There should be more sharing with these communities that are really struggling with stuff like that.

SHIRLEY: But in Madison there are all these big businesses that are paying taxes that we don't have here.

SUE: Exactly, but it should be a shared thing. I mean, why can't we look at that? Or at least put a state office building up here, with all the communication.

[*Agreement all around: "That would help."/ "That's a thought."/ "Great idea."/ "Absolutely."*]

SALLY: We could. I've worked for the state of Wisconsin, in a lot of offices, and a lot of offices could be—

DOROTHY: Outsource it to northern Wisconsin!

LAURA [*to me*]: You could be here all the time!

[*Laughter*]

KJC: That would be delightful—I would love it.

In the rural consciousness perspective, not only were the cities wealthier but they were also advantaged in terms of gas prices, utility bills, and infrastructure like sewers. These perceptions of injustice burned so brightly because they carried perceptions of blame. It was not just that cities were advantaged, but also that decision makers in them were intentionally overlooking the smaller communities in the state.

A man in the northwest logging group lamented, "I mean, rightfully so, you know, population centers, that's where the majority of the stuff has eventually got to go. It just makes sense. But you can't ignore everything up here either, you know." Likewise, a group of men at a diner in a rural northern-central tourist town almost laughed at the notion that the Obama administration stimulus proposal would help their community. They assumed none of the funds would focus on rural areas. One man said, "But the trickle down won't get to here because we don't have any business. So the trickle down will stop at Green Bay, Wausau [cities south of where they live] . . ."

Taxation was a seriously raw issue for many people in small communities. In general, the perception was that taxation hurt rural areas. At least one person in ten of the twenty-five groups outside the Milwaukee and Madison metro areas assumed that people in those cities are taxed at much lower rates than rural residents are.

Property taxes in particular were treated like an invasive species killing off native life forms. And people were sure it had come from the cities. Many rural folks blamed urbanites for driving up property values in their communities by purchasing expensive vacation homes. Some claimed this had driven locals out of their own communities or, at least, away from their lifetime dreams of finally buying a house on a local lake. They described these rising property values, driven by urbanites, as a threat to their personal and community identities (cf. Bell 1992, 76). For example, on the first morning that I met with the group of women in the rural northwest tourist town, one member showed me a list she had written in a small notebook of sixty people who had been forced out of their homes by urbanites buying expensive vacation homes. "The old-time families have left or are leaving," she said. "The character of the town is changing, and it is just too bad."

In Door County, the "thumb" of Wisconsin, I heard a similar thing from a woman taking part in a conversation after a church service:

> Having been raised and grown up here, it has gotten to the point that I think Door County is becoming very elitist. Thank God I have a home. I was lucky enough that my husband and I had worked for it and paid for it before he died. On my wages, I could not have bought a home by myself. The cost of all of the surrounding land has become so expensive because of all the people who don't live here more than six weeks out of the year, and build three-quarter-million-dollar homes, million-dollar homes, and basically visit, and so they've driven the property values so high that those people who have lived in a home their whole lives and were able to afford, can no longer afford because the tax rate has gone up so high. The wage scale is not that great in Door County. People say, "Well, you know, you make a good living." No. And they somehow get the impression that we go to the gas station and we pay less for our gas, and pay less for our food because we live here. Ah, wrong! We pay the same price [*laughter*], but we don't make the wages, and we're paying for what has been driven up, and it's—I see it as a real hardship. I'm fortunate, but I look at my children and my grandchildren and I wonder will they be able to live here and own a home? Maybe they'll be able to rent, but to live here and own a home and take pride in that? That's scary. Really is scary.

The sentiment that city people were oblivious to the economic hardships that rural residents face was simmering on the back burner in many of these conversations. People living in tourist communities acknowledged the income that tourism generated but resented the perception that people living "up north" led leisurely lives. A woman in a northwest rural town said to me, "Just remember that up here many people have two and three part-time jobs to survive." Across the state, one man explained to me that, yes, he lived in a beautiful wilderness area, but when the weather got nice enough to be outside, he hardly had time to enjoy it. It was during those summer months that he and most of the people he knew had to work multiple jobs to get by throughout the rest of the year: "I live on a lake—lived there twenty-three years. I've fished it three times. Just not enough time. When we want to fish, we go to Canada or Minnesota to get away from it all."

Four years earlier, some people in his breakfast group expressed exasperation at how clueless city people were about the economic realities of tourist towns.

NELSON: Yeah—people in town here, they sell their home in Milwaukee or Madison or Illinois and they come up here and buy one of these small businesses. Christ!

PETE: Yeah—wake up!

NELSON: You won't make any money for twenty years, if you can stay in business for that long, pay your taxes and everything else.

KJC: Wow.

NELSON: It's a different world up here than it is in the southern part of the state.

PETE: Looks great in the summer time!

NELSON: Yeah looks great.

PETE: Nine months are winter, and three months are tough sledding.

In Door County, the "tough sledding" sounded like this:

PAM: What you make in six months has to stretch all year.

BECKY: And many of 'em are working two and three jobs during this period of time.

PAM: Exactly.

BECKY: Yeah, they're not doing just one job.

PAM: You don't really have a summer—it consists of working. When my kids were home, I worked two jobs, so you know—it goes by quickly.

SHELLY: People always say, "You are so lucky to live [here] in the summertime!" Well, any of us who live here, live here and work here and never enjoy it. First of all we're irritated [*half-jokingly*] because we can't get to our job because of these tourists driving so slow.

KJC: I'm sorry! [*Apologizing for being a slow-driving tourist.*]

SHELLY: And then when we get there we work, leave that and go to another job and come home and then we are following another tourist to come home [*laughter*], and so we really don't get to enjoy what everybody else does, although I am so appreciative that I can live here, I really can't imagine—I just thank God every day that I am able to live here in [this town] where I was born.

DON [*sarcastically*]: You don't want to go to Milwaukee and live there?

SHELLY: No and I'm willing to give up a lot to do that, and I think a lot of us have done that.

The way they described it, making a living in a tourist community was a challenge, characterized by constant hardship and uncertainty. And they believed that urbanites just did not understand this.

People resented the economic hardships they faced, the fact that city people and those who held the reins of power did not seem to recognize these hardships, and, also, the unfulfilled promise of tourism. They did not necessarily like city people coming in to their communities but were willing to put up with it in order to make a living. In some places, however, people talked about city people infiltrating their communities, yet not helping the local economy in any way. Local residents would complain that tourists passed right through without spending any money. One example was the "all they leave on the sandbars is shit" comment noted earlier. Randall, from the group of loggers in the northwest corner of the state, also expressed this objection: "A lot of people tell me, well, if it wasn't for tourists, your taxes would be higher. Well, they don't spend much money here. They bring their own gas, they bring their own food, they might stay in a motel, you know. We're not really gaining anything from tourism."

In these conversations, the distinctiveness of rural economies was obvious to people living in them. In one case, a woman gave this a label—"the rural class." "If you look at the *rural class* [emphasis added] . . . we've never had jobs here, it's not like this is part of the economy that there are no jobs, but I think one of our big concerns is the coming tourist season and the decrease in funding from the state for tourist-related activities, cause so many people here rely entirely on tourists coming so it's just a real uneasy feeling about what's gonna happen this year."

Talk concerning rural economies ranged from this "uneasy feeling" to downright anger. Sometimes the resentment about the economic inequality between the major cities and small communities was so strong I wondered if I should end the conversation and get out. Other times it was downright comical. One group in west-central Wisconsin actually imagined a geographic line that represented this unfairness. . . .

This is the gang of men who played dice every morning before work. The first time I visited this group, when a local attorney led me through the curtain at the back of the diner to the group sitting at their L-shaped table, they stopped playing dice for a while and talked with me. At the end of our conversation, they asked me if I knew how to play Ship, Captain, and Crew. I said, proudly, "Why, yes I do." My Wisconsinness came in handy here, as I had played this dice game many times with my family growing up. They asked me to "turn off that machine [my recorder] and we'll shake for a buck" in their dollar round (before most of them left and went to work or their other tasks for the day), and I promptly lost. They asked me to "come back and shake dice" and "bring your quarters." It was clear that I was welcome to come back, but I had better plan on playing dice when I did.

On my third visit, there was a horse auction going on in town, and the group members joked with me about buying a horse. This led to some colorful comments about Madison. When several of them asked me if I was going to check out the auction, I answered:

KJC: I think I will go up once, yeah, I went up—I looked through the fence yesterday evening.

HENRY: Why don't you buy one of them horses? I got a trailer.

KJC: Not sure where I'd keep him. [They knew by this point that I lived right in Madison, a mile from the football stadium at the time, where there was room for them to park next time they come down for a game. But there is certainly no room to keep a horse.]

HENRY: Huh?

KJC: I'm not sure where I'd keep him!

HENRY: Keep him in Madison. That's where they keep all the bullshit.

After everyone got a good laugh out of that one, Henry continued on:

HENRY: Well, basically all you gotta do is buy the front end of the horse, they got the back end in Madison!

The group laughed, and I almost snorted my coffee, but then I started to get uncomfortable—not because of the anti-Madison comments, but because I had been winning round after round in the dice game. Most of the members of the group thought this was funny, but at least one was visibly irritated. To try to soften the situation, I joked,

KJC: I come and ask for your thoughts and I take your money!

RICHARD: I'll tell you what, that's good though. Because we have so little of it.

KJC: And it all goes to Madison anyway [*joking along with them*].

HOWARD: We expect nothing less from Madison!

RICHARD: It won't cost any postage to get it down there now!

This resentment was good-natured, but it was ubiquitous across the rural communities I visited. It didn't seem temporary, either, and wasn't just a product of the Great Recession. People talked about economic injustice as a fact of rural life.

ISN'T THIS REALLY JUST ABOUT RACE?

Many people in these small towns perceived that someone or something was responsible for the decline of their communities. Someone or something was siphoning off their money, they told me. They believed that wherever their tax dollars were going they sure were not going to their own towns.

Who or what was doing this? Who was getting their hard-earned money? "They" often had something to do with cities: decision makers, wealthy people, liberals, and the undeserving.

Cities represent a lot in American life. One thing they conjure up is race. In short, cities are often shorthand for people who are not white. When the dice game group in central Wisconsin referred to the line dividing rural Wisconsin from the metropolitan centers in the southern part of the state as the Mason-Dixon line, the racial implications of that term were probably not accidental.

The urban-versus-rural divide is undoubtedly in part about race. Cities have perhaps always "been the places where we have first and most fully confronted the task of living alongside people who do not necessarily belong to our own tribe" (Conn 2014, 4). There is a widening policy conflict between urban and rural areas, and it is no secret that it is driven in part by racial mobilization (Gimpel and Schuknecht 2003). Research on implicit racial priming tells us that the term "inner city" is racialized—that this term activates racial attitudes (Hurwitz and Peffley 2005). It is likely the term "urban" does so as well. This may be especially the case in Wisconsin, which is extremely racially segregated. Only 29 percent of the state's African American population lives outside the cities of Milwaukee and Madison, and most of the state has little experience to date with Latino immigration. Also, the Milwaukee metro area is extremely segregated with respect to African Americans and Latinos. According to a Brookings Institute analysis of 2005–9 data from the Census Bureau's American Community Survey, the Milwaukee metro area is one of the most racially segregated in the country (Frey 2010).

So yes, it is highly likely that when people refer to "those people in Milwaukee" they are often referring to racial minorities. But notice how complex this is. The urbanites that rural folks were referring to were not predominantly racial minorities. When white outstaters (i.e., those living outside the major metropolitan areas) complained of the laziness in the cities in these conversations, their comments were almost always directed at white people: government bureaucrats and faculty members at the flagship public university.

In that way, antiurban resentment is not simply resentment against people of color. At the same time, given the way arguments against government redistribution in the United States have historically been made by equating deservingness with whiteness, these conversations are about race even when race is not mentioned. Also, animosity toward public workers and wealthy folks in the city may be driven by conservative views on race. Since the cities, particularly Madison, are perceived as liberal and vote Democratic in elections, people who harbor racial resentment may indeed be equating city people with racial liberalism. Now, as in the past, racial animosity is directed toward groups of whites that help minorities, such as government employees and academics.

When rural folks did make openly racist comments, they did so about Native Americans, an overwhelmingly rural population in Wisconsin. There are eleven reservations in Wisconsin, located primarily in the northern third of the state. Hostility toward Native Americans did not arise often in these conversations, but it is no secret that relations between Native Americans and whites in Wisconsin have been tense historically and in recent history. Violent protests erupted in response to a series of federal court decisions in the 1980s, beginning in 1983. Those decisions affirmed spearfishing treaty rights to the Chippewa tribe and imposed no limits on how many fish tribal members could harvest (Bobo and Tuan 2006, chap. 2). White residents protested at boat landings, held demonstrations and rallies, and called for the end to treaty rights as well as the reservation system. Much of this opposition was rooted in racism, as social science research has documented (Bobo and Tuan 2006).

In recent years, these tensions have become salient to the broader population again, as the Walker administration has passed legislation that is facilitating the start of an iron ore mine in northwestern Wisconsin. To some, the mine signifies hundreds of jobs for people in the area who are sorely lacking them, but to others it means extensive disturbance to the way of life and natural environment and health of Native Americans on the adjacent Bad River Reservation (Seely 2011).

It is very possible that the lack of references to urban racial minorities in the conversations I observed is a manifestation of the threat hypothesis, or the idea that racial prejudice is heightened when people of different racial backgrounds are in proximity to one another (Key 1949; Blalock 1967). Given the extreme racial segregation in Wisconsin, there is little interaction here between whites and people of color. Thus the immediate racial tensions in most rural areas are not between whites and African Americans and Latinos but, instead, with Native Americans and, in a few communities, with Hmong refugees, who were relocated to Wisconsin in the decades since the Vietnam War.

The point I want to make is this: race is a part of rural consciousness. However, I ask the reader to notice the complexity of these perspectives and not think of them as simply about race. If we boil rural consciousness down to race, we ignore the ways in which these perspectives comprise many things: identities with place, a sense of oneself as a person of a particular place in the class hierarchy, identities as people with particular values, and sometimes ideology. Resentment is operating because people perceive they are not getting their fair share. They are making sense of this injustice by resenting those whom they think are getting more than they deserve, and perceptions of who works hard and who is deserving are infected with racism (Winter 2006, 2008). But those notions of distributive justice are *intertwined* with race—neither separate from nor synonymous with a simple distinction of white versus other.

Finally, if we conclude that rural consciousness is just racism dressed up in social science jargon, it allows us to overlook the role of antigovernment attitudes and preferences for small government here. Tea Party messaging appeals to racism (Burghart and Zeskind 2010; Parker and Barreto 2013), but it also resonates with many of the perceptions of inequality and alienation from government observed in the conversations presented [here]. As I have argued, attitudes about redistribution rest on a long history of racial discrimination in the United States. But that long history has enabled an accretion of meaning around attitudes of injustice.

This is how the politics of resentment operates—it works through seemingly simple divisions of us versus them, but it has power because in these divisions are a multitude of fundamental understandings: who has power, who has what values and which of those values are right, who gets what, and perceptions of the basic fairness of all of this. It is opposition to other people, and the overlap of urban and racially "other" is a powerful combination.

This is part of the reason racism is so persistent. Because it is intertwined with other fundamental attitudes, it can be invoked and expressed in seemingly socially acceptable ways (Mendelberg 2001). In the conversations I observed, when people expressed racist sentiments, they did so while weaving them with values and allegiances of which they were sufficiently certain and proud that they were willing to express them in front of me, a relative stranger. Take for example these comments to me, by a man in the group of loggers in northwest Wisconsin . . . :

RON: Yeah. You know. Well like him that just left, that was here before to get coffee?

KJC: Yeah.

RON: He's an American Indian. [One sentence deleted for confidentiality.]

KJC: Oh really?

RON: He's a good guy.

KJC: Yeah.

RON: Works hard. Yeah.

KJC: Well sure.

RON: But he won't live on the reservation where they get all the free housing and stuff, he's self-supporting, you know?

KJC: Yeah.

RON: And, there, there's too many programs down there for a bunch of people, you know to have it for them to want to go to work. You know? They got the casino down there shoving our money through 'em, they got the federal government shoving our money through 'em, and they wonder where they got drunken alcohol problems, they got nothing to do all day besides sitting around and do what they want to do. And they keep giving 'em money to do it, well how do you expect to get anything out of anybody? There's an old saying: A hungry dog hunts harder. Hey, you keep feeding a dog or a cat, they're not gonna hunt, they're not gonna look for food, they're gonna lay around and get fat.

If I said these comments in a classroom, I would expect to get accused of racism. But for Ron, this was about hard work and deservingness. To call this just plain racism misses the complexity of the sentiments involved here.

CONCLUSION

"Rural consciousness" is the term I am using to describe a strong sense of identity as a rural person combined with a strong sense that rural areas are the victims of injustice: the sense that rural areas do not get their fair share of power, respect, or resources and that rural folks prefer lifestyles that differ fundamentally from those of city people. . . .

When I argue that rural consciousness structures the way people understand politics, I am suggesting that something other than partisanship is driving their political preferences. Support for the Republican Party is not what causes people to have these complex, intertwined understandings of economic injustice, place identity, class identity, race, and values. And the complexities of this understanding do not inevitably lead to support for the Republican Party. You may have noticed that some of these rural groups contain a good number of Democrats. In fact, the northwestern and southwestern corners of Wisconsin, although predominantly rural, lean Democratic. Booth Fowler, one of the wisest scholars of politics in Wisconsin, reasons that this is due in part to high levels of poverty in those areas, the influence of the city of Superior and of Great Lake shipping unions in the northwest corner, and the effect of commuters or out-migrants from Madison in the southwest (Fowler 2008). Whatever the reason, it is clear that the correlation between where people live and how they vote are not set in stone. They are the product of people actively trying to make sense of their lives.

REFERENCES

Bachrach, Peter, and Morton Baratz. 1962. "Two Faces of Power." *American Political Science Review* 56: 947–52.

Bell, Michael. 1992. "The Fruit of Difference: The Rural-Urban Continuum as a System of Identity." *Rural Sociology* 57 (1): 65–82.

Blalock, Hubert M. 1967. *Toward a Theory of Minority-Group Relations*. New York: Wiley.

Bobo, Lawrence D., and Mia Tuan. 2006. *Prejudice in Politics: Group Position, Public Opinion, and the Wisconsin Treaty Rights Dispute*. Cambridge, MA: Harvard University Press.

Burghart, Devin, and Leonard Zeskind. 2010. *Tea Party Nationalism: A Critical Examination of the Tea Party Movement and the Size, Scope, and Focus of Its National Factions*. Kansas City, MO: Institute for Research and Education on Human Rights.

Conn, Steven. 2014. *Americans against the City: Anti-Urbanism in the Twentieth Century*. New York: Oxford University Press.

Creed, Gerald W., and Barbara Ching. 1997. "Recognizing Rusticity." In *Knowing Your Place: Rural Identity and Cultural Hierarchy*, edited by Barbara Ching and Gerald W. Creed, 1–28. New York: Routledge.

Dahl, Robert A. 1961. *Who Governs? Democracy and Power in an American City*. New Haven, CT: Yale University Press.

Epstein, Leon. 1958. *Politics in Wisconsin.* Madison: University of Wisconsin Press.

Fowler, Booth. 2008. *Wisconsin Votes: An Electoral History.* Madison: University of Wisconsin Press.

Frey, William H. 2010. "Census Data: Blacks and Hispanics Take Different Segregation Paths." http://www.brookings.edu/research/opinions/2010/12/16-census-frey.

Gimpel, James G., and Jason E. Schuknecht. 2003. *Patchwork Nation: Sectionalism and Political Change in American Politics.* Ann Arbor: University of Michigan Press.

Hurwitz, Jon, and Mark Peffley. 2005. "Playing the Race Card in the Post–Willie Horton Era." *Public Opinion Quarterly* 76 (2): 99–112.

Jarosz, Lucy, and Victoria Lawson. 2002. "'Sophisticated People vs. Rednecks': Economic Restructuring and Class Differences in America's West," *Antipode* 34 (1): 8–27.

Key, V. O., Jr. 1949. *Southern Politics in State and Nation.* New York: A. A. Knopf.

Mendelberg, Tali. 2001. *The Race Card: Campaign Strategy, Implicit Messages, and the Norm of Equality.* Princeton, NJ: Princeton University Press.

Parker, Christopher, and Matt A. Barreto. 2013. *Change They Can't Believe In: The Tea Party and Reactionary Politics in America.* Princeton, NJ: Princeton University Press.

Seely, Ron. 2011. "Mining in Wisconsin: Promise or Peril?" *Wisconsin State Journal,* October 9.

Winter, Nicholas. 2006. "Beyond Welfare: Framing and the Racialization of White Opinion on Social Security." *American Journal of Political Science* 50 (2): 400–20.

———. 2008. *Dangerous Frames: How Ideas about Race and Gender Shape Public Opinion.* Chicago: University of Chicago Press.

9.5

JAMES CAMPBELL

From *Polarized: Making Sense of a Divided America*

One way to measure the degree to which Americans have become more polarized is to use surveys to discover the proportion who consider themselves moderate in ideology. Campbell shows that many more Americans currently say that they are ideologically very liberal or very conservative than was the case in previous decades, with a shrinking proportion of moderates. He carefully shows that these measures from surveys reflect actual changes in American political attitudes with real consequences for politics.

Are Americans sharply divided in their politics or are they calmly gathered around a pragmatic political center? This is a tough question because the answer most probably lies somewhere in between. Americans are neither cantankerously polarized to the hilt nor blissfully of one mind. But the fact that Americans are not all at the outer edges of ideology or neatly clustered at the center does not mean that we can blithely split the difference and walk away thinking that the polarization questions are answered. We should be able to extract a more meaningful reading of polarization from the evidence.

IDEOLOGICAL DIFFERENCES

There is a long history of self-reported measures of political ideologies. Since at least the mid-1930s, surveys have asked respondents to declare their general ideological perspectives on politics as liberal or conservative. Data drawn from these questions played important roles in public opinion research in the late 1960s, but it was not until the early 1970s that surveys provided consistent question wordings offering response-options across the spectrum from liberal to moderate to conservative.

Where better to begin an investigation of the polarizati͏ than with what citizens themselves say about their own id͏ tions? After all, self-declarations are the basis for measurin

From James Campbell, *Polarized: Making Sense of a Divided America* (͏ University Press, 2016).

long-term political orientation of voters: individually in party identification and collectively in macropartisanship. The party identification of citizens is determined directly by asking respondents whether they think of themselves as Democrats, Republicans, independents, or something else rather than whether they routinely think or vote in a particular way or asking researchers how they would on some other basis classify a respondent's partisanship. The same measurement approach seems quite reasonable to follow with respect to ideology. Not all Republicans (or Democrats) think alike on all matters nor mean exactly the same thing in identifying with that party, and we would not expect that all conservatives (or liberals) are in lockstep either. Americans may not always label themselves correctly and no measure is without flaws, but the fact that individuals identify or associate themselves with a party or an ideology would seem highly credible, barring overwhelming evidence to the contrary.

Five Ideological Series

The direct evidence of ideological polarization is drawn from five highly respected national survey data series of ideological self-identifications. Each collected self-reported ideology data over a significant period. The five series include data from the American National Election Study (ANES), the General Social Survey (GSS), the CBS/*New York Times* polls (CBS/NYT), Gallup polls, and the National Exit Poll of voters conducted on election days. All have two important characteristics in common. Each series allows respondents to indicate whether they consider their views to be liberal or conservative, and each permits respondents to declare their views to be moderate or somewhere between liberals and conservatives.

Beyond these common characteristics, there are many differences. The surveys were conducted over different intervals and in different years. The longest series is ANES. It has been conducted, for the most part, in conjunction with biennial national elections and extends from 1972 to 2012 (19 observations). The joint CBS and *New York Times* surveys have been conducted more frequently but at irregular intervals. Their ideology question was asked in 304 surveys conducted between 1976 and 2015. For the sake of comparability with the other series, the medians of these polls within calendar years are used to collapse the 304 surveys into 40 annual observations. The GSS series is from 1974 to 2014 (missing a few years) and has 28 annual observations. Gallup got a late start in settling on its ideological question. Its data span from 1992 to 2014 (23 observations). The shortest of the five series is the exit polls. It covers the ten presidential election years from 1976 to 2012. Overall, the combined series covers the years from 1972 to 2015 and consists of 120 annual observations.

The five series differ in several other ways as well. Each has its own distinct-question wording and sampling frame. They also differ in their response s. CBS/NYT and the Exit Polls offer respondents three possible responses (liberal, moderate, or conservative). Others offer more gradations of liberal or conservative responses. Gallup's format allows respondents to place themselves on a five-point scale from "very liberal" to "very conservative." ANES and GSS present a seven-point scale (extremely liberal, liberal, or slightly liberal and the same on the conservative side). The five series also differ in how easily respondents can opt out of responding, with the ANES consistently generating the highest percentage of "don't knows" by explicitly offering respondents the "haven't thought much about it" option. . . .

Polarized Ideologies

What do these data reveal about ideological polarization in recent decades? What portions of these electorates were relatively polarized from one another? Polarization is measured here as the percentage of respondents claiming to be either liberal or conservative rather than moderate or not knowing their ideological orientation. A high percentage of liberals and conservatives would reflect a relatively polarized electorate. A high percentage of moderates or respondents unaware of their ideological perspectives would reflect a less polarized electorate. Figure [1] displays the combined percentage of liberals and conservatives (ideologicals) for each of the five series from 1972 to 2015.

As one would expect given the variety of question wordings, options offered, receptivity to "don't know" responses, and other differences as well as the normal sampling errors of surveys, there is variation across the series within each year. This is particularly the case in the 1970s and 1980s. In more recent years, the measures tend to converge. Some of the series start at higher levels of liberals and conservatives and others track greater changes in these levels over time. The GSS series is relatively flat in the high 50s. The ideological portion of the public was initially smaller in the ANES series and then grew at a higher rate. The CBS/*New York Times* and Exit Poll data fall in between.

Though they have their differences, the five different ideology series together support four important points about the extent and development of the public's polarization. First, at the outset in the 1970s and early 1980s, a large portion of the electorate already was fairly well polarized. At the low end of the range, ANES indicates that about 45% of Americans were neither moderates nor unaware of their ideological perspective. Generally about half the electorate in exit polls asserted liberal or conservative ideological orientations, and the CBS/NYT series normally found those declaring a liberal or conservative inclination to outnumber moderates. According to the GSS measure, nearly three of every five Americans declared an ideological viewpoint. Taken as a whole, those asserting liberal or conservative perspectives constituted anywhere from 45% to 60% of Americans in the 1970s. Whether this should be interpreted as high or low is open to question—at least at this point. What is not open to question is that roughly half of Americans or more claimed a non-centrist ideological viewpoint as early as the 1970s. Contrary to a good

FIGURE [1]   Ideologicals (Conservatives Plus Liberals) in the American Electorate, 1972–2015

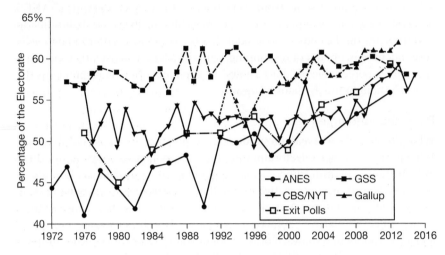

NOTE: The percentages are of all respondents. The data are from the American National Election Study, the General Social Survey, the CBS and *New York Times* Surveys, Gallup, and the national Exit Polls housed at the Roper Center.

deal of cavalier talk, *most* Americans were *not* moderates in the 1970s, probably no more than a bare majority were.

Second, the public has become more polarized and less centrist over time. In each series, the ideological portion of the electorate has grown. This is clearly visible in four of the five series, with the data plots moving to the upper right corner of the figure. . . .

There is no doubt more Americans adopted ideological orientations or became more cognizant of their orientations over the last few decades. There can be questions over whether the growth in polarization was as slight as the GSS series suggests or as strong as the Gallup and ANES series indicate, but there is no question that Americans became more polarized than they were, at least as reflected in their declared ideological viewpoints.

Third, though somewhat obscured by herky-jerky movements in the five data series, polarization has grown quite consistently since the 1970s. It has not been confined, as some might contend, to the contentious post-2000 period of the Bush II and Obama presidencies. Although the ideological clarity of more fully polarized parties may have pushed along polarization's increase in more recent times, the trend regression indicates that the public's polarization had increased significantly in the previous three decades and detects no substantial acceleration in this trend since 2000.

Fourth, while there is some variation in the pervasiveness of ideological orientations measured by the different series in the 1970s and 1980s (though all indicated that a large share of the electorate were ideological) and variation as well in the degree to which polarization grew in the intervening years (though all find some growth), there is a general consensus that nearly three of every five Americans now associate themselves with either a liberal or conservative perspective. The spread of the percentage of ideologicals in the five series in Figure [1] resembles a cone with a wide end on the left and a narrow end drawn to the upper right corner, approaching the 60% mark.

. . . Nearly half of Americans (49%) were either liberal or conservative in the early 1970s. This increased to about 56% by 2012. The ideological portion of the electorate expanded by approximately seven percentage points from the 1970s to the 2010s. This was accompanied, of course, by about a seven-percentage-point decline of non-ideologicals. These are the self-declared moderates and those who would not or could not associate themselves with an ideological view. A majority of the decline among the non-ideologicals occurred among those indicating that they did not know how to characterize their political perspectives. This was about five of the seven-point drop. Whether these respondents had been ideologicals all along and only became aware of it in more recent years, or whether they (or their successors) developed a less centrist perspective in later years is unclear. What is clear is that they had been unable or unwilling to identify themselves as liberals or conservatives in earlier years and now, rather than claiming moderation, they report their general political perspectives to be either liberal or conservative.

In effect, the nation changed from one in which ideologicals and non-ideologicals were about at parity in the 1970s (still a large number of ideologicals) to one in which those reporting an ideological perspective outnumbered centrists by 12 percentage points (56% to 44%) in the 2010s. If we were comparing election returns, the former would be a dead heat and the latter a near-landslide. This is substantial change.

Some to the Left, More to the Right

A good deal of the increase in polarization in recent decades has been the result of more Americans claiming to be conservative. The portions of the electorate who report themselves to be conservatives and liberals are presented respectively in Figures [2] and [3]. Self-declared conservatives made up nearly 31% of the electorate in the 1970s according to Figure [2]. By the 2010s, they were nearly 35% of the electorate. In four of the five series, the increase of conservatives is statistically significant and the increase just barely falls short of conventional significance levels in the fifth series (the exit polls). The change is greatest in the ANES series and weakest in the CBS/NYT data. The growing number of conservatives accounts for about four of the seven-percentage-point increase in ideologicals.

FIGURE [2]   Conservatives in the American Electorate, 1972–2015

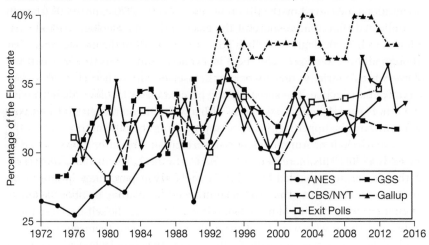

NOTE: The percentages are of all respondents. The data are from the American National Election Study, the General Social Survey, the CBS and *New York Times* Surveys, Gallup, and the national Exit Polls housed at the Roper Center.

FIGURE [3]   Liberals in the American Electorate, 1972–2015

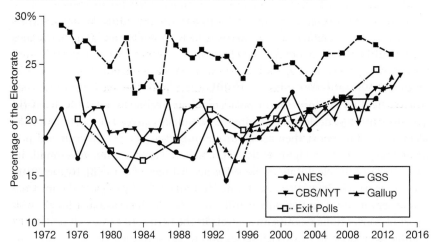

NOTE: The percentages are of all respondents. The data are from the American National Election Study, the General Social Survey, the CBS and *New York Times* Surveys, Gallup, and the national Exit Polls housed at the Roper Center.

The percentage of self-reported liberals in the electorate is plotted in Figure [3]. As a comparison to the previous figure shows, except for the GSS series in the early 1970s in which they are near parity, conservatives otherwise substantially outnumber liberals. From 1972 to 1990, the mean conservative advantage over liberals was about ten percentage points. Since 2000, the mean gap grew to about 13 points. Though there was no discernible increase in the percentage of liberals in one series (GSS), the percentage of liberals increased slightly in two others (ANES and CBS/NYT) and more substantially in two series (Gallup and the Exit Polls). The pooled series indicates a significant increase of about two and a half percentage points in liberal ranks since the 1970s. The liberal trend is about two-thirds as large as the trend toward conservatives. In short, from the 1970s to the 2010s, Americans became less moderate and more polarized, with an increase in the ranks of liberals and a larger increase in the ranks of conservatives.

▪   ▪   ▪

Operational Ideology

Free and Cantril in the late 1960s were the first to notice the apparent discrepancy of professed ideology and issue preferences as a challenge to the self-report measure. They noticed that a few self-reported liberals held conservative issue positions, but many more self-described conservatives adopted liberal issue positions. A good number of self-reported conservatives wanted to maintain or increase funding for education, public housing, and urban renewal and thought that the government should do more to reduce unemployment. These self-identified conservatives holding apparently inconsistent policy positions were labeled by Free and Cantril as "operational liberals."

Ellis and Stimson have updated and substantially extended Free and Cantril's interpretation of political ideology in the public. Like Free and Cantril decades before, Ellis and Stimson found that many conservatives surprisingly supported *more* government spending for a wide range of purposes—from healthcare and education to mass transportation and the environment. They constructed an index of operational ideology from responses to ten GSS questions asking respondents whether government was spending too much, too little, or about the right amount on ten different public problems. These included foreign aid, urban problems, crime, drug addiction, education, the environment, welfare, health, and "the conditions of blacks." Anyone who favored increased spending rather than cuts on more problems (other than defense) was classified as an operational liberal. Operational liberals who reported that they thought of themselves as conservatives were classified as "conflicted conservatives."

An example of the kind of question that Ellis and Stimson use in their operational ideology index is an ANES question about preferences on changes in spending for dealing with crime. Table [1] presents 2012 ANES responses of self-reported liberals, moderates, and conservatives to possible spending changes for anti-crime programs. The data demonstrate that a plurality of liberals, moderates, *and* conservatives favor devoting more resources to dealing with crime (though they might well differ over what "dealing" with crime entails as well as the source of the additional spending—including whether the additional spending might come from spending reductions elsewhere). Very few respondents of any ideological bent favor reductions in spending on anti-crime programs. Ellis and Stimson interpret the substantial percentage of self-declared conservatives favoring more spending on government programs, in this case anti-crime programs, as evidence of operational liberalism at odds with their symbolic attachment to the conservative label.

To demonstrate what they interpret as the robustness of operational ideology, Ellis and Stimson also examine responses to issues other than those involved with preferences about changes in government spending. Whether the government should guarantee jobs for everyone is one such issue. Responses to the ANES version of that question in 2012 are presented in Table [2]. Liberals presumably would favor the government guarantee and conservatives would oppose it. As the table shows, a large majority of self-reported conservatives, as expected, opposed the proposed policy, while a plurality of liberals favored it. There were, however, some liberals adopting the expected conservative position and some conservatives taking the expected liberal position. In this particular instance, a larger percentage of liberals (24%) strayed from the liberal line than conservatives (15%) from the conservative position. As this case demonstrates, there are a good number of individuals who hold issue positions that would appear to be contrary to or inconsistent with their self-reported ideology.

TABLE [1] Self-Reported Ideology and Preferences for Change in Spending on Crime, 2012

Self-Reported Ideology	*Preferred Change in Government Spending on Crime (%)*			
	Increased	*About the Same*	*Decreased*	*Total*
Liberal (24%)	45	44	11	100
Moderate/DK (39%)	59	36	5	100
Conservative (37%)	47	42	11	100
Total	51	40	9	100

NOTE: The data are from the 2012 ANES study. The question wording is: "Next I am going to read you a list of federal programs. For each one, I would like you to tell me whether you would like to see spending increased or decreased. What about dealing with crime. Should federal spending on dealing with crime be increased, decreased, or kept about the same (kept the same)?"

Based on their evaluation of the associations between self-reported ideology and an array of both spending and non-spending issue positions, much like those examined in Table [1], Ellis and Stimson conclude that, though "perhaps sincerely and deeply" identifying with the conservative label, nearly two-thirds of self-reported conservatives are actually misguided or "conflicted conservatives" who "support liberal public policies" and that "there is little evidence that conflicted conservatives are actually 'conservative' in any sense beyond self-identification." Despite strong evidence to the contrary . . . Ellis and Stimson conclude that "Americans tend to want to call themselves 'conservative' while they advocate big government liberalism." Put differently, and though they do not use the term, they essentially claim that as many as two-thirds of conservatives are really what might be called CINOs or "conservatives-in-name-only."

These are bold claims. Some might say outlandish. There is no question that some people misidentify their political ideologies, but the idea that *two-thirds* of conservatives would be so confused seems implausible, especially in light of the considerable evidence of the self-reported ideology measure's validity. Many self-declared conservatives would no doubt be deeply insulted by the proposition that they were so ill-informed and misguided—or mesmerized by a shiny conservative label—that they could not accurately describe their own general political perspectives. Still, as seemingly radical as the claims are, they are made by highly regarded scholars examining a good deal of professionally gathered survey data. They deserve to be taken seriously. The question is whether they should be believed.

TABLE [2]   Self-Reported Ideology and Preferences on the Issue of Government Guaranteed Jobs, 2012

Self-Reported Ideology	Government Guaranteed Jobs and Standard of Living (%)			
	Favor	Neutral	Opposed	Total
Liberal (25%)	46	29	24	100
Moderate/DK (38%)	36	29	35	100
Conservative (38%)	15	14	71	100
Total	31	23	46	100

NOTE: The data are from the 2012 ANES study. The question wording is: "Some people feel the government in Washington should see to it that every person has a job and a good standard of living. Suppose these people are at one end of a scale, at point 1. Others think the government should just let each person get ahead on their own. Suppose these people are at the other end, at point 7. And, of course, some other people have opinions somewhere in between, at points 2, 3, 4, 5, or 6. Where would you place yourself on this scale, or haven't you thought much about this?" Categories 1, 2, and 3 were grouped as favoring guaranteed jobs. Categories 5, 6, and 7 were grouped as opposing government guaranteed jobs. Category 4 was scored as neutral on the issue.

Mountain or Mole Hill?

How serious are these critiques of the self-reported ideology measure? Do they discredit their use for assessing polarization in the electorate? More specifically, are the claims that Americans are really more "operationally liberal" while being "symbolically conservative," that is, liberal with a conservative veneer, well supported? Are these claims against self-reported ideology a formidable mountain or a concocted mole hill?

Based on the analysis that follows, the answer is that *none* of these criticisms, including the "conflicted conservative" and "operational liberal" claims, raise serious concerns about the basic declaration by respondents of their own political perspectives. There are variations in ideological outlooks, different degrees to which they are held, local variations, and various competing influences for how much they influence policy positions, but these variations and competing influences are just that and not evidence that the underlying political perspective is anything other than what respondents say they are, especially in light of the substantial evidence of the measure's validity and reliability.

First, it is a certainty that ideological labels mean different things to different people at different times. All liberals and all conservatives may not even prioritize their values in the same way. This is to be expected. In itself, this does not amount to a challenge to the ideological concept or measure. Any two conservatives in the public are likely to disagree over what it means exactly to be a conservative, just as any two conservatives (or, for that matter, liberals) in Congress are likely to disagree about what that ideological label requires. I would venture to guess that all Democrats (or Republicans) do not share the same idea of what it means to be a Democrat (or Republican) or that all Communists, Libertarians, or self-declared moderates are on the same page regarding their essential attributes. Beyond the political realm, all Catholics or Protestants or Jews or Muslims do not have exactly the same idea about what it means to be members of those religions. Any group affiliation, particularly those based on beliefs rather than on a physical characteristic, is likely to allow some ambiguity or variation in its membership criteria. Moreover, there may be some significant variation in these definitions by time, region, and degree. What it means to be a liberal in 1950 in Mississippi may be a good deal different from what it means to be one in 2015 in New York. Any social group involves a somewhat moveable "big tent." This variation does not mean that the grouping is an empty symbol.

The Ellis and Stimson study illustrates the dangers inherent in imposing a definition of what it means to be an adherent of an ideology and then attempting to reconstitute ideological attachments from various attitudes and behaviors. Their operational ideology measure appears to assume that conservatism is reflected in the opposition to any increase at any time in government spending on a broad array of domestic programs and that liberalism is observed in

the support for increased spending for these programs under any circumstance (the assumption is reversed for defense spending). Respondents favoring an increase in spending in one area may qualify as conservative, but only
if they favor cuts in more programs. Many die-hard, true-blue conservatives
who favor limited, efficient, frugal, affordable, and sensible government for
truly public purposes, however, favor increased spending to improve the
nation's health (e.g., cancer and heart disease research, infectious disease
treatments), to improve the nation's educational system (e.g., school vouchers,
more and better teachers), or to halt a rising crime rate (see Table [1]). From
time to time, they might even also have some reservations about the need for
ever higher defense budgets. Are they any less conservative because they want
government to wisely spend more money to cure cancer or keep the streets
safe? Of course not. That a large majority of self-described conservatives do
not qualify as operational conservatives by Ellis and Stimson's litmus test
might be better regarded as evidence that the operational ideology measure is
itself problematic rather than that self-declared conservatives are not what
they claim themselves to be. To be clear, this is not to question the assumption
that conservatives favor less spending on domestic policies in general than
liberals. They most certainly do. It is, however, to question where the lines
in spending are drawn between conservatives, moderates, and liberals, both
in individual policy areas and in a collection of policy areas. Conservatives do
not always favor less spending than the status quo on everything (other than
defense) as the operational ideology index supposes.

Beyond variations in the meaning of ideologies, differences in the degrees to
which ideologies are held and the contexts in which the opinions are given, and
various complications in the construction of the operational questions,
respondents professing an ideological perspective may stray from their ideologically expected position for many other reasons. Even for highly committed
ideologues, ideology is not the be-all and end-all. Other considerations often
come into play in deciding where someone stands on an issue. Different perceptions, strategies, and priorities may lead people with strong ideological
principles in common to take somewhat different policy positions on occasion. A conservative may have a personal commitment to reducing crime or
fighting cancer or protecting the environment, for instance, and this may
override, on occasion, a general and deeply held commitment to government
frugality and restraint. Or, an ideological commitment may temper the extent
of support for various spending priorities. In either case, neither the ideological nor public policy preference precludes the other. They can, and do, harmoniously coexist.

▪   ▪   ▪

Self-reported ideology is a credible measure of the general political perspectives of Americans. There is solid evidence that a plurality, *not* a majority,
of Americans are moderates (or don't knows) and their numbers have been on

the *decline*. Many more Americans are conservative than liberal and though both ideological perspectives have been growing, growth has been a bit greater at the conservative end of the ideological spectrum than at the liberal end. The aggregate distribution of these perspectives indicates: (1) that Americans in the 1970s were already fairly well polarized, and (2) that the extent of polarization in the American public has grown significantly since that time.

10

PARTICIPATION

10.1

JANELLE WONG, S. KARTHICK RAMAKRISHNAN,
TAEKU LEE, AND JANE JUNN

From *Asian American Political Participation: Emerging Constituents and Their Political Identities*

Asian American is an increasingly influential demographic category in American politics. This study analyzes the relationship between self-identification as an Asian American and the propensity to participate in politics. The researchers find evidence that those who primarily identify themselves as Asian American, as opposed to a specific ethnic group like Filipino or Korean, have a higher probability of voting and participating in other forms of political activity.

NATIONAL ORIGIN, PAN-ETHNICITY, AND RACIAL IDENTITY

Identities are at once paradoxically personal and collective. My identity is what defines me personally and uniquely. Yet if my identity is Asian American, it is a fingerprint of individuality shared by roughly 15 million others. Consider for a moment any other trait or aspect you give as an answer to the defining identitarian question, "Who am I?" That answer will surely be shared.

The mystery that wraps this riddle is that the juxtaposition of Asian and American together does not lend itself to obvious interpretation, especially

From Janelle Wong et al., *Asian American Political Participation: Emerging Constituents and Their Political Identities* (New York: Russell Sage Foundation, 2011), Chapter 5.

under the rubric of a unitary, coherent collective identity. Lisa Lowe writes, "The American of Asian descent remains the symbolic 'alien,' the *metonym* for Asia who by definition cannot be imagined as sharing in America" (1996, 6). In some versions of Asian American, one identity dominates the other; in other versions, they coexist somewhere between détente and pluralist heaven, each retaining a willful integrity with respect to the other, and yet elsewhere they reconstitute in a hybrid identity—uniquely Asian American and neither Asian nor American.

Asian American is uncommonly diverse: Bengali, Chinese, Filipino, Indian, Indonesian, Japanese, Korean, Lao, Malay, Pakistani, Thai, Vietnamese, to mention just a few of the national origin groupings lumped together under this pan-ethnic rubric. An Asian American is Buddhist, Catholic, Confucian, Hindu, Muslim, Protestant, or one who eschews religious affiliation altogether. An Asian American may be a brand-new immigrant, just minutes through customs at Seattle-Tacoma International Airport, or the great-great-grandchild of immigrants from distant shores.

Sometimes an ethnic or racial label may emerge or crystallize as a result of identity-making work of doing politics together. . . .

■   ■   ■

Table [1] shows the distribution across the six major national origin groups in response to the following question: "People of Asian descent in the U.S. use different terms to describe themselves. In general do you think of yourself as . . . i) An Asian American, ii) A [Ethnic Group] (e.g., Korean), iii) A [Ethnic Group American] (e.g., Korean American), and iv) An Asian." The options were rotated so that respondents had an equal chance of getting one of these four group labels that relate to social identity. We gave respondents the option

TABLE [1]   Racial-Ethnic Self-Categorization (All Mentions)

	India	China	Philippines	Japan	Korea	Vietnam	Total
Ethnic American	36	40	46	44	64	69	47
Ethnic group	28	38	40	36	70	37	40
Asian American	21	20	15	13	43	20	21
Asian	12	17	15	12	48	16	19
American	6	4	3	5	2	1	4
Other	3	2	5	4	0	2	3

Survey question: "People of Asian descent in the U.S. use different terms to describe themselves. In general, do you think of yourself as . . . ?" [check all that apply; do not read "American" or "Other"]

SOURCES: Authors' compilation of data from the 2008 National Asian American Survey (Wong et al. 2011).

of saying yes or no to more than one of these categories, and we also recorded other answers that the respondent gave, including American and Other responses that were more open-ended. To avoid any confusion between the labels as offered in the survey and the terms we use throughout this book (such as Asian American, Vietnamese, and so on) we mark survey responses to the social identity question in italics. For example, in the case of a Filipino respondent, the four identity labels are *Filipino, Filipino American, Asian*, and *Asian American*.

As we can see in Table [1], nearly half of all survey respondents said they think of themselves as *Ethnic American*, with 47 percent saying yes to this descriptor. A slightly smaller proportion (40 percent) say they think of themselves as part of their *Ethnic Group*, while 21 percent identifies as *Asian American*, and 19 percent as *Asian*. Because respondents could select more than one label, the proportions total more than 100 percent for the overall survey sample as well as for the various national-origin groups.

Looking across national-origin groups, we find some important differences. Those of Vietnamese and Korean descent are the ones most likely to identify as *Ethnic American* (that is, for example, Vietnamese American) (69 percent and 64 percent, respectively). A similarly large proportion of those with Korean ancestry (70 percent) say they identify as *Korean* alone. On identification with *Ethnic Group*, the other notable finding is that Indians stand out as the ones least likely to adopt this descriptor (28 percent). Indians are also more likely to identify as *Asian American* than Filipinos and Japanese Americans (21 percent versus 15 percent and 13 percent, respectively), and just as likely to identify with this pan-ethnic label as Chinese and Vietnamese Americans. This finding is important because it runs counter to the bias that many scholars have pointed out in the scholarship and politics surrounding Asian American activism and identity, with Indians and other immigrants from South Asia seen as wholly distinctive from other Asian American groups, and relatively marginal to Asian American identity and politics (Shankar and Srikanth 1998; Kibria 1998; Dave et al. 2000). What we find here is that Indian Americans are not at all distinctive with respect to adopting the *Asian American* label. Indeed, they are just as likely to adopt the pan-ethnic label as Chinese Americans, and are much more likely to do so than Japanese Americans, the group who arguably is most central to the historical development of an Asian American identity.

Finally, another important aspect of self-categorization that emerges from a comparison across national origins is that Koreans are much more likely to identify with multiple categories than members of other national origin groups. On average, Koreans in our survey identified with 2.2 categories. The next closest frequency is among Vietnamese, who on average identify with 1.4 categories. For the remaining groups, the average number of categories identified with ranges from 1.1 to 1.2. This discrepancy has important consequences because Koreans have the highest levels of identification in all four categories, with levels often twice as high as those found for other groups. Depending on the research question, it may make sense to standardize the four categories by the total number of mentions within each group before making comparisons across groups. Such a comparison would reveal, for instance, that the gap between *Ethnic Group* identification and *Asian American* identification is greatest for Filipinos and Japanese Americans, and least for Indian Americans. Regardless of the measure used, however, the data in Table [1] present a fairly clear storyline on self-categorization: a relatively small proportion of Asians in the United States self-identify as *Asian American*, a larger proportion as *Ethnic Group*, and the largest proportion as *Ethnic American*, which combines their national origin and American identities.

Self-identifying with a label itself, however, provides a limited view of identity and its link to politics. Take the example of the potential political significance of the pan-ethnic label *Asian American*. Perhaps during the height of the Asian American movement of the late 1960s and 1970s, the label carried clear political meaning (Wei 1993). Even in its height, this movement originated from elite educational institutions (Takagi 1998) and several decades of dramatic demographic change have occurred since then. Its current use more likely simply reflects popular usage of the label as a social convention. Rather than being a measure of a politicized pan-ethnicity, individuals who identify with the label *Asian American* may instead be acquiescing with and assimilating into dominant norms and conventions.

Several findings are worth noting, however, with respect to the relationship between the categories of self-identification and a sense of linked fate. The concept of linked fate has a distinguished pedigree in research on racial politics. The belief that one's personal lot in life is intimately intertwined with the lot of others in one's ethnic group has been shown to be an important feature of African American public opinion. Several studies have shown that it is this sense of linked fate that helps African Americans (and, to a large extent, Latinos) to overcome some of the political divisions that one might anticipate based on education and income within each of the groups. . . .

The National Asian American Survey includes two measures of linked fate. We asked respondents, "Do you think what happens generally to other groups of Asians in this country affects what happens in your life?" This measure is nearly identical to the measure that has been used in prior studies of African Americans. At the same time, given the high level of *Ethnic Group* and *Ethnic American* identification among Asian Americans, we also included a question on linked fate that has the respondent's ethnic group as the reference category.

Interestingly, those who say they think of themselves as Asian Americans are the most likely to say that their fate in politics is somewhat or very linked to other Asians in the United States. Among the four identity categories we measure, 54 percent of those who classify themselves as *Asian American* feel a sense of linked fate. This proportion is larger than among those who call themselves *Asian* (47 percent), *Ethnic American* (45 percent), or *Ethnic Group* (44 percent). Similarly, when asked the same question about a sense of linked fate but this time with respect to their ethnic group (rather than to the pan-ethnic *Asian American* group), the findings by identity self-category follow a similar but slightly less dramatic pattern. Fifty-seven percent of those who call themselves Asian Americans agree that they have some or very strong linked fate with those in their ethnic group, followed by 54 percent of those who categorize themselves as Asian, 53 percent of those who say they are *Ethnic American*, and 52 percent who select the *Ethnic Group* term. However, in contrast to the findings above about the relatively strong sense of linked fate among those who choose the identity label of Asian American, we find that those who chose the *Ethnic Group* identity are the ones most likely to say they would vote for a co-ethnic candidate (66 percent) for political office. *Ethnic Americans* were next at 64 percent, *Asian Americans* at 62 percent, and *Asians* at 61 percent. These differences are modest, of course.

In addition to asking the higher-order question of how racial self-identification may relate to a sense of linked fate among Asian Americans, we also need to examine the more basic question of how linked fate varies across national origin groups. Table [2] displays the differences by national origin group on the two linked fate measures in the NAAS.

To the first question asking whether respondents think what happens generally to other groups of Asians in the United States affects what happens in

TABLE [2]   Pan-Ethnic and Ethnic Linked Fate

	India	China	Philippines	Japan	Korea	Vietnam	Total
Pan-ethnic linked fate							
Fate very linked	7	9	8	7	13	7	9
Fate somewhat linked	32	32	16	26	40	27	28
Fate not very linked	4	7	13	7	4	6	7
Fate not linked	49	43	60	50	35	47	48
Don't know	8	10	3	10	7	13	8
Ethnic linked fate							
Fate very linked	10	11	10	12	19	17	12
Fate somewhat linked	33	31	19	27	43	30	30
Fate not very linked	7	8	16	9	4	3	8
Fate not linked	42	40	50	43	28	42	42
Don't know	8	10	5	9	7	10	8

Survey questions: "Do you think what happens generally to other groups of Asians in this country affects what happens in your life?" "Do you think what happens generally to other [respondent's ethnic group] Americans affects what happens in your life?"
NOTE: Rates are in percentages.
SOURCE: Authors' compilation of data from the 2008 National Asian American Survey (Wong et al., 2011).

their lives, 44 percent agree to a sense of linked fate, but fewer than 10 percent feel that their fate is very linked to other Asians in this country. The variation among national origin groups is most substantial among Korean Americans: 57 percent agree with the concept of linked fate with other Asians in the United States; 13 percent of Koreans feel their fate is very closely linked. Filipinos and Vietnamese, by contrast, are the least likely to exhibit a linked fate orientation.

When the referent for the linked fate question is given as people who share the same ethnic or national-origin group, the overall sense of linked fate is somewhat stronger: half of the NAAS respondents agree that what happens to others in their national-origin group affects what happens in their life, and one in eight believe that this link is strong. Again, Korean Americans are the strongest supporters of a sense of ethnic-group linked fate, nearly two-thirds agreeing and almost one in five agreeing strongly. On ethnic-group linked fate, Filipinos and Vietnamese no longer look so different from Asian Indians, Chinese, and Japanese Americans.

One final observation on Table [2] is the degree of similarity in the distribution of responses to our two linked fate measures. Despite differences in emphasis, the rank-order of responses is identical: the modal response is that fates (ethnic or pan-ethnic) are unlinked, followed in frequency by the view that fates are somewhat linked. Far less common are the views that fates are very linked or not very linked, or that the respondent simply does not know how to answer the question.

■ ■ ■

ETHNIC AND RACIAL IDENTITY AND POLITICAL ACTIVISM

. . . [We now] begin to consider the relationship between ethnic and racial identity and political participation. . . . this analysis lays out the basic relationship between measures of racial identification in terms of identity labels and forms of political participation. Although the NAAS measures numerous acts of participation, as detailed in the introductory chapter, we focus on several dimensions of political activity, including an overall voting index, a standard measure of protest activity, and three measures of political participation beyond voting.

The results of this initial analysis are suggestive (Table [3]). For the two measures of identity that connote some degree of integration or incorporation—*Asian American* and *Ethnic American* identity—the association between identity and four of our five key measures of participation appears to be positive. At the bivariate level, those who self-identify as *Asian American* or *Ethnic American* appear to vote, contribute money, contact government officials, and work with others in their community at higher levels than those who self-

TABLE [3]   Ethnic and Self-Identified Categories by Political Participation

	Likely Voter	Political Contributor	Contact Government Officials	Protester	Community Activist
Asian American	49	15	10	4	24
Ethnic American	48	15	11	5	21
Ethnic group	42	9	6	4	17
Asian	44	9	7	4	16

NOTE: Rates are in percentages.
SOURCE: Authors' compilation of data from the 2008 National Asian American Survey (Wong et al., 2011).

TABLE [4]   Rates of Political Participation by Ethnic Identification

	Likely Voter	Political Contributor	Contact Government Officials	Protester	Community Activist
Pan-ethnic linked fate					
Yes	46	15	11	6	24
No	45	11	8	4	20
Ethnic linked fate					
Yes	46	15	11	6	23
No	45	11	8	3	20
Commonality with Asians					
Yes	45	14	10	5	23
No	47	8	5	3	15
Political commonality with others					
Yes	46	14	10	5	23
No	39	6	3	2	12
Discriminated against					
Yes	44	17	13	6	27
No	46	10	7	4	18
Victim of hate crime					
Yes	42	16	17	8	29
No	46	12	9	4	21
All	43	13	9	4	21

NOTE: Rates are in percentages, representing the proportion of those with a specific score on the identity measure (linked fate, commonality with other Asians, and so forth) who also took part in the political activity.
SOURCE: Authors' compilation of data from the 2008 National Asian American Survey (Wong et al., 2011).

identify with their *Ethnic Group* or as *Asian*. Those who self-identify as *Asian American* or *Ethnic American* engage in these activities at more or less comparable rates vis-à-vis each other; similarly, those who identify as *Asian* or with their *Ethnic Group* appear to engage in these four activities at comparable rates. The relationship between racial or ethnic identification and protest activity appears to be minimal.

Although only a modest relationship (if any) is apparent between identity choices and the five forms of political engagement we analyze here, differences in participation by some other indicators of racial and ethnic identity are important. Table [4] summarizes the differences in level of participation in voting, contributing, contacting, protesting, and working with others in the community to solve problems by the two measures of linked fate, commonality with Asians and other racial groups, and experiences with discrimination and hate crimes.

In terms of voting, evidence of differences between respondents with varying levels of racial and political identity beyond the identity labels is scant. Only a sense of political commonality with other racial and ethnic groups has a positive relationship. In contrast, both of the commonality items—with Asians in this country and with other racial groups—are important with respect to contributions, with those holding a sense of commonality much more active in this form of engagement. Likewise, experiences with discrimination and hate crimes are also positively associated with making political contributions. Contacting officials shows a similar pattern to contributing, with strong relationships for the commonality and bias measures. This is also the case for activity with others in the community to solve problems. The same patterns are apparent, but to a lesser degree, for protest activity.

REFERENCES

Dave, Shilpa, Pawan Dhingra, Sunaina Maira, Partha Mazumdar, Lavina Dhingra Shankar, Jaideep Singh, and Rajini Srikanth. 2000. "De-Privileging Positions: Indian Americans, South Asian Americans, and the Politics of Asian American Studies." *Journal of Asian American Studies* 3 (1): 67–100.

Kibria, Nazli. 1998. "The Racial Gap: South Asian American Racial Identity and the Asian American Movement." In *A Part, Yet Apart: South Asians in Asian America, Asian American History and Culture*, edited by Lavina Dhingra Shankar and Rajini Srikanth. Philadelphia: Temple University Press.

Lowe, Lisa. 1996. *Immigrant Acts: On Asian American Cultural Politics*. Durham, NC: Duke University Press.

Shankar, Lavina Dhingra, and Rajini Srikanth, eds. 1998. *A Part, Yet Apart: South Asians in Asian America*. Philadelphia: Temple University Press.

Takagi, Dana Y. 1998. *The Retreat from Race: Asian-American Admissions and Racial Politics*. New Brunswick, NJ: Rutgers University Press.

Wei, William. 1993. *The Asian American Movement*. Philadelphia: Temple University Press.

10.2

From *Bowling Alone: The Collapse and Revival of American Community*

Social capital refers to networks of interpersonal interaction that support civic life and make democratic politics vibrant and meaningful. It is built, for example, when people participate in voluntary organizations. Putnam argues that there has been a steady decline in social capital in the United States since the 1960s, especially interactions occurring within social and political organizations. In this excerpt he describes the value of social capital and why its decline is worrisome.

. . . In recent years social scientists have framed concerns about the changing character of American society in terms of the concept of "social capital." By analogy with notions of physical capital and human capital—tools and training that enhance individual productivity—the core idea of social capital theory is that social networks have value. Just as a screwdriver (physical capital) or a college education (human capital) can increase productivity (both individual and collective), so too social contacts affect the productivity of individuals and groups.

Whereas physical capital refers to physical objects and human capital refers to properties of individuals, social capital refers to connections among individuals—social networks and the norms of reciprocity and trustworthiness that arise from them. In that sense social capital is closely related to what some have called "civic virtue." The difference is that "social capital" calls attention to the fact that civic virtue is most powerful when embedded in a dense network of reciprocal social relations. A society of many virtuous but isolated individuals is not necessarily rich in social capital.

■   ■   ■

By virtually every conceivable measure, social capital has eroded steadily and sometimes dramatically over the past two generations evidence is overwhelming. . . . Americans have had a grow visceral level of disintegrating social bonds.

Are we right? Does social capital have salutary effe communities, or even entire nations? Yes, an impressive

From Robert D. Putnam, *Bowling Alone: The Collapse and Revival of A* York: Simon and Schuster, 2000).

of research suggests that civic connections help make us healthy, wealthy, and wise. Living without social capital is not easy, whether one is a villager in southern Italy or a poor person in the American inner city or a well-heeled entrepreneur in a high-tech industrial district.

If we are to believe that social capital benefits individuals and communities, we must first understand how social capital works its magic. High levels of trust and citizen participation operate through a variety of mechanisms to produce socially desirable outcomes. Obviously the mechanism(s) at work will vary by the circumstance and outcome in question. But in general social capital has many features that help people translate aspirations into realities.

First, social capital allows citizens to resolve collective problems more easily. Social scientists have long been concerned about "dilemmas" of collective action. Such dilemmas are ubiquitous, and their dynamics are straightforward. People often might all be better off if they cooperate, with each doing her share. But each individual benefits more by shirking her responsibility, hoping that others will do the work for her. Moreover, even if she is wrong and the others shirk, too, she is still better off than if she had been the only sucker. Obviously if every individual thinks that the others will do the work, nobody will end up taking part, and all will be left worse off than if all had contributed.

Supporting government through a tax system is a dilemma of collective action. So is limiting lawn sprinklers and long showers during arid summers. These and other coordination challenges go by various names—"collective-action problems," "the prisoner's dilemma," "the free-rider problem," and "the tragedy of the commons," to name a few. But they all share one feature: They are best solved by an institutional mechanism with the power to ensure compliance with the collectively desirable behavior. Social norms and the networks that enforce them provide such a mechanism.

Second, social capital greases the wheels that allow communities to advance smoothly. Where people are trusting and trustworthy, and where they are subject to repeated interactions with fellow citizens, everyday business and social transactions are less costly. There is no need to spend time and money making sure that others will uphold their end of the arrangement or penalizing them if they don't. Economists such as Oliver Williamson and political scientists such as Elinor Ostrom have demonstrated how social capital translates into financial capital and resource wealth for businesses and self-governing units. Indeed, the Nobel Prize–winning economist Kenneth Arrow has concluded, "Virtually every commercial transaction has within itself an element of trust, certainly any transaction conducted over a period of time. It can be plausibly argued that much of the economic backwardness in the world can be explained by a lack of mutual confidence."[1]

A third way in which social capital improves our lot is by widening our awareness of the many ways in which our fates are linked. People who have ⟨activ⟩e and trusting connections to others—whether family members, friends, ⟨or fellow⟩ bowlers—develop or maintain character traits that are good for the rest of society. Joiners become more tolerant, less cynical, and more empathetic to the misfortunes of others. When people lack connections to others, they are unable to test the veracity of their own views, whether in the give-and-take of casual conversation or in more formal deliberation. Without such an opportunity, people are more likely to be swayed by their worst impulses. It is no coincidence that random acts of violence, such as the 1999 spate of schoolyard shootings, tend to be committed by people identified, after the fact, as "loners."

The networks that constitute social capital also serve as conduits for the flow of helpful information that facilitates achieving our goals. For example, . . . many Americans—perhaps even most of us—get our jobs through personal connections. If we lack that social capital, economic sociologists have shown, our economic prospects are seriously reduced, even if we have lots of talent and training ("human capital"). Similarly, communities that lack civic interconnections find it harder to share information and thus mobilize to achieve opportunities or resist threats.

Social capital also operates through psychological and biological processes to improve individuals' lives. Mounting evidence suggests that people whose lives are rich in social capital cope better with traumas and fight illness more effectively. Social capital appears to be a complement, if not a substitute, for Prozac, sleeping pills, antacids, vitamin C, and other drugs we buy at the corner pharmacy. "Call me [or indeed almost anyone] in the morning" might actually be better medical advice than "Take two aspirin" as a cure for what ails us.

To clarify how these mechanisms operate in practice, consider the following stylized example, which, while technically fabricated, depicts reality for many parents. Bob and Rosemary Smith, parents of six-year-old Jonathan, live in an urban community that is full of both delights and troubles. Bob and Rosemary support public education in principle, and they would like their first-grader to be exposed to children from diverse backgrounds, an opportunity that the public schools provide. But the Smiths' local elementary school is a shambles: teachers are demoralized, paint is chipping off the walls, and there is no money for extracurricular activities or computer equipment. Worried about Jonathan's ability to learn and thrive in this environment, Bob and Rosemary have a choice. They can pull their child out of the public schools and pay dearly to put him in a private school, or they can stick around and try to improve the public school. What to do?

Let's suppose that the Smiths want to stick around and start a Parent-Teacher Association at Jonathan's school. The chances that they will be able to do so will depend upon two things: the existence of other concerned parents who are also likely to join; and the likelihood that such an association will be effective in improving conditions at the school. Here social capital comes in. The more the Smiths know and trust their neighbors, the greater their ability to recruit and retain reliable members of the new PTA. In cohesive neighborhoods filled with lots of overlapping connections, individuals more easily learn who can be counted on, and they can make better use of moral suasion to ensure continued attention to the problems at hand.

Let's assume the Smiths succeed in starting the PTA, and several months later it has an active membership of seventeen parents. What does this new institution, this addition to the stock of social capital, do for the individuals involved and for the community at large? For one, belonging to the PTA almost certainly inculcates civic skills in parents. People who might never have designed a project, given a presentation, lobbied a public official, or even spoken up at a meeting are pressed to do so. What's more, the PTA serves to establish and enforce norms of commitment and performance on the part of school officials, teachers, and perhaps even students. It also allows for the deepening of interpersonal bonds and "we-ness" between families and educators. On a more personal note, the PTA meetings are bound to establish, or strengthen, norms of reciprocity and mutual concern among parents. These connections will almost certainly pay off in myriad unexpected ways in the future. If Bob loses his job, he will now have fifteen other adults upon whom he can call for employment leads or even for simple moral support. If Rosemary decides to start a lobbying group to press for better child health facilities in the city, she will have fifteen other potential lobbyists to aid in her cause. At the very least, Bob and Rosemary will have another couple or two with whom they can catch a movie on Friday nights. All these gains—civic skills, social support, professional contacts, volunteer labor, moviegoing partners—arose because the Smiths wanted to put computers in their kid's school.

Community connectedness is not just about warm fuzzy tales of civic triumph. In measurable and well-documented ways, social capital makes an enormous difference in our lives. . . . Social capital makes us smarter, healthier, safer, richer, and better able to govern a just and stable democracy.

NOTE

1. Kenneth J. Arrow, "Gifts and Exchanges," *Philosophy and Public Affairs* 1 (Summer 1972): 357.

11

INTEREST GROUPS

11.1

MARTIN GILENS

From *Affluence and Influence: Economic Inequality and Political Power in America*

Do interest groups represent only wealthy interests in Washington, D.C.? Does lobbying by organized interests undermine or bolster the interests of the poor and marginalized? Gilens presents evidence that the poorest Americans receive some representation of their policy preferences from certain interest groups, especially unions. The political power of those interest groups has been waning, however, mostly because the social bases of those groups are shrinking relative to population size.

INTEREST GROUPS AND DEMOCRATIC RESPONSIVENESS

■ ■ ■

No list of "powerful interest groups in Washington" could hope to be definitive, but a plausible place to start is the "Power 25" list of lobbying organizations produced by *Fortune* magazine: Every few years since 1997, *Fortune* has surveyed Washington insiders (including members of Congress, congressional staff, White House aides, and lobbyists themselves), asking them to rate the influence of dozens of different lobbying organizations. Baumgartner et al. found that their index of relative interest group resources was strongly related

From Martin Gilens, *Affluence and Influence: Economic Inequality and Political Power in America* (Princeton: Princeton University Press, 2012), Chapter 5.

to the difference in the number of Power 25 groups identified with each side of their policy issues.[1]

The basis for my own coding of interest group involvement, then, is based on an expanded version of *Fortune*'s Power 25 list. I began by combining the Power 25 lists from surveys conducted during both the Clinton and the G. W. Bush administrations (since the perceived power of different interest groups may be influenced by changes in partisan control of government). I then added to this combined list the ten industries with the highest lobbying expenditures (that were not already represented in the Power 25 list) based on lobbying disclosure data compiled by opensecrets.org. (Industries that exert most of their lobbying efforts directly rather than through industry-wide organizations tend not to appear in the Power 25 list. For example, financial and investment firms, oil companies, and telecommunications companies all spend heavily on lobbying but not through industry-wide organizations.) This resulted in the expanded list of forty-three interest groups. . . .

■　■　■

Individual Interest Groups and the Public's Policy Preferences

Insight into the potential power of interest groups to redress the inequalities in Americans' influence over government policy may be gained by examining the existing cases in which interest groups appear to push policy in a direction favorable to the less well-off. A congruence of preferences between interest groups and lower-income Americans might arise for three reasons. First, a group might adopt a position for reasons unconnected with the needs or preferences of the poor. For example, if the American Hospital Association helps obtain increased government funding for teaching hospitals, the least well-off members of the public may benefit most (since they are more likely to lack health insurance and rely on uncompensated care from large urban hospitals). In this (hypothetical) case, the AHA would have no particular concern with helping to meet the needs or promote the policy preferences of the less well-off; this confluence of preferences between an interest group and the disadvantaged is merely a happy coincidence.

In other cases, however, interest groups appear to serve as conduits of influence for members of the public. The clearest such cases concern mass-membership organizations that exist to advance some particular set of policy goals and recruit members and attract donations on the basis of those goals. Citizens groups like the Sierra Club, the American Civil Liberties Union, and the National Rifle Association are examples of groups that serve as mechanisms through which like-minded members of the public exert influence over government policy.[2] To the extent that policy stances of such citizens groups reflect the preferences of poor or middle-class Americans, they offer a potential avenue of influence to counter the power exerted by more affluent Americans.

Finally, some interest groups that are not primarily mechanisms for the expression of their members' policy preferences might nevertheless have an ideological commitment to benefit the less advantaged. . . . Some of these organizations are citizens groups of the type described above. But others are funded through grants and donations, through commercial activities, or through the dues of members who join for reasons other than political advocacy. In these latter categories are labor unions (which workers in unionized businesses often have no choice but to join) and organizations like the AARP which attract members largely on the basis of the "selective incentives" they provide.[3] While most of the forty million members of the AARP may agree with most of the organization's policy positions, AARP membership brings with it a wide range of services and discounts on everything from health insurance to hotels. Moreover, membership dues make up a small part of the AARP's income (with the majority coming from licensing agreements for AARP-branded health plans, life insurance, financial planning, and so on).[4] Because members join for largely nonideological reasons, and because the AARP does not rely on dues to fund its operations, the extent to which the group's positions are constrained by and reflective of its members' policy preferences is much weaker than it is for pure mass-membership advocacy groups like the Sierra Club or the ACLU.

To what extent, then, do the interest groups that tend to align with the preferences of low- or middle-income Americans plausibly reflect the *influence* of the less advantaged over government policy, and to what extent are these congruent preferences merely happy coincidences that arise from interest groups' pursuit of their own agendas? The correlations between the positions coded for each of the forty-three interest groups on my expanded Power 25 list and the preferences of Americans at the 10th, 50th, and 90th income percentiles are shown in Table [1]. The associations shown offer some useful insights into the dynamics of interest groups vis-à-vis the preferences of lower- and higher-income Americans, and I discuss some of these general patterns below. But it is important to keep in mind that these data provide a very partial account of the full constellation of organized groups working to shape federal policy, and that my set of proposed policy changes excludes most of the narrow and typically obscure issues that constitute much of government policy making. I also leave for future studies the analysis of alliances among interest groups—alliances that might, at least under the right circumstances, allow less-powerful interest groups to leverage their resources in ways that might advance the preferences of the less well-off.[5]

The top section of Table [1] shows the four "pure" mass-membership advocacy organizations among the groups on my list. The policy positions of the Christian Coalition and the National Right to Life Committee are positively related to the preferences of the poor and negatively related to the preferences of the affluent. But none of these associations is especially strong, suggesting only a modest tendency for the preferences of the poor to coincide with the positions of these two interest groups, and at best a modest tendency for policy to align more closely with the preferences of the poor as a result of these groups' efforts.

TABLE [1] Correlations between Public Preferences and Interest Group Positions

		Income Percentile		
	N	10th	50th	90th
Mass membership advocacy organizations				
Christian Coalition	211	.19**	.04	−.15*
National Right to Life Committee	95	.21*	.04	−.24*
National Rifle Association	143	−.24**	−.23**	−.28***
American Israel Public Affairs Committee	99	−.12	−.24*	−.24*
Unions				
AFL-CIO	301	.42***	.38***	.14*
American Federation of State, County, and Municipal Employees	134	.38***	.33***	.12
International Brotherhood of Teamsters	154	.40***	.38***	.21**
United Auto Workers	173	.53***	.48***	.24**
Other organizations that tend to side with the poor				
AARP	301	.52***	.50***	.41***
National Governors' Association	85	.58***	.46***	.39***
Universities	26	.63***	.57**	.37
National Education Association	118	.48***	.41***	.34***
Organizations that tend to side with the affluent				
American Hospital Association	136	.14	.15	.27**
National Federation of Independent Business	245	−.09	−.02	.21***
Securities and investment companies	275	−.10	−.02	.18**
Organizations that tend to side against the poor				
Chamber of Commerce	392	−.20***	−.19***	−.03
National Association of Manufacturers	280	−.33***	−.34***	−.20***
Health Insurance Association	152	−.26***	−.17*	−.10
National Restaurant Association	105	−.39***	−.31***	−.19
Telephone companies	134	−.28***	−.28***	−.07
American Farm Bureau Federation	212	−.20**	−.18**	−.02
Computer software and hardware	159	−.18*	−.17*	.01
Automobile companies	202	−.29***	−.31***	−.17*
Defense contractors	232	−.35***	−.36***	−.23***
Electric companies	194	−.37***	−.38***	−.27***

TABLE [1]   *(continued)*

	N	Income Percentile		
		10th	*50th*	*90th*
Other organizations				
Airlines	180	−.13	−.15*	.00
American Bankers Association	171	−.12	−.10	.01
American Council of Life Insurance	87	−.15	−.14	−.10
American Medical Association	127	.09	.06	.16
Association of Trial Lawyers	70	.02	−.11	−.08
Credit Union National Association	82	−.11	−.08	−.08
Independent Insurance Agents of America	96	−.02	−.08	.01
Motion Picture Association of America	57	−.20	−.27*	−.18
National Association of Broadcasters	69	−.29*	−.29*	−.20
National Association of Home Builders	174	.05	.05	.12
National Association of Realtors	128	.05	.08	.13
National Beer Wholesalers Association	170	−.13	−.09	.05
Oil companies	216	−.37***	−.40***	−.33***
Pharmaceutical Research and Manufacturers	159	−.04	−.02	.07
Recording Industry Association	105	−.05	−.04	.02

*p < .05; **p < .01; ***p < .001

N indicates the number of proposed policy changes in dataset on which each organization took a position. Excludes the American Legion and Veterans of Foreign Wars, which took positions on fewer than twenty of the proposed policy changes.

The strongest positive associations between interest groups' positions and the preferences of the less well-off are shown in the next two sections of Table [1]. The four unions in my expanded Power 25 list show consistently strong tendencies to share the preferences of low- and middle-income Americans, with much weaker (but still positive) associations with the preferences of the affluent. Unions tended to side with the poor and the middle class in opposing free-trade policies and cuts in capital gains and corporate income taxes, and in supporting increases in the minimum wage and the right to strike for groups like firefighters, police officers, and college teachers. Some of these favored changes were supported at lower levels by the affluent (like raising the minimum wage), while others had majorities of the well-off and the poor on opposite sides (like teachers' right to strike).

Based on unions' strong tendency to share the preferences of the less well-off and the large number of policy areas they are engaged in (the AFL-CIO in particular took positions on a large number of issues), unions would appear to be among the most promising interest group bases for strengthening the policy influence of America's poor and middle class. Optimism in this regard must be tempered, however, by the steep decline in private-sector unionization rates over the past sixty years. In addition unions tend to be active on issues on which other powerful interest groups are aligned on the other side. Of the 1,357 proposed policy changes in my dataset on which at least one interest group took a position, interest groups were found on both sides of the issue only 30 percent of the time. In contrast, among the 311 proposed changes on which at least one union took a stand, interest groups were found on both sides 77 percent of the time. Because unions tend to be opposed by other interest groups far more frequently than the average for all interest groups, they are less likely to be able to prevail. Of course poor and middle-class Americans would be even less likely to find their preferences reflected in federal policy were it not for unions' lobbying efforts. Other scholars have examined the obstacles and successes of unions' political efforts in considerable detail.[6] My data are consistent with much of this literature in suggesting both that unions are among the most important forces moving federal policy in a direction desired by the less well-off and that unions' success in these efforts is likely to be fairly limited.

The third section of Table [1] lists the four remaining interest groups that show strong positive associations with the preferences of the less well-off. The positions of the AARP in support of Medicare and Social Security are often consistent with the preferences of Americans at all income levels, but when preferences diverge (for example, over various market-oriented reforms to these programs), the AARP tends to reflect the desires of those with low and moderate incomes. The considerable power attributed to the AARP as an advocacy organization suggests its important role in maintaining and strengthening government benefits for older Americans, but the exact basis for that power is difficult to discern. The AARP has a large membership and enormous financial resources, but it also advocates positions that strong majorities of the public tend to favor. This rather unique combination of characteristics (and the extent to which the AARP's income derives from its commercial activities) suggests that it cannot serve as a viable model for expanding the role of interest groups in giving a voice to lower-income Americans.

The other three interest groups in this section of Table [1]—universities, the National Governors' Association, and the National Education Association—took positions on relatively few policy issues compared with the interest organizations discussed above. Universities (which share with low- and middle-income Americans their strong support for increasing federal assistance to college students) are engaged on only 26 of my 1,779 proposed policy changes. Of these three organizations, only the National Governors' Association might be viewed as a mechanism of middle- or lower-class influence over federal policy. To the extent that the policy preferences of America's governors reflect their desire to advance the interests of their constituents (either from an ideological commitment or to improve their political prospects), the National Governors' Association lobbying might be an avenue through which less-affluent Americans' preferences help shape federal policy. On the other hand, given the absence of responsiveness of federal policy to the preferences of low- and middle-income Americans, it seems likely that governors too would favor the preferences of their more affluent constituents. If so, the congruence between the NGA's positions and the preferences of the less well-off should be attributed not to the influence of middle-class constituents but to the economic benefits states gain from federal spending on public works and programs like Medicaid and TANF.

The remainder of the interest groups in Table [1] are business organizations, divided into three sections. The first consists of the few business groups whose positions tend to reflect the preferences of the well-off (although none of these associations is particularly strong). The second set is those business organizations whose positions tend to conflict with the preferences of the poor and whose relationship with the preferences of the affluent are less negative or indistinguishable from zero. Finally, at the bottom of the table are those business groups that took positions that were more or less equally strongly (and negatively) related to the preferences of Americans across the income spectrum (or unrelated to preferences at any income level).

Of the twenty-eight business organizations in the bottom three sections of Table [1], none has positive and statistically significant associations with the preferences of either poor or middle-income Americans (in contrast, about a dozen of the correlations with each of these two income groups are negative and significant).

In sum, the diverse universe of organized interests (represented in a very partial way in Table [1]) does include groups seeking to promote the preferences of less-well-off Americans. Unfortunately for those concerned about representational inequality, these groups tend to be narrowly focused, disproportionately opposed by other organized interests, and/or declining in size and strength. Still the broader picture as reflected in the statistical analyses presented above is that interest groups sometimes enhance and sometimes diminish the likelihood that low- and middle-income Americans will see their preferences reflected in government policy. As earlier chapters indicated, only affluent Americans appear to have substantial influence over federal policy. This chapter shows that the influence of these citizens, and the lack of influence of the less well-off, cannot be attributed to the operation of interest groups.

Pluralist accounts of interest groups from the 1950s and 1960s often stressed the positive function of organized interests in facilitating popular representation and giving ordinary citizens a voice in government.[7] Pluralism's critics, on the other hand, have tended to focus on the advantages that groups with money and well-defined, narrow interests enjoy.[8] Rather than facilitating responsiveness to the public, these critics argue, the interest group system embodies and perpetuates inequality. Neither of these extreme depictions is consistent with my findings. Organized interests do sometimes push government policy in a direction favored by the public as a whole or by one or another economic subgroup of the public, just as they sometimes push policy in a direction the public opposes. But the interest group system, at least as captured by my coding of the most influential interest groups, appears on balance to neither facilitate nor undermine the public's influence over government policy.

NOTES

1. Correlation = 0.73, $p < 0.001$; Baumgartner et al., *Lobbying and Policy Change*.
2. Berry, *The New Liberalism*.
3. Ainsworth, *Analyzing Interest Groups*; Olson, *The Logic of Collective Action*.
4. AARP, "Aarp Consolidated Financial Statements 2007–2008." For 2007, membership dues accounted for about 21 percent of the AARP's operating revenue, with 59 percent coming from royalties, advertising income from AARP publications, and investments.
5. Baumgartner et al., *Lobbying and Policy Change*.
6. E.g., Masters and Delaney, "Organized Labor's Political Scorecard."
7. Dahl, *Who Governs?*; Truman, *The Governmental Process*.
8. Lindblom, *Politics and Markets*; Olson, *The Logic of Collective Action*; Schattschneider, *The Semisovereign People*.

REFERENCES

AARP. "Aarp Consolidated Financial Statements 2007–2008." http://assets.aarp.org /www.aarp.org_/articles/aboutaarp/AnnualReports/hq_main.html.

Ainsworth, Scott H. 2002. *Analyzing Interest Groups: Group Influence on People and Policies*. New York: Norton.

Baumgartner, Frank R., Jeffrey M. Berry, Marie Hojnacki, David C. Kimball, and Beth L. Leech. 2009. *Lobbying and Policy Change: Who Wins, Who Loses, and Why*. Chicago: University of Chicago Press.

Berry, Jeffrey M. 1999. *The New Liberalism: The Rising Power of Citizen Groups*. Washington, DC: Brookings Institution Press.

Dahl, Robert A. 1961. *Who Governs? Democracy and Power in an American City*. Yale Studies in Political Science. New Haven, CT: Yale University Press.

Lindblom, Charles Edward. 1977. *Politics and Markets: The World's Political Economic Systems*. New York: Basic Books.

Masters, Marick F., and John T. Delaney. 2005 "Organized Labor's Political Scorecard." *Journal of Labor Research* 26, no. 3 (2005): 365–92.

Olson, Mancur, Jr. 1965. *The Logic of Collective Action: Public Goods and the Theory of Groups*. Cambridge, MA: Harvard University Press.

Schattschneider, E. E. 1960. *The Semisovereign People*. New York: Holt Rinehart and Winston.

Truman, David B. 1951. *The Governmental Process: Political Interests and Public Opinion*. New York: Knopf.

11.2

KEN KOLLMAN

From *Outside Lobbying: Public Opinion and Interest Group Strategies*

Kollman contrasts two types of lobbying: inside and outside. The inside game is more private and is played among people in Washington. The outside game is played by interest group leaders who bring people from outside Washington into the business of persuading members of Congress. Outside lobbying both signals existing public opinion to lawmakers and tries to shape that public opinion to an interest group's advantage.

INTRODUCTION

Outside lobbying is defined as attempts by interest group leaders to mobilize citizens outside the policymaking community to contact or pressure public officials inside the policymaking community. It represents a viable and effective strategy for many interest groups trying to influence representative government between elections. What better way is there to win favorable legislation in Congress, for example, than to mobilize a significant number of constituents to contact key legislators? Old-fashioned inside lobbying, the personal access and contact with legislators so necessary for maintaining good relations with government, may have only limited effectiveness today. Just as elected officials in Washington feel the need to monitor and assuage public opinion through polls and public relations, modern lobbying increasingly requires sophisticated methods of public mobilization. Lobbying in Washington is not just a game among well-paid lawyers, ideological activists, and legislators in the Capitol. The outside public is increasingly involved.

Mass expressions of public concern directed toward the federal government are rarely spontaneous. Behind most telephone calls, letters, faxes, and e-mails to members of Congress, behind marches down the Mall in Washington, D.C., and behind bus caravans to the Capitol, there are coordinating leaders, usually interest group leaders, mobilizing a select group of citizens to unite behind a common message. At the most basic level, an interest group leader seeks to persuade policymakers that what the members of the group want (as specified by the leader) is good public policy and/or good politics.

From Ken Kollman, *Outside Lobbying: Public Opinion and Interest Group Strategies* (Princeton, NJ: Princeton University Press, 1998).

And the leader uses outside lobbying to demonstrate first, that the members of the group are in fact united behind the leader, and second, that many other constituents agree with what the group leader wants. Faced with organized groups of constituents making noise about this or that policy issue, not many members of Congress could afford to ignore these efforts completely. Any leader who can organize thousands of citizens to write letters to their congressional representative, for example, can with some probability organize a good number of voters on election day to support or oppose the incumbent. For all the apparent benefits of outside lobbying to an interest group—sending a strong message to policymakers or reinforcing to voters that the group represents a credible source of political information—it is surprising nonetheless that outside lobbying is not undertaken more often by groups with an interest in controversial policy issues.

Outside lobbying, however, is in fact applied selectively, and lobbyists and interest group leaders spend precious hours and resources crafting careful public campaigns of persuasion. On some policy issues, groups on all sides use outside lobbying intensively. On other policy issues, only groups on one side of the issue use outside lobbying. There are many issues, even those considered extremely important to specific interest groups, where no groups use outside lobbying. And of course, groups try to time their public appeals for maximum effect. As every lobbyist (or salesperson, parent, or leader) knows, persuasion is a subtle business, and careless lobbying strategies can backfire. It is not always the case that outside lobbying, even when it generates a substantial public response, wins over the policymakers targeted.

The selective application and timing of outside lobbying strategies raises important questions. Obviously, outside lobbying is not always influential, even when interest group leaders on only one side of an issue use it. Who or what captures the attention of Washington policymakers? When are demonstrations of popular support effective in influencing policymakers? How do outside lobbying campaigns compare to financial donations or inside lobbying in influencing policymakers? V. O. Key raised similar questions nearly four decades ago, and he found answers difficult to come by. In the 1961 book *Public Opinion and American Democracy*, he expresses doubts about the influence of outside lobbying activities. "Their function in the political process," he writes in reference to "propagandizing campaigns" by interest groups, "is difficult to divine" (528). Outside lobbying activities are "rituals in obeisance to the doctrine that public opinion governs" and are "on the order of the dance of the rainmakers. . . . Sometimes these campaigns have their effects—just as rain sometimes follows the rainmakers' dance. Yet the data make it fairly clear that most of these campaigns do not affect the opinion of many people and even clearer that they have a small effect by way of punitive or approbative feedback in the vote" (528).

Why and when, Key is really asking, do policymakers pay attention to outside lobbying? Certainly many organizational leaders consider outside lobbying potentially influential; otherwise, they would not do it. The leaders of the major labor unions, peak business organizations, and civil rights and environmental groups use outside lobbying regularly enough to indicate that they believe outside lobbying is more than the dancing of rainmakers. Even corporate leaders use outside lobbying occasionally. And policymakers admit that organized groups of constituents influence their decisions. One congressional staff member justified his boss's vote to repeal catastrophic health insurance in 1990, little more than a year after voting for the insurance bill, by explaining, "It was a no-brainer. He got over five thousand letters for the repeal of the insurance, and literally eight letters in favor of the current insurance. He didn't have much choice really. He had to vote for repeal."

But beyond the relatively uninteresting claims that interest group leaders consider outside lobbying effective and that policymakers sometimes consider it influential, the topic deserves more attention than it receives. If, as most observers claim, interest groups wield considerable power in Washington, and if interest groups spend resources using outside lobbying fairly regularly, then outside lobbying should be an important part of the process by which these groups wield their power. Precisely when, why, or how outside lobbying operates to enhance group influence, however, is not well understood.

Our evaluations of the normative effects of outside lobbying are similarly imprecise. We know very little about whether outside lobbying serves to improve the correspondence between what constituents want and what their representatives do or whether it merely confuses representatives with meaningless information or reinforces inequalities in access to representatives that accrue from campaign contributions and other less edifying activities of interest groups. Surprisingly, many depictions of outside lobbying in the national press are as unfavorable as those of lobbying in general. The image of fat-cat lobbyists shoving money in the pockets of legislators has been supplemented by negative images of farmers, teachers, truckers, or public employees demonstrating at the Capitol or flooding Congress with telephone calls for a bigger slice of the budgetary pie, or of business lobbyists spending money to generate so-called astroturf (in contrast to real grass-roots support) to save a valuable tax provision. The press depiction of interest group activities has had either a large influence on Americans or has tapped into deeply negative sentiments among the general population. Recent polls show that a vast majority of Americans are cynical about the power of special interests. In the 1992 American National Election Study (ANES), when asked whether "the government is pretty much run by a few big interests looking out for themselves or [if] it is run for the benefit of all the people," 78 percent of those offering a response answered, "a few big interests." Common wisdom, it appears, holds that some interest groups have their way in Washington, and that outside lobbying either reinforces existing inequalities in access or is irrelevant to the real game of special interest lobbying.

The cynicism of the press and the general public toward interest groups is not shared by many political scientists. Studies have tended to describe a more sanguine climate of bargaining and information gathering between interest groups and policymakers in Washington. Descriptions of interest group activities and influence from the last four decades range from the near impotence of business lobbyists during legislative conflicts over free trade to subtle forms of persuasion and pressure that influence legislation marginally. Many studies of policymaking or interest groups have concluded that other pressures on policymakers besides interest group lobbying—colleagues in the House or Senate, public opinion in the district, the White House, party leaders—were more important in determining policy. Even those who ascribe considerable power to special interests suggest that that power is wielded subtly or silently, without the intense lobbying activity so common in Washington.

One reason the press and the general public may tend to exaggerate the influence of interest groups is that the news overemphasizes dramatic instances of graft, exploited campaign finance loopholes, or extraordinary pressure exerted on members of Congress by organizations like the National Rifle Association. Successful outside lobbying campaigns and increasingly large campaign contributions due to the reporting of the Federal Election Commission attract attention and are visible manifestations of group power. Inside lobbying in the form of interpersonal contacts, while an everyday occurrence for nearly all interest groups, is harder for the mass media to observe on a regular basis and has more of the flavor of relationship building and coordination among lobbyists and legislators than of outright pressure. Thus, the media fail to report adequately on the effects of inside strategies, and if they were to do so, it would probably bring the popular evaluation of interest group power more into balance.

In contrast, some of the conclusions of political scientists about the muted influence of interest groups may have something to do with the lack of research on outside lobbying. Researchers have tended to focus on inside lobbying, campaign contributions, and especially organizational formation. For each of these subjects, conclusions of researchers have highlighted the limitations of organized interests. Inside lobbying rarely changes legislators' positions on policy issues. Campaign contributions seem to correlate only weakly with legislative or electoral success. And groups are hard to form because of collective action problems. Given all the obstacles interest groups presumably face, one wonders why there are more than seven thousand registered organizations in Washington, and why so many of them spend precious resources trying to influence policymakers. Interest groups work hard to influence legislation, and it is difficult to believe that their money and efforts go to waste.

Part of the problem for political scientists may be that they fail to see the role that outside lobbying serves in enhancing the inside lobbying of interest groups. Interest groups choose lobbying strategies at the same time policymakers are trying to please constituents. Groups thus choose strategies intended to convince policymakers that group goals align with constituent goals. If successfully wielded, these strategies can enable interest group leaders to be quite influential in shaping public policies. While this seems apparent, outside lobbying does not get the attention it deserves in interest group research. Simply put, outside lobbying has rarely been studied systematically. The kinds of interest group activities the mass media tend to highlight are precisely those that political scientists tend to understudy, and the differences in coverage among the two affect conclusions about interest group power. This reading, in attempting to answer three questions—Why do groups use outside lobbying? When does outside lobbying work? Who benefits from outside lobbying?—is an effort to rectify the imbalance in interest group research.

Of course, interest group leaders are not the only ones who find it in their interests to mobilize citizens to pressure American policymakers. Political party leaders, politicians (especially the president), and even newspapers and mass media personalities actively encourage citizens to contact their elected representatives. The question of when it is advantageous in a democracy to mobilize citizens to pressure policymakers is considerably more general than the more specific question of when interest groups should do so. Many of the ideas in this reading about outside lobbying by interest groups should certainly apply to other actors in the political system.

Overview

Outside lobbying is important because it is a common means (perhaps the most common means except for elections) for elite policymakers to experience pressure in the form of popular participation. Were it not for outside lobbying from interest groups, many policy decisions would take place solely among a relatively insulated group of Washington insiders. Instead, interest group leaders call upon people outside of Washington to remind policymakers that a sizable portion of their constituents is paying attention. At least potentially, outside lobbying can pressure policymakers to adopt more popularly supported policies than they would in the absence of outside lobbying.

Outside lobbying accomplishes two tasks simultaneously. First, at the elite level it communicates aspects of public opinion to policymakers. The many forms of outside lobbying—publicizing issue positions, mobilizing constituents to contact Congress, protesting or demonstrating—have the common purpose of trying to show policymakers that the people the group claims to represent really do care about some relevant policy issue. These tactics say, in effect, "See, we told you constituents were angry about policy X, and now you can hear it from them."

I refer to this role for outside lobbying as *signaling* because it has many characteristics of basic signaling models in game theory. An interest group (the sender) tries to signal its popular support (its type) to a policymaker (the receiver). . . . When do the signals sent by interest group leaders actually influence policymakers' behavior?

The noteworthy characteristic of outside lobbying, however, is that it is not just an elite-level phenomenon. It is intended to influence members of the mass public as well. The second role for outside lobbying is to influence public opinion by changing how selected constituents consider and respond to policy issues. I shall call this its *conflict expansion* role in reference to the theoretical legacy of Schattschneider, who wrote in 1960 that the "most important strategy of politics is concerned with the scope of the conflict. . . . Conflicts are frequently won or lost by the success that the contestants have in getting the audience involved in the fight or in excluding it, as the case may be" (3–4). As Schattschneider emphasized, political elites, when faced with intransigent opposition, can bring attention to their cause, invite constituents to participate in the policy process, and hope to swing momentum to their side.

For both of these roles, the salience of policy issues to constituents, an often-overlooked characteristic of public opinion, lies at the center of interest group politics. It is not the popularity of policies that is mostly communicated or altered through outside lobbying. For one, the popularity of policies tends to stay relatively fixed over long periods of time, even given the outside lobbying activities of interest groups. But even more important, policymakers tend to have good information on the popularity of policies, primarily through opinion polls, but also because such popularity stays relatively constant and they can learn about it over time. Salience, however, defined as the relative importance people attach to policy issues, is an aspect of public opinion that policymakers perpetually running for reelection want to know but cannot learn about from ordinary opinion polls and experience. Policymakers want to know what proportion of constituents, when voting in the next election, will weigh the actions of their elected representatives on a particular policy issue. More salient policy issues will weigh more heavily on voting decisions than will less salient policy issues, and policymakers rely to a considerable extent on interest groups for current information on which issues rank high on salience. Because they can mobilize constituents to speak for themselves and can occasionally increase the salience of issues to those constituents, interest group leaders have a comparative advantage in sending credible signals on this precious information.

In sum, interest group leaders can turn their informational and leadership advantages into policy influence. They can try through inside lobbying to convince policymakers that voters care about an issue and are on the side of their group on the issue. But outside lobbying goes a step further in making a costly, public demonstration that, one, the issue is in fact salient to voters and, two, the interest group can make the issue even more salient.

The distinction between the two roles can be quite fuzzy, especially in practice. Consider two analogous situations. An opposition leader in an authoritarian regime wants to hold a large rally in the capital. The rally, if it successfully gathers hundreds of thousands of people as planned, accomplishes the two tasks just specified. It both communicates to the current regime the swelling sentiment among the population that the current regime is offensive *and* coordinates or mobilizes the opposing citizens on a particular course of action:

support the opposition leader and work to topple the current government. To the government the rally signals the status of the opposition, and to the citizens in the rally it reinforces the notion that the effort to topple the regime is important and worthy of risky collective action.

Outside lobbying is also similar to the marketing behavior of business entrepreneurs promoting new product ideas to consumers and investors at the same time. Entrepreneurs do their own brand of inside lobbying among investors, hawking their product ideas and wooing support among a small group of people. At the same time, they gauge consumer demand for their products, communicate that level of demand to potential investors, and even try to stimulate more demand among consumers. Success among one audience (consumers) will likely lead to success among the other audience (investors). Just as investors try to assess potential consumer response to the entrepreneur's marketing efforts because future investments will succeed or fail based on consumer behavior, elected officials look to constituents' responses to outside lobbying because reelection efforts may hinge on the interest group success in mobilizing constituents. For interest groups, as with entrepreneurs, there are two audiences in mass marketing, but the overall goals converge because one audience relies very much on the other audience. . . .

The duality of purpose makes outside lobbying a powerful tool in the hands of interest groups. It can simultaneously fan the flames of constituent anger and bring the heat of those flames to the attention of representatives far away, whose job it is to put out or contain the fire. However, while the two roles can get mixed together in practice, there are important conceptual distinctions between them. In the signaling role, the salience of a policy issue must be considered *exogenous* in that there is something fixed and unknown to policymakers about salience that the group claims to be able to demonstrate through outside lobbying. Perhaps it is the potential salience of an issue that interest groups want to communicate. In this case, the "fixed" element of public opinion being communicated is the latent salience of an issue. The group is confident it can expand the conflict to a certain point, and it wants to communicate that confidence through outside lobbying. In the conflict expansion role, the salience of a policy issue is *endogenous,* in that the strategy is intended to influence the very characteristic of public opinion that is being communicated in the signaling role.

■   ■   ■

Communication costs in particular are relevant to the study of outside lobbying because the costs of successful outside lobbying are related systematically to the existing state of public salience on an issue. Precisely because outside lobbying is costly, and the strategies of interest groups conditional on those costs offer clues to the underlying public salience groups are trying to communicate, outside lobbying can influence policymakers. Policymakers learn about salience by making inferences from the revealed efforts of interest groups.

When group leaders are confident they can expand the conflict—raise public awareness of an issue or frame issues in different ways to their advantage—additional considerations besides the advantages of signaling to policy-makers become important. What information should a group present to constituents to convince them the issue is worth costly collective action? When in the course of legislation should conflict expansion happen for maximum impact? How should a group frame the advantages of one policy over another policy? In general, when there are opportunities to expand the conflict, deci-sion making over strategies turns on how potential increases in salience (or sometimes popularity) will benefit interest group goals, rather than on how the current level of popular support will play with policymakers.

As a first cut at understanding conflict expansion, we might think it benefits groups that do not have ready access to policymakers. Much of our under-standing of this comes from Schattschneider. Schattschneider believed not only that outsider groups would want to outside lobby, but also that such groups tend to have advantages in the realm of public opinion. According to Schattschneider, "It is the weak who want to socialize conflict, i.e., to involve more and more people in the conflict until the balance of forces is changed" (1960, 40), the assumption being that groups with concentrated wealth or power would eschew politics involving broad popular participation and do not stand to gain from increased salience.

Schattschneider's ideas, however, do not completely square with contem-porary interest group politics. In an age when all kinds of organizations, including large corporations, wealthy trade associations, and professional groups outside lobby on policy issues of great concern to millions of Ameri-cans, clearly there are times when the strong and those groups with consider-able inside access want to expand the scope of the conflict as well. . . .

Two aspects of the policy context that influence outside lobbying are discussed in detail in that chapter: the stage of legislation and the policy alter-natives confronting policymakers. The stage of legislation—whether a policy problem is just being introduced to the government or whether well-defined alternatives are being considered by legislators—will have a large effect on both signaling and conflict expansion decisions (Kingdon 1984). In decisions over lobbying strategies or tactics, groups facing policies in earlier stages, when they merely try to raise consciousness on a new policy issue, will be less concerned about popular support for their policy positions than will groups facing policies in later stages, when they fight to swing a few key votes in a congressional committee. The stage of legislation shapes the way public opin-ion constrains interest group strategies mostly by varying the benefits groups attain in signaling the current salience of an issue versus in trying to increase the salience of that issue or the popularity of specific policies.

Policy alternatives, or more specifically the relative popularity of policy alternatives, matter a great deal because they also determine whether increas-ing salience is a good idea for a group. What may not be overwhelmingly popular—say, needle exchange programs—may be more popular than the most prominent policy alternative, increased spending on drug rehabilitation programs. Thus, as for influencing outside lobbying decisions, the popularity of policies must be regarded as relative, not absolute, a consideration that carries implications about whether a group benefits from conflict expansion.

■ ■ ■

Most us would presumably like to see outside lobbying coming from groups supporting popular policies on salient issues. Instead, the empirical conclusions of this study are mixed. I find that outside lobbying, contrary to the view that most of it produces phony grass-roots support, is far from artificial. It is actually a good way for policymakers to learn what their constituents care about. My data show that outside lobbying on average works as a policymaker might hope: it communicates fairly accurately the salience of policy issues to large numbers of constituents, and it often influences the salience of policy issues to benefit the more popular side of an issue. At the same time, however, and more often than we would like, outside lobbying springs forth from intense groups pursuing relatively unpopular policies (especially early in the legislative process), and in this regard, it falls somewhat short in reinforcing the majority's preferences. Outside lobbying, in sum, does not distort the policymaking process nearly as much as many people like to claim, but it does a better job in communicating salience information than in bolstering popular pressure for majoritarian policies.

■ ■ ■

TACTICS AND STRATEGIES

The Story of the Hat Trick

One beautiful August morning in 1989, Leona Kozien took the bus from near her home in Chicago to the Copernicus Center for senior citizens on the city's northwest side. Kozien, who was sixty-nine years old, had no idea at the time that she was going to become a brief media star and a figure of political lore. All she knew was that she was angry with the politicians in Washington. In particular, she felt betrayed by her congressman, Dan Rostenkowski, chairman of the Ways and Means Committee of the House of Representatives. Kozien was upset by a new policy from Washington that caused her husband to pay a surtax for catastrophic health care insurance. In her mind, it was an unfair attempt by the federal government to make senior citizens pay unreasonably for health care.

Rostenkowski knew many seniors were angry, but he did not know the extent of the anger. Since the unveiling of the policy a year earlier, a policy that he and the largest seniors lobby, the American Association of Retired Persons (AARP), had sponsored and supported all through the legislative process, he had been reluctant to meet with smaller senior citizens' groups, even those from his own district. National groups separate from the AARP, especially the National Committee to Preserve Social Security and Medicare, run by James Roosevelt, son of President Franklin D. Roosevelt, had been mobilizing grass-roots opposition to the policy for more than a year. The AARP then decided to oppose the new policy. Partly as a concession and partly as a compromise, Rostenkowski had agreed to meet with a few of the leaders of local senior citizens groups. The meeting was held at the Copernicus Center, right in the heart of Rostenkowski's district.

After prodding by her husband (who could not attend), Kozien joined approximately one hundred seniors who waited in the main hall of the center for Rostenkowski to emerge from the meeting with the group leaders. She and other seniors had been given signs to wave at Rostenkowski. The signs indicated displeasure with the current policy: Congressman Rostenkowski, Don't Tax the Seniors, and Read My Lips: Catastrophic Act Is a Seniors Tax.

While Rostenkowski met with group leaders, Kozien and her own group were holding a meeting of their own in the main hall. Participants were taking turns telling the rest of the group why the catastrophic health policy was bad for seniors. The group waiting for Rostenkowski agreed that the catastrophic "tax" had to go, but they also agreed on something else. They wanted Rostenkowski to speak to them in person.

"A lot of people felt they were owed something," one local interest group leader recalls. "They just wanted to see him. He was right there, and they felt this was their opportunity [to tell him what they thought of the policy]."

Rostenkowski emerged from his meeting and headed for the exit. The group waiting for him booed and hissed. Before the congressman could get to the door, a television crew stopped him to ask questions about events in Poland, a topic of keen interest to many of his constituents. This pause gave a small group of seniors enough time to run out of the building and surround Rostenkowski's car. Kozien led the charge.

Kozien shouted, "Where's his car parked? I'm going to make him talk to us!"

A small mob followed Kozien outside, and pretty soon there were fifteen to twenty seniors surrounding the congressman's car, while television crews stood nearby. Rostenkowski, meanwhile, fought through the crowd and got in the car.

"Coward!" "Shame!" "Impeach Rottenkowski!" The seniors stood in front of the car and waved placards. The congressman's driver honked the horn and moved the car a few inches. The front bumper brushed against Kozien's thigh, and she staggered a bit. Some man shouted, "You knocked her down! You hurt her!" This same man then turned to Kozien and said quietly, "Lay down under the car."

"Are you crazy? No way, he'd run me over!" retorted Kozien, who was barely over five feet tall. The car moved again, and this time Kozien fell on the hood of the car. Her face was inches from Rostenkowski's, with glass separating them.

She was still carrying her placard, and from inside the car, Rostenkowski saw her placard, her face, and her body sprawled across the windshield.

"Killer! Killer!" the crowd shouted.

Rostenkowski then got out of the car and ran through a parking lot while angry seniors chased after him. The driver maneuvered through the crowd, drove around the block, and caught up with Rostenkowski down the street from the center. Rostenkowski jumped in, and the car sped off.

"It was a funny picture," recalled one local politician present, "because it was a true chase. The seniors would move faster, and Rosty would move faster. He gets in the car, and they stand in front of the car."

The scene made for dramatic television. The Chicago film crews, delighted with the footage, distributed it immediately to the national networks. All three major television news shows carried the story prominently that evening, earning the interest group leaders what they call "a hat trick," in reference to a hockey player scoring three goals in one game.

Kozien, meanwhile, the activist and agitator for that day, was an unlikely hero. She had never before been active in politics. She knew little about the seniors groups at the Copernicus Center. Her relatives called that evening, expressing amazement at their "crazy Aunt Leona." Over the next several years politicians, prior to speaking at senior citizen events, would ask her to accompany them onstage. She always refused.

She likewise downplayed her heroism. "We just wanted answers. Had he answered our questions, there would have been no incident." Yet the incident was a bonanza for the leaders of the interest groups. The image of Kozien on the hood of Rostenkowski's car was used for years afterward on network news to symbolize the potency of the senior citizen lobby.

The catastrophic insurance program, which had passed the House in June 1988 by a vote of 328 to 72, was soon after repealed. The vote was not even close. The House voted 360 to 66 in favor of repeal in October 1989. Incidentally, Rostenkowski stood firm, voting to oppose repeal.

Many members of Congress had heard from people like Kozien, though presumably not from atop the hoods of their cars. Two Florida legislators reported getting more than seventy-five thousand pieces of mail, each opposing the policy. One staffer reported to me that his boss received more than two thousand mail pieces in favor of repeal, and eight mail pieces against repeal. The turn of events on catastrophic health insurance had people shaking their heads.

To some, the outside lobbying gave a large voice to a small number of people. "It was a case of the House of Representatives being stampeded by a small, vocal group of seniors," said Pete Stark, a Democratic congressman from California. "Ambushed is how a lot of people here feel now," Tim Penny, a Democrat from Minnesota, said at the time. "Every member of Congress was getting accosted at town meetings," said Senator John McCain, Republican from Arizona.

Others were more positive about the outcome, preferring to think that the outside lobbying tapped into a widespread sentiment. "We made a mistake last year [in 1988]," said Brian Donnelly, a Democratic congressman from Massachusetts. "This time, we listened to the voters."

Significance of the Story

The story of the Rostenkowski incident in north Chicago, while hardly typical of stories of outside lobbying, is useful for several reasons. For one, it shows in dramatic fashion how interest groups can instigate or facilitate collective action through outside lobbying. Contrary to what interest group leaders were claiming afterward, the mobbing of Rostenkowski was not all that spontaneous. The meeting between Rostenkowski and the interest group leaders was set up by the interest group leaders, and seniors from around the neighborhood were encouraged to attend by the interest group leaders. The interest groups leaders, not Rostenkowski's staff, had invited the networks to the meetings at the Copernicus Center. Rostenkowski's staff wanted to avoid media attention. And the interest group leaders made the placards and distributed them to Kozien and other seniors.

Interest group leaders also knew that the seniors attending were unusually angry about the new policy, and the leaders wanted to communicate that anger forcefully and make it seem less than fully staged. The seniors at the Copernicus Center were to represent the tip of the iceberg of constituent opinion. As for the seniors, their reactions could not have been better for the group leaders. The leaders provided a small, low-cost spark and let it turn into a conflagration. The behavior of Kozien and others was spontaneous and chaotic enough to indicate that the seniors were just plain mad. After all the preparations, events got out of control at the right time and at the right level. "Just barely out of control" might be the optimum level of behavioral response interest group leaders want from constituents in an outside lobbying campaign.

Therefore, what was communicated loudly and clearly to policymakers was the ease with which interest group leaders mobilized Kozien and her fellow seniors. The low costs involved for the interest groups to get hundreds of seniors to stampede the car of a powerful committee chairman counted for much more than the stampede itself. In trying to signal the "true" level of public salience over an issue, an interest group that succeeds with little effort can gain credibility. I shall discuss this important point in more detail in the next chapter.

Most of the conflict expansion on the issue had occurred well before that fateful day. National seniors organizations like the Gray Panthers and the National Committee to Preserve Social Security and Medicare had been running advertisements for months, and they had successfully framed the issue as one of unfair taxation for all seniors as opposed to one of health care benefits for a vast majority of seniors. By one reasonable interpretation, through the summer of 1989 interest groups had increased the level of salience among seniors on the issue. Then, as the salience of the issue peaked in late summer, interest group leaders had only to signal to policymakers the salience of the issue among those seniors who opposed the new policy. The Rostenkowski incident was timed perfectly. The conflict had been expanded, and the time had come to let policymakers know about it.

The story also neatly illustrates the roles assumed by the main players described in the previous chapter. Interest group leaders, the ones who had invited people like Kozien in the first place, set the stage for the famous confrontation (though they got lucky when it succeeded beyond their expectations). A policymaker, in this case a powerful House committee chairman, found himself the target of outside lobbying efforts by interest group leaders and constituents. And the ordinary constituents like Kozien, who behaved in both an organized and disorganized manner, made the lives of policymakers more difficult through simple expressions of anger.

The story is useful as well for highlighting the potential influence of outside lobbying. The renegade senior citizens groups, those distinguishing themselves early on from the AARP on the catastrophic health care policy, appear to have had an effect on Rostenkowski's colleagues in the House. As Table [1] indicates, 240 members of the House switched their votes from supporting catastrophic coverage in June 1988 to supporting repeal of catastrophic coverage sixteen months later. This is a remarkable instance of collective reconsideration. Only 124 members, or approximately half of the number that switched votes, voted the "same" way for both bills—that is, 124 either voted against the original bill and for repeal, or they voted for the original bill and against repeal. The latter vote, on the amendment to repeal the Catastrophic Coverage Act, was the first time Congress had ever voted to repeal a major social benefit it had created.

"An event of about 150 elderly people changed the tide of the thing," recalled Jan Schakowsky, at the time a leader of the Illinois State Council of Senior

TABLE [1]   Reconsidering Catastrophic Health Insurance: Number of Members of the House of Representatives Voting For or Against Original Bill and Repeal

	Original Bill	
Repeal	*Yea*	*Nay*
Yea	240	64
Nay	60	1

NOTE: This takes into account turnover from the 100th to 101st Congress, in that only members who voted on both bills are included. One member, Larry Hopkins, a Republican from Kentucky, voted against the original proposal and against repeal. The original bill was HR 2470, Catastrophic Health Insurance/Rule. The repeal was HR 3299, Amendment to Budget Reconciliation, Repealing Catastrophic Health Insurance Surtax.

Citizens, one of the groups that mobilized seniors on that day. "It was a pivotal event." It was pivotal not because it changed Rostenkowski's mind (which it did not), but because it had such an influence on his colleagues. As the story and its aftermath remind us, a well-publicized event among a small number of people can send very strong signals about, and enhance the reputation of, a group numbering many thousands or even millions of people. More than five years later, members of Congress referred to the Rostenkowski incident as cementing the reputation of the senior citizens lobby. This, according to people in Washington who are inclined to slight hyperbole, is one group in the population they do not want to cross.

Another revealing aspect of the story is that the Rostenkowski event happened because of a grave miscalculation on the part of the chairman and his colleagues. They enacted the original policy because they were led to believe that seniors were behind it, but they gambled and lost when interest groups tapped into a undiscovered level of antipathy among certain groups of seniors.[1] In general, legislators try to estimate the policy preferences and issue salience among their constituents, yet these estimates are shots in the dark on many controversial issues. They never know how some groups will respond, or which issues their next electoral opponent will use against them. They need to do the near impossible: anticipate how latent constituent opinion will manifest itself in the coming years. Rostenkowski was probably warned when he led his committee to recommend the original policy. Like anyone facing a difficult decision, however, he listened to the people who had previously established a credible reputation for electoral power, the AARP. Yet until Kozien and her fellow seniors let him know loudly and clearly their preferences, he could not have been certain about the consequences of his previous actions. The response among seniors led Rostenkowski and other policymakers to move toward repeal.

The Rostenkowski story is unusual, of course. Rarely are outside lobbying efforts as successful. Famous examples, such as this one, become lore around the Capitol. Another example from the early 1980s still generates discussion around Washington. During the successful outside lobbying efforts in 1982 by the American Bankers Association to repeal tax withholding from interest-bearing accounts, 22 million postcards from depositors flooded into Congress within days of the passage of the tax bill containing the provision. Every congressional district responded, according to the staff of Robert Dole, the chair of the Senate Finance Committee at the time. The marvel is that bankers, of all people, were able to make an issue more salient through conflict expansion, and at the same time were able to signal that salience to policymakers with a successful outside lobbying campaign. They did all of this without hiding their identities as bankers, indicating that latent salience among constituents is a great resource for all groups, not just for those with popular images or credibility as electoral powerhouses.

NOTE

1. In truth, even the AARP was caught off guard. Dissident elderly groups, those opposed to the policy all along, began stirring opposition until the AARP changed its policy on the issue. Then, once the AARP was opposed to the policy, it galvanized further action by the dissident elderly groups.

BIBLIOGRAPHY

Key, V. O. 1961. *Public Opinion and American Democracy*. New York: Alfred Knopf.
Kingdon, John. 1984. *Agendas, Alternatives, and Public Policies*. Boston: Little, Brown.
Schattschneider, E. E. 1960. *The Semi-Sovereign People*. Hinsdale, IL: Dryden Press.

11.3

LARRY M. BARTELS

From *Unequal Democracy: The Political Economy of the New Gilded Age*

Different income groups (rich, middle class, poor) pressure the government through organizations that represent their respective interests. Bartels argues that the policies of the national government resulting from this pressure have had a major impact on income inequality in the United States. Income inequality has increased over the last three and half decades, with most of the increases occurring during Republican presidential administrations. Bartels argues that this reflects the success of organizations pressuring the government in favor of the rich, the different economic philosophies of the two major parties, and the different political interests of partisan voters.

THE PARTISAN POLITICAL ECONOMY

> . . . as our economy grows, market forces work to provide the greatest rewards to those with the needed skills in the growth areas. . . . This trend . . . is simply an economic reality, and it is neither fair nor useful to blame any political party.
>
> —Treasury Secretary Henry Paulson, 2006[1]

The tendency to think of economic outcomes as natural and inevitable is politically significant because it discourages systematic critical scrutiny of their causes and consequences. If escalating inequality is "simply an economic reality," it seems pointless to spend too much energy worrying about how and why it arises. Moreover, if "there has always been extreme income inequality" under Republicans and Democrats alike, it seems pointless to hope that public policies might mitigate that inequality. As prominent policy analyst Lawrence Mead rather breezily put it, in a response to the report of the American Political Science Association's Task Force on Inequality and American Democracy, . . . "The causes [of growing economic inequality] are not well understood and have little tie to government."[2]

My aim . . . is to refute the notion that the causes of economic inequality in contemporary America "have little tie to government." Indeed, I suggest that

From Larry M. Bartels, *Unequal Democracy: The Political Economy of the New Gilded Age* (Princeton, NJ: Princeton University Press, 2008).

the narrowly economic focus of most previous studies of inequality has caused them to miss what may be the most important single influence on the changing U.S. income distribution over the past half-century—the contrasting policy choices of Democratic and Republican presidents. Under Republican administrations, real income growth for the lower- and middle-income classes has consistently lagged well behind the income growth rate for the rich—and well behind the income growth rate for the lower and middle classes themselves under Democratic administrations.

. . . [T]he dramatic differences in patterns of income growth under Democratic and Republican presidents are quite unlikely to have occurred by chance; nor can they be attributed to oil price shocks or changes in the structure of the labor force or other purely economic factors, or to cyclical corrections by each party of the other party's policy excesses. Rather, they reflect consistent differences in policies and priorities between Democratic and Republican administrations. In the first half of the post-war era, these differences were expressed primarily in macroeconomic policies and performance, with Democrats presiding over significantly less unemployment and significantly more overall economic growth than Republicans. Since the 1970s some of these macroeconomic differences have been muted, but significant partisan differences in tax and transfer policies have continued to produce significant partisan disparities in patterns of post-tax income growth, with the middle class and, especially, the working poor experiencing significantly more income growth under Democratic presidents than under Republican presidents.

The cumulative effect of these partisan differences has been enormous. My projections based on the historical performance of Democratic and Republican presidents suggest that income inequality would actually have *declined* slightly over the past 50 years . . . had the patterns of income growth characteristic of Democratic administrations been in effect throughout that period. Conversely, continuous application of the patterns of income growth observed during periods of Republican control would have produced a much greater divergence in the economic fortunes of rich and poor people than we have actually experienced.

▪ ▪ ▪

The average rate of real income growth during 1948–2005 was higher for affluent families than for those lower in the income distribution. . . . What may be surprising is that this pattern of differential growth is entirely limited to periods in which Republicans controlled the White House.

. . . Figure [1] provides a graphical representation of . . . the starkly different patterns of income growth under Democratic and Republican administrations. . . . Under Democratic presidents, poor families did slightly better than richer families (at least in proportional terms), producing a modest net decrease in income inequality; under Republican presidents, rich families

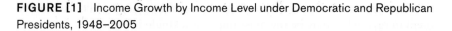

FIGURE [1] Income Growth by Income Level under Democratic and Republican Presidents, 1948–2005

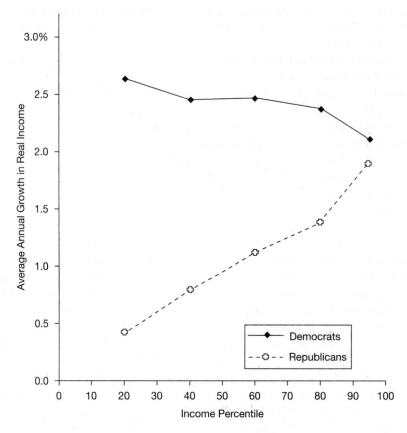

did vastly better than poorer families, producing a considerable net increase in income inequality. In both cases, the patterns are essentially linear over the entire range of family incomes represented in the figure (that is, for incomes ranging from about $25,000 to $200,000 in 2005).

▪ ▪ ▪

A Partisan Coincidence?

The partisan differences in characteristic rates of income growth documented in Figure [1] would seem to be of immense economic and political significance— if they are real. They suggest that middle-class and poor families in the postwar era have routinely fared much worse under Republican presidents than they have under Democratic presidents. By this accounting, economic inequality in contemporary America is profoundly shaped by partisan politics.

But to what extent are these patterns really attributable to partisan politics rather than to accidental historical factors? One way to address this question

FIGURE [2] Income Inequality under Democratic and Republican Presidents, 1947–2005

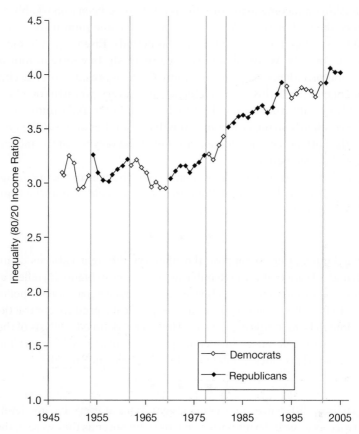

is to examine their consistency across a range of presidents and circumstances. To that end, Figure [2] shows the level of income inequality in each year of the post-war period as reflected in one standard measure of inequality, the ratio of incomes at the 80th percentile of the income distribution to those at the 20th percentile.

By this measure, income inequality was essentially constant from the late 1940s through the late 1960s, with families at the 80th percentile of the income distribution earning about three times as much as families at the 20th percentile. Inequality increased fairly steadily through the 1970s and 1980s before leveling off once again in the 1990s. These broad temporal trends reinforce the impression that growing inequality is significantly related to long-term technological and social changes.

Despite these long-term forces, distinguishing between Democratic and Republican administrations (the white [diamonds] and black diamonds in the figure, respectively) reveals the regularity with which Democratic presidents reduced and Republican presidents increased the prevailing level of economic inequality, regardless of the long-term trend. Indeed, the effect of presidential partisanship on income inequality turns out to have been remarkably consistent since the end of World War II. The 80/20 income ratio increased under each of the six Republican presidents in this period—Eisenhower, Nixon, Ford, Reagan, George H. W. Bush, and George W. Bush. In contrast, four of five Democratic presidents—all except Jimmy Carter—presided over declines in income inequality. If this is a coincidence, it is a very powerful one.[3] Even in the highly inegalitarian economic climate of the 1990s, Bill Clinton managed to produce slightly stronger income growth for families at the 20th percentile than at the 80th percentile, though families at the very top of the income distribution did even better.

The strikingly consistent partisan pattern of changes in income inequality in Figure [2] seems hard to attribute to a mere coincidence in the timing of Democratic and Republican administrations.

▪   ▪   ▪

It may be tempting to suppose that the very different patterns of income growth under Democratic and Republican presidents in Figure [1] reflect a cycle of partisan equilibration in which Democrats pursue expansionary policies in reaction to Republican contractions and Republicans produce contractions as an antidote to Democratic expansions. However, a detailed analysis of the timing of partisan differences in income growth provides no support for that notion. Table [1] provides tabulations of average income growth.

▪   ▪   ▪

[T]he partisan differences in average growth rates at every income level were about twice as large in terms with no partisan turnover as they were in the first terms of new partisan regimes. Democratic presidents generally presided over similar income growth rates for families in every part of the income distribution, regardless of whether they were in their first or second terms; but average income growth was consistently higher (by a little more than half a percentage point) when Democrats succeeded Democrats than when Democrats succeeded Republicans. Conversely, most families (except the most affluent) did better under first-term Republican presidents than in subsequent Republican administrations; these differences, too, were on the order of half a percentage point.

▪   ▪   ▪

[T]he partisan pattern of post-tax income growth in Figure [3] is strikingly similar to the partisan pattern of pre-tax family income growth in Figure [1]. Households at every income level did about equally well under Carter and Clinton, with average growth rates ranging from 1.4% to 1.6%. On the other hand, Republican presidents presided over weaker income growth for

TABLE [1] The Impact of Partisan Turnover on Partisan Differences in Real Income Growth Rates, 1948–2005

Average annual real pre-tax income growth (%) for families at various points in the income distribution (with standard errors in parentheses). Partisan control measured from one year following inauguration to one year following subsequent inauguration. "Partisan turnover" refers to first-term Democrats who succeeded Republicans or first-term Republicans who succeeded Democrats.

	All Presidents	*Democratic Presidents*	*Republican Presidents*	*Partisan Difference*
Partisan turnover				
20th percentile	1.38 (.75)	2.28 (1.00)	.71 (1.08)	1.57 (1.52)
40th percentile	1.52 (.54)	2.07 (.75)	1.11 (.76)	.96 (1.09)
60th percentile	1.60 (.47)	2.00 (.63)	1.30 (.67)	.71 (.95)
80th percentile	1.80 (.45)	2.19 (.62)	1.51 (.63)	.68 (.91)
95th percentile	1.89 (.45)	1.93 (.69)	1.86 (.61)	.07 (.92)
N	28	12	16	28
No partisan turnover				
20th percentile	1.46 (.68)	2.95 (1.19)	.16 (.61)	2.80 (1.29)
40th percentile	1.56 (.56)	2.80 (.88)	.48 (.63)	2.31 (1.06)
60th percentile	1.86 (.51)	2.86 (.82)	.97 (.57)	1.89 (.98)
80th percentile	1.87 (.48)	2.55 (.78)	1.27 (.57)	1.28 (.95)
95th percentile	2.10 (.62)	2.28 (1.07)	1.95 (.70)	.34 (1.25)
N	30	14	16	30

SOURCE: Calculations based on data from Census Bureau Historical Income Tables.

households in the top half of the income distribution and little or no income growth for households in the bottom half of the income distribution. As with the partisan differences in pre-tax growth presented in Figure [1], these partisan differences in post-tax growth are concentrated in the second year of each administration, when the policy initiatives adopted in the "honeymoon" period immediately following Inauguration Day are most likely to take effect.[4]

▪ ▪ ▪

Democrats, Republicans, and the Rise of Inequality

Economists associate the escalation of inequality over the past 30 years with important structural changes in the American economy, including demographic shifts, globalization, and technological change. I see no reason to doubt that these factors have played an important role in increasing the income gap between rich and poor people in the contemporary United States; but if this is "simply an economic reality," as Treasury Secretary Paulson asserted,

FIGURE [3] Post-Tax Income Growth under Democratic and Republican Presidents, 1980–2003

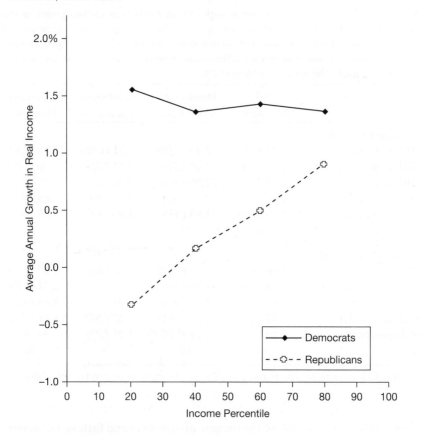

it does not follow that nothing can be done to mitigate the economic and social consequences of that reality. Nor does the fact that "there has always been extreme income inequality," as Ben Stein observed, imply that presidents and their policy choices can have no significant effect on the extent of inequality at any given time.

The cumulative impact of these partisan policy choices is illustrated in Figure [4]. The dotted line in the center of the figure represents the actual course of inequality over the past half-century, as measured by the ratio of family incomes at the 80th and 20th percentiles of the income distribution. (This portion of the figure is simply repeated from Figure [2].) The solid upper line represents the projected course of the 80/20 income ratio over the same period given the pattern of income growth that prevailed under Republican presidents during this period, while the lower line represents the projected course of the 80/20 income ratio under Democratic presidents. . . .

The projections in Figure [4] imply that continuous Democratic control would have produced an essentially constant level of economic inequality over the past

FIGURE [4] Projected Income Inequality under Republican and Democratic Presidents, 1947–2005

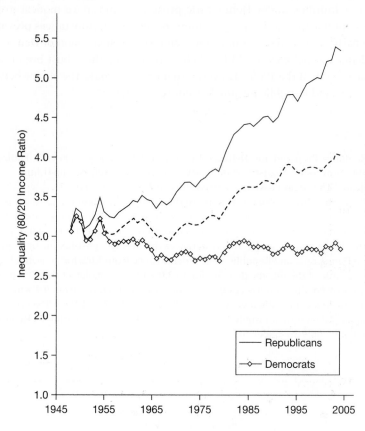

three decades, despite all the technological, demographic, and global competitive forces emphasized in economists' accounts of escalating inequality. In contrast, continuous Republican control would have produced a much sharper polarization between rich and poor than has actually occurred over the past 30 years, with the 80/20 income ratio reaching a level about one-third higher than it actually did.[5]

The projections presented in Figure [4] are based on an arguably unrealistic assumption: that if either party had uninterrupted control of the White House, it would do all the time what it in fact does only half the time. It is impossible to know whether either party would actually have the political will or the political power to produce economic redistribution of the cumulative magnitude suggested by these projections. Nevertheless, the cumulative differences portrayed in Figure [4] convey the fundamental significance of partisan politics in ameliorating or exacerbating economic inequality over the past half-century.

In the first 25 years of the post-war era, the partisan differences in income growth patterns documented [here] implied robust growth for middle-class and poor families under Democratic presidents and more modest growth under Republicans. In the less propitious economic circumstances prevailing in the early twenty-first century, not even a steady succession of Democratic presidents and policies would be likely to reproduce the robust broad-based income growth of the 1960s. However, that does not make the choice between Democrats and Republicans any less consequential.

NOTES

1. Remarks Prepared for Delivery by Treasury Secretary Henry H. Paulson at Columbia University, August 1, 2006, www.treas.gov/press/releases/hp41.htm.

2. Mead, "The Great Passivity," *Perspectives on Politics* 2 (2004): 671.

3. The probability of observing no more than one exception to the partisan pattern of increasing inequality under Republicans and decreasing inequality under Democrats in a random sequence of 11 increases and decreases would be $12 \div 2{,}048 = .006$.

4. In "honeymoon" years, the differences in average post-tax income growth between Democratic and Republican presidents range from 5.0% for households at the 20th percentile of the income distribution to 3.0% for households at the 80th percentile. The corresponding differences in nonhoneymoon years range from 0.9% to -0.3%.

5. The 80/20 income ratio increased by 27% between 1975 and 2005. The projections in Figure [4] suggest that it would have increased by 45% under continuous Republican control but by only 3% under continuous Democratic control.

12

POLITICAL PARTIES

12.1

JOHN H. ALDRICH

From *Why Parties? A Second Look*

Political parties are multifaceted organizations, and scholars have struggled to describe them and their functions in ways that make sense across eras and countries. In this important piece, Aldrich writes that, above all, parties are designed to serve the needs of ambitious politicians seeking public office. Parties have to be understood as solutions to a variety of collective dilemmas. They help government officials coordinate their actions so they can make public policy, candidates coordinate their behavior to win office, and voters overcome their collective action problems during elections.

POLITICS AND PARTIES IN AMERICA

■ ■ ■

The Political Party

■ ■ ■

My basic argument is that the major political party is the creature of the politicians, the partisan activist, and the ambitious office seeker and office-holder. They have created and maintained, used or abused, reformed or ignored the political party when doing so has furthered their goals and ambitions. The political party is thus . . . an institution shaped by these political actors.

From John H. Aldrich, *Why Parties? A Second Look* (Chicago: University of Chicago Press, 2011), Chapter 1.

Whatever its strength or weakness, whatever its form and role, it is the ambitious politicians' creation.

These politicians, we must understand from the outset, do not have partisan goals per se. Rather, they have more personal and fundamental goals, and the party is only the instrument for achieving them. Their goals are several and come in various combinations. Following Richard Fenno (1973), they include most basically the desire to have a long and successful career in political office, but they also encompass the desire to achieve policy ends and to attain power and prestige within the government. These goals are to be sought in government, not in parties, but they are goals that at times have best been realized *through* the parties. The parties are, as we will see, shaped by these goals in their various combinations, and particularly in the problems politicians most typically encounter when seeking to achieve their goals. Thus, there are three goals, three problems, and three reasons why politicians often turn to the organized party in search for a sustainable way to solve these problems and thus be more likely to achieve these goals.

Ambitious politicians turn to the political party to achieve such goals only when parties are useful vehicles for solving problems that cannot be solved as effectively, if at all, through other means. Thus I believe that the political party must be understood not only in relation to the goals of the actors most consequential for parties, but also in relation to the electoral, legislative, and executive institutions of the government. Fiorina was correct: only given our institutions can we understand political parties.

The third major force shaping the political party is the historical setting. Technological changes, for instance, have made campaigning for office today vastly different than it was only a few decades ago, let alone in the nineteenth century. Such changes have had great consequences for political parties. In the nineteenth century, political parties were the only feasible means for organizing mass elections. Today's technologies allow an individual member of Congress to create a personal, continuing campaign organization, something that was simply unimaginable a century ago. But there is, of course, more to the historical context than technology.

Normative understandings have changed greatly. Even Ronald Reagan, who claimed that "government is not the solution to our problems, government *is* the problem," also held to the value of a "social safety net" provided by the government that is far larger than even the most progressive politician of the nineteenth century could have imagined. Ideas, in short, matter a great deal. Founders had to overcome antipathy verging on disgust over the very idea of political parties in order to create them in the first place, and Martin Van Buren's ideas about the nature and value of the "modern mass party" greatly shaped the nature of Jacksonian Democracy and political parties generally for more than a century. Neither Van Buren nor anyone else set out to create a system of competing mass parties (although he and others of that era recognized the importance of sustained partisan competition, they merely—but always—wanted to win that competition). But the creation of the modern mass party led quickly to the creation of the first modern mass two-party system.

History matters in yet another way, beyond the ideas, values, and technological possibilities available at any given historical moment. The path of development matters as well. Once a set of institutional arrangements is in place, the set of equilibrium possibilities is greatly reduced, and change from the existing equilibrium path to a new and possibly superior one may be difficult or impossible. In other words, once there are two major parties, their presence induces incentives for ambitious politicians to affiliate with one party or the other, and some of these incentives emerge only because of the prior existence of these two parties.

The combination of these three forces means that the fundamental syllogism for the theory of political parties to be offered here is just what Rohde and Shepsle (1978) originally offered as the basis for the rational-choice-based new institutionalism: political outcomes—here political parties—result from actors' seeking to realize their goals, choosing within and possibly shaping a given set of institutional arrangements, and so choosing within a given historical context.

■   ■   ■

Previous Approaches to the Study of American Political Parties

Parties as Diverse Coalitions, Aggregating and Articulating
the Interest in and of the Public

There are three basic views or understandings of major political parties in America. The first is most often associated with V. O. Key Jr. (e.g., 1964), Frank Sorauf (1964; now Hershey 2009), Samuel Eldersveld (1964, 1982), and others. The major American party, to them, is a broad and encompassing organization, a coalition of many and diverse partners, that is commonly called umbrella-like. In seeking to appeal to a majority of the public, the two parties are based on similar values, roughly defining the "American creed." McClosky (1969) said of political (which is to say partisan) elites, "The evidence suggests that it is the [political elites] rather than the public who serve as the major repositories of the public conscience and as the carriers of the Creed. Responsibility for keeping the system going, hence, falls most heavily upon them" (286). His basic finding was that such elites share most elements of this "creed."

On many policy issues, however, there are clear and sometimes sharply drawn lines between the two parties. What Benjamin I. Page (1978) referred to as "partisan cleavages" are possible, even likely. On civil rights, as on many other issues, the Democratic Party has been more liberal than the Republican Party for decades, and on New Deal economic issues even a generation longer.

■   ■   ■

Each party is a coalition of many and diverse groups. This is most evident in the New Deal coalition Roosevelt forged in creating a working Democratic majority in the 1930s. It consisted of the then-solid South, cities, immigrants, blacks, ethnic and religious groups of many types, the working class and unions, and so on. Over half a century later this "coalition of minorities" has frayed considerably; some parts of it have exited from the coalition entirely, and the remnants are no longer capable of reaching majority size in presidential elections. Although some elements have left entirely or their loyalties have weakened, they have been replaced by others. For example, the Democratic coalition may no longer be home to as much of the South or as many blue-collar voters, but teachers' unions, women's groups, and organizations representing blacks, Hispanics, gays, environmentalists, and many others have been added since the 1960s to the panoply of voices seeking to be heard at their national convention. The Republican Party may once have been defined more easily by what wasn't included in the New Deal coalition, but it too has attracted a range of groups and interests. At Republican conventions one can find both Wall Street and Main Street fiscal conservatives, and westerners who seek to remove government interference in their lives (and lands), but also southerners who are social conservatives, the latter including pro-life groups, fundamentalist Christians, and so on, who seek active government intervention in behalf of their central concerns.

Although there are good reasons why these groups are allied with their particular parties, there is still great diversity within each party. There are even apparent contradictions latent—and at critical moments active—within each party. Blacks and white southerners may have found alliance comfortable when both were so deeply affected by the Great Depression, but when civil rights made it onto the national agenda in the 1950s and 1960s, the latent tensions in their respective views became active and divisive. Recent Republican conventions may have been noncontroversial, but fundamentalists and Wall Street business leaders, or other pairings, may well find that latent disagreements will become just as divisive when circumstances and the political agenda change. As of this writing, "tea party" and other conservative activists are engaging the Republican "regulars" on many such fronts.

In this view James Madison was correct. There is no small set of fixed interests; there are, rather, many and diverse interests in this extended Republic. He argued that a fundamental advantage of the new Constitution in creating a stronger federation was that the most evident and serious concern about majority rule—that a cohesive majority could tyrannize any minority—would be alleviated because there could be no cohesive majority in an extended republic. So too could no political party, no matter how large, rule tyrannically, because it must also be too diverse.

In a truly diverse republic, the problem is the opposite of majority tyranny. The problem is how to form *any* majority capable of taking action to solve pressing problems. A major political party aggregates these many and varied interests sufficiently to appeal to enough voters to form a majority in elections and to forge partisan-based, majority coalitions in government. In this view, parties are intermediaries that connect the public and the government. Parties also aggregate these diverse interests into a relatively cohesive, if typically compromise, platform, and they articulate these varied interests by representing them in government. The result, in this view, is that parties parlay those compromise positions into policy outcomes, and so they—a ruling, if nonhomogeneous and shifting, government majority—can be held accountable to the public in subsequent elections.

▪   ▪   ▪

The Responsible Party Thesis

. . . [T]he second view, that of responsible parties, is primarily normative and aspirational, with critique of the empirics of party politics thrown in. This thesis is most directly associated with E. E. Schattschneider (1942) and the Committee for a More Responsible Two-Party System, sponsored by the American Political Science Association, that he chaired (1950). But this view has deeper historical roots. Woodrow Wilson's *Congressional Government* (1881), for example, included a plea for parties more in the responsible party mold, and as Ranney (1975) and Epstein (1986) report, prominent political scientists at the beginning of the twentieth century were much enamored of this doctrine.

Ranney (1975, 43) lists four criteria that define responsible parties. Such parties (1) make policy commitments to the electorate, (2) are willing and able to carry them out when in office, (3) develop alternatives to government policies when out of office, and (4) differ sufficiently between themselves to "provide the electorate with a proper range of choice between alternative actions."[1] This doctrine derives from an idealized (and more closely realized) form of the British system, what Lijphart (1984, 1999) calls the "Westminster model." As a normative standard, it has several obvious defects. For example, it reduces choices for the public to exactly two. If the United States is a diverse and extended Madisonian republic, it is not obvious that the public would find its views adequately articulated by exactly two options, no matter how clear and distinct. A mélange of compromise proposals may be more suitable. Alternation of parties in office may also make policy trajectories shift dramatically back and forth. And if one party does capture a longtime working majority, majority tyranny could follow. This is a normative standard that thus places great weight on the accountability of elected officials, through their party's control of office, and less weight on interest articulation. In more practical terms, it is an idealization that fits more readily with a unified, essentially unicameral assembly that combines the legislative and executive branches and that is elected all at once. It fits more poorly with a government designed around the principles of separated but intermingled powers, with officials elected at different times from differently defined constituencies for the Madisonian purpose of making ambition check ambition.

. . . When the parties' candidates did address issues, it is often felt, they were too similar. Conservative Republicans in the 1940s and 1950s complained that the dominant, moderate wing of their party engaged in "me-too-ism"; whatever Democrats said, the moderate Republicans responded "me too!" Or as George Wallace, the once and future Democrat, claimed in his third-party presidential campaign in 1968, "there ain't a dime's worth of difference" between the two parties. It was not always so, responsible party advocates claimed. In other eras parties were stronger, and they were stronger in the sense of responsible parties. At the very least they were sufficiently united in office to "be willing and able to carry out" whatever policy commitments the majority party chose. They may not have been then, and today may not truly be, responsible parties, consistent with that doctrine, but they once were stronger, more effective, and more easily held accountable. Perhaps they could become so again.

■　　■　　■

Parties and Electoral Competition

The third view of parties focuses on the importance of this competition for office. Of course both earlier views also saw electoral competition as a central characteristic of partisan politics. But this third view sees competition for office as the singular, defining characteristic of the major American political party. The most rigorous advocates of this position are Anthony Downs (1957) and Joseph A. Schlesinger (1991; see also Demsetz 1990). Both are rational choice theorists, positing that actors are goal seekers and that their actions, and eventually the institutional arrangements they help shape, are the product of their attempts to realize their goals. At the center of their theory are the partisan elites: the aspiring office seekers and the successful officeholders. Their theories rest, moreover, on a simple assumption about the goal of each such partisan elite, office seeking and holding per se. That is, party leaders are motivated to win elections. As a result a party is, in the words of Downs (1957, 25), "a team seeking to control the governing apparatus by gaining office in a duly constituted election." The political party therefore is the organization that team uses to realize its goals. Electoral victory is paramount; other motives are at most secondary. Most important, as Downs puts it, parties formulate policies to win elections rather than winning elections to promulgate policies. In a two-party system, the "health" of the system is measured by how competitive the two parties are for a wide range of elective offices over a long period. In Schlesinger's view (1991), the hallmark of a party is its ability to channel the competing career ambitions of its potential and actual officeholders, forming them into an effective electoral machine. More accurately, he argued that each office and its partisan seeker serves as one "nucleus" of a party, and a strong party is one that has many strong nuclei connected to each other for the purpose of supporting its ambitious partisan office seekers.

The genius of democracy, in this view, is rather like the genius Adam Smith found in the free market. In Smith's case individuals acting in their own self-

interest turn out to be guided, as if by some unseen hand, to act in the economic interests of the collective. In Schlesinger's case ambitious politicians,
seeking to have a long and successful career, are all led by the necessity of
winning broad support in the face of stiff competition to reflect the desires of
those citizens who support them. Without competition for office—without at
least minimally strong political parties—career ambition is not necessarily
harnessed to reflect the desires of the public. In elections, political parties
serve the Madisonian principle of having ambition clash with, and thereby
check, ambition. Seeking popular support in the face of competition yields
officeholders who find it in their self-interest to respond to the wishes of the
public so that that public will continually reelect them, thereby satisfying
their career ambition. All else about parties flows from this Schumpeterian
view. Office seekers will try to create a strong electoral machine for mobilizing the electorate, but only if competition forces them to do so. Thus will the
party-as-organization flow from competition for office. So too will the party-
in-government flow naturally from electoral competition—but only so long as
it is in the long-term career interests of office seekers and holders to do so. Only
so long, that is, as there is a shared, collective interest in working together in
office, and doing so to remain in office. And that collective interest must come
from a common electoral fate.

These, then, are the three major views or understandings of political parties.
I will offer a fourth. . . . [I]t will be one that takes career ambitions of elective
office seekers and holders as one of its central building blocks. It will differ,
however, in seeing office seeking as only one of several goals held by those
with political ambitions. To be sure, winning elections is an intermediary
end on its way to achieving power and policy in addition to being an end in
itself. Motivations for policy ends and for power and prestige in office, that is,
require electoral victory. But for many, winning office per se is not the end of
politics but the beginning. As we will see, this leads naturally and inevitably
to drawing from the other views of parties, and it will be necessary to trace the
historical . . . path of development. . . .

A Theory of Political Parties

These and other astute observers might come to very different conclusions,
but they all agree that the political party is—or should be—central to the
American political system. Parties are—or should be—integral parts of all
political life, from structuring the reasoning and choice of the electorate,
through all facets of campaigns and seemingly all facets of the government,
to the very possibility of effective governance in a democracy.

▪   ▪   ▪

The "Fundamental Equation" of the New Institutionalism Applied to Parties

That parties are complex does not mean they are incomprehensible. Indeed
complexity is, if not an intentional outcome, at least an anticipated result of

those who shape the political parties. Moreover, they are so deeply woven into the fabric of American politics that they cannot be understood apart from either their own historical context and dynamics or those of the political system as a whole. Parties, that is, can be understood only in relation to the polity, to the government and its institutions, and to the historical context of the times.

The study of political parties is also necessarily a study of a major pair of political institutions. Indeed, the institutions that define the political party are unique, and as it happens they are unique in ways that make an institutional account especially useful. Their establishment and nature are fundamentally extralegal; they are nongovernmental political institutions. Instead of statute, their basis lies in the actions of ambitious politicians who created them and who maintain them. They are, in the parlance of the new institutionalism, *endogenous institutions*—in fact, the most highly endogenous political institutions of any substantial and sustained importance.

By endogenous I mean it was the actions of political actors that created political parties in the first place, and it is the actions of political actors that shape and alter them over time. And political actors have chosen to alter their parties dramatically at several times in our history, reformed them often, and tinkered with them constantly. Of all major political bodies in the United States, the political party is the most variable in its rules, regulations, and procedures—that is to say, in its formal organization—and in its informal methods and traditions. It is often the same actors who write the party's rules who then choose the party's outcomes, sometimes at nearly the same time and by the same method. Thus, for example, on one night, national party conventions debate, consider any proposed amendments, and then adopt their rules by a majority vote of credentialed delegates. The next night these same delegates debate, consider any proposed amendments, and then adopt their platform by majority vote, and they choose their presidential nominee by majority vote the following night.

Who, then, are these critical political actors? Many see the party-in-the-electorate as comprising major actors. To be sure, mobilizing the electorate to capture office is a central task of the political party. But America is a republican democracy. All power flows directly or indirectly from the great body of the people, to paraphrase Madison's definition. The public elects its political leaders, but it is that leadership that legislates, executes, and adjudicates policy. The parties are defined in relation to this republican democracy. Thus it is political leaders, those Schlesinger (1975) has called "office-seekers"—*those who seek and those who hold elective office*—who are the central actors in the party.

Ambitious office seekers and holders are thus the first and most important actors in the political party. A second set of important figures in party politics comprises those who hold, or have access to, critical resources that office seekers need to realize their ambitions. It is expensive to build and

maintain the party and campaign organizations necessary to compete effectively in the electoral arena. Thomas Ferguson, for example, has made an
extended argument for the "primary and constitutive role large investors
play in American politics" (1983, 3; see also Ferguson 1986, 1989, 1991). Much
of his research emphasizes this primary and constitutive role in party politics in particular, such as in partisan realignments. The study of the role of
money in congressional elections has also focused in part on concentrations
of such sources of funding, such as from political action committees (e.g.,
Sorauf 1988), which political parties have come to take advantage of (for
early accounts see Herrnson 1988; Kayden and Mayhe 1985). Elections are
also fought over the flow of information to the public. The electoral arm of
political parties in the eighteenth century was made up of "committees of
correspondence," which were primarily lines of communication among
political elites and between them and potential voters, and one of the first
signs of organizing of the Jeffersonian Republican Party was the hiring of a
newspaper editor. . . . The press was first a partisan press, and editors and
publishers from Thomas Ritchie . . . to Horace Greeley long were critical
players in party politics. Today those with specialized knowledge relevant
to communication, such as pollsters, media and advertising experts, and
computerized fund-raising specialists, enjoy influence in party, campaign,
and even government councils that greatly exceeds their mere technical
expertise. . . .

In more theoretical terms, this second set of party actors include those
Schlesinger (1975) has called "benefit seekers," those for whom realization of
their goals depends on the party's success in capturing office. Party activists
shade from those powerful figures with concentrations of, or access to, large
amounts of money and information, as described above, to the legions of volunteer campaign activists who ring doorbells and stuff envelopes and are,
individually and collectively, critical to the first level of the party—its office
seekers. All are critical because they command the resources, whether money,
expertise, and information, or merely time and labor, that office seekers need
to realize their ambitions. As a result, activists' motivations shape and constrain the behavior of office seekers, as their own roles are, in turn, shaped
and constrained by the office seekers. . . . [T]he changed incentives of party
activists have played a significant role in the fundamentally altered nature of
the contemporary party, but the impact of benefit seekers will be seen scattered throughout this account.

Voters, however, are neither office seekers nor benefit seekers and thus are
not a part of the political party at all, even if they identify strongly with a party
and consistently support its candidates. Voters are indeed critical, but they are
critical as the targets of party activities. Parties "produce" candidates, platforms, and policies. Voters "consume" by exchanging their votes for the party's
product (see Popkin et al. 1976). Some voters, of course, become partisan
benefit-seekers by becoming activists, whether as occasional volunteers, as

sustained contributors, or even as candidates. But until they do so, they may be faithful consumers, "brand name" loyalists as it were, but they are still only the targets of partisans' efforts to sell their wares in the political marketplace.

Why, then, do politicians create and recreate the party, exploit its features, or ignore its dictates? The simple answer is that it has been in their interests to do so. That is, this is a *rational choice* account of the party, an account that presumes that rational, elective office seekers and holders use the party to achieve their ends.

I do not assume that politicians are invariably self-interested in a narrow sense. This is not a theory in which elective office seekers simply maximize their chances of election or reelection, at least not for its own sake. They may well have fundamental values and principles, and they may have preferences over policies as means to those ends. They also care about office, both for its own sake and for the opportunities to achieve other ends that election and reelection make possible. . . . Just as winning elections is a means to other ends for politicians (whether career or policy ends), so too is the political party a means to these other ends.

Why, then, do politicians turn to create or reform, to use or abuse, partisan institutions? The answer is that parties are designed as attempts to solve problems that current institutional arrangements do not solve and that politicians have come to believe they cannot solve. These problems fall into three general and recurring categories.

The Problem of Ambition and Elective Office Seeking

Elective office seekers, as that label says, want to win election to office. Parties regulate access to those offices. If elective office is indeed valuable, there will be more aspirants than offices, and the political party and the two-party system are means of regulating that competition and channeling those ambitions. Major party nomination is all but a necessary condition for election in America, and partisan institutions have been developed—and have been reformed and re-reformed—for regulating competition. Intrainstitutional leadership positions are also highly valued and therefore potentially competitive. There is, for example, a fairly well-institutionalized path to the office of Speaker of the House trod by Speakers from Sam Rayburn to Nancy Pelosi. It is, however, a Democratic Party institution. Elective politicians, of course, ordinarily desire election more than once. They are typically careerists who want a long and productive career in politics. Schlesinger's ambition theory (1966), developed and extended by others (see especially Rohde 1979), is precisely about this general problem. Underlying this theory, though typically not fully developed, is a problem. The problem is that if office is desirable, there will be more aspirants than there are offices to go around. When stated in rigorous form, it can be proved that in fact there is no permanent solution to this problem. And it is a problem that can adversely affect the fortunes of a party. In 1912 the Republican vote was split between William Howard Taft and Theodore Roosevelt. This split enabled Woodrow Wilson to win with 42 percent of the popular vote. Not only was Wilson the only break in Republican hegemony of the White House in this period, but in that year Democrats increased their House majority by sixty-five additional seats and captured majority control of the Senate. Thus failure to regulate intraparty competition cost Republicans dearly.

For elective office seekers, regulating conflict over who holds those offices is clearly of major concern. It is ever present. And it is not just a problem of access to government offices but is also a problem internal to each party as soon as the party becomes an important gateway to office.

The Problem of Making Decisions for the Party and for the Polity

Once in office, partisans determine outcomes for the polity. They propose alternatives, shape the agenda, pass or reject legislation, determine how to implement what they enact, and oversee that implementation. The policy formation and execution process, that is, is highly partisan. The parties-in-government are more than mere coalitions of like-minded individuals, however; they are enduring institutions. Very few incumbents change their partisan affiliations. Most retain their partisanship throughout their careers, even though they often disagree (i.e., are not uniformly like-minded) with some of their partisan peers. When the rare incumbent does change parties, it is invariably to join the party more consonant with that switcher's policy interests. This implies that there are differences between the two parties at some fundamental and enduring level on policy positions, values, and beliefs. When incumbents do change parties, they almost invariably lament (often correctly) that they did not change their ideas or beliefs, but it was their party that changed and thus moved away from them. They were surprised by these important but occasional changes, reflecting the prevailing belief of partisan stability.

Thus, parties are institutions designed to promote the achievement of collective choices—choices on which the parties differ and choices reached by majority rule. As with access to office and ambition theory, there is a well-developed theory for this problem: social choice theory. Underlying this theory is the well-known problem that no method of choice can solve the elective officeholders' problem of combining the interests, concerns, or values of a polity that remains faithful to democratic values, as shown by the consequences flowing from Arrow's theorem (Arrow 1951). Thus, in a republican democracy politicians may turn to partisan institutions to solve the problem of collective choice. In the language of politics, parties may help achieve the goal of attaining policy majorities in the first place, as well as the often more difficult goal of maintaining such majorities. To the extent that this problem tends to reside most often in policy choices, it tends to be the problem that is confronted most often by legislative parties, although it certainly applies to electoral and organizational aspects of the parties, as well.

The Problem of Collective Action

The third problem is the most pervasive and thus the furthest-ranging in substantive content. The clearest example, however, is also the most important. To win office, candidates need more than a party's nomination. Election requires not only persuading members of the public to support that candidacy but also mobilizing as many of those supporters as possible. Mobilizing is perhaps the quintessential problem of collective action. How do candidates get supporters to vote for them—at least in greater numbers than vote for the opposition—as well as get them to provide the cadre of workers and contribute the resources needed to win elections? The political party has long been the solution.

As important as wooing and mobilizing supporters are, collective action problems arise in a wide range of circumstances facing elective office seekers. Party action invariably requires the concerted action of many partisans to achieve collectively desirable outcomes. Jimmy Carter was the only president in the 1970s and 1980s to enjoy unified party control of government. Democrats in Congress, it might well be argued, shared an interest in achieving policy outcomes. And yet Carter was all too often unable to get them to act in their shared collective interests. In 1980 not only he but the Democratic congressional parties paid a heavy price for failed cooperation. The theory here, of course, is the theory of public goods . . . and its consequence, the theory of collective action. . . .

The Elective Office Seekers' and Holders' Interests Are to Win

Why should this crucial set of actors, the elective office seekers and officeholders, care about these three classes of problems? The short answer is that these concerns become practical problems to politicians when they adversely affect their chances of winning. Put differently, politicians turn to their political party—that is, use its powers, resources, and institutional forms—when they believe doing so increases their prospects for winning desired outcomes, and they turn from it if it does not.

Ambition theory is about winning per se. The breakdown of orderly access to office risks unfettered and unregulated competition. The inability of a party to develop effective means of nomination and support for election therefore directly influences the chances of victory for the candidates and thus for their parties. The standard example of the problem of social choice theory, the "paradox of voting," is paradoxical precisely because all are voting to win desired outcomes, and yet there is no majority-preferred outcome. Even if there happens to be a majority-preferred policy, the conditions under which it is truly a stable equilibrium are extremely fragile and thus all too amenable to defeat. In other words, majorities in Congress are hard to attain and at least as hard to maintain. And the only reason to employ scarce campaign resources to mobilize supporters is that such mobilization increases the odds of victory. Its opposite, the failure to act when there are broadly shared interests—the problem of collective action—reduces the prospects of victory, whether at the ballot box or in government. Scholars may recognize these as manifestations of theoretical problems and call them "paradoxes," or "impossibility results," to emphasize their generic importance. Politicians recognize the consequences of these impossibility results by their adverse effects on their chances of winning—of securing what it is in their interests to secure.

So why have politicians so often turned to political parties for solutions to these problems? Their existence creates incentives for their use. It is, for example, incredibly difficult to win election to major office without the backing of a major party. It is only a little less certain that legislators who seek to lead a policy proposal through the congressional labyrinth will first turn to their party for assistance. But such incentives tell us only that an ongoing political institution is used when it is useful. Why form political parties in the first place? . . . A brief statement of three points will give a first look at the argument.

First, parties are institutions. This means, among other things, that they have some durability. They may be endogenous institutions, yet party reforms are meant not as short-term fixes but as alterations to last for years, even decades. Thus, for example, legislators might create a party rather than a temporary majority coalition to increase their chances of winning not just today but tomorrow and into the future. Similarly, a long and successful political career means winning office today, but it also requires winning elections throughout that career. A standing, enduring organization makes that goal more likely.

Second, American democracy chooses by plurality or majority rule. Election to office therefore requires broad-based support wherever and from whomever it can be found. So strong are the resulting incentives for a two-party system to emerge that the effect is called Duverger's Law (Duverger 1954). It is in part the need to win vast and diverse support that has led politicians to create political parties.

Third, parties may help officeholders win more, and more often, than alternatives. Consider the usual stylized model of pork barrel politics. All winners get a piece of the pork for their districts. All funded projects are paid for by tax revenues, so each district pays an equal share of the costs of each project adopted, whether or not that district receives a project. Several writers have argued that this kind of legislation leads to "universalism," that is, adoption of a "norm" that every such bill yields a project to every district and thus passes with a "universal" or unanimous coalition. Thus everyone "wins." Weingast proved the basic theorem (1979). His theorem yields the choice of the rule of universalism over the formation of a simple majority coalition, because in advance each legislator calculates the chances of any simple majority coalition's forming as equal to that of any other. As a result, expecting to win only a bit more than half the time and lose the rest of the time, all legislators prefer consistent use of the norm of universalism. But consider an alternative. Suppose some majority agree to form a more permanent coalition, to control outcomes now and into the future, and develop institutional means to encourage fealty to this agreement. If they successfully accomplish this, they will win regularly. Members of this institutionalized coalition would prefer it to universalism, since they always win a project in either case, but they get their projects at lower cost under the institutionalized majority coalition, which passes fewer projects. Thus, even in this case with no shared substantive interests at all, there are nonetheless incentives to form an enduring voting coalition—to form a political party. And those in the excluded minority have incentives to counterorganize. United, they may be more able to woo defectors to their side. If not, they can campaign to throw those rascals in the majority party out of office.

In sum, these theoretical problems affect elective office seekers and office-holders by reducing their chances of winning. Politicians therefore may turn to political parties as institutions designed to ameliorate them. In solving these theoretical problems, however, from the politicians' perspective parties are affecting who wins and loses and what is won or lost. And it is to parties that politicians often turn, because of their durability as institutionalized solutions, because of the need to orchestrate large and diverse groups of people to form winning majorities, and because often more can be won through parties. Note that this argument rests on the implicit assumption that winning and losing hang in the balance. Politicians may be expected to give up some of their personal autonomy only when they face an imminent threat of defeat without doing so or only when doing so can block opponents' ability to build the strength necessary to win.

This is, of course, the positive case for parties, for it specifies conditions under which politicians find them useful. Not all problems are best solved, perhaps even solved at all, by political parties. Other arrangements, perhaps interest groups, issue networks, or personal electoral coalitions, may be superior at different times and under different conditions (see Hansen 1991, for example). The party may even be part of the problem. In such cases politicians turn elsewhere to seek the means to win. Thus this theory is at base a theory of ambitious politicians seeking to achieve their goals. Often they have done so through the agency of the party, but sometimes, this theory implies, they will seek to realize their goals in other ways.

The political party has regularly proved useful. The permanence of parties suggests that the appropriate question is not "When parties?" but "How much parties and how much other means?" That parties are endogenous implies that there is no single, consistent account of the political party—nor should we expect one. Instead, parties are but a (major) part of the institutional context in which current historical conditions—the problems—are set, and solutions are sought with permanence only by changing that web of institutional arrangements. Of these the political party is by design the most malleable, and thus it is intended to change in important ways and with relatively great frequency. But it changes in ways that have, for most of American history, retained major political parties and, indeed, retained two major parties.

NOTE

1. Ranney is quoting Polsby and Wildavsky (1971, 225).

REFERENCES

APSA Committee on Political Parties. 1950. "A Report of the Committee on Political Parties." *American Political Science Review* 44 (September): i–xii, 1–99.

Arrow, Kenneth J. 1951. *Social Choice and Individual Values*. New York: Wiley.

Demsetz, Harold. 1990. "Amenity Potential, Indivisibilities, and Political Competition." In *Perspectives on Political Economy*, edited by James E. Alt and Kenneth A. Shepsle, 144–60. New York: Cambridge University Press.

Downs, Anthony. 1957. *An Economic Theory of Democracy*. New York: Harper and Row.

Duverger, Maurice. 1954. *Political Parties: Their Organization and Activities in the Modern State*. New York: Wiley.

Eldersveld, Samuel J. 1964. *Political Parties: A Behavioral Analysis*. Chicago: Rand McNally.

———. 1982. *Political Parties in American Society*. New York: Basic Books.

Epstein, Leon D. 1986. *Political Parties in the American Mold*. Madison: University of Wisconsin Press.

Fenno, Richard F. 1973. *Congressmen in Committees*. Boston: Little, Brown.

Ferguson, Thomas. 1983. "Party Realignment and American Industrial Structures: The Investment Theory of Political Parties in Historical Perspective." In *Research in Political Economy*, vol. 6, edited by Paul Zarembka, 1–82. Greenwich, CT: JAI Press.

———. 1986. "Elites and Elections, or: What Have They Done to You Lately?" In *Do Elections Matter?*, edited by Benjamin Ginsberg and Alan Stone, 164–88. Armonk, NY: Sharpe.

———. 1989. "Industrial Conflict and the Coming of the New Deal: The Triumph of Multinational Liberalism in America." In *The Rise and Fall of the New Deal Order, 1930–80*, edited by Steve Fraser and Gary Gerstle, 3–31. Princeton, NJ: Princeton University Press.

———. 1991. "An Unbearable Lightness of Being: Party and Industry in the 1988 Democratic Primary." In *Do Elections Matter?*, 2nd ed., edited by Benjamin Ginsberg and Alan Stone, 237–54. Armonk, NJ: Sharpe.

Hansen, John Mark. 1991. *Gaining Access: Congress and the Farm Lobby*. Chicago: University of Chicago Press.

Herrnson, Paul S. 1988. *Party Campaigning in the 1980s*. Cambridge, MA: Harvard University Press.

Hershey, Marjorie Randon. 2009. *Party Politics in America*. New York: Pearson Longman.

Kayden, Xandra, and Eddie Mayhe Jr. 1985. *The Party Goes On: The Persistence of the Two-Party System in the United States*. New York: Basic Books.

Key, V. O., Jr. 1964. *Politics, Parties, and Pressure Groups*. 5th ed. New York: Crowell.

Lijphart, Arend. 1984. *Democracies: Patterns of Majoritarian and Consensus Government in Twenty-One Countries*. New Haven, CT: Yale University Press.

———. 1999. *Patterns of Democracy: Government Forms and Performance in Thirty-Six Countries*. New Haven, CT: Yale University Press.

McClosky, Herbert. 1969. "Consensus and Ideology in American Politics." In *Empirical Democratic Theory*, edited by Charles F. Cnudde and Deane E. Neubauer, 268–302. Chicago: Markham. Originally published in *American Political Science Review* 58 (June 1964): 361–82.

Page, Benjamin I. 1978. *Choices and Echoes in Presidential Elections: Rational Man and Electoral Democracy.* Chicago: University of Chicago Press.

Polsby, Nelson W., and Aaron B. Wildavsky. 1971. *Presidential Elections: Strategies of American Electoral Politics.* 3rd ed. New York: Scribner.

Popkin, Samuel, John W. Gorman, Charles Phillips, and Jeffrey A. Smith. 1976. "Comment: What Have You Done for Me Lately? Toward an Investment Theory of Voting." *American Political Science Review* 70 (September): 779–805.

Ranney, Austin. 1975. *Curing the Mischiefs of Faction: Party Reform in America.* Berkeley and Los Angeles: University of California Press.

Rohde, David W. 1979. "Risk-Bearing and Progressive Ambition: The Case of the United States House of Representatives." *American Journal of Political Science* 23 (February): 1–26.

Rohde, David W., and Kenneth A. Shepsle. 1978. "Thinking about Legislative Reform". In *Legislative Reform: The Policy Impact*, edited by Leroy N. Rieselbach. Lexington, MA: Lexington Books.

Schattschneider, E. E. 1942. *Party Government.* New York: Rinehart.

Schlesinger, Joseph A. 1966. *Ambition and Politics: Political Careers in the United States.* Chicago: Rand McNally.

———. 1975. "The Primary Goals of Political Parties: A Clarification of Positive Theory." *American Political Science Review* 69 (September): 840–49.

———. 1991. *Political Parties and the Winning of Office.* Chicago: University of Chicago Press.

Sorauf, Frank J. 1964. *Party Politics in America.* Boston: Little, Brown.

———. 1988. *Money in American Elections.* Glenview, IL: Scott Foresman/Little, Brown.

Weingast, Barry R. 1979. "A Rational Choice Perspective on Congressional Norms." *American Journal of Political Science* 23 (May): 245–62.

Wilson, Woodrow. 1881. *Congressional Government: A Study in American Society.* Baltimore: Johns Hopkins University Press.

12.2

ANGUS CAMPBELL, PHILIP E. CONVERSE, WARREN E. MILLER,
AND DONALD E. STOKES

From *The American Voter: An Abridgement*

In this selection from the classic book The American Voter, *the authors depict partisanship as a deep psychological attachment to one of the two major parties, an attachment that largely determines individual voting decisions and shapes the way individuals evaluate policies and politicians. The authors demonstrate a way to measure partisanship in the population using surveys. Even though the original book was published in 1960, this conceptualization of partisanship and the method of measuring it are still widely used by scholars all over the world.*

THE IMPACT OF PARTY IDENTIFICATION

A general observation about the political behavior of Americans is that their partisan preferences show great stability between elections. . . . Often a change of candidates and a broad alteration in the nature of the issues disturb very little the relative partisanship of a set of electoral units, which suggests that great numbers of voters have party attachments that persist through time.

The fact that attachments of this sort are widely held is confirmed by survey data on individual people. In a survey interview most of our citizens freely classify themselves as Republicans or Democrats and indicate that these loyalties have persisted through a number of elections. Few factors are of greater importance for our national elections than the lasting attachment of tens of millions of Americans to one of the parties. These loyalties establish a basic division of electoral strength within which the competition of particular campaigns takes place. And they are an important factor in assuring the stability of the party system itself.

The Concept and Measurement of Party Identification

Only in the exceptional case does the sense of individual attachment to party reflect a formal membership or an active connection with a party apparatus. Nor does it simply denote a voting record, although the influence of party allegiance on electoral behavior is strong. Generally this tie is a psychological identification, which can persist without legal recognition or evidence of formal

From Angus Campbell et al., *The American Voter: An Abridgement* (New York: John Wiley & Sons, 1964).

membership and even without a consistent record of party support. Most Americans have this sense of attachment with one party or the other. And for the individual who does, the strength and direction of party identification are facts of central importance in accounting for attitude and behavior.

The importance of stable partisan loyalties has been universally recognized in electoral studies, but the manner in which they should be defined and measured has been a subject of some disagreement. In keeping with the conception of party identification as a psychological tie, these orientations have been measured in our research by asking individuals to describe their own partisan loyalties. Some studies, however, have chosen to measure stable partisan orientations in terms of an individual's past voting record or in terms of his attitude on a set of partisan issues. We have not measured party attachments in terms of the vote or the evaluation of partisan issues precisely because we are interested in exploring the *influence* of party identification on voting behavior and its immediate determinants. When an independent measure of party identification is used, it is clear that even strong party adherents at times may think and act in contradiction to their party allegiance. We could never establish the conditions under which this will occur if lasting partisan orientations were measured in terms of the behavior they are thought to affect.

Our measurement of party identification rests fundamentally on self-classification. Since 1952 we have asked repeated cross sections of the national population a sequence of questions inviting the individual to state the direction and strength of his partisan orientation.[1] The dimension presupposed by these questions appears to have psychological reality for virtually the entire electorate. The partisan self-image of all but the few individuals who disclaim any involvement in politics permits us to place each person in these samples on a continuum of partisanship extending from strongly Republican to strongly Democratic. The sequence of questions we have asked also allows us to distinguish the Independents who lean toward one of the parties from those who think of themselves as having no partisan coloration whatever.

The measure these methods yield has served our analysis of party identification in a versatile fashion. To assess both the direction and intensity of partisan attachments it can be used to array our samples across the seven categories shown in Table [1], which gives the distribution of party identification in the electorate during the years from 1952 to 1958.

In using these techniques of measurement we do not suppose that every person who describes himself as an Independent is indicating simply his lack of positive attraction to one of the parties. Some of these people undoubtedly are actually repelled by the parties or by partisanship itself and value their position as Independents. Certainly independence of party is an ideal of some currency in our society, and it seems likely that a portion of those who call themselves Independents are not merely reporting the absence of identification with one of the major parties.

Sometimes it is said that a good number of those who call themselves Independents have simply adopted a label that conceals a genuine psychological

TABLE [1]   The Distribution of Party Identification

	Oct. 1952	Sept. 1953	Oct. 1954	Apr. 1956	Oct. 1956	Nov. 1957	Oct. 1958
Strong Republicans	13%	15%	13%	14%	15%	10%	13%
Weak Republicans	14	15	14	18	14	16	16
Independent Republicans	7	6	6	6	8	6	4
Independents	5	4	7	3	9	8	8
Independent Democrats	10	8	9	6	7	7	7
Weak Democrats	25	23	25	24	23	26	24
Strong Democrats	22	22	22	19	21	21	23
Apolitical, don't know	4	7	4	10	3	6	5
Total	100%	100%	100%	100%	100%	100%	100%
Number of cases	1614	1023	1139	1731	1772	1488	1269

commitment to one party or the other. Accordingly, it is argued that a person's voting record gives a more accurate statement of his party attachment than does his own self-description. Our samples doubtless include some of these undercover partisans, and we have incorporated in our measure of party identification a means of distinguishing Independents who say they lean toward one of the parties from Independents who say they do not. We do not think that the problem of measurement presented by the concealed partisan is large. Rather it seems to us much less troublesome than the problems that follow if psychological ties to party are measured in terms of the vote.

This question can be illuminated a good deal by an examination of the consistency of party voting among those of different degrees of party identification, as is done in Table [2]. The proportion of persons consistently supporting one party varies by more than sixty percentage points between strong party identifiers and complete Independents. For the problem of the undercover partisan, the troublesome figure in Table [2] is the 16 percent of full Independents who have voted for the candidates of one party only. The importance of this figure diminishes when we remember that some of these persons have voted in very few presidential elections and could have supported one party consistently because of the way their votes fell, free of the influence of a genuine party tie.

▪ ▪ ▪

The measurement of party identification in the period of our research shows how different a picture of partisan allegiance voting behavior and

TABLE [2] Relation of Strength of Party Identification to Partisan Regularity in Voting for President, 1956[*]

	Strong Party Identifiers	Weak Party Identifiers	Independents Leaning to Party	Independents
Voted always or mostly for same party	82%	60%	36%	16%
Voted for different parties	18	40	64	84
Total	100%	100%	100%	100%
Number of cases	546	527	189	115

[*] The question used to establish party consistency of voting was this: "Have you always voted for the same party or have you voted for different parties for President?"

self-description can give. Despite the substantial Republican majorities in the elections of 1952 and 1956, the percentages of Table [1] make clear that the Democratic Party enjoyed a three-to-two advantage in the division of party identification within the electorate in these same years. Moreover, Table [1] documents the stability of this division of party loyalty in a period whose electoral history might suggest widespread change. Except for the shifting size of the group of respondents refusing to be assigned any position on the party scale, there is not a single variation between successive distributions of party identification that could not be laid to sampling error.

The great stability of partisan loyalties is supported, too, by what we can learn from recall data about the personal history of party identification. We have asked successive samples of the electorate a series of questions permitting us to reconstruct whether an individual who accepts a party designation has experienced a prior change in his party identification. The responses give impressive evidence of the constancy of party allegiance.

The fact that nearly everyone in our samples could be placed on a unitary dimension of party identification and that the idea of prior movements on this dimension was immediately understood are themselves important findings about the nature of party support within the electorate. In view of the loose, federated structure of American parties it was not obvious in advance that people could respond to party in these undifferentiated terms. Apparently the positive and negative feelings that millions of individuals have toward the parties are the result of orientations of a diffuse and generalized character that have a common psychological meaning even though there may be a good deal of variation in the way party is perceived.

Party Identification and Political Attitude

The psychological function of party identification undoubtedly varies among individuals. Our interest here centers primarily on the role of party as a supplier of cues by which the individual may evaluate the elements of politics. The fact that most elements of national politics are far removed from the world of the common citizen forces the individual to depend on sources of information from which he may learn indirectly what he cannot know as a matter of direct experience. Moreover, the complexities of politics and government increase the importance of having relatively simple cues to evaluate what cannot be matters of personal knowledge.

In the competition of voices reaching the individual the political party is an opinion-forming agency of great importance. This is not to say that party leaders are able as a matter of deliberate technique to transmit an elaborate defense of their position to those in the electorate who identify with the party. To the contrary, some of the most striking instances of party influence occur with only the simplest kind of information reaching the party's mass support. For example, a party undoubtedly furnishes a powerful set of cues about a political leader just by nominating him for President. Merely associating the party symbol with his name encourages those identifying with the party to develop a more favorable image of his record and experience, his abilities, and his other personal attributes. Likewise, this association encourages supporters of the opposite party to take a less favorable view of these same personal qualities. Partisans in each camp may incorporate into their view of the candidates whatever detailed information they can, and the highly-involved may develop an elaborate and carefully drawn portrait. But the impact of the party symbol seems to be nonetheless strong on those who absorb little of politics and whose image of the candidates is extremely diffuse.

Apparently party has a profound influence across the full range of political objects to which the individual voter responds. The strength of relationship between party identification and the dimensions of partisan attitude suggests that responses to each element of national politics are deeply affected by the individual's enduring party attachments.

■   ■   ■

In the period of our studies the influence of party identification on attitudes toward the perceived elements of politics has been far more important than the influence of these attitudes on party identification itself. We are convinced that the relationships in our data reflect primarily the role of enduring partisan commitments in shaping attitudes toward political objects. Our conviction on this point is rooted in what we know of the relative stability and priority in time of party identification and the attitudes it may affect. We know that persons who identify with one of the parties typically have held the same partisan tie for all or almost all of their adult lives. But within their experience since coming of voting age many of the elements of politics have changed.

▪ ▪ ▪

What is more, even the elements of politics that carry over from one election to another may be evaluated anew in later campaigns by part of the electorate. The involvement of many Americans in politics is slight enough that they may respond *de novo* to issues and personalities that have been present in earlier elections but that are salient to them only at the height of a presidential campaign. For many voters the details of the political landscape may be quite blurred until they are brought more into focus during the campaign period. The formative influence of party identification on these re-evaluations would not be essentially different from its influence on responses to newer elements of politics.

Because the influence of party identification extends through time, its workings cannot be fully disclosed by the relationships seen at a particular moment. For this reason, our statement of causal priorities is in the end an inference, but one for which the evidence is strong. If the inference is correct, the differences in attitude between those of differing partisan loyalties enlarge considerably our understanding of the configuration of forces leading to behavior.

▪ ▪ ▪

Our hypothesis that party identification influences the voting act by influencing attitudes toward the objects to which this act relates needs to be modified for the person who has only the faintest image of these objects. If someone has little perception of the candidates, of the record of the parties, of public issues or questions of group interest, his attitudes toward these things may play a less important intervening role between party identification and the vote. Like the automobile buyer who knows nothing of cars except that he prefers a given make, the voter who knows simply that he is a Republican or Democrat responds directly to his stable allegiance without the mediating influence of perceptions he has formed of the objects he must choose between.

Party Identification and Electoral Choice

The role of general partisan orientations in molding attitudes toward the elements of politics is thus very clear. As a consequence of this role, party identification has a profound impact on behavior. . . . From the strength and direction of attitudes toward the various elements of politics we could order the individuals in our samples according to the probability of their voting Republican. That is, we could form an array extending from those most likely to vote Democratic to those most likely to vote Republican. Let us now make explicit the impact party identification has on behavior through its influence on attitude, by showing a separate array for each of five groups defined by our party identification scale. For each of the distributions shown in Figure [1] the

FIGURE [1] Probable Direction of Vote by Party Identification Groups, 1956

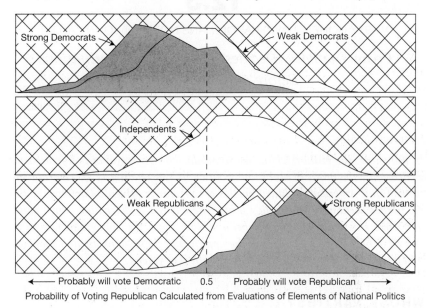

◄────── Probably will vote Democratic   0.5   Probably will vote Republican ──────►

Probability of Voting Republican Calculated from Evaluations of Elements of National Politics

horizontal dimension is the probability an individual will vote Republican; to the left this probability is low (that is, the likelihood the individual will vote Democratic is high), and to the right the probability that the individual will vote Republican is high. The effect of party is seen at once in the changing location of the distributions along this probability dimension as we consider successively Strong Democrats, Weak Democrats, Independents, Weak Republicans, and Strong Republicans. The moving positions of these arrays show clearly the impact of party identification on the forces governing behavior.

NOTE

1. The initial question was this: "Generally speaking, do you think of yourself as a Republican, a Democrat, an Independent, or what?" Those who classified themselves as Republicans or Democrats were also asked, "Would you call yourself a strong (Republican, Democrat) or a not very strong (Republican, Democrat)?" Those who classified themselves as Independents were asked this additional question: "Do you think of yourself as closer to the Republican or Democratic Party?" The concept itself was first discussed in George Belknap and Angus Campbell, "Political Party Identification and Attitudes toward Foreign Policy," *Public Opinion Quarterly*, XV (Winter 1952), 601–623.

12.3

MARTY COHEN, DAVID KAROL, HANS NOEL, AND JOHN ZALLER

From *The Party Decides: Presidential Nominations Before and After Reform*

In this piece, the authors challenge John Aldrich's portrayal of political parties as driven by the needs of ambitious politicians (see reading 12.1). They contend instead that American political parties are primarily driven by activists within the parties seeking certain policy goals. These activists determine which candidates will run under the party label and thus shape the policy direction of the party. Ambitious politicians seek the approval of these activists, and they need that approval before they can seek the approval of voters.

WHOSE PARTIES?

■ ■ ■

The Schwartz–Aldrich Model

In an important but unpublished essay, Schwartz (1989) imagined how a three-person legislature with no parties might structure its business. There would be a great temptation, Schwartz observed, for two legislators to gang up on the third by passing bills that help their constituents while shifting costs to constituents of the third. Schwartz called the winning coalition a "long coalition" to signify that it would form over a great many issues, always to the benefit of the same majority and the detriment of the same loser. The long coalition would be stable, because the two winning legislators would have every reason to continue cooperating over all business of mutual advantage. Voters, for their part, would be happy to reelect the two majority legislators because their interests would be well served by the long coalition. Schwartz generalized his argument to a large legislature, showing that the appeal of a "long coalition" of permanent winners would remain strong.

■ ■ ■

Schwartz's account is obviously quite spare, omitting important features of party organization in elections, local communities, and, the subject of most interest to us, presidential elections. In *Why Parties?* Aldrich builds on the Schwartz framework to fill in many of these features.

From Marty Cohen et al., *The Party Decides: Presidential Nominations Before and After Reform* (Chicago: University of Chicago Press, 2008), Chapter 2.

The most important idea in Aldrich's *Why Parties?*—the idea that comes up over and over and drives almost everything else—is that parties can be explained in terms of the benefits they provide to the ambitious politicians who form them. This is a change from Schwartz, who assumed that politicians formed parties in order to increase the flow of benefits to their districts. Aldrich thus writes that: "the major political party is the creature of the politicians, the ambitious office seeker and the officeholder. They have created and maintained, used or abused, reformed or ignored the political party when doing so has furthered their goals and ambitions. The political party is thus an 'endogenous' institution—an institution shaped by these political actors" (1995, 4).

. . . Aldrich's ambitious office seekers are more than single-minded seekers of office: They also care about good public policy and about power and prestige within government. Yet, as Aldrich goes on to argue, politicians must win election before they can accomplish any of their other goals. Thus, Aldrich's parties, like those of Schumpeter, Downs, and Schlesinger, aim first of all to please voters.

What, then, are the benefits that politicians get from the parties they create? One of the most important is the reputation that parties develop with voters. Many voters pay too little attention to politics to learn what individual politicians stand for. By associating with a party that is well known, a politician wins the support of voters who know only the party. Parties also build electoral machinery that aids individual politicians. A party coalition thus attracts voter support in one election after another, providing politicians with a basis for long professional careers.

But before a party can develop a reputation with voters, its officeholders must somehow come together as a coalition. This does not happen easily. In a legislature that contains many points of view, there are likely to be many potential majorities rather than just one. Thus, one majority may favor B over A, and another majority may favor C over B, but then a third majority may favor A over C. In this way, one majority can beat another in a potentially endless cycle. Stopping cycling, even on different versions of the same bill, may take huge effort. But, as Aldrich points out, the formation of a long coalition—a group of legislators who vote together on many issues—saves legislators the "transaction costs" of creating stable majorities for each new bill and at the same time creates a partisan group that lasts long enough to acquire a reputation with voters.

A signature argument in *Why Parties?* is that parties serve the electoral needs of ambitious politicians in different ways now than in the past. Until about 1960, party organization consisted largely of patronage workers who mobilized voters for politicians in elections. (Patronage jobs are government jobs that are filled by followers of the winning party.) In the current period, patronage has largely disappeared, so parties help candidates through polling, training, fund-raising, and other electoral services. To use Aldrich's terminology, the "mass mobilization party" of the last century has given way to a contemporary party that is "in service" to politicians' needs. With the services thus provided, candidates create their own campaign organizations and follow their own political strategies, making for a candidate-centered style of party politics. But this difference does not seem fundamental: Neither the mass mobilization party nor the in-service party tries to constrain politicians or hold them to any particular policy position; both kinds of parties aim to help politicians do what prevailing theories say politicians want to do—get elected to office and stay in office.

The motives of party workers have also changed over time. Patronage workers of bygone years cared little about issues, but nowadays, party activists care greatly. In an incisive analysis, Aldrich explains why activists are more ideologically extreme than most voters and pressure politicians through the nomination process to take their extreme views. This seems a significant change: Rather than helping politicians to win election, activists constrain politicians in ways that can make election more difficult. The activists also provide helpful electoral resources, but the resources come at the cost of pressure that limits the flexibility of candidates to take the policy positions that will most please voters. Despite the pressure, however, Aldrich's argument remains that the modern party is "in service" to its officeholders, who are "the actual leaders of the party" (1995, 183).

We take the Schwartz-Aldrich model of politician-centered parties to be the most important contemporary treatment of American parties in the political science literature. It not only subsumes a vast amount of prior theorizing . . . it makes novel contributions of its own. Yet we also believe that a key feature of nearly all contemporary party theory—the central focus on the ambitious politician—is questionable. Departing from the bulk of recent theorizing, we think that a focus on group and activist demands for policy would provide a more useful starting point for theorizing about parties.

Volunteer Policy Demanders

We now commence to make that argument, beginning with an observation by Paul Allen Beck. After outlining the formal legal machinery of parties, Beck describes the role of regular party workers, as follows:

> The party organization is a grouping of people, most of them contributing their time and energy on a purely voluntary basis. Even paid professional party workers who increasingly staff the national and state offices share many of the attributes of volunteers. The statutes ignore these men and women of the party, their goals and ambitions, their interactions and relationships, the contributions they make to the organization, and the price they exact for their contributions. Yet, the activity and motivations of those men and women are closer to the real world of party politics than all the statutory paragraphs put together. (1997, 106)

A few pages later, Beck adds that "the desire to use the party as a means to achieve policy goals appears to be the major incentive attracting individuals to party work these days" (113).

We could not agree more with these observations. America has been, at least since the time of Tocqueville, a country in which citizens have flocked to voluntary civic and political institutions. Every activity that any number of people really cared about—whether social, political, religious, recreational, or self-improving—has become an object of cooperation among like-minded citizens. Some of these associations have grown into major social movements, others have remained merely local clubs. As Beck's remarks make clear, political parties are another important outlet for Americans' traditional impulse to get out and work for what they care about.

The notion that parties are, and may long have been, powered by large numbers of policy-oriented individuals does not explain why parties exist, or whether parties are organized as Traditional Party Organizations or in some other way, or what contribution activists make to parties. It is not, in short, a theory of parties. But it can be the foundation for one.

A Group-Centered Theory of Parties

The central idea in the Schwartz-Aldrich model is that officeholders form parties to organize legislative business, mobilize voters, and assure stable careers. Parties exist, in other words, because they serve the needs of the politicians who create them.

But why only politicians? What about interest groups, social movements, sectional interests, and citizen activists who are also prominent in political parties? Might these actors have needs that parties could serve? Might they wish to form parties? No one denies such groups play a big role in party politics. Yet they are absent or secondary in contemporary theorizing about party organization. The attitude seems to be that party organization can be studied separately from the political forces that underlie it. This seems mistaken. Parties are a central political institution—arguably *the* central institution—for organizing society's diverse demands and interests. The myriad political actors that care intensely about these matters do not stand idly by while politicians organize parties and choose nominees for office. To the contrary, they insert themselves into the middle of the process, trying mightily to shape every important aspect of parties and often succeeding.

Much of the energy in American politics comes from these "intense policy demanders." Examples are business and labor, slaveholders and abolitionists, feminists and religious traditionalists, greenbackers and gold bugs, farm groups, environmentalists, gun owners, civil rights workers, southern white segregationists, immigrant and ethnic organizations, and people commonly known as liberal and conservative activists. Many of the party workers described above by Beck would probably fall into this last category. Intense policy demanders agitate, organize, and work late into the night to get policies they want. Because these groups are often motivated by deep feelings of justice and moral necessity, they are not deterred by long odds.

We define intense policy demanders by three criteria. They are (1) animated by a demand or set of demands, (2) politically active on behalf of their demands, and (3) numerous enough to be influential. Formal organization is often present but not essential.

Many intense policy demanders are identifiable by social, economic, or demographic characteristics, but what is relevant for our theory is that they have the same policy demands. In some cases, intense policy demanders from the same social or demographic category make opposing demands. When this happens, we say that two (or more) groups of intense policy demanders exist. For example, most members of feminist organizations are intense policy demanders for a liberal view of women's rights. But some women do not care much about feminism, and some women actively oppose liberal feminism. In our theory, the relevant group is not "women," but "feminist women" and "traditional women." So it is with all intense policy demanders: They are defined by their demands, not their social or demographic characteristics.

Having said carefully what we mean by intense policy demanders, we now wish to provide a shorthand expression for it. The shorthand is *group*. When we use the word *group* in this book, we will generally mean a *group of intense policy demanders, as defined by common demands*. The group may be a formally organized interest group, but also unorganized numbers of farmers, religious leaders, or ideological activists who make common demands.

Few if any groups of intense policy demanders are big enough to get what they want working alone. So they seek allies. But in joining party coalitions, groups do not put the good of the party ahead of their own goals. Parties are a means to an end, and the end is the group's own policy agenda. Groups cooperate in party business only insofar as cooperation serves their interests.

The most important party business is the nomination and election of office seekers *who will serve the interests of the party's intense policy demanders*. The italicized phrase marks the key difference between our theory and most other contemporary theorizing about parties. In our theory, parties—that is, the groups that constitute parties—do not care about winning for the sake of winning office. They care about the policy gains. And they make those gains not simply by the election of someone nominally affiliated with their party. They make them by the election of someone committed to the maximum feasible achievement of group goals.

In making nominations, the groups that constitute parties go beyond merely pressuring candidates to adopt positions closer to their own than most voters might prefer. They define basic party positions, decide how much electoral risk to take in pursuit of these positions, and choose which candidates to put forward under the party banner. Their purpose is to place reliable agents in

government offices. Thus, intense policy demanders expect that their nominees will, if elected, provide loyal service on matters large and small. A variety
of evidence indicates that they are not often disappointed in this expectation.
For example, Karol (1999, 2001, 2009) shows that when groups within a party
change their positions on issues, or when a new group joins a party coalition,
top politicians routinely change their views to agree with the new group position. For example, when business and labor groups changed their positions on
free trade around 1970, top Democratic and Republican officeholders changed
with them. When social conservatives joined the Republican party in the 1980s,
numerous top Republicans turned from pro-choice positions to pro-life ones.
Groups did not punish this behavior as flip-flopping; they encouraged it with
praise and support. In a different but related vein, Hall and Deardorff describe
how special-interest lobbyists, most of whom have close relationships with a
party, approach their work: "The proximate political objective of [lobbying] is
not to change legislators' minds but to assist natural allies in achieving their
own, coincident objectives" (2006, 69). In other words, lobbyists mainly just
fill in details for goals that they and the officeholders share.

Our argument about the centrality of group demands in party politics has
roots in an older tradition of theorizing by Arthur Bentley, E. E. Schattschneider, V. O. Key, and others. But it has been several decades since mainstream
political science has taken seriously a group theory of parties. We therefore
see value in working more fully through its logic. That done, we shall proceed
to testing, as best we can, whether the modern politician-centered or the more
venerable group-centered model gives a better account of how parties behave
in presidential nominations. A large part of this book is concerned with this
question.

Our development of the logic for group-centered parties takes the form of
the "why parties?" analysis of Schwartz and Aldrich, except that it has a different starting point—instead of an imaginary legislature made up of politicians, we begin with an imaginary society having groups of intense policy
demanders as well as politicians.

Why Groups Organize Parties

In our imaginary society, government consists of a policy dictator who is
elected and serves a four-year term. Society has an abundance of ambitious
politicians willing to promise whatever it takes to win this office.

Groups in our stylized society form when any large number of people wants
either to change the status quo through government action or defend a status
quo that is under attack. The number of intense policy demanders therefore
varies across time and political circumstance. Intense policy demanders are
the main source of campaign donations and campaign labor.

Voters in this society often hold strong political views but do not always
attend to politics. As a result, some government actions fall into an "electoral
blind spot" in which policies and their effects are invisible to voters. A degree

of voter blindness is central to our analysis because it creates the possibility for politicians, or groups that may influence them, to convert public policies and resources to group purposes. If, for example, voters do not follow the details of regulatory politics, officeholders can sell regulatory policy to intense policy demanders in exchange for campaign resources. Selling policy to groups is tricky, because no one can estimate what voters will notice and punish. But exploitation of voter inattentiveness by groups of intense policy demanders is the principal reason groups become active in politics, whether in party politics or in other ways.

Having now outlined the main features of an imaginary society, let us figure out how its politics might work. We begin our analysis as the country is about to have its first election. With intense policy demanders controlling most campaign resources, the outcome will depend on whether they back a candidate. Would it make political sense to do so? Or would the intense policy demanders do better to wait to deploy their resources until the dictator has been chosen?

Let us suppose the groups decide to sit out the election. If, after the election, a group wants something, it will have to induce the dictator to go along. For policies that would make most voters better off, simple persuasion would be effective. But for policies the public doesn't favor and may even oppose, something more will be needed—the promise to donate money to the dictator's reelection. But the dictator may demand a high price, and if one group won't meet her price, she can do business with another group and adopt its policies instead. If the groups try to form an alliance against her, the dictator might refuse them all. Suppose, for example, a group wants extra trash pickups from the government trash service. The dictator might go along with the demand in exchange for campaign donations. Alternatively, the dictator might reassign trash workers to political duties that would help toward reelection. Either way, voters get less trash pickup for the taxes they pay, but probably not enough less to notice, and the dictator gets extra campaign support. The bottom line, then, is that an incumbent politician can drive hard bargains with groups that try to buy policy from her and may not sell on any terms.

Suppose, then, that one of the groups foresees this problem and decides to back someone in the initial election who will be friendly to its needs once she gets into office. With many politicians in the race and only one group offering campaign funds, the group has the upper hand and is almost sure to find a politician who will promise what it wants in exchange for campaign resources. Or better yet, the group may be able to find a politician with a proven record of working for the group or, in the group's ideal world, the politician may be an actual member of the group and hence share its values. Political scientists typically treat politicians as separate from the groups that back them for office, but the separation becomes somewhat artificial if, as groups might like to do, they choose politicians from their own group. A politician committed to group values will still value reelection, but she will be more likely to take initiatives and risks for the group than would one with a different background.

From this analysis, we infer that at least one group will decide to become active in the initial election by sponsoring—that is, nominating—a candidate for office. The advantages of being able to select the politician at the nomination stage, as [opposed to] buying her support at the postelection stage, are simply too great to pass up. But if one group becomes active, other groups will not want to stay on the sidelines while the first group picks the policy dictator. Many groups will therefore enter the electoral fray, which will create a new problem: If each group backs its own candidate, only one group will win and the rest will lose. These are bad odds.

The groups will therefore consider forming a coalition. They will consider, that is, combining forces behind a single politician who is committed to a program that gives each of the groups what it wants. If all the groups support the same candidate, they can be almost sure of winning, and they can probably do so for relatively little cost. However, the question arises: Can all the groups work together in a coalition?

This is another tricky issue. If each group wants a policy others don't care about—for example, one wants more trash pickup, another wants looser enforcement of liquor laws—cooperation is easy. The coalition just gives each group most, though perhaps not all, of what it wants. Qualification is necessary because no group can get so much that it unduly burdens other groups, and all group benefits must remain within the voters' blind spot. For example, the group getting extra trash pickup cannot get so much service that other groups don't get their trash picked up or that voters suffer a noticeable drop in service.

But conflict between groups need not be a barrier to a party coalition unless the conflict is severe. Indeed, if public resources are available to underwrite party pacts, a coalition can be the means for resolving group conflict.

From this analysis, we conclude that groups can often get more from government by funneling their resources through a party coalition to nominate and elect officeholders friendly to their interests than by buying policies one at a time from independent officeholders after they have taken office.

Having decided to unite behind a nominee, the groups must choose one. Who they choose reflects who is in the coalition and who is not. Coalitions need to include enough groups to attract a majority of voters in the election, but not so many that it dilutes too much the benefits that any one group can get from being in the coalition.

A long coalition in a legislature can define itself bill by bill as it takes votes. A nominating coalition doesn't vote on individual bills, nor can it bind its nominee to any particular positions, since the nominee will be legally free to do whatever she wants once she gets into office. Hence, the parties must pick a nominee whose record or background demonstrates that the nominee can be trusted on all issues that groups in the coalition care about. In other words, the nominee must be acceptable to all members of the coalition. . . .

In our analysis, we have focused on election of a policy dictator, but our analysis would apply as well to the election of multiple officeholders. If, for example, we analyzed a case in which groups needed the support of scores of legislators as well as a president to enact policy, the efficiency gains from getting control of all these politicians at the nomination stage, when they were weak and disorganized, would be even more important than in the election of a policy dictator.

The advantage of party formation might be especially valuable to groups that sometimes come under popular attack. No group could expect an independent politician to stand up boldly for its interests when a majority is aroused against it. But if a politician has been selected to share group values, it will be individually rational for the politician to accept at least some electoral risk on behalf of the group. The problem with independent politicians is that they will jump ship in moments of danger; groups can expect greater steadfastness from politicians selected to share their values.

A final advantage of forming a party coalition, especially if no other party yet exists, is the opportunity to bias electoral procedures in favor of the group's party. We are not suggesting fraud, which is failure to follow rules, but rules that have a tilt to them. For example, if the party were strongest in cities, it might require voters to cast their ballots at urban locations. By such means, the first party to get control of government can create a permanent bias for its candidates. Even better than tilting the playing field is preventing an opposition party from forming in the first place. If only one party exists, it can quietly settle group differences internally, thereby increasing the range of policies in which voters will be blind to what groups are getting. As we argue in a later chapter, America's first party saw the opportunity for one-party politics and tried to seize it. The conditions under which party competition develops or fails to develop is an important but understudied problem in party politics (see, however, Masket, in press; Mickey 2008; Trounstine 2008).

In his original "Why Parties?" argument, Schwartz assumed that losing politicians would appeal to voters to win seats to become the majority. We make a similar assumption, except for groups. We assume, that is, that some initially inactive citizens will be directly hurt or angered by policies of the first party, become active as intense policy demanders, and form an opposition party. The result will be regular competition and rotation in office among group-dominated parties. Each party resembles one of Schwartz's long coalitions—a group of actors who vote together on a long list of issues.

It is natural to think of parties in a two-party system as majoritarian. Ours, however, are not. They want to win elections, but they do not necessarily wish to represent a majority of voters. As a by-product of their wish to govern, parties must offer a degree—perhaps a large degree—of responsiveness to popular majorities, but responsiveness to voters is not why parties exist. They exist to achieve the intense policy demands of their constituent groups. One might criticize parties for lack of deference to majority will, but their groups would not much care. Intense policy demanders nearly always believe their demands are just and that it is their duty to work for these demands whether or not most voters agree with them.

The theoretical analysis reported in this section grew out of our study of presidential nominations. We observed that party insiders seemed to control presidential nominations, but we could find no contemporary theory of party that would count their influence as party influence. Our theory of party has been created to explain why we believe it really is *party* influence.

REFERENCES

Aldrich, John H. 1995. *Why Parties? The Origin and Transformation of Political Parties in America*. Chicago: University of Chicago Press.

Beck, Paul Allen. 1997. *Party Politics in America*. 8th ed. New York: Longman.

Hall, Richard L., and Alan V. Deardorff. 2006. "Lobbying as Legislative Subsidy." *American Political Science Review* 100: 69–85.

Karol, David. 1999. "Realignment without Replacement: Issue Evolution and Ideological Change among Members of Congress." Paper given at the Midwest Political Science Association, Chicago, April 1999.

———. 2001. "How and Why Parties Change Positions on Issues: Party Policy Change as Coalition Management in American Politics." Paper given at the American Political Science Association, San Francisco, September 2001.

———. 2009. *Party Position Change in American Politics: Coalition Management*. New York: Cambridge University Press.

Mickey, Robert. 2008. *Paths Out of Dixie: The Democratization of Authoritarian Enclaves in America's Deep South, 1944–1972*. Princeton, NJ: Princeton University Press.

Schwartz, Thomas. 1989. *Why Parties?* Research memorandum, Department of Political Science, UCLA.

Trounstine, Jessica. 2008. *Political Monopolies in American Cities: The Rise and Fall of Bosses and Reformers*. Chicago: University of Chicago Press.

12.4

KEN KOLLMAN

"Who Drives the Party Bus?"

In this original essay, Kollman critiques the fundamental argument of the book
The Party Decides *(see reading 12.3) in light of Donald Trump's candidacy for*
president as the Republican nominee in 2016, and his subsequent victory and
behavior in office. It is not enough, Kollman argues, to say that Trump was
unusual or that sometimes unexpected things happen. The problem, he says, is
that the authors of The Party Decides *have the wrong theory of how political*
parties operate.

There has been much discussion among journalists, pundits, and academics
about the book *The Party Decides*. The book, published in 2008 by Marty Cohen,
David Karol, Hans Noel, and John Zaller, four political science scholars whom I
respect, made the following set of arguments: the two major political parties
have at their core major funders, politicians, and party leaders who share values
and ideologies, and who steer the parties; this core group for, say, the Republicans, has determined who wins the party's nomination as the presidential candidate. The candidate with the most endorsements among the key party insiders
has won the nomination in recent times. The party elites have historically
stacked the deck heavily in favor of establishment candidates and have kept
insurgents from gaining the nomination. The book has been widely read as not
only predicting that candidates like Donald Trump cannot win the nomination,
but also as highlighting the power of party insiders to get their way on nominations, platforms, and the distribution of money among party candidates.

Donald Trump's rise to become the Republican presidential candidate and
then president in 2016 directly contradicted the predictions of *The Party Decides*.
At least one of its authors gives a reasonable response. The party elites failed to
coordinate on an alternative to Trump. In response to criticism, Hans Noel
wrote in the *New York Times*, "Party leaders might have pushed aside Mr. Trump
if they'd had an easy choice among the acceptable candidates. Since they didn't,
the Trump distraction kept them from choosing anyone."[1]

When confronted with contradictory evidence for a theory, one could simply
claim that serendipity happens. Trump's rise was unexpected. Shrug the shoulders, concluding that unusual events happen. Trump's rise does not mean that
the overall theory is wrong. Perhaps if we were able to rerun the primary sea-

son many times, 95 out of 100 of those times Trump would not win the nomination, and thus never have become president. The likely event is that the favorite among party insiders would win. History throws unexpected events at us. The theory will predict better than other theories, but it will not always be correct.

The authors of *The Party Decides* probably have the right prediction most of the time—the most endorsed candidate usually wins the party's nomination for Republicans and Democrats. But the Trump nomination has exposed the real problem in their theory. The problem with *The Party Decides* is that it has the wrong theory of political parties.

Roughly two theories animate the academic study of political parties. To compare the theories, think of one as a story about a train and the other as a story about a bus. According to one view, exemplified by *The Party Decides*, the party elites structure the institutions of primary elections and caucuses and use their vast resources to determine the direction of the party. These party elites build the railroad tracks, place the train cars on the tracks, and then find the candidates to drive the trains in the direction predetermined.

The alternative view, as promulgated by political scientists Anthony Downs and John Aldrich, has political parties as more malleable and ultimately leaderless until candidates emerge. The candidates themselves, upon their choosing and their campaigning for office and ultimately governing, define what the party stands for and where it should go. The party is a bus that awaits a driver, and the candidate-driver can go in many different directions.

Another key difference between the theories is this: *The Party Decides* authors believe that the party elites, which include members of Congress, billionaire contributors, interest group leaders, and other stakeholders, can solve their internal conflicts *before* the nominating process and envision who or what kind of leader they need. Many experts on political parties believe that candidate nominating contests and campaigns are the *means* by which the various conflicting groups within parties temporarily solve their internal squabbles.

It takes an appealing candidate to bring together disparate factions within political parties. Funders and party intellectuals cannot unite parties because they create the factions that need to be brought together. Winning elections is what unites party factions.

Nixon, Reagan, Bill Clinton, George W. Bush, and Barack Obama were all successful at running for election in a manner that united their parties' factions. They found the rhetoric and policy ideas that brought success. No current theory of parties is able to predict events like the Trump surge well in advance. But a theory that places candidates at the center of decision-making better captures what actually happens in parties and gives more insight into the Trump phenomenon.

Trump, through his candidacy, proposed a way to solve the challenging contradictions within the Republican Party, and it proved surprisingly popular among primary voters and the general electorate. The party elites then played catch-up. The party ended up capturing the presidency. Sometimes parties are driven in an unpredicted direction and sometimes they win elections unexpectedly. Who drives the political parties? Candidates, not party elites.

NOTE

1. Hans Noel, "Why Can't the GOP Stop Trump?" *New York Times*, March 1, 2016. Available at http://www.nytimes.com/2016/03/01/opinion/campaign-stops/why-cant-the -gop-stop-trump.html (accessed November 3, 2016).

13

ELECTIONS

13.1

JOHN R. KOZA, BARRY FADEM, MARK GRUESKIN, MICHAEL S. MANDELL, ROBERT RICHIE, AND JOSEPH F. ZIMMERMAN

From *Every Vote Equal: A State-Based Plan for Electing the President by National Popular Vote*

In two recent elections, the presidential candidate with the most popular votes (Gore in 2000 and Clinton in 2016) lost to the candidate with fewer popular votes but a majority of electoral college votes (Bush in 2000 and Trump in 2016). Koza et al. lay out a bold proposal for avoiding this kind of outcome in the future. Their proposal does not require a constitutional amendment. Rather, it would require enough states that all together have more than 270 electoral votes to agree through a compact to elect the national popular vote winner as president. Each state in the group making the compact would agree to nominate for the electoral college only those electors pledged to vote for the candidate with the most popular votes nationwide.

What the U.S. Constitution Says—and Does Not Say—about Presidential Elections

The politically most important aspects of the system for electing the President of the United States are not established by the U.S. Constitution. Instead, the Constitution delegates the power to make those decisions to the states.

The Constitution specifies that the President and Vice President are to be chosen every four years by a small group of people (currently 538) who are individually referred to as "presidential electors." The presidential electors

From John R. Koza et al., *Every Vote Equal: A State-Based Plan for Electing the President by National Popular Vote* (Los Altos, CA: National Popular Vote Press, 2013).

are collectively referred to as the "Electoral College" (although this term does not appear in the Constitution).

■   ■   ■

Over the years, the states have used the Constitution's built-in flexibility concerning presidential elections in a remarkable variety of ways. Many of the most familiar features of present-day presidential elections (notably, voting by the people and the state-by-state winner-take-all rule) did not come into widespread use until decades after the Founders died.

■   ■   ■

. . . [B]y 1836, all but one state had adopted the concept of popular election of presidential electors using the statewide winner-take-all rule.

All the states used the statewide winner-take-all rule in the lengthy period between 1868 and 1968 with three isolated exceptions (namely legislative appointment in Florida in 1868 and Colorado in 1876 and district-level elections in Michigan in 1892).

Maine (in 1969) and Nebraska (in 1992) broke this pattern and adopted laws that awarded one electoral vote to the presidential candidate carrying each congressional district (and two electoral votes to the candidate carrying the state). In the 11 presidential elections in which the congressional-district approach has been used in Maine, the presidential candidate carrying the state also carried both of the state's two districts. In the six elections in which the congressional-district approach has been used in Nebraska, there has been one occasion where one of Nebraska's three districts was won by a candidate who did not carry the state (namely, Barack Obama in 2008).

The present-day state laws in Maine and Nebraska are reminders of the flexibility that the Founders built into the U.S. Constitution. These laws are reminders that the manner of awarding electoral votes is strictly a matter of state law. They are also reminders that a federal constitutional amendment is not necessary to change the way states award their electoral votes. Most importantly, they are reminders that the winner-take-all rule may be repealed by any state in the same manner as it was originally enacted, namely by passage of a different state law.

■   ■   ■

• **Voters Are Effectively Disenfranchised in Four-Fifths of the States in Presidential Elections.** One of the consequences of the statewide winner-take-all rule (i.e., awarding all of a state's electoral votes to the presidential candidate who receives the most popular votes in each separate state) is that presidential candidates do not campaign in states in which they are comfortably ahead or hopelessly behind. Presidential candidates ignore such states because they do not receive additional or fewer electoral votes based on the margin by which they win or lose those states. The result is that presidential candidates concentrate their public appearances, organizational efforts, advertising, polling, and policy attention on states where the outcome of the popular vote is not a foregone conclusion. In practical political terms, a vote matters in presidential politics only if it is cast in a closely divided battleground state. To put it another way, the value of a vote in presidential elections depends on whether *other* voters in the voter's state happen to be closely divided. Between 1988 and 2008, about two-thirds of the states were ignored by presidential campaigns. Four-fifths of the states were ignored in 2012. Twelve of the 13 least-populous states are spectator states, including six that have regularly gone Republican (Alaska, Idaho, Montana, Wyoming, North Dakota, and South Dakota) and six that have regularly gone Democratic (Hawaii, Vermont, Maine, Rhode Island, Delaware, and the District of Columbia).

- **The Current System Does Not Reliably Reflect the Nationwide Popular Vote.** The statewide winner-take-all rule makes it possible for a candidate to win the presidency without winning the most popular votes nationwide. This has occurred in four of the nation's 56 presidential elections—1 in 14 (as detailed in section 1.2.2 [not included]). In the past six decades, there have been six presidential elections in which a shift of a relatively small number of votes in one or two states would have elected (and, of course, in 2000, did elect) a presidential candidate who lost the popular vote nationwide.
- **Not Every Vote Is Equal.** The statewide winner-take-all rule creates variations of 1,000-to-1 and more in the weight of a vote (as detailed in section 1.2.3 [not included]).

▪ ▪ ▪

THE AGREEMENT AMONG THE STATES TO ELECT THE PRESIDENT BY NATIONAL POPULAR VOTE

▪ ▪ ▪

The authors' proposal, namely an interstate compact entitled the "Agreement Among the States to Elect the President by National Popular Vote," would not become effective in any state until it is enacted by states collectively possessing a majority of the electoral votes (that is, 270 of the 538 electoral votes).

The National Popular Vote compact would not change a state's internal procedures for operating a presidential election. After the 50 states and the District of Columbia certify their popular vote counts for President in the usual way, a grand total of popular votes would be calculated by adding up the popular vote count from all 51 jurisdictions.

The Electoral College would remain intact under the National Popular Vote compact. The compact would simply change the Electoral College from an institution that reflects the voters' state-by-state choices (or, in the case of

Maine and Nebraska, district-by-district choices) into a body that reflects the voters' nationwide choice. Specifically, the National Popular Vote compact would require that each member state award its electoral votes to the presidential candidate who received the largest number of popular votes in all 50 states and the District of Columbia. Because the compact would become effective only when it encompasses states collectively possessing a majority of the electoral votes, the presidential candidate receiving the most popular votes in all 50 states and the District of Columbia would be guaranteed enough electoral votes in the Electoral College to be elected to the Presidency.

The National Popular Vote compact would reform the Electoral College while retaining our federalist system of state control over elections.

Note that every state's popular vote would be included in the nationwide total regardless of whether it is a member of the compact. Membership in the compact is not required for the popular votes of a state to count. That is, every vote in every state would be equal under the compact.

Note also that the political complexion of the particular states belonging to the compact would not affect the outcome—that is, the presidential candidate receiving the most popular votes in all 50 states and the District of Columbia would be assured sufficient electoral votes to be elected to the presidency.

Text of the National Popular Vote Compact

This section presents the entire text (888 words) of the proposed "Agreement Among the States to Elect the President by National Popular Vote."

Article I—Membership

I-1   Any State of the United States and the District of Columbia may become a member of this agreement by enacting this agreement.

Article II—Right of the People in Member States to Vote for President and Vice President

II-1   Each member state shall conduct a statewide popular election for President and Vice President of the United States.

Article III—Manner of Appointing Presidential Electors in Member States

III-1   Prior to the time set by law for the meeting and voting by the presidential electors, the chief election official of each member state shall determine the number of votes for each presidential slate in each State of the United States and in the District of Columbia in which votes have been cast in a statewide popular election and shall add such votes together to produce a "national popular vote total" for each presidential slate.

III-2   The chief election official of each member state shall designate the presidential slate with the largest national popular vote total as the "national popular vote winner."

III-3   The presidential elector certifying official of each member state shall certify the appointment in that official's own state of the elector slate nominated in that state in association with the national popular vote winner.

III-4   At least six days before the day fixed by law for the meeting and voting by the presidential electors, each member state shall make a final determination of the number of popular votes cast in the state for each presidential slate and shall communicate an official statement of such determination within 24 hours to the chief election official of each other member state.

III-5   The chief election official of each member state shall treat as conclusive an official statement containing the number of popular votes in a state for each presidential slate made by the day established by federal law for making a state's final determination conclusive as to the counting of electoral votes by Congress.

III-6   In event of a tie for the national popular vote winner, the presidential elector certifying official of each member state shall certify the appointment of the elector slate nominated in association with the presidential slate receiving the largest number of popular votes within that official's own state.

III-7   If, for any reason, the number of presidential electors nominated in a member state in association with the national popular vote winner is less than or greater than that state's number of electoral votes, the presidential candidate on the presidential slate that has been designated as the national popular vote winner shall have the power to nominate the presidential electors for that state and that state's presidential elector certifying official shall certify the appointment of such nominees.

III-8   The chief election official of each member state shall immediately release to the public all vote counts or statements of votes as they are determined or obtained.

III-9   This article shall govern the appointment of presidential electors in each member state in any year in which this agreement is, on July 20, in effect in states cumulatively possessing a majority of the electoral votes.

Article IV—Other Provisions

IV-1   This agreement shall take effect when states cumulatively possessing a majority of the electoral votes have enacted this agreement in substantially the same form and the enactments by such states have taken effect in each state.

IV-2   Any member state may withdraw from this agreement, except that a withdrawal occurring six months or less before the end of a President's term shall not become effective until a President or Vice President shall have been qualified to serve the next term.

IV-3   The chief executive of each member state shall promptly notify the chief executive of all other states of when this agreement has been enacted and has taken effect in that official's state, when the state has withdrawn from this agreement, and when this agreement takes effect generally.

IV-4   This agreement shall terminate if the electoral college is abolished.

IV-5   If any provision of this agreement is held invalid, the remaining provisions shall not be affected.

13.2

Citizens United v. Federal Election Commission (2010)

Justice Anthony Kennedy's majority opinion in this controversial Supreme Court decision establishes the key precedent that in matters of political speech, all organizations, including corporations and unions, are accorded First Amendment rights similar to those granted to individuals. Campaign finance regulations that treat corporations and unions as different from people and other kinds of organizations are at odds with the intent of the First Amendment. Thus, this decision strikes down portions of a campaign finance law that makes distinctions among the types of political organizations that can air political advertisements.

JUSTICE KENNEDY delivered the opinion of the Court.

Federal law prohibits corporations and unions from using their general treasury funds to make independent expenditures for speech defined as an "electioneering communication" or for speech expressly advocating the election or defeat of a candidate. Limits on electioneering communications were upheld in *McConnell v. Federal Election Comm'n.* The holding of *McConnell* rested to a large extent on an earlier case, *Austin v. Michigan Chamber of Commerce* (1990). *Austin* had held that political speech may be banned based on the speaker's corporate identity.

In this case we are asked to reconsider *Austin* and, in effect, *McConnell.* It has been noted that *"Austin* was a significant departure from ancient First Amendment principles," *Federal Election Comm'n v. Wisconsin Right to Life, Inc.* (2007) *(WRTL).* We agree with that conclusion and hold that *stare decisis* does not compel the continued acceptance of *Austin.* The Government may regulate corporate political speech through disclaimer and disclosure requirements, but it may not suppress that speech altogether. We turn to the case now before us.

Citizens United is a nonprofit corporation. It brought this action in the United States District Court for the District of Columbia. A three-judge court later convened to hear the cause. The resulting judgment gives rise to this appeal.

Citizens United has an annual budget of about $12 million. Most of its funds are from donations by individuals; but, in addition, it accepts a small portion of its funds from for-profit corporations.

From *Citizens United v. Federal Election Commission*, 558 U.S. 310 (2010).

In January 2008, Citizens United released a film entitled *Hillary: The Movie*. We refer to the film as *Hillary*. It is a 90-minute documentary about then-Senator Hillary Clinton, who was a candidate in the Democratic Party's 2008 Presidential primary elections. *Hillary* mentions Senator Clinton by name and depicts interviews with political commentators and other persons, most of them quite critical of Senator Clinton. *Hillary* was released in theaters and on DVD, but Citizens United wanted to increase distribution by making it available through video-on-demand.

Video-on-demand allows digital cable subscribers to select programming from various menus, including movies, television shows, sports, news, and music. The viewer can watch the program at any time and can elect to rewind or pause the program. In December 2007, a cable company offered, for a payment of $1.2 million, to make *Hillary* available on a video-on-demand channel called "Elections '08." Some video-on-demand services require viewers to pay a small fee to view a selected program, but here the proposal was to make *Hillary* available to viewers free of charge.

To implement the proposal, Citizens United was prepared to pay for the video-on-demand; and to promote the film, it produced two 10-second ads and one 30-second ad for *Hillary*. Each ad includes a short (and, in our view, pejorative) statement about Senator Clinton, followed by the name of the movie and the movie's Website address.

Citizens United desired to promote the video-on-demand offering by running advertisements on broadcast and cable television.

Before the Bipartisan Campaign Reform Act of 2002 (BCRA), federal law prohibited—and still does prohibit—corporations and unions from using general treasury funds to make direct contributions to candidates or independent expenditures that expressly advocate the election or defeat of a candidate, through any form of media, in connection with certain qualified federal elections.

BCRA §203 amended §441b to prohibit any "electioneering communication" as well. An electioneering communication is defined as "any broadcast, cable, or satellite communication" that "refers to a clearly identified candidate for Federal office" and is made within 30 days of a primary or 60 days of a general election. The Federal Election Commission's (FEC) regulations further define an electioneering communication as a communication that is "publicly distributed."

Corporations and unions are barred from using their general treasury funds for express advocacy or electioneering communications. They may establish, however, a "separate segregated fund" (known as a political action committee, or PAC) for these purposes. The moneys received by the segregated fund are limited to donations from stockholders and employees of the corporation or, in the case of unions, members of the union.

Citizens United wanted to make *Hillary* available through video-on-demand within 30 days of the 2008 primary elections. It feared, however, that both the film and the ads would be covered by §441b's ban on corporate-funded independent expenditures, thus subjecting the corporation to civil and criminal penalties under §437g. In December 2007, Citizens United sought declaratory and injunctive relief against the FEC. It argued that (1) §441b is unconstitutional as applied to *Hillary;* and (2) BCRA's disclaimer and disclosure requirements, BCRA §§201 and 311, are unconstitutional as applied to *Hillary* and to the three ads for the movie.

The District Court denied Citizens United's motion for a preliminary injunction. The court held that §441b was facially constitutional under *McConnell,* and that §441b was constitutional as applied to *Hillary* because it was "susceptible of no other interpretation than to inform the electorate that Senator Clinton is unfit for office, that the United States would be a dangerous place in a President Hillary Clinton world, and that viewers should vote against her." The court also rejected Citizens United's challenge to BCRA's disclaimer and disclosure requirements. It noted that "the Supreme Court has written approvingly of disclosure provisions triggered by political speech even though the speech itself was constitutionally protected under the First Amendment."

As the foregoing analysis confirms, the Court cannot resolve this case on a narrower ground without chilling political speech, speech that is central to the meaning and purpose of the First Amendment. It is not judicial restraint to accept an unsound, narrow argument just so the Court can avoid another argument with broader implications. Indeed, a court would be remiss in performing its duties were it to accept an unsound principle merely to avoid the necessity of making a broader ruling. Here, the lack of a valid basis for an alternative ruling requires full consideration of the continuing effect of the speech suppression upheld in *Austin.*

Citizens United stipulated to dismissing count 5 of its complaint, which raised a facial challenge to §441b, even though count 3 raised an as-applied challenge. The Government argues that Citizens United waived its challenge to *Austin* by dismissing count 5. We disagree.

First, even if a party could somehow waive a facial challenge while preserving an as-applied challenge, that would not prevent the Court from reconsidering *Austin* or addressing the facial validity of §441b in this case. And here, the District Court addressed Citizens United's facial challenge. In rejecting the claim, it noted that it "would have to overrule *McConnell*" for Citizens United to prevail on its facial challenge and that "[o]nly the Supreme Court may overrule its decisions." The District Court did not provide much analysis regarding the facial challenge because it could not ignore the controlling Supreme Court decisions in *Austin* or *McConnell.* Even so, the District Court did "pas[s] upon" the issue. Furthermore, the District Court's later opinion, which granted the FEC summary judgment, was "[b]ased on the reasoning of [its] prior opinion," which included the discussion of the facial challenge. After the District Court addressed the facial validity of the statute, Citizens United raised its challenge to *Austin* in this Court. In these circumstances, it is necessary to consider Citizens United's challenge to *Austin* and the facial validity of §441b's expenditure ban.

Second, throughout the litigation, Citizens United has asserted a claim that the FEC has violated its First Amendment right to free speech. All concede that this claim is properly before us. Citizens United's argument that *Austin* should be overruled is "not a new claim." Rather, it is—at most—"a new argument to support what has been [a] consistent claim: that [the FEC] did not accord [Citizens United] the rights it was obliged to provide by the First Amendment."

Third, the distinction between facial and as-applied challenges is not so well defined that it has some automatic effect or that it must always control the pleadings and disposition in every case involving a constitutional challenge. The distinction is both instructive and necessary, for it goes to the breadth of the remedy employed by the Court, not what must be pleaded in a complaint. The parties cannot enter into a stipulation that prevents the Court from considering certain remedies if those remedies are necessary to resolve a claim that has been preserved.

Citizens United has preserved its First Amendment challenge to §441b as applied to the facts of its case; and given all the circumstances, we cannot easily address that issue without assuming a premise—the permissibility of restricting corporate political speech—that is itself in doubt. As our request for supplemental briefing implied, Citizens United's claim implicates the validity of *Austin*, which in turn implicates the facial validity of §441b.

When the statute now at issue came before the Court in *McConnell*, both the majority and the dissenting opinions considered the question of its facial validity. The holding and validity of *Austin* were essential to the reasoning of the *McConnell* majority opinion, which upheld BCRA's extension of §441b. *McConnell* permitted federal felony punishment for speech by all corporations, including nonprofit ones, that speak on prohibited subjects shortly before federal elections.

The *McConnell* majority considered whether the statute was facially invalid. An as-applied challenge was brought in *Wisconsin Right to Life, Inc. v. Federal Election Comm'n*, and the Court confirmed that the challenge could be maintained. Then, in *WRTL*, the controlling opinion of the Court not only entertained an as-applied challenge but also sustained it. Three Justices noted that they would continue to maintain the position that the record in *McConnell* demonstrated the invalidity of the Act on its face. The controlling opinion in *WRTL*, which refrained from holding the statute invalid except as applied to the facts then before the Court, was a careful attempt to accept the essential elements of the Court's opinion in *McConnell*, while vindicating the First Amendment arguments made by the *WRTL* parties.

As noted above, Citizens United's narrower arguments are not sustainable under a fair reading of the statute. In the exercise of its judicial responsibility, it is necessary then for the Court to consider the facial validity of §441b. Any other course of decision would prolong the substantial, nation-wide chilling effect caused by §441b's prohibitions on corporate expenditures. Consideration of the facial validity of §441b is further supported by the following reasons.

First is the uncertainty caused by the litigating position of the Government. As discussed above, see Part II–D, *supra*, the Government suggests, as an alternative argument, that an as-applied challenge might have merit. This argument proceeds on the premise that the nonprofit corporation involved here may have received only *de minimis* donations from for-profit corporations and that some nonprofit corporations may be exempted from the operation of the statute. The Government also suggests that an as-applied challenge to §441b's ban on books may be successful, although it would defend §441b's ban as applied to almost every other form of media including pamphlets. The Government thus, by its own position, contributes to the uncertainty that §441b causes. When the Government holds out the possibility of ruling for Citizens United on a narrow ground yet refrains from adopting that position, the added uncertainty demonstrates the necessity to address the question of statutory validity.

Second, substantial time would be required to bring clarity to the application of the statutory provision on these points in order to avoid any chilling effect caused by some improper interpretation. It is well known that the public begins to concentrate on elections only in the weeks immediately before they are held. There are short timeframes in which speech can have influence. The need or relevance of the speech will often first be apparent at this stage in the campaign. The decision to speak is made in the heat of political campaigns, when speakers react to messages conveyed by others. A speaker's ability to engage in political speech that could have a chance of persuading voters is stifled if the speaker must first commence a protracted lawsuit. By the time the lawsuit concludes, the election will be over and the litigants in most cases will have neither the incentive nor, perhaps, the resources to carry on, even if they could establish that the case is not moot because the issue is "capable of repetition, yet evading review." Here, Citizens United decided to litigate its case to the end. Today, Citizens United finally learns, two years after the fact, whether it could have spoken during the 2008 Presidential primary—long after the opportunity to persuade primary voters has passed.

Third is the primary importance of speech itself to the integrity of the election process. As additional rules are created for regulating political speech, any speech arguably within their reach is chilled.

This regulatory scheme may not be a prior restraint on speech in the strict sense of that term, for prospective speakers are not compelled by law to seek an advisory opinion from the FEC before the speech takes place. As a practical matter, however, given the complexity of the regulations and the deference courts show to administrative determinations, a speaker who wants to avoid threats of criminal liability and the heavy costs of defending against FEC enforcement must ask a governmental agency for prior permission to speak. These onerous restrictions thus function as the equivalent of prior restraint by giving the FEC power analogous to licensing laws implemented in 16th- and 17th-century England, laws and governmental practices of the sort that the First Amendment was drawn to prohibit.

This is precisely what *WRTL* sought to avoid. *WRTL* said that First Amendment standards "must eschew 'the open-ended rough-and-tumble of factors,' which 'invit[es] complex argument in a trial court and a virtually inevitable appeal.'" Yet, the FEC has created a regime that allows it to select what political speech is safe for public consumption by applying ambiguous tests. If parties want to avoid litigation and the possibility of civil and criminal penalties, they must either refrain from speaking or ask the FEC to issue an advisory opinion approving of the political speech in question. This is an unprecedented governmental intervention into the realm of speech.

The ongoing chill upon speech that is beyond all doubt protected makes it necessary in this case to invoke the earlier precedents that a statute which chills speech can and must be invalidated where its facial invalidity has been demonstrated.

The First Amendment provides that "Congress shall make no law . . . abridging the freedom of speech." Laws enacted to control or suppress speech may operate at different points in the speech process.

The law before us is an outright ban, backed by criminal sanctions. Section 441b makes it a felony for all corporations—including nonprofit advocacy corporations—either to expressly advocate the election or defeat of candidates or to broadcast electioneering communications within 30 days of a primary election and 60 days of a general election. Thus, the following acts would all be felonies under §441b: The Sierra Club runs an ad, within the crucial phase of 60 days before the general election, that exhorts the public to disapprove of a Congressman who favors logging in national forests; the National Rifle Association publishes a book urging the public to vote for the challenger because the incumbent U.S. Senator supports a handgun ban; and the American Civil Liberties Union creates a Web site telling the public to vote for a Presidential candidate in light of that candidate's defense of free speech. These prohibitions are classic examples of censorship.

Section 441b is a ban on corporate speech notwithstanding the fact that a PAC created by a corporation can still speak. A PAC is a separate association from the corporation. Even if a PAC could somehow allow a corporation to speak—and it does not—the option to form PACs does not alleviate the First Amendment problems with §441b. PACs are burdensome alternatives; they are expensive to administer and subject to extensive regulations. For example, every PAC must appoint a treasurer, forward donations to the treasurer promptly, keep detailed records of the identities of the persons making donations, preserve receipts for three years, and file an organization statement and report changes to this information within 10 days.

PACs have to comply with these regulations just to speak. This might explain why fewer than 2,000 of the millions of corporations in this country have PACs.

Section 441b's prohibition on corporate independent expenditures is thus a ban on speech. As a "restriction on the amount of money a person or group can spend on political communication during a campaign," that statute "necessarily reduces the quantity of expression by restricting the number of issues discussed, the depth of their exploration, and the size of the audience reached." Were the Court to uphold these restrictions, the Government could repress speech by silencing certain voices at any of the various points in the speech process. If §441b applied to individuals, no one would believe that it is merely a time, place, or manner restriction on speech. Its purpose and effect are to silence entities whose voices the Government deems to be suspect.

Speech is an essential mechanism of democracy, for it is the means to hold officials accountable to the people. The right of citizens to inquire, to hear, to speak, and to use information to reach consensus is a precondition to enlightened self-government and a necessary means to protect it. The First Amendment "'has its fullest and most urgent application' to speech uttered during a campaign for political office."

For these reasons, political speech must prevail against laws that would suppress it, whether by design or inadvertence. Laws that burden political speech are "subject to strict scrutiny," which requires the Government to prove that the restriction "furthers a compelling interest and is narrowly tailored to achieve that interest."

Premised on mistrust of governmental power, the First Amendment stands against attempts to disfavor certain subjects or viewpoints. Prohibited, too, are restrictions distinguishing among different speakers, allowing speech by some but not others. As instruments to censor, these categories are interrelated: Speech restrictions based on the identity of the speaker are all too often simply a means to control content.

By taking the right to speak from some and giving it to others, the Government deprives the disadvantaged person or class of the right to use speech to strive to establish worth, standing, and respect for the speaker's voice. The Government may not by these means deprive the public of the right and privilege to determine for itself what speech and speakers are worthy of consideration. The First Amendment protects speech and speaker, and the ideas that flow from each.

The Court has upheld a narrow class of speech restrictions that operate to the disadvantage of certain persons, but these rulings were based on an interest in allowing governmental entities to perform their functions. The corporate independent expenditures at issue in this case, however, would not interfere with governmental functions, so these cases are inapposite. These precedents stand only for the proposition that there are certain governmental functions that cannot operate without some restrictions on particular kinds of speech.

By contrast, it is inherent in the nature of the political process that voters must be free to obtain information from diverse sources in order to determine how to cast their votes. At least before *Austin*, the Court had not allowed the exclusion of a class of speakers from the general public dialogue.

We find no basis for the proposition that, in the context of political speech, the Government may impose restrictions on certain disfavored speakers. Both history and logic lead us to this conclusion.

The Court has recognized that First Amendment protection extends to corporations. Under the rationale of these precedents, political speech does not lose First Amendment protection "simply because its source is a corporation." The Court has thus rejected the argument that political speech of corporations or other associations should be treated differently under the First Amendment simply because such associations are not "natural persons."

At least since the latter part of the 19th century, the laws of some States and of the United States imposed a ban on corporate direct contributions to candidates. Yet not until 1947 did Congress first prohibit independent expenditures by corporations and labor unions in §304 of the Labor Management Relations Act 1947. In passing this Act Congress overrode the veto of President Truman, who warned that the expenditure ban was a "dangerous intrusion on free speech."

In its defense of the corporate-speech restrictions in §441b, the Government notes the antidistortion rationale on which *Austin* and its progeny rest in part, yet it all but abandons reliance upon it. It argues instead that two other compelling interests support *Austin*'s holding that corporate expenditure restrictions are constitutional: an anticorruption interest, and a shareholder-protection interest.

The Government contends that *Austin* permits it to ban corporate expenditures for almost all forms of communication stemming from a corporation. If *Austin* were correct, the Government could prohibit a corporation from expressing political views in media beyond those presented here, such as by printing books.

Political speech is "indispensable to decision making in a democracy, and this is no less true because the speech comes from a corporation rather than an individual." This protection for speech is inconsistent with *Austin*'s antidistortion rationale. *Austin* sought to defend the antidistortion rationale as a means to prevent corporations from obtaining "an unfair advantage in the political marketplace" by using "resources amassed in the economic marketplace." But *Buckley* rejected the premise that the Government has an interest "in equalizing the relative ability of individuals and groups to influence the outcome of elections." *Buckley* was specific in stating that "the skyrocketing cost of political campaigns" could not sustain the governmental prohibition. The First Amendment's protections do not depend on the speaker's "financial ability to engage in public discussion."

The rule that political speech cannot be limited based on a speaker's wealth is a necessary consequence of the premise that the First Amendment generally prohibits the suppression of political speech based on the speaker's identity.

Either as support for its antidistortion rationale or as a further argument, the *Austin* majority undertook to distinguish wealthy individuals from corporations on the ground that "[s]tate law grants corporations special advantages—such as limited liability, perpetual life, and favorable treatment of the accumulation and distribution of assets."

Austin's antidistortion rationale would produce the dangerous, and unacceptable, consequence that Congress could ban political speech of media corporations. Media corporations are now exempt from §441b's ban on corporate expenditures. Yet media corporations accumulate wealth with the help of the corporate form, the largest media corporations have "immense aggregations of wealth," and the views expressed by media corporations often "have little or no correlation to the public's support" for those views. Thus, under the Government's reasoning, wealthy media corporations could have their voices diminished to put them on par with other media entities. There is no precedent for permitting this under the First Amendment.

Austin interferes with the "open marketplace" of ideas protected by the First Amendment. It permits the Government to ban the political speech of millions of associations of citizens. Most of these are small corporations without large amounts of wealth. This fact belies the Government's argument that the statute is justified on the ground that it prevents the "distorting effects of immense aggregations of wealth." It is not even aimed at amassed wealth.

The censorship we now confront is vast in its reach. The Government has "muffle[d] the voices that best represent the most significant segments of the economy." By suppressing the speech of manifold corporations, both for-profit and nonprofit, the Government prevents their voices and viewpoints from reaching the public and advising voters on which persons or entities are hostile to their interests. Factions will necessarily form in our Republic, but the remedy of "destroying the liberty" of some factions is "worse than the disease."

The purpose and effect of this law is to prevent corporations, including small and nonprofit corporations, from presenting both facts and opinions to the public. When that phenomenon is coupled with §441b, the result is that smaller or nonprofit corporations cannot raise a voice to object when other corporations, including those with vast wealth, are cooperating with the Government. That cooperation may sometimes be voluntary, or it may be at the demand of a Government official who uses his or her authority, influence, and power to threaten corporations to support the Government's policies. Those kinds of interactions are often unknown and unseen. The speech that §441b forbids, though, is public, and all can judge its content and purpose. References to massive corporate treasuries should not mask the real operation of this law. Rhetoric ought not obscure reality.

Even if §441b's expenditure ban were constitutional, wealthy corporations could still lobby elected officials, although smaller corporations may not have the resources to do so. And wealthy individuals and unincorporated associations can spend unlimited amounts on independent expenditures. Yet certain disfavored associations of citizens—those that have taken on the corporate form—are penalized for engaging in the same political speech.

When Government seeks to use its full power, including the criminal law, to command where a person may get his or her information or what distrusted source he or she may not hear, it uses censorship to control thought. This is unlawful. The First Amendment confirms the freedom to think for ourselves.

What we have said also shows the invalidity of other arguments made by the Government. For the most part relinquishing the antidistortion rationale, the Government falls back on the argument that corporate political speech can be banned in order to prevent corruption or its appearance. In *Buckley*, the Court found this interest "sufficiently important" to allow limits on contributions but did not extend that reasoning to expenditure limits. When *Buckley* examined an expenditure ban, it found "that the governmental interest in preventing corruption and the appearance of corruption [was] inadequate to justify [the ban] on independent expenditures."

The *Buckley* Court, nevertheless, sustained limits on direct contributions in order to ensure against the reality or appearance of corruption. That case did not extend this rationale to independent expenditures, and the Court does not do so here.

The anticorruption interest is not sufficient to displace the speech here in question. Indeed, 26 States do not restrict independent expenditures by for-profit corporations. The Government does not claim that these expenditures have corrupted the political process in those States.

For the reasons explained above, we now conclude that independent expenditures, including those made by corporations, do not give rise to corruption or the appearance of corruption.

The Government contends further that corporate independent expenditures can be limited because of its interest in protecting dissenting shareholders from being compelled to fund corporate political speech. This asserted interest, like *Austin*'s antidistortion rationale, would allow the Government to ban the political speech even of media corporations. Assume, for example, that a shareholder of a corporation that owns a newspaper disagrees with the political views the newspaper expresses. Under the Government's view, that potential disagreement could give the Government the authority to restrict the media corporation's political speech. The First Amendment does not allow that power. There is, furthermore, little evidence of abuse that cannot be corrected by shareholders "through the procedures of corporate democracy."

Those reasons are sufficient to reject this shareholder-protection interest; and, moreover, the statute is both underinclusive and overinclusive. As to the first, if Congress had been seeking to protect dissenting shareholders, it would not have banned corporate speech in only certain media within 30 or 60 days before an election. A dissenting shareholder's interests would be implicated by speech in any media at any time. As to the second, the statute is overinclusive because it covers all corporations, including nonprofit corporations and for-profit corporations with only single shareholders. As to other corporations, the remedy is not to restrict speech but to consider and explore other regulatory mechanisms. The regulatory mechanism here, based on speech, contravenes the First Amendment.

Our precedent is to be respected unless the most convincing of reasons demonstrates that adherence to it puts us on a course that is sure error.

For the reasons above, it must be concluded that *Austin* was not well reasoned. The Government defends *Austin*, relying almost entirely on "the quid pro quo interest, the corruption interest or the shareholder interest," and not *Austin*'s expressed antidistortion rationale.

Austin is undermined by experience since its announcement. Political speech is so ingrained in our culture that speakers find ways to circumvent campaign finance laws. Our Nation's speech dynamic is changing, and informative voices should not have to circumvent onerous restrictions to exercise their First Amendment rights. Speakers have become adept at presenting citizens with sound bites, talking points, and scripted messages that dominate the 24-hour news cycle. Corporations, like individuals, do not have monolithic views. On certain topics corporations may possess valuable expertise, leaving them the best equipped to point out errors or fallacies in speech of all sorts, including the speech of candidates and elected officials.

Rapid changes in technology—and the creative dynamic inherent in the concept of free expression—counsel against upholding a law that restricts political speech in certain media or by certain speakers. Today, 30-second television ads may be the most effective way to convey a political message. Soon, however, it may be that Internet sources, such as blogs and social networking Web sites, will provide citizens with significant information about political candidates and issues. Yet, §441b would seem to ban a blog post expressly advocating the election or defeat of a candidate if that blog were created with corporate funds. The First Amendment does not permit Congress to make these categorical distinctions based on the corporate identity of the speaker and the content of the political speech.

Due consideration leads to this conclusion: *Austin* should be and now is overruled. We return to the principle established in *Buckley* and *Bellotti* that the Government may not suppress political speech on the basis of the speaker's corporate identity. No sufficient governmental interest justifies limits on the political speech of nonprofit or for-profit corporations.

Given our conclusion we are further required to overrule the part of *McConnell* that upheld BCRA §203's extension of §441b's restrictions on corporate independent expenditures. The *McConnell* Court relied on the antidistortion interest recognized in *Austin* to uphold a greater restriction on speech than the restriction upheld in *Austin,* and we have found this interest unconvincing and insufficient. This part of *McConnell* is now overruled.

Modern day movies, television comedies, or skits on Youtube.com might portray public officials or public policies in unflattering ways. Yet if a covered transmission during the blackout period creates the background for candidate endorsement or opposition, a felony occurs solely because a corporation, other than an exempt media corporation, has made the "purchase, payment, distribution, loan, advance, deposit, or gift of money or anything of value" in order to engage in political speech. Speech would be suppressed in the realm where its necessity is most evident: in the public dialogue preceding a real election. Governments are often hostile to speech, but under our law and our tradition it seems stranger than fiction for our Government to make this political speech a crime. Yet this is the statute's purpose and design.

Some members of the public might consider *Hillary* to be insightful and instructive; some might find it to be neither high art nor a fair discussion on how to set the Nation's course; still others simply might suspend judgment on these points but decide to think more about issues and candidates. Those choices and assessments, however, are not for the Government to make. "The First Amendment underwrites the freedom to experiment and to create in the realm of thought and speech. Citizens must be free to use new forms, and new forums, for the expression of ideas."

The judgment of the District Court is reversed with respect to the constitutionality of 2 U.S.C. §441b's restrictions on corporate independent expenditures.

It is so ordered.

13.3

Shelby County, Alabama v. Holder (2013)

A key part of the Voting Rights Act of 1965 was struck down in this 5–4 Supreme Court decision. The majority reasoned that the act singled out specific states and counties in the United States for special treatment in election administration based on 1960s data on racial discrimination. For Congress to continue to single out these same areas in the 2010s was in violation of the basic federal principles in the Constitution regarding states' equal authority to operate their own elections. This decision will likely grant states greater leeway in regulating the conduct of their elections, including requirements for voter eligibility. Critics of this decision claim that it negates the gains made in voting rights and once again gives states and counties license to discriminate against groups of voters as they had before the Voting Rights Act.

CHIEF JUSTICE ROBERTS delivered the opinion of the Court.

The Voting Rights Act of 1965 was enacted to address entrenched racial discrimination in voting, "an insidious and pervasive evil which had been perpetuated in certain parts of our country through unremitting and ingenious defiance of the Constitution." Section 2 of the Act, which bans any "standard, practice, or procedure" that "results in a denial or abridgement of the right of any citizen . . . to vote on account of race or color," applies nationwide, is permanent, and is not at issue in this case. Other sections apply only to some parts of the country. Section 4 of the Act provides the "coverage formula," defining the "covered jurisdictions" as States or political subdivisions that maintained tests or devices as prerequisites to voting, and had low voter registration or turnout, in the 1960s and early 1970s. In those covered jurisdictions, §5 of the Act provides that no change in voting procedures can take effect until approved by specified federal authorities in Washington, D.C. Such approval is known as "preclearance."

The coverage formula and preclearance requirement were initially set to expire after five years, but the Act has been reauthorized several times. In 2006, the Act was reauthorized for an additional 25 years, but the coverage formula was not changed. Coverage still turned on whether a jurisdiction had

From *Shelby County, Alabama v. Holder*, 570 U.S. ___ (2013).

a voting test in the 1960s or 1970s, and had low voter registration or turnout at that time. Shortly after the 2006 reauthorization, a Texas utility district sought to bail out from the Act's coverage and, in the alternative, challenged the Act's constitutionality. This Court resolved the challenge on statutory grounds, but expressed serious doubts about the Act's continued constitutionality. Petitioner Shelby County, in the covered jurisdiction of Alabama, sued the Attorney General in Federal District Court in Washington, D.C., seeking a declaratory judgment that §§ 4(b) and 5 are facially unconstitutional, as well as a permanent injunction against their enforcement. The District Court upheld the Act, finding that the evidence before Congress in 2006 was sufficient to justify reauthorizing §5 and continuing §4(b)'s coverage formula. The D.C. Circuit affirmed. After surveying the evidence in the record, that court accepted Congress's conclusion that §2 litigation remained inadequate in the covered jurisdictions to protect the rights of minority voters, that §5 was therefore still necessary, and that the coverage formula continued to pass constitutional muster.

The Voting Rights Act of 1965 employed extraordinary measures to address an extraordinary problem. Section 5 of the Act required States to obtain federal permission before enacting any law related to voting—a drastic departure from basic principles of federalism. And §4 of the Act applied that requirement only to some States—an equally dramatic departure from the principle that all States enjoy equal sovereignty. This was strong medicine, but Congress determined it was needed to address entrenched racial discrimination in voting, "an insidious and pervasive evil which had been perpetuated in certain parts of our country through unremitting and ingenious defiance of the Constitution." As we explained in upholding the law, "exceptional conditions can justify legislative measures not otherwise appropriate." Reflecting the unprecedented nature of these measures, they were scheduled to expire after five years. See Voting Rights Act of 1965, §4(a), 79 Stat. 438.

Nearly 50 years later, they are still in effect; indeed, they have been made more stringent, and are now scheduled to last until 2031. There is no denying, however, that the conditions that originally justified these measures no longer characterize voting in the covered jurisdictions. By 2009, "the racial gap in voter registration and turnout [was] lower in the States originally covered by §5 than it [was] nationwide." Since that time, Census Bureau data indicate that African-American voter turnout has come to exceed white voter turnout in five of the six States originally covered by §5, with a gap in the sixth State of less than one half of one percent.

At the same time, voting discrimination still exists; no one doubts that. The question is whether the Act's extraordinary measures, including its disparate treatment of the States, continue to satisfy constitutional requirements. As we put it a short time ago, "the Act imposes current burdens and must be justified by current needs."

In Northwest Austin, we stated that "the Act imposes current burdens and must be justified by current needs." 557 U.S., at 203. And we concluded that "a departure from the fundamental principle of equal sovereignty requires a showing that a statute's disparate geographic coverage is sufficiently related to the problem that it targets." Ibid. These basic principles guide our review of the question before us.

The Constitution and laws of the United States are "the supreme Law of the Land." U.S. Const., Art. VI, cl. 2. State legislation may not contravene federal law. The Federal Government does not, however, have a general right to review and veto state enactments before they go into effect. A proposal to grant such authority to "negative" state laws was considered at the Constitutional Convention, but rejected in favor of allowing state laws to take effect, subject to later challenge under the Supremacy Clause. Outside the strictures of the Supremacy Clause, States retain broad autonomy in structuring their governments and pursuing legislative objectives. Indeed, the Constitution provides that all powers not specifically granted to the Federal Government are reserved to the States or citizens. Amdt. 10. This "allocation of powers in our federal system preserves the integrity, dignity, and residual sovereignty of the States."

But the federal balance "is not just an end in itself: Rather, federalism secures to citizens the liberties that derive from the diffusion of sovereign power." Ibid. (internal quotation marks omitted). More specifically, "the Framers of the Constitution intended the States to keep for themselves, as provided in the Tenth Amendment, the power to regulate elections." Of course, the Federal Government retains significant control over federal elections. For instance, the Constitution authorizes Congress to establish the time and manner for electing Senators and Representatives. But States have "broad powers to determine the conditions under which the right of suffrage may be exercised."

Not only do States retain sovereignty under the Constitution, there is also a "fundamental principle of equal sovereignty" among the States. . . . Over a hundred years ago, this Court explained that our Nation "was and is a union of States, equal in power, dignity and authority." *Coyle v. Smith*, 221 U.S. 559, 567 (1911). Indeed, "the constitutional equality of the States is essential to the harmonious operation of the scheme upon which the Republic was organized."

The Voting Rights Act sharply departs from these basic principles. It suspends "all changes to state election law—however innocuous—until they have been precleared by federal authorities in Washington, D.C." States must beseech the Federal Government for permission to implement laws that they would otherwise have the right to enact and execute on their own, subject of course to any injunction in a §2 action. The Attorney General has 60 days to object to a preclearance request, longer if he requests more information. If a State seeks preclearance from a three-judge court, the process can take years.

And despite the tradition of equal sovereignty, the Act applies to only nine States (and several additional counties). While one State waits months or years and expends funds to implement a validly enacted law, its neighbor can typically put the same law into effect immediately, through the normal legislative process. Even if a noncovered jurisdiction is sued, there are important differences between those proceedings and preclearance proceedings; the preclearance proceeding "not only switches the burden of proof to the supplicant jurisdiction, but also applies substantive standards quite different from those governing the rest of the nation." All this explains why, when we first upheld the Act in 1966, we described it as "stringent" and "potent."

We recognized that it "may have been an uncommon exercise of congressional power," but concluded that "legislative measures not otherwise appropriate" could be justified by "exceptional conditions." We have since noted that the Act "authorizes federal intrusion into sensitive areas of state and local policymaking," and represents an "extraordinary departure from the traditional course of relations between the States and the Federal Government." As we reiterated in Northwest Austin, the Act constitutes "extraordinary legislation otherwise unfamiliar to our federal system."

In 1966, we found these departures from the basic features of our system of government justified. The "blight of racial discrimination in voting" had "infected the electoral process in parts of our country for nearly a century." Several States had enacted a variety of requirements and tests "specifically designed to prevent" African-Americans from voting. Case-by-case litigation had proved inadequate to prevent such racial discrimination in voting, in part because States "merely switched to discriminatory devices not covered by the federal decrees," "enacted difficult new tests," or simply "defied and evaded court orders." Shortly before enactment of the Voting Rights Act, only 19.4 percent of African-Americans of voting age were registered to vote in Alabama, only 31.8 percent in Louisiana, and only 6.4 percent in Mississippi. Id., at 313. Those figures were roughly 50 percentage points or more below the figures for whites. Ibid. In short, we concluded that "[u]nder the compulsion of these unique circumstances, Congress responded in a permissibly decisive manner." We also noted then and have emphasized since that this extraordinary legislation was intended to be temporary, set to expire after five years. At the time, the coverage formula—the means of linking the exercise of the unprecedented authority with the problem that warranted it—made sense. We therefore concluded that "the coverage formula [was] rational in both practice and theory." It accurately reflected those jurisdictions uniquely characterized by voting discrimination "on a pervasive scale," linking coverage to the devices used to effectuate discrimination and to the resulting disenfranchisement. The formula ensured that the "stringent remedies [were] aimed at areas where voting discrimination ha[d] been most flagrant."

Nearly 50 years later, things have changed dramatically. Shelby County contends that the preclearance requirement, even without regard to its disparate coverage, is now unconstitutional. Its arguments have a good deal of force. In the covered jurisdictions, "[v]oter turnout and registration rates now approach parity. Blatantly discriminatory evasions of federal decrees are rare. And minority candidates hold office at unprecedented levels." The tests and devices that blocked access to the ballot have been forbidden nationwide for over 40 years. Those conclusions are not ours alone. Congress said the same when it reauthorized the Act in 2006, writing that "[s]ignificant progress has been made in eliminating first generation barriers experienced by minority voters, including increased numbers of registered minority voters, minority voter turnout, and minority representation in Congress, State legislatures, and local elected offices." The House Report elaborated that "the number of African-Americans who are registered and who turn out to cast ballots has increased significantly over the last 40 years, particularly since 1982," and noted that "[i]n some circumstances, minorities register to vote and cast ballots at levels that surpass those of white voters." H.R. Rep. No. 109–478, p. 12 (2006). That Report also explained that there have been "significant increases in the number of African-Americans serving in elected offices"; more specifically, there has been approximately a 1,000 percent increase since 1965 in the number of African-American elected officials in the six States originally covered by the Voting Rights Act.

The 2004 figures come from the Census Bureau. Census Bureau data from the most recent election indicate that African-American voter turnout exceeded white voter turnout in five of the six States originally covered by §5, with a gap in the sixth State of less than one half of one percent. The preclearance statistics are also illuminating. In the first decade after enactment of §5, the Attorney General objected to 14.2 percent of proposed voting changes. In the last decade before reenactment, the Attorney General objected to a mere 0.16 percent.

There is no doubt that these improvements are in large part because of the Voting Rights Act. The Act has proved immensely successful at redressing racial discrimination and integrating the voting process.

When upholding the constitutionality of the coverage formula in 1966, we concluded that it was "rational in both practice and theory." The formula looked to cause (discriminatory tests) and effect (low voter registration and turnout), and tailored the remedy (preclearance) to those jurisdictions exhibiting both. By 2009, however, we concluded that the "coverage formula raise[d] serious constitutional questions."

As we explained, a statute's "current burdens" must be justified by "current needs," and any "disparate geographic coverage" must be "sufficiently related to the problem that it targets." Id., at 203. The coverage formula met that test in 1965, but no longer does so. Coverage today is based on decades-old data and eradicated practices. The formula captures States by reference to literacy tests and low voter registration and turnout in the 1960s and early 1970s. But such tests have been banned nationwide for over 40 years. And voter registration and turnout numbers in the covered States have risen dramatically in the years since. Racial disparity in those numbers was compelling evidence justifying the preclearance remedy and the coverage formula. There is no longer such a disparity. [H]istory did not end in 1965. By the time the Act was reauthorized in 2006, there had been 40 more years of it. In assessing the "current need" for a preclearance system that treats States differently from one another today, that history cannot be ignored. During that time, largely because of the Voting Rights Act, voting tests were abolished, disparities in voter registration and turnout due to race were erased, and African-Americans attained political office in record numbers. And yet the coverage formula that Congress reauthorized in 2006 ignores these developments, keeping the focus on decades-old data relevant to decades-old problems, rather than current data reflecting current needs.

The Fifteenth Amendment commands that the right to vote shall not be denied or abridged on account of race or color, and it gives Congress the power to enforce that command. The Amendment is not designed to punish for the past; its purpose is to ensure a better future. See *Rice v. Cayetano*, 528 U.S. 495, 512 (2000). ("Consistent with the design of the Constitution, the [Fifteenth] Amendment is cast in fundamental terms, terms transcending the particular controversy, which was the immediate impetus for its enactment.") To serve that purpose, Congress—if it is to divide the States—must identify those jurisdictions to be singled out on a basis that makes sense in light of current conditions. It cannot rely simply on the past. We made that clear in Northwest Austin, and we make it clear again today.

There is no valid reason to insulate the coverage formula from review merely because it was previously enacted 40 years ago. If Congress had started from scratch in 2006, it plainly could not have enacted the present coverage formula. It would have been irrational for Congress to distinguish between States in such a fundamental way based on 40-year-old data, when today's statistics tell an entirely different story. And it would have been irrational to base coverage on the use of voting tests 40 years ago, when such tests have been illegal since that time. But that is exactly what Congress has done.

Striking down an Act of Congress "is the gravest and most delicate duty that this Court is called on to perform." We do not do so lightly. That is why, in 2009, we took care to avoid ruling on the constitutionality of the Voting Rights Act when asked to do so, and instead resolved the case then before us on statutory grounds. But in issuing that decision, we expressed our broader concerns about the constitutionality of the Act. Congress could have updated the coverage formula at that time, but did not do so. Its failure to act leaves us today with no choice but to declare §4(b) unconstitutional. The formula in that section can no longer be used as a basis for subjecting jurisdictions to preclearance.

Our decision in no way affects the permanent, nationwide ban on racial discrimination in voting found in §2. We issue no holding on §5 itself, only on the coverage formula. Congress may draft another formula based on current conditions. Such a formula is an initial prerequisite to a determination that exceptional conditions still exist justifying such an "extraordinary departure from the traditional course of relations between the States and the Federal Government." Our country has changed, and while any racial discrimination in voting is too much, Congress must ensure that the legislation it passes to remedy that problem speaks to current conditions.

The judgment of the Court of Appeals is reversed.

It is so ordered.

13.4

RICHARD L. FOX AND JENNIFER L. LAWLESS

From "Gendered Perceptions and Political Candidacies: A Central Barrier to Women's Equality in Electoral Politics"

Using data from a survey of more than 2,000 people who were considered potential political candidates, Fox and Lawless provide evidence that shows that men's and women's self-perceptions differ in ways that matter a great deal in terms of political ambition. Men and women largely agree on the traits required to be successful in electoral politics, but women systematically believe that they themselves have fewer of those traits than men believe themselves to have. These differences go a long way toward explaining the persistence of a large gender disparity among elected politicians in the United States.

As of the 1970s, women occupied almost no major elective positions in U.S. political institutions. Ella Grasso, a Democrat from Connecticut, and Dixie Lee Ray, a Democrat from Washington, served as the only two women elected governor throughout the decade. Not until 1978 did Kansas Republican Nancy Kassebaum become the first woman elected to the Senate in her own right. By 1979, women comprised fewer than 5% of the seats in the U.S. House of Representatives, and only about 10% of state legislative positions across the country.

Although women's numeric representation is not quite as grave today, a striking gender imbalance persists. When the 111th Congress convened in January 2009, 83% of its members were men. Men occupy the governor's mansion in 44 of the 50 states, and they run City Hall in 93 of the 100 largest cities across the country. At least as important as women's continued under-representation in U.S. politics is evidence that points to stagnation in the numbers of women holding state and federal office. Since 2000, the number of women elected to state legislatures, which act as key launching pads to higher office, has reached a plateau. More Republican women won election to state assemblies in 1989 than in 2009. And even though the U.S. House of Representatives continues to experience incremental gains in female members, more women filed to run for Congress in 1992 than have ever since.

From Richard L. Fox and Jennifer L. Lawless, "Gendered Perceptions and Political Candidacies: A Central Barrier to Women's Equality in Electoral Politics," *American Journal of Political Science* 55, no. 1 (2011): 59–73.

Beginning in the 1970s, an academic subfield emerged to address women's political participation and representation. In particular, scholars began to offer a series of explanations for women's slow ascension into electoral politics. Much of the earliest research identified overt discrimination by voters and electoral gatekeepers as a critical impediment for women candidates (Diamond 1977; Githens and Prestage 1977; Rule 1981; Welch 1978). Other investigators pointed to "situational" factors as a prime explanation for the dearth of women in politics. Because women tended not to work in the fields of law and business—fields from which most congressional and state legislative candidates emerge—they often lacked the objective qualifications and economic autonomy to pursue elective office (Welch 1977). Political scientists also focused on structural barriers, most notably the incumbency advantage, which inhibited electoral opportunities for previously excluded groups such as women (Studlar and Welch 1990; Welch and Karnig 1979). Finally, scholars posited a broad socialization explanation for women's underrepresentation. Often reinforcing situational and structural obstacles, a culture of traditional gender role expectations hindered women's candidate emergence. Because women and men were expected to conform to traditional sex roles—women as the primary caretaker of the family and men as the public-oriented breadwinner—the notion of even well-situated women serving in positions of political power was anathema (Fowlkes, Perkins, and Tolleson Rinehart 1979; see also Jennings and Farah 1981).

Scholars in the women and politics subfield today continue to tackle the issue of women's underrepresentation. Indeed, since the 1970s, we have developed a much fuller understanding of the factors that impede women's election to public office. In the contemporary electoral environment, for instance, the explanatory power of overt discrimination has been largely discarded (e.g., Fox 2006; Lawless and Pearson 2008; Seltzer, Newman, and Leighton 1997).[1] Situational factors have also lost some of their strength in accounting for the low number of women in politics; women have substantially increased their presence in the pipeline professions that lead to political careers (American Bar Association 2006; Catalyst 2008). Even the power of institutional inertia has been called into question. Certainly, incumbency continues to pose a serious obstacle, particularly at the federal level (Palmer and Simon 2006). But 21 states enacted state legislative term limits throughout the 1990s, and scholars uncovered no evidence that combating incumbency with term limits improved women's representation (Kousser 2005). Thus, although structural barriers, situational factors, and, to a lesser degree, discrimination undoubtedly contribute to gender disparities in U.S. political institutions, the story is far more complicated.

As women's numeric representation continues to lag, despite their gains in educational and professional spheres, it is imperative to return to the one explanation that continues—at least in part—to elude us. We argue that one of the most fundamental barriers to women's representation derives from the patterns of traditional gender socialization to which scholars have long referred, but have been limited in studying empirically. Scholars suggest that women's historical exclusion from the political sphere, coupled with tenacious traditional gender role expectations, foster a masculinized ethos in electoral politics (e.g., Carroll 1994; Enloe 2004). Flammang (1997) argues, for instance, that men's dominance in political institutions that traditionally resisted women's inclusion makes it difficult for women to embrace themselves as politicians. Further, whereas men are taught to be confident, assertive, and self-promoting, cultural attitudes toward women as political leaders continue to leave an imprint suggesting to women—if even only subtly—that it is often inappropriate or undesirable to possess these characteristics. A political consequence of these patterns of gender socialization is that, over time, men develop a greater sense of efficacy as candidates. As Thomas posits, traditional socialization results in women's "lower levels of confidence about becoming candidates for political office" (2005, 12). Even women who are well positioned to offer themselves for public office often cannot envision themselves as candidates.

The theoretical connection between women and men's perceived efficacy as candidates and prospects for gender equality and parity in politics, therefore, is well established. And the implications of women's lower self-evaluations are far-reaching. As long as women are more likely than men to express doubts about their ability to run for office, then gender parity in politics will never materialize. Moreover, the degree of comfort and freedom women articulate regarding their entry into electoral politics serves as an important barometer of their full integration into all aspects of political life in the United States. Yet virtually no research systematically examines the ways that traditional gender socialization affects women and men's perceptions of themselves as candidates. In our previous work, which focuses explicitly on gender differences in the decision to run for office, we find that "the most potent explanation" for the gender gap in political ambition is that women are less likely than men to view themselves as "qualified" to enter the electoral arena (Lawless and Fox 2010). But we acknowledge that we can do little more than establish this important "qualifications gap." We can pinpoint neither the specific factors on which women and men rely, nor the calculus they employ, to arrive at their sense of efficacy as candidates. Moreover, we cannot examine the extent to which gendered perceptions, as opposed to concrete differences in women and men's politically relevant credentials, experiences, and proximity to the political sphere, drive gender differences in self-efficacy. Hence, the next critical step in evaluating the evolution of women's candidacies and gauging prospects for women's full inclusion in the political system is to make a systematic assessment of the degree to which socialized beliefs about candidate efficacy persist.

[We] use data from the second wave of the Citizen Political Ambition Panel Study—a national survey of more than 2,000 "potential candidates" in 2008—

to provide the first thorough analysis of the manner in which gender affects efficacy to run for office. Our findings reveal that, despite comparable credentials, professional backgrounds, and political experiences, highly accomplished women from both major political parties are substantially less likely than similarly situated men to perceive themselves as qualified to seek elective office. Importantly, we show that women and men rely on the same factors when evaluating themselves as candidates; but women are less likely than men to believe they meet these criteria. Not only are women more likely than men to doubt that they have the skills and traits necessary to succeed in electoral politics, but they are also more likely to doubt their abilities to engage in the mechanics involved in a political campaign. These empirical findings are critical because the perceptual differences we uncover account for much of the gender gap in potential candidates' self-efficacy and ultimately hinder women's prospects for political equality.

THE GENDER GAP IN EFFICACY AS A CANDIDATE: BACKGROUND AND HYPOTHESES

Many of the perceptions women and men hold about the political process are deeply engrained by a culture that tends to reinforce traditional sex-role expectations and women's marginalization in politics (Enloe 2004; Freedman 2002). These perceptions are essential when investigating women and men's self-efficacy as candidates because they suggest that, regardless of the concrete qualifications and credentials women and men possess, they may not view themselves the same way. Among individuals who have already entered politics as candidates and elected officials, for instance, researchers uncover a gendered perceptual lens through which women and men perform their leadership roles and pursue their policy goals (Thomas 2005). Limited research also points to gender differences in how elected officials conceive of climbing the political career ladder (Bledsoe and Herring 1990; Fulton et al. 2006). And our earlier work provides anecdotal evidence that perceptions underpin gender differences in potential candidates' attitudes about their qualifications to run for office (Lawless and Fox 2010). For the most part, though, studies of political ambition tend to overlook gendered perceptions and examine, instead, the manner in which the political opportunity structure influences the decision to run for office. Consequently, Githens (2003) identifies potential candidates' perceptions of the electoral process and their prospects for participating in it as a critical, yet unexplored question in the study of women's candidate emergence.

In gauging how socialized gendered perceptions may affect efficacy to serve as a candidate, we rely on an array of empirical studies from political science, social psychology, business, economics, and education. This body of literature establishes at least two types of gendered perceptions that, even among successful professionals, may inhibit women's views of themselves and their prospects for electoral success.

Perceptions of Politically Relevant Skills and Traits. The first type of gendered perceptions that may affect efficacy to serve as a candidate pertains to individuals' assessments of their skills and traits. Evaluating oneself as a potential candidate, after all, involves personal reflection of talents and shortcomings. Though not directly related to politics, investigators from a variety of disciplines provide evidence to suggest that these self-assessments will ultimately depress women's levels of efficacy.

Turning first to gender differences in skills-based measures, researchers find that women are more likely than men to diminish and undervalue their professional skills and achievements. Studies of gender differences in academic abilities provide a clear example. By the time of adolescence, male students rate their mathematical abilities higher than female students do, despite no sex differences in objective indicators of competence (Wigfield, Eccles, and Pintrich 1996). In the areas of language arts, male and female students offer comparable self-assessments, although objective indicators reveal that female students are actually higher achieving in these fields (Pajares 2002). Many of these misconceptions persist into adulthood, percolating up even to high-level professionals who have succeeded in traditionally male domains (Beyer and Bowden 1997; Brownlow, Whitener, and Rupert 1998). Controlling for a series of job-related functions and work experience, for instance, female MBAs accepted salary offers that were lower than the offers accepted by their male counterparts (Bowles, Babcock, and McGinn 2005). In the absence of clear compensation standards, women are also more likely than men to express lower career-entry and career-peak pay expectations (Bylsma and Major 1992).

Gender differences exist not only in how women and men perceive their objective skills, but also in the confidence they exhibit regarding their credentials, backgrounds, propensity to take risks, and willingness to compete. Studies reveal that, in general, men are more likely than women to express confidence in skills they do not possess and overconfidence in skills they do possess (Kling et al. 1999). Men tend to be more "self-congratulatory," whereas women tend to be more modest about their achievements (Wigfield, Eccles, and Pintrich 1996). Men tend to overestimate their intelligence, while women tend to underestimate theirs (Beloff 1992; Furnham and Rawles 1995). Men often fail to incorporate criticism into their self-evaluations, whereas women tend to be strongly influenced by negative appraisals of their capabilities (Roberts 1991). Further, a review of 150 studies in psychology concludes that in almost all personal and professional decisions, women exhibit significantly higher levels of risk aversion than do men (Byrnes, Miller, and Schafer 1999). Perhaps because of this tendency, investigators find, when comparing professional performance in competitive and noncompetitive environments, that men are more likely than women to seek out competitive environments and to exude confidence when competing (Gneezy, Niederle, and Rustichini 2003; Niederle and Vesterlund 2007, 2010).

It follows, therefore, that any gender gap in potential candidates' self-efficacy may be driven by differences in how women and men perceive their politically relevant skills and traits.

Perceptions of Campaigns and the Electoral Environment. The second type of gendered perceptions that likely affect efficacy to serve as a candidate concerns the political environment in which women and men would compete. Not only must prospective candidates consider how they will be treated in the political sphere, but they also must assess how they would feel about engaging in the nuts and bolts of a campaign. Even though women perform as well as men on Election Day, women's historic exclusion from the political sphere may underscore their perceptions and work to women's detriment.

A small body of literature pertaining to perceptions of the political environment suggests that when women perceive gender bias in public life, they often withdraw. Political scientists have identified this pattern both within the bureaucracy (Dolan 2000; Naff 1995) and elective offices (Blair and Stanley 1991). This withdrawal, which may be a rational response to dealing with a political environment that has traditionally not embraced women, can also reinforce women's exclusion and perpetuate the notion that the electoral arena is biased against them. Indeed, as recently as 2008, pollsters uncovered that 51% of Americans believed that the country was not "ready to elect a woman to high office" (Pew 2008). Further, 40% of women did not think Hillary Rodham Clinton was treated fairly in her presidential campaign (Lifetime Network 2008). These aggregate levels of perceived bias likely contribute to the gender gap in candidate efficacy.

Gender differences in attitudes toward competition, coupled with the experiences of actual candidates, may further lead women to doubt their abilities to succeed. After all, female congressional candidates face more primary competition than do their male counterparts (Lawless and Pearson 2008). Geographic differences facilitate women's election in some congressional districts, but lessen their chances of success in others (Palmer and Simon 2006). Female candidates often recount bias in the press coverage they receive (Rausch, Rozell, and Wilson 1999). And women perceive fundraising as more difficult than men do (Fox 1997), ultimately devoting more time to it (Jenkins 2007). Certainly, women and men who have achieved high levels of professional success have, to some extent, already exhibited a willingness to compete. But if women are cognizant of a more difficult electoral process, then they may be more inclined than men to doubt that they would excel at typical campaign activities.

When assessing their efficacy as potential candidates, perceptions of gender bias, heightened electoral competition, and more challenging campaign dynamics may lead many women to conclude—perhaps rightfully so—that they have to be better than the average man to succeed. Accordingly, women may be less likely than men to express self-efficacy and consider themselves qualified to run for office.

Based on our review of research from a variety of disciplines, we test two central hypotheses. First, we expect to uncover a baseline gender gap in potential candidates' efficacy to run for office, regardless of their objective qualifications and credentials:

> *Gender Gap in Self-Efficacy Hypothesis:* There is a gender gap in self-efficacy among potential candidates, even after controlling for detailed measures of professional experiences, credentials, and political proximity.

Second, we expect that the deeply internalized perceptions of gender roles and politics that lead men to envision the notion of emerging as a candidate will lead women to doubt their abilities to enter the political sphere. We break this hypothesis into two parts:

> *Gendered Perceptions Hypothesis*: The gender gap in self-efficacy will be explained by:

> a. gender differences in potential candidates' perceptions of their political skills and traits.
> b. gender differences in potential candidates' perceptions of the campaign and electoral environments in which they would compete.

In short, and to borrow from Githens, we expect the "gendered nature of evaluative standards" (2003, 43) to remain problematic even for women who have already achieved high levels of success. Operationalizing these hypotheses allows for the first in-depth assessment of the manner in which patterns of traditional gender socialization influence potential candidates' views of their suitability to run for elective office.

RESEARCH DESIGN AND DATASET: THE CITIZEN POLITICAL AMBITION PANEL STUDY

We rely on data from the second wave of the Citizen Political Ambition Panel Study to examine potential candidates' self-efficacy. This national panel—the first wave of which we conducted in 2001, and the second wave of which we completed in 2008—serves as the only broad random sample of equally credentialed women and men who are well positioned to serve as future candidates for all elective offices. We drew our 2001 "candidate eligibility pool" from the professions that yield the highest proportion of political candidates for congressional and state legislative positions: law, business, education, and political activism (Dolan and Ford 1997; Moncrief, Squire, and Jewell 2001). We disproportionately stratified by sex, so the sample includes roughly equal numbers of women and men. The women and men are comparable in education, profession, income, and region, and they also hold similar employment roles, high degrees of professional success, and heightened levels of political interest and participation.[2]

The 2,036 respondents who completed the 2008 survey are a representative subsample of the original eligibility pool. Controlling for sex, race, and profession, individuals who expressed political ambition in 2001 were no more likely than respondents who had never considered a candidacy to complete the 2008 survey. Similarly, potential candidates who reported high levels of political interest and activism at the time of the 2001 survey were no more likely than those who did not to respond to the 2008 questionnaire (regression results not shown). No significant demographic or professional factors distinguish the 2001 and 2008 samples. Further, the women and men who completed the second survey are well matched in race, education, income, and geography. Women are, however, more likely to be Democrats, while men are more likely to be Republicans. The women are also, on average, three years younger than the men, a probable result of women's relatively recent entry into the fields of law and business. Our empirical analyses are sensitive to these differences and always control for them.

Our method and sample allow for a comprehensive assessment of gender differences in self-efficacy. The results from the 2001 survey uncovered the gender gap in respondents' perceptions of their qualifications to run for office. But the survey was limited in the extent to which it could shed light on the reasons for the gender gap. The original survey did not ask questions about respondents' objective credentials, political experiences, or proximity to the political arena. Similarly, it failed to gauge respondents' assessments of their own politically relevant skills and traits, or their perceptions of electoral competition. Thus, we included in the 2008 survey detailed batteries of questions about proximity to politics, political skills and traits, attitudes toward campaigning, and perceptions of electoral competition and the political process. Accordingly, our analysis relies on the data collected from only those respondents who completed the 2008 survey.

FINDINGS AND ANALYSIS

Establishing the Gender Gap in Self-Efficacy in the Candidate Eligibility Pool

To examine gender differences in how potential candidates assess their self-efficacy to run for office, we asked respondents a series of questions about their political qualifications. The broad measure of efficacy on which we rely gauges where potential candidates place themselves on a continuum from "not at all qualified" to "very qualified" to launch a candidacy. The data presented in the top half of Table [1] reveal that men are roughly 50% more likely than women to consider themselves "very qualified" to seek an elective position. Women are twice as likely as men to assert that they are "not at all

TABLE [1]   Gender and Self-Efficacy in the Candidate Eligibility Pool

	Women	*Men*
How qualified are you to run for public office?		
Very Qualified	21%	33%
Qualified	35	40
Somewhat Qualified	32	21
Not at All Qualified	12	6
How qualified are you to hold public office?		
Very Qualified	27%	40%
Qualified	36	40
Somewhat Qualified	27	17
Not at All Qualified	9	4
N	862	1,003

NOTE: Chi-square tests comparing women and men are significant at least at $p < .05$ for all comparisons.

qualified" to run for office. Similar gender gaps appear when we consider women and men's assessments of whether they are qualified to perform the job of an elected official. Whereas 80% of men contend that they are "qualified" or "very qualified" to do the job of an officeholder, fewer than two-thirds of women assess themselves this way. Women are more than twice as likely as men to rate themselves as "not at all qualified" to perform the job. This gender gap in self-efficacy, which exists across professions, is roughly equal for Democrats and Republicans.[3] Further, the gap does not result from women envisioning running for higher offices than men. In fact, women are more likely than men to refer to local offices when expressing levels of political ambition (difference significant at $p < .01$).

The . . . gender gap in respondents' self-efficacy demonstrates that women are less likely than men to perceive themselves as qualified to enter the electoral environment. We would expect, however, that respondents who are politically involved may be more likely than those who are not to have a sense of efficacy to serve as candidates. In order to confirm the *Gender Gap in Self-Efficacy Hypothesis*, therefore, the gap must withstand a series of controls for measures of political proximity, campaign experience, and politically relevant credentials.

▪   ▪   ▪

[Our] results indicate that differences in women and men's assessments of their political qualifications do not derive from differences in their actual credentials. The sex of the potential candidate remains a . . . predictor of self-efficacy and withstands the series of rigorous controls. Whereas the "average" male respondent has a 0.077 likelihood of considering himself "not at all qualified" to run for office, the "average" female respondent's likelihood of assessing this way is 0.122.[4] At the other end of qualifications spectrum, a typical male potential candidate has a 0.174 predicted probability of considering himself "very qualified" to run for office, compared to a typical female potential candidate's predicted probability of 0.106. Put somewhat differently, women are nearly 60% more likely than similarly situated men to consider themselves "not at all qualified" to run for office; men are nearly two-thirds more likely than their female counterparts to evaluate themselves as "very qualified" to enter the electoral arena. Comparing the effect of sex relative to other factors highlights its importance; the independent, substantive effect of sex exceeds all of the political proximity and professional credentials variables. Indeed, the only predictor of qualifications with a larger relative effect than sex—albeit only slightly larger—is political recruitment.

■　■　■

When comparing women and men in the candidate eligibility pool, we confirm the *Gender Gap in Self-Efficacy Hypothesis*. The landscape for women candidates may be a shifting terrain with more women seeking and winning office than was the case 20 years ago. And women may have made progress in acquiring the backgrounds, experiences, and connections on which politicians traditionally have relied. Yet women remain less likely than men to report a sense of self-efficacy as a candidate. Because the gender gap persists despite professional and political similarities, we must move beyond objective credentials and assess respondents' perceptions of themselves navigating the political sphere.

EXPLAINING THE GENDER GAP IN SELF-EFFICACY IN THE CANDIDATE ELIGIBILITY POOL

Our *Gendered Perceptions Hypothesis* asserts that the gender gap in self-efficacy results from differences in women and men's perceptions of themselves and the electoral arena. Thus, we asked respondents 17 questions about a variety of activities and characteristics associated with being a candidate for elective office. The first series of questions we posed focuses on respondents' assessments of their political skills and traits. These measures allow us to test the first part of our hypothesis—that personal self-assessments drive the gender gap in self-efficacy. The second set of questions pertains to assessments of the political arena in which candidates compete. Here, we can examine the second part of the hypothesis—that perceptions of the political environment significantly affect efficacy to serve as a candidate. . . .

Turning first to perceptions of political skills and traits, women in our pool of potential candidates rate themselves less favorably than do men across the board. We uncover one of the largest gender differences when we focus on perceptions of political traits; women are 19 percentage points more likely than men to doubt that they have thick enough skin to run for office. Women are also less likely than men to perceive themselves as possessing all six of the skills about which we inquired. These perceptual differences are striking in light of women and men's actual skills and experiences. Women and men in the sample are . . . indistinguishable from one another in terms of the key skills necessary to run for office. Thirty-three percent of women and 35% of men have conducted extensive policy research; 65% of women and 69% of men regularly engage in public speaking; and 69% of women and 64% of men report experience soliciting funds. . . .

The gender differences are just as robust when we focus on respondents' perceptions of the electoral arena. . . . Women are significantly more likely than men to view most of the mechanics of running for office, particularly negative campaigning, as deterrents to a candidacy. Further, despite the fact that women and men in the sample are similarly dispersed geographically, women are more likely than men to perceive a biased and competitive electoral environment. . . .

It is important to recognize that the gender gap in self-efficacy may be a result not only of women's under-assessments of their skills and traits, but also men's tendency to overestimate their political skills. This phenomenon would be consistent with findings from the aforementioned studies in the fields of business and education. In a similar vein, men's longer-term presence and success in top positions in business and law may result in heightened levels of confidence about entering the political arena, also a male-dominated environment. In either case, though, women and men perceive political reality and their ability to succeed in the political system through a gendered lens.

▪   ▪   ▪

CONCLUSION AND DISCUSSION

Based on the results of the second wave of the Citizen Political Ambition Panel Study, we establish and explicate the gender gap in self-efficacy among potential candidates. The women and men we surveyed share professional and educational backgrounds. They are well matched in objective indicators and experiences typical of actual candidates and officeholders. And they rely on the same calculus when evaluating their qualifications to run for office. Yet women are significantly more likely than men to dismiss their qualifications, and significantly less likely than their male counterparts to express self-efficacy to enter the electoral arena. Once we account for gender differences in perceptions of the skill sets and characteristics necessary to run for office, however, the gender gap in self-efficacy decreases considerably. In fact, a potential candidate's sex does not exert an independent effect on the likelihood of assessing as "not at all qualified" to run for office. The empirical findings delineate several factors that work to women's detriment; gender differences in perceptions of political skills and traits, as well as what it would be like to engage in the mechanics of a campaign, depress women's self-efficacy.

Our findings strongly suggest that traditional gender role socialization continues to perpetuate a culture in which women remain unaccustomed to entering the electoral arena. Women's lower self-assessments of their political skills are consistent with a political culture that has not embraced women in the public sphere. In addition, women's perceptions of their politically relevant traits reflect a heightened level of discomfort with entering politics, also a likely result of traditional gender role orientations that discourage women's candidacies.

■   ■   ■

[Our] results provide strong support for the *Gendered Perceptions Hypothesis*. Women and men who are equally and objectively qualified to run for office perceive neither themselves nor the political arena the same way. Similar professional credentials, economic autonomy, and political experience, alone, cannot close the gender gap in self-efficacy. These findings are vital because the socialized perceptual differences we uncover translate into a formidable hurdle women must overcome when behaving as strategic politicians and navigating the candidate emergence process. Self-efficacy, after all, is a statistically and substantively significant predictor of whether a respondent ever considered running for office, actually ran for office, took any concrete steps that tend to precede a campaign, or expressed interest in running for office at some point in the future (regression results not shown).

NOTES

1. In dismissing the impact of discrimination, we do not mean to overlook the pockets of bias that researchers continue to uncover or the complex role that gender continues to play in electoral politics. Surveys of local party officials reveal that some electoral gatekeepers appear to prefer male candidates (Niven 1998; Sanbonmatsu 2006). Examinations of campaigns show that gender stereotypes affect media coverage (Fowler and Lawless 2009; Fox 1997). And voters continue to rely on stereotypical conceptions of women and men's traits, issue expertise, and policy positions (Koch 2000; Lawless 2004).

2. See online supplemental information for a description of the research design and sample.

3. Republican women are twice as likely as Republican men to self-assess as "not at all qualified" (10% of women, compared to 5% of men), and 32% of Republican men, compared to 20% of Republican women, consider themselves "very qualified" to run for office. Among Democrats, 12% of women, compared to 7% of men, self-assess as "not at all qualified," and 35% of men, but only 20% of women, consider themselves "very qualified" to run for office.

4. Our analysis is based on setting all continuous independent variables to their sample means and dummy variables to their sample modes.

REFERENCES

American Bar Association. 2006. *Charting Our Progress: The Status of Women in the Profession Today.* Chicago: American Bar Association Commission of Women in the Profession.

Beloff, Halla. 1992. "Mother, Father and Me: Our IQ." *Psychologist* 5: 309–11.

Beyer, Sylvia, and Edward M. Bowden. 1997. "Gender Differences in Self-Perceptions: Convergent Evidence from Three Measures of Accuracy and Bias." *Personality and Social Psychology Bulletin* 23 (2): 157–72.

Blair, Diane D., and Jeanie R. Stanley. 1991. "Personal Relationships and Legislative Power: Male and Female Perceptions." *Legislative Studies Quarterly* 16 (4): 495–507.

Bledsoe, Timothy, and Mary Herring. 1990. "Victims of Circumstances: Women in Pursuit of Political Office." *American Political Science Review* 84 (1): 213–23.

Bowles, Hannah Riley, Linda C. Babcock, and Kathleen McGinn. 2005. "Constraints and Triggers: Situational Mechanics of Gender in Negotiation." *Journal of Personality and Social Psychology* 89 (6): 951–65.

Brownlow, Sheila, Rebecca Whitener, and Janet M. Rupert. 1998. "I'll Take Gender Differences for $1000! Domain-Specific Intellectual Success on 'Jeopardy.'" *Sex Roles: A Journal of Research* 38 (3): 269–86.

Bylsma, Wayne H., and Brenda Major. 1992. "Two Routes to Eliminating Gender Differences in Personal Entitlement: Social Comparisons and Performance Evaluations." *Psychology of Women Quarterly* 16 (2): 193–200.

Byrnes, James, David C. Miller, and William D. Schafer. 1999. "Gender Differences in Risk-Taking: A Meta-Analysis." *Psychological Bulletin* 125 (3): 367–83.

Carroll, Susan J. 1994. *Women as Candidates in American Politics.* 2nd ed. Bloomington: Indiana University Press.

Catalyst. 2008. "Catalyst 2008 Census of the Fortune 500." New York: Catalyst. December 10.

Diamond, Irene. 1977. *Sex Roles in the Statehouse.* New Haven, CT: Yale University Press.

Dolan, Julie. 2000. "The Senior Executive Service: Gender, Attitudes and Representative Bureaucracy." *Journal of Public Administration Research and Theory* 10 (3): 513–29.

Dolan, Kathleen, and Lynne E. Ford. 1997. "Change and Continuity among Women State Legislators: Evidence from Three Decades." *Political Research Quarterly* 50 (1): 137–51.

Enloe, Cynthia. 2004. *The Curious Feminist.* Berkeley: University of California Press.

Flammang, Janet. 1997. *Women's Political Voice: How Women Are Transforming the Practice and Study of Politics.* Philadelphia: Temple University Press.

Fowler, Linda L., and Jennifer L. Lawless. 2009. "Looking for Sex in All the Wrong Places: Press Coverage and the Electoral Fortunes of Gubernatorial Candidates." *Perspectives on Politics* 7 (3): 519–37.

Fowlkes, Diane L., Jerry Perkins, and Sue Tolleson Rinehart. 1979. "Gender Roles and Party Roles." *American Political Science Review* 73 (3): 772–80.

Fox, Richard L. 1997. *Gender Dynamics in Congressional Elections.* Thousand Oaks, CA: Sage.

Fox, Richard L. 2006. "Congressional Elections: Where Are We on the Road to Gender Parity?" In *Gender and Elections: Shaping the Future of American Politics,* edited by S. Carroll and R. Fox. New York: Cambridge University Press, 97–166.

Freedman, Estelle. 2002. *No Turning Back*. New York: Ballantine Books.

Fulton, Sarah A., Cherie D. Maestas, L. Sandy Maisel, and Walter J. Stone. 2006. "The Sense of a Woman: Gender, Ambition, and the Decision to Run for Congress." *Political Research Quarterly* 59 (2): 235–48.

Furnham, Adrian, and Richard Rawles. 1995. "Sex Differences in the Estimation of Intelligence." *Journal of Social Behavior and Personality* 10: 741–48.

Githens, Marianne. 2003. "Accounting for Women's Political Involvement: The Perennial Problem of Recruitment." In *Women and American Politics*, edited by S. Carroll. New York: Oxford University Press, 33–52.

Githens, Marianne, and Jewel L. Prestage. 1977. *A Portrait of Marginality: The Political Behavior of the American Woman*. New York: Longman.

Gneezy, Uri, Muriel Niederle, and Aldo Rustichini. 2003. "Performance in Competitive Environments: Gender Differences." *Quarterly Journal of Economics* 118 (3): 1049–74.

Jenkins, Shannon. 2007. "A Woman's Work Is Never Done? Fundraising Perceptions and Effort Among Female State Legislative Candidates." *Political Research Quarterly* 60 (2): 230–39.

Jennings, M. Kent, and Barbara G. Farah. 1981. "Social Roles and Political Resources: An Over-Time Study of Men and Women in Party Elites." *American Journal of Political Science* 25 (3): 462–82.

Kling, Kristen C., Janet Hyde, Carolin Showers, and Brenda N. Buswell. 1999. "Gender Differences in Self-Esteem: A Meta-Analysis." *Psychological Bulletin* 125 (4): 470–500.

Koch, Jeffrey W. 2000. "Do Citizens Apply Gender Stereotypes to Infer Candidates' Ideological Orientations?" *Journal of Politics* 62 (2): 414–29.

Kousser, Thad. 2005. *Term Limits and the Dismantling of State Legislative Professionalism*, New York: Cambridge University Press.

Lawless, Jennifer L. 2004. "Women, War, and Winning Elections: Gender Stereotyping in the Post September 11th Era." *Political Research Quarterly* 53 (3): 479–90.

Lawless, Jennifer L., and Richard F. Fox. 2010. *It Still Takes a Candidate: Why Women Don't Run for Office*. New York: Cambridge University Press.

Lawless, Jennifer L., and Kathryn Pearson. 2008. "The Primary Reason for Women's Under-Representation: Re-Evaluating the Conventional Wisdom." *Journal of Politics* 70 (1): 67–82.

Lifetime Networks. 2008. "New Lifetime Every Woman Counts Poll Sheds Light on Women's Reactions to Historic Presidential Election, Their Agenda for New Leaders and the Future of Female Candidates." *PR Newswire,* November 24.

Moncrief, Gary F., Peverill Squire, and Malcolm E. Jewell. 2001. *Who Runs for the Legislature?* Upper Saddle River, NJ: Prentice Hall.

Naff, Katherine C. 1995. "Subjective vs. Objective Discrimination in Government: Adding to the Picture of Barriers to the Advancement of Women." *Political Research Quarterly* 48 (3): 535–58.

Niederle, Muriel, and Lise Vesterlund. 2007. "Do Women Shy Away from Competition? Do Men Compete Too Much?" *Quarterly Journal of Economics* 122 (3): 1067–1101.

Niederle, Muriel, and Lise Vesterlund. 2010. "Explaining the Gender Gap in Math Test Scores: The Role of Competition." *Journal of Economic Perspectives* 24 (2).

Niven, David. 1998. "Party Elites and Women Candidates: The Shape of Bias." *Women & Politics* 19 (2): 57–80.

Pajares, Frank. 2002. "Gender and Perceived Self-Efficacy in Self-Regulated Learning." *Theory Into Practice* 41 (2): 116–25.

Palmer, Barbara, and Dennis Simon. 2006. *Breaking the Political Glass Ceiling: Women and Congressional Elections.* New York: Routledge.

Pew Research Center. 2008. "Men or Women? Who's the Better Leader?" *Social and Demographic Trends,* August 25.

Rausch, John D., Mark Rozell, and Harry L. Wilson. 1999. "When Women Lose: A Case Study of Media Coverage of Two Gubernatorial Campaigns." *Women & Politics* 20 (4): 1–22.

Roberts, T. 1991. "Gender and the Influences of Evaluation on Self-Assessment in Achievement Settings." *Psychological Bulletin* 109 (2): 297–308.

Rule, Wilma. 1981. "Why Women Don't Run: The Critical Contextual Factors in Women's Legislative Recruitment." *Western Political Quarterly* 34 (March): 60–77.

Sanbonmatsu, Kira. 2006. *Where Women Run: Gender and Party in the American States.* Ann Arbor: University of Michigan.

Seltzer, R. A., J. Newman, and M. Leighton. 1997. *Sex as a Political Variable.* Boulder, CO: Lynne Rienner.

Studlar, Donley T., and Susan Welch. 1990. "Multi-Member Districts and the Representation of Women: Evidence from Britain and the United States." *Journal of Politics* 52 (2): 391–412.

Thomas, Sue. 2005. "Introduction: Women and Elective Office: Past, Present, and Future." In *Women and Elective Office,* 2nd ed., edited by S. Thomas and C. Wilcox. New York: Oxford University Press, 3–25.

Welch, Susan. 1977. "Women as Political Animals? A Test of Some Explanations for Male-Female Political Participation Differences." *American Journal of Political Science* 21 (4): 711–30.

Welch, Susan. 1978. "Recruitment of Women to Public Office." *Western Political Quarterly* 31 (2): 372–80.

Welch, Susan, and Albert K. Karnig. 1979. "Correlates of Female Office Holding in City Politics." *Journal of Politics* 41 (2): 478–91.

Wigfield, Allan, Jacquelynne S. Eccles, and Paul R. Pintrich. 1996. "Development between the Ages of 11 and 25." In *Handbook of Educational Psychology,* edited by D. C. Berliner and R. C. Calfee. New York: Macmillan, 148–85.

13.5

CHRISTOPHER ACHEN AND LARRY M. BARTELS

From *Democracy for Realists: Why Elections Do Not Produce Responsive Government*

Achen and Bartels take a pessimistic view of whether voters in a democracy understand enough to choose their leaders wisely. The authors summarize decades of research showing that voters misunderstand the basic elements of democracy, that they are swayed at election time by irrelevant information, and that they often choose leaders against their own interests. This selection challenges us to depart from "romantic" views about democracy and instead to confront the reality that elections often do not work to produce effective, responsive government.

In the conventional view, democracy begins with the voters. Ordinary people have preferences about what their government should do. They choose leaders who will do those things, or they enact their preferences directly in referendums. In either case, what the majority wants becomes government policy—a highly attractive prospect in light of most human experience with governments. Democracy makes the people the rulers, and legitimacy derives from their consent. In Abraham Lincoln's stirring words from the Gettysburg Address, democratic government is "of the people, by the people, and for the people." That way of thinking about democracy has passed into everyday wisdom, not just in the United States but in a great many other countries around the globe. It constitutes a kind of "folk theory" of democracy, a set of accessible, appealing ideas assuring people that they live under an ethically defensible form of government that has their interests at heart.[1]

Unfortunately, while the folk theory of democracy has flourished as an ideal, its credibility has been severely undercut by a growing body of scientific evidence presenting a different and considerably darker view of democratic politics. That evidence demonstrates that the great majority of citizens pay little attention to politics. At election time, they are swayed by how they feel about "the nature of the times," especially the current state of the economy, and by political loyalties typically acquired in childhood. Those loyalties, not the facts of political life and government policy, are the primary drivers of

From Christopher Achen and Larry M. Bartels, *Democracy for Realists: Why Elections Do Not Produce Responsive Government* (Princeton, NJ: Princeton University Press, 2016).

political behavior. Election outcomes turn out to be largely random events from the viewpoint of contemporary democratic theory. That is, elections are well determined by powerful forces, but those forces are not the ones that current theories of democracy believe should determine how elections come out. Hence the old frameworks will no longer do.

We want to persuade the reader to think about democracy in a fundamentally different way. . . .

TWO CONTEMPORARY APPROACHES TO DEMOCRACY

What are the conventional notions of democracy that we argue have outlived their time? We consider two main types of theory, one popular with broad swatches of democratic society and a second whose appeal is largely confined to scholars specializing in the study of elections.[2]

The first model, which we refer to as the *populist* ideal of democracy, emphasizes the role of ordinary citizens in "determining the policies" of democratic communities (Dahl 1998, 37–38). As we will see, this populist notion of popular sovereignty has inspired a good deal of sophisticated academic thinking derived from Enlightenment concepts of human nature and the political views of 19th-century British liberalism. In its less rarified forms it has also undergirded the folk theory of democracy celebrated in much Fourth of July rhetoric. As the homespun poet of democracy Carl Sandburg (1936) proclaimed, "The People, Yes."

But *how* precisely shall the people govern according to the populist theory? [There are] two different accounts of how populist democracy might work. In one, the public "decide[s] issues through the election of individuals who are to assemble in order to carry out its will," as an unsympathetic critic of this account put it (Schumpeter 1942, 250). In the other, the people rule through "direct democracy," choosing policies themselves via initiative and referendum procedures. Both representative democracy and direct democracy loom large in popular understanding of democratic self-government. But as we shall see, the assumptions undergirding both versions of populist democracy are highly unrealistic.

The second contemporary model in defense of democracy is less widely popular, though more persuasive to most political scientists. This model focuses on elections as mechanisms for *leadership selection*. In contrast to the populist model, which he characterized as "the classical doctrine of democracy," Joseph Schumpeter (1942, 269) famously defined the democratic method as "that institutional arrangement for arriving at political decisions in which individuals acquire the power to decide by means of a competitive struggle for the people's vote."[3] Dispensing with the notion that "the people itself decide issues" by electing those who will "carry out its will," Schumpeter (1942, 284–285) insisted that "democracy does not mean and cannot mean that the people actually rule in any obvious sense of the terms 'people' and 'rule.' Democracy means only that the people have the opportunity of accepting or refusing the men who are to rule them."

Schumpeter gave little attention to the criteria by which voters would—or *should*—choose among potential rulers. However, subsequent scholars have fleshed out his account. The most influential model of democratic selection in contemporary political science is the *retrospective theory of voting*, which portrays "the electorate in its great, and perhaps principal, role as an appraiser of past events, past performance, and past actions" (Key 1966, 61). In this view, election outcomes hinge not on ideas, but on public approval or disapproval of the actual performance of incumbent political leaders. This model of democratic accountability appeals to skeptical scholars because it puts much less pressure on the voters to have elaborate, well-informed policy views. Ordinary citizens are allowed to drive the automobile of state simply by looking in the rearview mirror. Alas, we find that this works about as well in government as it would on the highway. Thus, we . . . argue that this second model of democracy, like the first, crumbles upon empirical inspection.

Hence we must think again. . . . A dramatically different framework is needed to make sense of how democracy actually works. We . . . argue that voters, even the most informed voters, typically make choices not on the basis of policy preferences or ideology, but on the basis of who they are—their social identities. In turn, those social identities shape how they think, what they think, and where they belong in the party system. But if voting behavior primarily reflects and reinforces voters' social loyalties, it is a mistake to suppose that elections result in popular control of public policy. . . . The [argument] may not be very comfortable or comforting. Nonetheless, we believe that a democratic theory worthy of serious social influence must engage with the findings of modern social science.

▪   ▪   ▪

THE CRITICAL TRADITION

The folk theory of democracy celebrates the wisdom of popular judgments by informed and engaged citizens. The reality is quite different. Human beings are busy with their lives. Most have school or a job consuming many hours of the day. They also have meals to prepare, homes to clean, and bills to pay. They may have children to raise or elderly parents to care for. They may also be coping with unemployment, business reverses, illness, addictions, divorce, or other personal and family troubles. For most, leisure time is at a premium. Sorting out which presidential candidate has the right foreign policy toward Asia is not a high priority for them. Without shirking more immediate and more important obligations, people cannot engage in much well-informed, thoughtful political deliberation, nor should they.

Recognizing that actual people are far from the unrealistic ideal citizens of the folk theory, disappointed observers have often adopted a judgmental tone, implicitly assuming that the folk theory provides the appropriate moral standard for citizens, which few meet. At the end of the 19th century, for example, James Bryce (1894, 250) observed "how little solidity and substance there is in the political or social beliefs of nineteen persons out of every twenty. These beliefs, when examined, mostly resolve themselves into two or three prejudices and aversions, two or three prepossessions for a particular leader or party or section of a party, two or three phrases or catchwords suggesting or embodying arguments which the man who repeats them has not analyzed." He might have added that the remaining one in twenty exhibit the limits of rationality, too. Nevertheless, however unaware of his own human limitations Bryce may have been, in our view he was not wrong about the fact of widespread citizen inattention. Indeed, the past century of political science has done remarkably little to alter the basic outlines of his portrait of public opinion. Even in the midst of the Progressive Era, the fundamental veracity of that portrait and its troubling implications for folk democratic theory were clear enough to those willing to see them. The great political scientist and Harvard University president A. Lawrence Lowell (1913, 233), for example, noted with respect to democracy that "there has probably never existed a political system of which men have not tried to demonstrate the perfection," but he dismissed as "fallacious" all theories "based on the assumption that the multitude is omniscient" and "all reforms that presuppose a radical change in human nature."

Three other distinguished scholars of the era also saw the tension between conventional democratic ideals and dreary reality. Schumpeter (1942, 262) acidly observed that citizens are especially prone "to yield to extra-rational or irrational prejudice and impulse" in the political sphere. By comparison with other realms of life, he argued (Schumpeter 1942, 261), "the typical citizen drops down to a lower level of mental performance as soon as he enters the political field. He argues and analyzes in a way which he would readily recognize as infantile within the sphere of his real interests."

Walter Lippmann (1914; 1922; 1925) faced more squarely than other commentators of his time the inevitable limits of human cognitive ability in politics. "Once you touch the biographies of human beings," he wrote (1914, 215), "the notion that political beliefs are logically determined collapses like a pricked balloon." He saw that the cherished ideas and judgments we bring to politics are stereotypes and simplifications with little room for adjustment as the facts change (1922, 16): "For the real environment is altogether too big, too complex, and too fleeting for direct acquaintance. We are not equipped to deal with so much subtlety, so much variety, so many permutations and combinations. And although we have to act in that environment, we have to reconstruct it on a simpler model before we can manage it." Lippmann remains the deepest and most thoughtful of the modern critics of the psychological foundations of the folk theory of democracy.

Reinhold Niebuhr (1932; 1944) noted that human judgment is not just over-whelmed by the complexity of the political world, as Lippmann emphasized, but in addition is profoundly warped by self-interest and the will to power. And he perceived clearly that the idealistic justification of democracy as human rationality in pursuit of the common good serves only too well to provide cover for those who profit from the distortions and biases in the policy-making processes of actual democracies: "The will to power uses reason as kings used courtiers and chaplains to add grace to their enterprise" (Niebuhr 1932, 44).

These and other critical thinkers struggled to put democracy on an intellectually respectable foundation, taking account of human nature as they knew it. But in the era in which they wrote, few could hear. It was all too easy and convenient to dismiss the entire intellectual lineage as elitist and cynical, a mere literary tradition based on nothing but jaundiced interpretations of personal experience. Subsequent scholarly generations have also disliked the various racial and religious prejudices of the time, which these men sometimes shared. By the 1950s and 1960s, skeptical writers like Wallas, Lowell, John Dickinson (1930), and even Lippmann and Niebuhr were no longer much read by students of politics.

Meanwhile, however, new tools emerged for investigating political behavior, most notably scientific survey research, whose findings were much harder to glibly dismiss. The pioneering survey research of Paul Lazarsfeld and his colleagues at Columbia University (Lazarsfeld, Berelson, and Gaudet 1948; Berelson, Lazarsfeld, and McPhee 1954), of Angus Campbell and his colleagues at the University of Michigan (Campbell et al. 1960), and of other early analysts of electoral choice produced a rather bleak portrait of habitual, socially determined political behavior, once again calling into question whether citizens could perform the role that the folk theory of democracy seemed to require of them.

Philip Converse (1964) extended this seminal work, building a new, more formidable case for skepticism regarding the idealized image of democratic citizens, this time substituting random national samples for the insightful but less systematic observations of Bryce, Lippmann, Niebuhr, and Schumpeter. Converse's essay set off a vibrant decades-long critical discussion of his methodology and the inferences he drew from his findings, but few public opinion scholars disputed the central point he made—that judged by the standards of the folk theory, the political "belief systems" of ordinary citizens are generally thin, disorganized, and ideologically incoherent.

. . . Converse's argument is, if anything, even better supported a half century later than it was when he wrote. A vast amount of supporting evidence has been added to his dispiriting comparison of actual human political cognition with the expectations derived from the folk theory of democracy. Well-informed citizens, too, have come in for their share of criticism, since their well-organized "ideological" thinking often turns out to be just a rather mechanical reflection of what their favorite group and party leaders have instructed them to think. Faced with this evidence, many scholars in the final chapters of their books continue to express idealistic hope that institutional reform, civic education, improved mass media, more effective mobilization of the poor, or stronger moral exhortation might bring public opinion into closer correspondence with the standards of the folk theory. But in sober moments most acknowledge the repeated failures of all those prescriptions.

Thus, scholars, too, persist uneasily in their schizophrenia, recognizing the power of the critical arguments but hoping against hope that those arguments can somehow be discredited or evaded, allowing the lackluster reality of democratic practice to be squared with conventional idealistic democratic thinking. Often, their attempts to bolster the tattered theoretical status quo bring them back to Winston Churchill's claim that "democracy is the worst form of government except all those others that have been tried from time to time."[4] But that is a distinctly un-idealistic defense of democracy—and no defense at all of the folk theory of democracy.

■　　■　　■

Our view is that conventional thinking about democracy has collapsed in the face of modern social-scientific research.

■　　■　　■

Unfortunately . . . Converse (1964) found that "the vast majority of Americans" are "thoroughly innocent of ideology" (Kinder 1983, 391)—and that finding has been "largely sustained" by subsequent scholarship (Kinder 1983, 401). The available evidence suggests that citizens of other advanced democracies are similar to Americans in this respect. Thus, Converse's work raises a significant challenge not only to the spatial model, but to a great deal of scholarly and popular thinking about how policy decisions might be justified on democratic grounds.

. . . A substantial body of scholarly work demonstrat[es] that most democratic citizens are uninterested in politics, poorly informed, and unwilling or unable to convey coherent policy preferences through "issue voting." How, then, are elections supposed to ensure ideological responsiveness to the popular will? In our view, they do not. The populist ideal of electoral democracy, for all its elegance and attractiveness, is largely irrelevant in practice, leaving elected officials mostly free to pursue their own notions of the public good or to respond to party and interest group pressures.

■　　■　　■

We conclude that group and partisan loyalties, not policy preferences or ideologies, are fundamental in democratic politics. Thus, a realistic theory of democracy must be built, not on the French Enlightenment, on British liberalism, or on American Progressivism, with their devotion to human rationality and monadic individualism, but instead on the insights of the critics of these traditions, who recognized that human life is group life.

▪   ▪   ▪

THE CHALLENGE: TAKING ON THE DIVINE RIGHT OF THE PEOPLE

. . . Democracy is the justifying political ideology of our era. It is inevitably very difficult for any of us to recognize the intellectual constraints and contradictions entailed by our own preconceptions and normative commitments to it. As one of the preeminent contemporary scholars of American politics, James Stimson (2004, 170), wrote, "The word 'democracy' is bound up with symbolism, belief, patriotism, and a quasi-religious commitment. It is imbued with our self-identity as Americans. Democracy is the civil religion of America." Dahl (1961, 317) put it even more bluntly: "To reject the democratic creed is in effect to refuse to be an American."

Some useful perspective on this aspect of contemporary thinking about democracy may be provided by recalling political thought in early modern times regarding the divine right of kings. The idea that kings were divinely anointed had a long history in human thought, and not just in the West; Chinese emperors, too, needed "the mandate of heaven." The idea was highly functional, providing a sturdy basis for political stability—as many astute observers recognized. However, the chronic gap between kingly ideals and realities was a source of severe ideological strain.

The doctrine of "The King's Two Bodies" (Kantorowicz 1957) provided useful leeway for understanding and accommodating the fact that mortal rulers were often manifestly less than divine in bearing and behavior. On this view, the king always intended to rule well and justly, but he was sometimes misled. As Edmund Morgan (1988, 30) described the situation in 17th-century England, "A host of ambitious schemers, according to the Commons' view, continually caught the king's natural ear and misinformed him in order to procure benefits to themselves. But the king in his body politic always wanted what was best for his subjects, all his subjects, and surely no subject could know better what that was than the combined representatives of all his subjects. 'If anything fall out unhappily,' said Sir Robert Phelips, 'it is not King Charles that advised himself, but King Charles misadvised by others and misled by misordered counsel.'" In their time, these ideas were widely credited among thoughtful people and important scholars. But of course, genuine political progress depended on abandoning this entire way of thinking.

In our view, the ideal of popular sovereignty plays much the same role in contemporary democratic ideology that the divine right of kings played in the monarchical era. It is "a quasi-religious commitment," in Stimson's terms, a fiction providing legitimacy and stability to political systems whose actual workings are manifestly—and inevitably—rather less than divine. The fiction feels natural within the Enlightenment mind-set of rationality and human perfectibility. Thoughtful people and important scholars believe it. And its credibility is bolstered by the undeniable practical successes of many of the political systems that invoke it.

The fiction of popular sovereignty is so much the sturdier—and more useful to our own ambitious schemers and powerful interests who profit from its fallacies—for being notoriously hard to pin down. As Henry Maine (1885, 185) wrote long ago, "the devotee of Democracy is much in the same position as the Greeks with their oracles. All agreed that the voice of an oracle was the voice of a god; but everybody allowed that when he spoke he was not as intelligible as might be desired." Thus, policies and practices that are unjust or simply unsuccessful can always be attributed to some mistranslation or temporary deflection of the people's will, with "special interests" trotted out to play the role played by "ambitious schemers" in 17th-century England. We even have our own "two bodies" doctrine: when majorities go seriously astray, it is not the people that "advised themselves," but rather the people misadvised by others and misled by misordered counsel. "The people are never corrupted," said Rousseau, "but sometimes deceived."

In all these ways, conventional thought has avoided the painful task of grappling seriously with all the evidence undermining the standard versions of democratic theory. "Well, yes, there are problems," we say, and then we turn back to the impossible dream. In consequence, cheerful illusions and wish fulfillment have dominated both popular and scholarly thought about democracy for two centuries. Democratic theory has sailed along as if no iceberg had struck and the engine room were not taking on water. But the damage to the intellectual structure is very real.

Both the allure and the cost of romanticism in this domain were eloquently described by political philosopher John Dunn (1999, 342–343) in an essay on democratic political accountability:

> To be ruled is both necessary and inherently discomfiting (as well as dangerous). For our rulers to be accountable to us softens its intrinsic humiliations, probably sets some hazy limits to the harms that they will voluntarily choose to do to us collectively, and thus diminishes some of the dangers to which their rule may expose us. To suggest that we can ever hope to have the power to make them act just as we would wish them to suggests that it is really we, not they, who are ruling. This is an illusion, and probably a somewhat malign illusion: either a self-deception, or an instance of being deceived by others, or very probably both.

Dunn went on to say that "a political science that did justice to democracy (in all its ambiguity) would have to be one in which the presence of these per-

ceptions and sentiments was recognized and explained, and their consequences accurately assessed, not one in which their existence was denied or
dismissed as irrational in the first instance."

The history of democratic thought—including much contemporary political
science—is marked by an addiction to romantic theories. As with any addiction, the first step toward recovery is to admit that we have a problem.

NOTES

1. We thank Jane Mansbridge for emphasizing the centrality of this concept in our
argument.

2. These two models by no means exhaust the variety of meanings of democracy
around the world, or even within the United States. For example, the (overlapping)
traditions of *participatory democracy, face-to-face democracy,* and *deliberative democracy* have received a great deal of attention from academic theorists (Pateman 1970;
Barber 1984; Habermas 1994; Fishkin 1995; Benhabib 1996; Gutmann and Thompson
1996; Sanders 1997; Macedo 1999; Cohen 2003), and they have been implemented with
more or less success in a variety of settings, especially in small groups and local communities (Mansbridge 1980; Mendelberg and Oleske 2000; Fung 2004; Karpowitz 2006).
However, notwithstanding some creative attempts to employ small-scale deliberative
exercises as simulations of how mass publics *would* decide controversial issues in a
deliberative fashion (Fishkin 1991; 2009), these models seem to us to be less relevant for
understanding democratic politics on a national scale than those we consider here.

3. Pateman (1970, 3–5, 16–20) correctly pointed out that no such "classical theorists"
exist; but she acknowledged that "one could extract something which bears a family
resemblance to Schumpeter's definition of the "classical theory" from the 19th-century
works of Jeremy Bentham and James Mill, among others. Some popular writers in the
Progressive Era, such as William Allen White (1910), nicely exemplify the viewpoint
that Schumpeter criticized. The high hopes for public opinion surveys as a guiding
force for democratic policy-making reflect the same Progressive logic (Gallup 1940/1968).

4. The authors of *The American Voter* adopted this view (Campbell et al. 1960, 545).
An updated version of Churchill's argument is that democracy promotes freedom,
human development, and material well-being (Dahl 1989; Mueller 1999; Przeworski
et al. 2000). Demonstrating causal effects in this domain is very hard, but even if they
exist, this line of argument generally does not speak to *how* democracy matters and
how it should be organized to work better.

REFERENCES

Barber, Benjamin R. 1984. *Strong Democracy: Participatory Politics for a New Age.*
  Berkeley: University of California Press.
Benhabib, Seyla. 1996. "Toward a Deliberative Model of Democratic Legitimacy." In
  Democracy and Difference: Contesting the Boundaries of the Political, edited by
  Seyla Benhabib, 67–94. Princeton, NJ: Princeton University Press.
Berelson, Bernard R., Paul F. Lazarsfeld, and William N. McPhee. 1954. *Voting: A
  Study of Opinion Formation in a Presidential Campaign.* Chicago: University of
  Chicago Press.
Bryce, James. 1894. *The American Commonwealth.* 3rd ed., vol. 2. New York: Macmillan.

Campbell, Angus, Philip E. Converse, Warren E. Miller, and Donald E. Stokes. 1960. *The American Voter.* New York: John Wiley.

Cohen, Joshua. 2003. "Deliberation and Democratic Legitimacy." In *Debates in Contemporary Political Philosophy: An Anthology,* Derek Matravers and Jon Pike, edited by Derek Matravers and Jon Pike, 342–60. London: Routledge.

Converse, Philip E. 1964. "The Nature of Belief Systems in Mass Publics." In *Ideology and Discontent,* edited by David E. Apter, 206–61. Glencoe, IL: Free Press.

Dahl, Robert A. 1961. *Who Governs? Democracy and Power in an American City.* New Haven, CT: Yale University Press.

———. 1989. *Democracy and Its Critics.* New Haven, CT: Yale University Press.

———. 1998. *On Democracy.* New Haven, CT: Yale University Press.

Dickinson, John. 1930. "Democratic Realities and Democratic Dogma." *American Political Science Review* 24: 283–309.

Dunn, John. 1999. "Situating Democratic Political Accountability." In *Democracy, Accountability, and Representation,* edited by Adam Przeworski, Susan C. Stokes, and Bernard Manin, 329–44. New York: Cambridge University Press.

Fishkin, James S. 1991. *Democracy and Deliberation: New Directions for Democratic Reform.* New Haven, CT: Yale University Press.

———. 1995. *The Voice of the People: Public Opinion and Democracy.* New Haven, CT: Yale University Press.

———. 2009. *When the People Speak: Deliberative Democracy and Public Consultation.* New York: Oxford University Press.

Fung, Archon. 2004. *Empowered Participation: Reinventing Urban Democracy.* Princeton, NJ: Princeton University Press.

Gallup, George. 1940/1968. *The Pulse of Democracy: The Public Opinion Poll and How It Works.* New York: Greenwood.

Gutmann, Amy, and Dennis Thompson. 1996. *Democracy and Disagreement: Why Moral Conflict Cannot Be Avoided in Politics, and What Should Be Done about It.* Cambridge, MA: Belknap.

Habermas, Jürgen. 1994. "Three Normative Models of Democracy." *Constellations 1*: 1–10.

Kantorowicz, Ernst H. 1957. *The King's Two Bodies: A Study in Mediaeval Political Theology.* Princeton, NJ: Princeton University Press.

Karpowitz, Christopher. 2006. "Having a Say: Public Hearings, Deliberation, and American Democracy." PhD dissertation, Department of Politics, Princeton University.

Key, V. O., Jr. 1966. *The Responsible Electorate: Rationality in Presidential Voting 1936–1960.* Cambridge, MA: Harvard University Press.

Kinder, Donald R. 1983. "Diversity and Complexity in American Public Opinion." In *Political Science: The State of the Discipline,* edited by Ada Finifter, 389–425. Washington, DC: American Political Science Association.

Lazarsfeld, Paul F., Bernard Berelson, and Hazel Gaudet. 1948. *The People's Choice: How the Voter Makes Up His Mind in a Presidential Campaign.* 2nd ed. New York: Columbia University Press.

Lippmann, Walter. 1914. *A Preface to Politics.* New York: Mitchell Kennerley.

———. 1922/1946. *Public Opinion.* New York: Penguin.

———. 1925. *The Phantom Public.* New York: Harcourt, Brace.

Lowell, A. Lawrence. 1913. *Public Opinion and Popular Government.* New York: Longmans, Green.

Macedo, Stephen, ed. 1999. *Deliberative Politics: Essays on Democracy and Disagreement.* New York: Oxford University Press.

Maine, Henry Sumner. 1885. *Popular Government: Four Essays*. London: John Murray.

Mansbridge, Jane J. 1980. *Beyond Adversary Democracy*. New York: Basic Books.

Mendelberg, Tali, and John Oleske. 2000. "Race and Public Deliberation." *Political Communication* 17: 169–91.

Morgan, Edmund S. 1988. *Inventing the People: The Rise of Popular Sovereignty in England and America*. New York: Norton.

Mueller, John E. 1999. *Capitalism, Democracy, and Ralph's Pretty Good Grocery*. Princeton, NJ: Princeton University Press.

Niebuhr, Reinhold. 1932. *Moral Man and Immoral Society*. New York: Scribner's.

———. 1944. *The Children of Light and the Children of Darkness*. New York: Scribner's.

Pateman, Carole. 1970. *Participation and Democratic Theory*. Cambridge: Cambridge University Press.

Przeworski, Adam, Michael E. Alvarez, José Antonio Cheibub, and Fernando Limongi. 2000. *Democracy and Development: Political Institutions and Well-Being in the World, 1950–1990*. New York: Cambridge University Press.

Sandburg, Carl. 1936. *The People, Yes*. New York: Harcourt, Brace.

Sanders, Lynn M. 1997. "Against Deliberation." *Political Theory* 25: 347–76.

Schumpeter, Joseph A. 1942. *Capitalism, Socialism and Democracy*. New York: Harper & Brothers.

Stimson, James A. 2004. *Tides of Consent: How Public Opinion Shapes American Politics*. New York: Cambridge University Press.

White, William Allen. 1910. *The Old Order Changeth: A View of American Democracy*. New York: Macmillan.

14

THE MEDIA

14.1

MATTHEW A. BAUM

From *Soft News Goes to War: Public Opinion and American Foreign Policy in the New Media Age*

Soft news refers to mass media programming that is primarily intended to entertain rather than provide news, but that also includes—as a by-product of the entertainment—information about politics and international events. Baum analyzes the degree to which people who are relatively uninterested in politics receive information about politics from soft news sources. He finds that international crises especially find their way into "water cooler" conversations—and thus the public's broader consciousness—because people learn about these events from soft news.

SUMMARY AND HYPOTHESES

Driven by market competition and the relatively low cost of producing soft news, broadcasters are finding human interest and other entertainment values in places where their predecessors saw only dry news. One implication is that soft news, as opposed to traditional news programming, may actually increase the likelihood that typical individuals—particularly those not normally interested in politics—will be exposed to information about at least *some* of the major issues of the day, especially those that become water-cooler events, albeit in a format that is less public-policy-oriented and less apt to provide a context for understanding an issue.

From Matthew A. Baum, *Soft News Goes to War: Public Opinion and American Foreign Policy in the New Media Age* (Princeton, NJ: Princeton University Press, 2003).

613

Under normal, everyday circumstances, these developments might not result in a public more attuned to political issues than were earlier generations. Given well-documented increases in political apathy and cynicism about politics, it is not surprising to find that typical individuals are no more interested in politics than their parents or grandparents were. This suggests that individuals have reacted to the explosion of available information by becoming increasingly selective regarding what information warrants their attention. Most of the time, the highly segmented modern television marketplace presumably allows individuals to *escape* news and information more effectively than in prior decades. Soft news programs, for instance, generally avoid such "mundane" political topics as foreign affairs, in favor of more salacious issues like celebrity sex scandals, murder trials, and fashion shows. Hence, with minimal effort, television viewers can remain blissfully uninformed about the day-to-day political issues facing the nation, including foreign policy.

When, however, potential water-cooler events emerge—and cross over from network evening newscasts to the soft news media—a far broader audience will likely confront such issues, albeit perhaps as the subject of an entertainment-oriented talk show or entertainment newsmagazine show. Moreover, unlike the relatively arcane or complex presentation of political information offered by traditional news outlets, soft news programs will focus on aspects of such issues of interest to their particular niche of the viewing audience.

For instance, during the Persian Gulf War, while CNN and the major networks filled the airwaves with graphic images of precision bombs and interviews with military experts, the daytime talk shows hosted by Oprah Winfrey, Geraldo Rivera, and Sally Jesse Raphael, as well as the original tabloid TV newsmagazine, *A Current Affair*, focused on episodic stories of the personal hardships faced by spouses of soldiers serving in the Gulf and on the psychological trauma suffered by families of Americans being held prisoner in Iraq as "human shields." In this context, learning about the war was an incidental by-product of seeking entertainment (e.g., human drama or a fight between good and evil). War-related information was effectively piggybacked to entertainment-oriented information, and thereby made available to viewers at virtually no additional cost. In other words, when *The Oprah Winfrey Show* presented a program dealing with the Gulf War, substantive information about the war was "piggybacked," via cheap framing (e.g., human impact and injustice), to information presented primarily for its entertainment value. In choosing to watch Oprah, viewers also, at no additional cost, received substantive information about the Persian Gulf War.[1]

The incidental nature of soft news coverage of foreign crises is illustrated in the following comment by Barry Berk of *Access Hollywood*, regarding that program's rationale for covering some foreign crisis issues, despite the program's primary mission of providing their audience with information about movies and celebrities:

I think rather than just say [to a celebrity], "Why did you like that script?" or "Why do you want to make this movie?" . . . it's a way to get to know the celebrities better. And let [the audience] know there's another level there; that they [celebrities] do have opinions; that they're citizens and they're parents, and they have concerns. And they get very upset about the prospect that we're bombing Iraq. Or "good for them, I'm glad we're going in there." You know, they have opinions. I think people find that interesting.[2]

Hence, when a foreign crisis emerges, the numerous programming formats that comprise the modern television marketplace may focus their diverse lenses upon a single issue, albeit varying aspects of that issue. When the mass media unify their focus, I expect the contemporary public, in the aggregate, to be significantly more attentive to such an issue, compared to the publics of prior decades. In today's news environment, when an issue crosses over from traditional news outlets to the soft news media, politically uninterested citizens are far more likely to be exposed and pay attention to the issue—as an incidental by-product of seeking entertainment—relative to most typical political issues, which rarely reach beyond traditional news programming.

Most importantly, this mechanism does not depend on any overall increase in the public's interest in or knowledge about politics or foreign affairs.[3] Indeed, the basis for predicting increased attentiveness is entirely independent of the expected benefit for typical individuals of political information in general or information about foreign affairs in particular. Once someone is exposed to an issue in her preferred programming format, her cost-benefit calculus for paying attention to additional information about the issue is altered. For such an individual, this issue is no longer a typical mundane, and perhaps baffling, political news item.

▪ ▪ ▪

WHAT ARE CRISES AND WHEN DO THEY BECOME WATER-COOLER EVENTS?

▪ ▪ ▪

[D]ue in part to the increasing prevalence of soft news outlets, foreign military crises—as well as some other issues which are decidedly not "high politics"— are increasingly likely to attract the attention of typical individuals. In general, issues that can be readily framed in stark and dramatic terms, thereby priming widely accessible frames, without generating significant cognitive conflict between simultaneously accessible yet contradictory causal narratives, are most likely to be covered by the soft news media. Such issues are thereby most likely to attract the attention of even politically uninterested individuals. These are the issues that occasionally become water-cooler events.

A direct marketing revolution in television has systematically altered the cost-benefit calculus for a large segment of the public, which is not predisposed to follow politics. By transforming mundane political coverage into entertainment, the soft news media have successfully employed piggybacking and cheap framing strategies in order to capture a substantial segment, or niche, of the television audience. This has the perhaps unintended effect of increasing the likelihood that politically uninterested individuals will be exposed to information about those political issues that cross over from hard to soft news outlets.

. . . [T]he class of issues most likely to become water-cooler events [are] "dramatic crises" because these events typically possess the several characteristics necessary to appeal to the soft news media. Nonetheless, not all crises, nor even all dramatic crises, are covered by the soft news media or become water-cooler events. Indeed, it seems unlikely that there exists any foolproof formula for determining ex ante which issues will pass this attentiveness threshold. Rather, given the extraordinary complexity of the modern political, media, and public opinion environments, perhaps the best we can hope for in the near term is an improved understanding of the various factors that raise or lower the probability that a given issue or event will capture the public's imagination.

NOTES

1. The contrast between war coverage on *The Oprah Winfrey Show* and the emphasis of traditional news programming on military tactics and precision bombing campaigns also illustrates the increasing niche orientation of the traditional and soft news media. The former orientation may be intended, in part, to have a greater appeal for the largely female audience that typically watches *The Oprah Winfrey Show*, while the latter type of coverage has traditionally held greater appeal for a male audience.

2. Barry Berk, interview with author, Los Angeles, Calif., June 20, 2000.

3. I do, however, present some evidence in the concluding chapter [not included] that exposure to soft news outlets can enhance some individuals' knowledge about particular foreign crisis events.

14.2

MARISA A. ABRAJANO

From *Campaigning to the New American Electorate: Advertising to Latino Voters*

It has become increasingly important for candidates for federal office—Congress or the presidency—to make explicit appeals to the interests of Latino voters to win elections. Campaign advertisements in Spanish and appeals made in media tailored toward Latinos have become common even in locations with relatively few Latinos. As Abrajano argues, these behaviors of direct appeal to immigrant groups with new citizenship status follow a long tradition in American politics.

CAMPAIGNING TO ETHNIC AND RACIAL MINORITIES IN THE UNITED STATES
■ ■ ■

Candidates, particularly at the local level, have competed for the votes of immigrants since the 1800s (Erie 1990; Dahl 1961; Katznelson 1981). Perhaps the most infamous political machine of all, Tammany Hall, led by William Marcy "Boss" Tweed, pioneered numerous efforts aimed at persuading immigrants to join the powerful Irish machine. These newcomers arrived in droves to the port city of New York, and by 1930, Jews and Italians made up 36 percent of the population of New York City. Party bosses appealed to these groups by offering them party posts and providing "coal, food and rent money to needy Jews and Italians on the Lower East Side" (Erie 1990, 102). Other actions were less substantive in nature; for example, Tammany's "Big Tim" Sullivan "shamelessly 'recognized' the new immigrants with symbolic gestures and donned a yarmulke to solicit Jewish votes" (103). Tammany bosses were also known to eat "corned beef and kosher meat with equal nonchalance" (McNickle 1993, 17) and to advertise in the Yiddish press to reach out to these new immigrants. To gain the support of Italian immigrants, the Irish sponsored legislation to honor Columbus Day as a holiday. Substantively, Congressman James Michael Curley of Boston advocated against literacy tests as one of the requirements for U.S. citizenship and also fought for less-restrictive immigration laws.

From Marisa A. Abrajano, *Campaigning to the New American Electorate: Advertising to Latino Voters* (Palo Alto, CA: Stanford University Press, 2010), Chapter 3.

Not all immigrants were bowled over by these efforts. Instead of joining the Irish-led political machines, many offered their support to Tammany challengers. Jews became increasingly involved with the Socialist Party, particularly because of their concerns over labor and reform politics. Italian immigrants, though, lent their support to the Republicans.

As the earliest accounts on minority campaigning demonstrate, candidates have long believed that appealing to voters based on ethnic group membership is an effective and powerful strategy in gaining their support. The rationale for this behavior could be attributed to the perception that group membership is salient to the political decisions that individuals make. But as the responses from immigrant Jews and Italians indicate, such campaign appeals did not necessarily lead to unconditional support. Some immigrant groups were concerned about substantive matters, especially those that affected their community. Thus, although efforts to target ethnic minorities date back to the late nineteenth century, it is unclear what consequences these efforts may have had on the political well-being of the immigrant or minority group in question.

Historical Efforts at Latino Outreach

Latinos have been a presence on the American landscape for hundreds of years. In 1848, following the Mexican-American War, the northern portion of Mexico was annexed to the United States and, thus, many individuals of Mexican descent became part of the American fabric. The first documented effort aimed at the Latino electorate can be traced back to the 1960 presidential election. John F. Kennedy, the Democratic contender, established Latino outreach efforts by way of his Viva Kennedy clubs. Concentrated primarily in the Southwest and Midwest, these grassroots associations focused on organizing Mexican Americans to support Kennedy. The clubs also indirectly served to incorporate and familiarize them with the electoral process. According to community leader Rodolfo Ramos, "The best thing we did with Viva Kennedy Clubs was that we organized independent local Democratic institutions" (Pycior 1997, 117). And although these clubs were officially part of the Kennedy presidential campaign, they operated independently from the state party Democratic committees (Garcia 2000). Moreover, much like presidential candidates do today, Kennedy sought endorsements from Latino elected officials, such as State Senator Henry Gonzalez of Texas and Los Angeles City Councilman Edward Roybal.

The fact that Kennedy was a Roman Catholic gave him a considerable advantage with this ethnic group, as most Mexican Americans are also of the Catholic faith (Pew Hispanic Center 2007). According to Garcia (2000), Kennedy's religious affiliation "represented a cultural bridge to the Mexican American community . . . it meant that he valued family and tradition" (59). Without a doubt, this shared faith was something that Kennedy and the Democrats intended to capitalize on. Moreover, because "[Kennedy's] wife Jacqueline understood and spoke Spanish, [it] meant that Kennedy could communicate with Mexican Americans and understand their needs" (Garcia 2000, 59).

The Kennedy campaign took advantage of Jacqueline Kennedy's Spanish-language proficiency to create the first-ever televised Spanish-language ad. In a commercial that lasted slightly longer than a minute, she expressed the following sentiments:

> Dear friends, the wife of senator John Kennedy, candidate for the U.S. presidency, is talking to you. In these very dangerous times, when the world peace is threatened by communism, it is necessary to have in the White House a leader able to guide our destinies with a firm hand. My husband has always cared for the interests of all the portions of our society who need the protection of a humanitarian government. For the future of our children and to reach a world where true peace shall exist, vote for the Democratic Party on the eighth of November. Long live Kennedy![1]

The primary emphasis in this landmark political ad is on the personal qualities and traits of the candidate; there is also a subtle reference to Kennedy's commitment to underrepresented groups such as Latinos. Aside from the issue of communism, no mention is made about the policies that concerned Latinos during this time (for example, civil rights). His decision to target the Latino electorate turned out to be a prudent one; Kennedy captured 85 percent of the Latino vote, and some political analysts attributed Kennedy's victory in the close election to the support he received from Latinos (Schmal 2004).

Kennedy's outreach efforts are noteworthy for one main reason. The Viva Kennedy campaign brought Latinos, primarily Mexican Americans at that time, to the national spotlight. Latinos were thus recognized as a constituency that presidential candidates needed to court. In the 1968 Democratic presidential primaries, Eugene McCarthy and Robert F. Kennedy battled for the support of Latinos in the key states of Texas and California. Kennedy's campaign enlisted the aid of the Mexican American Political Association (MAPA) and its president, Bert Corona, to target thousands of potential supporters in East Los Angeles. Kennedy also made a series of campaign appearances in San Antonio, Chicago, and Los Angeles. Another key endorsement came from César Chávez, civil rights advocate and founder of the United Farm Workers, who used his extensive network to mobilize Latino voters. The concerted outreach efforts resulted in Kennedy's victory in California; according to media reports, "Mexican Americans contributed most of the slender margin by which Kennedy beat McCarthy in California" (Pycior 1997, 225). The organizational and political skills exhibited by Latinos through the Viva Kennedy clubs secured their position as an important part of the Democratic base; these clubs also enabled many Latinos to familiarize themselves with the electoral process.

By 1980, Democrats were not the only ones who had established Latino outreach efforts. Along with incumbent Democratic president Jimmy Carter, Republican challenger Ronald Reagan developed a specific campaign for the Latino electorate (Subervi-Velez and Connaughton 2008; Segal 2003). Because Reagan was then the governor of California, he likely recognized the importance of the Latino electorate. Latino rates of electoral participation, however, were quite low, with only 29.9 percent of Latinos turning out to vote in the 1980 presidential election. It is estimated that 60.1 percent of Latinos nationwide supported Carter, but among Hispanic voters in Florida, who are mostly Cuban American, 80 percent voted for Reagan (Schmal 2004). Thus, although both candidates made efforts to reach out to Latinos, Reagan's decisive victory over Carter (50.9 versus 41.1 percent) meant that the Latino vote was not as pivotal as it was in the 1960 presidential race.

Four years later, Reagan stepped up his Latino outreach efforts even more and, with the help of the Republican National Committee (RNC), crafted the "Hispanic Victory Initiative '84: A Proposed Strategy for the Reagan-Bush '84 Hispanic Campaign" (Subervi-Velez and Connaughton 2008). One of the highlights from this sixty-six-page document is a statement indicating that although campaigns may be able "to reach [Latinos] in English . . . you have to convince them in Spanish." Lionel Sosa, the political consultant that spearheaded Reagan's Latino outreach efforts, was confident that Latinos would be willing to support the Republican party—it was just a matter of reaching out to them and convincing them to do so. The two Spanish-language ads developed by Reagan and the RNC, "Democrat All the Way" and "New Tradition," reflected these sentiments. The theme of these ads focused on the notion that although Latinos traditionally have been aligned with the Democrats, they should consider supporting Reagan because of his leadership skills. No specific mention is made, however, about the types of policies enacted or supported by Reagan that would benefit Latinos. Given his success with Cuban Americans in the previous election, Reagan also paid special attention to this community by emphasizing his tough anticommunist position toward Cuba. Moreover, Vice President George H. W. Bush assisted in these campaign efforts by speaking Spanish at various events to attack Mondale.[2]

The Democratic candidate in this election, Walter Mondale, also targeted Latino voters. Adopting Kennedy's campaign slogan, Mondale courted Latinos in both the primary and general elections through his Viva Mondale campaign. He made great efforts in the primary season to reach out to Latinos in California, because they were considered to be a critical swing group in the state. During the general election campaign, Mondale continued these efforts by promising Latinos in Texas that he would appoint coethnics to his cabinet.[3] A surge in the number of national network television news stories covering Latino voters was also evident in this election season, up from seven stories in 1980 to twelve in 1984.[4] As in the previous presidential race, Reagan defeated his opponent by a considerable margin (18.3 percent); he also continued to win the support of the Cuban population in Florida, capturing

82 percent of their votes. But the Latino electorate as a whole continued to cast their ballots in favor of the Democratic candidate, 66 percent versus 32.6 percent.

In the 1988 presidential election, both candidates, George H. W. Bush and Michael Dukakis, made even greater efforts to gain the support and allegiance of Latino voters. The Bush campaign developed a grassroots organization, Hispanics for Bush, in order to target specific campaign messages to Latinos. Altogether, the campaign created four Spanish-language ads that were broadcast on Spanish-language media; some were also dubbed into English and aired on shows with large Latino audiences. The Dukakis campaign created five Spanish-language ads for the general election, a strategy many considered advantageous because the candidate was fluent in Spanish (Subervi-Velez and Connaughton 2008). But, somewhat surprisingly, the campaign spent less than $1 million broadcasting these ads (Segal 2003, 7). The explanation for this low figure was attributed to the well-accepted belief at the time that Latinos were already strong Democratic voters who were unlikely to defect and vote for Bush. Despite these efforts, however, Bush soundly defeated Dukakis by a margin of 7.8 percentage points. Latinos remained supportive of the Democratic candidate, with 70.2 percent of the Latino vote going to Dukakis.

Part of Bush's re-election campaign in 1992 involved targeting the Latino electorate. His challenger in the general election, Bill Clinton, also recognized the importance of the Latino vote. Clinton mostly relied on English-language media to communicate to Latinos and created only one Spanish-language ad, which was aired in the New York media market as a response to a negative ad broadcast by Bush. In contrast, Bush allocated millions to Spanish-language media, mostly in the markets of Illinois, Colorado, New Mexico, and Texas. Both candidates relied on endorsements from either Latino relatives or prominent Latino elected officials; Bush received endorsements from his Latino family members (his daughter-in-law and grandson), whereas Clinton turned to Henry Cisneros, then mayor of San Antonio. It was Clinton who received the lion's share of the Latino vote (71 percent). And although he was similar to his Republican predecessors, Bush captured just 70 percent of the Latino vote in Florida.

The 1996 presidential race also witnessed both the incumbent and the challenger, Republican Bob Dole, developing outreach efforts toward the Latino electorate. Clinton's campaign allocated more than $1 million to Spanish-language ad buys in New Mexico, Nevada, and Arizona. Clinton's political ads focused on jobs and national unity; he also created several attack ads focusing on Dole's positions on immigration and bilingual education. Although Dole targeted Latino voters in Florida, his record on immigration and bilingual education hampered these efforts. As a result, Dole's share of the Latino vote (21 percent) was the smallest of any Republican presidential candidate in the past twenty-five years. Approximately 10 percent of Latino voters supported the third-party candidate, Ross Perot.

Media coverage on Latinos was low in the 1996 election—only one television news story focused on the Latino electorate during that campaign season.[5] Perhaps the decrease was due to the dynamics of this presidential election, because Clinton had a good relationship with the Latino electorate. In fact, this was a landmark election for the Democrats, as it marked the first time since 1976 that a Democrat captured Florida. One reason for this shift has been attributed to the inroads that Clinton made with Cuban Americans. He received 35 percent of their votes, a 15 percent increase from his 1992 share of the Cuban vote. Latinos also proved to be pivotal in Clinton's historic victory in Arizona. He captured 90 percent of the Latino vote there, and the last time Democrats had won that state was 1948.

▪   ▪   ▪

Spanish-Language Campaigns in House Races, 2000–2004

During the 2000–2004 election cycles, twenty-one House races saw at least one candidate using Spanish-language ads. In total, twenty-six candidates advertised in Spanish, with only one candidate advertising in all three election cycles that I examine (see the next section, on New Mexico's 1st congressional district, for a more detailed discussion). Table [1] lists those House races with candidates that advertised in Spanish, along with the same information presented in Table 3.1 [not included]. As in the statewide races, House candidates that used Spanish-language ads competed in a district with a considerable number of Latino voters; in fact, many of these districts were majority and even super-majority Latino districts. At the low end of the population scale were California's 9th and Florida's 8th congressional districts—in each district Latinos constituted approximately 17 percent of the population. At the high end, 77.5 percent of the 28th congressional district in Texas are Latino, and in the 4th district of Illinois, Latinos make up 74.5 percent of the population. The content of the ads targeting the House districts reflects the same general pattern as those used in the statewide races—the majority of the ads featured images of Latinos, as well as simple policy and character statements.

Forty percent of the elections were considered to be competitive, whereas the number of statewide races deemed competitive was considerably higher (75 percent). This difference could perhaps be attributed to the nature of House elections, because House members have smaller constituencies than do senators, and many representatives are long-time incumbents. As such, they may advertise in Spanish as a gesture of goodwill to their Latino constituents more than as a bid for votes. Of the twelve noncompetitive elections in which at least one candidate advertised in Spanish, five were incumbents. They were Luis Gutierrez (IL-4), Ed Pastor (AZ-2), Ileana Ros-Lehtinen (FL-18), Silvestre Reyes (TX-16), and Xavier Becerra (CA-30). Also note that in these five elections, the challengers did not create a Spanish-language advertising campaign. And with the exception of Ileana Ros-Lehtinen, all the incumbents are Democrats. Yet, Republican incumbents, such as Henry Bonilla (TX-23), Steve Pearce (NM-2), and Joe Skeen (NM-1), did not advertise in Spanish, even when their Democratic challengers chose to do so. Thus, there appears to be some partisan bias, because Democrats, at least in these three election cycles, were more apt to use this media outlet than were Republicans. This difference can perhaps be attributed to the long-standing relationship that Democrats have had with the Latino electorate. It is also interesting to note that of the sixteen Latino candidates competing in these elections, only one—former congressman Henry Bonilla (TX-23)—did not target his Latino electorate through Spanish-language ads.

Case Study: New Mexico's 1st Congressional District

During the 2000–2004 election cycles, Heather Wilson of New Mexico's 1st congressional district was the lone candidate who consistently developed a Spanish-language advertising campaign. Some characteristics of her district offer insight on why Wilson used such a campaign in each of these election cycles. Her district is 42.6 percent Latino, 25.5 percent of whom are Spanish speaking (U.S. Census Bureau 2000a). Moreover, only 1.2 percent of the population consists of foreign-born individuals (U.S. Census Bureau 2000a). Thus, more than half of the Latinos in her district could be exposed to her Spanish-language ads, and, more importantly, they are likely to be eligible voters (given that virtually all Latinos in this district are U.S. born). Finally, that Wilson faced a formidable competitor in all of her reelection bids, as evidenced by a margin of victory of 10 percent or less in each election, can also help explain why she regularly employed a targeted Latino campaign. The one recurring theme in her Spanish-language ads was a mention of the personal qualities of either Wilson or her opponent, and although Latinos were not featured in her 2000 commercials, she did include them in her subsequent campaign ads. Wilson also discussed policy in her Spanish-language ads, with a preference for simple and explained policy messages over complex policy statements.

This case study offers a number of insights about candidates' Latino-specific campaigns, and it helps support the theory of information-based advertising. Wilson's concerted efforts to campaign to Latinos, despite the fact that she is a Republican, reinforces the conventional wisdom that Latinos are considered a valuable swing group. And although Latinos have traditionally been aligned with the Democratic party, Wilson exemplifies the efforts made by the Republican party to appeal to this group of voters. She made her appeal by communicating messages that primarily focused on her or her opponent's personal characteristics and on easily understood policy statements. Specifically recognizing Latinos in her Spanish-language ads, either by featuring them or by having them speak in the ad, is another regular component of her campaign strategy. That the content of these Spanish-language ads focused more on character and cultural appeals, with less of an emphasis on substantively

TABLE [1] House Races Using Spanish-Language Advertising (2000–2004)

State and District	Year	Candidate	Types of Ads Advertised	Competitive Election?	Percent Latino in District
AZ-2	2000	E. Pastor (D)	Simple, Character	No	62.5
CA-9	2004	C. Bermudez (R)	Simple, Latino	No	17.3
CA-20	2000	C. Dooley (D)	Simple, Latino	Yes	63.7
		R. Rodriguez (R)	Latino		
	2004	J. Costa (D)	Simple, Latino, Character	No	
		L. Quigley (D)	Complex		
CA-30	2000	X. Becerra (D)	Simple, Character	No	64.3
CA-39	2002	L. Sanchez (D)	Latino	No	61.2
		T. Escobar (R)	Simple, Latino		
FL-8	2002	M. Diaz-Balart (R)	Latino, Explained, Simple, Character	Yes	17.6
		E. Diaz (D)	Explained, Latino		
FL-18	2004	I. Ros-Lehtinen (R)	Simple	No	70.5
IL-4	2000	L. Gutierrez (D)	n/a	No	74.5
NM-1	2000	H. Wilson (R)	Explained, Simple, Character	Yes	42.6
		J. Kelly (D)	n/a		
	2002	H. Wilson (R)	Character, Latino	Yes	
	2004	H. Wilson (R)	Explained, Simple, Latino, Character	Yes	

State and District	Year	Candidate	Types of Ads Advertised	Competitive Election?	Percent Latino in District
NM-2	2000	M. Montoya (D)	Latino	Yes	47.3
	2002	S. Pearce (R)	Latino, Complex, Explained, Simple, Character	No	
	2004	J. Smith (D)	Character; Explained, Latino	No	
		G. King (D)	Character, Latino		
NM-3	2000	T. Udall (D)	Latino	Yes	36.3
TX-16	2004	S. Reyes (D)	Character, Latino	No	78
TX-23	2000	W. Garza (D)	Character, Simple, Latino	No	65.1
TX-28	2004	H. Cuellar (D)	Explained, Latino	Yes	77.5
		C. Rodriguez (D)	Latino		
TX-32	2004	M. Frost (D)	Complex, Latino	No	36.2
		P. Sessions (R)	Character, Latino		

SOURCE: *The American Almanac of American Politics* (2000–2004) for competitive election information; U.S. Census for the percentage of Latinos in a district; ad content was discerned using data from the Wisconsin Advertising Project dataset, 2000–2004

motivated policy messages, lends some initial support for the theory of information-based advertising. Of course, this case study is not conclusive evidence, because the focus is only on the content of Wilson's Spanish-language ads. Nonetheless, it offers a glimpse into the campaign strategies used by the same candidate in three different races.

Summary

Clearly, politicians competing for both national and statewide races realize the importance of developing a specific campaign strategy directed toward Latinos. In a growing number of states across our nation, a successful bid for most elected offices requires that some effort be made to win the support of the Latino electorate. Particularly in states in which Latinos make up more than a third of the population, and therefore a sizeable part of the electorate, it is almost a given that candidates competing in statewide offices need to secure their allegiance. Just as California's Latinos were pivotal to Robert Kennedy's bid for the Democratic presidential nomination, Latinos play an equally, if not more, prominent role in today's elections. . . .

Those seeking elected office have long understood the importance of targeting specific groups within the electorate whom they believe may behave in a politically homogeneous manner. Although appeals to our nation's newest arrivals have resulted in candidates swapping corned beef for tamales, the motivations for such behavior appear to remain the same—candidates believe that campaigning to immigrants based on their ethnicity or culture is effective. That is, politicians believe that such efforts signal to these ethnic groups that politicians understand them and care about them. Candidates hope that, in turn, these groups will respond positively to the campaigns and will cast their ballots in favor of the candidate who appeals to them in this way.

This conventional wisdom appears to have carried over to the campaigns developed for the country's largest immigrant and minority group today. Given the technological advances in communication and the access that Latinos have to myriad Spanish-language media outlets, aspiring politicians can use these media sources to target ethnic messages to Latinos. Just as candidates have allocated the bulk of their campaign resources to televised political advertising for the general public, candidates have also turned to this medium in reaching out to Latino voters.

NOTES

1. This ad is titled "Mrs. JFK" and is available at http://www.livingroomcandidate.org/commercials/1960.

2. ABC Evening News, November 5, 1984.

3. CBS Evening News, November 4, 1984.

4. Television News Archive, Vanderbilt University.

5. ABC Evening News devoted 2 minutes and 10 seconds to discussing the Latino vote on June 29, 1996.

REFERENCES

Dahl, Robert. 1961. *Who Governs?* New Haven, CT: Yale University Press.

Erie, Steven P. 1990. *Rainbow's End: Irish-Americans and the Dilemmas of Urban Machine Politics, 1840–1985.* Berkeley, University of California Press.

Garcia, Ignacio M. 2000. *Viva Kennedy: Mexican Americans in Search of Camelot.* College Station, Texas A&M University Press.

Katznelson, Ira. 1981. *City Trenches: Urban Politics and the Patterning of Class in the United States.* New York, Pantheon Press.

McNickle, Chris. 1993. *To Be Mayor of New York: Ethnic Politics in the City.* New York, Columbia University Press.

Pew Hispanic Center. 2007. "Changing Faiths: Latinos and the Transformation of American Religion." Report. Washington, DC, Pew Hispanic Center and Pew Forum on Religion & Public Life.

Pycior, Julie L. 1997. *LBJ and Mexican Americans: The Paradox of Power.* Austin, The University of Texas Press.

Schmal, John P. 2004. "Electing the President. The Latino Electorate (1960–2000)." *La Prensa*, April 30. http://www.laprensa-sandiego.org/archive/april30-04/elect.htm.

Segal, Adam J. 2003. "The Hispanic Priority: The Spanish-Language Television Battle for the Hispanic Vote in the 2000 U.S. Presidential Election." Report. Hispanic Voter Project, Washington Center for the Study of American Government. Washington, DC, Johns Hopkins University,

Subervi-Velez, Federico A., and Stacey L. Connaughton. 2008. "Democratic and Republican Mass Communication Campaign Strategies: A Historical Overview." In *The Mass Media and Latino Politics: Studies of U.S. Media Content, Campaign Strategies and Survey Research: 1984–2004*, edited by Federico Suservi-Velez, 273–90. New York, Routledge.

U.S. Census Bureau. 2000a. "United States Foreign-Born Population." Population Division. March. http://www.census.gov/population/www/socdemo/foreign/cps2000.html.

15

POLICY

15.1

KENNETH SCHEVE AND DAVID STASAVAGE

From *Taxing the Rich: A History of Fiscal Fairness
in the United States and Europe*

*A common argument is that democratic governments will inevitably tax the rich
more than the poor because there are fewer rich than poor, and the latter will
vote in favor of taxes on the former. Scheve and Stasavage say that this logic
cannot explain why taxes on the rich have gone up and then down over time in
the world's democracies. Their theory says that taxes on the rich have tended to
go up when many people feel like the government has been unequal in its treatment of different classes, favoring the rich over the poor. The poor and middle
classes react by supporting policies to increase taxes on the rich. Increasing
taxes on the rich often happens also during times of war, when many people feel
like the rich do not do their fair share to contribute to war efforts.*

WHY MIGHT GOVERNMENTS TAX THE RICH?

When and why do countries tax the rich? It's hard to think of a timelier question today or one for which there are more sharply colliding views. We know
that taxes on the rich today aren't what they were half a century ago, but how
did we get from there to here? We know even less about how those high taxes
of the twentieth century happened in the first place. Was it the effect of dem-

From Kenneth Scheve and David Stasavage, *Taxing the Rich: A History of Fiscal Fairness in the
United States and Europe* (Princeton, NJ: Princeton University Press, 2016).

ocracy, or a response to rampant inequality? Much of what is written today about taxing the rich takes the form of advocacy that is focused above all on the present. We do something different by taking a step back and showing what the long history of taxing the rich can teach us about our current situation.

What a country decides about taxes on the rich has profound consequences for its future economic growth and the distribution of economic resources and opportunities. Given the stakes, it's surprising how few comparative studies exist of taxation of the rich over the long run. Many people have asked this question only for recent decades, or for a single country. The last book to treat the question extensively was published more than a century ago, by Edwin Seligman.

We argue that societies do not tax the rich just because they are democracies where the poor outnumber the rich or because inequality is high. Nor are beliefs about how taxes influence economic performance ultimately decisive. Societies tax the rich when people believe that the state has privileged the wealthy, and so fair compensation demands that the rich be taxed more heavily than the rest.

When it comes to thinking of what tax policy is best, few would disagree with the notion that governments should be—in part—guided by fairness. It is a term used frequently by those on both the political left and right. How can this be? History suggests that the concept of fairness is up for grabs. Standards of fairness in taxation vary greatly across countries, over time, and from individual to individual.

When scholars write about fairness and taxation they most often adopt a normative point of view; that is, they ask what governments should do. But fairness isn't just a normative standard; it also matters for what governments do in practice because it influences the policy opinions of citizens. Ordinary people are more likely to support heavy taxation of the rich if it adheres to the fairness standards that they themselves hold. While many theories of politics assume people are concerned only with maximizing their own income, there is abundant evidence that humans are also concerned about issues of equity and fairness. These concerns don't mean that people aren't also concerned about self-interest—no one likes paying taxes—or even that self-interest isn't their prime concern. Individuals may also care about the efficiency of a tax system and whether it taxes people so heavily that they stop producing at all. Opinions about tax policy can be informed by both self-interest and efficiency, as well as fairness.

Political support for taxing the rich is strongest when doing so ensures that the state treats citizens *as equals*. Treating citizens as equals means treating them with "equal concern and respect," to use the phrase adopted by Ronald Dworkin. The idea that people should be treated as equals is, of course, part of the bedrock of modern democracy. This criterion narrows the field for what counts as an effective fairness justification for a tax. It cannot be an argument that refers to how people are inherently different or how some are inherently more worthy than others. Nor, of course, can it refer to pure self-interest. Even so, simply saying that people should be treated "as equals" or "with equal concern and respect" does not allow us to proceed deductively to identify the precise tax policies that satisfy this criterion. There are multiple ways to plausibly treat people as equals in taxation, and this is what debating tax fairness is all about. We take an inductive approach and focus on the three arguments that have been the most common and the most persuasive in political debate: *equal treatment, ability to pay*, and *compensatory* arguments. We refer to these arguments as three ways to treat people *as equals*.

The greatest political support for taxing the rich emerges when *compensatory* arguments can be credibly applied in policy debates. This happens when it is clear that taxing the rich more heavily than the rest serves to correct or compensate for some other inequality in government action. Compensatory arguments are most likely to emerge in democracies precisely because the very idea of democracy is that citizens should be treated as equals. If the rich have been privileged by some government intervention while others have not, then it is fair that they should be taxed more heavily to compensate for this advantage. Symmetrically, if the state has asked others to sacrifice while the rich have not borne the same burden, then again taxation of the rich can compensate. Compensatory arguments push policy toward heavier taxation of the rich, but in many cases the straightest route to fairness is to remove the initial privilege in the first place. Therefore, compensatory arguments are most powerful in cases when a government is obliged to take an unequal action that somehow favors the rich.

The compensatory theory is not the only fairness-based argument for taxing the rich. Over the past few centuries, the most common fairness-based argument for taxing the rich has been the *ability to pay* doctrine. According to this doctrine, a dollar in taxes for someone earning a million dollars a year represents less of a sacrifice than it does for someone earning a more average salary. Ability to pay arguments have existed since at least the sixteenth century, and they underpin the contemporary theories of optimal taxation most favored by economists.

For many, the ability to pay doctrine suffices as a reason to tax the rich more heavily than the rest. Others object to this notion. They may question how the ability to pay doctrine can be applied in practice. How much more should a rich person pay? They may also ask why ability to pay says nothing about how disparities in income or wealth emerged in the first place. Maybe the rich were just more talented or exerted more effort than others? People who criticize the ability to pay doctrine do not deny that a dollar in taxes represents less of a sacrifice for a rich person than for someone else; they simply do not accept that this is the right criterion by which to judge fairness.

In the face of doubts about ability to pay, a salient alternative is to suggest that the fairest system involves *equal treatment* for all. Both rich and poor should pay the same tax rate—a "flat tax." We use the phrase "equal treat-ment" to refer to fairness arguments suggesting that the same exact policy be adopted for all. Since the sixteenth century, opponents of progressive tax-ation have suggested that the basis of a republic is equal treatment for all, as illustrated by the norm of one person one vote. Therefore the same exact pol-icy should be applied to taxation. The logic that equal treatment requires a flat tax is not perfect; having all pay a lump-sum tax, where each person pays the same amount, would also respect equal treatment, yet many today would consider such a tax unfair. Nevertheless, arguments based on equal treat-ment have carried great power in debates about taxing the rich.

Some of the earliest examples of *compensatory* arguments involve sugges-tions that the rich ought to pay a higher rate of income tax because the poor bear the brunt of indirect taxes on common consumption goods. The idea is that to maintain themselves, the poor must consume a greater share of their income each year. However, over the last two centuries the most powerful compensatory arguments have involved a different sort of tax—military con-scription. This one simple fact goes a long way toward explaining both the rise of heavy taxation of the rich in the early and mid-twentieth century and the subsequent move away from this policy over the last several decades. The mass wars of the twentieth century were fought in a way that had a strong economic rationale but which privileged the rich along two dimensions. First, labor was conscripted to fight while capital was not. Second, owners of cap-ital benefited from high wartime demand for their products. Heavy taxation of the rich (owners of capital) became a way to mitigate these effects and to restore at least some degree of equality of treatment by the government. This was what those on the political left claimed and what those on the right were forced to concede. It was a powerful new argument for progressive forms of taxation, and it shifted mass and elite opinion on the question of taxing the rich in a leftward direction. Other scholars before us have investigated the effect of war on tax fairness, particularly in the United States and the United Kingdom. We show that this war effect can be explained by the compensa-tory theory of progressive taxation and that it is a more general phenomenon across countries and time.

Compensatory arguments are less credible in the case of more limited wars of the sort that the United States has fought of late. If the bulk of the popula-tion is not sacrificing for war, then how is it credible to ask the rich to pay a special sacrifice as compensation?

Finally, the choice between limited war or mass mobilization has been dependent on the state of military and related technologies. In the twentieth century the advent of the railroad made mass mobilization possible. When mass mobilization did eventually occur in 1914, compensatory arguments for taxing the rich emerged. In the twenty-first century the advent of precision weapons and drone technology means that mass armies are no longer neces-sary and may even be undesirable. Therefore, we are unlikely to see a repeat of the twentieth-century forces that led to heavy taxation of the rich. The compensatory theory explains why it was the wars of the early and mid-twentieth century that brought heavy taxation of the rich and not prior or subsequent wars.

Over the last two centuries, when circumstances have made compensatory arguments less credible, debates about taxation of the rich have boiled down to a conflict between the two competing visions of ability to pay and equal treatment, as well as efficiency. The outcome of this conflict has generally been for the rich to not be taxed much more heavily than the rest of the population. But, when circumstances have allowed for wartime compensatory arguments to be made, opinion has shifted in favor of taxing the rich. While those who adhere to ability to pay have continued to support taxing the rich, many of those who have preferred equal treatment have thought that the compensatory argument must be taken into account to achieve this goal. In such situations political parties of the left have used compensatory arguments to reinforce their arguments for taxing the rich. Political parties of the right have been forced to cede ground in order to remain electable.

It is also the case that political parties can and have used compensatory arguments instrumentally. If you personally are already convinced by the ability to pay rationale for taxing the rich, you may gain greater support for your proposal by making compensatory arguments that win broader support. Once external circumstances change and compensatory arguments lack credibility, then debates about taxing the rich return to a conflict between the competing notions of equal treatment, efficiency, and ability to pay.

THE RISE (AND DEMISE?) OF TAXES ON THE RICH

We can learn a great deal by studying changes in taxation over the long run. A look at broad trends can help us tease out the most important factors at play. To do this we, and the research assistants who helped us, have collected information on taxation in twenty countries, located principally in North America and Western Europe, over a period of two centuries. We focus on these countries for feasibility in data collection, but the conclusions we draw apply more generally. In an ideal world we would know all taxes due by a rich person and an average person in each year for each of the cases; unfortunately this is not possible. For most countries, even statutory rates of taxation are not widely published and must instead be verified by consulting original legislation. This is a time-consuming process.

We have been able to construct a unique database tracking statutory top marginal rates of income and inheritance taxation across the twenty countries. By statutory top marginal rates we mean the tax rate that would apply by law on the last dollar of income (or wealth) for someone in the highest tax bracket. This information is mostly drawn from original legislation. The top marginal rate provides an indication of what a rich person would be likely to pay. However, a focus on top statutory rates alone can provide misleading conclusions, and to deal with this problem we have also collected much additional information. First, we have the full schedules of tax rates (i.e., not just those at the top) for half of the countries. This shows whether an increase in the top rate represented a move to tax just the rich or whether it was just part of a move to tax everyone more heavily. A look at these schedules also reveals something more specific about who was being taxed. Rather than simply referring to "the rich" and "the rest," we can refer to individuals earning incomes or having fortunes of a specific size relative to the national average. What do we mean by a "rich" person? Extensive research has shown that much of the recent rise in inequality has been attributable to movements within the top 1.0 percent of the income distribution or even between the top 0.1 percent and the rest of the population. We adopt a similar categorization. Our focus on the rich also means that we are asking a question that is related to but distinct from those asked by the many scholars who have focused more generally on the politics of redistribution and/or social insurance.

Second, we also compare statutory rates with effective rates of taxation. This is critical because effective rates are what people actually pay. The effective rate for the income tax is found by taking total income tax paid and then dividing this by gross income. Information on effective rates is, on the whole, not easy to come by, particularly for a broad set of countries over a long time period. We do, however, have long-run effective rates of income taxation for six of the study countries. Using these we show that top statutory rates tend to be good proxies for how much the rich actually pay. There are important exceptions to this, however, that will be pointed out.

As a way of introducing the data, Figure [1] shows the average top statutory marginal rate of income and inheritance taxation in all twenty countries from 1800 to the present. The picture invites us to think of the world in three stages. First taxes on the rich were very low, then they rose to dramatic heights, and then they fell again, very dramatically. But a look at Figure [1] does not immediately suggest why this was the case. The rise of progressive taxation coincided with a period of democratization across the western world. But it also coincided with an era of massive military conflict as well as other changes to the political and economic landscape. To be sure, the rich had been taxed in wars of past centuries, but all evidence suggests this twentieth-century taxation was something entirely new. . . . Our conclusion that there was little taxation of the rich during the nineteenth century remains unaltered when one takes into consideration a broader range of taxes, including property taxes and annual taxes on wealth.

One way in which Figure [1] may be misleading is that it takes no account of the growth of government over time. Perhaps the rich were more heavily taxed in the twentieth century, compared to the nineteenth, because citizens demanded more from government, and all had to contribute? Average tax revenue as a percentage of gross domestic product increased from 9 percent to

FIGURE [1]   Average Top Rates of Income and Inheritance Taxation, 1800–2013

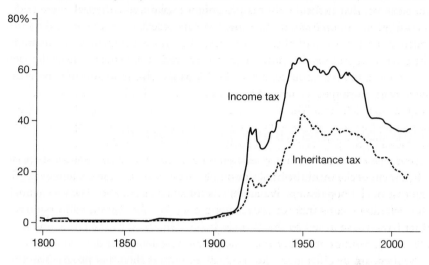

20 percent from 1900 to 1950, consistent with this conjecture. However, government revenue continued to increase over the remainder of the twentieth century—to an average of 43 percent of gross domestic product—while top rates on the rich declined over this period. The rich have been taxed less even though governments have increased in size. Scholars who work on public spending sometimes speak of a "ratchet" effect whereby each of the two world wars led to a permanent increase in the size of government. When it comes to long-run trends in taxing the rich there has been no ratchet; the period of high taxes on the rich was temporary. . . .

Another point missing from the figure is a discussion of how governments spent their money. This certainly ought to have some impact on what taxes citizens support and whether they consider them "fair." In an ideal world we would use two centuries of evidence to chart how much the rich and the rest benefited from government spending across the twenty countries. That, however, is a task that lies beyond the data that we have available. Fortunately, history has provided us with a convenient laboratory for studying taxation separately from the impact of the government transfers that are commonplace today. Prior to 1945 the governments in our study spent relatively little apart from providing basic public goods and fighting wars. Looking at taxation alone will therefore not give us a biased picture. Moreover, . . . after 1945, wartime compensatory arguments applied to spending every bit as much as they applied to taxation. Therefore, a look at government spending only reinforces our main conclusions.

Combining the information on top tax rates with extensive political data allows testing of several alternative arguments about when and why governments have taxed the rich. Data on when governments expanded the suffrage, as well as other institutional details, might explain why the rich were taxed more heavily in some cases than others. We also use data on income and wealth inequality to ask whether countries taxed the rich when inequality was high.

... The main lesson is not that war mattered; it is instead that if the rich were taxed so heavily during wartime, then this tells us something about the broader question of fairness in taxation.

COMMON IDEAS ABOUT TAXING THE RICH

Taxation of the rich is a hotly debated topic. So it should come as no surprise that there are several theories that might explain why some societies tax the rich heavily. Each of them is inadequate for the task at hand. The very plausible assumptions underlying these hypotheses are first that individuals do not like paying taxes; second that decisions are influenced by the prevailing type of political representation; and finally that decisions also depend on beliefs about economic efficiency. The received wisdom is then that progressive taxation is natural in a democracy because the bulk of the population wants it, unless people believe that the adverse incentive effects of doing so will be too great, or unless democracy somehow becomes "captured" by the rich.

"Democracies Tax the Rich More Heavily"

There may be many ways in which citizens can pressure governments to tax the rich, but having the vote certainly shouldn't harm their chances of doing so. In a democracy it should be numbers that count, and the poor and middle classes outnumber the rich. Among political scientists and economists today it is common to suggest that democracies are more likely to redistribute income from the rich to the rest, and progressive taxation is one means of doing so. Current scholars are in good company in making this argument. Sometime between the years 1521 and 1524, Francesco Guicciardini composed a dialogue among several fictitious speakers debating the merits of popular government in Florence. One of the opponents of democracy spoke as follows:

> As far as methods of taxation are concerned, I can assure you that the people's [sic] will normally be much worse and more unjust, because by nature they like to overburden the better-off; and since the less well off are more numerous, it is not difficult for them to do this.

Five centuries later, in a new era of expanding democracy, Edwin Seligman expressed a very similar opinion, but unlike Guicciardini, he saw this as an entirely good thing. Seligman's view was that as societies became more infused with democratic ideals, people naturally favored progressive taxation because it is simply the sensible and desirable thing to do. An alternative view from this time was that within democracies, the choice for progressive taxation was an outcome of political conflict. In 1926, William Shultz suggested the following:

> In legislatures, progressive taxes are proposed by representatives from "poorer" districts, they are fought tooth and nail by representatives of the propertied classes, and usually they are passed by legislatures only when the political influence of the poorer majority of the electorate outweighs the influence of the richer minority. By means of new radical parties or radical blocs growing up within older parties, the poorer classes of the nations have come to exercise more or less control over legislatures, and in this country and abroad progressivity in tax rates is an established order. This is an incidental parliamentary victory of the poorer classes over the richer—just as the retention of proportional rates would have been a defeat—in the present veiled economic and political struggle between the two.

Many subsequent scholars have emphasized the effect of universal suffrage on redistribution, and on progressive tax policies as part of the equation. What does the evidence say? There is some support for the idea that the introduction of income taxation was associated with the expansion of the suffrage. However, we ask not only whether governments have created an income tax, but also whether they have used it to tax the rich heavily. . . .

The evidence shows that democracy's effect on progressive taxation has been overstated. As noted, though the expansion of the suffrage and the adoption of progressive taxation happened around the same time in many countries, one needs to distinguish between the adoption of progressive taxation and the choice of high marginal tax rates for the rich. After the basic principle of progressive taxation was adopted, many countries took a very long time before choosing top statutory marginal tax rates that we would think of today as being high. Some countries never took this step at all. One explanation for this finding is that granting ordinary people the vote didn't result in progressive taxation because they didn't want it. They may have subscribed to a version of treating citizens as equals that is inconsistent with this policy.

It is also possible to extend the analysis by looking at institutions other than suffrage. Universal suffrage might arguably only have an impact on progressive taxation when elections of representatives are direct, when the ballot is secret, and when there are not additional institutional obstacles in place to prevent a majority from expressing its will. We investigated a host of such possibilities and came up with surprisingly little. Democracy alone was insufficient to produce heavier taxation of the rich.

"Democracies Tax the Rich When Inequality Is High"

Many observers remark that our current situation seems abnormal. Inequality is rising just as taxes on the rich are low and perhaps falling further. The implicit assumption behind this claim is that governments in "normal" times will raise taxes on the rich to fight inequality. There are three reasons they might do this.

The first reason is that as the amount of income or wealth of those at the top increases relative to the rest of society, voters will find it in their self-interest to tax the rich more heavily as long as the negative incentive effects from doing so are not too large. Voters might also favor this choice if they subscribe to the ability to pay doctrine.

The second reason why people might demand taxation of the rich when inequality is high is if they believe that inequality of outcomes derives from inequality of opportunity.

The third reason why governments might tax the rich when inequality is high is that they fear the consequences of inequality for the political system. They fear that inequalities of income and wealth will lead to the political process being captured by a wealthy elite or oligarchy. This is a very old idea. It was a common fear expressed by the U.S. Founding Fathers. It was also a view emphasized by the proponent of progressive taxation in Francesco Guicciardini's discourse on sixteenth-century Florence's progressive income tax, the *decima scalata*. Excess inequality of wealth would undermine the republic by sapping citizens of their virtue, perhaps even leading to tyranny. Finally, some authors, such as Jean-Jacques Rousseau, have emphasized that extreme inequality is a danger for a republic both because the rich can overcome legal restraints and also because the poor are more likely to revolt. As Rousseau suggested:

> The greatest evil has already been done where there are poor people to defend and rich people to restrain. The full force of the laws is effective only in the middle range; they are equally powerless against the rich man's treasures and the poor man's misery; the first eludes them, the second escapes them; the one tears the web, the other slips through it.

The big question is whether voters prompt democratically elected governments to take corrective policy actions so that levels of inequality remain in the "middle range" to which Rousseau referred.

Evidence from top incomes and top wealth shares suggests that democracies do not, in fact, tax the rich more heavily when inequality is high. . . . [T]here is only very weak evidence that governments, on average, respond to high prevailing levels of inequality by increasing taxes on the rich. Second, high taxes on the rich are indeed associated with lower subsequent levels of inequality. This means that high top tax rates can be a powerful tool to address inequality, but the mere presence of inequality is insufficient to prompt governments to pursue this strategy. This also implies that ability to pay arguments were insufficient to carry the day. Therefore we must think of why governments might respond to inequality in some cases but not others.

"Democratic Politics Can Be Captured by the Rich"

The rich in a democracy have one vote just like everyone else. But it would of course be naïve to think that wealth would bring zero additional advantage. A modified version of the democracy hypothesis is to suggest that democracy only results in greater taxation of the rich when the rich are unable to use their wealth to capture the political process. As we noted previously, theorists of republican government have long feared that inequalities in wealth would lead to the wealthy imposing their policies. It is possible today to think of multiple channels through which this effect might take place. The rich will logically be in a better position to lobby and give campaign contributions. They may also be better informed about how specific policies will influence them. Maybe they are also simply more likely to travel in the same circles as those who make policy.

When considering this problem many observers are quick to refer to the example of the United States today. For decades American political campaigns have relied on very substantial campaign contributions, and this phenomenon has only increased since the U.S. Supreme Court's 2010 *Citizens United* decision. Perhaps this is why careful studies by survey researchers, such as Martin Gilens and Larry Bartels, show that members of the U.S. Congress tend to vote in a manner that is most consistent with the views of their high-income constituents, as opposed to the general electorate. The fact that the American government taxes the rich less heavily than it did may simply be a result of this broader phenomenon of capture. Some authors have examined this issue extensively, finding clear support for a link between money contributed and policy choice. Others have claimed that capture helps to explain developments with regard to specific taxes, such as the estate tax.

The capture hypothesis seems ideally suited for explaining recent events in the United States; private campaign finance is abundant and private expenditures on lobbying are arguably even more significant. But if reference to campaign finance and lobbying is to be a convincing explanation for the big picture, then this hypothesis should also hold true for other democracies that have reduced taxes on the rich. A number of countries have actually gone further than the United States by abolishing inheritance taxation entirely. Top rates of income taxation have also come down dramatically elsewhere. The problem for the capture hypothesis is that these developments have included countries where the role of private money in politics is much more limited. So, even though Canadian electoral campaigns have, until recently, been publicly financed, the Canadian government abolished its inheritance tax in 1971. Sweden took a similar step in 2004 despite the fact that there is far less money in Swedish politics than in the United States.

Now, just because we fail to find a relationship between how campaigns are financed and how heavily the rich are taxed does not mean that there is no truth to the capture hypothesis. Nor does it mean that campaign lobbying by the wealthy has had no effect on taxation of the rich in the United States in recent decades. As an example, lobbying by members of the financial sector is no doubt preserving the policy through which hedge fund managers are able to classify their income as carried interest so as to reduce taxes due. Overall, though, the capture hypothesis is inadequate for explaining the broad variation in tax rates across many countries over time. Convincing evidence for the capture hypothesis would have to show that in a broad set of cases where democracies failed to tax the rich heavily, this failure was attributable to the persistence of elite power in a manner that has been suggested by Daron Acemoglu and James Robinson. Such an account would also have to show that it was variation in the extent of capture that explained variations in taxing the rich between countries over time.

"Governments Avoid Taxing the Rich When They Think It Is Self-Defeating"

A major claim in many arguments against taxing the rich is that this policy is self-defeating. Levying high taxes on the rich, it is suggested, will prompt them to work less, invest less, and, in a world of mobile capital, to shift their wealth abroad. Therefore it is better to not do it in the first place. Our goal is not to assess the plausibility of these claims. We instead ask how much force these arguments have had in the political arena and whether they can account for changes in top rates of taxation over time. It may be that knowledge about these incentive effects changes over time, perhaps because of new theories or new evidence about how the economy functions. For example, when an economy's growth rate slows, people may infer that taxes on the rich should be cut because incentive effects are having a negative impact. . . . We fail to find evidence that governments in recent decades have, on average, cut top tax rates as growth slows.

Another possibility is that until recent decades, people simply didn't believe incentive effects could be a major drag on the economy. Even astute observers sometimes suggest this. History shows that nothing could be further from the truth. It is indeed the case that as economic theory has advanced, scholars have been able for the first time to construct mathematical models in which incentive effects from taxation are directly incorporated. The most salient contribution here is that by James Mirrlees in the early 1970s. However, it is certainly not true that incentive arguments began with Mirrlees, and he made no attempt to claim this. As early as 1897, we can find a clear statement by Francis Edgeworth that what might seem an ideal policy based on equalization of incomes should be more nuanced because of incentive effects. As Edgeworth put it: "The *acme* of socialism is thus for a moment sighted; but it is immediately clouded over by doubts and reservations." . . . Arguments about incentive effects actually extend back to the sixteenth century. Since the first date at which modern progressive tax systems were proposed, opponents have argued that they would harm investment and employment. However, we find little evidence to suggest that changes in beliefs about the importance of these effects can account for the major changes in policy that we observe during the nineteenth and twentieth centuries.

TREATING CITIZENS AS EQUALS

A basic principle of democracy is that people ought to be treated as equals, but when it comes to taxation, people often disagree about what "as equals" means. We argue that the most politically powerful arguments for taxing the rich have been compensatory arguments; the rich should be taxed to compensate for the fact that they have been unfairly privileged by the state. Compensatory arguments have come in different guises, . . . but over the last two centuries the most powerful compensatory arguments have been those associated with mass mobilization for war.

The arrival of an era of mass warfare in 1914 created the possibility for powerful new arguments for taxing the rich. If labor was conscripted then fairness demanded that capital be conscripted as well. Having the rich pay higher taxes than the rest was one way to achieve this goal. Mass warfare has been the main force shaping the development of progressive tax policies during the last century. In emphasizing this, we are in keeping with other recent work that emphasizes the effect of war on domestic politics. However, this doesn't just tell us something about war; it also tells us that the most politically powerful arguments for taxing the rich are those based on compensation to restore treatment as equals.

The two world wars of the twentieth century involved mobilization of manpower on an unprecedented scale by both great powers and smaller states. Armies had once been recruited from a small segment of the population as volunteers or through limited conscription. Suddenly they were selected by universal conscription from the broad population. When raising a very large army, a state may find it necessary to recruit in this manner because the tax burden for paying volunteers would be unbearable. There is also a fairness argument for universal conscription. As Margaret Levi has demonstrated, universal conscription itself emerged from prior systems of limited conscription as a result of demands for equal treatment.

The problem with even a system of universal conscription is that it does not truly ensure equal treatment, even in an ex ante sense before a draft lottery is run. In virtually any universal conscription system there are reasons for exemption from service, and it is likely that the rich will be more apt to have access to these opportunities than the rest. Age presents yet another reason for exemption in any universal conscription system, and it is well known that age is highly correlated with wealth. Finally, universal conscription satisfies only a state's need for labor while saying nothing about how capital is to be raised for the war effort. If those with capital benefit from increased demand for the products of companies in which they have invested, then this too can violate widely shared commitments to equal treatment.

During the twentieth century, the inability of even a system of universal conscription to ensure citizens were being treated as equals gave proponents of progressive taxation a new and powerful compensatory argument for taxing the rich. If there was unequal sharing of the war burden, then the rich should be taxed more heavily than the rest. In other words, instead of having to rely only on arguments involving ability to pay, advocates of progressive taxation could now say that without heavily taxing the rich they would not be doing their fair share for the war effort. The clearest exposition of this argument was offered by the Labour Party in the UK in its call for a "conscription of wealth" to match the conscription of labor. During the two world wars this same argument was made in many other venues.

Mass mobilization for war presented new possibilities for making compensatory arguments for taxing the rich. Because such arguments could only be made for a limited time, the compensatory theory helps explain not only why taxes on the rich went up but also why they eventually came down. As we show, in the wake of World War II compensatory arguments emphasizing war sacrifice were ubiquitous in former belligerent countries. As had been the case after World War I, compensatory arguments remained prominent in discussions of how to repay war debts and, to a much greater degree than after World War I, with the provision of veterans' benefits. But ultimately, after mass mobilization wars ended, such arguments faded from view. Instead, high taxes on the rich became a new status quo that had to be defended strictly by referring to "ability to pay" or by saying that taxing the rich was "fair" without explaining why. In this environment it was inevitable that taxes on the rich would eventually come down. This does not explain the exact moment when taxes on the rich came down, but it does show why this evolution was inevitable.

If mass warfare created a new compensatory argument for taxing the rich, we need to recognize that not all wars open up this possibility. Some commentators have found it odd that the Bush administration lowered taxes on the rich during the recent wars in Iraq and Afghanistan. Others have even wondered why there aren't calls for a new conscription of wealth. Yet there is a fundamental problem with such an argument. Most of the U.S. population has not been asked to sacrifice during these recent wars, so why should the rich be singled out for sacrifice? Today the United States fights limited wars in which a small percentage of the population is mobilized and those in the armed forces are recruited voluntarily. Therefore, arguments about conscripting wealth no longer carry the same weight.

There is also a final critical element to our interpretation of the history of progressive taxation. The way that countries like the United States have fought wars is to a very great extent dependent on the state of military technology and on the type of enemies being fought. The emergence of the railroad first made it possible to mobilize armies on the scale that occurred during the two world wars. Over the last fifty years technological developments have pushed in the opposite direction. It is still possible to field a mass army, but the invention of weapons like the cruise missile, the laser guided bomb, and the drone mean that it is no longer necessary to do so.

Our finding about military technology and international rivalry is important for two reasons. First, it tells us more about the deeper reasons why steeply progressive taxation happened when it did, and why it is more difficult to achieve political support for it today. Compensatory arguments did not become credible by accident. They became credible because the pattern of international rivalry and military technology changed the type of wars that states fought. Second, our finding also sheds more light on the question of whether taxation of the rich during the twentieth century, and perhaps even trends in inequality, was accidental, as Thomas Piketty has prominently argued. While agreeing with his emphasis on war, our conclusions suggest that rather than high taxation of the rich being a simple accident, it was ultimately driven by long-run trends involving international rivalries and the technologies available for fighting wars.

THE FUTURE FOR TAXING THE RICH

Mass warfare mattered because it gave birth to new ideas and new arguments for why taxing the rich was fair. The extent of war mobilization was itself dictated by prevailing war technologies of the time. What does all this suggest for today's debates about taxing the rich? First, as technological change has led to a more limited form of warfare, there is unlikely to be a simple repeat of the twentieth-century conditions in which powerful compensatory arguments led to very high top marginal rates of income and inheritance taxation.

What about the effect of rising inequality? Won't this fuel demands for taxing the rich? Today it is most common to hear arguments in favor of taxing the rich simply because inequality is high and getting higher. In essence this is an invocation of the ability to pay doctrine. Yet two centuries of evidence show that governments, on average, do not tax the rich just because inequality is high. The rich are taxed when people believe not just that inequality is high but also that it is fundamentally unfair because the deck is stacked in favor of the rich, and the government did the stacking. In other words, they believe in compensatory arguments.

Based on current trends, future debates about taxing the rich will likely follow the familiar cleavage between those who adhere to ability to pay and those who emphasize equal treatment and/or economic efficiency. It is unlikely that such a debate will result in significant increases in taxes on those in the top 1.0 percent or the top 0.1 percent. Change would instead depend on whether proponents of taxing the rich are able to develop compensatory arguments for an era of peace. . . . [T]hose who want to tax the rich might do better to look at the type of compensatory arguments made in the nineteenth century rather than the twentieth. This was an era where many argued that income taxes needed to be progressive to offset the regressive incidence of other state levies. Such old arguments in a new era could lead to moderately increased taxes on the rich, though not to a repeat of the twentieth century. Change may also ultimately depend on whether those who want to tax the rich are themselves able to appeal to the logic of equal treatment. In some cases today those who are at the very top are paying a lower effective rate of tax than those who are merely well off. There is no need to appeal to ability to pay or rising inequality to argue against this. Such outcomes go against the basic equal treatment principles of fairness that opponents of taxing the rich have themselves espoused.

15.2

SUZANNE METTLER

From *The Submerged State: How Invisible Government Policies Undermine American Democracy*

Many Americans are critical of government redistribution to help the poor. In her book, Mettler argues that the lack of support is caused by a basic disparity between perception and reality. A large proportion of middle-class Americans, according to surveys, do not recognize the degree to which their material well-being flows from government subsidies or payouts. Mettler writes about the "submerged state"—the large portion of the American economy that results from explicit government policy but is not openly acknowledged by the middle- and upper middle-class beneficiaries. This lack of understanding about government's role in their own lives can affect the degree to which they support candidates promoting governmental help for the poor. Relatively well-off Americans who benefit from government redistribution often criticize relief for the poor as undeserved handouts from government.

[T]he *submerged state*: existing policies that lay beneath the surface of U.S. market institutions and within the federal tax system. . . .

The "submerged state" includes a conglomeration of federal policies that function by providing incentives, subsidies, or payments to private organizations or households to encourage or reimburse them for conducting activities deemed to serve a public purpose. Over the past thirty years, American political discourse has been dominated by a conservative public philosophy, one that espouses the virtues of small government. Its values have been pursued in part through efforts to scale back traditional forms of social provision, meaning visible benefits administered fairly directly by government. In the case of some programs geared to the young or working-age people, the value of average benefits has withered and coverage has grown more restrictive.[1] Ironically, however, the more dramatic change over this period has been the flourishing of the policies of the submerged state, which operate through indirect means such as tax breaks to households or payments to private actors who provide services. Since 1980 these policies have proliferated in number, and the average size of their benefits has expanded dramatically.

From Suzanne Mettler, *The Submerged State: How Invisible Government Policies Undermine American Democracy* (Chicago: University of Chicago Press, 2011).

Most of these ascendant policies function in a way that directly contradicts Americans' expectations of social welfare policies: they shower their largest benefits on the most affluent Americans. Take the Home Mortgage Interest Deduction (HMID), for example, which is currently the nation's most expensive social tax break aside from the tax-free status of employer-provided health coverage. Let us assume that a family buys a median-value home and to finance it borrows $230,000 at an interest rate of 6.25 percent for thirty years. The richer the household, the larger the benefit: in the first year, the average family, with an income between $16,751 and $68,000, would owe around $3,619 less in taxes; those in the next income group, with earnings up to $137,300, would reap an extra $5,146; and so forth, on up to the wealthiest 2 percent of families, with incomes over $373,650, who would enjoy a savings of $6,673. Of course, in reality, these differences are likely to be much greater. Low- to moderate-income Americans usually do not have enough deductions to itemize, so they would forgo this benefit and receive instead only the standard deduction. Meanwhile, the most affluent are likely to purchase far more expensive homes; if a family in the top income category opts for a more upscale home and borrows $500,000 for a mortgage, it will reap a benefit of $14,506 from the HMID; if this family purchases a truly exclusive property and borrows $1 million for a mortgage, it will qualify to keep a whopping $29,012! This pattern of upward redistribution is repeated in numerous other policies of the submerged state: federal largesse is allocated disproportionately to the nation's most well-off households. Such policies consume a sizable portion of revenues and leave scarce resources available for programs that genuinely aid low- and middle-income Americans.

Yet despite their growing size, scope, and tendency to channel government benefits toward the wealthy, the policies of the submerged state remain largely invisible to ordinary Americans: indeed, their hallmark is the way they obscure government's role from the view of the general public, including those who number among their beneficiaries. Even when people stare directly at these policies, many perceive only a freely functioning market system at work. They understand neither what is at stake in reform efforts nor the significance of their success. As a result, the charge leveled by opponents of reforms—that they amount to "government takeovers"—though blatantly inaccurate, makes many Americans at least uncomfortable with policy changes, if not openly hostile toward them.

Exacerbating these challenges, at the same time as the submerged state renders the electorate oblivious and passive, it actually promotes vested interests, and it has done so especially over the past two decades. The finance, real estate, and insurance industries all thrived until the recent recession, and in turn they invested heavily in strengthening their political capacity, making them better poised to protect the policies that have favored them. As a result, reform has required public officials to engage in outright combat or deal making with powerful organizations. Such politics disgust most Americans and hardly epitomize the kind of change Obama's supporters expected when he won office.

▪ ▪ ▪

American politics today is ensnared in the paradox of the submerged state. Our government is integrally intertwined with everyday life from health care to housing, but in forms that often elude our vision: governance appears "stateless" because it operates indirectly, through subsidizing private actors. Thus, many Americans express disdain for government social spending, incognizant that they themselves benefit from it. Even if they do realize that benefits they utilize emanate from government, often they fail to recognize them as "social programs." People are therefore easily seduced by calls for smaller government—while taking for granted public programs on which they themselves rely. Meanwhile, economic inequality has soared in the United States over the past forty years, reaching levels not seen since 1929, yet over this same period, policymakers have adamantly protected submerged state policies that bestow their greatest rewards on the affluent.[2] Ordinary citizens fail to realize the upward bias of such policies. Political leaders who do seek to reform them, to make their benefits more accessible to Americans of low and moderate incomes, face charges of mounting a "government takeover." If against the odds they manage to succeed, the policies achieved, especially if they still cloak government's role, prove difficult to sustain.

▪ ▪ ▪

As long as the submerged state persists in its shrouded form, American democracy is imperiled. Contrary to popular claims, the threat to self-governance is not the size of government, but rather the hidden form so much of its growth has assumed, and the ways in which it channels public resources predominantly to wealthy Americans and privileged industries.

GOVERANCE UNSEEN

▪ ▪ ▪

The Origins of the Submerged State

How did so much of U.S. governance come to be so heavily obscured from view? Policymakers built the foundation of the submerged state as we know it today during the early and mid-twentieth century, first largely by happenstance and then as a means of brokering political agreements. During the last thirty years of conservative governance, the submerged state has flourished. The composition of its policies has appealed to conservatives and liberals alike, such that in an era of increasingly sharp partisan divisions, it has offered a rare format for agreement on new policy initiatives. Also, some of the aggressive growth of the submerged state occurred automatically, as policies established long ago offered increasingly larger benefits due to changes such as the rise in housing values or health care costs—while political leaders looked the other way. As a result of both trends, the submerged state has expanded—even while some visible policies that aid poor and middle-income Americans atrophied. Since the 1970s, programs geared mostly for seniors, such as Social Security and Medicare, have remained strong, but various of those for younger people—for example, Pell Grants, unemployment insurance, and welfare—feature benefits that have deteriorated in value or coverage that has grown more restrictive.[3] On balance, in the lives of most Americans other than seniors, the impact of visible governance has diminished while that of the submerged state has grown.

Some of the earliest provisions of the submerged state either predated group mobilization in relevant domains or occurred beyond its radar screen. For example, when the framers of the original income tax code in 1913 opted to exclude mortgage interest from taxable income, they were not responding to group pressure. Rather, in omitting consumer debt from taxation, they followed a tradition that dated back to the Civil War period, while also seeking administrative simplicity that would aid in effective implementation.[4] During the 1910s and 1920s, policymakers enacted several other major social tax breaks, including the deduction of state and local taxes and charitable contributions.[5] Ironically, these components—minor footnotes early on—have ballooned to become vast entitlements today, and they are fiercely defended by the industries that benefit from them.

During the post–World War II period, innovations in the submerged state epitomized the fruit of political compromise. On some issues, policy enactment appears to have been possible only when the demands of vested interests were met through policy designs that accommodated them and thus prompted key moderate Democrats or Republicans to vote in favor of legislation.[6] For example, when the Johnson administration encountered steadfast opposition to student loan policy from bankers—more than from any other group—it finally invited a group of them to the White House to discuss the terms on which they would be willing to accept such a policy. These negotiations broke the logjam, leading to a final bill that included several features favorable to the banks in exchange for their support.[7]

In recent decades of conservative dominance and political polarization, the submerged state entered into its new stage of aggressive growth. Increasingly, the design of its policies became not a last resort but rather the template of choice for new policy initiatives. In an era when direct visible social policies have been under attack, submerged policies contain several attributes that have enabled them to overcome partisan divisions and institutional gridlock. They have gained favor for four reasons: first, Republicans and conservative Democrats find them attractive; second, other Democrats have proven willing to go along; third, institutional features of Congress make them easier to enact than new direct spending programs; and fourth, over time they have cultivated the support of interest groups that defend them vigorously.

The submerged state has long fused well with conservatives' political values and priorities. While hallmark programs of the visible state originated at the hands of mainstream Democrats, from the very beginning Republicans and a few conservative Democrats took the lead in submerged state-building. Christopher Howard reports that southern Democrats and conservative Republicans helped enact the income tax back in 1913, complete with its early tax expenditures, and in 1926 pro-business Republican Senator George McLean (R-CT) nonchalantly introduced the amendment that henceforth excluded employer pensions from taxation. In the early 1970s, Senator Russell Long judged President Richard Nixon's welfare reform plan to be too generous. He devised an alternative policy—the Earned Income Tax Credit (EITC)—that aimed to help the working poor through tax relief, and it passed easily as part of a larger tax bill in 1975.[8]

Conservatives' leadership in the construction of the submerged state is not accidental. All elected officials, if they wish to stay in office, need to find ways to represent citizens, to respond to the needs of those who elected them and those whose votes they would like to attract. The challenge for conservatives is doing this without expanding the visible state. Conservative politicians favor submerged state policies primarily because they enable them to deliver goods and services to core constituencies while neither creating vast new direct spending programs nor enlarging the federal bureaucracy in the process.

Submerged policies appeal to some contemporary conservatives because they can appear to restrain government spending. Tax expenditures, at first blush, might seem consistent with this goal because they reduce the amount government collects in revenues. Of course, in fact they do not reduce government obligations—they only limit the funds available to it for spending on other programs. But some policymakers assume that curtailing revenues provides a means by which to reduce spending, an approach that became known as "starve the beast." As articulated by Reagan in 1981: "Over the past decade we've talked about curtailing spending so that we can lower the tax burden. . . . But there were always those who told us that taxes couldn't be cut until spending was reduced. Well, you know, we can lecture our children about extravagance until we run out of voice and breath. Or we can cure their extravagance simply by reducing their allowance."[9] Some policymakers also believe that submerged policies, by bestowing rewards on some people, may quell popular demands for more extensive visible social provision for all citizens. Republican Senator Robert Packwood, chair of the Senate Finance Committee, implied this in 1983 when he defended the tax-free status of employer health insurance: "I think the one reason we do not have any significant demand for national health insurance in this country among those who are employed is because their employers are paying for their benefits, by and large. And we will never go to the situation in Great Britain so long as that system exists, and I hate to see us nibble at it for fear you are going to have the demand that the Federal Government take over and provide the benefits that would otherwise be lost."[10] The submerged state is thus supported in part because it is thought to deter direct government spending, both by reducing revenues and by appeasing those who might otherwise be vocal proponents.

Submerged state policies can also appear to embody the principle of privatization, meaning the contracting out of government responsibilities to the private sector on the assumption that it can deliver goods and services more efficiently. As such, they seem to reflect the kinds of market-based approaches that Reagan championed and that have become commonplace in American politics ever since his presidency. It is the case that the officials on the front lines of service delivery for such policies are not government bureaucrats but, instead, representatives of institutions such as health insurance companies and banks. Yet, in fact, such policies function not through free-market principles of laissez-faire but rather through public subsidization of the private sector. Some submerged policies, such as tax breaks, subsidize individuals to participate in activities that promote the profitability of particular industries; others, such as student loans, function by delivering public funds directly to the private sector. In either case, they encourage people to act differently than if they were left to pure market forces; for example, consumers are more likely to purchase bigger houses than they would if home-owner tax advantages did not exist, and this fuels the real estate industry. Nonetheless, these features of the submerged state help explain why conservatives have not acted to restrain even its policies that have grown to be hugely expensive, and why they have continued to initiate new ones.

Another critical factor that has enabled the submerged state to flourish in recent decades is that over time, a wider array of Democrats became willing accomplices—and leaders—in its creation. During the New Deal and Great Society periods, Democrats initiated the creation of new direct spending programs. When in the 1980s that approach to governance began to seem politically infeasible, they looked to the submerged state instead to find ways to aid low- and middle-income people. They increasingly acquiesced and supported policies such as tax expenditures because, to quote one member of Congress, they became "the only game in town."[11] After Democratic candidate Walter Mondale lost his bid for the presidency in 1984, the Democratic Leadership Council (DLC) formed in an effort to take control of the party away from liberals. The DLC championed tax expenditures, and in 1988 its affiliates in Congress pushed successfully for large increases in the EITC and for other new tax credits for the working poor.[12] While Republicans had proposed tuition tax breaks as far back as the early 1960s, it was Democratic President Bill Clinton who finally called for their successful enactment in the form of the HOPE and Lifetime Learning Tax Credits, which he signed into law. Once Democrats controlled both Congress and the White House in 2009, tax expenditures constituted their policy tool of choice, as numerous new and expanded tax breaks were tucked into bills intended to encourage particular activities and to stimulate the flagging economy.

With Congress so deeply and closely divided between the two major political parties in recent decades, submerged policies—particularly in the case of tax expenditures—have also proven easier to enact than other policies because the institutional hurdles are much lower. Direct new spending programs must overcome multiple hurdles in the budget process, gaining the approval of two separate committees in each chamber for authorization and appropriation. New tax breaks, by contrast, only need to pass muster with the tax committees, and they can be folded into large revenue bills, attracting little attention in floor votes.[13]

Over time, each well-established wing of the submerged state has been tended by the trade associations and other interest groups that represent its core industries—such as the National Association of Realtors and National Association of Home Builders in the case of the Home Mortgage Interest Deduction (HMID). Such groups have carefully cultivated and tended relationships with elected officials on both sides of the aisle. They have long made their positions known through lobbying in Washington, D.C., and by activating their constituencies; in recent decades, as the cost of campaigns has escalated, they have devoted substantial amounts to donations. Such influence serves as another important reason why substantial components of the submerged state enjoy strong bipartisan support, resilient enough to withstand the sharp partisan divisions around most other issues.

In short, over the past thirty years, by nurturing and protecting the submerged state, conservatives did not downsize government; rather, they took the lead in restructuring and actually enlarging it, but in ways that elude the public. Liberals, with few alternatives, willingly followed suit. Meanwhile interest groups worked to maintain strong support for their favored policies from members of both parties.

The Size and Scope of the Submerged State

As a result of these attributes, submerged state policies of many varieties have proliferated in number and in scope during the conservative period of the past three decades. To illustrate such trends, this section will focus on social tax expenditures. When Reagan took office in 1981, 81 of these existed; by 2010, Obama's second year in office, the number had risen by 86 percent, to 151. The number of such policies increased steadily but slowly during the 1980s and 1990s, then grew more rapidly from 2000 to the present—both when Republicans controlled both chambers of Congress and the White House and more recently when Democrats did.[14]

The amount of total revenue lost to social tax expenditures soared between 1981 and 2010, in 2010 dollars, as shown in Figure [1]. The temporary decline in the late 1980s is attributable primarily to the effect of tax reform in 1986. It is important to note that even in this major legislation policymakers treated

FIGURE [1] Revenue Lost from All Social Tax Expenditures, 1981–2010 (2010 Dollars)

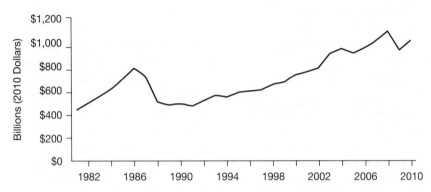

SOURCES: Joint Committee on Taxation, "Estimates of Federal Tax Expenditures for Fiscal Years" (various years), http://www.jct.gov/publications.html; Congressional Budget Office, "Tax Expenditures: Current Issues and Five-Year Budget Projections for Fiscal Years 1982–1986" (1981), http://www.cbo.gov/ftpdocs/51xx/doc5185/doc29-Entire.pdf.

social tax expenditures as sacrosanct, leaving intact all of the most costly ones. The reason why their overall value dipped was because tax reform lowered regular tax rates, and when households owe less, the worth of individual tax breaks is effectively reduced.[15] Nonetheless, after a few years of stasis, the actual cost of tax breaks began to grow steadily and rapidly again, increasing by more than 130 percent by 2008. In that year, just before the recession temporarily reduced their value, they cost the nation $1.086 trillion, and recently their cost has nearly returned to that level.

The three most expensive social tax expenditures were each created long ago—starting with the case of the Home Mortgage Interest Deduction in 1913—and have expanded tremendously in terms of their value in recent decades. Figure [2] shows the value, in 2010 dollars, of the HMID, and the nontaxable status of health insurance and retirement benefits. Notably, while each diminished briefly in the late 1980s and early 1990s for the reasons mentioned above, they then once again resumed their growth, which was mitigated only briefly by the recession in 2008.

Their low profile notwithstanding, submerged state policies consume a large portion of federal resources relative to many social programs that are much more visible. Figure [3] shows the size of the three most expensive social tax expenditures compared to the value of a few well-known direct social programs. The HMID consumes four times the amount of the primary federal housing program for low-income Americans, called Section 8 Housing vouchers. Despite the amount of attention often given in public discourse to welfare (now called Temporary Assistance for Needy Families), it costs the

FIGURE [2] Revenue Lost from Three Major Tax Expenditures, 1981–2010
(2010 Dollars)

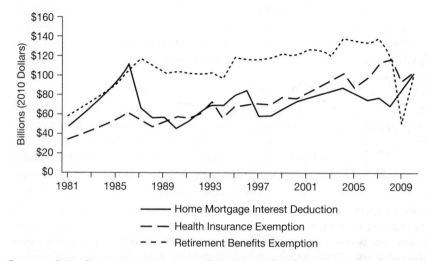

Home Mortgage Interest Deduction
— — Health Insurance Exemption
- - - Retirement Benefits Exemption

SOURCES: Joint Committee on Taxation, "Estimates of Federal Tax Expenditures for Fiscal Years" (various years), http://www.jct.gov/publications.html; Congressional Budget Office, "Tax Expenditures: Current Issues and Five-Year Budget Projections for Fiscal Years 1982–1986" (1981), http://www.cbo.gov/ftpdocs/51xx/doc5185/doc29 -Entire.pdf.

FIGURE [3] Selected Visible and Submerged Social Expenditures, 2007
(2010 Dollars)

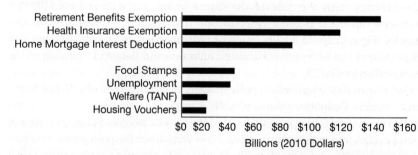

SOURCES: Joint Committee on Taxation, "Estimates of Federal Tax Expenditures, 2007– 2011" (2007), http://www.jct.gov/publications.html?func=startdown&id=1198; Office of Management and Budget, *Analytical Perspectives: Budget of the United States Government FY 2009* (2008), tables 3.2, 8.5, http://www.gpoaccess.gov/usbudget/fy09/pdf/spec .pdf; Congressional Budget Office, Budget Factsheets for TANF, Food Stamps, and Unemployment (March 2007).

nation less than one-fifth the amount of subsidizing employer-provided health insurance and less than one-seventh the expense of employer-provided retirement benefits. Neither the costs of food stamps, the most utilized program for low-income people, nor of unemployment insurance, which provides economic security for Americans of all income levels, amounts to as much as half the value of even the least expensive of these programs.

Fostering Economic Inequality

Because the submerged state typically distributes its rewards through more complex and circuitous processes than do more direct policies, its major beneficiaries are often not obvious. To the extent that lawmakers discuss the submerged state publicly, they usually imply that its policies facilitate widely held goals, such as the expansion of health care coverage or growth of retirement savings for average citizens. In some instances, such images are reasonably accurate depictions of policy effects, as exemplified by the Earned Income Tax Credit, which subsidizes the earnings of the working poor, or the tuition tax credits signed into law by Clinton, which aided middle-income Americans in paying for college. Most submerged policies, however, actually exacerbate inequality: they shower their most generous benefits on affluent people, and they generate detrimental side effects that adversely impact those who are less well-off. Some of the largest winnings, moreover, are accrued not by individuals and households but rather by the third-party organizations and businesses that benefit from the economic activities such policies promote.

Figure [4] illustrates how the three most costly tax expenditures distribute their benefits across income groups. Each bestows its bounty in an upwardly redistributive fashion, with the largest amounts going to those in the upper-income groups. The most skewed distribution accompanies the Home Mortgage Interest Deduction and the tax-free status of retirement benefits: in 2004, 69 percent and 55 percent of the benefits from each of these policies, respectively, were conferred on Americans with household incomes of $100,000 or more—the top 15 percent of the income distribution.[16] The tax-free nature of employer-sponsored health insurance is somewhat less biased, though still 30 percent of the benefit was allocated to families in the top 15 percent of the income distribution.

On the rare occasions when policymakers ever talk about the Home Mortgage Interest Deduction, they typically convey the impression that it helps make home-ownership possible for middle-income people. Scholars have not found evidence to support this effect, however; rather the policy merely offers an extra financial advantage to those who were already positioned to buy a home.[17] HMID offers particularly generous aid, as we have seen, to the wealthy. Whereas the median new home value in the nation has fluctuated between $200,000 and $260,000 since 2006, the HMID applies to mortgages up to $1,000,000; those who can afford to buy the most expensive homes and qualify for the largest mortgages reap by far the largest benefits from the policy.[18]

FIGURE [4]   Percent of Tax Subsidies Claimed by Households, by Income, 2004

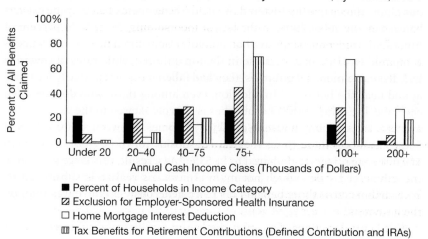

■ Percent of Households in Income Category
☑ Exclusion for Employer-Sponsored Health Insurance
☐ Home Mortgage Interest Deduction
⊞ Tax Benefits for Retirement Contributions (Defined Contribution and IRAs)

SOURCES: Leonard E. Burman et al., "Tax Code, Employer-Sponsored Insurance, and Tax Subsidies," in *Using Taxes to Reform Health Insurance*, edited by Leonard E. Burman and Henry J. Aaron (Washington, DC: Brookings Institution Press, 2008); Joint Committee on Taxation, "Estimates of Federal Tax Expenditures for Fiscal Years 2005–2009" (2005), http://www.jct.gov/publications.html?func=startdown&id=1200; Leonard E. Burman et al., "Distributional Effects of Defined Contribution Plans and Individual Retirement Accounts," Tax Policy Center Discussion paper No. 16 (2004), http://www.urban.org/uploadedPDF/311029TPC DP16.pdf.

Moreover, both the HMID and other benefits for home owners operate as artificial incentives that encourage people to purchase more expensive and larger homes than they would in their absence. As a result, such policies inflate prices, making home-ownership more out-of-reach for non-owners. For those who are financially capable of buying a home, housing equity provides their primary source of wealth, and that further widens the economic gap between owners and renters. In addition, the lost government revenues leave lawmakers with insufficient funds to maintain or create policies that could more effectively enhance the social welfare of low- and moderate-income citizens.[19]

The employer-provided and government-subsidized benefits of the submerged state are also tilted to higher-income Americans and have become more so over time. During the 1940s, increasing numbers of jobs offered workers such benefits, and before long, the majority of Americans enjoyed coverage. As health care costs soared in recent years, however, fewer and fewer jobs granted health coverage to employees: the percentage of Americans possessing it diminished in every consecutive year from 2000 to 2009, falling from 68 to 59 percent over the period.[20] In addition, the extent of the plans that are still offered by employers has diminished.[21] While higher-income people have long been most likely to gain employment in positions that offer health

insurance and have had the good fortune of being covered by more generous plans, the inequality fostered by such arrangements has become exacerbated recently. As of 2009, in the lowest income quintile, only 16 percent of
Americans under age sixty-five had employer-sponsored health insurance—
compared to 85 percent of those in the top quintile; while rates of coverage
had declined among all quintiles, they had fallen most precipitously for those
at and near the bottom.[22] In addition, even among those who do have such
coverage, the value of the tax subsidies is sharply skewed to the wealthy: the
average subsidy for households with incomes between $200,000 and
$500,000 is over three times the average subsidy for those in the $10,000 to
$20,000 range, $4,791 compared to $1,535.[23] As a result, this large portion of
the submerged state, which not many Americans realize is subsidized by
government, showers its benefits far more generously on the haves than on
the have-nots.

Well beyond its impact on individuals and families, the submerged state
exacerbates economic inequality by promoting some entire sectors of the
economy over others, at government expense. In delivering subsidies to particular industries and creating incentives for people to participate in specific
market activities, its policies protect and enhance profit-making capabilities
in those areas. From 1980 until the current recession, the core sectors that it
nurtures—finance, insurance, and real estate—outpaced growth in other
sectors of the American economy.[24] The fortunes of these industries ema-
nated not from "market forces" alone but rather from their interplay with the
hidden policies that promoted their growth and heaped extra benefits on
them.

Such patterns are exemplified by the rise in profitability of the student loan
sector. Americans' need for student aid escalated during the 1980s and 1990s
as the rise in tuition rates exceeded inflation. Amid the growing partisan divide in Congress, policymakers could forge agreement more easily on terms
for student loans, for which they needed to do little more than expand borrowing limits and loosen eligibility requirements, than they could on Pell
Grants, the direct form of tuition assistance for low-income students, for
which rate increases would have involved the highly conflictual and many-
staged process of legislative approval for increased spending.[25] As a result of
these trends, growing numbers of students borrowed, the average amount of
their loans soared, and lending became increasingly lucrative. Student lender
Sallie Mae, created by the federal government in 1973 and permitted to
become a private company in 1996, saw the value of its stocks rise by nearly
2000 percent over the next decade, compared to the Standard and Poor 500's
average gain of 228 percent. Its CEO became the most highly compensated in
the nation, with approximately $37 million in salary, bonuses, and stock
awards in 2006.[26]

Similarly, government subsidies for health insurance appeared more complicit in the development of the "winner take all" society than in providing for

the health care of the nation's citizens. Health insurance companies enjoyed soaring profits that did not abate even with the recession: the five largest insurers reported $12.2 billion in profits in 2009, a 56 percent increase from 2008.[27] For the CEOs of the top seven health insurance companies, average total compensation, including stock options, soared to $10.6 million.[28] Meanwhile, among ordinary Americans, the ranks of the uninsured escalated, reaching 16.7 percent in 2010, and the insured faced mounting costs.[29]

Whereas most Americans assume social welfare policy exists in order to provide economic security to average people and to lessen inequality, the policies of the submerged state have aided and abetted the upward distribution of riches, with more and more of the largesse accrued to those at the very top. The sectors that it nurtures, in turn, have invested in strengthening their political capacity, fortifying their ability to defend existing arrangements.

NOTES

1. Suzanne Mettler and Andrew Milstein, "American Political Development from Citizens' Perspective: Tracking Federal Government's Presence in Individual Lives over Time," *Studies in American Political Development* 21 (Spring 2007): 110–30.

2. Thomas Piketty and Emmanuel Saez, "Income Inequality in the United States, 1913–1998," *Quarterly Journal of Economics* 118 (February 2003): 1–39.

3. Mettler and Milstein, "American Political Development from Citizens' Perspective."

4. Christopher Howard, *The Hidden Welfare State: Tax Expenditure and Social Policy in the United States* (Princeton, NJ: Princeton University Press, 1997), 48–54.

5. Ibid., 176–77.

6. Paul Starr and Gosta Esping-Andersen, "Passive Intervention," *Working Papers for a New Society*, July/August 1979, http://www.princeton.edu/~starr/articles/articles68-79 /Starr_Esping-Andersen_Passive_Intervention.pdf (accessed October 19, 2010).

7. Muhammad Attaullah Chaudhry, "The Higher Education Act of 1965: An Historical Case Study" (PhD diss., Oklahoma State University, 1981), 97–99; Jose Chávez, "Presidential Influence on the Politics of Higher Education: The Higher Education Act of 1965" (PhD diss., University of Texas at Austin, 1975), 121–23.

8. Howard, *Hidden Welfare State*, 46, 61, 64–70.

9. Ronald Reagan, "Address to the Nation on the Economy," February 5, 1981, http://www.reagan.utexas.edu/archives/speeches/1981/20581c.htm (accessed February 29, 2011).

10. Quoted in Howard, *Hidden Welfare State*, 190–91.

11. Pete Stark (D-CA), referring to the Targeted Jobs Tax Credit, quoted in Christopher Howard, "Tax Expenditures," in *The Tools of Government: A Guide to the New Governance*, ed. Lester M. Salamon (New York: Oxford University Press, 2002), 428.

12. Howard, *Hidden Welfare State*, 151–52.

13. Ibid., 179–80.

14. Office of Management and Budget, *Analytical Perspectives: Budget of the United States Government*, FY 1997, 2002, 2007, 2011; Joint Committee on Taxation, "Estimates of Federal Tax Expenditures for Fiscal Years 1990–1994" (1989); Congressional Budget Office, "Tax Expenditures: Current Issues and Five-Year Budget Projections for Fiscal Years 1982–1986" (1981).

15. C. Eugene Steuerle, *Contemporary U.S. Tax Policy*, 2nd ed. (Washington, DC: Urban Institute Press, 2008), 128, 130, 132, 133, 248; Hacker, *Divided Welfare State*, 160–63. Tax reform also increased the standard deduction, so fewer people qualified to itemize deductions.

16. U.S. Census Bureau, "Annual Social and Economic (ASEC) Supplement" (2005), last modified August 28, 2007, http://pubdb3.census.gov/macro/032007/hhinc/new06 _000.htm.

17. Edward L. Glaeser and Jesse M. Shapiro, "The Benefits of the Home Mortgage Interest Deduction," NBER Working Paper no. 9284 (October 2002), http://papers.nber .org/papers/w9284 (accessed October 24, 2010).

18. U.S. Census, "Median and Average Sale Prices of New Homes Sold in the United States," http://www.census.gov/const/uspricemon.pdf (accessed October 20, 2010).

19. Starr and Esping-Andersen, "Passive Intervention."

20. Elise Gould, "Employer-Sponsored Health Insurance Erosion Accelerates in the Recession: Public Safety Net Catches Kids but Fails to Adequately Insure Adults," *EPI Briefing Paper*, November 16, 2010, Briefing Paper #283, http://www.epi.org/publications /entry/bp283 (accessed December 2, 2010).

21. Jacob S. Hacker, *The Divided Welfare State: The Battle over Public and Private Social Benefits in the United States* (New York: Cambridge University Press, 2002), 36– 39; Jacob S. Hacker, *The Great Risk Shift: The Assault on American Jobs, Families, Health Care, and Retirement, and How You Can Fight Back* (New York: Oxford University Press, 2006), 139.

22. Gould, "Employer-Sponsored Health Insurance Erosion Accelerates in the Recession."

23. Len Burman, Surachai Khitatrakun, and Sarah Goodell, "Tax Subsidies for Private Health Insurance: Who Benefits and at What Cost?" Robert Wood Johnson Foundation, Synthesis Project, Update, July 2009, http://www.rwjf.org/files/research/072209policy synthesis3update.brief.pdf (accessed January 15, 2011).

24. Frank Levy and Peter Temlin, "Inequality and Institutions in 20th Century America," Industrial Performance Center, MIT, Working Paper Series, MIT-IPC-07-002 (2007), 36–37, http://papers.ssrn.com/sol3/papers.cfm?abstract_id=984330.

25. National Center for Public Policy and Higher Education, *Losing Ground: A National Status Report on the Affordability of American Higher Education* (San Jose, CA: National Center for Public Policy and Higher Education, 2002), 8–9, 12, 22–30.

26. Bethany McLean, "Sallie Mae: A Hot Stock, A Tough Lender," CNNMoney.com, December 14, 2005, http://money.cnn.com/2005/12/14/news/fortune500/sallie_fortune _122605/index.htm (accessed January 29, 2011); "Top 100 Executives by Total Compensation," *Washington Post* (2006), http://projects.washingtonpost.com/post200/2006 /executives-by-compensation/ (accessed January 29, 2011).

27. "Fortune 500: Health Care: Insurance and Managed Care, 2009," CNNMoney .com (2010), http://money.cnn.com/magazines/fortune/fortune500/2010/industries /223/index.html (accessed October 25, 2010).

28. Dan Bowman, "2009 Health Insurance CEO Compensation," *Fierce Health Payer*, May 11, 2010, http://www.fiercehealthpayer.com/special-reports/2009-health-insurance -ceo-compensation (accessed October 28, 2010).

29. Mike Lillis, "Census: Number of Uninsured Americans Skyrocketed Last Year," *The Hill*, September 16, 2010, http://thehill.com/blogs/healthwatch/health-reform -implementation/119271-census-number-of-uninsured-americans-skyrocketed-last -year (accessed October 26, 2010).

15.3

WALTER RUSSELL MEAD

From *Special Providence: American Foreign Policy and How It Changed the World*

There are four strains of American foreign policy, Mead argues: Hamiltonian, Wilsonian, Jeffersonian, and Jacksonian. Contemporary American leaders invoke specific memories of American history related to one or more of these strains to justify their foreign policy decisions. Mead argues that foreign policy has had an enormous influence on domestic politics throughout American history, much more than is ordinarily supposed.

INTRODUCTION

. . . In little more than two hundred years, the United States has grown from a handful of settlements on the Atlantic seaboard to become the most powerful country in the history of the world. Both foreigners and Americans themselves take this remarkable development for granted. Throughout the U.S. rise to world power, most observers have believed that the country did not care very much about foreign policy and was not very good at it. Even today in the United States, most policy-makers and pundits think that foreign policy played only a very marginal role in American life before World War II, and that there is very little to be gained by studying the historical records of our past.

. . . I found myself increasingly drawn to question this conventional wisdom. I wondered if American success in the rough-and-tumble contest of nations wasn't due just to dumb luck, the special providence for drunks, fools, and the United States of America that Bismarck believed watched over us. I also wondered if the American foreign policy system had a logic of its own, a different logic from the one that governed the foreign policy of the traditional great powers of Europe.

Two discrepancies led me to ask these questions. First, there was the odd fact that while much conventional discussion of foreign policy assumes at least tacitly that democracy is at best an irrelevance and at worst a serious obstacle in foreign affairs, in the twentieth century democratic states were generally more successful in foreign policy than either monarchies or dictatorships.

From Walter Russell Mead, *Special Providence: American Foreign Policy and How It Changed the World* (New York: Alfred A. Knopf, 2001).

The clearest examples come from Germany and Japan. Under nondemocratic regimes, both Germany and Japan followed risky, aggressive foreign policies that ultimately brought them to misery and ruin. Starting under much less favorable external circumstances after World War II, democratic German and Japanese governments made their countries rich, peaceful, and respected. Was it possible that something about democracy actually improves the ability of governments to conduct their foreign affairs?

Second, I could not escape the fact that the two most recent great powers in world history were what Europeans still sometimes refer to as "Anglo-Saxon" powers: Great Britain and the United States. Besides having a large number of cultural similarities, these two countries have historically looked at the world in a different way than have most of the European countries. The British Empire was, and the United States is, concerned not just with the balance of power in one particular corner of the world but with the evolution of what we today call "world order." A worldwide system of trade and finance made both Britain and the United States rich; those riches were what gave them the power to project the military force that ensured the stability of their international systems. Both Britain and the United States spent less time thinking about the traditional military security preoccupations of European power diplomacy and more time thinking about money and trade. "A nation of shopkeepers!" Napoleon scoffed about Britain—but the shopkeepers got him in the end.

Could it be that the British shopkeepers and American democrats know something about foreign policy that Napoleon and Bismarck didn't?

These questions led me to the study of the history of American foreign policy. . . .

For one thing, . . . foreign policy has played a much more important role in American politics throughout our history than I expected. Our contemporary battles over the North American Free Trade Agreement (NAFTA) and the World Trade Organization (WTO) are the latest installments in a long line of American political contests over trade issues. Long before World War II or even World War I, foreign policy questions were deciding American elections, reshaping American politics, and driving the growth of the American economy.

I also found that American thinking about foreign policy has been relatively stable over the centuries. The arguments over foreign policy in George Washington's administration—and some of the bitterest political battles Washington engaged in were over foreign policy—are clearly related to the debates of our own time.

Americans through the centuries seem to have had four basic ways of looking at foreign policy, which have reflected contrasting and sometimes complementary ways of looking at domestic policy as well. *Hamiltonians* regard a strong alliance between the national government and big business as the key both to domestic stability and to effective action abroad, and they have long focused on the nation's need to be integrated into the global economy on favorable terms. *Wilsonians* believe that the United States has both a moral obligation and an important national interest in spreading American democratic and social values throughout the world, creating a peaceful international community that accepts the rule of law. *Jeffersonians* hold that American foreign policy should be less concerned about spreading democracy abroad than about safeguarding it at home; they have historically been skeptical about Hamiltonian and Wilsonian policies that involve the United States with unsavory allies abroad or that increase the risks of war. Finally, a large populist school I call *Jacksonian* believes that the most important goal of the U.S. government in both foreign and domestic policy should be the physical security and the economic well-being of the American people. "Don't Tread on Me!" warned the rattlesnake on the Revolutionary battle flag; Jacksonians believe that the United States should not seek out foreign quarrels, but when other nations start wars with the United States, Jacksonian opinion agrees with Gen. Douglas MacArthur that "There is no substitute for victory."

These four schools have shaped the American foreign policy debate from the eighteenth century to the twenty-first. They are as important under George W. Bush as they were under George Washington and from everything that I can see, American foreign policy will continue to emerge from their collisions and debates far into the future.

. . . The long economic boom of the 1990s spawned some triumphalist literature about the American way of capitalism and the growth of American power. . . . After each of the three great wars of the twentieth century—the two world wars and the Cold War—many voices in America proclaimed an "end to history." With the powers of evil defeated, the United States and its allies, some argued each time, would go on in the postwar period to build a new world order of justice, peace, and democracy.

History, alas, has a way of hanging on. More than a decade after the Cold War, it now seems clear that the twenty-first century is bringing the United States new challenges and new problems. Not all countries will become democratic; not all democratic countries will agree with the United States about how the world should be run. Foreign policy will not become a field of dreams; our choices will sometimes be painful ones, and together with new opportunities and adventures this century may well bring new wars and new problems that are even worse than those of the bloody century just past.

. . . American foreign policy will not bring history to an end, but it has done a remarkably good job of enabling the United States to flourish as history goes on. I do not know how long the present moment of American supremacy will last, or if the world is due for a second American century. I am not even sure that another century of American global hegemony is what the American people should hope for. But the long and successful record of this country's unique—and uniquely complex—foreign policy system gives me solid grounds for believing that whatever else happens in the world, our foreign policy tradition offers the American people real hope for a prosperous and democratic future.

ACKNOWLEDGMENTS

Marisa Abrajano: Excerpts from *Campaigning to the New American Electorate: Advertising to Latino Voters* Marisa Abrajano. Copyright © 2010 by the Board of Trustees of the Leland Stanford Jr. University. All rights reserved. Used with the permission of Stanford University Press, www.sup.org.

Christopher Achen and Larry Bartels: *Democracy for Realists: Why Elections Do Not Produce Responsive Government* by Christopher Achen and Larry Bartels. Published by Princeton University Press. © 2016. Reprinted by permission of Princeton University Press via Copyright Clearance Center.

John Aldrich: *Why Parties: A Second Look* by John Aldrich. Copyright 1995, 2011 by The University of Chicago. Reprinted by permission of The University of Chicago Press.

Larry M. Bartels: *Unequal Democracy.* © 2008 by Russell Sage Foundation. Published by Princeton University Press. Reprinted by permission of Princeton University Press.

Matthew Baum: *Soft News Goes to War.* © 2003 by Princeton University Press. Reprinted by permission of Princeton University Press.

Angus Campbell: "The Impact of Party Identification" from *The American Voter: An Abridgement* by Angus Campbell, Phillip E. Converse, Warren Edward Miller, Donald E. Stokes. Reprinted by permission of Jean Campbell.

James Campbell: From *POLARIZED: Making Sense of a Divided America* by James E. Campbell. Copyright © 2016 by Princeton University Press. Reprinted by permission.

Brandice Canes-Wrone: *Who Leads Whom? Presidents, Policy, and the Public.* Copyright © 2006 by The University of Chicago. Reprinted by permission of The University of Chicago Press.

Daniel Carpenter: *The Forging of Bureaucratic Autonomy.* Princeton University Press. Reprinted by permission of Princeton University Press.

Marty Cohen: *The Party Decides: Presidential Nominations Before and After Reform* by Marty Cohen. Copyright © 2008 by The University of Chicago. Reprinted by permission of The University of Chicago Press.

Gary W. Cox and Mathew D. McCubbins: From *Setting the Agenda: Responsible Party Government in the U.S. House of Representatives.* Copyright © 2005 Gary W. Cox and Mathew D. McCubbins. Reprinted with the permission of Cambridge University Press.

Katherine Cramer: From *The Politics of Resentment: Rural Consciousness in Wisconsin and the Rise of Scott Walker.* Copyright © 2016 The University of Chicago. Reprinted by permission of the University of Chicago Press.

Robert A. Dahl: *How Democratic Is the American Constitution?* by Robert A. Dahl. Copyright © 2002 by Yale University. Reprinted by permission of Yale University Press.

James Druckman and Lawrence Jacobs: From *Who Governs: Presidents, Public Opinion, and Manipulation.* Copyright © 2015 The University of Chicago. Reprinted by permission of the University of Chicago Press.

Lee Epstein, et al.: *Circuit Effects: How the Norm of Federal Judicial Experience Biases the Supreme Court*, 157 U. PA. L. REV. 833, 833–41, 864–65, 868–75, 877–78 (2009). Reprinted by permission of the University of Pennsylvania Law Review.

Richard F. Fenno: *Home Style: House Members in Their Districts, 1st Edition,* © 2003, pp. 1–2, 8-10, 18, 24, 27–28. Reprinted by permission of Pearson Education, Inc., Upper Saddle River, NJ.

Richard Fox and Jennifer Lawless: "Gendered Perceptions and Political Candidacies: A Central Barrier to Women's Equality in Electoral Politics." *American Journal of Political Science*, 55: 59–73. Copyright © 2011. Reproduced with permission of Blackwell Publishing Ltd.

Sean Gailmard and John Patty: *Learning While Governing: Expertise and the Accountability in the Executive Branch.* Copyright © 2013 by The University of Chicago. Reprinted by permission of The University of Chicago Press.

Martin Gilens: *Affluence and Influence.* Princeton University Press. Reprinted by permission of Princeton University Press.

Justin Grimmer, Sean Westwood, and Solomon Messing: "From *The Impression on Influence: Legislator Communication, Representation, and Democratic Accountability* by Justin Grimmer, Sean J. Westwood, and Solomon Messing. Copyright © 2015 by Princeton University Press. Reprinted by permission.

Christopher Hammons: From "State Constitutions, Religious Protection, and Federalism," *University of St. Thomas Journal of Law and Public Policy*, Volume 7, Issue 2, Spring 2013. Reprinted by permission of the author.

Garrett Hardin: From "The Tragedy of the Commons" by Garrett Hardin, *Science*, December 13, 1968. Reprinted with permission from American Association for the Advancement of Science via the Copyright Clearance Center.

William G. Howell: *Power without Persuasion.* Copyright 2003 by Princeton University Press. Reprinted by permission of Princeton University Press.

Samuel Kernell: From *Going Public: New Strategies of Presidential Leadership*, pp. 1–4, 114–115, 122–123, 129, copyright © 1997 CQ Press, a division of SAGE Publications, Inc. Reprinted by Permission of Sage Publications, Inc.

D. Roderick Kiewiet and Mathew McCubbins: *The Logic of Delegation* by D. Roderick Kiewiet and Mathew McCubbins. Copyright © 1991 by The University of Chicago. Reprinted by permission of The University of Chicago Press.

Donald Kinder and Cindy Kam: *Us Against Them: Ethnocentric Foundations of American Opinion* by Donald Kinder and Cindy Kam. Copyright © 2010 by The University of Chicago. Reprinted by permission of The University of Chicago Press.

Ken Kollman: *Outside Lobbying.* © 1998 Princeton University Press. Reprinted by permission of Princeton University Press.

John Koza, Barry Fadem, Mark Grueskin and Michael S. Mandell: *Every Vote Equal: A State-based Plan for Electing the President by Popular Vote*. Reprinted by permission of National Popular Vote Press.

Arthur Lupia and Mathew D. McCubbins: From *The Democratic Dilemma: Can Citizens Learn What They Need to Know?* Copyright © 1998 Cambridge University Press. Reprinted with the permission of Cambridge University Press.

David Mayhew: *Congress: The Electoral Connection* by David Mayhew. Copyright © 1974 by Yale University. Reprinted by permission of Yale University Press.

Mathew D. McCubbins and Thomas Schwartz: "Congressional Oversight Overlooked: Police Patrols versus Fire Alarms". *The American Journal of Political Science*, Feb. 1984. Reproduced with permission of Blackwell Publishing Ltd.

Walter Russell Mead: Excerpt from *Special Providence: American Foreign Policy and How It Changed the World* by Walter Russell Mead, copyright © 2001 by The Century Foundation. Used by permission of Alfred A. Knopf, an imprint of the Knopf Doubleday Publishing Group, a division of Random House LLC. All rights reserved.

Suzanne Mettler: *The Submerged State: How Invisible Government Policies Undermine American Democracy* by Suzanne Mettler. Copyright © 2011 by The University of Chicago. Reprinted by permission of The University of Chicago Press.

Susan Moffitt: *Making Public Policy: Participatory Bureaucracy in American Democracy* by Susan Moffitt. Copyright © 2014 Cambridge University Press. Reprinted with the permission of Cambridge University Press.

Richard E. Neustadt: Reprinted with the permission of Simon & Schuster Publishing Group from the Free Press edition of *Presidential Power and The Modern Presidents: The Politics of Leadership from Roosevelt to Reagan* by Richard E. Neustadt. Copyright © 1990 by Richard E. Neustadt. All rights reserved.

Mancur Olson, Jr.: "A Theory of Groups and Organizations" reprinted by permission of the publisher from *The Logic of Collective Action: Public Goods and the Theory of Groups* by Mancur Olson, pp. 5–48, Cambridge, Mass.: Harvard University Press, Copyright © 1965, 1971 by the President and Fellows of Harvard College.

Jeremy Pope and Shawn Treier: "Voting for a Founding: Testing the Effect of Economic Interests at the Federal Convention of 1787," *Journal of Politics*, Vol. 77, No. 2, 2015. Copyright © 2015 The University of Chicago. Reprinted by permission of the University of Chicago Press.

Robert D. Putnam: Reprinted with the permission of Simon & Schuster Publishing Group from *Bowling Alone: The Collapse and Revival of American Community* by Robert D. Putnam. Copyright © 2000 Robert D. Putnam. All rights reserved.

William Riker: "Chapter 6: Is the Federal Bargain Worth Keeping?" from *Federalism: Origin, Operation, Significance*. Reprinted by permission of the Estate of William Riker.

Gerald N. Rosenberg: *The Hollow Hope: Can Courts Bring about Social Change?* by Gerald N. Rosenberg. Copyright © 1991, 2008 by The University of Chicago. Reprinted by permission of The University of Chicago Press.

Kenneth Scheve and David Stasavage: From *Taxing the Rich: A History of Fiscal Fairness in the United States and Europe* by Kenneth Scheve and David Stasavage. Copyright © 2016 by Princeton University Press. Reprinted by permission.

Michael Tesler: *Post-Racial or Most-Racial: Race and Politics in the Obama Era* by Michael Tesler. Copyright © 2016 by The University of Chicago. Reprinted by permission of the University of Chicago Press.

James Q. Wilson: *Bureaucracy: What Government Agencies Do and Why They Do It* by Wilson, James Q. Reproduced with permission of BASIC BOOKS via Copyright Clearance Center.

Janelle S. Wong, Kathrick Ramakrishnan, Taeku Lee, and Jane Junn: *Asian American Political Participation: Emerging Constituents and Their Political Identities*. Pp. 152, 161–166, 177–179 © 2011 Russell Sage Foundation, 112 East 64th, Street, New York, NY 10065. Reprinted with permission.

John R. Zaller: From *The Nature and Origins of Mass Opinion*. Copyright © 1992 Cambridge University Press. Reprinted with the permission of Cambridge University Press.